Psychology

A DISCOVERY EXPERIENCE

Stephen L. Franzoi

Marquette University

SOUTH-WESTERN
CENGAGE Learning

Australia • Brazil • Mexico • Singapore • Spain • United Kingdom • United States

SOUTH-WESTERN
CENGAGE Learning

Psychology: A Discovery Experience
Stephen L. Franzoi

SVP Global Product Management - Research, School & Professional: Frank Menchaca

General Manager, K-12 School Group: CarolAnn Shindelar

Acquisitions Editor: Jeff Werle

Senior Developmental Editor: Karen Caldwell

Consulting Editor: Hyde Park Publishing Services, LLC

Production Management and Composition: PreMediaGlobal

Senior Art Director: Michelle Kunkler

Senior Media Developer: Mike Jackson

Manufacturing Planner: Kevin Kluck

Senior IP Project Manager: Michelle McKenna

Internal Design: Ke Design, Mason, OH

Cover Designer: Tippy McIntosh

Cover image: © Corbis, Tetra Images

Essential Question Icon: © art4all/Shutterstock

For product information and technology assistance, contact us at **Cengage Learning Customer & Sales Support, 1-800-354-9706**

For permission to use material from this text or product, submit all requests online at **www.cengage.com/permissions**
Further permissions questions can be emailed to **permissionrequest@cengage.com**

The 16 Career Cluster icons are being used with permission of the: States' Career Clusters Initiative, 2006, www.careerclusters.org

Student's Edition ISBN-13: 978-1-305-11429-6
Student's Edition ISBN-10: 1-305-11429-9

South-Western Cengage Learning
5191 Natorp Boulevard
Mason, OH 45040
USA

Cengage Learning is a leading provider of customized learning solutions with office locations around the globe, including Singapore, the United Kingdom, Australia, Mexico, Brazil, and Japan. Locate your local office at: **www.cengage.com/global**.

Cengage Learning products are represented in Canada by Nelson Education, Ltd.

For your course and learning solutions, visit **www.cengage.com/school**.

Visit our company website at **www.cengage.com**.

Printed in the United States of America
1 2 3 4 5 6 7 18 17 16 15 14

From the Author

A typical high school psychology textbook is often dull and boring. This is surprising, because the history of psychology is filled with exciting stories about discoveries of the human mind. As a high school student, psychology has a great deal to offer you because seeking knowledge about yourself and others will help you make better decisions and choices in your life.

In *Psychology: A Discovery Experience*, I will be introducing you to the science of psychology as a journey of discovery undertaken both by researchers and by yourself. By encouraging you to consider how psychological knowledge relates to your own life, this book will make the learning of psychology a very personal discovery experience for you.

There are two ways in which I will encourage you on this journey. First, each chapter has "Self-Discovery" questionnaires that ask you to consider how psychology relates to your life. These questionnaires are used by psychologists in their research. As you learn about this research, you also learn something about yourself. Second, I will share some of my life experiences with you. By actively applying psychological knowledge to my own life, I am hoping that you will do the same and have a better understanding of yourself and others.

By taking this journey with me, I guarantee that you will learn some valuable information about yourself, your friends, your family, and the many other people that share your everyday life. Are you ready to begin?

Your partner and guide,

Stephen L. Franzoi
Professor of Psychology
Marquette University

Acknowledgments

While I was writing this text, many people provided me with invaluable assistance and understanding.

I first want to thank my family for their support and for also providing me with wonderful examples that I use throughout the text. I also wish to thank the people at South-Western for providing me with the opportunity to make my book a reality. The editors and consultants worked closely with me throughout the entire writing process. Their invaluable assistance helped make this text reader-friendly for high school students.

About the Author

Stephen L. Franzoi is a Professor of Psychology at Marquette University in Milwaukee, Wisconsin. Dr. Franzoi received his Ph.D. from the University of California at Davis, and has served as assistant editor of *Social Psychology Quarterly* and associate editor of *Social Problems*. At Marquette University, Professor Franzoi teaches psychology courses and is also the author of college textbooks in introductory psychology and social psychology. He is an active researcher in the area of body esteem. Over the years, Dr. Franzoi has discussed his research in many popular media outlets, including *The New York Times, USA Today*, National Public Radio, and the "Oprah Winfrey Show." He and his wife are the proud parents of Amelia and Lillian.

PSYCHOLOGY CONSULTANTS AND ADVISORY BOARD

REVIEWERS

Katherine Gaskins
Granger High School
West Valley City, Utah

Rhonda Gephart
Bear River High School
Garland, Utah

Erin Gould
Wauwatosa East High School
Wauwatosa, Wisconsin

Susan Hoereth
Ben Davis High School
Indianapolis, Indiana

John Hofer
Franklin High School
Franklin, Ohio

Steve Kutcher
Waukesha West High School
Waukesha, Wisconsin

Rhinehart Lintonen
Elkhorn Area High School
Elkhorn, Wisconsin

Yolande Martinez-Jolitz
Germantown High School
Germantown, Wisconsin

Greg Miller
Bishop Chatard High School
Indianapolis, Indiana

Don Morabito
Great Valley High School
Malvern, Pennsylvania

Maria Mueller
Mason High School
Mason, Ohio

Keith Neth
Millard North High School
Omaha, Nebraska

Tina Raduege
West Allis Central High School
West Allis, Wisconsin

Richard D. Reinders
Cedarburg High School
Cedarburg, Wisconsin

Judie Roberts
Skyline High School
Salt Lake City, Utah

Cynthia Davis Smith
Northridge High School
Layton, Utah

Florencia Sparks
Coronado High School
Henderson, Nevada

Joe Stucker
Brownsburg High School
Brownsburg, Indiana

Craig Watkins
Medina County Career Center
Medina, Ohio

James White
Legacy High School
North Las Vegas, Nevada

Renita Williams
Newport News Public Schools
Newport News, Virginia

Lark Woodbury
Layton High School
Layton, Utah

Terese Wright
West Allis Central High School
West Allis, Wisconsin

BRIEF CONTENTS

CONTENTS

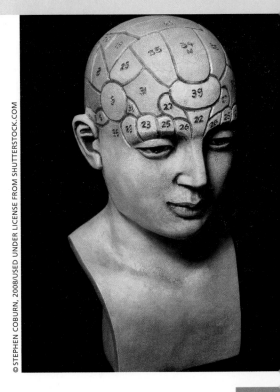

CONTENTS

UNIT 3   DEVELOPMENTAL DOMAIN 213

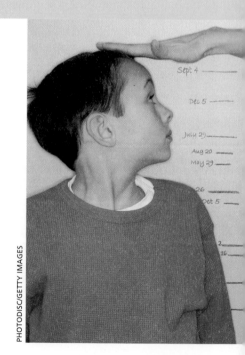

PHOTODISC/GETTY IMAGES

CONTENTS

©TOMASZ TROJANOWSKI, 2009/USED UNDER LICENSE FROM SHUTTERSTOCK.COM

CONTENTS

CONTENTS

IMAGE SOURCE BLACK/JUPITER IMAGES

DISCOVER

CHAPTER OPENERS

begin each chapter with an entertaining and informative story that leads into the central topic of the chapter.

DISCOVER IT

uses thought-provoking questions that show how the next lesson relates to students' own lives.

SELF-DISCOVERY

provides students with a guided method for introspection through self-report questionnaires and activities.

LESSONS

4.1 Basic Principles of Sensation

4.2 Vision

4.3 Hearing and Your Other Senses

ESSENTIAL QUESTION
Go to page XXIV

CHAPTER 4

Sensation

"We live on the leash of our senses."

—DIANE ACKERMAN, AMERICAN POET, B. 1948

In the spring of 2003, 27-year-old Aron Ralston was alone when he climbed up the side of a canyon in Utah's Canyonlands National Park. An 800-pound boulder shifted and pinned his right arm between the boulder and the rocky wall. For three days he tried to free his arm. By then he had used up all his food and water. Realizing his hope of being rescued was remote, Aron decided to cut off his pinned arm. He applied a tourniquet, and then he used his pocketknife to cut off his crushed forearm just below the elbow. After freeing himself from the boulder, Aron crawled through the canyon, and then rappelled to the canyon floor. He walked six miles until he met hikers, who notified nearby rescuers.

How did Aron cope with the pain of cutting through his own flesh and bone? "I'm not sure how I handled it," Aron later said. "I felt pain and I coped with it. I moved on." Following surgeries and rehabilitation, Aron resumed his outdoor adventures.

LESSON 4.1 Basic Principles of Sensation

OBJECTIVES

• Explain the concepts of sensory thresholds and compare the different theories.

• Describe sensory adaptation.

DISCOVER IT | *How does this relate to me?*

Can you sometimes overhear other students talking quietly in another part of the cafeteria? Do you see better in the dark after standing still for a few minutes when you first turn the lights out? Do you sometimes tune out distracting noises around you? Do you wonder how your senses interact with your environment? Psychologists look for answers to these questions when researching how physical stimuli affects sensory perceptions and a person's mental state.

KEY TERMS

• sensation
• psychophysics
• absolute threshold
• signal-detection theory
• difference threshold
• Weber's law
• sensory adaptation

SELF-DISCOVERY

Would You Like to "See" Your Blind Spot?

You can experience your own blind spot by closing your right eye and lining up the cross with your left eye. Now slowly move your head back and forth. When the image of the happy face is between 6 and 18 inches away from your eye, it crosses your blind spot and disappears from sight. One reason you are seldom aware of your blind spot is that when an image falls on the blind spot of one eye, it falls on the receptors of the other, so you detect the image. Another reason you don't often see the blind spot—even with one-eyed vision—is because it is located off to the side of your visual field so objects near this area are never in sharp focus. Perhaps the most important reason you don't see the blind spot is that your visual system somehow fills in the place where the image disappears. When you try this blind spot demonstration, the place where the happy face used to be isn't replaced by a "hole" or by "nothingness" but, by the white surrounding it.

a relevant and real personal journey.

PLANNING A CAREER IN PSYCHOLOGY

presents the skills, education, and work experience needed for a variety of careers in psychology relating to the National Career Clusters.

Apply Psychology Concepts

30. Your family rents a cabin on a lake and your Mom discovers on the second day that she has lice in her hair! Immediately on hearing this unsettling news, your scalp feels itchy. Explain your reaction based on signal-detection theory.

31. What is the blind spot in your field of vision, and why doesn't it cause many problems for you?

32. How does gate-control theory explain why rubbing or massaging a sore muscle reduces the pain?

PSYCHOLOGY APPLICATIONS

require students to apply the concepts to a stated question or scenario.

LAB TEAMS

is a group-oriented activity that provides students with hands-on learning of a specific concept.

PLANNING A CAREER IN PSYCHOLOGY

ealth Science

Psychobiologist and Comparative Psychologist

Do you have an interest in how the brain and nervous system affects behavior? Do you wonder how animals learn? Do you like research? If so, you may be interested in a career in psychobiology or comparative psychology.

Psychobiology and comparative psychology have many names. These include behavioral neuroscience, biopsychology, and physiological psychology. Psychologists in these two career areas study behavior by examining physiological processes.

Careers in psychobiology and comparative psychology may be in teaching or research. Psychologists in this field may work for medical centers, private or nonprofit research and development firms, or for government-funded organizations.

Psychologists in psychobiology may study either animals or human behavior, but comparative psychologists mainly study non-humans. In studying animals, they may study the behavior of dolphins and whales in an oceanic laboratory, or compare and contrast the similarities and differences between animals today and those from the ancient world in order to understand evolution.

Psychobiologists might study the effects of certain chemicals or pharmaceuticals on human behavior, examine the effects of damage or disease to the brain on cognitive functions, or examine the neural system to understand its effect on learning, memory, or sensory perceptions. Individuals with a bachelor's of science degree in psychology who focus their studies on psychobiology or comparative psychology usually continue with their

schooling to the Ph.D. level. They may also go on to medical or veterinary school, or health-related graduate professional schools.

Employment Outlook
Careers for psychologists are expected to grow 15 percent until 2016. This is a faster than average rate.

Needed Skills and Education
Most psychobiologists and comparative psychologists have a Ph.D. in psychology. While working toward this degree, many individuals gain research experience in th[e field] ice by working under the supervision of s[ ] the field.

Students interested in these two ca[ ] logy, biology, physics, neuroscience, [ ] animal physiology. More specific coll[ ] research methods, experimental design[ ] comparative psychology, and behavioral[ ]

Skills and aptitudes helpful in this career[ ] ing, oral and written communication, me[ ] compiling and evaluating data, perceptiv[ ] well as computer and research skills.

How You'll Spend Your Da[y]
The way psychologists in this career spe[ ] depending on the area of expertise. They[ ] or more a week in a laboratory or have s[ ] with research animals or human test sub[ ]

Earnings
The median hourly earnings of psycholo[ ] $59,440. The lowest 10 percent earn $3[ ] 10 percent earn more than $102,730.

What About You?
Do these two careers sound interesting t[ ] Internet search for colleges and universit[ ] specializing in these two fields.

STOCKBYTE/GETTY IMAGES

LAB TEAMS

Sensory Adaptation Demonstration

Try a little demonstration. Place a substance with a strong odor—an onion, perfume, or shaving lotion, for example—near your nose for a few minutes. Its odor will seem less intense over time. Next, remove the substance for five minutes and then smell it again. Now it should smell as strong as it did when you first smelled it.

DISCOVER

INTERACTIVE FIGURES

bring concepts to life and help students understand complex psychology topics. These interactive figures are available on the Instructor Resource CD and the student website.

DIGGING DEEPER WITH PSYCHOLOGY eCOLLECTION

links students to a unique online database of current Psychology resources that allow students to research topics and issues in depth.

Inner ear | Middle ear | Outer ear

Stirrup
Oval window
Anvil
Hammer
Auditory nerve
Pinna
Cochlea
Sound waves
Eardrum
Auditory canal

INTERACTIVE FIGURE

DIGGING DEEPER
with Psychology eCollection

Have you ever wondered why it is hard to "get over it" when someone hurts your feelings? Have you ever held a grudge? Do you know people who think the deck is stacked against them and that they can't get a break? Scientists have traced this behavior, called injustice collecting, back through human evolution. Psychologists maintain that this process is a self-protection impulse. They believe nursing grudges might have, at one time, helped people survive. By monitoring fairness and being alert to those who weren't contributing, it allowed people to protect scarce resources. Access the Gale Psychology eCollection at *www.cengage.com/school/psych/franzoi* and read the hypotheses about injustice collecting proposed by evolutionary psychologists such as Tooby and Cosmides. Write a brief report describing the research and findings on injustice collecting and answer the question: Why do psychologists research the development of behaviors in the past? As an additional project, describe an instance when you or someone you know had a grudge and explain how it was resolved.

Source: Pelusi, Nando. "Injustice collecting: you can't let go of a grudge, says Nando Pelusi, Ph.D., because there are deep-seated emotional payoffs. (NEANDERTHINK)." *Psychology Today* 39.6 (Nov–Dec 2006): 64(2).

THE DVD COLLECTION

enhances the classroom experience and demonstrates how psychology concepts are applied to daily life.
(ABC News Videos, Psychology Research in Action)

COCHLEA

WHAT'S THE FREQUENCY?
RING TONES ONLY KIDS CAN HEAR
ABC News Videos

metro

Courtesy: PREVI
Psychology and Research in Action

the ultimate learning experience.

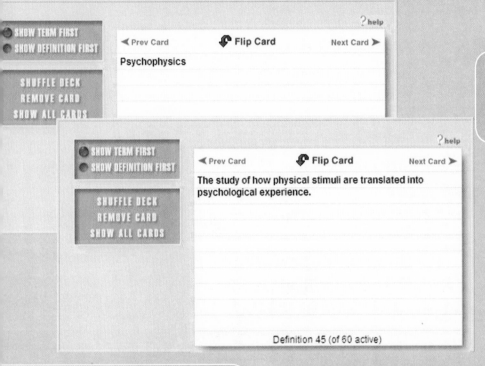

STUDENT COMPANION WEBSITE

extends your learning experience well beyond the classroom with interactive figures, study tools, flash cards, and the Psychology e-Collection resource database.

iMPACT INTERACTIVE TEXT CD-ROM

is a fully functioning text on CD that offers key learning tools such as hypertext linking, key term definitions, and forms for completing self assessment opportunities.

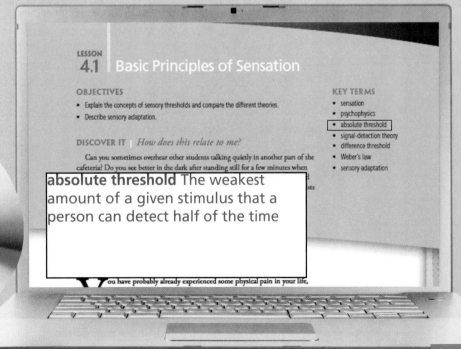

DISCOVER

Sensory Crossovers

Have you ever heard a sound and experienced it as a flash of light? This *seeing* of sound is fairly common and is most often experienced when the eyes are closed and the sound is unexpected. A much more sophisticated *colored hearing* is a type of sensory experience known as synesthesia (pronounced sin-ess-THEE-zhah). Synesthesia is a rare and extraordinary sensory condition in which people perceive stimuli in other senses, such as *tasting* color or shapes, *hearing* someone's touch, or *feeling* the sounds of musical instruments on their bodies. Scientists estimate that about one in 2,000 people are synesthetes, with females outnumbering males 6 to 1.

The most common form of synesthesia is *colored hearing*. Most people with this condition report that they see sounds internally (in the mind's eye), but a few see colors projected outside the body, usually within arm's reach. Recent brain scans of synesthetes who report colored hearing indicate that visual areas of their brains show increased activation in response to sounds.

In another type of synesthesia, a person experiences specific letters, numbers, and/or words as vivid patterns or particular colors. For example, a person with this form of synesthesia might see the letter B as orange, the letter T as green, and the letter R as red. Some neuroscientists believe that this type of synesthesia occurs partly because the areas of the brain that process colors are near the areas that process letters and numbers, and that synesthetes may have more extensive neural connections between these two nearby brain areas.

Think Critically
What is synesthesia?

Your Other Senses

In gathering sensory information from your surroundings, you primarily rely on your vision and hearing, which scientists call the higher senses in humans. In contrast, the senses of smell, taste, touch, and proprioception are classified as minor senses because they are not considered as crucial to sustaining life. However, as you will learn in this section, your minor senses are very important in many areas of daily living.

SMELL

The stimuli for smell are airborne molecules. When you smell hot chocolate you are sensing molecules that have left the hot chocolate and traveled through the air to your nose. These molecules then enter your nasal passages and reach tiny receptor cells at the top of the nasal cavity. These receptor cells then transmit neural impulses containing smell information through the **olfactory nerve** to the brain. Once your brain has processed these neural signals, you experience the hot chocolate's aroma (see Figure 4-6 on page 110).

Many people prefer perfume-like fragrances and dislike foul and sulfurous odors. Smells that individuals most like are those that help survival. Ancient peoples survived in part through their sense of smell, because poisonous vegetation or foods smelled rotten.

The number of receptor cells in the nasal cavity determines smell sensitivity. Animals with more receptors than other animals have a much keener sense of smell. While humans have about 10 million olfactory receptors, dogs have 200 million receptors.

Although the human sense of smell is not as sensitive as that of many other species, we can often identify one another by smells. For example, blindfolded mothers can identify with close to 95 percent accuracy the clothing worn by their own children through smell alone. Similarly, infants quickly learn to identify their

olfactory nerve The nerve that transmits neural impulses containing smell information from the nose to the brain

Research indicates that women's smell sensitivity is better than that of men.

NEW SCIENCE

identifies and explores the latest developments in the field of psychology.

PSYCHOLOGY eCOLLECTION

offers instant online access to hundreds of reference sources allowing you to stay current with the latest psychology developments. Access is provided free on the companion website.

content you've been asking for.

What is Positive Psychology?

Within the past 10 years, the insights of humanistic psychology have inspired a new generation of psychologists to develop a related scientific approach called positive psychology, which studies how people find mental health and happiness in their everyday living. Positive psychologists study what it means to be a well-adjusted person and what makes people happy and optimistic in their daily living. For example, when does a positive view of life help you overcome hurdles to success? When does an overly positive outlook cause you to ignore real problems that need your attention? How can you take positive steps to reach important life goals, reduce social injustice in the world, and improve your life and the life of others? These are some of the questions positive psychology seeks to answer.

Throughout this text, information will be presented about positive psychology topics that relate to the chapter material. Much of the information will inform you about recent studies and theories coming directly from this new area of psychology. Other information will inform you about older studies that investigated the psychology of happiness and positive living before positive psychology was created as a separate psychological perspective.

Think Critically

How will reading about positive psychology help you in your daily life?

POSITIVE PSYCHOLOGY

offers a look at this new psychological approach and how scientists use positive mental health and happiness as a tool in everyday life.

Make Academic Connections

33. **Cross-Cultural Studies** A study of more than 660 college students in four countries found cross-cultural differences among the students in the colors they associated with emotionally charged words. The students were asked what color they identify with the words anger, envy, fear, and jealously. Polish students associated anger, envy, and jealously with the color purple. German students associated envy and jealously with the color yellow. American students associated envy with the colors black, green, and red. Russian students associated these emotions with the colors black, purple, and yellow. Make a list of four emotions and the colors you associate with these emotions. For example, you could list the emotion of love and the color pink. Ask 11 people of different ages, genders, and cultural heritages or diverse backgrounds what color they associate with the emotions on your list. If possible, include one person who is colorblind. Make a chart of your findings, and then explain the conclusions you infer from your findings.

34. **Art** Download pictures from the Internet or use your drawing skills to create an illustration of the parts of either the eye or ear. Label each part. Then write an explanation of each part.

35. **History** Use the library or Internet to research Gustav Fechner, the pioneer in psychophysics. Examine his theory and analyze how he concluded that there is a relationship between bodily and mental experiences. Provide examples that illustrate absolute threshold. Make sure your sources are educational, news, or government web sites. Write a summary of your findings.

36. **Research** Use the library or Internet to search for studies on how loud noises affect hearing and hearing loss. Use the search term "loud noise effects." Make sure the studies you cite are from educational, news, or government sources. Write a paper that evaluates your findings.

MAKE ACADEMIC CONNECTIONS

relates psychology concepts to other courses of study.

CASE STUDY

Shyness, Self-Efficacy, and the Illusion of Transparency

INTRODUCTION Joanne, a junior in high school, was doing well in all her courses. Academically, she had high self-efficacy, meaning she felt very capable of successfully accomplishing whatever challenges her teachers presented to her. However, Joanne's a-efficacy outside the classroom in other areas was sorely lacking. In social situations she felt shy, awkward, and very unsure of herself. A simple greeting by another classmate was often all it took to make Joanne blush and feel like everybody was watching her. Joanne's utter lack of social confidence troubled her and she wanted to try to become less socially anxious and more socially self-confident. But how?

After reading some books on shyness, Joanne discovered that it is a very common experience. She also learned that when people become socially anxious they often overestimate the degree to which others can detect their anxiety.

Psychologists call this false belief that your thoughts, feelings, and emotions are more transparent to others than is actually the case the illusion of transparency.

HYPOTHESIS Joanne decided to use this knowledge about the illusion of transparency to become less socially anxious and increase her feelings of self-efficacy in social situations. She hypothesized that people were probably not that aware of her nervousness when meeting her and talking to her.

METHOD Joanne decided to approach a classmate in school and have a brief casual conversation about a TV show that most students watched every week. Joanne made sure to remind herself about the illusion of transparency just before approaching the classmate. The conversation lasted less than a minute, it seemed to go well, and the classmate even laughed when Joanne mentioned a humorous incident in the TV show. Throughout the next few weeks Joanne repeatedly reminded herself about the illusion of transparency before talking to fellow classmates.

RESULTS Joanne's hypothesis was confirmed! People mostly never seemed to notice her nervousness while talking to her. Even more surprising was the fact that Joanne noticed that her anxiety began decreasing the more she forced herself to approach other people and engage them in conversation. After awhile, Joanne no longer had to "force herself" to start conversations.

- The headache is severe, new, and unlike past headaches.
- The headache is the "worst" you have ever experienced.
- The headache becomes much worse over time.
- Headache occurs with exertion, coughing, or sneezing.

Critical Analysis

1. What does this case study suggest about people's ability to change their personalities?

2. What might prevent some people from decreasing their own levels of shyness?

CASE STUDIES

present intriguing and challenging situations drawn from actual psychological studies related to chapter concepts. They investigate the hypothesis, method, and results of each study. Critical Analysis questions provide opportunities for students to refine their critical thinking skills.

Correlation to APA National Standards for High School Psychology Curricula

I. METHODS DOMAIN

Standard Area IA: Introduction and Research Methods

IA-1.1	Describe and compare the biological, behavioral, cognitive, sociocultural, humanistic, and psychodynamic perspectives.	Lesson 1.1, Lesson 1.2
IA-2.1	List and explain the major subfields of psychology.	Lesson 1.1, Lesson 1.2
IA-3.1	Describe the elements of an experiment.	Lesson 2.1, Lesson 2.2
IA-3.2	Explain the importance of sampling and random assignment in psychological research.	Lesson 2.1
IA-3.3	Describe and compare quantitative and qualitative research strategies.	Lesson 2.2
IA-4.1	Define descriptive statistics and explain how they are used by behavioral scientists.	Lesson 2.3
IA-4.2	Explain and describe measures of central tendency and variability.	Lesson 2.3
IA-4.3	Describe the concept of correlation and explain how it is used in psychology.	Lesson 2.2
IA-4.4	Recognize how inferential statistics are used in psychological research.	Lesson 2.3
IA-5.1	Identify ethical issues in psychological research.	Lesson 2.1
IA-6.1	Discuss psychology's roots in philosophy and natural science.	Lesson 2.1, Lesson 2.2
IA-6.2	Describe the emergence of experimental psychology.	Lesson 1.1
IA-6.3	Recognize the diversity of psychological theories in the 20th and 21st centuries.	Lesson 1.2
IA-6.4	Describe psychology's increasing inclusiveness of diverse interests and constituents.	Lesson 1.1

II. BIOPSYCHOLOGICAL DOMAIN

Standard Area IIA: Biological Bases of Behavior

IIA-1.1	Identify the neuron as the basis for neural communication.	Lesson 3.1
IIA-1.2	Describe how information is transmitted and integrated in the nervous system.	Lesson 3.1
IIA-1.3	Analyze how the process of neurotransmission can be modified by heredity and environment.	Lesson 3.1
IIA-2.1	Classify the major divisions and subdivisions of the nervous system.	Lesson 3.1
IIA-2.2	Differentiate the functions of the various subdivisions of the nervous system.	Lesson 3.1
IIA-3.1	Identify the structure and function of the major regions of the brain.	Lesson 3.2
IIA-3.2	Recognize that specific functions are centered in specific lobes of the cerebral cortex.	Lesson 3.2
IIA-3.3	Describe lateralization of brain functions.	Lesson 3.2
IIA-4.1	Explain how research and technology have provided methods to analyze brain behavior and disease.	Lesson 3.2
IIA-5.1	Describe how the endocrine glands are linked to the nervous system.	Lesson 3.1
IIA-6.1	Assess the effects of heredity and environment on behavior.	Lesson 3.3
IIA-7.1	Explain how evolved tendencies interact with the present environment and culture to determine behavior.	Lesson 4.1, Lesson 4.3, Lesson 15.2

APA NATIONAL STANDARDS CHART

Standard Area IIB: Sensation and Perception

IIB-1.1	Explain the concepts of threshold, adaptation, and constancy.	Lesson 4.1, Lesson 5.1
IIB-1.2	Describe the operation of sensory systems.	Lesson 4.1, Lesson 4.2, Lesson 4.3, Lesson 5.1
IIB-1.3	List forms of energy for which we do and do not have sensory receptors.	Lesson 4.2, Lesson 4.3
IIB-1.4	Relate knowledge of sensory processes to applications in areas such as engineering psychology, advertising, music, architecture, and so on.	Lesson 4.3, Lesson 5.1
IIB-2.1	Explain Gestalt concepts and principles, such as figure-ground, continuity, similarity, proximity, closure, and so on.	Lesson 5.1
IIB-2.2	Describe binocular and monocular depth cues.	Lesson 5.1
IIB-2.3	Describe the influence on perception of environmental variables, motivation, past experiences, culture, and expectations.	Lesson 5.2
IIB-3.1	Explain what is meant by attention.	Lesson 15.1

Standard Area IIC: Motivation and Emotion

IIC-1.1	Apply motivational concepts to the behavior of humans and other animals.	Lesson 6.1
IIC-2.1	Describe the interaction of internal cues and learning on basic drives.	Lesson 6.1, Lesson 6.2
IIC-2.2	Describe the situational cues giving rise to anger and fear.	Lesson 6.3
IIC-2.3	Describe the situational cues and individual characteristics giving rise to curiosity and anxiety.	Lesson 6.1, Lesson 6.2, Lesson 6.3
IIC-3.1	Describe one or more theories of motivation, such as expectancy value, cognitive dissonance, arousal, Maslow's hierarchy of needs, and drive reduction.	Lesson 6.1
IIC-4.1	Explain how common motives and emotions develop.	Lesson 6.1, Lesson 6.2
IIC-5.1	Use expectancy-value theory to explain their own and others' behavior.	Lesson 6.1
IIC-6.1	Describe theories of emotion, such as James-Lange, Cannon-Bard, or cognitive theories.	Lesson 6.3
IIC-6.2	Explaining how emotions and behaviors are related.	Lesson 6.3
IIC-7.1	Describe differences in perception between individuals differing in motivation.	Lesson 4.1
IIC-7.2	Explain how learning, memory, problem-solving, and decision-making strategies are influenced by motivation and emotion.	Lesson 6.1

Standard Area IID: Stress, Coping, and Health

IID-1.1	Identify and explain major sources of stress.	Lesson 7.1, Lesson 7.2
IID-2.1	List and explain possible physiological reactions to stress.	Lesson 7.1
IID-3.1	List and explain possible psychological reactions to stress.	Lesson 7.1, Lesson 7.2
IID-4.1	Identify and explain cognitive strategies to deal with stress and promote health.	Lesson 7.2
IID-4.2	Identify and explain behavioral strategies to deal with stress and promote health.	Lesson 7.3

III. DEVELOPMENTAL DOMAIN
Standard Area IIIA: Life Span Development

IIIA-1.1 Describe physical, social, and cognitive changes from the prenatal period throughout the life span. — Lesson 8.1, Lesson 8.2, Lesson 9.2, Lesson 10.3

IIIA-1.2 Examine the nature of change over the life span. — Lesson 8.2, Lesson 10.2, Lesson 10.3

IIIA-1.3 Identify the complex cognitive structures found in the early development of infants and young children. — Lesson 8.1, Lesson 8.2, Lesson 8.3

IIIA-1.4 Apply life span principles to personal experience. — Lesson 9.1, Lesson 10.3

IIIA-2.1 Explain the distinguishing characteristics of the longitudinal and cross-sectional methods of study. — Lesson 8.1

IIIA-3.1 Explain various developmental models. — Lesson 8.2, Lesson 8.3, Lesson 9.2, Lesson 10.3

IIIA-3.2 Recognize how biological and cultural notions of gender shape the experiences of men and women. — Lesson 8.2, Lesson 10.2

IIIA-3.3 Examine the development of ethnic identity. — Lesson 9.2

IIIA-3.4 Explore developmental theories as they relate to cultural bias. — Lesson 8.2, Lesson 9.2, Lesson 10.1

IIIA-4.1 Describe the role of critical periods in development. — Lesson 10.1

Standard Area IIIB: Personality and Assessment

IIIB-1.1 Define personality as the individual's unique way of thinking, feeling, and acting. — Lesson 11.1, Lesson 11.2

IIIB-1.2 Explain the role of personality constructs as a framework for organizing behavioral phenomena. — Lesson 11.1, Lesson 11.2

IIIB-2.1 Explain the characteristics of the psychodynamic, cognitive-behavioral, humanistic, and trait approaches. — Lesson 11.1, Lesson 11.2

IIIB-2.2 Identify important contributions to the understanding of personality. — Lesson 11.1

IIIB-3.1 Distinguish between objective and projective techniques of personality assessment. — Lesson 11.3

IIIB-3.2 Describe tests used in personality assessment. — Lesson 11.3

IV. COGNITIVE DOMAIN
Standard Area IVA: Learning

IVA-1.1 Discuss learning from a psychological viewpoint. — Lesson 12.1, Lesson 12.2

IVA-1.2 Recognize learning as a vehicle to promote adaptation through experience. — Lesson 12.1, Lesson 12.2, Lesson 12.3

IVA-2.1 Describe the classical conditioning paradigm. — Lesson 12.1

IVA-3.1 Describe the operant conditioning paradigm. — Lesson 12.2

IVA-4.1 Explain how observational learning works. — Lesson 12.3

IVA-4.2 Describe cognitive learning approaches. — Lesson 12.2

IVA-5.1 Identify biological contributions to learning. — Lesson 12.1, Lesson 12.2

IVA-5.2 Speculate on the role of culture in determining what behaviors will be learned. — Lesson 12.1, Lesson 12.2, Lesson 12.3

| IVA-5.3 | Explore how biological and cultural factors interact to impede or enhance learning. | Lesson 12.2, Lesson 12.3 |
| IVA-5.4 | Describe the collaborative nature of some forms of learning within cultures. | Lesson 12.3 |

Standard Area IVB: Memory

IVB-1.1	Characterize the difference between surface and deep elaborate processing.	Lesson 13.1
IVB-1.2	Identify other factors that influence encoding.	Lesson 13.1, Lesson 13.2
IVB-2.1	Describe the operation of sensory memory.	Lesson 13.1
IVB-2.2	Describe the operation of short-term memory and working memory.	Lesson 13.1
IVB-2.3	Describe the operation of long-term memory.	Lesson 13.1, Lesson 13.2
IVB-3.1	Analyze the importance of retrieval cues in memory.	Lesson 13.2
IVB-3.2	Explain the role that interference plays in retrieval.	Lesson 13.3
IVB-3.3	Relate difficulties created by reconstructive memory processes.	Lesson 13.2
IVB-4.1	Identify the brain structures most important to memory.	Lesson 13.2, Lesson 13.3
IVB-5.1	Identify factors that interfere with memory.	Lesson 13.2
IVB-5.2	Describe strategies for improving memory based on our understanding of memory.	Lesson 13.2
IVB-6.1	Describe the processes that lead to inaccuracies in memory.	Lesson 13.2

Standard Area IVC: Thinking and Language

IVC-1.1	Define thinking as a mental process involved in the manipulation and understanding of information.	Lesson 14.3
IVC-1.2	Recognize that information is classified into categories containing similar properties known as concepts.	Lesson 14.3
IVC-2.1	Identify problem solving as a directed and productive example of thinking.	Lesson 14.3
IVC-2.2	Explain the use of creative thinking in problem solving.	Lesson 14.3, Lesson 16.2
IVC-2.3	Analyze the obstacles that inhibit problem solving and decision making.	Lesson 14.3
IVC-3.1	Define language as symbols and sounds that convey meaning and facilitate communication.	Lesson 14.1
IVC-3.2	Recognize that language is organized in a hierarchical structure.	Lesson 14.1
IVC-4.1	Discuss the effects of development on language acquisition.	Lesson 14.2
IVC-4.2	Evaluate the theories of language acquisition.	Lesson 14.1, Lesson 14.2
IVC-4.3	Speculate on whether animals acquire and use language.	Lesson 14.1
IVC-5.1	Examine the influence of language on thought and behavior.	Lesson 14.1

Standard Area IVD: States of Consciousness

IVD-1.1	Define states of consciousness.	Lesson 15.1
IVD-1.2	Describe levels of consciousness.	Lesson 15.1
IVD-2.1	Describe the sleep cycle.	Lesson 15.2
IVD-2.2	Compare theories that explain why we sleep.	Lesson 15.2
IVD-2.3	Assess types of sleep disorders.	Lesson 15.2
IVD-3.1	Demonstrate an understanding of individual differences in dream content and recall.	Lesson 15.2
IVD-3.2	Compare different theories about the use and meaning of dreams.	Lesson 15.2

IVD-4.1   Describe several hypnotic phenomena.   Lesson 15.3

IVD-4.2   Explain possible uses of hypnosis in psychology.   Lesson 15.3

IVD-5.1   Characterize the major categories of psychoactive drugs and their effects.   Lesson 15.4

IVD-5.2   Evaluate the effects of narcotic, depressant, stimulant, and hallucinogenic drugs. Lesson 15.4

Standard Area IVE: Individual Differences

IVE-1.1   Define and understand the nature of test constructs, such as intelligence,
          personality, and creativity.   Lesson 16.1, Lesson 16.2

IVE-1.2   Describe basic statistical concepts in testing.   Lesson 16.1

IVE-2.1   Explain how intelligence and personality may be influenced by heredity and
          environment.   Lesson 16.3

IVE-3.1   Link intelligence to the use of cognitive skills and strategies.   Lesson 16.1

IVE-3.2   Describe theories of intelligence.   Lesson 16.2

IVE-4.1   Explain why intelligence tests predict achievement.   Lesson 16.1

IVE-4.2   Explain issues of using conventional intelligence tests.   Lesson 16.1

V. VARIATIONS IN INDIVIDUAL AND GROUP BEHAVIOR DOMAIN
STANDARD AREA VA: PSYCHOLOGICAL DISORDERS

VA-1.1   Distinguish the common characteristics of abnormal behavior.   Lesson 17.1

VA-1.2   Cite examples of abnormal behavior.   Lesson 17.1, Lesson 17.2,
                                                                                              Lesson 17.3

VA-1.3   Relate judgments of abnormality to contexts in which those judgments occur.   Lesson 17.1

VA-1.4   Describe major explanations for the origins of abnormality.   Lesson 17.1

VA-2.1   Identify the purpose of different research methods.   Lesson 2.2

VA-3.1   Discuss major categories of abnormal behavior.   Lesson 17.2, Lesson 17.3

VA-3.2   Explore the challenges associated with accurate diagnosis.   Lesson 17.2, Lesson 17.3

VA-4.1   Consider factors that influence vulnerability to abnormal behavior.   Lesson 17.2

VA-4.2   Discuss the stigma associated with abnormal behavior.   Lesson 17.1

VA-4.3   Speculate about means for promoting greater understanding
         of abnormal behavior.   Lesson 17.1

Standard Area VB: Treatment of Psychological Disorders

VB-1.1   Describe availability and appropriateness of various modes of treatment
         for individuals with psychological disorders.   Lesson 18.1, Lesson 18.2,
                                                                                              Lesson 18.3

VB-1.2   Describe characteristics of effective treatment and prevention.   Lesson 18.2, Lesson 18.3

VB-2.1   Identify therapists according to training.   Lesson 18.1

VB-2.2   Describing strategies for locating appropriate therapists.   Lesson 18.1

VB-3.1   Describe the intersection between mental health and law.   Lesson 17.3

VB-3.2   Examine the influence of ethics and professional practice.   Lesson 2.1

APA NATIONAL STANDARDS CHART

Standard Area VC: Social and Cultural Dimensions of Behavior

VC-1.1	Demonstrate an understanding of person perception.	Lesson 19.1
VC-1.2	Describe how attributions affect our explanations of behavior.	Lesson 19.1
VC-1.3	Identify sources of attitude formation.	Lesson 19.2, Lesson 20.1
VC-1.4	Assess some methods used to change attitudes.	Lesson 19.2
VC-2.1	Identify basic social and cultural categories.	Lesson 1.2, Lesson 20.3
VC-2.2	Discuss how social and cultural categories affect behavior.	Lesson 20.1
VC-3.1	Describe effects of the presence of others on individual behavior.	Lesson 19.3
VC-3.2	Describe how social structure can affect intergroup relations.	Lesson 20.3
VC-3.3	Explore the nature and effects of bias and discrimination.	Lesson 19.1, Lesson 20.3
VC-3.4	Describe circumstances under which conformity and obedience are likely to occur.	Lesson 20.1
VC-3.5	Discuss the nature of altruism in society.	Lesson 19.3
VC-3.6	Discuss the significance of aggression.	Lesson 19.3
VC-3.7	Discuss factors influencing attraction.	Lesson 19.1

CH	Page(s)	ELP Standard	Essential Question	Activity
1	17	1-B-1	Are the groups you belong to more like a collectivist society or an individualist society?	By studying the language of a society, we can often tell whether the society is collectivist or individualist. For example, in an individualist society, words or phrases often used might include "independence, personal goals, subjective opinion, my thoughts," and so on. In a collectivist society, words or phrases often used might include "group, conformity, group goals, social assembly," and so on. Identify whether your first language reflects a collectivist or individualist society. Justify your answer, citing specific words or phrases and their meaning. Prepare a short speech that explains how the words you chose reflect either a collectivist or individualist society.
2	34, 38	1-A-2	Think of a situation where you observed a human behavior or an environmental phenomenon. What scientific method would you use to explain or examine that situation? Would your examination be observational, correlational or experimental?	Practice naturalistic observation (a form of observational research) in your school. Observe student behavior in a situation such as the school cafeteria or at a school-sponsored event. Record your observations, and then use your critical thinking skills to draw conclusions about the behavior of the students. Write a short report that explains your conclusions and how you reached them.
3	73, 85	2-C-1, 2-C-2	Do you think if identical twins raised in the same family were asked to conduct specific tasks (such as reading or talking) during a positron emission tomography (PET) scan, the results would add to the validity of the argument for nature, for nurture, neither, or both?	Using the language of a psychologist and scientist, justify your opinion in a paper with information from the text and supported by research on nature versus nurture. Cite at least one source in addition to the text. Research can be either from the library or Internet. Make sure your source is a valid and reliable scientific and/or educational source.
4	97, 99, 105	2-D-1	Why is sensory adaptation important to you when you study?	Pay attention to what you are doing right now and describe in a few sentences the sensations you are experiencing. Include sensations from all five senses and your body position and movement. Include the colors of the electromagnetic energy your brain perceives, the sound waves your auditory system perceives, the temperature your skin feels, etc. Develop a chart that lists each sense, body position, and sensation. Add a column that describes the absolute threshold of each stimulus. Compare your chart with that of at least one other classmate.

CH	Page(s)	ELP Standard	Essential Question	Activity
5	129, 139	4-F-6	How might perpetual sets from your culture of origin influence where you shop, what you like to eat, or whether or not you can experience extrasensory perception (ESP)?	Before watching the news tonight or reading a newspaper or Internet news, sit in a quiet place and take a couple deep and relaxing breaths. Give yourself the suggestion that you want to know something newsworthy that will be reported on the news. Allow your thoughts to wander until something seems to clarify itself. It may be that you have a sense or a thought of something or you may experience a visual sense of something. Jot down a few notes about your experience, and then watch or read the news to see if your ESP is correct. Do you think your perpetual set of ideas about ESP influenced your experiment? How? Discuss your findings with a student from a culture of origin different from yours.
6	167	4-G-4	What physiological changes do your emotions produce?	Spend an entire day paying attention to your emotions and the physiological sensations that accompany those emotions. Take notes that record your experiences. Include in your notes (1) the time of day, (2) the emotion, (3) the situation that provoked the emotion, and (4) your physical response to the emotion. Be prepared to discuss your findings in class.
7	183, 191, 201	3-C-4	Do you think there is a correlation between life-changing events, such as moving to a new country and learning a new language, and stress on the body?	Make a list of the things that cause stress in your life. Then develop a piece of art (drawing or something three-dimensional) that depicts your body's reaction to the stressors including any illnesses caused by stress, any psychological reactions you experienced such as problems focusing, and how you managed the stress such as your social support and/or your exercise program. Be prepared to give a short presentation about your visual to the class.
8	233	2-D-2	How have you used both assimilation and accommodation in this class?	During class lectures and interactions, make a list of any terms from this chapter that are unfamiliar to you and with which you need clarification. Look up each term in the text or a dictionary. Using your own words, write a short definition for the term. Then use the term in a sentence that shows you understand the meaning.
9	257	3-C-3	Which level of Kohlberg's stages of moral development are you now experiencing?	Write a short biography that describes the difference between your life as an adolescent and as an adult. Use information from the text to distinguish the two. Include information such as the difference between the physical and social aspects of your life; how your emotions and self-confidence have grown; your moral development; and how your personal and ethnic development has changed. Present a short summary of your biography to the class.

CH	Page(s)	ELP Standard	Essential Question	Activity
10	289	3-F-1	How do different cultures view the aging process?	Compare and contrast the cultural view of aging from the point of view of your culture of origin with that of your adopted country. Prepare a short speech that describes the similarities and differences. Deliver the speech to your classmates.
11	307, 316	2-E-3	According to psychoanalytic theories of personality, how does the unconscious mind shape behavior?	Create a pamphlet that explains Sigmund Freud's psychoanalytic theory and Carl Jung's analytic theory. Use illustrations to support the print information in your pamphlet. Create your pamphlet with or without the aid of computer software.
12	339, 362	2-I-5	What types of learning play a part in adjusting to life in a new country?	Use the notes you took in class on this chapter to develop an overview lesson to teach the material to another person. Include information on Pavlov's research; the principles of classical conditioning; classical conditioning in everyday behavior; the principles of reinforcement; the principles of punishment; the reinforcement schedule; the social learning theory; and observational learning of aggression.
13	381	4-F-7	What is the difference between explicit and implicit memory?	Develop a mnemonic for each key word and concept in this chapter to help you remember the key words and concepts. When designing your mnemonic, use places that will help you remember the word or concept and its meaning and/or key points. For example, to remember the storage memory process, you might create a storage bin that when opened you remember that storage is a memory process in which information is entered and maintained in memory for a period of time. Discuss your mnemonic with other students to help each other develop this memory system.
14	410	3-D-1, 3-D-2	Does language determine thinking?	Write a commercial for one of your favorite products that uses only generic masculine language, and then rewrite the same commercial that uses alternative gender-neutral terms. Deliver your commercial to another student or to the class. Make sure your nonverbal communication matches your message.
15	454	3-G-1	What is the effect of alcohol and other drugs on the human body and mind?	Use computer software or markers and poster board to create a poster that explains the effects of the various psychoactive drugs on the human body.

CH	Page(s)	ELP Standard	Essential Question	Activity
16	475	3-G-2	What types of intelligences did Howard Gardner identify in his theory of multiple intelligences?	Write an editorial that expresses your opinion and ideas about the value of education to intelligence. Refer to the types of intelligences Gardner identified in his theory of multiple intelligence. Be prepared to read and defend your editorial in class.
17	501, 506, 518	2-I-4	What are psychological disorders?	Using index cards, write the key terms from this chapter on one side and the corresponding definition on the other. Do the same with key concepts. Test your knowledge of the chapter by reading the front of a card, and then providing the definition of the key word or explanation of the key concept. Now turn the card over and check your answer. Pair up with a classmate and do the activity together by one partner showing the other the front of a card. The second partner has to provide the answer. Partners then trade roles.
18	533, 541, 546	2-C-3, 2-C-4	What are the three main mental health professionals, and what does each one do?	Imagine you are a psychologist who is the leader for group therapy that meets for depression. Your job is to provide information about the different types of therapies available to individuals in the group. Using the key terms and key concepts from this chapter as guidelines, write a dialogue with group members asking questions and you providing answers.
19	563	3-F-2	How does physical appearance affect your impressions of others?	Using magazine photographs or those downloaded from the Internet, collect 10 or 12 different photos that depict the physical attractiveness stereotype from your culture of origin and that of men and women in your adopted country. Using key terms from this chapter, write a short speech about your conclusions, including how your attitudes—and those of others—have been formed. Prepare to give your speech in class.
20	591	3-H-3	How do conformity, compliance, and obedience differ?	Imagine you are the leader of a group that was formed to speak to high school students about breaking the prejudice habit. Write an article that explains how you will lead the group to help high school students understand the power of social influence and conformity. Be prepared to narrate your article in class.

Methods Domain

How do your friends and parents react when they learn that you are taking a psychology course? Based on many people's strong interest in "pop psychology" TV talk shows and self-help books, some of your friends and family members probably are wondering what you might learn in the coming months. Other people might dismiss psychology as merely "warmed-over common sense."

One reason some people think of psychology as simply a restating of common knowledge is that it studies topics that are very personal and familiar. You think about your own thoughts, feelings, and actions and those of others. Yet, what is different about the way psychologists learn about human behavior compared to your everyday observations? The first two chapters in this book will look at how the scientific theories and methods used in psychology are both similar to and different from the analysis you use on yourself every day.

Introduction to Psychology

ESSENTIAL QUESTION
Go to page XXIV

"A journey of a thousand miles starts from beneath one's feet."

—LAO-TSU, 6TH CENTURY B.C., CHINESE PHILOSOPHER

DIGITAL VISION/GETTY IMAGES

As the studio audience applauded, Oprah Winfrey stood squarely facing the camera and emphatically stated: "Short men! Short men! What do you think of them? . . . Today I'm going to talk to short men who have felt insecure about their height at different times in their lives. . . . And we will also talk to a social psychologist who studies the effect of height on a man's self-esteem."

Why was I a guest on *The Oprah Winfrey Show*? In the way of an answer, let me describe a bit of what happened on the show. The three short male guests were all outgoing, seemingly well-adjusted adults who had been shunned, taunted, and discriminated against throughout their lives due to their short stature.

My role on the show was being the expert psychologist, providing scientific insight into why these men were sometimes treated badly and how they reacted to this discrimination. At one point I mentioned that research suggests that women in our society prefer to date men who are about four inches taller than themselves. After this comment, Oprah responded, "There's a psychological feeling of protection when the guy is taller . . . We admit it, it's a terrible thing. But if I date a shorter guy I feel like I'm his mother!" A female audience member agreed and disclosed that, "I like to hug 'up' rather than hug 'down.'" Sharply challenging these comments, another woman declared, "My husband is short and he has a great personality. It doesn't matter how tall you are!"

OBJECTIVES

- Define psychology.
- Identify and describe the early pioneers and schools of thought in psychology.

DISCOVER IT | *How does this relate to me?*

The value and the appeal of psychology is that it studies both the ordinary and extraordinary events of everyday living. Psychologists try to find answers to questions that you have undoubtedly thought about—or will think about—at some point in your life. You have probably wondered, for example, how your physical appearance—such as your height, age, or skin color—influences people's reactions to you. The science of psychology will not deliver the final and ultimate answers to life's wonders, but it can provide you with very useful information in your personal search for knowledge. In this text, you will learn how psychology has expanded understanding of how people think, feel, and behave. You will be encouraged to apply this knowledge to better understand yourself and others. This is your own journey of discovery.

KEY TERMS

- psychology
- psychiatry
- structuralism
- functionalism
- Gestalt psychology

Psychologists are considered experts on topics such as romance, attractiveness, prejudice, and mental health. My expertise in the psychology of physical appearance was the reason I was asked to appear on *The Oprah Winfrey Show*. My comments on the show were based on science, but the comments Oprah and the audience members made were not. Their comments were based on their opinions and experience. Up to now your exposure to psychology may come from television shows like *The Oprah Winfrey Show*. In this text, you will learn about psychology that is based on science. You will learn about many different people who represent psychology as it exists today. These psychologists seek to understand the human mind and behavior. Different from psychiatry, psychology has a long history of pioneers in different schools of thought with the same objective—to understand why you behave the way you do.

Psychology Defined

The term **psychology** comes from the Greek words *psyche*, meaning "mind," and *logos*, meaning "study." In its broadest sense, psychology is the scientific study of mental processes and behavior. This means that psychologists are interested in using scientific methods (see Chapter 2) to understand how we and other living creatures think, feel, and act.

People often confuse psychology with **psychiatry**, which is a branch of medicine concerned with the diagnosis and treatment of psychological disorders. Psychiatry is practiced by physicians. Psychology also deals with the diagnosis and treatment of such disorders (see Chapters 17 and 18), but this is only one area of specialization in psychology. Psychology has a much broader scope than psychiatry. Whereas psychiatrists go to medical schools for their training and obtain the M.D. (doctor of medicine), psychologists attend graduate schools in psychology and obtain the Ph.D. (doctor of philosophy) or, in some cases, the Psy.D. (doctor of psychology).

CHECKPOINT *What is psychology?*

Early Pioneers and Schools of Thought

Many people have contributed to the development of psychology, and any history of the discipline will omit some of those who made valuable contributions. In the following text, you will be introduced to the individuals who have been ranked by prominent historians as some of the most important psychologists of all time and the schools of thought they founded.

STRUCTURALISM

Most historians identify Wilhelm Wundt (pronounced "Vill-helm Voont," 1832–1920) as the "world's first psychologist." In 1879, Wundt established the first institute for research in experimental psychology at the University of Leipzig in Germany. Over the next 40 years, more than 100 students obtained doctoral degrees in psychology under his supervision. Wundt's research focused on the study of consciousness by having specially trained observers report on the contents of their own current conscious experiences. His approach to studying consciousness was called **structuralism** because it tried to identify the basic parts, or structure, of the conscious mind.

In studying the mind's structure, Wundt used a procedure called *introspection* in which trained observers would look at, smell, or touch something and then try to describe in detail what they were experiencing. Unfortunately for Wundt, introspection and structuralism did not lead to any lasting scientific discoveries. Despite this fact, Wundt's influence on the first generation of psychologists was far reaching. In fact, most psychologists today still have a connection to him through their

psychology The scientific study of mental processes and behavior

psychiatry A branch of medicine concerned with the diagnosis and treatment of psychological disorders

structuralism An early approach to psychology that tried to identify the basic parts, or structure, of the conscious mind

professors who were educated by someone who was, in turn, educated by one of Wundt's students.

FUNCTIONALISM

In the United States, the first important psychologist to influence the young science of psychology was William James (1842–1910). Although both James and Wundt studied consciousness, James was not interested in identifying the structure of the mind. Instead he was interested in discovering how the conscious mind works to help humans survive in their environment. James's approach to psychology was called **functionalism**. Functionalism did lead to some important insights into different areas of psychology. In Chapter 6, for example, you will examine James's theory of how our emotions help us survive.

ARCHIVES OF THE HISTORY OF AMERICAN PSYCHOLOGY—THE UNIVERSITY OF AKRON

ARCHIVES OF THE HISTORY OF AMERICAN PSYCHOLOGY—THE UNIVERSITY OF AKRON

Wilhelm Wundt (left), the founder of psychology

William James (right), the first major American psychologist

GESTALT PSYCHOLOGY

In Germany, Max Wertheimer (1880–1943), criticized Wundt and structuralism for trying to understand the mind by identifying and analyzing its individual parts. Instead Wertheimer argued that "the whole is different from the sum of its parts." This means that your perceptions are not the result of your mind simply responding to a combination of individual elements, or stimuli. Instead your mind actively organizes these elements into a meaningful whole, or gestalt. *Gestalt* is a German word that means "shape" or "form." Based on this idea of the mind, Wertheimer developed a third approach to psychology. His approach is called **Gestalt psychology**, which is an approach to psychology that studies how the mind actively organizes stimuli into meaningful wholes.

As an example of how the mind organizes stimuli into a gestalt, look at the four dots in Figure 1-1a on the following page. Most people perceive the dots as corners of an invisible square rather than as separate objects. Do you? When three of the dots are increased in size in Figure 1-1b, most people see the configuration of a triangle and a separate dot. This dot example illustrates how your perceptions emerge as understandable wholes, not separate, meaningless parts. Besides creating new ways of thinking about perception (see Chapter 5, p. 121), Gestalt psychology also

functionalism An early approach to psychology that tried to discover how the conscious mind works to help humans survive in their environment

Gestalt psychology An early approach to psychology that studied how the mind actively organizes stimuli into meaningful wholes

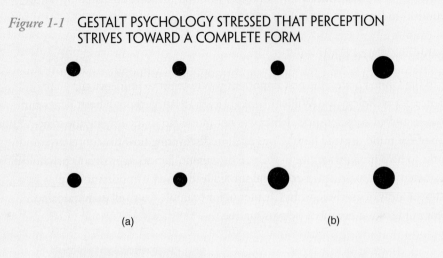

Figure 1-1 GESTALT PSYCHOLOGY STRESSED THAT PERCEPTION STRIVES TOWARD A COMPLETE FORM

(a) These four dots are likely to be perceived as a square. (b) However, if three of the dots become twice as big while the fourth remains the same size, the four dots are likely to be perceived as a triangle (of larger dots) and a single dot.

(a)

(b)

analyzed learning, problem solving, and social behavior. This early school of thought was influential in the later development of cognitive psychology. This is the branch of psychology concerned with the study of mental states.

WOMEN AND CULTURALLY DIVERSE PIONEERS

During the first 75 years of psychology's existence, women and minorities generally were prevented from becoming psychologists because of the prejudice and discrimination within the larger society. Those women and people from culturally diverse backgrounds who were fortunate enough to pursue careers in psychology often had to rely on outdated equipment and rundown laboratories to conduct their research. Despite such obstacles, many people made valuable contributions to the development of psychology.

Mary Whiton Calkins is a woman who faced prejudice and discrimination. She completed all requirements for a Ph.D. at Harvard University in 1895. Yet despite a unanimous recommendation by William James and her other professors, Calkins's doctorate was denied because the university did not grant degrees to women. Instead, Harvard offered Calkins a Ph.D. from its "sister college," Radcliffe. She declined the degree, stating that accepting it would mean that she also accepted the college's discriminatory policies. Pursuing the few career paths open to her, Calkins became a professor at all-female Wellesley College. There, she established one of the first psychology laboratories in the United States where she pioneered research in short-term memory. In 1905 she became the first woman president of the American Psychological Association.

Despite similar levels of discrimination against psychologists of culturally diverse heritages during these early years, a number of individuals overcame these obstacles and made significant contributions to psychology. For example, in 1920 J. Henry Alston, an African American, discovered how people sense heat and cold from their skin receptors (see Chapter 4, p. 111).

In the 1930s and 1940s, Kenneth Clark and Mamie Phipps Clark made groundbreaking research in the field of social psychology. Their study of the self-concepts of African American children provided the scientific justification for the U.S. Supreme Court to end the practice of racially segregated education (check out the Closer Look feature on page 10). In 1971 Kenneth Clark became the first African American president of the American Psychological Association.

Hispanic psychologists have also made many important contributions. George Sanchez, a Latin American, was an early critic of using culturally biased psychological tests in assessing minority school children. John Garcia, also a Latin American, pioneered research on taste aversion in the 1960s (see Chapter 12, p. 346).

Today in the United States almost half of all psychologists holding doctoral degrees are women, and they make up two-thirds of all new Ph.D.s. Also, members of culturally diverse groups now account for 16 percent of the new doctoral degrees earned each year. Today, many women and ethnic minorities have important leadership positions within psychology. Some of you reading this textbook will be part of this new and diverse generation of psychologists.

CHECKPOINT *Who were three pioneers in psychology, and what schools of thought did they develop?*

ARCHIVES OF THE HISTORY OF AMERICAN PSYCHOLOGY—THE UNIVERSITY OF AKRON

LIBRARY OF CONGRESS, KENNETH BANCROFT CLARK COLLECTION [LC-USZ62-115760]

Mary Whiton Calkins (left) was the first female president of the American Psychological Association.

Kenneth and Mamie Clark (right) were instrumental in shaping the U.S. Supreme Court's 1954 decision to integrate the nation's educational institutions.

Two Psychologists Helped Desegregate Schools in the United States

In the 1930s and 1940s, psychologists Kenneth Clark and Mamie Phipps Clark used different colored dolls to measure African American children's racial awareness and preferences. In interviews with children ranging in age from 3 to 7, the Clarks showed each child two dolls—one with light-colored skin and one with dark-colored skin. Then the Clarks made the following requests:

Give me the doll that you want to play with.

Give me the doll that is a nice doll.

Give me the doll that looks bad.

Give me the doll that is a nice color.

The Clarks found that about two-thirds of the African American children preferred the white-colored doll. The children identified this doll as the "nice" doll, the doll with the "nice" color, and the doll they wanted to play with. For these children, the black-colored doll looked "bad" in comparison. These preferences occurred even though the children clearly understood that they themselves were members of the "black-colored" group. As Kenneth Clark later recalled:

> "What was surprising was the degree to which the children suffered from self-rejection. . . . I don't think we had quite realized the extent of the cruelty of racism and how hard it hit. . . . Some of these children, particularly in the North, were reduced to crying when presented with the dolls and asked to identify with them. They looked at me as if I were the devil for putting them in this predicament. Let me tell you, it was a traumatic experience for me as well." (Kluger, 1976, p. 400)

The sort of self-rejection that the Clarks found in the African American children was later cited by the U.S. Supreme Court as evidence that the cultural beliefs justifying racially segregated education were damaging to the self-esteem of African American children. The Court's 1954 *Brown vs. Board of Education* decision outlawed such segregation. The Clarks' research and its effect on American society is just one example of how psychologists have helped create positive changes in our world.

Think Critically

How did the Clarks' study help change the law in the United States?

In Your Own Words

Define psychology and discuss the school of thought of one of the psychologists mentioned in the text. For example, you may choose to write about William Wundt's research—structuralism—that focused on the study of consciousness by having specially trained observers report on the contents of their own current conscious experiences.

Review Concepts

1. Psychology is the scientific study of mental processes and behavior, whereas _____ is a branch of medicine concerned with the treatment of psychological disorders.

   a. structuralism   c. functionalism
   b. psychiatry   d. gerontology

2. Who was the world's first psychologist?

   a. Wolfgang Köhler   c. William James
   b. George Sanchez   d. Wilhelm Wundt

3. Who developed Gestalt psychology?

   a. Mary Whiton Calkins   c. Max Wertheimer
   b. John Garcia   d. Kenneth and Mamie Clark

4. **True or False** Women and people of culturally diverse heritages were readily accepted in the field of psychology in its early days.

5. **True or False** Kenneth and Mamie Clark were psychologists who helped change education in the United States.

6. **True or False** Psychologists are interested in using scientific methods to understand how humans, and other living creatures, think, feel, and act.

7. **True or False** Today in the United States almost half of all psychologists holding doctoral degrees are women, and they make up two-thirds of all new Ph.D.s.

Think Critically

8. Support the statement: You can better understand yourself through the study of psychology.

9. Analyze why Wilhelm Wundt has such an influence on modern-day psychologists.

10. Explain what Max Wertheimer meant by "the whole is different from the sum of its parts."

11. How did Harvard University discriminate against Mary Whiton Calkins?

12. Compare and contrast structuralism and functionalism.

Contemporary Perspectives and Areas of Specialization

KEY TERMS

- psychoanalysis
- behaviorism
- humanistic psychology
- positive psychology
- cognitive psychology
- psychobiology
- sociocultural psychology
- individualism
- collectivism

OBJECTIVES

- Identify and describe the current perspectives in psychology.
- Identify and describe the areas of specialization in psychology.

DISCOVER IT | *How does this relate to me?*

Consider the following situations: (1) You wake up after having a strange and interesting dream, wondering what could explain it. (2) You are confused why another classmate has ideas so different from your own. (3) You wonder whether some people can guess what you are thinking or feeling without you telling them. How might knowledge about psychology help you better understand these different experiences? As you will discover, there are a number of different perspectives and fields of specialization within psychology that could provide insights into many areas of your life.

Psychologists have different areas of specialization and follow different schools of thought. Their area of specialization might influence which school of thought they follow. A psychologist who works in your school district might follow a different school of thought than a psychologist who conducts research at a college or university. The school psychologist is more interested in how students behave in their environment. The research psychologist at a college or university might be more interested in understanding how biology plays a role in students' behavior.

Contemporary Perspectives

Some of the ideas developed by psychology's early pioneers are reflected in current schools of thought within modern psychology. The most important approaches to studying psychology today are psychoanalysis, behaviorism, humanistic psychology, cognitive psychology, psychobiology, and sociocultural psychology.

PSYCHOANALYSIS

An early pioneer in psychology, Sigmund Freud's ideas are still reflected in contemporary perspectives. Freud (1856–1939) was an Austrian physician trained as a neurologist. Because Freud was a physician, his proper title is "psychiatrist" and not "psychologist." Despite this technicality, psychology claims him as an important founder of one of the early schools of thought, **psychoanalysis**. This approach to psychology studies how human behavior is determined by hidden or unconscious motives and desires. Based on his work with patients who suffered from emotional problems, Freud developed his theory that all human behavior is determined by hidden or unconscious motives and desires. Psychoanalysis has provided important insights into such topics as dreams, childhood development, aggression, sexuality, creativity, motivation, personality, and psychotherapy.

Later psychoanalysts such as Carl Jung, Karen Horney, Alfred Adler, and Erik Erikson made their own important changes and modifications to Freud's original version of psychoanalysis. In its various modified forms, psychoanalysis remains a perspective that still has an influence in psychology, as you will discover throughout this text.

BEHAVIORISM

Just as psychoanalysis is closely associated with Sigmund Freud, so is behaviorism closely connected with John Watson (1878–1958). **Behaviorism** is an approach to psychology that studies observable behavior rather than hidden mental processes. Watson, an American researcher, studied rats, dogs, and other animals, which caused him to question the usefulness of studying the inner workings of the mind. Watson argued that psychology should instead study only behavior that could be directly observed. Watson's behaviorism sought to describe, explain, predict, and control behavior, while it criticized the "fuzziness" of the other scientific approaches within psychology. Behaviorism was most influential within psychology from the 1920s through the 1950s.

psychoanalysis An approach to psychology that studies how human behavior is determined by hidden or unconscious motives and desires

behaviorism An approach to psychology that studies observable behavior rather than hidden mental processes

INFOBIT
As a teenager, John Watson was a poor and disruptive student who was arrested twice by authorities. Then, at the age of 16, he talked his way into taking a psychology course at a local college and quickly fell in love with this new science. Watson is an excellent example of how the love of learning can dramatically change a person's life.

LIBRARY OF CONGRESS, SIGMUND FREUD COLLECTION, [LC-US262-72266]

ARCHIVES OF THE HISTORY OF AMERICAN PSYCHOLOGY—THE UNIVERSITY OF AKRON

Sigmund Freud (left), the founder of psychoanalysis

John Watson (right), the founder of behaviorism

B. F. Skinner's research found that people and other animals tend to repeat behaviors that are followed by positive consequences and avoid behaviors that bring negative consequences.

COURTESY OF B. F. SKINNER FOUNDATION

Another important psychologist who shaped behaviorism during the second half of the twentieth century was B. F. Skinner (1904–1990). Skinner stressed the role of consequences in controlling behavior. His research found that people and other animals tend to repeat behaviors that are followed by positive consequences and avoid behaviors that bring negative consequences. For example, if you are rewarded for being helpful, you are likely to repeat such actions in the future, but you are unlikely to do so if your helpfulness is punished.

HUMANISTIC PSYCHOLOGY

Because many psychologists were dissatisfied with both the psychoanalytic and the behaviorist views of human nature, a third force exerted its influence on psychology in the 1950s. This was **humanistic psychology**, which emphasizes people's inborn desire for personal growth and their ability to consciously make choices. Carl Rogers (1902–1987) and Abraham Maslow (1908–1970) were the primary developers of this perspective. Both argued—like William James before them—that psychology should study people's unique mental experience of the world. Humanistic psychology stresses the importance of positive life experiences in people's lives and the basic goodness of people. Both within psychology and throughout the larger culture, humanistic psychology has had a broad impact by stressing the important role that positive life experiences play in people's lives.

A relatively new approach related to humanistic psychology but that relies much more on rigorous scientific methods has emerged. This approach, called **positive psychology**, studies how people find mental health and happiness in their everyday living. Check out the Positive Psychology feature on the next page and look for this feature throughout this book to learn more about this new discipline.

humanistic psychology
An approach to psychology that emphasizes human beings' inborn desire for personal growth and their ability to consciously make choices

positive psychology
A relatively new approach to psychology that studies how people find mental health and happiness in their everyday living

What Is Positive Psychology?

Within the past 10 years, the insights of humanistic psychology have inspired a new generation of psychologists to develop a related scientific approach called positive psychology, which studies how people find mental health and happiness in their everyday living. Positive psychologists study what it means to be a well-adjusted person and what makes people happy and optimistic in their daily living. For example, when does a positive view of life help you overcome hurdles to success? When does an overly positive outlook cause you to ignore real problems that need your attention? How can you take positive steps to reach important life goals, reduce social injustice in the world, and improve your life and the lives of others? These are some of the questions positive psychology seeks to answer.

Throughout this text, information will be presented about positive psychology topics that relate to the chapter material. Much of the information will inform you about recent studies and theories coming directly from this new area of psychology. Other information will inform you about older studies that investigated the psychology of happiness and positive living before positive psychology was created as a separate psychological perspective.

Think Critically
How will reading about positive psychology help you in your daily life?

COGNITIVE PSYCHOLOGY

The word cognitive comes from the Latin for "to know." **Cognitive psychology** is a psychological approach that attempts to understand behavior by studying how the mind organizes and makes sense of information and experiences. For example, how do you remember a new friend's phone number? Or how do you decide whether a defendant is guilty or innocent while serving on a jury? Cognitive theories provide insights into these kinds of mental processes. Two leaders of cognitive psychology were George A. Miller, who made important discoveries in human memory, and Ulric Neisser, who coined the term *cognitive psychology* and wrote one of the first books in the field.

The rise of cognitive psychology occurred about the same time as the development of computer technology. Cognitive psychologists argued that the mind was like a computer. The mind, like a computer, receives input from the environment. It then transforms, stores, and later retrieves this input using a host of "programs," which then generate specific response outputs. Today this perspective provides valuable insights into many of the topics you will examine throughout this text.

cognitive psychology
An approach to psychology that studies how the mind organizes and makes sense of information and experiences

PSYCHOBIOLOGY

The development of new techniques and instruments allowed scientists to examine the brain and other biological structures. When technology opened the way for psychologists to study the biological origins of behavior, **psychobiology** became a new area of study. Psychobiology studies how the brain and other biological structures and substances influence behavior.

Psychobiologists do study humans, but a good deal of their research uses animals. Animals have simpler brains, but psychobiologists hope that the knowledge gained in the animal studies will lead to greater understanding of how humans think and behave. For example, researchers are attempting to better understand memory loss in Alzheimer's disease, which is the most common form of dementia, or loss of memory, in the elderly. A researcher grafts tissue from the brains of rat fetuses into the brains of elderly rats. If this procedure improves the older rats' memory, it may provide a crucial clue to curing Alzheimer's disease in humans. You will learn more about some of the discoveries uncovered by this biological approach in Chapter 3.

SOCIOCULTURAL PSYCHOLOGY

Sociocultural psychology examines how your social surroundings and culture shape your thinking and behavior. For example, social-cultural research indicates that you are often slower in reacting to dangerous situations when you are in a crowd than when you are alone because the presence of other people complicates your decision-making. Research also shows that your willingness to help others depends on what you learn from your culture. Your culture helps you determine who deserves help and who does not.

psychobiology An approach to psychology that studies how the brain and other areas of our biology influence behavior

sociocultural psychology An approach to psychology that studies how social surroundings and culture shape thinking and behavior

According to sociocultural research, why might you be slower in reacting to danger when in a crowd than when you are alone?

©FLASHON STUDIO, 2008/USED UNDER LICENSE FROM SHUTTERSTOCK.COM

One aspect of culture that has a great deal of importance in understanding the psychology of human behavior is the way in which people relate to groups within society. Some cultures tend to have an individualist orientation. **Individualism** is a philosophy of life stressing that personal goals are more important than group goals and that people should try to be relatively free of group influence. The United States, Canada, Australia, and many Western European nations are examples of countries with individualist cultures. This country's Declaration of Independence represents a bold statement that individual rights are more important than group rights. Commonly heard phrases such as, "The squeaky wheel gets the grease" and "Do your own thing" reflect individualist thinking.

In contrast to individualism, many cultures around the world have more of a collectivist orientation. **Collectivism** is a philosophy of life stressing that group needs are more important than individual needs and that people should be willing to submit to the influence of their group. Asian, African, and Latin and South American nations tend to have a collectivist orientation. In Japan a popular phrase is, "The nail that sticks up shall be hammered down." Currently 70 percent of the world's population lives in cultures that have a collectivist orientation. Table 1-1 lists some of the differences between these two philosophies of life.

individualism A philosophy of life stressing that the individual is more important than the group

collectivism A philosophy of life stressing that the group is more important than the individual

Table 1-1 DIFFERENCES BETWEEN COLLECTIVIST AND INDIVIDUALIST CULTURES

Collectivist Cultures	Individualist Cultures
Identity is given by one's group.	Identity is achieved by one's own striving.
Individuals are socialized to be emotionally dependent on their social group, and conformity is valued.	Individuals are socialized to be emotionally independent of their social group, and independence is valued.
Personal and group goals are generally consistent; when inconsistent, group goals have priority.	Personal and group goals are often inconsistent; when inconsistent, personal goals have priority.
Trust is placed in group decisions.	Trust is placed in individual decisions.

Although cultures differ in their individualist–collectivist philosophies, one is not necessarily better than the other. Later in this text you will examine how the psychology of people from different cultures affect their behavior. For example, in Unit 3 you will discover that within collectivist societies, child-rearing practices tend to emphasize conformity, obedience, and knowing one's proper place. In more individualist societies, parents stress independence and self-reliance.

 **CHECKPOINT** *What are the six main contemporary perspectives within psychology?*

Are Individualist or Collectivist Values More Important to You?

Directions: Listed below are 12 values. Please rank them in their order of importance to you, with "1" being the "most important" and "12" being the "least important."

1. Pleasure (Satisfying Desires)
2. Honor of Parents and Elders (Showing Respect)
3. Creativity (Uniqueness, Imagination)
4. Social Order (Stability of Society)
5. A Varied Life (Filled with Challenge and Change)
6. National Security (Protection of My Nation from Enemies)
7. Being Daring (Seeking Adventure, Risk)
8. Self-discipline (Self-control, Resisting Temptation)
9. Freedom (Freedom of Action and Thought)
10. Politeness (Courtesy, Good Manners)
11. Independence (Self-reliance, Choice of Own Goals)
12. Obedience (Following Orders, Meeting Obligations)

See page 27 for scoring instructions.

Think Critically

Does your ranking of these values fit this pattern? If you know someone from another culture, how do they rank these values?

DIGITAL VISION/GETTY IMAGES

Areas of Specialization in Psychology

Now that you have learned something about the different schools of thought within psychology, you might be wondering who employs psychologists and what they do in these jobs. About one-fourth of all psychologists who received their Ph.D.s during the past 25 years are employed at colleges, universities, or institutes where they teach and conduct research in their areas of specialization (see Figure 1-2). Their goals are to acquire psychological knowledge through scientific methods and to teach this knowledge to students. Six areas of specialization for these research psychologists are as follows:

1. **Biopsychology** (also called *psychobiology*)   Studies behavior by examining biological processes, especially those occurring in the brain

2. **Developmental psychology**   Studies how people mature and change physically, cognitively, and socially throughout the life span

3. **Experimental psychology**   Studies basic psychological processes such as sensation, perception, learning, motivation, emotion, and states of consciousness

4. **Cognitive psychology**   Studies all aspects of thinking, including problem solving, decision making, memory, reasoning, and language

5. **Personality psychology**   Studies how people are influenced by relatively stable internal traits

6. **Social psychology**   Studies how people are influenced by others

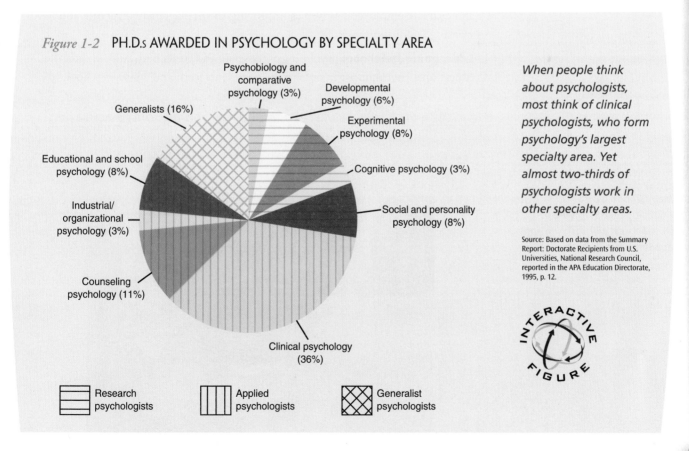

Figure 1-2 PH.D.s AWARDED IN PSYCHOLOGY BY SPECIALTY AREA

Psychobiology and comparative psychology (3%)

Developmental psychology (6%)

Generalists (16%)

Experimental psychology (8%)

Educational and school psychology (8%)

Cognitive psychology (3%)

Industrial/organizational psychology (3%)

Social and personality psychology (8%)

Counseling psychology (11%)

Clinical psychology (36%)

Research psychologists

Applied psychologists

Generalist psychologists

When people think about psychologists, most think of clinical psychologists, who form psychology's largest specialty area. Yet almost two-thirds of psychologists work in other specialty areas.

Source: Based on data from the Summary Report: Doctorate Recipients from U.S. Universities, National Research Council, reported in the APA Education Directorate, 1995, p. 12.

INTERACTIVE FIGURE

Psychology Specialties

With a partner, choose one of the specializations in psychology as described in this section. Use the library or Internet to research this field of psychology, and then make an illustrated chart that lists information about this field.

In addition to psychologists within these six areas, a little more than half the psychologists who received their Ph.D.s during the past 25 years have careers in specialty areas where they use existing psychological knowledge to solve and prevent problems (refer back to Figure 1-2). These applied psychologists most often work in mental health centers, schools, industries, governmental agencies, or private practice. Four major applied specialties include:

1. **Clinical psychology** Diagnoses and treats people with psychological disorders, such as depression and schizophrenia.

2. **Counseling psychology** Diagnoses and treats people with personal problems that do not involve psychological disorders, including marriage counseling, social skills training, and career planning.

3. **Industrial–organizational psychology** Focuses on ways to select, motivate, and evaluate employees, as well as improving the management structure and working conditions.

4. **Educational and school psychology** Assesses and treats both students and the educational environment in order to help students learn and adjust in school.

CHECKPOINT *What are the 10 major areas of specialization within psychology?*

Many schools have a psychologist on staff who helps students deal with learning and adjustment issues.

LIQUIDLIBRARY/JUPITER IMAGES

1.2 ASSESSMENT

In Your Own Words

Choose one of the contemporary perspectives in psychology and write about the most important points of that approach to studying psychology. Include the founder's name if one is given. For example, you could write your essay on Sigmund Freud and psychoanalysis.

Review Concepts

1. Which is an approach to psychology that studies observable behavior rather than hidden mental processes?
   - a. psychoanalysis
   - b. humanistic psychology
   - c. behaviorism
   - d. cognitive psychology

2. Which attempts to understand behavior by studying how the mind organizes and makes sense of information and experiences?
   - a. psychoanalysis
   - b. positive psychology
   - c. cognitive psychology
   - d. sociocultural psychology

3. Which of the four major applied specialties in psychology diagnoses and treats people with personal problems that do not involve psychological disorders?
   - a. counseling
   - b. clinical
   - c. industrial–organizational
   - d. educational

4. Which approach studies how human behavior is determined by hidden or unconscious motives and desires?
   - a. behaviorism
   - b. psychoanalysis
   - c. humanistic psychology
   - d. sociocultural psychology

5. **True or False** Behaviorism is closely associated with Sigmund Freud.

6. **True or False** Psychobiology studies behavior by examining biological processes, especially those occurring in the brain.

7. **True or False** Positive psychology studies why people are so unhappy.

8. **True or False** Humanistic psychology emphasizes people's inborn desire for personal growth and their ability to make choices consciously.

Think Critically

9. Why are dreams and early childhood trauma important to psychoanalysis?

10. In what ways might your own life be affected by sociocultural psychology?

11. What do B.F. Skinner and John Watson have in common?

12. Do you believe Rogers and Maslow are correct in their approach? Explain your answer.

Who Is Happy and Why?

INTRODUCTION In 1776, Thomas Jefferson wrote in our country's Declaration of Independence that everybody has the inalienable rights of life, liberty, and "the pursuit of happiness." While Americans have the right to pursue happiness, are we any happier than people from other countries? If so, what are some of the causes of these differences? Positive psychologists have been trying to find answers to these questions.

HYPOTHESIS Money will only have a positive effect on happiness in countries where citizens do not have enough of it to cover their basic needs.

METHOD Psychologists David Myers and Ed Diener (1995) conducted research in 24 countries, with some countries being poor and others being relatively rich.

RESULTS As you can see in the figure below, people in richer countries were happier than people in poorer countries. Yet additional research finds that the happiness differences between wealthy and middle-income people are very small, with wealthy people being only a little happier. This research suggests that money increases happiness only if you do not have enough of it to cover your basic needs of food, safety, and shelter. Once you meet your basic needs, increasing your wealth does not make you much happier. In fact, those who still strongly desire wealth are relatively unhappy. Perhaps placing too much importance on worldly possessions takes time and energy away from friends and family who ultimately determine most people's happiness levels.

Critical Analysis

Do you need an abundance of money to make you happy? Why or why not?

Gross National Product and Happiness

In a 24-nation study, happiness was related to a country's overall wealth. Additional research suggests that money has an effect on happiness only if people do not have enough of it to cover their basic needs. After meeting basic needs, those who still strongly desire wealth tend to be relatively unhappy.

Source: Myers, D., & Diener, E. (1995). Who is Happy? *Psychological Science, 6*, 10–19. Reprinted by permission of Blackwell Publishing Ltd.

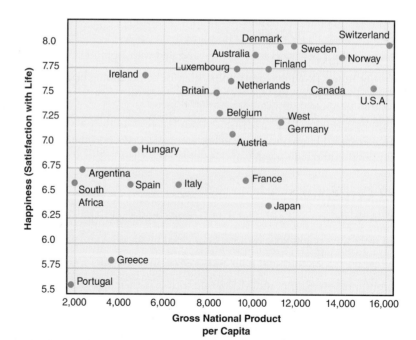

Forensic Psychologist

Television shows have made the work of forensic psychologists well known. Working for the FBI—or other law enforcement agencies—forensic psychologists in these shows study the actions of criminals, and then create a psychological profile that helps police catch the person who has committed the crime. Although this is the best-known job in this career, it is not the only one.

Forensic psychologists use their knowledge and understanding of people's behavior in many areas of the criminal justice system. They may work with defense attorneys to determine whether a defendant was insane at the time the crime took place; they may be asked to judge the competence of a defendant's ability to stand trial; or they may be asked to help attorneys select a jury.

Psychologists in this career may study how prison conditions affect inmates; treat mentally ill inmates; analyze inmates' criminal minds in order to apprehend other criminals or to help stop future criminal acts. The court may ask the forensic psychologist to counsel someone who was involved in a vehicle accident; teach anger management classes; or counsel juveniles on probation.

Other areas open to forensic psychologists include teaching in colleges and universities and research.

Forensic psychologists work for private firms, educational institutions, and nonprofit and government agencies. Some forensic psychologists work with local, state, or federal governments to write new policies or work with legislators to help groups of people.

Employment Outlook

Careers for forensic psychologists are expected to grow, with the highest growth among psychologists who work with the courts, attorneys, lawmakers, and in research and teaching.

Needed Skills and Education

Education and skills required depend on the area of forensic psychology and the type of job within the career field. Some entry-level positions, such as a probation/parole office or residential youth counselor, require a bachelor's degree. A master's degree is required to work in institutions, such as a correctional facility, where the psychologist will be supervised by a forensic psychologist with a Ph.D. Most forensic psychologists have a Ph.D., which is required for most jobs in this field.

If you are interested in becoming a forensic psychologist, you will need classes in criminal justice and investigation; law; and psychology, especially in clinical, social, and cognitive psychology. Reading, interpersonal relationship, computer, research, writing, and teaching skills also may be needed.

How You'll Spend Your Day

In all areas of this career, you will spend time researching, reading, and writing. The number of hours required at work varies depending on the area chosen. Psychologists who work with law-enforcement agencies to provide psychological profiles of criminals may work long hours in the field. Others who work with attorneys or with the courts may work 40 hours or fewer each week.

Earnings

Annual earnings for entry-level positions range from $19,000 to $20,600; mid-level positions range from $20,000 to $25,000. Annual salaries for forensic psychologists with Ph.D.s start at $35,000.

What About You?

Does this career interest you? Contact your local law enforcement agencies or courts, or use the Internet to interview a forensic psychologist. Write a summary of your interview that includes your personal thoughts about the career.

RUBBERBALL/JUPITER IMAGES

CHAPTER SUMMARY

1.1 What Is Psychology?

- Psychology is the scientific study of mental processes and behavior.

- People often confuse psychology with psychiatry. Psychiatry is a branch of medicine concerned with the diagnosis and treatment of psychological disorders. Psychology has a much broader scope.

- Wilhelm Wundt is considered the world's first psychologist. Wundt established the first research in experimental psychology at the University of Leipzig in Germany. Wundt's approach to studying consciousness was called structuralism, which tries to identify the basic parts, or structure, of the conscious mind.

- William James was the first important psychologist in the United States. James' approach to psychology was called functionalism, which studies how the conscious mind functions to help humans survive in their environment.

- Max Wertheimer developed a third approach to psychology called Gestalt psychology. This approach studied how the mind actively organizes stimuli into meaningful wholes.

- In the early days of psychology, women and people of culturally diverse heritages met with discrimination. Despite this fact, a number of individuals made significant contributions, including Mary Whiton Calkins (a woman), Henry Alston (an African American), Kenneth Clark and Mamie Phipps Clark (African Americans), George Sanchez (Hispanic), and John Garcia (Hispanic).

- Today in the United States almost half of all psychologists holding doctoral degrees are women, and they make up two-thirds of all new Ph.D.s.

1.2 Contemporary Perspectives and Areas of Specialization

- Psychologists have different areas of specialization and follow different schools of thought. Ideas developed by early pioneers are reflected in modern psychology.

- The major schools of thought include psychoanalysis, behaviorism, humanistic psychology, cognitive psychology, psychobiology, and sociocultural psychology.

- One aspect of sociocultural psychology examines how human behavior differs depending on whether the culture is one of individualism or collectivism.

- Psychologists have different areas of specialization. Four of the applied specialties are clinical psychology, counseling psychology, industrial–organizational psychology, and educational and school psychology. Psychologists in these fields are employed at colleges, universities, or other teaching facilities. Others are employed in mental health centers, schools, industries, government agencies, or in private practice.

CHAPTER ASSESSMENT

Review Psychology Terms

Select the term that best fits the definition. Some terms will not be used.

_____ 1. Studies how human behavior is determined by hidden or unconscious motives and desires

_____ 2. Tries to identify the basic parts, or structure, of the conscious mind

_____ 3. Studies how the mind organizes and makes sense of information and experiences

_____ 4. A branch of medicine concerned with the diagnosis and treatment of psychological disorders

_____ 5. Emphasizes people's inborn desire for personal growth and ability to consciously make choices

_____ 6. Stresses personal goals over group goals

_____ 7. The scientific study of mental processes and behaviors

_____ 8. Examines how social surroundings and culture shape thinking and behavior

_____ 9. Stresses group goals over personal goals

_____ 10. Studies observable behavior

_____ 11. Study that is interested in discovering how the conscious mind works to help humans survive in their environment

_____ 12. Studies how people find mental health and happiness in everyday living

_____ 13. Studies how the brain and other biological structures and substances influence behavior

_____ 14. Studies how the mind actively organizes stimuli into meaningful wholes

a. behaviorism

b. cognitive psychology

c. collectivism

d. functionalism

e. Gestalt psychology

f. humanistic psychology

g. individualism

h. introspection

i. positive psychology

j. psychiatry

k. psychoanalysis

l. psychobiology

m. psychology

n. sociocultural psychology

o. structuralism

Review Psychology Concepts

15. Of the following four psychologists, select the one responsible for establishing the world's first institute for research in experimental psychology at a university: William James, Sigmund Freud, Wilhelm Wundt, or Max Wertheimer.

16. Of the following psychologists, select the founders of humanistic psychology: Miller and Neisser, Jung and Erikson, Freud and James, or Rogers and Maslow.

17. Which has the broader scope of study—psychology or psychiatry? Explain your answer.

18. On what did Wilhelm Wundt's research focus? What was his school of psychology called? Why was it called this?

19. Why was William James's theory called functionalism?

20. Which approach to psychology studies how the mind actively organizes stimuli into meaningful wholes?

21. What are two reasons you should remember Mary Whiton Calkins?

22. For what research is John Garcia known?

23. Who are the founders of psychoanalysis and behaviorism, and what is the difference between the two approaches?

24. How is positive psychology related to humanistic psychology?

25. Which approach to psychology looks at how you remember a friend's phone number?

26. How do animals contribute to psychobiology?

27. Individualism and collectivism are part of which approach to psychology?

28. What do educational and school psychologists do?

29. What do sociopsychologists study?

30. Is the United States an individualist or collectivist culture? Justify your answer with examples.

Apply Psychology Concepts

31. Psychoanalysis contends that all human behavior is determined by hidden or unconscious motives and desires. Identify a behavior in your own life that might be determined by such unconscious thinking.

32. When John Watson developed behaviorism, he argued that psychology should study only behavior that could be directly observed. Why was behaviorism such a drastic departure from the approaches of structuralism, functionalism, and psychoanalysis? If you were a behaviorist and wanted to study why some people help others in need while other people do not, what sort of things would you look for when observing people's behavior?

33. Imagine that you were born and raised in a collectivist culture instead of an individualist culture. Based on your understanding of individualism and collectivism, how might your thinking about yourself and how might your thinking about other people be different?

34. Identify and briefly describe the types of psychologists you would most likely find primarily at colleges and universities. Identify and briefly describe two types of psychologists who commonly use existing psychological knowledge to solve and prevent problems in settings away from colleges and universities.

Make Academic Connections

35. **Language Arts** Use the library or Internet to research one of the early pioneers mentioned in this chapter. Write a biography about the person. Include information on the person's early life, career, and important contributions to psychology.

36. **Art** Make a bulletin-board sized chart that lists the early pioneers of psychology and their schools of thought. Leave room for adding information as you go through the text this year. Download photos from the Internet of the psychologists and add these to your chart. Include a summary of each perspective and information that evaluates the limitations of each perspective in assessing behavior and mental processes. Include information from the biography you wrote in item 35.

37. **Careers** What would your life be like if you chose psychology as a career? Write an essay that describes the type of psychologist you could become. Explain why you chose this school of psychology and what you would do in this career.

38. **Science** Choose a person currently in the news from the newspaper, news magazine, or electronic news. Analyze how each psychological approach could explain the person's behavior, such as aggression, altruism, and so on. Write a summary of your analysis.

39. **Writing** Create a brochure for an ideal psychological center for high school students. In your brochure, describe the services available and the types of psychologists on staff, including their school of thought, what they do, and how they help students. Have at least three different types of psychologists on staff.

40. **History** Use the library or Internet to research the form psychology took before the twentieth century and the very early philosophers such as Aristotle or John Locke. Write a fact sheet about your findings, including information about these philosophers that relates to their ideas about how the mind works and human behavior.

41. **Sociology** Use the library, Internet, or personal interviews to explore reasons why psychology had more limited participation from women and ethnic minorities in its early stage. Write a paper on your findings. Include source materials. Make sure your Internet sources are educational, news, or government web sites.

42. **Cross-Cultural** Select one of the Hispanic psychologists discussed in this chapter. In your own words, describe the psychologist's accomplishments.

DIGGING DEEPER
with Psychology eCollection

When most people think of psychology, they think of the science of "trying to figure out why people do the things they do." Psychology is the study of behavior and the reasons for that behavior. Some psychological studies focus on everyday events and motivations; others study unusual or rare phenomena. The purpose of all research to is to add to our knowledge of human thought and behavior. In one thought-provoking study, psychologist Kathleen McGowan compared the behaviors and motivations of people who refused to give in to what seemed inevitable. Access the Gale Psychology eCollection at *www.cengage.com/school/psych/franzoi* and find out what McGowan discovered about what she calls "champions of the lost cause." Write a brief report describing McGowan's research and answer the question: What can we learn about human behavior from this study? As an additional project, select—from personal experience or research—an instance where someone refused to back down despite overwhelming odds and analyze why you believe they did what they did.

Source: McGowan, Kathleen. "The boy who wants to live forever . . . and other champions of the lost cause: obsession, defiance, grit, the line between indomitable genius and hopeless holdout is blurred. We all have the capacity to chase unlikely dreams, but for some people, the pursuit becomes its own reward." *Psychology Today*. 40.2 (March–April 2007): 76(7).

SELF-DISCOVERY: YOUR SCORE

Are Individualist or Collectivist Values More Important to You?

Scoring instructions: Six of these values are more associated with individualist cultures and the other six values are more connected to collectivist cultures. The individualist and collectivist values are listed in alternating order. Numbers 1, 3, 5, 7, 9, and 11 are individualist values. Numbers 2, 4, 6, 8, 10, and 12 are collectivist values.

People from individualist cultures such as the United States, Canada, England, or Australia tend to have more individualist values than collectivist values. This order tends to be reversed for those from collectivist cultures such as Mexico, Japan, Korea, or China.

CHAPTER 2

Scientific Methods in Psychology

ESSENTIAL QUESTION
Go to page XXIV

BLEND IMAGES/JUPITER IMAGES

"Since the beginning of the 20th century, people's innate desire to understand themselves—and the human condition—has found a new avenue toward the answer: the scientific method."

—JACQUELINE SWARTZ, CANADIAN JOURNALIST

In the early 1960s, psychologist Leonard Eron was conducting research on aggression in children. After asking parents questions on a survey, Eron was surprised to discover that the most aggressive children were those who watched a lot of violent shows on television. "What was going on here?" Eron wondered.

Scientific discovery is a form of problem solving. Scientific problem solving is highly valued because it increases our ability to understand, predict, and control things in our world. The question that Eron asked after reading the parents' surveys set him on a 30-year scientific exploration of television violence. His work also inspired other psychologists to conduct their own studies. In this chapter you will examine the scientific methods that psychologists use in their research. In doing so, you will learn more about Eron's research and whether watching television violence encourages people to behave more aggressively in their everyday living.

OBJECTIVES

- Explain critical thinking and why it is important in psychology.
- Describe the stages in the psychological research process.

DISCOVER IT | *How does this relate to me?*

You may read or hear about new scientific discoveries every week. A good deal of this scientific knowledge has a direct influence on your life. For example, before graduating from high school you will be given a number of tests designed to measure your ability to use vocabulary and math skills. Scientific studies find that students with high ability in these areas earn better grades in school and are more successful in their later careers than students who struggle with their vocabulary and math. Scientific studies also have led to discoveries of better ways to teach vocabulary and math. Your teachers use this scientific knowledge to help you develop your skills. What is involved in scientific research? What are the steps that scientists follow when studying issues related to psychology? In this chapter you will learn about the scientific process that is used to uncover the wonders of the mind.

KEY TERMS

- scientific methods
- critical thinking
- theory
- hypothesis
- sample
- random selection
- variables
- operational definition
- replication

Did you ever try building something that came with a set of plans? I remember making my first model airplane. I was so excited about getting it to look like the image on the box, that I ignored the directions and simply slapped the pieces together as fast I could. Unfortunately, this slapdash method did not lead to a very pleasing result. Through such experiences, I learned the value of designing a plan of action when undertaking projects.

Psychologists must follow a plan to effectively study the mind and behavior. **Scientific methods** consist of a set of procedures used to gather, analyze, and interpret information in a way that reduces error and leads to dependable conclusions.

Science and Critical Thinking

Psychologists approach the study of the mind by engaging in **critical thinking**, which is the process of deciding what to believe and how to act based on a careful evaluation of the evidence. An important aspect of critical thinking is thinking about

scientific methods A set of procedures used to gather, analyze, and interpret information in a way that reduces error and leads to dependable conclusions

critical thinking The process of deciding what to believe and how to act based on a careful evaluation of the evidence

other explanations for events. For example, when Eron's research found that aggressive children watched a lot of violent television shows, the natural explanation was that aggressive children simply liked to watch violence on television. However, Eron considered another possibility. He considered the possibility that watching violent television shows caused children to behave more aggressively. Were parents unknowingly teaching their children to behave more aggressively by letting them watch a lot of television violence?

Critical thinking skills are necessary in conducting scientific research. They are important in making you both a wise consumer of psychological knowledge and a smart decision-maker in your own life. Thinking critically about any kind of evidence that is presented to you can greatly improve your own ability to make good decisions. Spend a few minutes answering the questions in the Self-Discovery feature on page 31 to learn something about your own interest in thinking critically.

The following guidelines will help you to use critical thinking skills:

1. **Be willing to ask questions**   Knowledge begins with questioning the nature of things. Think of the process of questioning as a sign of intelligence, not a lack of it.

2. **Analyze assumptions**   Instead of simply accepting what others assume is true, think about possible exceptions and contradictions.

3. **Examine the evidence**   Don't just accept a conclusion without evidence. Ask for and analyze the evidence that supports and contradicts the various opinions and beliefs being expressed by yourself and others.

4. **Be cautious of emotional decisions**   There is nothing wrong with being emotionally involved with a particular decision. However, avoid basing your decision on what you would like to be true rather than what you know to be true.

5. **Tolerate uncertainty**   Realize that sometimes there are no clear answers to questions. Develop a tolerance for uncertainty. Don't be afraid to admit that the evidence suggests not one correct solution, but many possible ones.

CHECKPOINT   *What is critical thinking?*

Developing the ability to think critically will help you make good decisions throughout your life.

BLEND IMAGES/JUPITER IMAGES

Do You Enjoy Critical Thinking?

Directions: Read the following eight items and decide whether you agree or disagree with each statement.

1. I really enjoy a task that involves coming up with new solutions to problems.

2. Thinking is not my idea of fun.

3. The notion of thinking abstractly is appealing to me.

4. I like tasks that require little thought once I've learned them.

5. I usually end up deliberating about issues even when they do not affect me personally.

6. It's enough for me that something gets the job done; I don't care how or why it works.

7. I prefer my life to be filled with puzzles that I must solve.

8. I only think as hard as I have to.

One important thing to remember is that your critical thinking ability is like a muscle: the more you use it, the stronger it becomes. Even people who don't enjoy critical thinking can do so if the topic is important or interesting to them. The more you critically analyze events in your life, the stronger you become as a critical thinker.

See page 59 for scoring instructions.

Source: From "The Need for Cognition" by J. T. Cacioppo and R. E. Petty in *JOURNAL OF PERSONALITY AND SOCIAL PSYCHOLOGY*, 1982, 42, 116–131 (Table 1, pp. 120–121). Copyright © 1982 by the American Psychological Association. Adapted with permission.

PHOTODISC/GETTY IMAGES

Stages in the Psychological Research Process

Conducting research is an active process and involves many decisions. Research also occurs in a series of stages, which are summarized in Figure 2-1. Let us examine each of these stages.

STAGE 1: SELECT A TOPIC AND SEARCH THE LITERATURE

Research begins by selecting a topic worth exploring. Scientists get their ideas from many sources, including someone else's research, an incident in the daily news, or some personal experience in the researcher's life. Once a topic has been selected, investigators search the scientific literature to determine whether anyone else has investigated the topic. The findings from these previous studies shape the current investigation. Today psychologists can quickly learn about previous studies by using a number of computer-based programs to find even the most recently published studies. In addition, psychologists often can instantly correspond with researchers at other universities through the Internet.

The psychological research process has four stages.

Figure 2-1 **STAGES IN THE PSYCHOLOGICAL RESEARCH PROCESS**

Stage 1: Selecting a Topic and Searching the Literature

Ideas come from a variety of sources, including existing theories, past research, current social events, and personal experiences. Once a topic has been selected, psychologists must not only become knowledgeable about past research findings in their area of interest, but also keep abreast of recently published studies and those reported at scientific meetings.

Stage 2: Developing a Theory and Formulating Hypotheses

Once the research literature has been digested, a theory is formulated and hypotheses that can be empirically tested must then be developed.

Stage 3: Selecting a Scientific Method and Submitting the Study for Ethical Evaluation

Research can be conducted in the laboratory or in the field, and the psychologist can employ a variety of methods, including correlational, experimental, and case study. All institutions seeking federal research funding must establish institutional review boards to evaluate the potential benefits and risks of proposed studies.

Stage 4: Collecting and Analyzing Data and Reporting Results

The three basic techniques of data collection are self-reports, direct observations, and archival information. Data is analyzed using statistics (see Lesson 2.3). Psychologists then report their results at professional meetings and by publishing articles in scientific journals.

STAGE 2: DEVELOP A THEORY AND HYPOTHESIS

Theory development is an important aspect of the second stage of the research process. A **theory** is an organized system of ideas that seeks to explain why two or more events are related. A theory provides a picture of reality concerning some phenomenon. This picture develops after extensive observation, critical thinking, and creative reflection.

The most important factor in determining the value of a theory is its predictive accuracy. In other words, can it reliably predict behavior? Scientists determine the *predictive accuracy* of a theory by developing a hypothesis. A **hypothesis** is an educated guess, or prediction, about the nature of things based on a theory. The researcher asks, "If the theory is true, what observations would we expect to make in our investigation?"

Psychologist William Dement's interest in dreaming is an example of a hypothesis developed from a theory. In the 1950s, Dement began researching what happens when humans dream. He first studied other researchers' work and their discovery that dreaming was associated with periods of rapid eye movement (REM) sleep. Dement developed a theory that dreaming was a basic need for all humans. He predicted that if people were awakened during REM sleep, they would stop dreaming. People who were not allowed to dream over a series of nights would experience some kind of pressure to increase their "dream time" during the next night's sleep. The data Dement collected with his test subjects supported his hypothesis that we all have a basic need to dream. (See Chapter 15 for the results of Dement's research.)

Like Dement, psychologists collect data to determine whether their hypothesis successfully predicts the outcome of their study. If the data supports the study's hypothesis, researchers have greater confidence that their theory is a good explanation of the topic. If the findings do not support the study's hypothesis, the theory needs revising. Figure 2-2 shows how a theory and a hypothesis influence each other.

theory An organized system of ideas that seeks to explain why two or more events are related

hypothesis An educated guess, or prediction, about the nature of things based on a theory

Figure 2-2 **THE THEORY-HYPOTHESIS RELATIONSHIP**

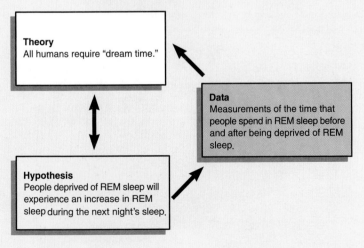

Theory
All humans require "dream time."

Data
Measurements of the time that people spend in REM sleep before and after being deprived of REM sleep.

Hypothesis
People deprived of REM sleep will experience an increase in REM sleep during the next night's sleep.

In research, a hypothesis is used to test a theory, with the data from a study providing the evidence to support or reject the hypothesis. The example in this figure applies the theory-hypothesis relationship to William Dement's research on dreaming.

STAGE 3: SELECT A SCIENTIFIC METHOD AND CONSIDER ETHICAL ISSUES

When a theory and hypothesis have been developed, researchers must next select a scientific method that allows the hypothesis to be tested. Psychological research generally occurs in one of two settings—the laboratory (a controlled environment) or the field (a natural setting).

In selecting a scientific method, researchers also must decide on who they will be studying, or a sample. A **sample** is a group of subjects who are selected to participate in a given study. A sample is selected from a much larger group, which is called a *population*. This consists of all the members of an identifiable group from which a sample is drawn. The closer a sample is in representing the population, the greater confidence researchers have in generalizing their findings beyond the sample. Researchers have the most confidence that their sample is an accurate representation of the population when everyone in the population has an equal chance of being selected for the sample. Such **random selection** of participants, although highly desirable, is not always possible. For example, in Eron's study of childhood aggression, his population consisted of all eight-year-old children in the United States, but his *sample* was much smaller and was not randomly selected. The sample consisted of only 856 eight-year-old students who attended school in Columbia County, New York.

Defining **variables** in the study also is an important part of the process of selecting a scientific method. Variables are the factors in the study that can be measured and that are capable of changing, or varying. When scientists describe a specific variable, they do so by using an **operational definition**, which is a very clear description of how a variable has been measured. For example, psychologists studying television violence and aggression among children may use the operational definition of aggression as any behavior that appears to have the goal of causing physical harm or physical discomfort to another person.

sample A group of subjects who are selected to participate in a research study

random selection A procedure for selecting a sample of people to study in which everyone in the population has an equal chance of being chosen

variables Factors in the study that can be measured and that are capable of changing, or varying

operational definition A very clear description of how a variable has been measured

Psychologists conducting a study about television violence and aggression among children need to specify an operational definition of aggression for the study.

©GEOM, 2008/ USED UNDER LICENSE FROM SHUTTERSTOCK.COM

As another example, when psychologists study hunger, they frequently use specialized instruments that measure movement of stomach muscles. These muscles trigger brain areas related to eating. In such studies, the operational definition of hunger is the beginning of movement in the stomach muscles. This clear definition tells other psychologists how the variables were measured in the study. This allows these psychologists to repeat the same scientific procedures in their own studies.

Sometimes researchers repeat an earlier study's scientific procedures using different participants in an attempt to duplicate the findings. This is known as **replication**. Replication is important in advancing scientific knowledge, because the findings from a single study are far less convincing than the same findings from a series of related studies.

To protect the health and safety of participants in psychological studies, all proposed studies are evaluated by a panel of both scientists and nonscientists. In assessing proposed studies, priority is always given to the welfare of the participants over any potential benefits of the research. This means that some studies simply cannot be conducted because of the risks. For example, no studies of television violence and aggression allow any actual physical aggression against participants to take place. With such a careful review process in place, human psychological research is very safe. Figure 2-3 lists some of the guidelines developed by the American Psychological Association for conducting research with human participants.

About 5 percent of all psychological studies use animals as subjects. Almost all of these studies involve little more than slightly changing the environments of animals and observing how these changes affect their behavior. A small number of studies,

replication Repeating an earlier study's scientific procedures, using different participants in an attempt to duplicate the findings

Figure 2-3 GUIDELINES FOR CONDUCTING RESEARCH WITH HUMAN PARTICIPANTS

In assessing proposed studies involving human subjects, priority is always given to ensuring their welfare over any potential benefits of the research. The guidelines also urge researchers to do the following:

1. Provide enough information to possible participants about the activities they will perform in the study so that they can freely give their informed consent.

2. Be truthful whenever possible. Deception should be used only when absolutely necessary.

3. Allow participants the right to decline to be a part of the study and the right to discontinue their participation at any point without being denied full payment for their participation.

4. Protect participants from both physical and psychological harm. If participants suffer any undesirable consequences, the researcher must do as much as possible to remove the damaging effects.

5. Ensure that any information provided by individual participants is kept confidential.

6. Debrief individuals once they have completed their participation. Explain all aspects of the research, answer all questions, and make sure they realize that their participation contributes to better scientific understanding.

Sources: Saks, E. R., Jeste, D. V., Granholm, E., Palmer, B. W., & Schneiderman, L. (2002). Ethical issues in psychosocial interventions research involving controls *Ethics & Behavior*, 12, 87–101; Street, L. L., & Luoma, J. B. (2002). Control groups in psychosocial intervention research: Ethical and methodological issues. *Ethics & Behavior*, 12, 1–30.

however, involve painful and dangerous procedures that would never be attempted on human participants. For example, research investigating the effect of drugs on the brain often begins with animal studies. This research has helped explain the causes of human mental illness and has helped the development of effective treatments. Animal research also has contributed greatly to explanations of how the brain works, as well as to the discovery of basic principles of perception, motivation, and learning. Both the American Psychological Association and a federal law known as the Animal Welfare Act have established standards for the humane care and treatment of laboratory animals. These standards ensure that

- Animals are properly cared for.
- Subjecting animals to painful or stressful procedures is used only when an alternative procedure is unavailable.
- Surgical procedures are performed under anesthesia, and techniques to avoid infection and minimize pain are followed.
- When an animal's life must be ended, it is done rapidly, with an effort to minimize pain.

Figure 2-4 lists some myths and facts about animal research.

Figure 2-4 MYTHS AND FACTS ABOUT ANIMAL RESEARCH

Myth: Most animal research is unnecessary.
Fact: Strong economic pressures weigh against the unnecessary use of animals in research. The extremely limited funds available to conduct animal research minimize the possibility that animals will be used for trivial purposes.

Myth: Other research methods can be used so that animals are not needed in research.
Fact: In most cases, no good alternatives exist. For example, computerized models of complex behavior still do not truly mimic actual behavior.

Myth: Most research animals are dogs, cats, monkeys, and chimpanzees.
Fact: These animals together account for less than 1 percent of the total number of animal subjects. Nearly 90 percent of the animals used in research are rats, mice, and other rodents.

Myth: Most animals in research suffer great pain and distress.
Fact: The vast majority of studies (more than 90 percent) do not cause pain or significant distress to the animal. In only 6 percent of experiments are anesthesia or painkillers withheld. In such instances, researchers withhold pain relief because it would interfere with the objectives of the research (for example, studying the effects of pain).

Myth: Animal research only benefits humans.
Fact: Knowledge of animal sexual and feeding behavior has helped save a number of species from extinction. Further, insights gained through animal research on taste aversion have been used by both ranchers and conservationists to condition animal predators in the wild to avoid killing livestock and endangered species.

STAGE 4: COLLECT AND ANALYZE DATA AND REPORT RESULTS

Once approval is granted by the review panel, it is time to collect the data. There are three basic techniques of data collection: (1) self-report, (2) direct observation, and (3) archival information. A self-report involves collecting data by asking people to answer questions about such things as people's perceptions, emotions, or attitudes. The disadvantage of self-report data is that it relies on people accurately describing these internal states—something they are not always willing or able to do. Because of this disadvantage, many researchers prefer to directly observe people's behavior, recording any changes that occur over time. Finally, researchers sometimes examine existing documents, or archives, to gather information. These accumulated records include census data, court records, and newspaper articles.

When the data is collected, the researchers must analyze and then report the results. Psychologists share their findings by making presentations at professional meetings and by publishing articles in scientific journals. This process of sharing discoveries allows psychologists to learn from one another, and that is why this final task is very important for the advancement of knowledge.

CHECKPOINT *What are the three basic techniques of data collection?*

2.1 ASSESSMENT

In Your Own Words

Write a summary of the stages in the psychological research process.

Review Concepts

1. A _____ is an organized system of ideas that seeks to explain why two or more events are related.

        a. theory   c. hypothesis

        b. replication   d. sample

2. The factors in a scientific study that can be measured and that are capable of changing are called

        a. critical thinking   c. variables

        b. samples   d. statistics

3. Explain the theory–hypothesis relationship.

4. **True or False** Animal research can benefit some animals as well as humans.

5. **True or False** Replication helps advance scientific knowledge.

Think Critically

6. Is psychology the only study in which you use critical thinking skills? Explain your answer.

7. Why do researchers use a sample of an identifiable group instead of the population in conducting research on the group?

KEY TERMS

- naturalistic observation
- participant observation
- case study
- correlational research
- survey
- correlation coefficient
- experiment
- independent variable
- dependent variable
- random assignment

OBJECTIVES

- Explain observational research.
- Explain correlational research.
- Explain experimental research.

DISCOVER IT | *How does this relate to me?*

Have you ever answered an Internet survey? What about a telephone call where you were asked a lot of questions? If so, you might have participated in a psychological study. These studies help research psychologists understand your behavior. For example, a survey on study skills among high school students could help researchers understand why some students have trouble studying.

Psychologists use many different scientific methods in conducting their research. In this lesson you will learn about the three basic methods. They are the observational, correlational, and experimental methods. As in all sciences, there are a number of different methods of conducting psychological research. The three methods discussed in this chapter are the most commonly used by researchers. The observational method seeks to describe behavior. The correlational method seeks to understand the relationship between two or more variables. The experimental method, or the experiment, seeks to explain the causes of behavior.

Observational Research

If scientists want to understand behavior, they must first describe it accurately. Observational research is a scientific method that has accurate description as its goal. Three different types of observational research are naturalistic observation, participant observation, and case study.

NATURALISTIC OBSERVATION

naturalistic observation A scientific method that describes how people or animals behave in their natural environment

Naturalistic observation is a scientific method that describes how people or animals behave in their natural environment. An example of a natural environment might be a day-care center where research psychologists observe and record how children play. Understanding play helps researchers understand how children develop. Other researchers might travel to the jungles of Africa to study how baboons defend themselves against enemies. This helps researchers understand the animals. Researchers observe and record the behavior, but they never manipulate, or try to change, it. This is true of all naturalistic observation research studies.

One example of a naturalistic observation study was done in the 1990s by Robert Levine and Ara Norenzayan. These psychologists analyzed the pace of everyday life in 31 cultures. They collected data on measurements of people's average walking speed on city sidewalks, the speed at which postal clerks responded to a simple request, and the accuracy of clocks in public settings. These observations involved the researchers observing how people behaved in their natural surroundings. Their findings showed that the pace of life was faster in colder and more economically developed cultures (such as Switzerland and Japan) than in those that were hotter and less economically developed (such as Mexico and Indonesia). Based on these observations, the researchers suggested that the difficulty working in hot temperatures may explain the slower-paced life in certain cultures around the world.

PARTICIPANT OBSERVATION

Another type of observational method is **participant observation**. Here, as in naturalistic observation, a researcher describes behavior as it occurs in its natural environment, but does so as a participant of the group being studied. One of the chief benefits of this research strategy is that it allows researchers to get closer to what they are studying. In 1956, psychologist Leon Festinger and his colleagues used this method in studying members of a doomsday cult who believed that the world was going to be destroyed on a specific date. The researchers joined the cult and observed the group's activities, detailing how the members reacted when the doomsday came and went with the world still intact.

participant observation
A scientific method in which a researcher describes behavior as it occurs in its natural environment, and does so as a participant of the group being studied

A researcher studies behavior in a natural environment.

CASE STUDY

Another form of observational research is a case study. A **case study** is an in-depth analysis of a single subject. This research method is used by psychotherapists who study people with psychological disorders. A psychologist who studies a patient suffering from a psychological disorder writes an extensive description of the person's disorder. This helps other psychologists better understand the factors, or the causes, that lead to and influence the disorder. Sigmund Freud's work (see Chapter 1) is perhaps the most famous example of this method.

The advantage of the case study is that it provides a more detailed analysis of a person than any other research method. One disadvantage is that researchers must be extremely cautious in generalizing from a single case to the population as a whole.

case study A scientific method involving an in-depth analysis of a single subject

> **CHECKPOINT** *Name three common observational methods psychologists use.*

CLOSER LOOK

Demand Characteristics in Research

When you walk into a library, you are expected to speak and walk softly. This expectation is specific to the situation. Expectations that are specific to a situation are called *demand characteristics*. Research settings also can have demand characteristics. When psychologists conduct research, they must be careful to not create demand characteristics among their research participants.

For example, you, as a researcher, could alter children's aggressive behavior in a playground setting. When the children see an older person observing their play activities, they may delay any aggressive behavior because they think you might punish them. This demand characteristic makes it very unlikely that you can trust that your observations are capturing the children's natural everyday behavior. Researchers go to great lengths to not draw attention to themselves when conducting observational research. In fact, they may conceal themselves when making observations or use hidden cameras to record events of interest.

Think Critically
What are demand characteristics in research?

Correlational Research

Observational research only describes variables in a study. Yet often psychologists want to know whether these variables are related, and, if so, how strongly. When changes in one variable relate to changes in another variable, psychologists say that the variables correlate. **Correlational research** assesses the nature of the relationship between two or more variables that are not controlled by the researcher.

A study of the relationship between children's television viewing habits and their aggressive behavior has two variables—the viewing habits and aggressive behavior. Psychologists conducting correlational research do not try to influence how much time any of the children in the study actually spend viewing violent shows. Instead, they gather information on the amount of time the children spend watching such programs and on the children's degree of aggressive behavior. Then the researchers determine how these two variables correlate. The important goal of correlational research is prediction, which allows psychologists to predict a change in one variable by knowing the value of another variable.

SURVEYS

Have you ever been at the mall and had someone with a clipboard come up to you and ask you questions? If so, you may have participated in a **survey**. A survey is a structured set of questions or statements given to a group of people to measure their attitudes, beliefs, values, or behaviors. Surveys often are used in correlational research.

The advantage of using surveys is that obtaining information is generally easy. The main disadvantage is that surveys rely on people's self-reports, which are sometimes faulty. Listed below are a few examples of survey questions that psychologists might ask parents to answer when studying the relationship between watching violent television shows and children's aggressive behavior.

1. During a typical week, how many hours of television does your child watch?

   _____ hours

2. Of the hours of television viewing listed above, what percent of those television shows (from 0 to 100 percent) have characters who are physically aggressive or violent?

   _____ percent (0 = no shows; 50 = half of the shows; 100 = all the shows)

3. Using the 7-point sliding scale below, indicate your child's tendency to behave aggressively in daily activities (fighting, pushing, punching others).

   Not at all   Very
   aggressive   1 2 3 4 5 6 7   aggressive

correlational research A scientific method that assesses the nature of the relationship between two or more variables that are not controlled by the researcher

survey A structured set of questions or statements given to a group of people to measure their attitudes, beliefs, values, or behaviors

THE CORRELATION COEFFICIENT

The statistic, or numerical value, that psychologists use to describe the relationship between two variables is known as the **correlation coefficient**. It often is abbreviated by using the *r* symbol, and can range from −1.00 to +1.00.

A correlation coefficient that is positive has a value greater than zero. A positive correlation tells you that as one variable increases in value, the other variable also increases in value. Using the example of television viewing and aggression, a correlation near +1.00 indicates that children who watch a lot of violent television are more aggressive than those who watch little violence on television.

The opposite of a positive correlation is a negative correlation. A correlation coefficient that is negative has a value less than zero. A negative correlation tells you that as one variable increases in value, the other variable decreases in value. A correlation that is near −1.00 tells you that children in the sample who watch a lot of violent television are less aggressive than those who watch little violence on television.

What does a correlation coefficient with a value of zero tell you? A correlation coefficient at or very near zero tells you that viewing television violence has no relationship to children's aggressive behavior. In other words, neither of the variables influences the other. Look at Figure 2-5. A zero correlation has dots scattered all around the graph, while a correlation near +1.00 or −1.00 has dots lining up on an imaginary straight line running between the X and Y axes of the graph. The farther the dots on the graph fall from the imaginary straight line, the lower the value of the correlation.

correlation coefficient
The statistic, or numerical value, that psychologists use to describe the relationship between two variables

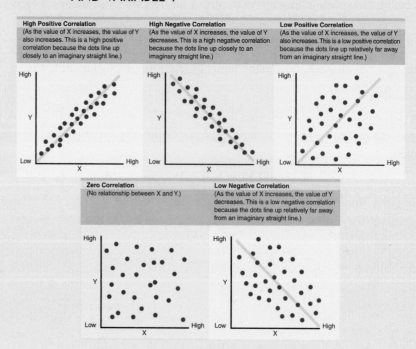

Figure 2-5 **PLOTTING THE RELATIONSHIP BETWEEN VARIABLE X AND VARIABLE Y**

The points on the graphs represent a pairing of variable X with variable Y for each participant in the study. In addition to the direction of the relationship between variable X and variable Y, correlations can have different values. The greater the scatter of values on the graph, the lower the correlation is. A perfect correlation occurs when all the values fall on an imaginary straight line.

High Positive Correlation
(As the value of X increases, the value of Y also increases. This is a high positive correlation because the dots line up closely to an imaginary straight line.)

High Negative Correlation
(As the value of X increases, the value of Y decreases. This is a high negative correlation because the dots line up closely to an imaginary straight line.)

Low Positive Correlation
(As the value of X increases, the value of Y also increases. This is a low positive correlation because the dots line up relatively far away from an imaginary straight line.)

Zero Correlation
(No relationship between X and Y.)

Low Negative Correlation
(As the value of X increases, the value of Y decreases. This is a low negative correlation because the dots line up relatively far away from an imaginary straight line.)

ADVANTAGES AND DISADVANTAGES OF CORRELATIONAL RESEARCH

The advantage of correlational research is prediction. You can predict a change in one variable by knowing the value of another variable. The major disadvantage of correlational research is that it cannot determine the cause of the relationship between two variables. Besides knowing that two variables are correlated with one another, it is extremely valuable to know which variable caused a change in the other. Does watching violent shows make children more aggressive, or are aggressive children more likely to watch violent shows? Correlational research also cannot rule out the possibility that a third, unmeasured variable is causing the changes in both variables being studied. For example, perhaps parents who spank their children (the unmeasured variable) also are more likely to allow their children to view violent television shows and to teach their children to be physically aggressive.

LAB TEAMS

Correlational Research

With three other students, use correlational research in a survey. Your survey should measure the attitudes, beliefs, values, or behaviors of students in your school. For example, you could study the correlation between the number of hours of sleep students obtain and their grades. Record your survey questions and findings.

CHECKPOINT *What is correlational research?*

Experimental Research

Correlational research can only tell whether a change in one variable is related to a change in another variable. Psychologists also want to discover whether a variable is causing the change in other variables. To do so, researchers conduct experimental research, or an **experiment**. In an experiment, researchers manipulate, or change, a variable to observe the effect on some other variable. The variable that is manipulated is called the **independent variable**. It is the one the researcher is testing as the possible cause of any changes that might occur in the other variables. The variable that may change in response to the manipulated changes in the independent variable is called the **dependent variable**. Once participants have been exposed to the independent variable, their behavior is carefully monitored to determine whether it changes in the predicted fashion with different levels of the independent variable. If it does, the experimenter concludes that the independent variable is the cause of the changes in the dependent variable.

A key feature of most experiments is that participants are randomly assigned to the different levels of the independent variable. In such **random assignment**, the experimenter, by some random procedure, decides which participants are exposed to which level of the independent variable. Due to this procedure, the experimenter

experiment A scientific method in which researchers manipulate, or change, a variable to observe the effect on some other variable

independent variable The variable that is manipulated in an experiment

dependent variable The variable that may change in response to the manipulated changes in the independent variable

random assignment A procedure ensuring that all research participants have an equal chance of being exposed to different levels of the independent variable

can be reasonably confident that the participants in the different experimental conditions don't differ from one another.

How might you conduct an experiment on whether watching television violence causes increased aggression in children? As depicted in Figure 2-6, your independent variable is the amount of television violence that you allow children to watch. The children in your experiment who are exposed to television violence are in the experimental group. The children who are treated the same way as the experimental group, except they are not exposed to the independent variable, are in the control group. The dependent variable is the level of aggression that you observe in both groups of children after they watch their television shows.

In one experiment conducted in a private school for boys, some boys were shown a violent film every night for one week (experimental group). Other boys were shown the same number of nonviolent films (control group). In this study the independent variable was exposure to violent films (high or no exposure). The researchers then observed and recorded the children's aggressive behavior (the dependent variable) over the next few days. Results indicated that boys who had been exposed to the violent films behaved more aggressively than the boys who watched the nonviolent films. Based on these findings, the psychologists concluded that exposure to violent films had indeed caused increased aggressiveness.

Now that you have learned about the different scientific methods that psychologists use, which is best? There is no one best method. In each investigation, the psychologist must decide what method would provide the best test of the hypotheses. The best overall strategy is to use many different scientific methods to study the same topic. Each method has strengths and weaknesses. Check out the New Science feature on page 45 to learn about how new technologies are used in research.

Figure 2-6 THE BASIC ELEMENTS IN AN EXPERIMENT

The power of experimental research is based on treating the experimental and control groups exactly alike except for the manipulation of the independent variable. Any later observed differences in the dependent variable between the two groups can then be confidently attributed to the effects of the independent variable.

Hypothesis		
Watching television violence causes increased aggression in boys.		
Random Assignment	Subjects are randomly assigned to experimental and control conditions.	
Manipulation of Independent Variable	**Experimental condition:** Boys watch a violent film every night for one week.	**Control condition:** Boys watch a nonviolent film every night for one week.
Measurement of Dependent Variable	The experimental group later engaged in greater aggressive behavior than did the control group.	
Conclusion		
Exposure to violent films causes increased aggression in boys.		

NEW SCIENCE

Virtual Environment Technology

Laboratory experiments provide psychologists with a high degree of control over what happens in a study. Field experiments provide a greater degree of realism to research participants. Some psychologists believe they found a possible remedy to the dilemma of choosing between greater control and greater realism. It's called virtual environment technology. Researchers create a virtual research environment with a computer. Once this virtual reality is created, participants wearing virtual reality equipment are "immersed" in the setting.

A commonly used piece of virtual reality equipment is a head-mounted, or binocular-style, device that allows an individual to view 3-D images and to "walk" through the virtual environment. This type of simulated environment is controlled completely by the experimenter, even more so than the traditional laboratory setting. Still it has a very "real-world" feel to it, similar to that of a field experiment.

Studies using virtual environment technology suggest that participants behave relatively naturally in such settings. Although still only used in a small percentage of studies, virtual environment technology is being used to investigate such topics as why people do or do not conform, fear of heights and other phobias, the reliability of eyewitness testimony, and the effects of violent video games. As this technology improves, psychologists hope to involve senses beyond sight and hearing, as well as to improve the ways people can interact with the virtual creations they encounter. This technology is not meant to replace traditional field and laboratory studies, but instead to provide another research technique that psychologists can use in their study of human thought and behavior.

COMSTOCK IMAGES/JUPITER IMAGES

2.2 ASSESSMENT

In Your Own Words

Write a paper that compares and contrasts the three types of observational research.

Review Concepts

1. Which of the following includes the researcher in the group being studied?
   - a. case study
   - b. correlational research
   - c. participant observation
   - d. naturalistic observation

2. Which refers to an in-depth study of a single subject?
   - a. case study
   - b. experiment
   - c. dependent variable
   - d. correlation coefficient

3. Surveys are most often used in
   - a. experiment
   - b. participant observation
   - c. naturalistic observation
   - d. correlational research

4. **True or False**   Researchers must be careful to create demand characteristics among their research subjects.

5. **True or False**   The correlation coefficient is a statistical measure that describes the nature of the relationship between two variables.

6. **True or False**   People taking surveys at the mall are conducting scientific research.

Think Critically

7. If you want to study students in a psychology class, why might you choose participant observation?

8. You are a psychologist writing a case study on a person with a behavior disorder. Why should you be careful about concluding that your findings apply to the population?

9. Why is prediction important in correlational research?

10. Why is there not one best scientific method? Explain your answer.

11. Which scientific method would you choose to study the habits of black bears in the wild? Support your answer with information from the text.

12. Evaluate the accuracy of a survey that asks students about their study habits. How could the results be misleading?

13. Contrast an independent variable with a dependent variable.

14. Explain why it is important to carefully monitor the behavior of participants in an experiment once they have been exposed to the independent variable.

2.3 | Statistical Reasoning

OBJECTIVES

- Define and explain descriptive statistics.
- Define and explain inferential statistics.

DISCOVER IT | *How does this relate to me?*

Your school newspaper reported that a certain running back on the football team is averaging 4.5 yards per carry. This fact is a statistic. Most scientific discoveries also involve statistics. Reports on scientific discoveries often mention statistical differences between groups of people tested in a study. A *statistical difference* in a study is any meaningful difference found between groups on a measured variable. You will be better able to understand and critically analyze statistical differences if you have a basic understanding of statistical reasoning.

KEY TERMS

- statistics
- descriptive statistics
- central tendency
- mean
- median
- mode
- normal distribution
- standard deviation
- inferential statistics

Statistics is a branch of mathematics that allows researchers to organize, describe, and make meaningful judgments from data they collect. Analyzing the statistics from their studies, or statistical analysis, is very important because doing so provides scientists with information to judge whether they should accept or reject their research hypotheses. When conducting research, psychologists use two basic kinds of statistics: descriptive and inferential. This chapter examines the purpose, logic, and value of these two different kinds of statistics.

Descriptive Statistics

After data is collected in a study, psychologists use **descriptive statistics**. These are numbers that summarize and describe the data in a practical and efficient manner. For example, after researchers survey parents about the number of hours their children spend watching television during a typical week, researchers might want to summarize the scores. Two important descriptive statistics are measures of central tendency and measures of variability.

statistics A branch of mathematics that allows researchers to organize, describe and make meaningful judgments from data they collect

descriptive statistics Numbers that summarize and describe data in a practical, efficient manner

MEASURES OF CENTRAL TENDENCY

When researchers summarize data, they use a number to describe the central location within the distribution of scores in a sample. This score is referred to as the **central tendency**. There are three measures of central tendency: mean, median, and mode. Figure 2-7 provides an example of these three measures of central tendency.

The **mean** is the arithmetic average of the distribution of scores for a particular variable. The mean is the most common measure of central tendency and the one that most people think of when they hear the word *average*. You find the mean by adding all the scores in the distribution and then dividing by the number of scores. In Figure 2-7, the mean number of hours that children watch television per week is 30 hours.

The second measure of central tendency is the **median**. This is the middle score in a distribution of scores after you rank the scores from the lowest to highest. Half the scores are above the median and half below it. In Figure 2-7, the median number of hours children watch television per week is 31 hours.

The **mode** is the third measure of central tendency. It is the score that occurs most frequently in a distribution. In Figure 2-7 the mode is 30 hours.

When the scores that are placed in a graph form a bell shape, it is called a normal distribution. In a **normal distribution**, the mean, median, and mode are identical in value. Most scores cluster around the average test score, and fewer scores are found far from the average score. In Figure 2-7 the mean and mode are identical (30), but the median score is slightly higher (31). This means that the television viewing data is not a perfect normal distribution.

Let's try an example with a normal distribution. Imagine that you ask 38 teachers at your school how many hours they slept the previous night. This is a variable in your study. You find that their responses yield the normal distribution as shown in Figure 2-8. As you can see, this distribution peaks at the center and tapers off

central tendency A number that describes the central location within a distribution of scores in a sample

mean The arithmetic average of the distribution of scores for a particular variable

median The middle score in a distribution of scores after you rank the scores from the lowest to highest

mode The score that occurs most frequently in a distribution

normal distribution The bell shaped curve that occurs on a graph when the mean, median, and mode are identical in value

---

Figure 2-7   MEASURES OF CENTRAL TENDENCY: CHILDREN'S AVERAGE WEEKLY TELEVISION VIEWING TIME

Survey Question: During a typical week, how many hours of television does your child watch? _____ hours

Data From Eleven Parents: 30, 23, 35, 37, 30, 18, 22, 34, 38, 31, 32

What is the mean?

The *mean* is the arithmetic average:

$30+23+35+37+30+18+22+34+38+31+32=330\div11=$ **30** is the mean score

What is the median?

The *median* is the middle score after the scores have been ranked from lowest to highest:

18 22 23 30 30 **31** 32 34 35 37 38 → **31** is the median score

What is the mode?

The *mode* is the score that occurs most frequently:

18 22 23 **30 30** 31 32 34 35 37 38 → **30** is the modal score

Figure 2-8 NORMAL DISTRIBUTION

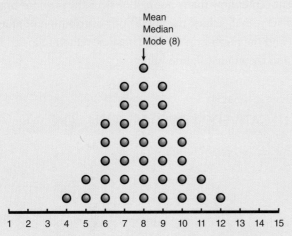

Reported Hours of Sleep Among Middle-Aged Adults

This graph of the distribution of high school teachers' previous night's sleep time illustrates the three measures of central tendency: mean, median, and mode. In a normal distribution, the mean, median, and mode have the same values.

outwardly while remaining symmetrical with respect to the center. You can clearly see the bell-shaped curve of this normal distribution.

When the mean, median, and mode have different values, your data set is described as having a skewed distribution. As an example, imagine that you ask 38 students at your school how many hours they slept the previous night, and their responses yield the distribution depicted in Figure 2-9. This distribution is positively skewed, meaning that your data contains a small number of very large values so that when the distribution of scores is drawn there is a long tail after the peak. The mode is to the left (lowest value), the median is in the middle (middle value), and the mean is to the right (highest value), pulled upward in value by the few very high scores.

Figure 2-9 POSITIVELY SKEWED DISTRIBUTION

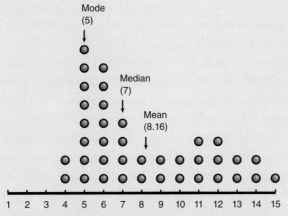

Reported Hours of Sleep Among Students

This graphic representation of the distribution of high school students' previous night's sleep time illustrates that in a negatively skewed distribution, the mean, median, and mode have different values. The mean has the lowest value and the mode has the highest value.

Reversing this trend gives you a distribution that is negatively skewed. This is shown in Figure 2-10. Here, imagine that you have asked 38 elderly adults living in a retirement center how many hours they slept the previous night. With a small number of very small values, the tail of your distribution of scores appears before the peak, and the mean is to the left (smallest value), followed by the median (middle value), and the mode (highest value).

This graphic representation of the distribution of elderly adults' previous night's sleep time illustrates that in a positively skewed distribution, the mean, median, and mode have different values. The mode has the lowest value and the mean has the highest value.

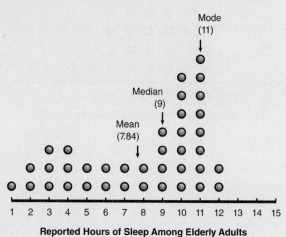

Figure 2-10 **NEGATIVELY SKEWED DISTRIBUTION**

Reported Hours of Sleep Among Elderly Adults

MEASURES OF VARIATION

In addition to knowing the value of the measures of central tendency in the data, it also is important to know something about the variation in the data. Measures of variability, or measures of variation, are statistics that tell you how closely distributed your scores are to some measure of central tendency.

The simplest measure of variation for a particular variable is the range of scores among all the participants tested, meaning the difference between the lowest and highest values in a distribution. To compute the range, you subtract the lower value from the higher value. In Figure 2-8 the range is 8: 12 – 4. In Figure 2-9 the range is 11: 15 – 4. In Figure 2-10, the range is 11: 12 – 1.

The range is easy to compute, but it doesn't take into account any of the other scores in the distribution. A more sensitive measure of variation is the **standard deviation**, which takes into account all the scores. The standard deviation also indicates the average difference between the scores and their mean. In other words, the standard deviation is a measure of how much the average score deviates from the mean. The value of the standard deviation tells you whether scores for a particular variable are packed close together or spread far apart. A low score indicates scores are packed together and a high score indicates scores are spread apart. When the standard deviation value is low, the mean provides a good representation of the entire data set for that variable. When the standard deviation is high, the mean is not a very good representation of all the data for that variable.

standard deviation
A measure of variation that indicates the average difference between the scores in a distribution and their mean

Inferential Statistics

After describing and summarizing the data using descriptive statistics, psychologists often use **inferential statistics**. These are mathematical methods used to determine whether the data support or do not support the research hypothesis. Psychologists use inferential statistics to estimate the likelihood that a difference found in the research sample also would be found if everyone in the population participated in the study. Researchers ask whether the difference found in the sample is due to chance, or if it reflects actual differences in the larger population.

For example, imagine that you have the following theory: *depriving people of sleep causes memory problems.* You hypothesize that people who are sleep deprived will perform more poorly on a memory task than those who are not sleep deprived. To test this hypothesis, you conduct an experiment in which 50 participants perform a memory task after going without sleep for 24 hours. Your control group in this experiment consists of another 50 participants who perform the same memory task after a normal night's sleep. Your independent variable is sleep deprivation and your dependent variable is performance on the memory task.

After scoring the memory task, you discover that the mean score for the sleep-deprived individuals is 15 points lower than the mean score for the control group. You also compute the standard deviation values for the two data sets and discover that both are relatively low and roughly equal to one another. This indicates that these mean scores provide a good representation of the entire data in the two samples. However, is this difference in the two sample means due to chance variation? Is this difference between the two groups large enough to support your hypothesis? These are the types of questions answered by inferential statistics.

inferential statistics
Mathematical methods used to determine whether the data support or do not support the research hypothesis

Researchers may test the theory that depriving people of sleep causes memory problems using inferential statistics.

©SIMONE VAN DEN BERG, 2008/USED UNDER LICENSE FROM SHUTTERSTOCK.COM

Figure 2-11 **STATISTICALLY SIGNIFICANT DIFFERENCES**

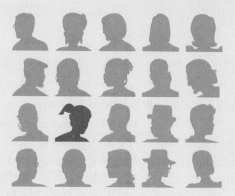

Researchers generally accept a difference as statistically significant if the likelihood of it having occurred by chance is less than 1 in 20.

When the deviation from the sample mean indicates low variability, and the difference between the two sample means is relatively large, it is likely that additional statistical calculations will indicate that these differences are statistically significant. In science, this means that the difference probably is not due to chance variation between the samples. Psychologists generally accept a difference as statistically significant if the likelihood of it having occurred by chance is less than 1 in 20—that is, a probability of less than 5 percent (indicated by the notation $p < 0.05$). However, keep in mind that this probability assessment is telling you how likely it is that this difference between the two sample means is due to chance. It does not tell you whether this difference is actually due to chance. Your probability assessment could be wrong. There are no certainties in science, just probability estimates.

In the sleep-deprivation study, further imagine that inferential statistics tell you that the likelihood of the difference between the group means being due to chance is 1 in 25 (a 4 percent probability level). As the researcher, you would conclude that sleep-deprived participants performed significantly worse on the memory task than non-sleep-deprived participants. More importantly, if your research participants reasonably represent the general population, you would generalize your findings beyond the sample. You now have support for your theory that sleep deprivation causes memory problems in the general population. On the other hand, if your inferential statistics indicate that the likelihood that the difference between the group means is due to a 1 in 5 chance (a 20 percent probability level), you would conclude that sleep-deprived and non-sleep-deprived participants did not significantly differ from one another on the memory task. Your theory—from which your hypothesis was derived—was not supported. These nonsignificant findings likely would cause you to closely reexamine your study for possible flaws. The findings also might prompt you to reconsider the ideas underlying your theory. Does the theory need revising?

Both descriptive and inferential statistics are important tools in the quest to answer scientific questions. However, again remember that in science, any conclusion is only a statement of the probable relationship between the events that are being investigated. There are no final truths in science. Every theory is always subject to revision when new data come to light that challenge the hypotheses derived from the original theory.

CHECKPOINT *How do psychologists use inferential statistics?*

2.3 ASSESSMENT

In Your Own Words

Explain the difference between descriptive statistics and inferential statistics.

Review Concepts

1. Which is the middle score in a distribution of scores after you rank the scores from lowest to highest?
   - a. mean
   - b. normal distribution
   - c. mode
   - d. median

2. When scores placed in a graph form a bell shape, it is called a
   - a. standard deviation
   - b. skewed distribution
   - c. normal distribution
   - d. central tendency

3. Statistics that tell you how closely distributed your scores are to some measure of central tendency are called
   - a. measures of variability
   - b. median
   - c. standard deviation
   - d. normal distribution

4. Which is the branch of mathematics that allows researchers to organize, describe, and make meaningful inferences from data they collect?
   - a. central tendency
   - b. statistics
   - c. normal distribution
   - d. inferential statistics

5. **True or False** The three measures of central tendency are the mean, median, and mode.

6. **True or False** The mean is the score that occurs most frequently in a distribution.

7. **True or False** Measures of central tendency and measures of variability are two important descriptive statistics.

8. **True or False** Inferential statistics help researchers determine whether the data collected supports the research.

Think Critically

9. Why do psychologists need to understand statistics?

10. Why might designing a graph of the central tendency be important to researchers?

11. Is a normal distribution more important in a study than a skewed distribution? Support your answer.

12. What is the danger in using inferential statistics?

13. Defend the reason scientists keep statistics.

14. In a normal distribution, what is the difference in value in the mean, median, and mode?

Violence in Computer Video Games

INTRODUCTION   Forty years of research strongly support the theory that allowing children to watch violent television shows increases the likelihood that they will later behave aggressively. Is there any evidence that playing violent computer video games has similar harmful effects?

HYPOTHESIS   Unlike television, computer video games are interactive. Computer-game players engage in make-believe aggression, receive rewards for their aggression, and closely identify with the characters they control. Psychologists who study computer video violence predict that children, teenagers, and young adults who play violent video games will be more aggressive in their daily living than those who do not play violent video games.

METHOD   During the past 15 years, psychologists have conducted many different studies on exposure to computer video violence and later aggression. More than 3,000 female and male participants have been studied in both experimental and correlational research.

RESULTS   Despite the denials from the video-game industry, the overall findings from these studies indicate that exposure to high video-game violence is associated with heightened aggression in the real world among young adults and children. The effects are the same for both girls and boys. Additional research indicates that even brief exposure to violent video games significantly increases aggressive thoughts, aggressive emotions, and—most importantly—aggressive behavior.

Another negative effect of playing violent computer games is emotional numbing, which means becoming unconcerned about aggression. For example, experiments with both children and young adults have found that those who had just played violent computer games were less concerned when they observed other people fighting than a control group who had not played these violent games. These findings suggest that people who play a lot of violent video games become used to violence in other areas of their lives.

Of course, these findings do not mean that all, or even most, children and young adults who regularly play violent video games will begin terrorizing their schools and neighborhoods. However, while exposure to such staged violence is not the main cause of aggression among young people, it is one cause that is relatively easy to control and reduce.

Critical Analysis

Imagine that a new computer video game is created in which players engage in make-believe helping, receive rewards for their helping, and closely identify with the characters they control. How would you design an experiment to discover whether children who play this computer game become more helpful in their daily lives?

Market and Survey Researcher

Marketing, Sales & Service

Market and survey researchers work in business and in the political arena. Their job is to design surveys, to gather information on the behavior and attitudes of people, and to analyze the findings. Surveys are conducted over the Internet, by telephone, through the mail, or in person by going door-to-door. Surveys also are conducted in shopping malls and other public places. After conducting interviews, researchers then analyze and evaluate the information, and make recommendations to their client or employer.

Who are these clients or employers? In the business world, an automotive company might hire a survey research firm to find out what young people want in a vehicle. The information gathered in the surveys along with recommendations of the researchers are used by companies to improve products or customer satisfaction. Political parties use survey researchers to learn which political candidate is ahead in an election, or what issues are the most important to people.

Employment Outlook

Careers in market and survey research are expected to grow faster than average through 2016. The demand will continue to increase as consumers become better informed and companies expand their markets. Global companies need professionals in this occupation to research and analyze foreign markets. Employment in this career is especially favorable for professionals with an MA or PhD degree in marketing or related fields.

Needed Skills and Education

A bachelor's degree usually is required. An MA or PhD may be required for market and survey research in technical areas. Quantitative skills are helpful. These skills require a knowledge of mathematics and the ability to measure and express values in numerical terms. Other helpful knowledge and experience include being able to analyze data and write reports. Good communication and people skills are also necessary.

Studies for this career include courses in business, marketing, consumer behavior, economics, psychology, communication, English, sociology, social science, and liberal arts.

How You'll Spend Your Day

A large percentage of people in this career are market research analysts who work in management and scientific and technical consulting services. These services may include marketing research and public opinion polls. Colleges, universities, and professional schools also employ survey researchers.

You will write questions for surveys that are geared to learn about specific behaviors of people. You may spend your day on the phone asking people to answer questions about their behaviors. You may research behaviors of the general public or a specific group. You also may conduct surveys in person, by mail, or over the Internet.

After you have completed your sampling survey, you will analyze all the data, and then write a report that evaluates the data and makes recommendations based on your findings.

Earnings

The median annual wage for market research analysts is $58,820. The median annual wage for survey researchers is $33,360.

What About You?

Does the occupation of market research analyst or survey researcher interest you? Write about you and this career, answering these questions: What makes the career sound interesting to you? What about the career does not sound interesting?

CHAPTER SUMMARY

2.1 The Scientific Process in Psychology

- Psychologists and other scientists approach the study of the mind by engaging in critical thinking which is the process of deciding what to believe and how to act based on a careful evaluation of the evidence.

- Scientific methods consist of a set of procedures used to gather, analyze, and interpret information in a way that reduces error and leads to dependable conclusions.

- A theory is an organized system of ideas that seeks to explain why two or more events are related. A hypothesis is a prediction about the nature of things based on a theory.

- Conducting research is an active process that involves many decisions. Researchers must select a method that allows the hypothesis to be tested. They also must consider any ethical issues related to the research project.

- Research takes place in a series of stages: select a topic and search the literature; develop a theory and hypothesis; select a scientific method and consider ethical issues; collect and analyze data and report results.

2.2 Commonly Used Scientific Methods

- Psychologists use many scientific methods in conducting research. Three of these methods are the observational method, the correlational method, and the experimental method.

- Observational research is a scientific method that has accurate description as its goal. Three different types are naturalistic observation, participant observation, and case study.

- Research psychologists are concerned with variables. They want to know whether the variables relate and how a change in one variable affects another variable. When changes in one variable relate to changes in another variable, psychologists say the variables correlate. Correlational research assesses the nature of the relationship between two or more variables that are not controlled by the researcher.

- Psychologists want to discover whether one variable causes a change in other variables. To do so, researchers conduct experiments using independent variables, which can be manipulated during an experiment, and dependent variables, which may change in response to the changes in the independent variables.

2.3 Statistical Reasoning

- Statistics is a branch of mathematics that allows researchers to organize, describe, and make meaningful inferences from data they collect.

- The two basic kinds of statistics researchers use are descriptive and inferential. Descriptive statistics are numbers that summarize and describe data in a practical, efficient manner. Inferential statistics are mathematical methods used to determine whether the data support or do not support the research hypothesis.

- Two important descriptive statistics are measures of central tendency and measures of variability. The central tendency is the typical, or average, score in a distribution of scores in a sample. The three measures of central tendency are the mean, median, and mode.

Review Psychology Terms

Select the term that best fits the definition. Some terms will not be used.

_____ 1. An educated guess, or prediction, about the nature of things based on a theory

_____ 2. The arithmetic average of the distribution of scores for a particular variable

_____ 3. A researcher records behavior as it occurs in a natural environment, but does so as a participant of the group being studied

_____ 4. The bell-shaped curve that occurs on a graph when the mean, median, and mode are identical in value

_____ 5. Assesses the nature of the relationship between two or more variables that are not controlled by the researcher

_____ 6. A number that describes the central location within a distribution of scores in a sample

_____ 7. A set of procedures used to gather, analyze, and interpret information in a way that reduces error and leads to dependable conclusions

_____ 8. A branch of mathematics that allows researchers to organize, describe, and make meaningful judgments from data they collected

_____ 9. The statistic, or numerical value, that psychologists use to describe the relationship between two variables

_____ 10. Structured sets of questions or statements given to a group of people to measure their beliefs, values, or behaviors

_____ 11. A scientific method involving an in-depth analysis of a single subject

_____ 12. Mathematical methods used to determine whether the data support or do not support the research hypothesis

_____ 13. Scientific method in which researchers manipulate, or change, a variable to observe the effect on some other variable

_____ 14. The process of deciding what to believe and how to act based on a careful evaluation of the evidence

a. case study
b. central tendency
c. correlation coefficient
d. correlational research
e. critical thinking
f. dependent variable
g. descriptive statistics
h. experiment
i. hypothesis
j. independent variable
k. inferential statistics
l. mean
m. median
n. mode
o. naturalistic observation
p. normal distribution
q. operational definition
r. participant observation
s. random assignment
t. random selection
u. replication
v. sample
w. scientific methods
x. standard deviation
y. statistics
z. survey
aa. theory
bb. variable

Review Psychology Concepts

15. Define replication.

16. Explain the difference between a theory and hypothesis.

17. How do critical thinking skills help scientific researchers in psychology?

18. List five ways to improve your critical thinking skills.

19. What is the difference between a sample and a population?

20. How does replication help advance scientific knowledge?

21. How is the health and safety of human and animal participants protected in psychological studies?

22. What are the three basic techniques of data collection?

23. Give a brief description of the three types of observational research methods used by psychologists.

24. What is an advantage and disadvantage of a case study?

25. What is the range of the correlation coefficient?

26. What are the advantages and disadvantages of correlational research?

27. What is the difference between an independent variable and a dependent variable?

28. How do inferential statistics differ from descriptive statistics?

29. Explain this statement: There are no final truths in science.

Apply Psychology Concepts

30. An important aspect of critical thinking is thinking about different explanations for events. Psychologist Leonard Eron's research found that aggressive children watched a lot of violent television shows. What is one explanation for this relationship between the aggressiveness of children and the degree to which they watch violence on television? What is an alternative explanation for this finding?

31. What is an operational definition in a psychological study? If you were going to investigate whether depriving people of sleep hurt their ability to learn new information, how might you operationally define both "sleep deprivation" and "learning" in your study?

32. Imagine that you wanted to study how rumors are created and spread among high school students. You decide that you are going to do a participant observation study. Explain what is involved in this type of study and how you might conduct this research.

33. How would you conduct an experiment on whether watching television violence causes increased aggression in children? In describing how you would design this experiment, identify your independent variable and your dependent variable.

Make Academic Connections

34. **Science** With a partner, design an experiment in which the hypothesis, population, sample, independent variable, dependent variable, and experimental and control groups are properly identified.

35. **Writing** Write an argument on a topic of interest to you. Use the library or Internet to find information on your topic. Cite a statistical finding to strengthen your argument.

36. **Mathematics** Gather data about a subject that interests you, such as basketball scores for the senior players at your school. Calculate the mean, median, and mode for the data.

37. **Language Arts** Write a research paper that either supports or does not support using animals in research studies. Cite at least one statistical finding and one quotation from an expert.

38. **Cultural Diversity** Use the library or Internet to research contributions made by ethnic minority psychologists. Create a graphic organizer of your findings.

39. **History** Use the library or Internet to research experiences of and opportunities for minority groups in psychology. Choose one or more of the experiences or opportunities and create a visual representation of your findings.

40. **Business and Marketing** Write a survey that allows you to collect data on consumers' buying behaviors. Questions might include in which stores consumers shop for clothes, what type of brands they usually buy, and why they typically purchase these brands. After you write your survey, ask six people of the same age group and gender the questions, and then ask six people of the same age group and the opposite gender the questions. Compare the data between the groups, and then write a report of your findings. Attach the survey questions to your report.

DIGGING DEEPER
with Psychology eCollection

One of the most interesting—and controversial—subjects of psychological study is dreaming. As you read in this chapter, psychologist William Dement studied dreaming in the 1950s. His work rendered a hypothesis that humans have a basic need to dream. Since Dement's research, many scientists have studied dreams. Through observation and experimentation, they have learned more about this fascinating behavior. Milton Kramer is a recent dream researcher. Experiments in his sleep laboratory have provided interesting confirmation for Dement's hypothesis as well as additional results. Access the Gale Psychology eCollection at *www.cengage.com/school/psych/franzoi* and discover what Kramer's research shows about dreams and dreaming. Write a brief report describing Kramer's findings and answer the question: Why is studying dreams important to understanding human behavior? As an additional project, apply Kramer's findings to your sleep and dreams or to those of someone you know.

Source: Kramer, Milton. "Dreamspeak." *Psychology Today* 33.5 (Sept 2000): 56.

SELF-DISCOVERY: YOUR SCORE

Do You Enjoy Critical Thinking?

Scoring Instructions: If you agree with items 1, 3, 5, and 7 and disagree with items 2, 4, 6, and 8, this suggests that you often enjoy engaging in critical thinking. If your response to these items are exactly in the opposite direction, this suggests that you find less enjoyment in critical thinking. Do your responses suggest that you are more or less of a critical thinker?

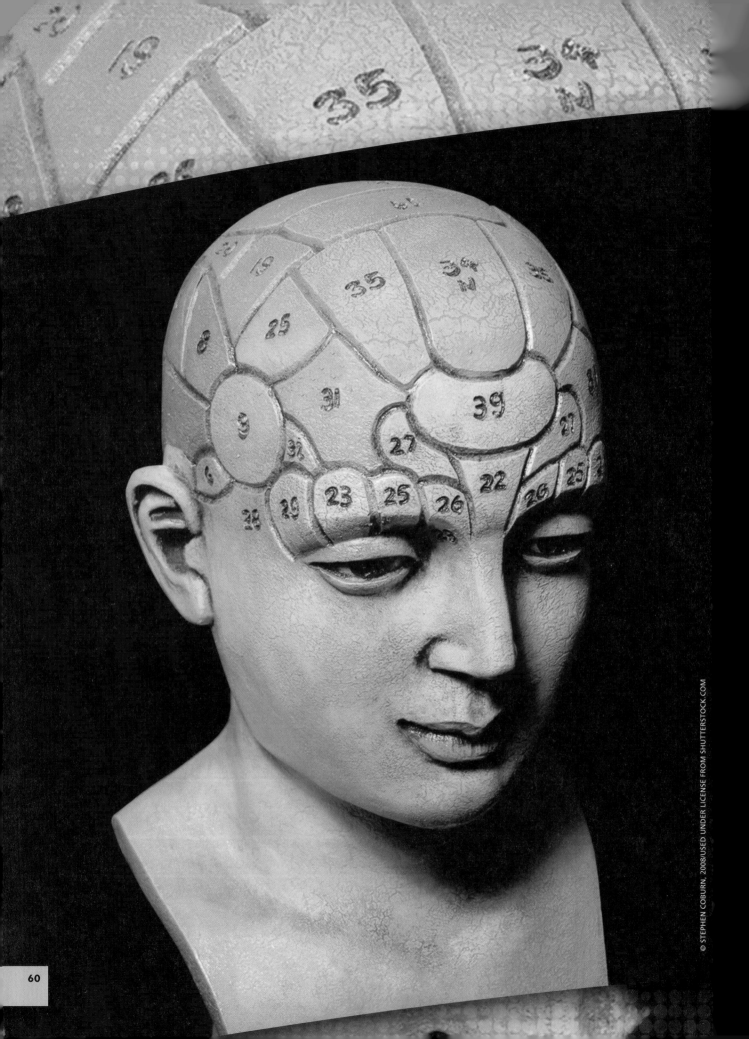

UNIT 2

Biopsychological Domain

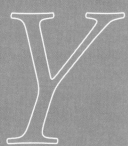our body is not only an object of beauty, it also is a wonderful instrument of action. Nowhere is the action of your body more complex and furious than way at the top, inside your skull. Yes, your brain is a marvel, and scientists are struggling to uncover its many complicated patterns. Specialized cells, called neurons, are located in your brain. These neurons send and receive information throughout your body. Each cell in your body contains thousands of genes which provide instructions for how every activity in the cell should be carried out. Chapter 3 in this unit will explain how the work of neurons and genes create the wonder of you.

This unit also will take you on a journey that will help you discover how you make sense of the world around you through your senses. Why are you sometimes tricked into falsely understanding various sights, sounds, tastes, smells, and touch sensations? What motivates you to eat certain foods yet avoid others? Your motivation both pushes you and pulls you toward many goals in life. This unit will examine the psychology behind your sensations, perceptions, motives, and emotions.

Finally, this unit will explore what happens when you experience stress in your life. How do your body and mind react while studying for that big exam, preparing for that important game or play, or having fun with your friends? Why do some people feel greater stress than others when faced with the same challenges in life? Psychologists have many important insights into the biopsychology of you.

ESSENTIAL QUESTION
Go to page XXIV

Neurological and Genetic Bases of Behavior

"It's like waking up, sort of like waking up in the world. You're waking, trying to push things together yourself, reaching back. And you wonder at times yourself just, well, what it is and what it isn't."

—HENRY MOLAISON AS QUOTED BY HILTS, 1995, P. 239

At the age of 16 Henry Molaison experienced his first major grand mal epileptic seizure. By age 27 he was having as many as 11 seizures per week and was unable to hold a job or live on his own. In desperation, Henry's doctor drilled two holes into Henry's skull above his eyes. The doctors inserted a silver straw deep into Henry's brain and sucked out a fist-sized piece of the *hippocampus*. The year was 1953 and neuroscientists knew very little about the hippocampus.

The surgery reduced Henry's epileptic seizures, but it had an additional unintended consequence. Prior to this surgery, no one realized that the hippocampus is the part of the brain that plays a critical role in forming new memories. Henry was now a man with a memory frozen in time. His memories of people and events prior to his surgery were intact. Yet now, when Henry stopped thinking about something that had just happened to him, the memory disappeared, as if it never occurred. During the final 55 years of his life (he died in 2008 at the age of 82), Henry Molaison did not remember that his parents had died or that people had walked on the moon. He also did not know that his tragic life circumstances dramatically increased scientists' understanding of the brain.

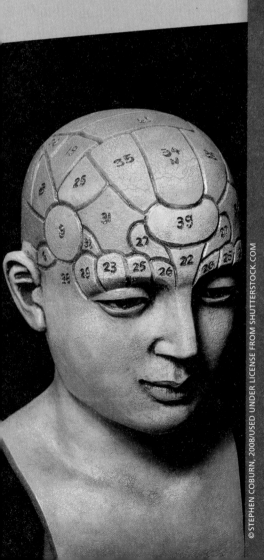

LESSON
3.1 | Neural and Hormonal Systems

OBJECTIVES

- Define neurons, and explain how they work and how they communicate with one another.
- Distinguish the parts of the nervous system.
- Describe the endocrine system.

DISCOVER IT | *How does this relate to me?*

Did you know that your body runs on electricity and that tiny chemical messengers are flowing throughout your body in your blood? Would you be surprised to learn that your nervous system has about as many specialized cells as the number of stars in the galaxy? These specialized nerve cells, or *neurons,* account for all human thought and action. In this lesson, you will gain an understanding of the neuron and nervous system as well as the endocrine system, which is connected to the nervous system.

KEY TERMS

- neurons
- spinal cord
- neurotransmitters
- central nervous system
- peripheral nervous system
- somatic nervous system
- autonomic nervous system
- sympathetic nervous system
- parasympathetic nervous system
- endocrine system
- hormones

The doctors who operated on Henry Molaison did not realize at the time that they were removing Henry's ability to form new memories. However, the neuroscientists who later studied Henry's memory problems learned a great deal about how the hippocampus works. Neuroscientists are concerned with the nervous system within the brain such as vision and hearing, and behavior produced by the brain.

Neurons and Neural Communication

Your body's nervous system regulates all your body functions and controls your emotions, movements, thinking, and behavior. The nervous system has specialized cells, called **neurons,** that send and receive information throughout the body. They are the nervous system's building blocks. The human nervous system contains anywhere from 90 to 180 billion neurons, with 98.8 percent residing in the brain. The remaining 1.2 percent (more than 1 billion neurons) are distributed throughout the spinal cord. The **spinal cord** is a bundle of nerves that connects the brain to the rest of the body. Your spinal cord runs along the length of your back.

Each neuron transmits information to about a thousand other neurons. This means there are trillions of different neuron connections in the brain. Although

neurons Specialized cells in the nervous system that send and receive information throughout the body

spinal cord A bundle of nerves that connects the brain to the rest of the body

neurons come in thousands of different shapes and sizes, researchers have identified three basic types. These are sensory neurons, motor neurons, and interneurons.

Sensory neurons pick up stimuli inside the body or in the world and send *input signals* to the brain. For example, stimuli sent from inside the body might be the body sending a message to the brain that you have a headache or strained muscle. Stimuli coming from the world might be another person's voice.

Motor neurons send signals in the opposite direction. They send *output signals* from the brain to glands, muscles, and organs. For example, motor neurons send commands for your fingers to move across the computer keyboard.

The majority of neurons are *interneurons*. These connect neurons to one another. One of the most important functions of interneurons is to connect the sensory neurons' input signals with the motor neurons' output signals.

THE STRUCTURE OF A NEURON

Most neurons have three basic parts, as illustrated in Figure 3-1. The central part is the *soma,* which is the Latin word for "body." This cell body contains the nucleus, or control center of the neuron. Attached to the soma are branchlike extensions, known as *dendrites* (the Greek word for "trees"). Dendrites receive information from other neurons and bring it to the soma. After organizing this information, the soma transmits it to a tube-like extension called an *axon* (Greek for "axle"). The axon carries the information down its "tube" in the form of an electrochemical impulse. Axons can range in length from 1/32 of an inch to more than 3 feet.

Use the idea of a tennis ball to help you understand the relative size and length of the soma, dendrites, and axon of some of the longer neurons. Visualize a tennis ball with a number of shoelaces attached to one side of it and a thin rope 14 miles long attached to the other side. The tennis ball is the soma, the shoelaces are the dendrites, and the long rope is the axon.

Figure 3-1 **STRUCTURE OF A NEURON**

The primary components of the neuron are the soma, dendrites, and axon.

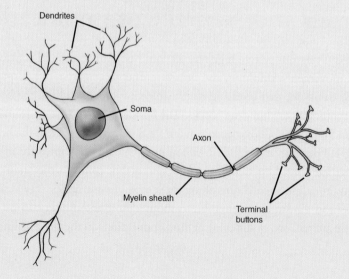

Many axons are covered with a protective coating of fatty cells known as a *myelin sheath*. This coating speeds up the passing of information. In certain diseases, such as multiple sclerosis (MS), the myelin sheath is slowly destroyed. As the myelin sheath is destroyed, the brain is unable to efficiently communicate with the body's muscles. The result is the loss of muscle control.

At the end of each axon are branches with knoblike tips called *terminal buttons*. These come close to, but do not touch, the dendrites of other neurons. The space between the axon's terminal buttons and the dendrites is less than a millionth of an inch wide. It is called the *synapse,* which in Greek means "to clasp."

Nerve tissue throughout the body is composed of two kinds of cells. These cells are neurons and supporting glial cells (*glial* in Greek means "glue"). Glial cells supply the neurons with support, nutrients, and insulation. Think of the brain as a house. Glial cells are the floors, walls, and supporting beams, while the neurons are the electrical wiring. Glial cells literally hold the brain together, while the neurons send and receive information throughout the brain structure. The myelin sheath that covers most axons is made up of glial cells. There are 10 times more glial cells in the nervous system than there are neurons, but they are much smaller than neurons and make up only about half the brain's total mass.

About 400,000 people in the United States suffer from MS, and each week about 200 more are diagnosed with this disease.

NEURON ACTIVITY

A neuron is always in either a resting or a firing state. There is no in-between condition. When the neuron is in a resting state, there is a tiny negative electrical charge—about one-twentieth of a volt—within the axon. The neuron is a storehouse of potential energy even in a resting state. The release of this energy depends on the combined stimulation received by all the dendrites from other nearby neurons. The combined stimulation must exceed a certain minimum intensity, or *threshold*. As the threshold is exceeded, the energy is released and the neuron transmits an electrochemical impulse down its axon. This occurs in about one-thousandth of a second.

Does this neural impulse speed seem fast? The speed of an electric current passing through a wire is three million times faster. The fact that electrical wire transmission is so much faster than neural impulse speed explains why there are machines that respond faster than our bodies.

How do the billions of neurons in the nervous system work together to coordinate the body's activities? To understand this process, you need to examine how neural impulses get from one neuron to another.

The end of each axon has terminal buttons that get close to, but do not touch, the dendrites of other neurons. These terminal buttons contain a number of tiny round sacs called *synaptic vesicles*. When a neural impulse arrives at the axon's terminal buttons, these synaptic vesicles release chemical messengers. These messengers are called **neurotransmitters**. Neurotransmitters travel across the synapse. When they arrive at the receiving neuron's dendrites, they fit into *receptor sites* like keys fit into locks. Just as specific keys can fit into only specific kinds of locks, each kind of neurotransmitter has a unique chemical makeup that allows it to fit into only one

neurotransmitters
Chemical messages that travel between nerve cells and muscles to trigger or prevent an impulse in the receiving cell

specific kind of receptor site. This neural communication process is illustrated in Figure 3-2.

Once a neurotransmitter fits into a receptor site, it either increases or decreases the odds that the neuron will fire. Messages from neurotransmitters called *excitatory messages* increase the chance of the neuron firing. Messages called *inhibitory messages*

Figure 3-2 **NEURAL COMMUNICATION**

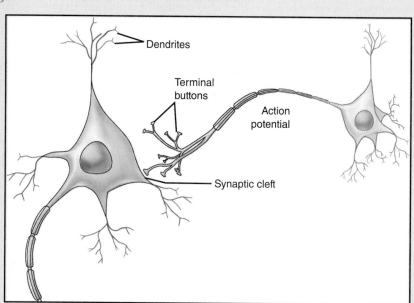

reduce the chance of the neuron firing. Neuron dendrites receive both excitatory and inhibitory messages at the same time from different receptor sites. Whether or not the neuron fires depends on which type of message is stronger. If a neuron receives many more excitatory than inhibitory messages, it will fire. If the neuron receives more inhibitory messages than excitatory ones, it will remain in a resting state.

MAJOR NEUROTRANSMITTERS

Understanding how neurotransmitters work in the brain helps scientists develop drugs that are similar to naturally occurring neurotransmitters. The major neurotransmitters that occur naturally in your brain include acetylcholine, dopamine, endorphins, and serotonin.

One of the most important neurotransmitters is *acetylcholine*. This neurotransmitter sends excitatory messages to your skeletal muscles, which help you to walk, talk, blink your eyes, and breathe. It also plays a critical role in the formation of memories. Researchers believe that the memory loss found in the brain disorder known as *Alzheimer's disease* is caused by a sharp reduction in the supply of acetylcholine. Alzheimer's disease afflicts 11 percent of people over the age of 65.

Another important neurotransmitter is *dopamine,* which controls large muscle movements and influences pleasure and motivation. Too much or too little dopamine in the brain results in a wide variety of negative effects. These range from jerky muscle movements to strange hallucinations experienced by people who suffer from serious psychological disorders.

One group of neurotransmitters known as *endorphins* is important in the experience of pleasure and the control of pain. The brain produces endorphins in response to injury and many forms of physical stress, such as intense exercise and childbirth labor. The increase in endorphins temporarily provides the body with a natural painkiller. These neurotransmitters are believed to cause the "runners' high" that many athletes experience following a strong workout.

One neurotransmitter that is especially important in regulating emotions, aggression, appetite, and sleep is *serotonin*. Depressed and anxious moods, aggressiveness, and food cravings are associated with low levels of serotonin in the brain. Milk contains an amino acid that helps the brain produce serotonin, so the age-old advice to drink a glass of milk before going to bed may be the ticket to a good night's rest. Table 3-1 summarizes the function of the four neurotransmitters described here.

Table 3-1 MAJOR NEUROTRANSMITTERS

Neurotransmitters	Involved In
Acetylcholine	Walking, talking, blinking, breathing, and memories
Dopamine	Large muscle movement, pleasure, and motivation
Endorphins	Pain suppression and pleasure
Serotonin	Emotions, aggression, appetite, anxious moods, and sleep

CHECKPOINT ▷ *What are neurons?*

The Nervous System

Neurons combine to form the *nervous system*. The nervous system is your body's primary information system. It is divided into two major portions—the *central nervous system* and the *peripheral nervous system*.

THE CENTRAL NERVOUS SYSTEM

The **central nervous system** consists of the brain and spinal cord (see Figure 3-3). It is covered by bone and three protective membranes, and is also shielded from injury by a clear solution known as *cerebrospinal fluid.* This protective fluid allows the brain to float inside the skull. In this floating state, the brain's three-pound "air weight" is reduced to only a few ounces, which lessens its pressure on the spinal cord.

As you read earlier in this chapter, the spinal cord is the slender, tube-shaped part of the central nervous system that connects the brain to the rest of the body. It is protected inside the bony spinal column and surrounded by cerebrospinal fluid. The nerves of the spinal cord transmit information from sensory neurons up to the brain and from the brain down to motor neurons that create movement. Every voluntary

central nervous system The brain and spinal cord

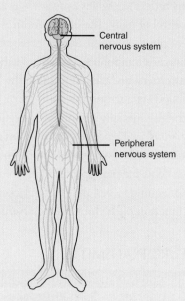

Figure 3-3 THE CENTRAL AND PERIPHERAL NERVOUS SYSTEMS

The human nervous system is divided into two major portions, the central nervous system, which consists of the brain and spinal cord, and the peripheral nervous system, which consists of the remaining nerves in the body.

Central
nervous system

Peripheral
nervous system

action, such as walking and moving your arms, requires a message from the brain to the spinal cord and from the spinal cord to the muscles.

The spinal cord extends from the base of the brain to slightly below the waist. The upper sections of the spinal cord control the upper parts of the body, while the lower sections control the lower body. If a portion of the spinal cord is ever severed, the person loses all sensation and muscle control below the injury. The higher up the spine an injury occurs, the greater the extent of paralysis. Some 11,000 Americans injure their spinal cords each year. When such injuries occur, the central nervous system cannot repair itself. However, advances in medical science provide hope that in the future such damage can be repaired.

THE PERIPHERAL NERVOUS SYSTEM

The **peripheral nervous system** is made up of all the nerves located outside the brain and spinal cord. Its function is to connect the brain and spinal cord with the organs and tissues of the body. It does this by conducting neural impulses into and out of the central nervous system.

The peripheral nervous system has two major divisions, the somatic nervous system and the autonomic nervous system. The **somatic nervous system** sends commands to the voluntary skeletal muscles by way of *motor neurons* and receives sensory information from the muscles and skin by way of *sensory neurons*. Commands to the skeletal muscles control your movement. Messages received from the muscles and the skin provide you with the sense of touch, the sense of position in your surroundings, and the perception of temperature and pain. As you read this text, the movement of your eyes and your ability to see the words and feel the book in your hands is being controlled by the somatic nervous system.

peripheral nervous system The nerves that connect the brain and spinal cord with the organs and tissues of the body

somatic nervous system A division of the peripheral nervous system that sends commands to voluntary skeletal muscles and receives sensory information from the muscles and the skin

The word *autonomic* means "self-governing." The **autonomic nervous system** controls movement of involuntary, nonskeletal muscles over which you have little or no control. These include the heart, lungs, and stomach muscles. The primary function of this self-governing system is to maintain *homeostasis,* the body's steady state of normal functioning.

The autonomic nervous system is divided into two separate branches—the *sympathetic* and *parasympathetic* systems (see Figure 3-4). These two branches work together in regulating many of your body functions. The **sympathetic nervous system** activates the body's energy resources to deal with threatening situations. If something angers or frightens you, the sympathetic system prepares you for "fight or flight" by slowing your digestion, accelerating your heart rate, raising your blood sugar, and cooling your body with perspiration.

The **parasympathetic nervous system** acts to conserve and maintain the body's energy resources. When the threat has passed, parasympathetic nerves slow the autonomic system back down to its normal level of functioning. Although the sympathetic and parasympathetic systems produce opposite effects, together they keep the nervous system as a whole in a steady state of normal functioning.

autonomic nervous system The division of the peripheral nervous system that controls movement of involuntary, nonskeletal muscles

sympathetic nervous system The part of the autonomic nervous system that activates the body's energy resources to deal with threatening situations

parasympathetic nervous system The part of the autonomic nervous system that conserves and maintains the body's energy resources

CHECKPOINT *How does the central nervous system differ from the peripheral nervous system?*

Figure 3-4 THE DUAL FUNCTIONS OF THE AUTONOMIC NERVOUS SYSTEM

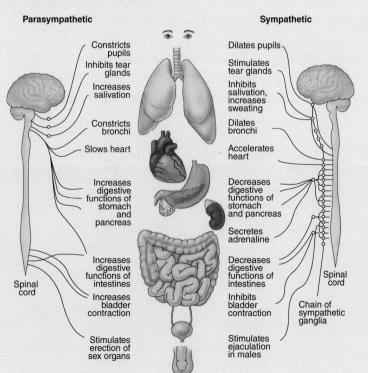

Parasympathetic

- Constricts pupils
- Inhibits tear glands
- Increases salivation
- Constricts bronchi
- Slows heart
- Increases digestive functions of stomach and pancreas
- Increases digestive functions of intestines
- Increases bladder contraction
- Stimulates erection of sex organs

Spinal cord

Sympathetic

- Dilates pupils
- Stimulates tear glands
- Inhibits salivation, increases sweating
- Dilates bronchi
- Accelerates heart
- Decreases digestive functions of stomach and pancreas
- Secretes adrenaline
- Decreases digestive functions of intestines
- Inhibits bladder contraction
- Stimulates ejaculation in males

Spinal cord

Chain of sympathetic ganglia

The sympathetic and parasympathetic divisions of the autonomic nervous system often stimulate opposite effects in the body's organs. The sympathetic nervous system prepares your body for action, while the parasympathetic nervous system calms the body

INTERACTIVE FIGURE

The Endocrine System

The **endocrine system** is a network of glands that manufactures and secretes hormones. **Hormones** are chemical messengers that regulate or stimulate the body. The endocrine system is interconnected with—but not actually part of—the nervous system. Hormones are secreted directly into the bloodstream by the endocrine system (see Table 3-2). They are carried by your blood throughout the body. The membrane of every cell has receptors for one or more of these chemical messengers. Hormones have a direct effect on many different body organs, including the brain.

The most influential endocrine gland is the *pituitary gland,* a pea-sized structure located in the base of the brain. The pituitary gland is controlled by a nearby brain area called the *hypothalamus,* which regulates body temperature. The pituitary often is referred to as the master gland because it releases about 10 different hormones that stimulate and regulate the rest of the endocrine system. One of these hormones influences growth. Around the age of 13, the pituitary gland increases its secretion of the growth hormone that acts directly on bone and muscle tissue to produce the adolescent growth spurt.

Other notable glands in the endocrine system are the thyroid gland, the adrenal glands, and the gonads (see Table 3-2). The thyroid gland is located in the neck. It produces the hormone thyroxin, which controls metabolism, or the rate at which the food you eat is transformed into energy. People with an underactive thyroid tend to be tired and depressed. People with an overactive thyroid tend to be very excitable and have short attention spans.

The adrenal glands secrete epinephrine (also called adrenaline) and norepinephrine (also called noradrenaline). These hormones work with and add to the effects of the sympathetic nervous system. They make the heart beat faster, slow digestion, and increase the rate at which the body uses energy. Have you ever noticed that it takes you a while to calm down after facing a stressful situation? That's because the adrenaline and noradrenaline levels remain high following stressful events.

The gonads are the two sex glands. The two male gonads are called testes, and they produce sperm cells. The two female gonads are known as ovaries, and they

endocrine system
A network of glands that manufactures and secretes hormones directly into the bloodstream

hormones Chemical messengers, carried by the bloodstream, that regulate or stimulate the body

Table 3-2 IMPORTANT GLANDS AND HORMONES IN THE ENDOCRINE SYSTEM

Gland	Hormone	Effects
Pituitary gland	Growth hormone	Stimulates growth (especially bones) and metabolic functions
Thyroid gland	Thyroxin	Stimulates and maintains metabolic processes
Adrenal glands	Epinephrine and norepinephrine	Increase metabolic activities and blood glucose; constrict certain blood vessels
Gonads (male testes and female ovaries)	Testosterone (males), estrogen, and progesterone (females)	Two sex glands; testosterone helps in the growth of muscles, bone, and male characteristics such as chest hair; estrogen and progesterone help in development of female physical characteristics and regulation of the female menstrual and reproductive cycles

produce ova, or eggs. The testes and ovaries also both produce testosterone, but the male gonads produce much more of this hormone. Testosterone is important in the growth of muscles, bone, and male characteristics such as chest hair. Female ovaries also produce estrogen and progesterone, hormones important to female adolescent physical development and the regulation of the menstrual and reproductive cycles.

CHECKPOINT *What is the endocrine system?*

INFOBIT
A number of well-known athletes have been accused of using steroids to enhance their performance. Steroids act like testosterone, adding muscle weight and increasing strength. However, these drugs can cause cancer, heart damage, strokes, and violent behavior. They are extremely dangerous.

3.1 ASSESSMENT

In Your Own Words

Write a paper comparing how communication to the body in the nervous system compares with communication to the body in the endocrine system.

Review Concepts

1. Which neurotransmitter is known to suppress pain?
   - a. acetylcholine
   - b. dopamine
   - c. endorphins
   - d. serotonin

2. Which nervous system activates the body's energy resources to deal with threatening situations?
   - a. sympathetic
   - b. somatic
   - c. parasympathetic
   - d. autonomic

3. Which gland stimulates growth?
   - a. pituitary
   - b. thyroid
   - c. adrenal
   - d. gonads

4. Which are specialized cells that send and receive information throughout the body?
   - a. spinal column
   - b. serotonin
   - c. inhibitory messages
   - d. neurons

5. Describe the spinal cord.

6. **True or False** Neurons are the building blocks of the nervous system.

7. **True or False** There are trillions of different neurons in the brain.

8. **True or False** Hormones are secreted by the nervous system.

Think Critically

9. Why is it important for psychologists to understand how the neural and hormonal systems work?

10. Why is paralysis greater with injuries that occur higher on the spinal cord?

11. Why does it take you a while to calm down after facing a stressful situation?

KEY TERMS

- electroencephalograph (EEG)
- computerized axial tomograph (CAT) scan
- magnetic resonance imaging (MRI)
- positron emission tomography (PET) scan
- functional magnetic resonance imaging (fMRI)
- hindbrain
- midbrain
- forebrain
- cerebral cortex
- cerebral hemispheres
- lobes

OBJECTIVES

- Identify the different technologies used to study the brain.
- Identify the three major brain regions.

DISCOVER IT | *How does this relate to me?*

You may have heard the following statement: "You use only 10 percent of your brain." The truth is that you could not behave normally if only 10 percent of your neurons were active. Your brain accounts for only about 2 percent of your total body weight, but it controls most of the complex aspects of your behavior and mental life. It is the most vital organ in your body and is constantly changing and altering its neural connections.

Remember Henry Molaison from the chapter opening? He lost memory function after surgery that removed part of his brain. How different his life would have been had he undergone medical treatment today rather than in the 1950s when so little was known about the brain. Modern technology allows neuroscientists to see how the brain functions without causing it any harm.

Studying the Brain

The most widely used technique to study the brain is the **electroencephalograph (EEG)**. The EEG records "waves" of electrical activity in the brain using metal electrodes placed on a person's scalp. EEG measurement has provided researchers with valuable information on brain functioning. The one drawback of the EEG is that it measures the electrical activity of many different areas of the brain at once, making it difficult to pinpoint the exact location of specific brain wave activity.

A more revealing look at the brain is obtained by *brain-imaging techniques,* which provide pictures—or scans—of the brain. One such technique is the **computerized axial tomograph (CAT) scan**. A CAT scan takes thousands of X-ray photographs of the brain while the patient lies still on a table. The patient's head is placed in the middle of a doughnut-shaped ring. Using a computer, the multiple X-ray images are

electroencephalograph (EEG) A brain-imaging technique that records "waves" of electrical activity in the brain

computerized axial tomograph (CAT) scan A brain-imaging technique that combines thousands of X-ray brain photographs to construct a picture of the brain.

combined to construct a picture of the brain. CAT scans are helpful in detecting brain abnormalities, such as swelling and enlargement of certain areas.

Another brain-imaging technique is **magnetic resonance imaging (MRI)**. This technology produces three-dimensional images of the brain's soft tissues by detecting magnetic activity from nuclear particles in brain molecules. MRI provides greater accuracy in the diagnosis of brain diseases than the CAT scan.

Both the CAT and MRI scans document the brain's structure. The **positron emission tomography (PET) scan** measures the amount of brain activity. Neural activity in different brain regions is measured by showing each region's use of glucose, a sugar that is the brain's chemical fuel. PET scans can reveal which parts of the brain are most active in such tasks as talking or listening to others, reading, listening to music, and solving math problems.

A newer technology called **functional magnetic resonance imaging (fMRI)** produces a picture of neural activity averaged over seconds, not minutes, and the images can identify much smaller brain structures than those in PET scans.

These brain-imaging techniques provide researchers with the means to make new discoveries about the brain. Neuroscientists' ability to "peek" into the brain provides the necessary information to prevent the type of surgery experienced by Henry Molaison. However, the ability to measure the workings of the human brain is raising growing concerns about how such technology might be abused by tapping into people's minds without their consent. The New Science feature on page 74 discusses potential privacy issues associated with brain imaging.

magnetic resonance imaging (MRI) A brain-imaging technique that produces three-dimensional images of the brain's soft tissues

positron emission tomography (PET) scan A brain-imaging technique that measures the average neural activity in different brain regions over a few minutes

functional magnetic resonance imagining (fMRI) A brain-imaging technique that measures the average neural activity in different brain regions over a few seconds

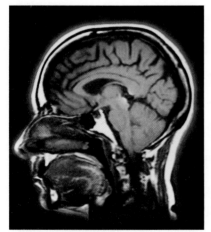

PHOTODISC/GETTY IMAGES

(Left) Brain image using a magnetic resonance imaging (MRI) scan. (Right) Positron emission tomography (PET) scan showing highlighted regions of the brain during auditory stimulation.

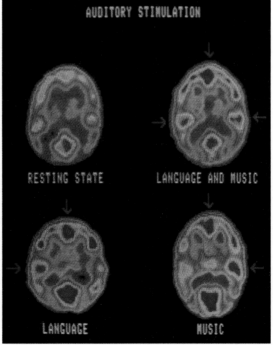

SCIENCE FACTION/GETTY IMAGES

CHECKPOINT ▶ *What are five technologies used to study the brain?*

Is Privacy an Issue in Brain Imaging?

Would you be concerned if brain-imaging techniques could "read" people's minds and determine such things as whether they are truthful or racially prejudiced? Is this possibility pure science fiction? Maybe not. Brain-imaging studies indicate that certain areas of the brain are more active when people are lying. Scientists are trying to determine whether this knowledge can be used to produce the world's most effective lie detector. Other brain-imaging studies have been able to detect unconscious racism among people, raising the possibility that one day we may be able to scan people's brains and identify who is likely to discriminate against others.

Privacy concerns raised by brain imaging are becoming an important topic of discussion in neuroscience. Such concerns may prompt the passage of new laws to protect the public from the misuse of this powerful new technology.

Think Critically

How might society apply brain-imaging techniques to determine if someone is telling the truth? What is your opinion of using brain imaging to determine if someone is telling the truth? Explain your answer.

The Three Major Brain Regions

The brain has three major regions. These are the hindbrain, midbrain, and forebrain (see Figure 3-5). The names come from the physical arrangement of the regions in the skull.

The **hindbrain** is found at the rear base of the skull and contains the *medulla, pons,* and *cerebellum.* It controls the most basic biological needs for life. The medulla, located at the top of the spinal cord, controls breathing, heart rate, swallowing, and digestion. It also allows you to maintain an upright posture. The pons, located just above the medulla, is concerned with sleep and arousal. Behind the medulla and pons is the cerebellum. This region of the brain is important in the regulation and coordination of body movement. The cerebellum also plays a role in learning.

The **midbrain** is located just above the hindbrain. It plays a critical role in attention and stimulation. It also combines sensory information and sends it to other brain regions. The most important structure in the midbrain is the *reticular formation.* The reticular formation is involved in the regulation and maintenance of consciousness and sleep. It extends into the hindbrain, where it makes up a portion of the pons. When you are startled by a loud noise, your heightened arousal is due

hindbrain The part of the brain found at the rear base of the skull that controls the most basic biological needs for life

midbrain The part of the brain above the hindbrain that plays a role in attention, stimulation, and consciousness

Figure 3-5 THE PARTS OF THE BRAIN

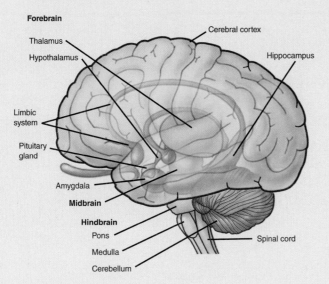

The three major regions of the brain are the hindbrain, the midbrain, and the forebrain.

to the reticular formation. It also allows you to sleep through familiar sounds. If the reticular formation is damaged, a permanent coma can result.

The **forebrain** is the area of the brain that is the most forward in the skull. It controls complex emotions, thoughts, and movement. The forebrain is made up of the thalamus, hypothalamus, and limbic system. The *thalamus* is the brain's sensory relay station. It sorts and sends messages from the eyes, ears, tongue, and skin to other parts of the brain.

The *hypothalamus* is located under the thalamus. One of its most important functions is to provide *homeostasis,* maintaining a constant internal body state. This small brain structure regulates eating, drinking, and sexual behavior. It also controls the release of hormones from the pituitary gland.

In the core of the forebrain is a series of interrelated doughnut-shaped neural structures called the *limbic system.* This system's two main structures are the *amygdala* and *hippocampus.* The amygdala controls fear and aggression. The hippocampus is important in memory formation. It is the area of the brain that was surgically removed in Henry Molaison to control his seizures.

THE CEREBRAL CORTEX

The **cerebral cortex** is the thinking center of the brain. Located in the uppermost portion of the forebrain, the cerebral cortex coordinates and integrates all other areas of the brain into a fully functioning unit. This is the part of the brain that sets us apart from all other animals and makes us human.

The cerebral cortex is divided into two rounded halves, called the **cerebral hemispheres.** These hemispheres are connected together at the bottom by the *corpus callosum.* This is a thick band of more than 200 million white nerve fibers that transmit information between the two hemispheres of the brain (see Figure 3-6). Your brain is cross-wired. The right hemisphere controls movement and feeling of the left side of the body, and the left hemisphere controls the right side of the body.

forebrain The part of the brain above the midbrain that controls emotional reactions, thought processes, movement, sensory information, and body temperature

cerebral cortex The thinking center of the brain which coordinates and integrates all areas of the brain into a fully functioning unit

cerebral hemispheres Two halves of the cerebral cortex

Figure 3-6 THE CORPUS CALLOSUM

The corpus callosum is the dense band of nerve fibers connecting the right and left cerebral hemispheres.

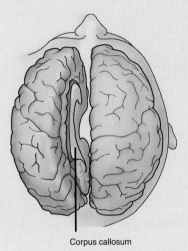

Corpus callosum

Lobes of the Cerebral Cortex   Both cerebral hemispheres are divided into four major sections called **lobes**. These are the frontal, parietal, temporal, and occipital lobes (see Figure 3-7). These lobes are not independent parts of the cortex, but regions named for the bones of the skull covering them.

The two *occipital lobes* are the visual regions of the brain. They are located at the back of the cerebral hemispheres and allow you to experience shapes, color, and motion. Damage to the occipital lobes can cause blindness, even if the eyes and optic nerves are healthy.

The *parietal lobes* are involved in touch sensation and how you experience yourself in the space around you. They are located in front of the occipital lobes. Damage to the parietal lobes can destroy your sense of touch, making it impossible to feel an object placed in your hands.

The two *temporal lobes* are important in hearing and language. They are located below the parietal lobes, near the temples. Damage to the left temporal lobe can cause difficulty understanding what words and sentences mean.

The two largest lobes in the human brain are the *frontal lobes*. They are involved in the coordination of movement and higher mental processes, such as planning, social skills, emotional control, and abstract thinking. The frontal lobes are located at the front of the cerebral hemispheres, just behind the forehead. Studies show that the left frontal lobe controls more positive feelings, while the right frontal lobe controls more negative moods. Damage to the frontal lobes can result in dramatic personality changes.

lobes The four major sections of both cerebral hemispheres

LAB TEAMS

Regions of the Brain

Work with a partner to design an image or model of the three regions of the brain. Identify each region and its purpose. In the cerebral cortex area, identify the possible consequences of damage to the different areas. Your image can be a drawing, computer image, or you can design a three-dimensional model.

Figure 3-7 THE CEREBRAL CORTEX

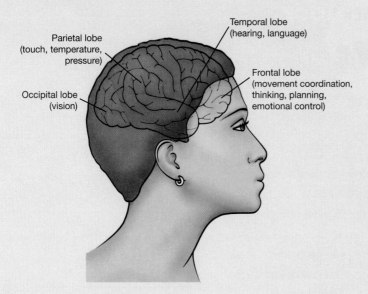

Parietal lobe
(touch, temperature,
pressure)

Temporal lobe
(hearing, language)

Frontal lobe
(movement coordination,
thinking, planning,
emotional control)

Occipital lobe
(vision)

Each hemisphere of the cerebral cortex can be divided into four lobes: the occipital lobe, the parietal lobe, the temporal lobe, and the frontal lobe.

Although damage to the brain can cause serious problems and even death (Table 3-3), your brain is remarkably flexible in repairing itself following an injury (see Closer Look on page 78).

The following lifelong strategies will help you maintain a healthy brain:

1. **Avoid harmful substances** Drug and alcohol abuse damage brain cells.

2. **Exercise on a regular basis** People who engage in strenuous physical activity throughout their lives are more likely to maintain high cognitive functioning.

3. **Eat sensibly** Poor eating habits are associated with an increased risk of stroke, which is the largest single cause of brain disabilities. Decrease the intake of saturated fat, and eat more fruits and vegetables.

4. **Challenge yourself mentally** Staying mentally active by reading regularly and learning new skills strengthens neural connections much like regular physical exercise strengthens the heart.

5. **Wear your seat belt and bike helmet** Motor vehicle accidents account for up to half of all brain injuries. Head injury is the most common cause of death in bicycle and motorcycle crashes.

Table 3-3 POSSIBLE CONSEQUENCES OF DAMAGE TO DIFFERENT AREAS OF THE CEREBRAL CORTEX

Damage To	Effects
Occipital Lobes	Blindness
Parietal Lobes	Loss of touch sensation
Temporal Lobes	Inability to understand the meaning of words and sentences
Frontal Lobes	Dramatic personality changes, inability to plan and reason

How Flexible Is Your Brain?

Would it surprise you to learn that roughly 200,000 neurons in your brain die each day of your life? How does your brain stay healthy with such neural loss? One reason is that your brain can grow new dendrites, which then make new connections with other neurons. In essence, the brain rewires itself. These new connections keep your brain functioning at a high level of efficiency. This rewiring of the brain is called *collateral growth*.

The ability to transfer brain functions from one part of the brain to the other is highest in childhood, during the peak years of dendrite growth. Adults also are able to rewire their brains. Collateral growth occurs in older adults when certain brain areas are destroyed by strokes or accidents.

Think Critically
What does the statement, "In essence, the brain rewires itself," mean?

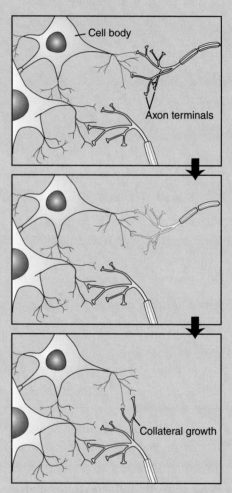

The brain can alter its neural connections when neurons are damaged. This collateral growth is highest in childhood, when dendrite growth is at its peak.

New Analysis of a Famous Case of Brain Damage

INTRODUCTION In 1848, Phineas Gage had a terrible accident. The foreman of a Vermont railroad company, Gage was using a three-and-a-half-foot iron rod to pack gunpowder into a boulder. A spark ignited the gunpowder and the rod flew into his left cheek, through his skull, and out the top of his head. Gage survived. His wounds healed within two months, but his personality changed. This once friendly, hardworking, emotionally mature adult became irresponsible, disrespectful, and unable to control his own impulses.

Doctors had different opinions about the extent and location of Gage's brain damage. Gage died 12 years after the accident with these differences unresolved. His case became famous for demonstrating how brain damage can affect people's thinking and behavior.

HYPOTHESIS In 1867, Gage's skull and the tamping iron that caused his injury were sent to John Harlow, the physician who first treated Gage following the accident. Harlow hypothesized that only the left hemisphere of Gage's brain was affected. Others who examined the skull believed there also was some right-hemisphere damage. Almost a century and a half later, scientists used modern technology to solve the debate.

METHOD In 2004, Peter Raitu and his coworkers used computer-generated three-dimensional reconstructions of a CAT scan of Gage's skull to assess which brain regions were destroyed or damaged. They compared their CAT-scan analysis with Dr. Harlow's reports and the examination of the original skull following Gage's death.

RESULTS The researchers' findings supported Harlow's conclusion that Gage's brain injury was limited to the left frontal lobe of the cerebral cortex.

Critical Analysis

Why might researchers today be interested in explaining a brain injury that occurred more than 150 years ago?

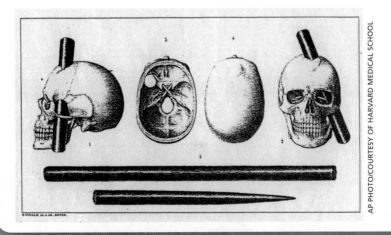

AP PHOTO/COURTESY OF HARVARD MEDICAL SCHOOL

Using measurements of Phineas Gage's skull and modern neuroimaging techniques, researchers have reconstructed Gage's accident and the likely path taken by the metal tamping rod as it traveled through his brain.

Split-Brain Patients Psychologist Roger Sperry (1913–1994) discovered that the right and left cerebral hemispheres have different abilities while studying *split-brain patients*. These were patients who had the nerves of their corpus callosum surgically cut in what was once a treatment for severe epileptic seizures. Epilepsy is a disorder where people have irregular electrical impulses in the brain that can cause the loss of body function and even loss of consciousness.

The surgery was drastic, but the patients did improve rapidly and their personalities stayed the same. However, by cutting the corpus callosum, these patients' right and left hemispheres no longer had a direct line of communication. Each hemisphere now had its own separate and private sensations, perceptions, and impulses to act.

When Sperry and his colleagues studied these split-brain patients, they learned a great deal about the functions of the right and left hemispheres. In one experiment, split-brain participants stared at a dot while the word HEART flashed across their visual field. The letters HE were in the left visual field of each eye (which is processed by the right hemisphere) and the letters ART were in the right visual field (which is processed by the left hemisphere). The word flashed so quickly that the patients' eyes could not move fast enough to process the entire word in each hemisphere. Participants were asked first to report verbally what they saw, and then to indicate with their left hands what they saw. People with an intact corpus callosum performed this task normally—the right and left hemispheres passed information between them and the word HEART was seen and reported. Split-brain patients verbally reported that they saw the word ART, but their left hands pointed to the word HE (see Figure 3-8). These findings suggested that the left hemisphere is involved with language abilities, while the right hemisphere is involved with spatial abilities.

Figure 3-8 **TESTING THE SPLIT BRAIN**

When the word HEART flashes across the visual field of split-brain patients, they verbally report seeing the portion of the word transmitted to their left hemispheres (ART). However, when asked to indicate with their left hands what they saw, they point to the portion of the word transmitted to their right hemispheres (HE).

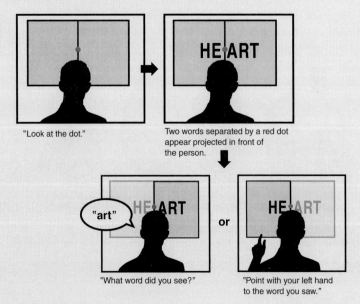

"Look at the dot."

Two words separated by a red dot appear projected in front of the person.

"art"

"What word did you see?"   or   "Point with your left hand to the word you saw."

Later studies of healthy brains using brain-imaging techniques provided additional insights into the different abilities of the two hemispheres. As depicted in Figure 3-9, the right hemisphere is superior to the left in completing visual and spatial tasks, recognizing music and other sounds, identifying faces, and perceiving and expressing emotions. The left hemisphere is superior at using language, employing logic, and providing explanations for events. The left hemisphere is often described as the brain's "interpreter." It is always trying to provide some rational meaning to behavior, even when there is none. The right hemisphere is most active when reading a map, listening to music, looking for a friend in a crowd, laughing, or crying (check out the Self-Discovery feature on page 82). The left hemisphere is more active when talking on the phone, working on a math problem, or explaining to your parents why you should be allowed to stay out later than usual this weekend.

© CORBIS

Which hemisphere of your brain is more active when you speak in front of a group?

Figure 3-9 SPECIALIZED ABILITIES OF THE TWO HEMISPHERES

Left-Hemisphere Dominance	General Function	Right-Hemisphere Dominance
Words Letters	VISION	Faces Emotional expression Geometric patterns
Language sounds	HEARING	Nonlanguage sounds Music
Verbal memory	MEMORY	Nonverbal memory
Speech Grammar Reading Writing Arithmetic	LANGUAGE	Emotional tone of speech
Logic Explaining events	REASONING ABILITY	
	SPATIAL ABILITY	Geometry Sense of direction Judgment of distance Mental rotation of objects

Study the abilities shown in the figure for right-brain versus left-brain dominance. Based on this information, which half of your brain do you think is dominant?

Are some people logical and scientific because they rely mostly on their left hemispheres ("left-brainers")? Do creative and artistic people mostly use their right hemispheres ("right-brainers")? Specific abilities are not completely located within one hemisphere and absent from the other. There also is no reliable evidence that you can train yourself to activate or suppress one hemisphere over the other. Describing people as "left-brainers" or "right-brainers" simplifies how the brain works. Whatever task you work on, both hemispheres are working to some extent. The healthy brain is a balance of a side-by-side exchange of information.

CHECKPOINT *What are the names of the four lobes that make up the cerebral cortex?*

Do You Use Different Patterns of Brain Activity to Recognize Faces?

Which of these faces looks happier to you?

Many people think the face on the right (photo b) is the happier one. Notice the smile is on the left side of her face. Most people accurately recognize visual stimuli in the left visual field, which is processed first in the right hemisphere. Exercises like this one suggest that the right hemisphere plays a larger role in recognition of facial expression than the left hemisphere. After a very brief interval, both hemispheres share information through an

(a)　　　(b)

PHOTODISC/GETTY IMAGES

intact corpus callosum. Before the hemispheres share the information, the right hemisphere has greater influence in recognizing facial features.

Is this true for everyone? No. Test the theory by asking as many people as possible to complete this exercise. Does anyone not show this right-hemisphere preference?

3.2 ASSESSMENT

In Your Own Words

Identify and describe the three major brain regions.

Review Concepts

1. A(n) _____ can produce a picture of neural activity over seconds with images that identify much smaller brain structures than those in a PET scan.
   - a. fMRI
   - b. EEG
   - c. CAT scan
   - d. MRI

2. Which refers to the four sections of the cerebral hemispheres?
   - a. hindbrain
   - b. lobes
   - c. cerebral cortex
   - d. midbrain

3. Which produces three-dimensional images of the brain's soft tissue?
   - a. MRI
   - b. EEG
   - c. CAT scan
   - d. PET scan

4. In which portion of the brain is the cerebral cortex located?
   - a. hindbrain
   - b. forebrain
   - c. midbrain
   - d. nobrain

5. Which lobes are important in hearing and language?
   - a. temporal
   - b. frontal
   - c. occipital
   - d. parietal

6. Explain the statement, "Your brain is cross-wired."

7. **True or False** Both CAT and MRI scans document the brain's structure.

8. **True or False** The brain has the ability to rewire itself.

9. **True or False** The frontal lobes control breathing and the heart rate.

10. **True or False** There is a right and left lobe in each brain hemisphere.

11. **True or False** A human brain is capable of repairing itself after an injury.

Think Critically

12. Why is studying the brain important to psychologists?

13. Why is the cerebral cortex so important?

14. Why should you avoid harmful substances, eat sensibly, exercise regularly, challenge yourself mentally, and wear your seat belt and bike helmet?

15. Why might someone call an artist a right-brain person and a scientist a left-brain person? Is this a correct assessment? Why or why not?

KEY TERMS

- heredity
- environment
- genes
- chromosome
- DNA
- fraternal twins
- identical twins

OBJECTIVES

- Explain how your genetic makeup is determined.
- Analyze the nature versus nurture debate.

DISCOVER IT | *How does this relate to me?*

Do you think you were born with the way you think and act? Or, do you think your experiences in life affect you more? Do you think singers like Beyonce, Madonna, or Frank Sinatra were born with good voices, or were they taught how to sing? What about athletes like tennis player Venus Williams, quarterback Tom Brady, or golfer Tiger Woods? Were their abilities born or made? Would it change your opinion about Albert Einstein if you learned he was born smart? What if you believed being smart was something you could learn? For many years psychologists have studied whether people are born with abilities or learn them from life experiences.

Heredity is the transmission of genetic characteristics from parents to their children. It determines your biological makeup. **Environment** refers to the world around you. Your environment includes your family, culture, education, and experiences. Some psychologists think heredity plays the most important role in forming behavior. Others think environment plays the larger role. Despite these differences of opinion, all psychologists agree it takes a combination of both heredity and environment to form behavior.

Heredity and Environment

heredity The transmission of genetic characteristics from parents to their children

environment The world around you

genes The basic biochemical units of heredity

In 2003, *geneticists* completed the Human Genome Project. Geneticists are scientists who study **genes**, the basic biochemical units of heredity. Genes are reproduced and passed along from parents to their children. The Human Genome Project identified 99.99 percent of the genetic material in humans. Every person has a unique genetic pattern, so researchers do not expect to ever reach 100 percent.

YOUR GENETIC MAKEUP

Genes are located on and transmitted by **chromosomes**. These are threadlike structures found in every cell of your body, except in red blood cells. All chromosomes contain strands of the molecule deoxyribonucleic acid, or **DNA**. Your DNA contains thousands of different genes. Figure 3-10 shows the genetic building blocks breaking down the human body from its 100 trillion cells to the genes that provide them with instructions on making protein, which is essential for life.

You inherited your particular genetic blueprint, or *genotype,* from your mother and father. Each sperm cell of a human male and egg cell of a human female contains 23 chromosomes. With the union of your father's sperm and your mother's egg at conception, all body cells that developed from this new cell (called the *zygote*) contained 46 chromosomes, or 23 pairs. Each of these body cells contained your genotype, with half the genetic material coming from each parent.

Among the 23 chromosomal pairs in the body cells, one pair known as the *sex chromosomes* determines whether you will become a boy or a girl. You inherit an X chromosome from your mother and either an X or a Y chromosome from your father. XX pairings result in the embryo developing female physical characteristics, while XY pairings result in male physical characteristics. Only the father's sex chromosome varies, so it is the father's genetic contribution that determines if a newborn is male or female.

Brothers and sisters with the same parents share 50 percent of the same genes. **Fraternal twins** (also known as *dizygotic twins*) develop from the union of two separate sperms and eggs. Their genes are no more similar as or different from brothers and sisters who are not twins. **Identical twins** (also called *monozygotic twins*) share the same genes. Identical twins develop from the union of the same egg and sperm that has split, so they have exactly the same genotype.

NATURE VERSUS NURTURE

How much heredity and environment contribute to behavior is known as the *nature versus nurture debate*. Nature refers to heredity, a person's biological makeup. Nurture refers to the environment, a person's life experiences, family, and education.

chromosomes Threadlike structures found in every cell of your body, except in red blood cells

DNA The means by which hereditary characteristics pass from one generation to the next

fraternal twins Dizygotic twins develop from the union of two separate sperms and eggs

identical twins Monozygotic twins develop from the union of the same egg and sperm that have split and have exactly the same genotype

Figure 3-10 **GENETIC BUILDING BLOCKS**

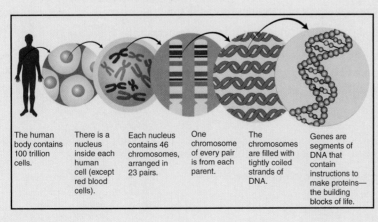

The human body contains 100 trillion cells.

There is a nucleus inside each human cell (except red blood cells).

Each nucleus contains 46 chromosomes, arranged in 23 pairs.

One chromosome of every pair is from each parent.

The chromosomes are filled with tightly coiled strands of DNA.

Genes are segments of DNA that contain instructions to make proteins—the building blocks of life.

Chromosomes are contained in the nucleus of each of the cells in your body. Each chromosome contains tightly coiled strands of DNA. Genes are DNA segments that are the biochemical units of inheritance.

Psychologist Auke Tellegen has studied identical twins reared apart from each other to help determine the extent to which heredity and the environment cause certain characteristics to develop. If identical twins living with different families have very similar characteristics, this finding would support the hypothesis that genes (nature) shape personal characteristics. However, if these twins do not have similar characteristics, this finding would support the hypothesis that the environment (nurture) shapes personal characteristics. The results of Tellegen's twin studies show that both genetic and environmental factors have different influences on personal characteristics and how people live their lives. For example, while identical twins are very similar in their tendencies to be leaders or followers, or to be excitable or calm (nature), they do not typically share tendencies to work hard or be lazy, or to seek close ties with others or be loners (nurture). In other words, you might be a "born leader" or be "naturally excitable," but you more likely need guidance in learning the value of hard work and the comfort of close friendships.

Do you know any identical twins who appear to be alike in every way?

BIG CHEESE PHOTO/JUPITER IMAGES

CHECKPOINT *Define heredity and environment.*

3.3 ASSESSMENT

In Your Own Words
Write a paper that describes the nature versus nurture debate.

Review Concepts
1. Which is the basic biochemical unit of heredity?

    a. hormones   c. chromosomes

    b. neurons   d. genes

2. Which refers to transmitting genetic characteristics from parents to children?

    a. environment   c. genes

    b. chromosome   d. heredity

3. Explain the development and genotype of fraternal twins and identical twins.

4. **True or False** You inherited your genetic blueprint from your parents.

5. **True or False** The Human Genome Project identified 100 percent of the genetic material in humans.

6. **True or False** A person's DNA contains thousands of different genes.

Think Critically
7. How does studying twins help psychology better understand human behavior?

8. Why was the Human Genome Project so important?

9. What is the importance of DNA?

Science Technician

ealth Science

Does assisting a psychologist in researching animal or human behavior sound interesting to you? Are you interested in how organisms or the environment affect behavior? Do you wonder how the criminal mind works? If so, you might find a career as a science technician to be fulfilling. Science technicians work alongside the research scientists who supervise them. Their responsibilities may include setting up, operating, and maintaining instruments used in experiments in laboratories. They also work with research subjects. They observe and record their observations, as well as draw conclusions about the experiments.

Science technicians work in all areas of science. Technicians interested in behavior may assist psychologists who conduct experiments with animal or human test subjects. Technicians interested in biology may work in medical research to learn more about how the brain functions. Technicians interested in chemistry may test products or pollution levels to learn how they affect life on the planet. Technicians interested in environmental science monitor the environment and its resources and measure how changes in resources affect behavior. Technicians interested in investigating crimes may assist forensic scientists in collecting physical evidence connected to crimes, or they may assist behavioral psychologists who work for federal, state, or local law-enforcement agencies.

Needed Skills and Education

Most employers want you to have a two-year associate's degree or specialized training in applied science or science-related technology. Some technicians have a four-year bachelor's degree.

Courses that will help you in this career are those in science including chemistry, physics, biology, psychology, and other related sciences. Math courses also are helpful. Technicians also require good written and oral communication skills; good interpersonal relationship skills; strong computer skills, especially in computer modeling; organizational abilities; good mechanical skills, analytical thinking skills; strong attention to detail; and the ability to interpret scientific results.

How You'll Spend Your Day

Science technicians work inside laboratories or in private offices. They work for private companies, governments, and for groups of research psychologists. Usually science technicians work regular hours. Sometimes technicians may have irregular hours while conducting an experiment that requires monitoring. Science technicians work directly with people or animals who are research subjects.

Earnings

The median hourly earnings of science technicians ranges between $15 and $32 an hour.

What About You?

Does the career of psychology science technician interest you? To help you make a decision about this good career choice, make two columns on a sheet of paper. Title the first column "Positive Aspects." Title the second column "Negative Aspects." List the positive aspects of the career as a science technician in the first column. List the negative aspects of the career as a science technician in the second column. When you have completed your list, look at what you have written in each column. Do you have more negatives or positives? If you have a lot of positive aspects, you will want to spend time researching careers as a science technician.

Employment Outlook

Careers as science technicians are expected to grow at an average rate through 2016 for all areas. The largest career opening for technicians may be in biotechnology, the study of living organisms.

CHAPTER SUMMARY

3.1 Neural and Hormonal Systems

- Neurons are specialized cells in the nervous system that send and receive information throughout the body. They are the nervous system's building blocks.

- Most (98.9 percent) neurons are in the brain. The remaining 1.2 percent (more than 1 billion) are distributed throughout the spinal cord.

- The spinal cord is a bundle of nerves that connects the brain to the rest of the body.

- Neurotransmitters are chemical messengers that travel between nerve cells and muscles to trigger or prevent an electrical impulse in a receiving cell. Neurotransmitters regulate physical movement, emotions, pain and pleasure, appetite, and sleep.

- Your nervous system is your body's primary information system. It is divided into the central nervous system and the peripheral nervous system. The central nervous system is made up of the brain and spinal cord. The peripheral nervous system consists of the remaining nerves in the body.

- Your endocrine system is a network of glands that manufactures and secretes hormones, which are chemical messengers that regulate or stimulate the body. Glands that secrete important hormones include the pituitary gland, thyroid gland, adrenal glands, and gonads.

3.2 The Brain

- To study the brain, scientists use different methods that include electroencephalograph (EEG), computerized axial tomography (CAT) scan, magnetic resonance imaging (MRI), positron emission tomography (PET) scan, and functional magnetic resonance imaging (fMRF).

- The three major brain regions include the hindbrain, midbrain, and forebrain.

- The cerebral cortex, which is located in the forebrain, is the thinking center of the brain. It is divided into two cerebral hemispheres, which are then divided into four lobes.

- The right and left brain have different specialized abilities. The right brain is superior to the left in completing visual and spatial tasks, recognizing music and other sounds, identifying faces, and perceiving and expressing emotion. The left hemisphere is superior at using language, employing logic, and providing explanations for events.

- While studying split-brain patients, Roger Sperry discovered that the right and left cerebral hemispheres have different abilities.

3.3 Genes and Behavior

- Heredity is the transmission of genetic characteristics from parents to their children. Inherited characteristics pass from one generation to the next through DNA.

- Environment is the world around you, which includes your family, culture, education, and experiences.

- Genes are the basic biochemical units of heredity. They are reproduced and passed along from parents to their children. Genes are located on and transmitted by chromosomes.

CHAPTER ASSESSMENT

Review Psychology Terms

Select the term that best fits the definition. Some terms will not be used.

____ 1. Chemical messengers that travel between nerve cells and muscles to trigger or prevent an impulse in the receiving cell

____ 2. The brain and spinal cord

____ 3. A brain-imaging technique that measures the average neural activity in different brain regions over a few seconds

____ 4. A bundle of nerves that connects the brain to the rest of the body

____ 5. Thinking center of the brain, which coordinates and integrates all areas of the brain into a fully functioning unit

____ 6. Part of the brain above the hindbrain that plays a role in attention, stimulation, and consciousness

____ 7. A brain-imaging technique that records "waves" of electrical activity in the brain

____ 8. Chemical messengers, carried by the bloodstream, that regulate or stimulate the body

____ 9. Part of the brain above the midbrain that controls emotional reactions, thought processes, movement, sensory information, and body temperature

____ 10. Transmission of genetic characteristics from parents to children

____ 11. Specialized cells in the nervous system that send and receive information throughout the body

____ 12. The world around you

____ 13. Part of the brain found at the rear base of the skull that controls the most basic biological needs for life

____ 14. Basic biochemical unit of heredity

____ 15. Part of the autonomic nervous system that conserves and maintains the body's energy resources

____ 16. A network of glands that manufactures and secretes hormones directly into the bloodstream

a. autonomic nervous system

b. central nervous system

c. cerebral hemispheres

d. chromosome

e. computerized axial tomography (CAT) scan

f. DNA

g. electroencephalograph (EEG)

h. endocrine system

i. environment

j. forebrain

k. functional magnetic resonance imaging (fMRI)

l. gene

m. heredity

n. hindbrain

o. hormones

p. lobes

q. magnetic resonance imaging (MRI)

r. midbrain

s. neurons

t. neurotransmitters

u. parasympathetic nervous system

v. peripheral nervous system

w. positron emission tomography (PET) scan

x. somatic nervous system

y. spinal cord

z. sympathetic nervous system

Review Psychology Concepts

17. The division of the peripheral nervous system that controls movement of involuntary, nonskeletal muscles.

18. The four major sections of both cerebral hemispheres.

19. A brain-imaging technique that measures the average neural activity in different brain regions over a few minutes.

20. Threadlike structure found in every cell of your body, except in red blood cells.

21. A division of the peripheral nervous system that sends commands to voluntary skeletal muscles and receives sensory information from the muscles and the skin

22. The means by which hereditary characteristics pass from one generation to the next

23. What purpose does the body's nervous system serve?

24. What are the three basic parts of a neuron?

25. Identify and describe the two types of messages from neurotransmitters.

26. What is the body's primary information system and what are its two major parts? Provide information on both.

27. Compare and contrast the following: somatic nervous system, autonomic nervous system, sympathetic nervous system, and parasympathetic nervous system.

28. How are hormones related to the endocrine system?

29. What is the advantage of the fMRI over other brain-imaging techniques?

30. In which part of the brain is the cerebral cortex located?

31. Identify the four brain lobes and describe the function of each.

32. Explain the term *split-brain* and describe how a healthy brain functions.

33. Compare and contrast heredity and environment.

34. What is the relationship between chromosomes and DNA and DNA and genes?

35. What is the difference between fraternal and identical twins?

Apply Psychology Concepts

36. Your brain is made up of glial cells and neurons. If you think of your brain as a house, identify and explain why certain parts of your house are your glial cells and why other parts of your house are your neurons.

37. When Christopher dives into a shallow pool of water he severs his spinal cord about four inches above his waist. Provide a general description of this spinal cord damage.

38. Susan is having a brain scan while she is looking at photographs of people's faces. Which lobes in her brain are likely to be particularly active as she looks at these faces, and where are these lobes located in the cerebral hemispheres?

39. You meet Kimberly's twin sister and discover that it is almost impossible to tell them apart. What is the name for this type of twin? What percent of genes do they share? How did they develop in their mother's womb?

Make Academic Connections

40. **Writing** Take a stand on the left-brain right-brain issue. Do you think there is a difference in the two hemispheres, or not? Write a research paper that supports your argument. Using the library or Internet for research, cite studies and researchers who have studied the issue. When using the Internet, use reliable web sites, such as educational or government sites.

41. **Art** Download pictures from the Internet, or use your drawing skills, to create a chart that illustrates the two hemispheres of the brain. Label each hemisphere and the attributes of that side.

42. **History** Use the Internet or library to research how views of the nervous system have evolved. Design a timeline of your findings. Include all major historical views on the timeline.

43. **Research** Use the library or Internet to research the connection between hormones and behavior problems. Write a summary of your findings.

44. **Science** Students with the reading disorder dyslexia are benefiting from brain research. Use the Internet or library to research how brain-scan images help researchers to know more about brain disorders such as dyslexia. Write a paper that predicts how future research may help people with brain disorders, such as dyslexia. Base your predictions on the work that is currently being done.

45. **Speech** Use the Internet or library to research a study on twin adoption to assess the influence of heredity and environment on behavior. Create a speech that explains and evaluates your findings.

46. **Computer Science** Use a computer graphics program to create a diagram that identifies the structure and function of different parts of a neuron. Label each of the three parts of a neuron. Provide information on the functions of each on a separate sheet of paper.

47. **Marketing** Use the Internet to research the results of different drugs on one of the following: Parkinson's disease, hyperactivity, or multiple sclerosis. Write a fact sheet that includes information on the drug, side effects of the drug, and improvements—and lack of improvements—with patients taking the drug.

DIGGING DEEPER
with Psychology eCollection

The debate about what influences our behavior more—nature or nurture—has raged for more than 100 years. Nature advocates argue that genetics dictate most of our actions, perceptions, and thought processes. Supporters of nurture insist that environment, such as living conditions, upbringing, education, and personal interactions, is the key ingredient. Much of the study on this topic has focused on identical twins. Because they have the same basic genetics, other variables can be studied. However, a closer look at identical twins brings both subtle and not-so-subtle differences to light and strengthens the argument for the nature camp. Sinja Gunjan conducted research with identical twins. Access the Gale Psychology eCollection at *www.cengage.com/school/psych/franzoi* and review Gunjan's findings about twins and behavior. Write a brief report describing the research findings and answer the question: Which influence has been strongest on you—nature (genetics) or nurture (environment)? Why? As an additional project, support your answers to the questions above with examples from your life.

Source: Gunjan, Sinja. "The identity dance: the battle between genes and the environment is over. As the dust settles, scientists piece together how DNA and life experience conspire to create personality." *Psychology Today* 37.2 (March–April 2004): 52(9).

Sensation

ESSENTIAL QUESTION
Go to page XXIV

"We live on the leash of our senses."

—DIANE ACKERMAN, AMERICAN POET, B. 1948

In the spring of 2003, 27-year-old Aron Ralston was alone when he climbed up the side of a canyon in Utah's Canyonlands National Park. An 800-pound boulder shifted and pinned his right arm between the boulder and the rocky wall. For three days he tried to free his arm. By then he had used up all his food and water. Realizing his hope of being rescued was remote, Aron decided to cut off his pinned arm. He applied a tourniquet, and then he used his pocketknife to cut off his crushed forearm just below the elbow. After freeing himself from the boulder, Aron crawled through the canyon, and then rappelled to the canyon floor. He walked six miles until he met hikers, who notified nearby rescuers.

How did Aron cope with the pain of cutting through his own flesh and bone? "I'm not sure how I handled it," Aron later said. "I felt pain and I coped with it. I moved on." Following surgeries and rehabilitation, Aron resumed his outdoor adventures.

OBJECTIVES

- Explain the concepts of sensory thresholds and compare the different theories.
- Describe sensory adaptation.

DISCOVER IT | *How does this relate to me?*

Can you sometimes overhear other students talking quietly in another part of the cafeteria? Do you see better in the dark after standing still for a few minutes when you first turn the lights out? Do you sometimes tune out distracting noises around you? Do you wonder how your senses interact with your environment? Psychologists look for answers to these questions when researching how physical stimuli affect sensory perceptions and a person's mental state.

KEY TERMS

- sensation
- psychophysics
- absolute threshold
- signal-detection theory
- difference threshold
- Weber's law
- sensory adaptation

You have probably already experienced some physical pain in your life, whether it be a broken bone or cut finger. Hopefully that is the extent of any pain you will experience, and you will never have to deal with the type of life-threatening dilemma Aron Ralston faced. Experiencing and managing pain is a natural part of life, however, and one of the topics of this chapter. Your journey of discovery in psychology continues by examining the important process of sensation, a physical feeling caused by stimulation to one or more of your senses.

Sensory Thresholds

Sensation is the process that detects stimuli from your body and environment. For example, while typing this sentence, I am eating a handful of peanut M&M's. I can hear their crunch while chewing, and I know this sound is a response to vibrations in the air, or sound waves. I am also noticing a sweet taste in my mouth, which is a response to the dissolving candy. I can even faintly smell the aroma of chocolate, which is a response to molecules in the air that I am inhaling through my nose. I also feel the last three M&M's® in my hand, which is a response to their physical pressure on my skin. I see that these remaining candies are colored red, blue, and brown, which is a response to the light waves reflecting from their surfaces.

sensation The process that detects stimuli from your body and environment

What is the process that allows you to experience sound, light, and other kinds of stimuli? Your sensory organs convert the physical properties of sound, light, and other kinds of stimuli into neural impulses. This conversion process takes place at structures called *sensory receptors*. Sensory receptors are the receptor sites for the senses. Connecting neurons in the sense organs then send this information to the brain. The brain then processes these neural impulses into what you experience.

You are aware of a stimulus in your environment only if you have sensory receptors that convert the stimulus into neural impulses. Human beings cannot see X-rays or hear very-high-frequency tones. You cannot taste certain chemicals because you do not have sensory receptors that convert these stimuli into neural impulses. Stimuli of which you are not aware are just as real as those that you do convert into neural impulses, but they are not a part of your sensory experience. Table 4-1 lists the stimuli and sensory receptors for what scientists identify as the primary senses.

Table 4-1 THE STIMULI AND SENSORY RECEPTORS FOR EACH PRIMARY SENSE

Sense	Stimulus	Sensory Receptors
Vision	Light waves	Light-sensitive rods and cones in the retina of the eye
Hearing	Sound waves	Pressure-sensitive hair cells in the cochlea of the inner ear
Taste	Molecules dissolved in fluid on the tongue	Taste cells in the taste buds of the tongue
Smell	Molecules dissolved in fluid in the nose	Sensitive ends of olfactory (smell) neurons
Touch	Pressure on the skin	Sensitive ends of touch neurons in the skin

ABSOLUTE THRESHOLD

German scientist Gustav Fechner (1801–1887) was a pioneer in **psychophysics**, the study of how physical stimuli are translated into psychological experience. Fechner introduced the term **absolute threshold** to describe the weakest amount of a given stimulus that a person can detect half of the time. Psychologists measure absolute thresholds by presenting a stimulus (for example, a light or a sound) to a person at different intensities and determining the lowest level detectable 50 percent of the time.

Some examples of absolute thresholds for various senses are listed in Table 4-2. The absolute threshold for any sense varies between people. For example, the sense of smell is less sensitive in people with allergies and among smokers.

SIGNAL-DETECTION THEORY

The idea behind the absolute threshold concept is that there is a minimum intensity level at which a stimulus is consistently detected. Yet according to **signal-detection theory**, the detection of a stimulus is also influenced by your decision-making strategy. Two important factors that shape decision-making are (1) your

psychophysics The study of how physical stimuli are translated into psychological experience

absolute threshold The weakest amount of a given stimulus that a person can detect half of the time

signal-detection theory A theory stating that detecting a stimulus is influenced by a person's decision-making strategy

Table 4-2 EXAMPLES OF ABSOLUTE THRESHOLDS

Stimulus	Absolute Threshold
Vision	A candle seen at 30 miles on a dark, clear night
Hearing	The tick of a watch at 20 feet under quiet conditions
Taste	One teaspoon of sugar in 2 gallons of water
Smell	One drop of perfume diffused into a three-room apartment
Touch	The wing of a fly falling on your cheek from a distance of 0.5 inch

Source: Adapted from Galanter, 1962.

expectations about the probability the stimulus will occur, and (2) the rewards and costs associated with detecting or not detecting the stimulus.

Suppose you think tonight there is going to be a meteor shower. You go outside looking for the meteors, with the expectation of seeing lots of shooting stars. Unfortunately you have the wrong night. Chances are because of your expectations—even though they are false—you will see some evidence of a meteor shower. You will detect more flashes of light in the sky than if you expected no meteor shower. Detecting these flashes also might be affected by how important this task is to you. If astronomy is your favorite hobby, you might see more flashes than if stargazing were less important.

A major contribution of signal-detection theory is that it established that there is not a single absolute threshold for any sense. Whether or not you perceive a particular stimulus depends on the situation, what expectations and motives you have, and your level of fatigue. Such knowledge is important because many signal-detection tasks carry life-and-death implications. Consider the task of a

What life-and-death implication would there be for an air traffic controller who fails to see an airplane on radar due to fatigue?

PHOTODISC/GETTY IMAGES

medical technician who is screening numerous X-rays every hour for possible signs of disease. On one X-ray there are faint markings made by a weak stimulus. The technician needs to decide whether these markings are normal or early signs of a serious illness. Studies prove that when people try to judge whether a weak stimulus is present or absent, fatigue sets in and attention diminishes after about 30 minutes. Although such fatigue effects won't cause any serious consequences when looking for shooting stars, they could prove disastrous in the medical lab.

DIFFERENCE THRESHOLD

In addition to detecting a weak stimulus, you also need to be aware of changes in the intensity of a stimulus and be able to discriminate between two similar stimuli. The smallest difference between two stimuli that can be detected half of the time is known as the **difference threshold** (also called the *just-noticeable difference*, or *jnd*). For example, what is the minimum amount of difference that you can detect in the sweetness of two soft drinks?

In 1834, Ernst Weber (1795–1878) made an important discovery related to the difference threshold. The size of the difference threshold depends on the intensity of the stimuli being compared. For example, when comparing two weights, the difference threshold is smaller for light weights compared to heavy weights. You will easily notice the weight difference when holding a 1-lb. bag versus a 2-lb. bag, but will not notice a difference between a 100-lb. bag and a 101-lb. bag. For both comparisons the weight difference is one pound, so why don't you notice the difference between the larger weights? According to **Weber's law**, to be noticed as different, two stimuli must differ by a constant minimum percentage rather than by

difference threshold
Smallest difference between two stimuli that can be detected half of the time

Weber's law The principle that to be noticed as different, two stimuli must differ by a constant minimum percentage rather than by a constant amount

According to Weber's law, you would notice a weight difference after about 3 percent of the current weight is either added or taken away.

a constant amount. The smallest noticeable change in weight is about 3 percent. Thus, you would need to add two more pounds to the 101-lb. bag to reach the difference threshold.

The values of the constant minimum percentile differences vary a great deal for the different senses. While you can detect a change in sound frequency of 0.3 percent (one-third of 1 percent), it requires a 7 percent increase to detect a difference threshold in smell, and a 20 percent increase to detect a difference in taste. This means that your sense of hearing is much more sensitive than your sense of taste.

CHECKPOINT > *What is the difference between absolute threshold and difference threshold?*

Sensory Adaptation

When I moved to New York City to attend graduate school I rode the subway each day. At first, the noise was so distracting that I had difficulty reading, and came home each day with a headache. Yet, very soon, the subway noise seemed to become softer, and I was comfortably reading and headache-free when riding. This example explains **sensory adaptation**, the tendency for sensory receptors to decrease in response to stimuli that continue at the same level. The most common explanation for sensory adaptation is that it is caused by nerve cells firing less frequently after high levels of stimulation.

Sensory adaptation is very important in everyday living. For example, while working on a task, you quickly tune out constant unchanging stimuli in your surroundings. In doing so, you are better able to detect more useful information. Sensory adaptation does have disadvantages. For example, while tuning out subway noises increased my ability to read, I sometimes didn't hear the conductor call out my stop, causing me to arrive late for class!

Sensory adaptation occurs for all your senses. For example, receptors in your skin decrease in response to the regular pressure your clothes have on your body. Auditory, or sound, adaptation occurs much more slowly than adaptation to odors, tastes, and skin sensations. You adapt to smells very quickly. Within one minute, odor adaptation is complete. You may still smell the odor, but not as intensely.

LAB TEAMS

Sensory Adaptation Demonstration

Try a little demonstration. Place a substance with a strong odor—an onion, perfume, or shaving lotion, for example—near your nose for a few minutes. Its odor will seem less intense over time. Next, remove the substance for five minutes and then smell it again. Now it should smell as strong as it did when you first smelled it.

sensory adaptation
The tendency for sensory receptors to decrease in response to stimuli that continue at the same level

CHECKPOINT > *What is sensory adaptation?*

In Your Own Words

Compare and contrast absolute threshold, signal-detection theory, and difference threshold.

Review Concepts

1. Which refers to Weber's Law?
   a. absolute threshold
   b. difference threshold
   c. signal-detection theory
   d. none of the above

2. Which scientist introduced the term *absolute threshold*?
   a. Aron Ralston
   b. Eugene Galanter
   c. Gustav Fechner
   d. Ernst Weber

3. Which refers to nerve cells firing less frequently after high levels of stimulation?
   a. critical thinking
   b. absolute threshold
   c. environmental threshold
   d. sensory adaptation

4. Which is the stimulus for vision?
   a. sound waves
   b. pressure on the skin
   c. light waves
   d. molecules dissolved on the tongue

5. With which of the following sensations does adaptation occur most slowly?
   a. sound
   b. odor
   c. taste
   d. skin sensations

6. **True or False** Absolute threshold refers to only four of your senses.

7. **True or False** According to the signal-detection theory, detection of a stimulus is influenced by your decision-making strategy.

8. **True or False** The major contribution of the signal-detection theory was the establishment of specific absolute thresholds for all senses.

9. **True or False** Psychophysics is the study of how physical stimuli are translated into psychological experience.

Think Critically

10. What is the result for a person who has damage to taste sensory receptors?

11. What argument would you use for the need to be well rested when trying to detect a weak stimulus?

12. Using an example from your own life, what argument can you make for sensory adaptation?

13. Using an example from your own life, defend Weber's Law.

LESSON
4.2 | Vision

OBJECTIVES

- Identify and illustrate the structures of the eye that are responsible for vision.
- Describe the way the brain perceives color.

DISCOVER IT | *How does this relate to me?*

Think about how you perceive your world around you. Unless you are visually impaired, you use your sense of sight more than any other sensory organ to provide you with information about your environment. Through your vision, you learn about your world and the objects in it—their size, shape, density, texture, even how close or far away objects are. How do messages received by your eyes convert into messages that are understood by the brain? Psychologists have asked this same question and found the answer.

KEY TERMS

- pupil
- iris
- lens
- retina
- optic nerve
- blind spot
- color blindness

L ight is a form of energy known as *electromagnetic energy*. This energy is all around you. It is created by the vibration of electrically charged *particles*, which are basic units of matter. Electromagnetic energy travels in waves of different lengths and intensities. A *wavelength* is the distance between two peaks of light waves. Your eyes detect wavelengths of visible light. As shown in Figure 4-1, the range of electromagnetic energy that you and other humans can see is very small. How do your eyes and brain work together to turn wavelengths into visual images? To answer this question, you must first understand the structure of the human eye.

Figure 4-1 **THE ELECTROMAGNETIC SPECTRUM**

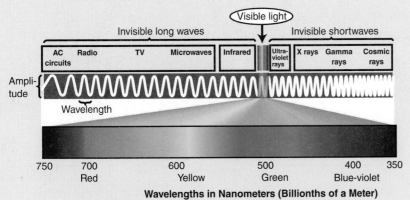

Humans sense only a narrow band of electromagnetic energy. Within this narrow band, light at different wavelengths is experienced as different colors.

pupil An opening in the iris that allows light to enter the eye

iris A ring of muscles that range in color from light blue to dark brown

lens A clear, elastic, disc-shaped structure that refocuses light

retina The light-sensitive surface at the back of the eye

Structures of the Human Eye

Light enters the eye through the **pupil**, which is an opening in the iris (see Figure 4-2). The **iris** is a ring of muscles that range in color from light blue to dark brown. In dim light, the iris opens, or dilates, the pupil, which lets in more light. In bright light, the iris closes, or constricts, the pupil, which lets in less light. After passing through the pupil, light enters a clear, elastic, disc-shaped structure called the **lens**. The lens refocuses the light with the aid of attached muscles. Images of distant objects in this light are seen clearly when these muscles stretch and flatten the lens. Relaxing the lens and making it more spherical allows you to clearly see near objects.

Once focused by the lens, the light image travels through the *vitreous humor*, which is a clear jelly-like liquid that occupies the space behind the lens. The light image is then projected onto a light-sensitive surface at the back of the eye known as the **retina**. The retina is actually a piece of the brain that migrates to the eye during early fetal development.

Below the retina's outer layer of cells is a layer of two basic kinds of receptor neurons, or photoreceptors, called *rods and cones* (see Figure 4-3 on page 101). The rods are extremely sensitive to light and are important in detecting patterns of black, white, and gray. The rods function best under low-light conditions so are most useful at night. In contrast, the cones require much more light to be activated and play a key role in color vision. Most cones are concentrated in a small area near the center of the retina known as the *fovea*, which is the area of central focus. A human retina contains about 125 million rods and 7 million cones. As you would expect, animals that are most active at night, such as owls and rats, have all-rod eyes. Daytime animals, such as lizards and chipmunks, have mostly cone-dominant eyes.

To observe how your eye responds to light, look into a mirror under a bright light. Notice that your pupils are small. Turn the light off for 30 seconds, and then turn it back on while looking into the mirror. Notice how much larger your pupils have become in response to the lack of light, then how quickly they constrict as they adjust to the light.

Figure 4-2 **MAJOR STRUCTURES OF THE HUMAN EYE**

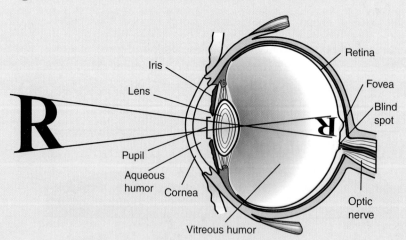

When light reaches the back of the eye and strikes the retina, it activates the rods and cones and generates neural signals that are sent to the **optic nerve**, which carries information from the retina to the brain. At the point where the optic nerve leaves the eye on the retina, there are no rods or cones, so there are no receptor cells. This means that you do not see images that fall into this area, which is called the **blind spot**. So why doesn't this blind spot impair your field of vision? Check out the Self-Discovery feature on page 102 to locate your own blind spot and find the answer to this question.

optic nerve Carries information from the retina to the brain

blind spot The area on the retina where the optic nerve leaves the eye and that contains no receptor cells

Figure 4-3   **HOW LIGHT TRAVELS THROUGH THE EYE**

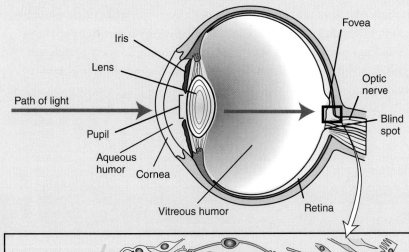

Light passing through the eye falls on the retina and then activates sensory receptors called photoreceptors—rods and cones. When activated, these two photoreceptors send neural impulses to the brain.

INTERACTIVE FIGURE

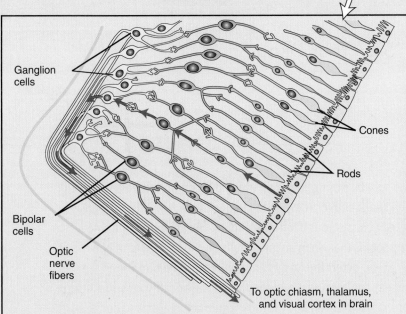

CHECKPOINT   *What is the path by which light travels through the eye?*

Color Vision

All the colors you see are red, blue, and green, or a mixture of these three. What does it mean when you say a leaf is green? Is the color in the leaf? No. An object appears as a particular color because it absorbs or reflects certain wavelengths of light. The color green is not actually in the leaf, nor is it in the light waves reflected from the leaf. The color is in your visual system. The leaf absorbs all the wavelengths of light except those that create the sensation of green in your mind. There is nothing naturally blue about short wavelengths or red about long wavelengths. Wavelengths are simply energy.

Colors are created by the cones in your eye responding to wavelengths and sending neural signals to your brain, which then creates the colors you see. Some cones are sensitive to wavelengths of light that you perceive as red, while other cones are sensitive to wavelengths you perceive as green or blue. Any object that you see in your surroundings is reflecting light to your eye containing a variety of different wavelengths. It is this mixture of wavelengths that makes the object appear as a specific color.

SELF-DISCOVERY

Would You Like to "See" Your Blind Spot?

You can experience your own blind spot by closing your right eye and lining up the cross with your left eye. Now slowly move your head back and forth. When the image of the happy face is between 6 and 18 inches away from your eye, it crosses your blind spot and disappears from sight. One reason you are seldom aware of your blind spot is that when an image falls on the blind spot of one eye, it falls on the receptors of the other, so you detect the image. Another reason you don't often see the blind spot—even with one-eyed vision—is because it is located off to the side of your visual field so objects near this area are never in sharp focus. Perhaps the most important reason you don't see the blind spot is that your visual system somehow fills in the place where the image disappears. When you try this blind spot demonstration, the place where the happy face used to be isn't replaced by a "hole" or by "nothingness" but, by the white surrounding it.

The experience of colors is created by the nervous system, so species differ in what they see when looking at the same object. For example, honeybees have three-color vision like humans, but their color receptors are sensitive to a much wider range of wavelengths in the electromagnetic spectrum. They are sensitive to light in the ultraviolet range. Pigeons have color vision based on five kinds of cones, so they see the world differently than do humans.

Some people's cones do not function properly. They are unable to see differences among colors, a condition known as **color blindness** (see Figure 4-4). Approximately 1 in 50 individuals is color blind, of which about 90 percent are male.

The term color blindness is misleading because most people classified as color-blind can see two out of the three primary colors. They are unable to see the third color because the cone that is sensitive to that color is not functioning. In contrast, only about 10 people out of 1 million have the rare form of color blindness where they have no functioning cones. These individuals see only shades of white, gray, and black generated by their rods.

color blindness A deficiency in the ability to distinguish among colors

Figure 4-4 **TEST FOR COLOR BLINDNESS**

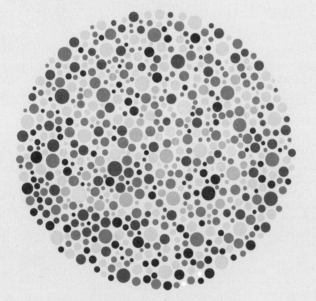

Do you see the red number 26 against a background of green dots? Individuals who do not see the number are red-green color blind.

CHECKPOINT > *How does the brain perceive color?*

In Your Own Words

Write a paragraph that explains how the iris works.

Review Concepts

1. Which refers to an opening in the iris?
   - a. blind spot
   - b. lens
   - c. retina
   - d. pupil

2. Which refers to the light-sensitive surface at the back of the eye?
   - a. lens
   - b. retina
   - c. iris
   - d. optic nerve

3. Which carries information from the retina to the brain?
   - a. pupil
   - b. color blindness
   - c. optic nerve
   - d. retina

4. Which is a ring of muscles that range in color from light blue to dark brown?
   - a. pupil
   - b. iris
   - c. lens
   - d. retina

5. Which is a clear, elastic, disc-shaped structure that refocuses the light with the aid of attached muscles?
   - a. pupil
   - b. iris
   - c. lens
   - d. retina

6. **True or False** All the colors you see are red, blue, and green, or a mixture of these three.

7. **True or False** Short wavelengths of light are always blue, whereas long wavelengths of light are always red.

8. **True or False** The blind spot is where all the receptor cells are found.

9. **True or False** Light enters the eye through the pupil.

10. **True or False** Most individuals who are color blind are female.

Think Critically

11. Explain how a blind spot on the eye is formed.

12. What is the function of the retina?

13. Explain the process in your eyes that creates the perception of color.

14. Why do different species differ in the way they perceive color?

15. Why is the term *color blind* misleading?

OBJECTIVES

- Explain and illustrate the human auditory system and the structure of the ear.
- Describe the senses of smell, taste, touch, and body position and movement.

KEY TERMS

- eardrum
- cochlea
- olfactory nerve
- taste buds
- gate-control theory
- kinesthetic sense
- vestibular sense

DISCOVER IT | *How does this relate to me?*

Think about how you hear the world around you. Unless your hearing is impaired, hearing is the sense you use most often after vision. You also have other senses that help you interpret your world—the sense of smell and taste, and skin senses. You rely less on these senses than on sight and hearing, yet they are important senses that help you interpret and understand your environment.

Vision and hearing are classified as higher senses in humans, meaning they are extremely important to survival. The senses of taste, smell, touch, and senses that detect body position and movement are classified as minor senses because they are not crucial to sustaining life.

The Auditory System

The auditory system controls your sense of hearing. Hearing begins with *sound waves*—vibrations in air, water, or solid material. The number of sound waves that pass through a given point in one second is called the sound's *frequency*. When your sensory system experiences the physical sensation of frequency, you also have the psychological experience of *pitch*. High-pitched sounds are high frequencies, and low-pitched sounds are low frequencies.

Loudness of sound is a psychological experience that corresponds to the height of a sound wave, called *amplitude*. Amplitude is measured in decibels (dB). The greater the amplitude, the higher the decibels, and the louder the sound. A whisper or the sound of rustling leaves has an amplitude of about 20 dB. Long exposure to sounds above 90 dB—such as those in rock concerts—can cause permanent hearing loss. Even brief exposure to sounds above 120 dB can be painful and may cause hearing damage. Putting your hands over your ears because a sound hurts them is smart because any sound that hurts your ears can cause hearing damage. Table 4-3 (see page 106) provides examples of common sounds and their decibel levels.

Most sounds are a combination of different waves of different frequencies. You experience this combination—or blending of frequencies—as *timbre*. Timbre is why you can recognize different friends' voices over the telephone. You also hear

> **INFOBIT**
> iPods and other MP3 players can reach 120 decibels. At that level, you risk damage to your hearing after only 7 1/2 minutes. How do you know if the volume is too loud? It's too loud if someone three feet away can hear your music, or if you need to remove the ear piece to hear someone talking to you.

Table 4-3 DECIBEL LEVEL OF SOME COMMON SOUNDS

Decibels	Source Exposure	Danger
180	Space shuttle launch	Hearing loss certain within 150 feet of launch pad
140	Jet aircraft motor	Any exposure dangerous
120	Sandblaster, thunderclap	Immediate danger
100	Heavy auto traffic, lawn mower	2 hours
60	Normal conversation	No danger
40	Quiet office	No danger
30	Quiet library	No danger
20	Soft whisper	No danger
0	Minimal detectable sound	No danger

the timbre of different musical instruments because of the blend of the different frequencies. Want to experience timbre? Try this. Clap your hands together while holding them flat, and then clap them again when they are cupped. Cupped-hand clapping produces a greater combination of low-frequency sound waves. The combination of sound waves produces a more complex sound.

THE EAR

The ear is divided into three major parts: the outer ear, middle ear, and inner ear (see Figure 4-5 on page 107). The outer ear is the part you see. This is the part of the ear that receives sound waves and sends them down a passageway called the *auditory canal*. At the end of the auditory canal is the **eardrum**, which is a thin, flexible membrane that vibrates in sequence with the sound waves.

The middle ear is an air-filled cavity that begins on the other side of the eardrum. As the eardrum vibrates, it sets in motion three tiny, interconnected bones—the *hammer, anvil,* and *stirrup*. When the eardrum vibrates from sound waves, these bones also vibrate against the **cochlea**, which is part of the inner ear.

The cochlea (pronounced COKE-lee-ah) is a coiled, fluid-filled tube that is lined with special hair-like auditory receptor cells. When these hair cells are stimulated by sound wave vibration, they trigger the firing of sensory neurons that form the *auditory nerve*. The auditory nerve then transmits sound information to the brain.

HEARING LOSS

There are two types of hearing loss, *conduction* and *sensorineural*. Conduction hearing loss occurs when there are physical problems sending sound waves through the outer or middle ear. Sensorineural hearing loss involves nerve problems in the inner ear.

Conduction hearing problems often involve a punctured eardrum or damage to any of the three bones in the middle ear. A common treatment for conduction hearing loss is hearing aids, which are tiny instruments worn just inside the outer ear. Hearing aids change sound waves into amplified vibrations and send them to the inner ear.

eardrum A thin, flexible membrane that vibrates in sequence with sound waves

cochlea The coiled, fluid-filled tube in the inner ear that contains hair-like auditory receptors

Figure 4-5 THE HUMAN EAR

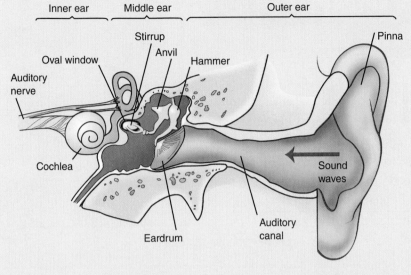

The outer ear picks up sound waves and sends them to the eardrum, and then to the middle ear where small bones vibrate and transmit to the inner ear.

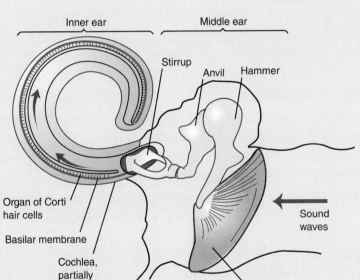

Sensorineural hearing loss is a more common problem. It often occurs because hair cells in the cochlea are damaged either by disease, injury, or aging. The only means of restoring hearing in people suffering from nerve deafness is a cochlear implant, which is a miniature electronic device that is surgically placed into the cochlea. The implant changes sound waves into electrical signals and sends them to the auditory nerve, which transmits them to the brain. Young children born with hearing loss are the best candidates for this implant.

CHECKPOINT How does hearing begin, and in which part of the ear does it occur?

Sensory Crossovers

Have you ever heard a sound and experienced it as a flash of light? This *seeing* of sound is fairly common and is most often experienced when the eyes are closed and the sound is unexpected. A much more sophisticated *colored hearing* is a type of sensory experience known as synesthesia (pronounced sin-ess-THEE-zhah). Synesthesia is a rare and extraordinary sensory condition in which people perceive stimuli in other senses, such as *tasting* color or shapes, *hearing* someone's touch, or *feeling* the sounds of musical instruments on their bodies. Scientists estimate that about one in 2,000 people are synesthetes, with females outnumbering males 6 to 1.

The most common form of synesthesia is *colored hearing.* Most people with this condition report that they see sounds internally (in the mind's eye), but a few see colors projected outside the body, usually within arm's reach. Recent brain scans of synesthetes who report colored hearing indicate that visual areas of their brains show increased activation in response to sounds.

In another type of synesthesia, a person experiences specific letters, numbers, and/or words as vivid patterns or particular colors. For example, a person with this form of synesthesia might see the letter B as orange, the letter T as green, and the letter R as red. Some neuroscientists believe that this type of synesthesia occurs partly because the areas of the brain that process colors are near the areas that process letters and numbers, and that synesthetes may have more extensive neural connections between these two nearby brain areas.

 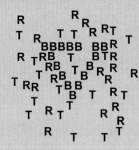 

Think Critically
What is synesthesia?

Your Other Senses

In gathering sensory information from your surroundings, you primarily rely on your vision and hearing, which scientists call the higher senses in humans. In contrast, the senses of smell, taste, touch, and proprioception are classified as minor senses because they are not considered as crucial to sustaining life. However, as you will learn in this section, your minor senses are very important in many areas of daily living.

SMELL

The stimuli for smell are airborne molecules. When you smell hot chocolate you are sensing molecules that have left the hot chocolate and traveled through the air to your nose. These molecules then enter your nasal passages and reach tiny receptor cells at the top of the nasal cavity. These receptor cells then transmit neural impulses containing smell information through the **olfactory nerve** to the brain. Once your brain has processed these neural signals, you experience the hot chocolate's aroma (see Figure 4-6 on page 110).

Many people prefer perfume-like fragrances and dislike foul and sulfurous odors. Smells that individuals most like are those that help survival. Ancient peoples survived in part through their sense of smell, because poisonous vegetation or foods smelled rotten.

The number of receptor cells in the nasal cavity determines smell sensitivity. Animals with more receptors than other animals have a much keener sense of smell. While humans have about 10 million olfactory receptors, dogs have 200 million receptors.

Although the human sense of smell is not as sensitive as that of many other species, we can often identify one another by smells. For example, blindfolded mothers can identify with close to 95 percent accuracy the clothing worn by their own children through smell alone. Similarly, infants quickly learn to identify their

olfactory nerve The nerve that transmits neural impulses containing smell information from the nose to the brain

Research indicates that women's smell sensitivity is better than that of men.

© BARTLOMIEJ MAGIEROWSKI, 2008/USED UNDER LICENSE FROM SHUTTERSTOCK.COM

Figure 4-6 THE OLFACTORY SYSTEM

Smell depends on odor molecules in the air reaching the nose and traveling to receptor cells, which send a neural impulse through the olfactory nerve to the brain.

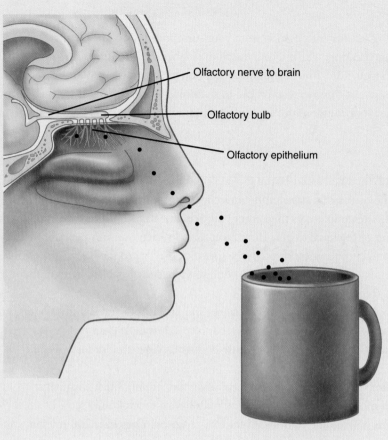

Olfactory nerve to brain

Olfactory bulb

Olfactory epithelium

mother's smell from that of other women. Brain scans taken while people are smelling objects find that smells trigger more brain activity in women than in men. This and other research indicates that women's smell sensitivity is better than that of men.

TASTE

Taste occurs when receptor cells in your mouth and throat trigger neural impulses to the brain. About 50 to 150 of these receptor cells are contained in each of the 10,000 **taste buds** that are located mainly on the tongue. The four most familiar taste sensations are sweetness (mostly sugars), sourness (mostly acids), saltiness (mostly salts), and bitterness (mainly chemicals that have no food value or are toxic). Most taste experiences are complex and result from the combined effects of receptor cells in the mouth and nose, which produce the different flavors you experience.

Has anyone ever told you that the taste buds sensitive to sweetness are on the front of your tongue and the taste buds for saltiness are on the sides? If so, don't believe them. As shown in Figure 4-7 (see page 111), this popular belief that the taste buds on different areas of the tongue detect different tastes is wrong. It is based on a mistranslation of a German paper that was written more than

taste buds Sensory receptor organs that contain the receptor cells for taste

Figure 4-7 THE TONGUE MAP MYTH

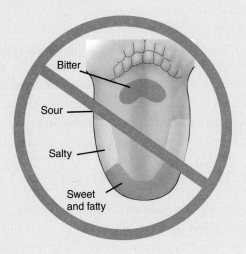

Bitter

Sour

Salty

Sweet
and fatty

Contrary to popular belief, different areas of the tongue are not more sensitive to one of the four primary tastes.

100 years ago. To set the record straight, the fact is that all your taste buds detect all taste qualities.

THE SKIN SENSES

Every living organism has a skin of some sort that defines its boundaries with the environment, and every living organism has a sense of touch. Your skin is your largest sensory organ. Your sense of touch is actually a combination of three skin senses: pressure, temperature, and pain.

The stimulus for *pressure* is physical pressure on the skin. Although the entire body is sensitive to pressure, some areas—such as your fingertips and face—have more receptors so are more sensitive.

Temperature sensations depend on which type of receptor is stimulated. Whether more warm or cold receptors are stimulated depends on the difference between your skin temperature and the temperature you are feeling. Your skin temperature must be either greater or less than what you are feeling. For example, if you wash your cold hands in 60°F water, the water feels warm. If your hands were already hot, the water feels cold.

What about *pain*? The chapter-opening story described how Aron Ralston cut off his own arm to save his life. What is so remarkable about Aron's actions is that he performed this self-surgery while ignoring all of his body's built-in defenses against the self-infliction of pain. Although pain is an unpleasant experience, it is important to survival because it serves as a warning system that signals danger and the risk of injury. Pain can

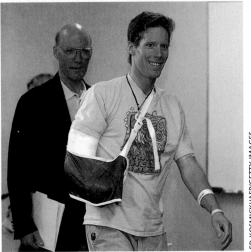

Aron Ralston cut off his own arm to save his life despite his body's built-in defenses against the self-infliction of pain.

INFOBIT
About 25 percent of people have a very large number of taste buds. These "supertasters" are extremely sensitive to bitter and sweet tastes. Supertasters' hypersensitivity to bitterness can cause them to avoid eating some very healthy foods, such as broccoli and other vegetables.

also force people to cope appropriately with an injury by causing them to seek treatment and to remain still to promote healing.

The most widely accepted theory of pain is **gate-control theory**. This theory proposes that the spinal cord contains a neurological "pain gate" that opens when pain signals arrive from different body areas. After these signals pass through the gate and reach the brain, you experience pain. Under some conditions, non-pain touch signals from the body temporarily close this pain gate. When the gate is closed incoming pain signals cannot reach the brain. Gate-control theory explains why rubbing, massaging, or even pinching a bruised or sore muscle eases the pain.

BODY POSITION AND MOVEMENT

The five senses already discussed are certainly important. However, if you did not possess two more senses, the *proprioceptive senses*, you would not be able to put food in your mouth or maintain proper balance. These two sources of sensory information detect body position and movement. One is the kinesthetic sense and the other is the vestibular sense.

The **kinesthetic sense** provides information about the movement and location of different parts of your body. Kinesthetic information comes from receptors in muscles, joints, and ligaments. You sometimes experience partial disruption of your kinesthetic system when your leg "falls asleep" and you have trouble walking.

The **vestibular sense** (or equilibrium) provides information on the position of your body in space by sensing gravity and motion. Vestibular sense information comes from tiny, hair-like receptor cells located in your inner ear. Whenever your head moves, these receptors provide information that helps you maintain your balance.

gate-control theory A theory describing how pain signals open a neurological "pain gate" in the spinal cord and how other touch signals close the gate

kinesthetic sense Provides information about the movement and location of different parts of your body

vestibular sense (or equilibrium) Provides information on the position of your body by sensing gravity and motion

CLOSER LOOK

Using Psychology to Reduce Pain

Pain accounts for 80 percent of all visits to the doctor, and it affects more than 50 million Americans per year. More than any of your other senses, your experience of pain can be significantly influenced by a variety of psychological factors. For example, distracting people's attention away from their pain to soothing music or a pleasant image (imagine yourself on a warm, sunny beach) is an effective strategy to reduce pain. Dentists and other health-care workers understand the benefits of distraction. This is why they provide music, videos, and a constant flow of conversation while performing painful procedures.

Think Critically

Why might soothing music cause you to feel less pain while having dental work?

4.3 ASSESSMENT

In Your Own Words

Name the three parts of the ear and explain the function of each.

Review Concepts

1. Which helps you maintain your balance?
   - a. pressure points
   - b. vestibular system
   - c. olfactory nerve
   - d. kinesthetic system

2. Loudness of a sound corresponds to the height of a sound wave called
   - a. amplitude
   - b. pitch
   - c. frequency
   - d. timbre

3. With which does hearing begin?
   - a. olfactory
   - b. pitch
   - c. frequency
   - d. sound waves

4. Which is not a part of the middle ear?
   - a. hammer
   - b. cochlea
   - c. anvil
   - d. stirrup

5. Which refers to smell?
   - a. olfactory
   - b. kinesthetic
   - c. taste buds
   - d. vestibular

6. What is the term for the senses that detect body position and movement?
   - a. olfactory
   - b. proprioceptive
   - c. sensorineural
   - d. auditory

7. Arrange the following in the order in which sound passes through them from first to last: eardrum; brain; outer ear; hammer, anvil, and stirrup; auditory nerve; cochlea; auditory canal.

8. **True or False** Every living organism has some sort of skin.

9. **True or False** Hearing loss in different individuals may be caused by different problems.

10. **True or False** The gate-control theory is a theory that explains the sense of taste.

Think Critically

11. Using either the example in the text or one from your own life, explain how the gate-control theory works and evaluate its effectiveness.

12. Why are taste experiences considered complex?

Why Do Some People Enjoy Eating Hot Chili Peppers?

INTRODUCTION Chili peppers have been a part of the human diet since at least 7500 B.C. Yet not everybody enjoys eating hot chili peppers and no one is born liking the burning sensation of these vegetables. It is an acquired taste. So why do some people like eating chili peppers?

HYPOTHESIS Psychologist Paul Rozin hypothesized that acquiring a taste for chili peppers depends on social influences. He further hypothesized that, for some people, eating chili peppers is an example of thrill seeking. Like riding a roller coaster, eating chili peppers is an activity in which extreme sensations can be enjoyed because people know that these sensations are not actually harmful.

METHOD Rozin set out to understand people's motivation for eating chili peppers and also how they learned to eat this hot food. Rozin conducted interviews and made observations in both Mexico and the United States.

RESULTS Rozin found evidence to support his hypothesis that the enjoyment of the irritation caused by eating chili peppers at least partly results from the user's appreciation that the sensation and the body's defensive reaction to it are harmless. Rozin also learned that children learn to enjoy eating chili peppers by observing their family members enjoying this food and having it gradually added to their diet. At first, the children may try the chili peppers to gain their family's approval. However, at some point the chili is liked for its own sake.

Critical Analysis

1. What does this case study suggest about people's motives for trying new and extreme food sensations?

2. What might encourage some young children to try a new food sensation?

PHOTODISC/GETTY IMAGES

Psychobiologist and Comparative Psychologist

Health Science

Do you have an interest in how the brain and nervous system affects behavior? Do you wonder how animals learn? Do you like research? If so, you may be interested in a career in psychobiology or comparative psychology.

Psychobiology and comparative psychology have many names. These include behavioral neuroscience, biopsychology, and physiological psychology. Psychologists in these two career areas study behavior by examining physiological processes.

Careers in psychobiology and comparative psychology may be in teaching or research. Psychologists in this field may work for medical centers, private or nonprofit research and development firms, or for government-funded organizations.

Psychologists in psychobiology may study either animals or human behavior, but comparative psychologists mainly study non-humans. In studying animals, they may study the behavior of dolphins and whales in an oceanic laboratory, or compare and contrast the similarities and differences between animals today and those from the ancient world in order to understand evolution.

Psychobiologists might study the effects of certain chemicals or pharmaceuticals on human behavior, examine the effects of damage or disease to the brain on cognitive functions, or examine the neural system to understand its effect on learning, memory, or sensory perceptions.

Individuals with a bachelor's of science degree in psychology who focus their studies on psychobiology or comparative psychology usually continue with their schooling to the Ph.D. level. They may also go on to medical or veterinary school, or health-related graduate professional schools.

Employment Outlook

Careers for psychologists are expected to grow 15 percent until 2016. This is a faster than average rate.

Needed Skills and Education

Most psychobiologists and comparative psychologists have a Ph.D. in psychology. While working toward this degree, many individuals gain research experience in the field of their choice by working under the supervision of someone with a Ph.D. in the field.

Students interested in these two careers need classes in psychology, biology, physics, neuroscience, chemistry, and comparative animal physiology. More specific college-level courses include research methods, experimental design and statistical inference, comparative psychology, and behavioral neuroscience.

Skills and aptitudes helpful in this career include critical thinking, oral and written communication, memory, organization, compiling and evaluating data, perceptiveness, and creativity, as well as computer and research skills.

How You'll Spend Your Day

The way psychologists in this career spend their day varies depending on the area of expertise. They may work 40 hours or more a week in a laboratory or have sporadic hours working with research animals or human test subjects.

Earnings

The median hourly earnings of psychologists are $59,440. The lowest 10 percent earn $35,280 while the highest 10 percent earn more than $102,730.

What About You?

Do these two careers sound interesting to you? Conduct an Internet search for colleges and universities that have programs specializing in these two fields.

STOCKBYTE/GETTY IMAGES

CHAPTER SUMMARY

4.1 Basic Principles of Sensation

- Sensation is the process that detects stimuli from your body and environment.

- Sensory receptors are the receptor sites for the senses.

- Gustav Fechner (1801–1887) was a pioneer in psychophysics, the study of how physical stimuli are translated into psychological experience. Fechner introduced the term absolute threshold to describe the weakest amount of a given stimulus that a person can detect half of the time. Psychologists measure absolute thresholds by presenting a stimulus (for example, a light or a sound) to a person at different intensities and determining the lowest level detectable 50 percent of the time.

- With signal-detection theory, the detection of a stimulus is influenced by your decision-making strategy. Two important factors that shape decision making are (1) your expectations about the probability the stimulus will occur, and (2) the rewards and costs associated with detecting or not detecting the stimulus.

- The difference threshold is the smallest difference between two stimuli that can be detected half of the time. Weber's Law is the principle that to be noticed as different, two stimuli must differ by a constant minimum percentage rather than by a constant amount.

- Sensory adaptation is the tendency for sensory receptors to decrease in response to stimuli that continue at the same level.

4.2 Vision

- The eye is responsible for vision. Light enters through the pupil, an opening in the iris that allows light to enter the eye. The light then enters a clear, elastic, disc-shaped structure called the lens. The lens reinforces the light with the aid of attached muscles as they stretch and flatten. Light then travels through the vitreous humor and is projected onto the retina, a light-sensitive surface at the back of the eye. When light reaches the back of the eye and strikes the retina, it activates the rods and cones and generates neural signals that are sent to the optic nerve, which carries information from the retina to the brain.

- The blind spot is an area on the retina where the optic nerve leaves the eye and that contains no receptor cells.

- Color blindness is a deficiency in the ability to distinguish among colors.

4.3 Hearing and Your Other Senses

- Hearing begins with sound waves, vibrations in air, water, or solid material. Sound comes through the ear.

- The ear is divided into three major parts—the outer ear, middle ear, and inner ear. The outer ear is the part you see. This is the part of the ear that receives sound waves and sends them down a passageway called the auditory canal. At the end of the auditory canal is the eardrum, a thin flexible membrane that vibrates in sequence with the sound waves.

- Your other senses include smell, taste, touch, skin-related, kinesthetic, and vestibular. The kinesthetic sense provides information about the movement and location of different parts of your body. Kinesthetic information comes from receptors in muscles, joints, and ligaments.

CHAPTER ASSESSMENT

Review Psychology Terms

Select the term that best fits the definition.

_____ 1. A theory stating that detecting a stimulus is influenced by a person's decision-making strategy

_____ 2. A thin, flexible membrane that vibrates in sequence with sound waves

_____ 3. An opening in the iris that allows light to enter the eye

_____ 4. Sensory receptor organs that contain the receptor cells for taste

_____ 5. The process that detects stimuli from your body and environment

_____ 6. Provides information about the movement and location of different parts of your body

_____ 7. Carries information from the retina to the brain

_____ 8. The weakest amount of a given stimulus that a person can detect half of the time

_____ 9. The coiled, fluid-filled tube in the inner ear that contains hair-like auditory receptors

_____ 10. The study of how physical stimuli are translated into psychological experience

_____ 11. The area on the retina where the optic nerve leaves the eye and that contains no receptor cells

_____ 12. A ring of muscles that range in color from light blue to dark brown

_____ 13. The tendency for sensory receptors to decrease in response to stimuli that continue at the same level

_____ 14. Provides information on the position of your body by sensing gravity and motion

_____ 15. The nerve that transmits neural impulses containing smell information from the nose to the brain

_____ 16. Smallest difference between two stimuli that can be detected half of the time

_____ 17. A deficiency in the ability to distinguish among colors

_____ 18. A clear, elastic, disc-shaped structure that refocuses light

_____ 19. The principle that to be noticed as different, two stimuli must differ by a constant minimum percentage rather than by a constant amount

_____ 20. A theory describing how pain signals open a neurological "pain gate" in the spinal cord and how other touch signals close the gate

_____ 21. The light-sensitive surface at the back of the eye

a. absolute threshold
b. blind spot
c. cochlea
d. color blindness
e. difference threshold
f. eardrum
g. gate-control theory
h. iris
i. kinesthetic sense
j. lens
k. olfactory nerve
l. optic nerve
m. psychophysics
n. pupil
o. retina
p. sensation
q. sensory adaptation
r. signal-detection theory
s. taste buds
t. vestibular sense
u. Weber's law

Review Psychology Concepts

22. Explain Weber's law.

23. Restate in your own words what a lens is.

24. What is the retina?

25. Why is it better for you to be in a quiet library than around jet aircraft?

26. Identify the difference between color blindness and blind spot.

27. Explain signal-detection theory and relate it to an example from your life.

28. Using your knowledge of the basic principles of sensation, design an ideal environment for doing your homework.

29. Explain why some species see color differently.

30. Predict the problem you would have if you responded to all the stimuli you are exposed to each day.

31. Why is pain important to survival?

32. Restate in your own words what the kinesthetic sense is, and give an example of why you need it.

33. Restate in your own words what the vestibular sense is, and give an example of why you need it.

34. Which two senses are considered the most important to human survival? Explain your answer.

Apply Psychology Concepts

35. Your family rents a cabin on a lake and your Mom discovers on the second day that she has lice in her hair! Immediately on hearing this unsettling news, your scalp feels itchy. Explain your reaction based on signal-detection theory.

36. What is the blind spot in your field of vision, and why doesn't it cause many problems for you?

37. How does gate-control theory explain why rubbing or massaging a sore muscle reduces the pain?

Make Academic Connections

38. **Cross-Cultural Studies** A study of more than 660 college students in four countries found cross-cultural differences among the students in the colors they associated with emotionally charged words. The students were asked what color they identify with the words anger, envy, fear, and jealously. Polish students associated anger, envy, and jealously with the color purple. German students associated envy and jealously with the color yellow. American students associated envy with the colors black, green, and red. Russian students associated these emotions with the colors black, purple, and yellow. Make a list of four emotions and the colors you associate with these emotions. For example, you could list the emotion of love and the color pink. Ask 11 people of different ages, genders, and cultural heritages or diverse backgrounds what color they associate with the emotions on your list. If possible, include one person who is colorblind. Make a chart of your findings, and then explain the conclusions you infer from your findings.

39. **Art** Download pictures from the Internet or use your drawing skills to create an illustration of the parts of either the eye or ear. Label each part. Then write an explanation of each part.

40. **History** Use the library or Internet to research Gustav Fechner, the pioneer in psychophysics. Examine his theory and analyze how he concluded that there is a relationship between bodily and mental experiences. Provide examples that illustrate absolute threshold. Make sure your sources are educational, news, or government web sites. Write a summary of your findings.

41. **Research** Use the library or Internet to search for studies on how loud noises affect hearing and hearing loss. Use the search term "loud noise effects." Make sure the studies you cite are from educational, news, or government sources. Write a paper that evaluates your findings.

42. **Science** Use the library or Internet to research the hearing abilities of one of the following animals: bat, cat, dog, dolphin, or grasshopper. Compare and contrast the chosen animal's hearing with human hearing. Try the search term "animal hearing." Make sure your sources are educational, news, or government web sites.

43. **Speech** Design a short oral demonstration that helps other students identify variables that influence the ability to divide attention. For example, you might play loud music while reading from a book, and then ask students to answer a list of five questions about the passage.

DIGGING DEEPER
with Psychology eCollection

Have you ever wondered why it is hard to "get over it" when someone hurts your feelings? Have you ever held a grudge? Do you know people who think the deck is stacked against them and that they can't get a break? Scientists have traced this behavior, called injustice collecting, back through human evolution. Psychologists maintain that this process is a self-protection impulse. They believe nursing grudges might have, at one time, helped people survive. By monitoring fairness and being alert to those who weren't contributing, it allowed people to protect scarce resources. Access the Gale Psychology eCollection at *www.cengage.com/school/psych/franzoi* and read the hypotheses about injustice collecting proposed by evolutionary psychologists such as Tooby and Cosmides. Write a brief report describing the research and findings on injustice collecting and answer the question: Why do psychologists research the development of behaviors in the past? As an additional project, describe an instance when you or someone you know had a grudge and explain how it was resolved.

Source: Pelusi, Nando. "Injustice collecting: you can't let go of a grudge, says Nando Pelusi, Ph.D., because there are deep-seated emotional payoffs. (NEANDERTHINK)." *Psychology Today* 39.6 (Nov–Dec 2006): 64(2).

Perception

ESSENTIAL QUESTION
Go to page XXV

"The eye sees only what the mind is prepared to comprehend."

—HENRI BERGSON, FRENCH PHILOSOPHER, 1859–1941

In the summer of 1910 while traveling by train, German psychologist Max Wertheimer noticed something many people before him had also noticed. When gazing out the window of a moving train, close, stationary objects—such as fences, trees, and buildings—appear to race in the opposite direction of the train, while distant objects—such as mountains and clouds—seem to slowly move along with the train. Wertheimer became so interested in understanding this experience—that came to be called motion parallax—that he began conducting experiments. These experiments led to the development of a new school of thought in psychology called Gestalt psychology.

Organizing Sensations into Perceptions

- Explain form perception.
- Describe depth perception, including binocular cues and monocular cues.
- Explain perceptual constancy and how it is influenced by prior experience.

DISCOVER IT | *How does this relate to me?*

Henri Bergson, a French philosopher, said, "The eye sees only what the mind is prepared to comprehend." What does this mean? You and a friend may both look at the same object, but see it differently. This is because your *perception* of the object is different from that of your friend's. Your perceptions influence your beliefs about the world around you. It is also true that your beliefs about the world influence your perceptions. In this section, you'll read about the scientific reasons behind perception—*why* and *how* you perceive things the way you do.

- perception
- form perception
- depth perception
- binocular cues
- monocular cues
- perceptual constancy

*S*ensation is the process that detects stimuli from your body and your environment, and **perception** is the process that organizes those stimuli into meaningful objects and events. Normally, you experience sensation and perception as one process, but they can be distinguished. For example, look at Figure 5-1 on page 122. At first, you may have a hard time seeing anything meaningful—that is, you may sense different shapes but perceive no meaningful pattern. To make sense of the shapes, your brain—through perception—organizes the different shapes into a meaningful pattern.

Form Perception

As you recall from Chapter 1, Gestalt psychology studies how your mind actively organizes stimuli into a meaningful whole, or *gestalt*. The process by which sensations are organized into meaningful shapes and patterns is called **form perception.** In form perception, the "whole is greater than the sum of its parts." For example, when you look at a beautiful painting, your perception helps organize the different sensations into a pattern that allows you to see the painting. Your perception of the painting is different from that of all the individual sensations you experience when looking at the painting.

perception The process that organizes stimuli into meaningful objects and events

form perception The process by which sensations are organized into meaningful shapes and patterns

Figure 5-1 DISTINGUISHING SENSATION FROM PERCEPTION

Can you identify anything meaningful in these patterned shapes? Detecting the different shapes involves the process of sensation. However, seeing a person riding a horse involves the process of perception. When looking at this picture, which process did you experience first, sensation or perception?

One basic rule of form perception is the *figure-ground relationship*—that is, when you focus on an object, it stands out from its surroundings. What you focus on is the *figure,* and everything else becomes the *ground.* For example, the words you are reading on this page are the figures, while the white surrounding the text is the ground. In Figure 5-2, the figure and ground are reversible, depending on what you are focusing on. When there are not enough cues to distinguish a figure from its ground, it is difficult to perceive the object you are seeking. The blending of objects into their surroundings is the basic idea behind camouflage.

The figure-ground relationship applies to all the senses. For example, you can hear one person's singing voice in a group. That person's voice is the figure and the rest of the group is the ground. Similarly, when you eat a slice of pumpkin pie and notice the taste of cinnamon, at that moment the cinnamon is the figure and the other pie tastes are the ground. Smelling barbecued chicken at a county fair among all the other aromas is another example of this basic rule of form perception.

Figure 5-2 REVERSIBLE FIGURE AND GROUND

What do you see? A white vase or two profiles? Can you keep one image in mind without the other intruding?

Once you distinguish figure from ground, you next organize the figure into a meaningful form. Gestalt psychologists identified simple principles—known as the *laws of grouping*—that describe how you group objects together into a meaningful whole. These principles are illustrated in Figure 5-3.

Similarity—You group objects together that are similar.

Proximity—You group nearby objects together.

Continuity—You perceive straight or curving lines as continuous, flowing patterns.

Closure—You close the gaps in a figure and perceive it as a whole.

Connectedness—You perceive similar objects that are linked as a single unit.

Common fate—You perceive similar objects moving together in the same direction (sharing a common fate) as belonging to a single group.

LAB TEAMS

Form Perception

Work with a partner. Use an object, such as a bottle, box, or pen. Place the object against five or six different backgrounds of different colors and patterns. Using the basic figure-ground relationship rule, record the different grounds, and then assess which grounds make it easier to perceive the figure.

CHECKPOINT *What is form perception?*

Figure 5-3 **GESTALT LAWS OF GROUPING**

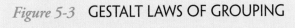

Similarity   **Proximity**   **Continuity**

There are many ways to perceive the objects shown here, but you tend to organize them into patterns that can be grouped together.

Connectedness   **Common Fate**

Closure

INTERACTIVE FIGURE

Depth Perception

Besides form perception, you also organize sensations in terms of the distance they are from you. In judging distance, your brain transforms the two-dimensional images that fall on your retinas into three-dimensional perceptions. This ability to perceive objects three-dimensionally is known as **depth perception** and it depends on the use of both *binocular cues* and *monocular cues*.

BINOCULAR CUES

Binocular cues are depth cues that require information from both eyes. Your eyes are about three inches apart, so slightly different images fall on each retina when you look at the same object. This degree of difference between the two images—which is greater when objects are closer to us—is known as the binocular cue of *retinal disparity.* Your brain fuses these two images into one and uses the cue of retinal disparity to judge the distance of objects. You can see the difference between the views of your eyes by holding both forefingers vertically in front of you, one at a distance of six inches and the other at arm's length. Now alternately close each eye while looking at both fingers. Notice that the closer finger appears to move farther side to side than the farther finger. If you focus on one finger with both eyes, you will see two images of the other finger. Three-dimensional (3-D) movies create the illusion of depth by presenting to each eye slightly different views of the same image. The stereogram in Figure 5-4 uses retinal disparity to create a similar illusion of depth. When you first look at the stereogram, you perceive a two-dimensional picture of meaningless shapes. However, by focusing your eyes well behind the surface of the page, each of your eyes will process a slightly different image and you will perceive a three-dimensional picture.

depth perception The ability to perceive objects three-dimensionally

binocular cues Depth cues that require information from both eyes

To see the three-dimensional images in this stereogram first hold this picture close to your face and focus your eyes as if you are looking at an object far behind the page. The stereogram picture will be blurry. Keeping that distant focus, slowly move the picture away from you until the details in the stereogram come into focus and you see the swordfish.

Figure 5-4 **PERCEIVING THREE-DIMENSIONAL IMAGES IN STEREOGRAMS**

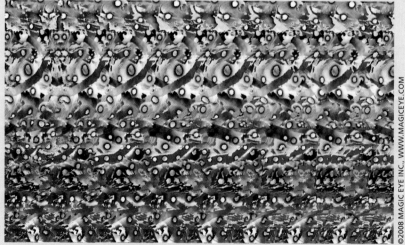

©2008 MAGIC EYE INC., WWW.MAGICEYE.COM

MONOCULAR CUES

Monocular cues are depth cues that require information from only one eye. Some of the more important monocular cues—illustrated in Figure 5-5 and in the photo on page 126—include the following:

Interposition—When one object partially blocks your view of another, you perceive the partially hidden object as more distant.

Familiar size—Familiar objects that cast small retinal images are perceived as distant, while familiar objects that make large retinal images are perceived as near.

Relative size—If you assume that two objects are similar in size, you perceive the object with the larger retinal image as being closer.

Height in the field of view—Objects you see closer to the horizon are perceived as farther away.

Texture gradients—You perceive objects as farther away when you see a change in their surface texture from rough, clear features to fine, unclear features.

Atmospheric blur—You perceive objects that appear hazy as farther away than sharp, clear objects.

> **monocular cues** Depth cues that require information from only one eye

Figure 5-5 MONOCULAR CUES

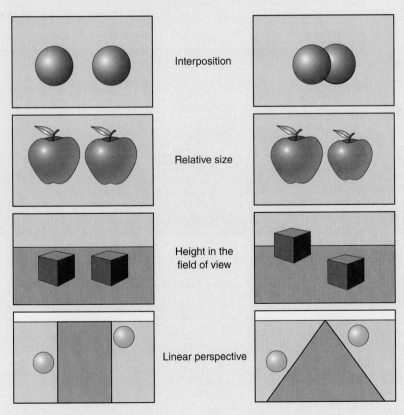

Interposition

Relative size

Height in the field of view

Linear perspective

Monocular cues are depth cues that require information from only one eye. Close one eye and test the monocular cues principle for yourself.

INTERACTIVE FIGURE

Linear perspective—When you see the convergence, or coming together, of what you assume are parallel lines, you perceive this convergence as indicating increasing distance.

Light and shadow—You perceive brighter objects as closer to you. Seeing different degrees of light and shadow on a single object provides clues about the object's three-dimensional shape.

Motion parallax—Motion parallax is a change in the position of an object caused by motion. For example, when you move your head from side to side, objects that move a greater distance in the opposite direction of your head are perceived as closer to you than objects that move a shorter distance. Also, as mentioned in the chapter-opening story, Max Wertheimer's attention to motion parallax led to the founding of Gestalt psychology. The next time you ride in a car, notice what Wertheimer experienced by looking out the window and focusing on objects to the side. Notice how closer objects appear to speed by in the opposite direction of your own movement, while objects farther away seem to move more slowly and in your same direction.

Which monocular cues does this photograph illustrate?

COURTESY OF FIGZOI

CHECKPOINT   *What is depth perception?*

Perceptual Constancy

Perceptual constancy is perceiving objects as not changing even though there is constantly changing sensory information. Once you form a stable perception of an object, you can recognize it from almost any distance and angle, regardless of it size, shape, brightness, or color.

Size constancy is perceiving an object as having the same size in spite of changes in the size of its retinal image when you view it from different distances. *Shape constancy* is the tendency to perceive an object as the same shape regardless of the angle from which you view it. When you look at your hand from different angles, you perceive it retaining its original shape in spite of changes in the shape of its retinal image.

With both size constancy and shape constancy, your ability to accurately judge objects depends on prior experience with those objects. You are better at assessing the true size and shape of familiar objects than unfamiliar objects (see photo below).

perceptual constancy
Perceiving objects as not changing even though there is constantly changing sensory information

CENGAGE LEARNING

If you traced the outline of the music CD in this photo, the tracing would show an oval. Is that how you would describe this object? Probably not. Shape constancy leads you to perceive and think of this CD as the flat circular object that it is.

CHECKPOINT *What is perceptual constancy?*

In Your Own Words

Choose a favorite photo. It could be a scene, an animal, an object, or a person. You might even use a photo of yourself. Look at the photo closely. Using the information you have read in this section, describe your perceptions of the photo and the process it took to arrive at your perceptions. Then analyze how you feel about the subject of the photo based on your perceptions. Address such concepts as form perception, figure-ground relationship, depth perception, and perceptual constancy. Explain how these concepts affect your feelings about the subject.

Review Concepts

1. Which refers to how your mind organizes stimuli into a meaningful whole?
   a. binocular cues
   b. monocular cues
   c. depth perception
   d. laws of grouping

2. Which refers to how an object stands out from its surroundings?
   a. similarity
   b. common fate
   c. figure-ground relationship
   d. perceptual constancy

3. Which is an example of perceiving parallel lines coming together as increasing distance?
   a. atmospheric blur
   b. linear perspective
   c. motion parallax
   d. light and shadow

4. **True or False** Binocular cues require information from both eyes.

5. **True or False** Perceptual constancy is perceiving objects in the same way even though there is constantly changing sensory information.

6. **True or False** Closure refers to seeing objects as separate pieces of the whole.

Think Critically

7. Use evidence from the text to support this statement: Your perception of a painting is different from all the individual sensations you experience when looking at the painting.

8. Distinguish between the figure and ground in the following examples: the taste of cinnamon in a pumpkin pie; the aroma of baking donuts in a bakery; a train whistle in city traffic; and a family member you are meeting at a busy airport.

9. Why is retinal disparity known as a binocular cue?

10. Why is it easier to assess the true size and shape of familiar objects than unfamiliar objects?

11. Explain the perceptual principle behind camouflage, and give an example.

12. What does depth perception allow you to do, and what does it depend on?

Perceptual Expectations and Misperceptions

OBJECTIVES

- Define perceptual set.
- Identify three perceptual illusions.

DISCOVER IT | *How does this relate to me?*

One Christmas during my high school years, my parents invited Great-Aunt Edith over for dinner. After the meal, as my sister was trying to coax our finicky dog to eat table scraps, she blurted out in frustration, "Oh eat it, you dumb dog!" However, what our aunt heard was "Oh, Edith, you dumb dog!" My sister had to do some quick explaining to convince Great-Aunt Edith that she wasn't being extremely disrespectful. Have you had similar incidents in your life where you or others have misperceived stimuli, resulting in misunderstandings?

KEY TERMS

- perceptual set
- perceptual illusion
- Müeller-Lyer illusion
- stroboscopic movement
- moon illusion

I n Chapter 4 you read about signal-detection theory and how expectations can influence whether you detect the presence of a stimulus. In this section, you will learn how the expectations you bring to a situation influence how you perceive the stimulus object. What were my Great-Aunt Edith's expectations? She had heard others use her name so often that when my sister spoke the phrase "eat it," my aunt heard "Edith."

Perceptual Sets

When you have an expectation of what or how something should be, you create a tendency to interpret sensory information in a particular way. This expectation is known as a **perceptual set**.

Look at the drawing of a duck in Figure 5-6. Based on your expectation of seeing a duck, you see a duck. In your mind, you organize the stimuli in this drawing so that you see what you expect to see. Ask a friend to look at this same drawing (cover up the caption), but tell them to "look at the rabbit." Chances are your friend will see the rabbit. This demonstrates how people develop different perceptions of the same stimuli based on different perceptual sets—or expectations—of what they expect to experience.

perceptual set An expectation that creates a tendency to interpret sensory information in a particular way

Figure 5-6   WHAT KIND OF A DUCK IS THIS?

Now that you have seen the duck, look again at this drawing, but now see the rabbit.

ILLUSTRATION FROM MIND SIGHTS: ORIGINAL VISUAL ILLUSIONS, AMBIGUITIES, AND OTHER ANOMALIES, WITH A COMMENTARY ON THE PLAY OF MIND IN PERCEPTION AND ART BY ROGER N. SHEPARD. COPYRIGHT © 1990 BY ROGER N. SHEPARD. REPRINTED BY PERMISSION OF HENRY HOLT AND COMPANY, LLC

Perceptual sets are influenced by culture. For example, look at Figure 5-7a. You probably see a confusing pattern of black shapes that may look somewhat like a boot. When you look at Figure 5-7b, you see the word FLY in the white spaces. Your experience with the English language causes you to focus attention on the white spaces in Figure 5-7b, while the black regions serve as background. If you were a native Chinese, you would see the white spaces in Figure 5-7a as the Chinese characters for the word FLY, but Figure 5-7b would likely look confusing.

Figure 5-7   CULTURAL INFLUENCE ON PERCEPTION

Figure 5-7a appears to be a confusing pattern of black figures to most English-speaking Westerners, but not to people who are familiar with Chinese. The exact opposite is true for Figure 5-7b.

(a)

(b)

Perceptual sets influence all types of sensations. The effects of perceptual sets demonstrate that what you perceive is much more than just detecting sensory stimuli—perception has to do with what's going on in your mind. For example, think about the shops where you buy your clothes. Your perception of where to shop depends on where your friends shop, on advertisements, and on what the music and film stars endorse.

DIGITAL VISION/GETTY IMAGES

Your perceptual sets influence where you shop for clothes. You choose the shops based on where your friends shop, on advertisements you like, endorsements of celebrities you admire, and because you expect to find what you like there.

CHECKPOINT *What are perceptual sets?*

Perceptual Illusions

Have you ever been sitting in a parked car when the vehicle parked next to you begins to back up, and you mistakenly perceived your car moving forward? When this happens, you have experienced a **perceptual illusion**. You experience a perceptual illusion because you misapply one or more of the *perceptual principles* examined in this chapter. In this case, it's the principle of motion parallax. That is, instead of your movement forward causing close objects to appear as though they are moving backward, the movement backward of the car next to you makes you feel like you are moving forward.

Illusions are incorrect interpretations of perceptual cues. When perceptional cues are misleading, your brain interprets—or misinterprets—the information. You see the size, shape, depth, and distance of an object differently from what it actually is. Vision is human's dominant sense, so scientists know more about visual illusions than any other sensory misperceptions.

MÜELLER-LYER ILLUSION

The **Müeller-Lyer illusion** is misperceiving the length of lines when either inward or outward facing "wings" are placed on the ends of the lines. As shown in Figure 5-8, on page 132 the vertical line b appears longer than line a, yet they are equal in length. This illusion occurs because you misapply size constancy. In the second illustration, figure a looks like the outside corner of a building and figure b looks like the inside corner of a room. Line b appears farther away than line a, which makes it appear longer. Fashion designers rely on the Müeller-Lyer illusion to make women's legs appear longer when they wear high-cut bathing suits rather than low-cut bathing suits.

perceptual illusion
A misperception of physical reality caused by misapplying one or more perceptual principles

Müeller-Lyer illusion
Misperceiving the length of lines when either inward or outward facing "wings" are placed on the ends of the lines

Figure 5-8 THE MÜELLER-LYER ILLUSION

In the Müeller-Lyer illusion, lines of equal length are perceived as unequal.

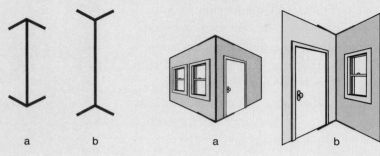

a   b   a   b

Figure 5-9 THE PONZO ILLUSION

The Ponzo illusion is an example of misapplying the monocular distance cue of linear perspective.

PONZO ILLUSION

Another perceptual illusion caused by the misapplication of size constancy is the *Ponzo illusion* shown in Figure 5-9. Do you see the line on top as longer than the one on the bottom? As in the Müeller-Lyer illusion, these two lines cast the same-sized retinal image. You experience the Ponzo illusion because you misapply the monocular distance cue of linear perspective. In other words, because you perceive the top line as being farther away than the bottom line, the line on top must be longer.

STROBOSCOPIC MOVEMENT

The most important visual illusion you experience when watching movies and playing video games is **stroboscopic movement**, which is the illusion of movement produced by a rapid pattern of stimulation on different parts of the retina. In motion pictures, stroboscopic movement is created by rapidly passing a series of still pictures (or film frames) past a light source, which projects these images onto a screen. As you watch these rapidly changing images, the memory of each lasts just long enough in your mind until the next one appears (see Figure 5-10 on p. 133). For this illusion of movement to occur, each film frame must replace the previous one 24 times per second. Check out the Closer Look feature about 3-D movies for more information on stroboscopic movement.

stroboscopic movement
The illusion of movement produced by a rapid pattern of stimulation on different parts of the retina

Figure 5-10 STROBOSCOPIC MOTION

IMAGE SELECT/ART RESOURCE, NY

Motion picture film consists of a series of still photographs. Presenting the pictures, one at a time, in quick succession, creates the illusion of movement.

CLOSER LOOK

3-D Movies and the Virtual Environment

When stroboscopic movement is combined with the nineteenth-century technology of stereoscope photography, the visual illusion offered by 3-D movies is created. Early black-and-white 3-D movies from the 1950s were filmed from two slightly different angles, and the two images were later projected onto the theater screen with different colored filters (red or blue) placed in front of each projector. So that each eye could receive a different view of the same scene, moviegoers wore special glasses with one red and one blue lens. The red lens washed out the red image, and the blue lens washed out the blue image. Viewers' brains merged these two images into one image, and using the cue of retinal disparity, they experienced three-dimensional movie vision. Later 3-D movies used different types of polarized light that allowed color to be shown.

The modern version of the 3-D movie is the *virtual environment*, in which a person can experience 3-D images and sounds while wearing a head visor. The visor sends clear, full wraparound 3-D images to each eye, and the ears receive digital stereo sound. The images and sounds transmitted by the visor are controlled by a computer that adjusts for head movements. Whenever the wearer's head turns, the scene shifts. As you read in Chapter 2, psychologists are beginning to use virtual-environment technology in their research to increase the realism of laboratory experiments. Some clinical psychologists also use this technology when treating clients who suffer from certain intense fears, such as the fear of flying or the fear of heights (see Chapter 18).

Think Critically

How might virtual-environment technology help clinical psychologists treat clients who suffer from a fear of flying or a fear of heights?

THE MOON ILLUSION

An illusion that is affected by depth perception is the **moon illusion**, in which the moon appears to be about 1½ times larger when near the horizon than when high in the sky. The same illusion also occurs for the sun. You know the moon does not actually shrink as it rises in the sky, and the retinal size of the moon also doesn't change (see Figure 5-11a). The earth's atmosphere also does not magnify the visual appearance of the horizon moon. Yet, as you watch the moon rise from the horizon to the night sky, it does appear to decrease in size, as represented in Figure 5-11b. There are various theories to explain this rather complicated illusion, and currently there is still widespread disagreement as to its causes.

moon illusion The moon appears to be about 1½ times larger when near the horizon than when high in the sky

CHECKPOINT *What is a perceptual illusion?*

Figure 5-11 **THE MOON ILLUSION**

(a) This is a representation of a time-lapse photograph of the horizon moon and zenith moon. Each moon image has the same diameter. (b) This is a representation of what you perceive as the moon illusion.

(a)

(b)

In Your Own Words

Write an essay that describes your feelings about an incident, person, place, or group. In the paper, analyze how perceptual sets play a part in your expectations and feelings about the incident, person, place, or group. Also make a prediction about how you might experience the incident, person, place, or group differently if you change your expectations. For example, you might write about your favorite vacation spot, or you might choose to write about your study group.

Review Concepts

1. Which is the illusion of movement produced by a rapid pattern of stimulation on different parts of the retina?
   - a. moon illusion
   - b. Ponzo illusion
   - c. stroboscopic movement
   - d. perceptual sets

2. Which is misperceiving the length of lines when either inward or outward facing "wings" are placed on the ends of the lines?
   - a. sun illusion
   - b. moon illusion
   - c. Ponzo illusion
   - d. Müeller-Lyer illusion

3. Which is an illusion affected by depth perception in which the sun appears to be about 1½ times larger when near the horizon than when high in the sky?
   - a. universal illusion
   - b. sun illusion
   - c. Earth illusion
   - d. moon illusion

4. **True or False** Perceptual sets are influenced by culture.

5. **True or False** The moon seems to increase in size as it rises because of a misperception of size constancy.

6. **True or False** Perceptual sets are influenced only by specific sensations.

7. **True or False** Perceptual illusions are caused by nearsightedness and farsightedness.

8. **True or False** You experience stroboscopic movement when watching movies or playing video games.

9. **True or False** All scientists agree on the causes of the moon illusion.

Think Critically

10. Were you surprised to see a duck in Figure 5-6? Did you have more trouble seeing the rabbit? Explain your answer in a sentence or two.

11. Describe in your own words a perceptual illusion that you have experienced.

12. Why do scientists know more about visual illusions than illusions that affect the other senses?

13. Evaluate this statement and provide an example that supports your evaluation: What is going on in your mind influences what you experience.

The Visual Cliff

INTRODUCTION   While psychologist Eleanor Gibson (1910–2002) was visiting a farm, she observed a farmer help a pregnant cow deliver two calves. When the first calf was born, the farmer placed the newborn on the steps of a nearby ladder and then helped the cow deliver the second calf. Later, when Gibson asked the farmer about placing the newborn calf on the ladder steps, he replied that doing so prevented the calf from wandering away, because cows fear heights. This experience prompted Gibson to design a study to find out whether humans are born with depth perception.

HYPOTHESIS   Gibson hypothesized that human infants, like newborn calves, are born with depth perception.

METHOD   To test this hypothesis, Gibson and Richard Walk (1960) designed the *visual cliff*. As shown in the figure, the visual cliff consists of a glass-covered tabletop with a "shallow" checkerboard on one end and a "deep" checkerboard on the other end that appears to drop off like a cliff. Infants between 6 and 14 months were placed on the middle of this table, and their mothers were instructed to try to coax them into crawling to one side or the other.

RESULTS   The mothers had little problem getting their children to crawl toward them on the shallow end of the visual cliff. However, most children refused to crawl past the visual cliff onto the deep end. It is possible that by the time they learned to crawl, these children had also learned to perceive depth. Newborn animals that can walk the day they are born—such as calves, lambs, chicks, kittens, pigs, and rats—also avoid the deep end of the visual cliff.

Later studies found that when younger non-crawling infants were moved from the shallow end of the visual cliff table to the deep end, their heart rates slowed. Heart slowing is a typical reaction when people are introduced to new situations. Although these younger babies may not have known how to react, they did perceive something different between the shallow and deep ends of the table. These findings suggest that infants may have depth perception at birth or shortly afterwards. However, fear and avoidance of dangerous depths may develop only after they learn to crawl and obtain firsthand experience with the dangers of height. For her contributions to the study of perception, Eleanor Gibson was awarded the National Medal of Science in 1992.

Critical Analysis

After Gibson obtained the results of her first study with crawling infants, why was it important to conduct additional studies that tested younger infants?

Unconscious and Extrasensory Perceptions

OBJECTIVES

- Define subliminal perception and summarize the findings of studies.
- Define parapsychology and summarize the research findings.

KEY TERMS

- subliminal perception
- extrasensory perception
- parapsychology

DISCOVER IT | *How does this relate to me?*

Do you think it is possible for advertisers to unconsciously convince you to buy their products by embedding hidden messages into commercials? Have you ever heard of subliminal messages? A subliminal message is a message that flashes onto a movie or television screen so quickly you don't consciously notice it, but your brain unconsciously registers the message. What do psychologists say about subliminal messages? What about extrasensory perception, or ESP? Can some people foretell the future? Is it possible to "read" other people's minds? Do police departments solve crimes by relying on people who claim to have ESP powers? Do you think ESP exists and affects people's thinking and behavior? What do psychologists say about ESP?

M any people who have some knowledge of subliminal messages in advertising believe that subliminal perception can influence your buying habits. Also, many people believe that extrasensory perception exists. Is there any reliable scientific evidence that either subliminal perception or extrasensory perception exists? This chapter explores both topics from a scientific perspective.

Subliminal Perception

As you read in Chapter 4, the *absolute threshold* of a stimulus is the level at which you can detect the stimulus half of the time. Can you detect a stimulus below your absolute threshold? Yes. At or slightly below this threshold you may detect the stimulus some of the time. For example, flashing on a computer screen a photo of a kitten for only 13/1000 of a second is just below your absolute threshold for conscious perception. Being just below your absolute threshold, you probably will not consciously perceive the kitten, but your brain may process the image and react to it, most likely in brain areas responsible for positive emotions. This processing of information that is below your threshold of conscious awareness is called **subliminal perception**.

Can subliminal perception influence your thoughts, feelings, and actions? Carefully controlled laboratory studies have successfully altered people's attitudes and behavior using subliminal stimuli. For example, participants who were repeatedly shown subliminal stimuli (abstract geometric figures or people's faces) later expressed a greater liking for those stimuli than participants who did not experience the subliminal messages.

In another study, some people were subliminally exposed to achievement words (such as *strive, succeed,* and *master*) while completing a word-search puzzle. This exposure caused them to spend more time working on the puzzle than people who were not subliminally exposed to these words. This and other research suggests that subliminal messages can influence a person's emotions and actions.

Do such findings mean that your desire to purchase specific products can be shaped by subliminal messages secretly placed in advertisements? One study explored this possibility with college students. Students first taste-tested two different types of cookies. Next, the researchers manipulated students' thirst by telling half of them to refresh their taste buds by drinking as much water as they desired. The other students received no water. Then, while answering questions on a computer, some students were subliminally exposed to neutral words, such as *pirate* or *won,* while other students were subliminally exposed to thirst-related words, such as *thirst* or *dry.* Following this computer exercise, all students were allowed to drink as much Kool-Aid as they desired during a second taste test.

Results showed that the subliminal thirst words did not influence the drinking behavior of students who had previously been allowed to drink water. Yet these subliminal thirst words did significantly increase beverage drinking among those who were already thirsty. In other words, the subliminal thirst words did not create a desire to drink beverages in people who were not thirsty, but they did increase the drinking behavior of already-thirsty people. This study suggests that when people

subliminal perception
Processing of information that is below your threshold of conscious awareness

One day, advertisers may be able to unconsciously encourage thirsty and hungry moviegoers to buy their products using subliminal perception.

PHOTODISC/GETTY IMAGES

are already motivated to behave in a certain way, subliminal messages may cause them to behave more strongly than they would otherwise have acted.

In many of these laboratory studies, the subliminal effects appear to be very short, lasting only a few seconds. Few studies have found evidence that people exposed to subliminal stimuli in the laboratory have any noticeable effects days later. If subliminal effects last only a short time, they are unlikely to influence how people purchase products unless the subliminal messages are presented in stores or places where products are purchased. For example, it is possible that if already thirsty customers in a restaurant are exposed to subliminal *thirsty* messages just before they order, they may be more likely to buy a super-size drink. Customers who are not thirsty are unlikely to be influenced by such subliminal messages. However, it is important to remind you that the ability of subliminal messages to influence people's behavior is still something that has only been demonstrated in laboratory experiments, not anywhere else. For more on subliminal messages, check out the Positive Psychology feature on page 140.

 *What is subliminal perception, and is there solid scientific evidence to support its existence?*

Extrasensory Perception

Some people believe that humans can perceive events in the world without using the normal senses. This **extrasensory perception (ESP)** is a controversial topic within psychology, with only a minority of psychologists believing in its possible existence. The field that studies ESP and other paranormal phenomena is known as **parapsychology**.

Parapsychologists are the psychologists who study a variety of extrasensory abilities. *Mental telepathy* is the supposed ability to perceive other people's thoughts. *Clairvoyance* is the supposed ability to perceive objects or events that are not physically present. *Precognition* is the supposed ability to perceive events in the future—that is, before they happen. *Psychokinesis* is the supposed ability to control objects through mental manipulation, such as causing a chair to move or a flipped coin to land either heads or tails.

Is there any scientific evidence to support ESP ability? Since the 1930s, parapsychologists have conducted many studies, and some of their findings seemed to suggest that ESP abilities might exist. In these studies, researchers ask participants to transmit telepathically highly distinct symbols (see Figure 5-12 on page 141) to people in distant locations. The problem with such studies is that the findings often cannot be replicated in later research. British scientists tested the ESP ability of almost 28,000 people by asking them to guess the outcome of four random electronic coin tosses. With such a large sample size, this study had the statistical power to detect the possible existence of even a very small ESP effect. However, the results found no evidence of ESP ability. Reviews of the findings from many different ESP studies also have failed to find solid evidence for the existence of ESP.

extrasensory perception (ESP) The ability to perceive events in the world without using the normal senses

parapsychology The field that studies ESP and other paranormal phenomena

Are Subliminal "Self-Help" Tapes Worthwhile?

Many people who have used subliminal tapes to increase their self-esteem or improve their memory believe that their lives have been changed in a positive way. Yet do these subliminal tapes really perform the way they're advertised?

This was the question that psychologist Anthony Pratkanis and his colleagues were interested in answering when they conducted a study of self-help tapes. Participants were first pre-tested for their level of self-esteem and memory recall ability and then given an audiotape containing various pieces of classical music. The tape manufacturers claimed that embedded within these self-help tapes were subliminal messages designed either to increase self-esteem (for example, "I have high self-worth and high self-esteem") or to increase memory (for example, "My ability to remember and recall is increasing daily."). However, the researchers purposely mislabeled half of the tapes, leading participants who received them to believe they had a memory tape when they really had a self-esteem tape, or vice versa. The remaining participants received the rest of the tapes, with correct labels.

During the next five weeks, these volunteers listened daily to their tapes at home. After this exposure period, they again were given self-esteem and memory tests, and they were also asked whether they believed the tapes had been effective. Was there any evidence that these subliminal tapes had their advertised positive effects?

Pratkanis and his coworkers found no self-esteem or memory increases: the subliminal tapes were completely ineffective. These findings, however, stood in sharp contrast to the participants' beliefs about the tapes. Those who thought they had received the self-esteem tape tended to believe their self-esteem had increased, and those who thought they had been given the memory tape were more likely to believe that their memory had improved. This was true even if they had received a mislabeled tape! According to the researchers, these findings indicate that users of subliminal self-help tapes expect self-improvement through their use, and actually convince themselves that the improvement has taken place, when, in fact, it has not.

These results have been replicated in other studies using different types of subliminal self-help tapes. Together they suggest that whatever benefits people receive from such self-help products have little to do with the content of the subliminal messages. Instead, people's expectations, combined with the time and money they have invested in these products ("I spent a lot on this tape, it must be good!"), appear to be the only influence operating here.

Think Critically

Why might people buy subliminal self-help tapes even if they know the results of studies that show these tapes do not help?

Figure 5-12 ESP TEST CARDS

COURTESY OF FIGZOI

In the 1930s, parapsychologist J. B. Rhine designed a special set of cards with easy-to-recall symbols as a way to test paranormal abilities.

What about the belief that psychics are successful at predicting the future and in helping various government agencies uncover hidden or secret information, such as aiding the police in solving crimes or uncovering spy plots? When police departments in the 50 largest cities in the United States were surveyed in the 1990s, only 35 percent reported ever having used psychics on a crime case, and none of those had found it helpful. Additional studies have compared the success rates of psychics, college students, and experienced crime detectives in solving crime cases. Results indicate that the psychics are no more successful than the students and detectives, and their success rate is no better than chance. Similar results have occurred when psychics have been tested in the world of intelligence gathering. After 20 years of testing "psychic spies," the Central Intelligence Agency concluded in a 1995 report that ESP claims were not supported by any reliable evidence.

Although there is little evidence to indicate that ESP is a valid means of perceiving the world, many people believe in its existence. The evidence upon which almost all these people base their beliefs comes from personal accounts, not scientific studies. Until the phenomenon known as ESP can be replicated reliably in carefully controlled scientific studies, it will remain only a highly speculative *extra sense* to most scientists.

NBC/EVERETT COLLECTION

Popular television shows like Medium *portray psychics successfully solving crimes for police departments. Research, however, indicates that the success rate of psychics in solving crimes is no better than chance.*

CHECKPOINT *What is extrasensory perception, and is there solid scientific evidence to support its existence?*

In Your Own Words

Write an essay both for and against the argument that subliminal perception exists.
Provide evidence for both sides.

Review Concepts

1. Which refers to the processing of information that is below your conscious awareness?
   - a. ESP
   - b. parapsychology
   - c. subliminal perception
   - d. extrasensory perception

2. Which refers to the ability to perceive events in the world without using the normal senses?
   - a. perceptual illusion
   - b. ESP
   - c. monocular cues
   - d. subliminal perception

3. Which refers to the field that studies paranormal phenomena?
   - a. sensory perception
   - b. parapsychology
   - c. social psychology
   - d. extrasensory perception

4. Which refers to the ability to perceive objects or events that are not physically present?
   - a. psychokinesis
   - b. precognition
   - c. mental telepathy
   - d. clairvoyance

5. Which refers to the supposed ability to perceive other people's thoughts?
   - a. psychokinesis
   - b. precognition
   - c. mental telepathy
   - d. clairvoyance

6. **True or False** Effects of subliminal perceptions last a lifetime.

7. **True or False** ESP can be replicated reliably in carefully controlled scientific studies.

8. **True or False** You cannot detect a stimulus below your conscious awareness.

9. **True or False** Research suggests that when people are already motivated to behave in a certain way, subliminal messages may cause them to behave more strongly than they otherwise would have acted.

10. **True or False** ESP is a controversial topic within psychology.

11. **True or False** Parapsychologists study a variety of extrasensory abilities.

Think Critically

12. Why might you be more influenced by *thirsty* subliminal messages if you are already thirsty?

13. Why do most scientists state that ESP does not exist?

14. Why do many people believe in ESP if there is little scientific evidence to indicate that ESP is a valid means of perceiving the world?

Statistician

Science, Technology, Engineering & Mathematics

Do you like mathematics? Do you enjoy studying the relationships among numbers? Are you also interested in human or animal behavior and the data collected in scientific research experiments? If so, you might enjoy a career as a statistician who works with a research psychologist.

Statisticians work with *statistics*, a mathematical way to analyze information as an aid to decision making. Statisticians help researchers analyze the data they collect by applying their knowledge of mathematics and statistics to the data. Through statistical analysis, both statisticians and psychologists are able to make inferences and draw conclusions about human and animal behavior.

In addition to being experts at analyzing data, statisticians also can help psychologists by providing expert advice on the collection of the data. Statisticians are also experts at using computer software to analyze, interpret, and write a report about their statistical findings.

Employment Outlook

Careers for statisticians are expected to grow at an average rate through 2016. Many statisticians work for the federal government, state and local governments, private industry, and colleges and universities. Jobs in the federal government are usually in the Department of Commerce, Agriculture, and Health and Human Services. In private industry, jobs are in the areas of scientific research and developmental services.

Job titles may vary depending on the specialty of the statistician. For example, statisticians working in public health and medicine may be called biostatisticians or biometricians.

Needed Skills and Education

A bachelor's degree in statistics or mathematics is required for careers as a statistician in the federal government. Most statisticians have a master's degree for working in the government or private industry. For teaching or working in research in colleges and universities, a Ph.D. is required.

If you are interested in this career, plan to major in statistics or mathematics. Courses in computer science and psychology also are helpful. Good interpersonal and communication skills are needed when you work with researchers to prepare and collect data and to help you interpret your analysis for researchers less familiar with mathematics.

How You'll Spend Your Day

Most statisticians work in an office environment. New statisticians often work with a senior statistician. Most work a 40-hour week, but may work overtime when needed.

Earnings

The median annual earnings for statisticians are $65,720. Some statisticians earn as little as $48,480, while some earn as much as $108,630.

What About You?

Does the occupation of statistician interest you? Use the Internet or library to research this career, and then make a list of 10 things about this career. Include such things as salary, job environment, type of work, and work environment. Give each item on your list a numerical value from 1 to 10, 1 being what you do not like about the career, 10 being what you really like about the career. Add the total. If your total is above 50, conduct more research on this career. If it is below 50, consider another career.

BLEND IMAGES/JUPITER IMAGES

CHAPTER SUMMARY

5.1 Organizing Sensations into Perceptions

- Perception is the process that organizes stimuli into meaningful objects and events. Form perception is the process by which sensations are organized into meaningful shapes and patterns.

- Depth perception is the ability to perceive objects three-dimensionally. Depth perception depends on binocular cues and monocular cues. Binocular cues are depth cues that require information from both eyes; monocular cues require information from only one eye. Binocular cues include retinal disparity; monocular cues include interposition, familiar size, relative size, height in the field of view, texture gradients, atmospheric blur, linear perspective, light and shadow, and motion parallax.

- Perceptual constancy is perceiving objects as not changing even though there is constantly changing sensory information. Once you form a stable perception of an object, you can recognize it from almost any distance and angle, regardless of its size, shape, brightness, or color.

5.2 Perceptual Expectations and Misperceptions

- Perceptual set is an expectation that creates a tendency to interpret sensory information in a particular way. Perceptual sets are influenced by culture, and they influence all types of sensations.

- Perception has to do with what's going on in your mind as well as the sensory stimuli you perceive.

- Perceptual illusion is a misperception of physical reality caused by misapplying one or more perceptual principles. Four types of perceptual illusion are the Müeller-Lyer illusion, the Ponzo illusion, stroboscopic movement, and the moon illusion.

5.3 Unconscious and Extrasensory Perceptions

- Subliminal perception is the processing of information that is below your threshold of conscious awareness. Laboratory studies show that the subliminal effects appear to be very short, lasting only a few seconds. Few studies have found evidence that people exposed to subliminal stimuli in the laboratory have any noticeable effects days later. If subliminal effects last only a short time, they are unlikely to influence how people purchase products unless the subliminal messages are presented in stores or places where products are purchased.

- Parapsychology is the field that studies extrasensory perception (ESP) and other paranormal phenomena.

- Extrasensory perception (ESP) is the ability to perceive events in the world without using the normal senses. Scientific studies do not support the existence of ESP because it cannot be reliably replicated in a controlled study.

CHAPTER ASSESSMENT

Review Psychology Terms

Select the term that best fits the definition. Some terms will not be used.

_____ 1. The moon appears to be about 1½ times larger when near the horizon than when high in the sky

_____ 2. A misperception of physical reality caused by misapplying one or more perceptual principles

_____ 3. Processing of information that is below your threshold of conscious awareness

_____ 4. The process that organizes stimuli into meaningful objects and events

_____ 5. The illusion of movement produced by a rapid pattern of stimulation on different parts of the retina

_____ 6. The ability to perceive events in the world without using the normal senses

_____ 7. Perceiving objects as not changing even though there is constantly changing sensory information

_____ 8. The process by which sensations are organized into meaningful shapes and patterns

_____ 9. An expectation that creates a tendency to interpret sensory information in a particular way

_____ 10. Depth cues that require information from only one eye

_____ 11. The ability to perceive objects three-dimensionally

_____ 12. The field that studies ESP and other paranormal phenomena

_____ 13. Misperceiving the length of lines when either inward or outward facing "wings" are placed on the ends of the lines

_____ 14. Depth cues that require information from both eyes

a. binocular cues

b. depth perception

c. extrasensory perception

d. figure-ground relationship

e. form perception

f. laws of grouping

g. monocular cues

h. moon illusion

i. Müeller-Lyer illusion

j. parapsychology

k. perception

l. perceptual constancy

m. perceptual illusion

n. perceptual set

o. Ponzo illusion

p. size constancy

q. shape constancy

r. stroboscopic movement

s. subliminal perception

Review Psychology Concepts

15. Restate in your own words what happens when perceptual cues are misleading.

16. Judge the importance of the retina on stroboscopic movement. Support your answer.

17. Does the moon illusion cause the moon to increase or decrease in size as it rises in the sky?

18. Argue that "the whole is greater than the sum of its parts" when looking at a painting.

19. Explain the figure-ground relationship.

20. Restate the laws of grouping in your own words.

21. Differentiate between binocular cues and monocular cues.

22. Distinguish between size constancy and shape constancy.

23. Use the library or Internet to find three examples of monocular depth cues—such as linear perspective and relative size—in pictures, paintings, or photographs.

24. Describe how police departments or government agencies have used people with extrasensory perception and these agencies' success using psychics.

Apply Psychology Concepts

25. How does size constancy allow you to correctly perceive that when a car drives away from you it is not actually getting smaller?

26. Consider the following statements: Some students refer to their parents as their "folks." A funny story is called a "joke." When people stick their pointed finger into your arm, you would say they gave you a "poke." Ok, now, answer this question: What do you call the white of an egg? In asking this question, how am I using the principle of perceptual set to influence your answer?

27. What does research tell us concerning the effectiveness of subliminal self-help tapes that are advertised as being able to improve memory or increase self-esteem?

28. What does research tell us about the ability of psychics to successfully predict the future and help various government agencies uncover hidden or secret information, such as aiding the police in solving crimes or uncovering spy plots?

Make Academic Connections

29. **Science** Using information from the text on perceptual principles, hypothesize how these principles might relate to stereotypes and prejudice.

30. **Cross-Cultural Studies** Choose a foreign country, and then use the library or Internet to research food in that country. Choose a food that people in that country think is delicious while you might think it sounds awful. Compare and contrast the similarities and differences in your perception of the chosen food with that of the perception of the people of the foreign culture.

31. **Mathematics** Conduct your own experiment with extrasensory perception. Choose one of the following or create your own experiment: (1) Gather six photographs of the same size. Turn them upside down, and then have someone else mix them up. After spending a few minutes looking at the upside down photographs, try to guess the name of the subject in each photograph. Record your answers. (2) Use a deck of cards. Turn each card upside down and mix them up. Before picking up each card, try to guess the number and suit of the card. Record your answers. (3) For three days, try to guess who is calling before you look at the number or answer the phone. Record your answers.

    Your record should include the number of photographs, cards, or phone calls and the number of times you answered correctly and the number of times you answered incorrectly. Once you have recorded all your answers, make a chart that illustrates how many times you were correct and how many times you were incorrect. Calculate your percentage of correctness. If you have six photographs and were correct three times and incorrect three times, you were correct 50 percent of the time.

32. **Art** Choose one of the laws of grouping and design a visual that illustrates the chosen principle. You can draw an illustration, create a three-dimensional design, or download an illustration from the Internet.

33. **Marketing** Use magazines, newspapers, or the Internet to find an advertisement for a product that interests you. Analyze how the advertisement uses sensory information to tempt the reader into buying the product. Analyze the advertisement and assess which words and illustrations attract which senses. Evaluate any subliminal messages you think exist in the advertisement, and how your perceptions play a role in your attraction to the product. Write an analysis of your findings.

34. **Speech** Use the Internet to search for stereograms, 3-D images hidden within another image. Download one of the stereograms. Find the hidden image, but do not tell other students what you found. Prepare a short speech on how you found the image, and post the stereogram in the room so other students can find the hidden image. Leave the stereogram posted until all students have seen the hidden image.

35. **Sociology** Obtain a photograph from your collection or download one from the Internet. Write a sentence or two about your perception of the photograph, explaining what you know or think is taking place in the photograph. Then ask six other people of different ages and cultural groups what they think is happening in the photograph. Record their answers. Write a summary of your findings.

36. **Language Arts** Find a passage in an article or book that uses labels to identify a person or groups of people. For example, how do political opponents talk about each other? How do sports teams talk about their rivals? Make a copy of your passages, and then highlight the words or phrases that label people. Write a paragraph that evaluates how these subliminal messages can affect the reader.

DIGGING DEEPER
with Psychology eCollection

You're psychic—a mind reader! In fact, we all are. Don't believe it? How many times have you said, "I know what he or she is thinking?" Your keen sense of observation has picked up subtle clues that help you interpret behavior such as the look on someone's face or how they are acting at a given time. Using your perceptions, you draw on your experiences to determine what they are feeling and thinking, a behavior known as empathic accuracy. According to psychologists, mind reading such as this is a form of intelligence. It is discussed more fully in Chapter 16. It helps us to understand other people's behavior and successfully decide what we should do. As we get older, we refine the skill through our growing number of experiences. Access the Gale Psychology eCollection at *www.cengage.com/school/psych/franzoi* and discover more about empathic accuracy. Write a brief report describing the research and findings on this topic and answer the question: Why might understanding how we are "in sync" with other people be an important area of research? As an additional project, describe an instance when you were a mind reader. Explain what happened, what you sensed, and what your actions were.

Source: Paul, Annie Murphy. "Mind reading: whether we know it or not, we're all street-corner psychics. Without the ability to divine other's thoughts and feelings, we couldn't handle the simplest social situations—or achieve true intimacy with others. (Cover story)." *Psychology Today* 40.5 (Sept-Oct 2007): 72(8).

Motivation and Emotion

ESSENTIAL QUESTION
Go to page XXV

"The greater the difficulty the more glory in surmounting it. Skillful pilots gain their reputation from storms and tempests."

—EPICTETUS, GREEK PHILOSOPHER, 55–135 C.E.

When I was eleven, my grandmother died. Right after hearing this very sad news, my best friend, Pete, came over to play. My father told me to tell Pete about my Gramma. I looked at my father, my Gramma's son, and saw that while his eyes looked hurt, they were dry. In that look, I knew I couldn't tell Pete anything, because if I did, the tears would come. Feeling trapped, I choked out the two-word phrase, "I can't!" and ran past my crying mother and sister. During the next few days, I did cry, but only when alone. I never saw tears flow down my father's cheeks or those of any other men in the family.

Why did I think and act the way I did upon hearing the news of my grandmother's death? Why did my mother and sister respond differently from my father and me? It wasn't a matter of us not loving Gramma. No, that wasn't it at all. It was a matter of boys and girls being taught different ways to express emotions.

IMAGE100/JUPITER IMAGES

6.1 | Theories of Motivation

OBJECTIVES

- Define motivation.
- Compare and contrast internal push theories.
- Differentiate among external pull theories.
- Understand Maslow's hierarchy of needs.

KEY TERMS

- motivation
- homeostasis
- drive-reduction theory
- Yerkes-Dodson law
- incentive theory
- incentive
- intrinsic motivation
- extrinsic motivation
- hierarchy of needs
- self-actualization

DISCOVER IT | *How does this relate to me?*

Do you ever wonder what motivates—or causes—you to behave in certain ways? Before a big test you may feel *pulled* to study by external forces, such as the need to get a good grade or to please your parents. Or you may feel *pushed* to study by an internal force because you enjoy learning and feel driven to know more about the subject. Psychologists have formed theories about what motivates people. Some theories state motivation is an internal push, while others think motivation is an external pull. Another theorist believes people are motivated by their needs, such as the need for safety or approval. What motivates you right now to read this chapter? Are you motivated by the internal push because you want to know what psychologists say about motivation, or the external pull because you want a good grade in this course? Or are you motivated because in learning the material and earning good grades you receive approval from your parents?

The push or pull to act in certain ways or to achieve particular goals is one of the topics in this section. In addition to learning about motivation, you also will consider theory and research about whether there is a hierarchy—a ranking or ladder—of human needs. Are some needs more important motivators than other needs? Can you identify needs in your own life that are greater than others?

What Is Motivation?

Motivation is an inner state that energizes behavior toward a goal. The study of motivation is to learn what moves a person or other animal to act in a particular way.

Your motivation may change all the time. Changes in motivation come from both changes in the world outside you and changes going on inside you. To understand changes going on inside you, imagine that you want to be an artist who

> **motivation** An inner state that energizes behavior toward a goal

paints. You have positive feelings associated with this desire, so you enroll as a student in a famous art institute. Your successes at the institute strengthen your motivation to be a painter. However, your paintings do not sell, so this failure weakens your career motivation. You may also have other life goals that get in the way of being a painter. You may want to have a family or to travel, which also may weaken your motivation to be a painter.

Theories of motivation focus on either *internal* or *external* influences on behavior. Internal theories assume that something inside you pushes you toward or away from some objects or activities. Genes play a role in internal motivation and may affect the way people behave. For example, research suggests that some individuals have inherited a gene from their parents that makes them vulnerable to developing a problem with drinking alcohol, or alcoholism. If these individuals have easy access to alcohol, this gene provides an internal push for them to drink alcohol regularly. External theories focus more on things that pull you in a certain direction. An external theory focuses on how alcoholism develops among individuals who are encouraged to consume alcohol by their peers. Both internal and external influences are important in understanding motivation.

CHECKPOINT   *What is motivation?*

Internal Push Theories

Psychologists have tried to understand motivation by examining different ways biological processes push you to behave. Three of these biologically based theories have highlighted instincts, drive reduction, and arousal regulation.

INSTINCT THEORIES

An *instinct* is an unlearned, inherited fixed pattern of behavior. Instincts are common in many animals. For example, many species of birds have an inborn ability to build a specific kind of nest. In the early 1900s, William McDougall (1908) proposed that much of human behavior is controlled by a variety of instincts. His list of 18 human instincts included greed, self-assertion, and curiosity. Other instinct theorists expanded this human list into the thousands. One problem with this approach was that instead of explaining human behaviors, these instinct theories only named them. For example, human aggression was explained as being caused by the instinct of aggressiveness. A second problem with instinct theories for humans was that most of the human behaviors that were identified as being caused by instincts, such as aggression, were actually found to be learned and shaped by experience.

Nest building among birds is an instinct, meaning that it is an unlearned, inherited fixed pattern of behavior. In contrast, humans' ability to create shelters is not inborn. It is flexible and learned.

©RYAN MORGAN, 2008/ USED UNDER LICENSE FROM SHUTTERSTOCK.COM

Although we now know that instincts do not explain human behavior, there is plenty of scientific evidence that genes may influence people to engage in certain patterns of behavior. How is a genetic explanation different from an instinct theory? Consider again the alcoholism example. Early instinct theorists explained alcoholism as being directly caused by an inherited instinct. In contrast, modern behavior geneticists (see Chapter 3) admit that there may be a genetic influence on alcoholism. They reject, however, that a genetic code predetermines that someone will become an alcoholic. Instead, they contend that certain genes might affect how a person's body responds to alcohol or what emotions a person might experience while drinking. These predispositions might increase a person's consumption of alcohol, but they would not predetermine that the person would become an alcoholic.

DRIVE-REDUCTION THEORY

Another theory psychologists developed to explain motivation is based on *drives*. A drive is a powerful need in the body, created by a physiological imbalance, that motivates behavior. This imbalance drives the person or animal to engage in some behavior to restore the internal balance, or homeostasis. **Homeostasis** is the tendency to keep physiological systems internally balanced by adjusting them in response to change. An example of homeostasis is your body's temperature-regulation system. An increase in body temperature causes the physiological response of sweating, which helps return your body's temperature to a lower level.

Drive-reduction theory is based on the concept of homeostasis. According to this theory, a physiological need creates a drive motivating you to satisfy the need and restore homeostasis. Once the need is met, the drive is reduced and the behavior that you started in response to the drive stops. For example, as shown in Figure 6-1, if you were denied water or other liquids for many hours your body's chemical balance would become disturbed, triggering a "thirst drive." This drive would push you to seek liquid to reduce the discomfort. After drinking enough liquid, homeostasis would be restored, the drive would be reduced and you would stop drinking.

homeostasis The tendency to keep physiological systems internally balanced by adjusting them in response to change

drive-reduction theory The idea that an imbalance in homeostasis creates a physiological need, which produces a drive that motivates the organism to satisfy the need

Figure 6-1 **DRIVE-REDUCTION THEORY**

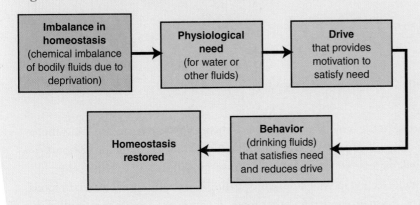

An imbalance in homeostasis creates a physiological need, which then produces a drive that moves you to engage in behavior to satisfy the need. When homeostasis is restored, the drive is reduced and no longer motivates behavior.

YERKES-DODSON LAW

Research indicates that people and animals generally perform to the best of their abilities when their nervous system is at an *optimum* level of arousal—not too much and not too little. A theory that states individuals perform best when maintaining an intermediate level of physiological arousal is called the **Yerkes-Dodson law**, which is named after the researchers who developed it. As shown in Figure 6-2, the Yerkes-Dodson law states that when your nervous system is underaroused or overaroused, you perform below your abilities. Why? When underaroused, you are bored and sluggish. When overaroused, you are nervous and tense.

Figure 6-2   **THE YERKES-DODSON LAW**

According to the Yerkes-Dodson law, people perform best when their nervous system is at an intermediate level of arousal.

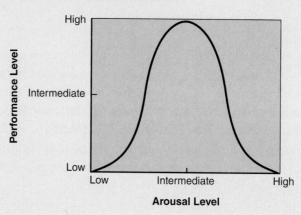

People differ in how easily external stimulation increases the arousal of their nervous system to its optimum level. Those who enjoy listening to loud music, riding roller coasters, watching scary movies, and eating spicy foods require greater external stimulation for their nervous system to reach its optimum level of arousal. Individuals who are more introverted and take fewer risks have a nervous system that reaches its optimum arousal level with much less external stimulation. The body's chemistry explains individual differences, but regardless of whether someone's nervous system needs high or low stimulation, it is important that it be regulated in order to function at an optimal level.

CHECKPOINT › *What are three internal push theories?*

External Pull Theories

In contrast to the biologically based push theories, external theories focus more on things that pull you in a certain direction. Not eating anything for 12 hours certainly will increase your hunger drive. However, will you try to reduce the uncomfortable feeling in your stomach by eating just anything? No. Certain foods pull you toward them more than other foods. Chances are you are more pulled to a sweet-smelling apple pie than to a bowl of plump caterpillars.

Yerkes-Dodson law
A theory that states individuals perform best when maintaining an intermediate level of physiological arousal

INCENTIVE THEORY

Incentive theory states that any stimulus that you think has either positive or negative outcomes for you will become an **incentive** for your behavior. An incentive is a positive or negative stimulus in the environment that attracts or repels you. You are motivated to behave in certain ways when you expect to gain positive incentives and/or avoid negative incentives through your actions.

The value of an incentive can change over time and in different situations. For example, gaining praise from your parents may have positive incentive value for you in some situations, but not in others. When you are home, your parents' praise may be a positive incentive. However, when your friends visit, you may go out of your way to avoid receiving parental praise, because your friends may tease you. In this instance, your parents' praise has negative incentive value. Biology also influences incentive value. That is why food is a stronger motivator when you are hungry than when you are full.

INTRINSIC VERSUS EXTRINSIC MOTIVATION

Psychologists identify two types of motivation that are tied to whether incentives are either intrinsic or extrinsic. The desire to perform a behavior for its own sake, perhaps because it is fun and interesting, is called **intrinsic motivation**. You may choose to read a book because you enjoy reading. The desire to perform a behavior because of promised rewards or the threats of punishment is called **extrinsic motivation**. Working at a job only because you receive payment is an example of extrinsic motivation. The work itself may not provide pleasure, but it does provide access to another outcome—money—that does bring pleasure.

In general, we value behaviors and activities that are intrinsically motivating more highly than those that are extrinsically motivating. Both types of motivation often operate at the same time. For example, you may read a lot in part because you enjoy the activity for its own sake, but also because doing so earns praise from adults and better grades in school. Check out the Positive Psychology feature on page 154 to learn more about intrinsic and extrinsic motivation.

incentive theory A theory proposing that any stimulus that has either positive or negative outcomes for you will become an incentive for your behavior

incentive A positive or negative stimulus in the environment that attracts or repels you

intrinsic motivation The desire to perform a behavior for its own sake

extrinsic motivation The desire to perform a behavior because of promised rewards or the threats of punishment

CHECKPOINT *What is the difference between intrinsic motivation and extrinsic motivation?*

©YURI ARCURS, 2008/ USED UNDER LICENSE FROM SHUTTERSTOCK.COM

If parents promise to give their children money for earning good grades, could this actually reduce the students' joy in performing these academic tasks?

Should Your Parents Pay You for Earning Good Grades in School?

Do your parents promise to give you money or some other desirable reward if you earn good grades in school? Did you know that when you receive a reward for a certain activity, the reward may either increase or decrease your intrinsic motivation for the activity? Receiving a reward may increase your sense of confidence and increase your enjoyment of the task (intrinsic motivation is increased). However, receiving a reward also may cause you to pay more attention to receiving this external reward in the future. You may now think that your behavior is more motivated by the reward (extrinsic motivation) than by your enjoyment of the task (intrinsic motivation). In such instances, your intrinsic motivation decreases and so does your enjoyment of the task.

In one study examining this effect, preschoolers who liked to draw were asked to draw a picture. Some of these preschoolers were told ahead of time that they would receive a reward for their picture, while others were told about the reward after completing the picture. The students who were told ahead of time they would receive a reward became less interested in drawing. By thinking about the reward while drawing, these students' enjoyment of drawing weakened.

Other studies found that students' interest in, and enjoyment of, math tends to decrease when rewards are emphasized at school and when parents give them money for good grades. In such situations, students shift their focus from their enjoyment of the activity to the external reward, which causes them to enjoy the activity less.

Not all external rewards undermine intrinsic motivation. Being praised by others is an external reward, and it often increases intrinsic motivation by increasing confidence. Giving praise rather than money for good grades is much more likely to increase students' intrinsic motivation and their love of learning.

Think Critically

1. Why might receiving a reward for an activity that you really enjoy decrease your enjoyment of the activity?

2. What type of external reward is less likely to undermine intrinsic motivation?

Maslow's Hierarchy of Needs

Abraham Maslow, one of the pioneers of humanistic psychology, believed all people have a basic need for personal growth—to become what is possible. As illustrated in Figure 6-3, Maslow proposed that you are born with a **hierarchy of needs**, a ladder of needs that rank from basic needs to higher-level needs. Maslow stated that your basic needs must be reasonably satisfied before you are motivated to satisfy higher-level needs. The needs further up the hierarchy are considered less basic because you can survive without satisfying them.

The most basic of these needs are physiological, or things your body needs to live such as food and water. Once these physiological needs are satisfied, you are motivated to move up the hierarchy, and the next set of needs—safety needs—are activated. These safety needs involve striving for a sense of safety, security, and the ability to be able to predict what is going to happen in your life.

Maslow stated that when food and safety are difficult to attain, they dominate your life, and higher-level needs don't motivate you. If you are starving and freezing, your decisions in life are strongly motivated by finding food and shelter and not by seeking approval and love from others. Homeless people's daily decisions are shaped by these basic food and safety needs. Similarly, children who have abusive parents often are so focused on protecting themselves from harm that making friends or doing well in school is relatively unimportant. If you are fortunate to have these first two levels of basic needs reasonably satisfied, you become motivated by more psychological needs.

The first psychological needs activated are the belongingness and love needs, which involve the desire for intimacy, love, and acceptance from others. Next on the hierarchy are esteem needs, which involve the desire for achievement, power, and recognition and respect from others.

Up to this point in the hierarchy, Maslow believed that you are motivated by a desire to overcome your feelings of being deprived of some kind of physical or psychological need. All the needs in the first four levels of the hierarchy are *deficiency needs*, or needs where you lack something. The absence of any of these needs interferes with your personal growth.

hierarchy of needs
Maslow's ladder of human needs in which more basic physiological and safety needs must be satisfied before you are motivated to satisfy higher-level psychological needs

Figure 6-3 **MASLOW'S HIERARCHY OF NEEDS**

Self-actualization needs
(realization of one's full potential)

Esteem needs
(achievement, power, etc.)

Belongingness and love needs
(intimacy, acceptance)

Safety needs
(security, predictability, etc.)

Physiological needs
(hunger, thirst, etc.)

Except for self-actualization, all of Maslow's needs in the hierarchy are motivated by a feeling of deprivation.

From Martin/Loomis, Annotated Instructor's Edition (with CD) for Martin/Loomis' Building Teachers: A Constructivist Approach, 1E. ©2007 Wadsworth, a part of Cengage Learning, Inc. Reproduced by permission. www.cengage.com/permissions.

The needs in the upper levels of the hierarchy are self-actualization needs that move you toward fulfilling your potential. **Self-actualization** is the ultimate goal of human growth. However, Maslow believed that very few people are ever motivated by self-actualization needs. Why? The biggest reason is that most people spend their entire lives trying to satisfy the needs lower in the motivational hierarchy.

Can you think of examples of how television commercials are designed to appeal to some of the needs identified in Maslow's hierarchy? Ads that highlight home security systems or safety features on automobiles appeal to your safety needs. Commercials showing people being better liked after they purchase certain shampoos, toothpastes, or cell-phone services appeal to belongingness needs. Commercials for the United States Army urging you to "Be all that you can be" appeal to self-actualization needs.

The simplicity of Maslow's needs hierarchy makes it an appealing theory of motivation. However, this simplicity is also one of its problems. Although research suggests that the motives lower in Maslow's hierarchy often do motivate behavior more than those higher in the hierarchy, this is not always true. In spite of these weaknesses the theory is still useful in identifying different human motives and providing an organized way to discuss how they might influence behavior.

self-actualization The ultimate goal of human growth is the realization of your full potential

 **CHECKPOINT** *What is Maslow's hierarchy of needs?*

6.1 ASSESSMENT

In Your Own Words

Compare and contrast the internal push and the external pull motivation theories. Provide a real-world example that illustrates each.

Review Concepts

1. Which refers to an external pull theory?
   - a. instinct
   - b. drive reduction
   - c. Yerkes-Dodson law
   - d. incentive

2. According to Maslow's hierarchy of needs, which is the highest goal to achieve?
   - a. safety
   - b. self-actualization
   - c. esteem
   - d. belonging and love

3. **True or False**   Motivation is always determined by biology.

Think Critically

4. Are genes internal or external influences of motivation? How might a person be affected by genes?

5. Are your motivations for taking this course intrinsic or extrinsic? Formulate your answer in a way that indicates you understand intrinsic and extrinsic motivation.

6.2 | Biological and Social Motives

OBJECTIVES

- Examine hunger and eating.
- Define and interpret eating problems.
- Identify and differentiate between the need to belong and the need to achieve.

DISCOVER IT | *How does this relate to me?*

How do you know when you are hungry? Does your stomach grumble? Is the smell of food more appealing? How hungry would you need to be to eat a juicy fat worm or a multi-legged insect? Is your need to eat biological or social? Is what you choose to eat biological or social? Maslow identified satisfying hunger as one of the most basic needs. What about the other needs in Maslow's hierarchy, such as the need for belonging or love? How do these needs affect your life?

The need to belong was identified by Maslow as the first psychological need activated when physiological needs have been satisfied adequately. The need to belong prompts you to want to be part of a group or family. How do you know when you need the company of others? Why do some people need to socialize more than others? What about another need Maslow identified—your need for achievement? Why do people differ in their need for achievement? In this section of the chapter you will examine all these questions and learn which are biological or social motives. First, before achievement, the need for hunger must be satisfied.

Hunger and Eating

You don't have to learn how to be hungry, but you also don't eat just to survive. Sitting down to eat provides social interaction with your friends or family. Hunger and the motivation to eat are controlled by both internal and external factors.

INTERNAL CONTROLS

Due to its importance for survival, it is not surprising that the internal controls over hunger and eating involve several independent and interacting bodily systems. Three of the major control systems for hunger and eating are the bloodstream, the stomach, and the brain.

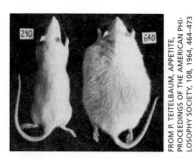

When a part of the hypothalamus in laboratory rats was destroyed, they could not control their eating and became very obese (rat on right). This research indicated that this brain area plays an important role in regulating eating.

FROM P. TEITELBAUM, APPETITE, PROCEEDINGS OF THE AMERICAN PHILOSOPHY SOCIETY, 108, 1964, 464–473

The blood is the pathway for many eating signals that flow to the brain. When the brain receives signals that food nutrients in the blood are low, you feel hungry. The two major types of food nutrients are fatty acids and the blood sugar glucose. As you eat and your stomach becomes full, it sends "fullness" signals to the brain. Your full stomach also releases the hormone gastrin, which signals the pancreas to begin releasing *insulin*, a blood hormone that decreases appetite. High insulin production causes your body cells to take in more glucose than they can use, and the excess is converted into fat.

In the brain, the hypothalamus (see Chapter 3) plays an important role in regulating eating. Certain neurons in the hypothalamus fire when blood nutrient levels are low, while others fire when nutrients are at high levels. Together, these neurons act like sensors that provide information to the frontal lobes of the brain, which then decide eating behavior.

EXTERNAL CONTROLS

Physiological responses that prepare the body for food, such as a surge in insulin, occur in response to cues normally related to eating. These cues are such things as the sight or smell of food, the time of day, other people eating, and the clattering of dishes. This means that hunger also is a response to environmental cues that indicate food is on the way, rather than simply being a response to specific changes occurring within the body.

Another control over eating is the incentive value of food. The early phases of eating depend on the taste of food, but as you continue eating the same food, its positive incentive value declines. The first taste of barbecued ribs may be wonderful, but they lose their appeal with each bite. Because of this, you tend to eat more when there is a variety of food available rather than just one type of food. Food variety matters in how much you eat.

Your culture also influences your food preferences. You have learned to like specific foods from your personal experiences and by observing what others around you eat. While you might not enjoy eating roasted insects, there are many cultures around the world where they are a delicacy. A major factor in determining food preferences is simply what foods are available for people who live in different areas of the world. Over time, eating practices become linked to a particular culture.

Your eating behavior also is influenced by how you think about food in relation to yourself. If you are always worrying and trying to control what and how much you eat, you are a *restrained eater*. If you are unconcerned about controlling your eating, you are an *unrestrained eater*. Restrained eaters put constant limits on the amount of food they allow themselves to eat and many of them frequently diet.

INFOBIT

In trying to control their eating urges, restrained eaters are much more likely than unrestrained eaters to try to eat only during regular mealtimes. There are at least two problems with this eating strategy. First, trying to avoid eating any food between meals often leads to overeating when hunger pangs become very strong. Second, restrained eaters are much more likely than unrestrained eaters to eat a full helping at mealtime even when they are not hungry.

PHOTODISC/GETTY IMAGES

Restrained eaters are constantly trying to control what and how much they eat. When such people are under stress, how might they react upon seeing the food displayed in this photo? Why are they more likely than unrestrained eaters to go on high-calorie binges?

Despite this, restrained eaters have more difficulty than unrestrained eaters avoiding "forbidden" yet desirable food, such as chocolate. This is especially true during times of stress.

CHECKPOINT *What are three major internal control systems for hunger and eating?*

Eating Problems

Some people gain too much weight for their optimum health while others lose too much weight. Is weight gain and loss biological or social? Both play a role.

WEIGHT GAIN

You inherited from your parents a tendency to be light or heavy. Part of this inherited weight tendency is your body's **set point**, meaning a level of body weight that the body works to maintain. Your set point may be determined by the number of fat cells in your body. Research indicates that when you gain or lose weight, you do not gain or lose fat cells. The number of fat cells stays the same, but the cells will increase or decrease in size. Individuals who inherit the tendency for more fat cells have a higher set point, which increases the chances of becoming overweight.

set point A level of body weight that the body works to maintain

Individuals who inherit fewer fat cells have a lower set point, and they are more likely to be thin.

Weight also depends on eating habits. Today, Americans' daily diet has increased by 300 calories compared to 15 years ago. Almost one-third of these calories come from junk food with little nutritional value. This increase in daily food consumption partly explains why two-thirds of Americans are now overweight. Even more alarming is the fact that one-fourth of Americans suffer from **obesity**, which is the excessive accumulation of body fat. Obesity contributes to numerous health conditions, including high blood pressure, heart disease, diabetes, arthritis, and sleep disorders. One study that charted the lives of more than one million Americans over the age of 14 found that people who were significantly overweight at age 40 died three years earlier than those who were normal weight.

Unfortunately, when people who are overweight or obese shed excess body fat by dieting, most are unsuccessful in keeping the weight off. Losing excess pounds and maintaining a healthier weight generally requires permanent changes in your eating and exercise habits. See Table 6-1 for tips that researchers offer on successful weight loss strategies.

obesity The excessive accumulation of body fat

Table 6-1 HEALTHY EATING AND EXERCISE HABITS

Avoid fad diets	Popular diet programs receive plenty of media attention and sell many books and DVDs, but they usually don't succeed in the long run and can even pose health risks for dieters.
Avoid exposure to tempting food cues	Do not bring tempting foods home, or at least, keep them out of sight. Do not go to the supermarket on an empty stomach, and avoid the sweets and snacks aisles.
Eat "big" and healthy foods	Eat bulky foods that are low in calories, such as grapes and soups. These foods will fill your stomach and reduce your hunger pangs. Whole grains, fruits, vegetables, and fish help monitor your appetite and reduce bad cholesterol that can clog your arteries.
Exercise regularly	Lack of exercise explains why most people fail to lose weight or keep off lost weight. Exercise burns fat stored in your body, reduces weight, strengthens your cardiovascular fitness, and improves your mood. 30 minutes of moderate exercise at least three times per week or four 10-minute brisk walks per day is helpful in losing weight.
Eat sensibly and slowly	Don't starve all day and eat a big meal at night. This pattern slows your metabolism down and results in weight gain, not weight loss. Skipping meals can also cause you to gorge yourself to feed your out-of-control hunger. Instead, eat smaller portions of food and skip desserts. Eat slowly to give your stomach time to tell you that you are full. Fast eaters don't receive those signals until they have already overeaten.
Reduce television viewing and computer time	Watching television and computer Internet surfing burn very few calories and take you away from much healthier exercise activities. Eating snacks is the common activity associated with television.
Be realistic and moderate	Being moderately heavy is less risky for you than being dangerously thin. You should never diet and try to lose weight to conform to the unrealistic and dangerous thinness standards promoted by the fashion and entertainment industries.

Eating the right amount of healthy foods is the best way to maintain a healthy weight.

WEIGHT LOSS

At the same time that Americans' weight levels in general have been increasing to dangerous levels, many young people experience pressure to reach extreme thinness. One eating disorder, **anorexia nervosa**, is diagnosed when a person weighs less than 85 percent of her or his expected weight but still expresses an intense fear of gaining weight or becoming fat. Another related eating disorder is **bulimia nervosa**, which involves regular episodes of intense, out-of-control eating, followed by drastic attempts to remove the food calories from the body. Attempts to purge the body of calories often involve vomiting, taking laxatives, or exercising to the point of exhaustion. A person who is anorexic also may be bulimic.

Both eating disorders occur 10 times more frequently among women than men, with about one percent of women in late adolescence and early adulthood being anorexic and three percent being bulimic. Because the body is being starved, both disorders pose severe health risks, including death, if left untreated.

Anorexia always begins as an attempt to lose weight. The self-induced vomiting typical of bulimia almost always occurs after a person fails to follow the eating restrictions of a weight-loss diet. Both eating disorders are almost always motivated by a desire to match ultra-thin cultural standards of beauty. Adolescent girls who suffer from eating disorders tend to be emotionally insecure and have mothers who obsess about both their own weight and their daughters' weight and appearance. In addition to social pressures to have a thin body, some people may be more likely to develop an eating disorder because of genetic and motivational influences. The Closer Look feature on page 162 contains information on warning signs of an eating disorder.

anorexia nervosa An eating disorder in which a person weighs less than 85 percent of her or his expected weight but still expresses an intense fear of gaining weight or becoming fat

bulimia nervosa An eating disorder in which a person engages in recurrent episodes of binge eating followed by drastic measures to remove the food calories from the body

CHECKPOINT > *Define anorexia and bulimia nervosa.*

Warning Signs of an Eating Disorder

People who suffer from an eating disorder often are careful to hide their illness from friends and loved ones. Listed below are some of the warning signs that a person is developing—or already has—an eating disorder. If one or more of these symptoms are present, encourage the person to consult both a physician and a mental health professional. This usually means someone besides a family physician, because most doctors have had little training or experience with eating disorders. However, family physicians can provide a preliminary medical examination and they often can make a referral to a specialist. If contacting a health professional is too difficult, start by talking to a school counselor, administrator, or teacher.

- Increased picky eating or food restriction, especially eating only "healthy foods" and becoming a vegetarian
- Regularly fasting and skipping meals, and engaging in dieting behavior involving calorie counting or portion control (weighing and measuring food amounts)
- Reluctance or refusal to eat with others and/or refusing to allow others to prepare foods
- Going to the bathroom immediately after eating or taking a shower following eating (toilets and showers are the most common sites to purge food)
- Unusual number of episodes described as "stomach flu" (provides an excuse for both food restriction and purging)
- Large amounts of food missing (evidence of bingeing, which often follows food restriction)
- Strong interest in diet books and Internet web sites related to eating disorders, especially web sites that encourage eating-disordered thinking and behavior

Think Critically

Why is it often difficult to notice that a person is suffering from an eating disorder?

©ARTSIOM KIREYAU, 2008/ USED UNDER LICENSE FROM SHUTTERSTOCK.COM

The Need to Belong and the Need to Achieve

Other important human motives are the need to belong and the need to achieve. Over the years, psychologists have studied both needs.

THE NEED TO BELONG

Survey studies find that young people spend about 75 percent of their waking time with other people. When with others, young people tend to be happier, more alert, and more excited than when they are alone.

The need to interact with others and be socially accepted is called the **need to belong** (also known as the *need for affiliation*). The need to belong is as real as the need for food. When this need is denied due to rejection by others, we often react with increased stress, anxiety, and decreased physical health. In fact, brain-imaging studies indicate that the same area in the brain's frontal lobes that triggers the emotional pain following rejection also triggers the emotional distress associated with physical pain. Why does the brain react to social rejection and physical injury in a similar way? Neuroscientists suggest that the pain experienced by both social rejection and physical injury is the brain's attempt to send a warning signal that your survival is being threatened.

Just as some people enjoy eating more than others, people also differ in their desire to seek the company of others. Studies find that people with a high need to belong seek out warm social relationships and want to be liked by others. In contrast, people with a low need to belong tend to be loners who are not very interested or comfortable socializing with others.

Whether you have a high or low need to belong is strongly shaped by life experiences. For example, in the United States and many other countries, females are more likely than males to be raised to think and act in ways that emphasize their emotional connectedness to other individuals. This might explain why women are more likely than men to remember birthdays, anniversaries, and who said what during conversations. Of course, this does not mean that all women have a higher need to belong than all men. There are many males who have higher affiliation needs than the average female. There are also many females who are less interested in seeking out others for close relationships than the average male. Spend a few minutes responding to the items in the Self-Discovery feature on page 164 to learn more about your need for having close relationships.

PHOTODISC/GETTY IMAGES

need to belong The need to interact with others and be socially accepted (also known as the *need for affiliation*)

How Important Are Your Close Relationships in Defining You?

Instructions: Below is a series of statements about your attitudes and beliefs about having close relationships with other people. Please read each statement and indicate the extent to which you agree or disagree with it using the following scale:

Strongly disagree   1   2   3   4   5   6   7   Strongly agree

_____ 1. My close relationships are an important reflection of who I am.

_____ 2. When I feel very close to someone, it often feels to me like that person is an important part of who I am.

_____ 3. I usually feel a strong sense of pride when someone close to me has an important accomplishment.

_____ 4. I think one of the most important parts of who I am can be captured by looking at my close friends and understanding who they are.

_____ 5. When I think of myself, I often think of my close friends or family also.

_____ 6. If a person hurts someone close to me, I feel personally hurt as well.

_____ 7. In general, my close relationships are an important part of my self-image.

_____ 8. Overall, my close relationships have very little to do with how I feel about myself.*

_____ 9. My close relationships are unimportant to my sense of what kind of person I am.*

_____ 10. My sense of pride comes from knowing who I have as close friends.

_____ 11. When I establish a close friendship with someone, I usually develop a strong sense of identification with that person.

See page 181 for scoring instructions.

Source: Cross, S. E., Bacon, P. L., & Morris, M. L. (2000). The relational-interdependent self-construal and relationships. *Journal of Personality and Social Psychology, 78,* 791–808. Copyright © 2000 by the American Psychological Association. Adapted with permission.

THE NEED TO ACHIEVE

The motives examined so far—hunger and affiliation—are observed in many other species. The need to achieve may be unique to humans. The **need to achieve** (also known as the *need for achievement*) is a desire to overcome obstacles and meet high standards of excellence. Psychologist David McClelland contends that the need to achieve develops when children adopt the achievement values of their parents and other important role models.

According to McClelland, your overall need for achievement is based both on your *desire to succeed* and your *fear of failure*. If your desire for success is considerably stronger than your fear of failure, you will have a high need to achieve. However, if your fear of failure is considerably stronger than your desire for success, you will have a low need to achieve.

need to achieve A desire to overcome obstacles and meet high standards of excellence

Do people with a high need to achieve approach all challenges equally? No. Individuals with a high need to achieve choose tasks that are moderately difficult and challenging rather than tasks that are almost impossible or very easy. They choose this way because their desire for success is stronger than their fear of failure. These individuals are attracted to achievement situations they can master if they work hard and carefully apply their skills. When they succeed at these tasks, people with a high need to achieve generally are thought of as being talented, hardworking, and deserving of praise and rewards. This positive feedback serves both to satisfy and strengthen their achievement desires. Almost impossible and very easy tasks are not very appealing to those with a high need to achieve, because the chance of success is either very low ("Why waste my time?") or almost guaranteed ("Where is the challenge?"). Further, if they do succeed at an almost impossible task, their achievement likely would be dismissed by others as sheer "dumb luck."

What about individuals with a low need to achieve? Do they completely avoid achievement situations? No. In people with a low need to achieve, fear of failure is stronger than their desire for success. They tend to pick achievement situations that are either very easy so that success is guaranteed or almost impossible so that they have a good excuse for failing. However, such situations almost guarantee they cannot take credit for any success they achieve. While they may protect themselves from embarrassment, they have little hope of winning praise or increasing their self-confidence.

One important reason people with a low need to achieve avoid achievement situations is because of past bad experiences. They have a history of working on tasks that are (1) so easy that they gain little satisfaction when they succeed, and (2) so difficult that their confidence is destroyed. To break this pattern of bad experiences, individuals with a low need to achieve must learn to choose achievement situations that are not too easy or too difficult for their abilities. By choosing moderately difficult tasks that can be mastered if they work hard, these individuals can discover the joys of achievement. Success can motivate them to develop a higher need for achievement.

CHECKPOINT *Explain the need to belong and the need to achieve.*

©CORBIS

Students with a high need to achieve have a high desire for success and a low fear of failure.

6.2 ASSESSMENT

In Your Own Words

Using evidence from the text, support this statement: Motivation to eat is both internal and external.

Review Concepts

1. Which is not a major control system for hunger and eating?
   - a. brain
   - b. ego
   - c. stomach
   - d. bloodstream

2. Which is not an external hunger cue?
   - a. low blood sugar
   - b. dishes clattering
   - c. smell of food
   - d. time of day

3. Which refers to the level of body weight that the body works to maintain?
   - a. anorexia nervosa
   - b. obesity
   - c. set point
   - d. bulimia nervosa

4. Which of the following tips will not help you lose excess pounds and maintain a healthier weight?
   - a. try fad diets
   - b. eat healthy foods
   - c. exercise regularly
   - d. reduce television viewing

5. **True or False** The need for achievement is unique to human beings.

6. **True or False** People tend to eat more when there is only one type of food available rather than a variety of foods.

7. **True or False** You inherited from your parents a tendency to be light or heavy.

8. **True or False** Young people tend to be happier when around other people.

Think Critically

9. Defend this statement: The need to belong is as real as the need for food.

10. Evaluate the need to achieve as being either low or high for the following people: a music star who is thought of as being talented; a worker who always keeps quiet in meetings; a writer who writes a lot of stories but never tries to have them published; a short woman who plays basketball and wins.

11. Support this statement with information from the text: High insulin levels cause weight gain.

12. Name the eating problem or problems that belong to the following symptoms: poses severe health risks; intense fear of gaining weight; purges after overeating; excessive accumulation of body fat; requires changes in eating habits to maintain a healthy weight.

6.3 | Emotion

OBJECTIVES

- Identify and compare and contrast three theories of emotion.
- Examine how emotions are communicated nonverbally.
- Assess culture, gender, and emotions.
- Identify two effective ways to manage anger.

DISCOVER IT | *How does this relate to me?*

Think about the push–pull of your motivations. Are your emotions involved? Would you be surprised to learn that your emotions help to either push you toward or pull you away from a goal or a person? Consider the emotions you are likely to experience when you near your high school graduation. Happiness at being done? Sadness because you are parting ways with friends? Anxiety about the uncertainty ahead of you? Excitement about your future possibilities? Why might the emotions you experience be influenced by your friends' and family's emotions? What physical changes occur in your body when you feel happiness, sadness, anxiety, excitement, or any other emotion? Do you think your body causes the emotion, or does the emotion cause your body's reaction? These are questions psychologists ask.

KEY TERMS

- emotion
- James-Lange theory
- Cannon-Bard theory
- two-factor theory
- facial-feedback hypothesis

P sychologists who study motivation also are interested in emotions, because they are two sides of the same coin. Emotions both reflect and trigger motives. For example, your happiness at succeeding at an important task reflects your high need to achieve, while it also triggers your motivation to seek even more challenging achievement situations in the future.

Emotions

Emotion is a positive or negative feeling state involving physiological arousal, conscious experience, and expressive behavior. An emotion is accompanied by automatic physiological changes, such as an increase in your blood pressure and heart rate. An emotion is created partly by how you consciously interpret the situation you are in, and an emotion is often related to specific expressed behaviors, such as different facial expressions and body postures.

emotion A positive or negative feeling state involving physiological arousal, conscious experience, and expressive behavior

EMOTIONS AND PHYSIOLOGICAL AROUSAL

Can you imagine riding a roller-coaster and not feeling your heart pounding or your blood pressure rising? What if there were no "butterflies" in your stomach as you prepare for an important first date with someone you like? The emotional impact of these events would be blunted without the physiological feedback.

The autonomic nervous system produces the body's reactions associated with emotions. As you read in Chapter 3, the autonomic nervous system is the part of the peripheral nervous system that commands movement of involuntary, nonskeletal muscles, such as the heart, lungs, and stomach muscles. The two branches of the autonomic nervous system—the sympathetic and parasympathetic nervous systems—play an important role in emotions (see Figure 6-4). The sympathetic nervous system uses energy and is active in (the "fight or flight" response) moving blood to the muscles and releasing stored energy. When you experience strong emotions such as anger and fear, this system prepares your body for action.

Figure 6-4 **THE DUAL FUNCTIONS OF THE AUTONOMIC NERVOUS SYSTEM**

The sympathetic nervous system prepares your body for action, while the parasympathetic nervous system calms the body.

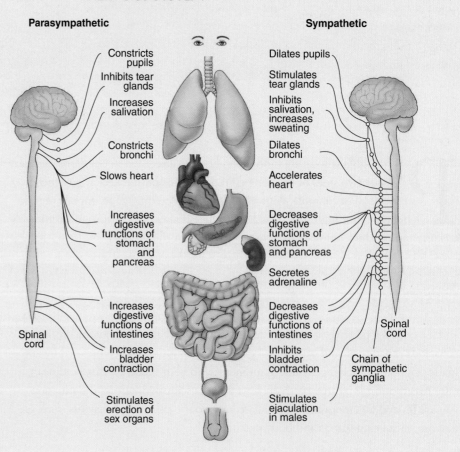

Parasympathetic

- Constricts pupils
- Inhibits tear glands
- Increases salivation
- Constricts bronchi
- Slows heart
- Increases digestive functions of stomach and pancreas
- Increases digestive functions of intestines
- Increases bladder contraction
- Stimulates erection of sex organs

Spinal cord

Sympathetic

- Dilates pupils
- Stimulates tear glands
- Inhibits salivation, increases sweating
- Dilates bronchi
- Accelerates heart
- Decreases digestive functions of stomach and pancreas
- Secretes adrenaline
- Decreases digestive functions of intestines
- Inhibits bladder contraction
- Stimulates ejaculation in males

Spinal cord

Chain of sympathetic ganglia

In contrast, the parasympathetic nervous system is geared toward conserving energy and refueling the body's resources. It accomplishes these goals by doing such things as stimulating digestion and decreasing blood flow to the muscles. The emotion of worrying is associated with low parasympathetic activity. If the parasympathetic system overreacts and reduces physiological activity too much, *emotional fainting* or passing out occurs.

TWO EARLY THEORIES

Two early theories tried to explain how bodily responses are related to the experience of emotions, the James-Lange theory and the Cannon-Bard theory.

In 1884, William James and Carl Lange independently proposed the same theory. They said that your emotions are caused by physiological changes in the autonomic nervous system, which are caused by something happening around you. Consider these two examples: someone honks a car horn when you're standing near; and you see someone you have a crush on. Your brain perceives the physiological responses to the horn as the emotion of fear. When you see a person you have a crush on, your palms sweat, your heart flutters, and your stomach churns, all signs of the emotion of love. These emotions are the product of different physiological changes that the brain automatically interprets in response to events around you. The **James-Lange theory** states that your heart pounds and your body trembles before you feel either fear or love.

In contrast to this view, Walter Cannon (1927) and Philip Bard (1934) offered a different explanation of emotions. Their **Cannon-Bard theory** proposes that feedback from physiological changes cannot cause emotions because these changes happen too slowly (taking 1–2 seconds) to explain the almost immediate experience of an emotion. This theory also argued that most emotions are physiologically too similar to one another to directly cause the many emotions people experience. The theory proposes that emotion-provoking events simultaneously cause both physiological responses and the experience of emotions. From this perspective, when the car's horn sounds, it causes your heart to race as you also experience a feeling of fear. Your increased heart rate is caused by your autonomic nervous system, while your subjective experience of fear is caused by higher-order thinking in your brain's cerebral cortex. Figure 6-5 illustrates how these two theories view the process of emotion differently.

Which of the two theories of emotion is more accurate? Research supports both theories. The Cannon-Bard theory is correct in claiming that physiological responses occur too slowly to explain many emotional responses. However, consistent with the James-Lange theory, research indicates that certain emotions, such as anger, fear, and happiness, are associated with specific physiological responses. These findings suggest that emotional reactions can be generated by both changes in your bodily states and by higher-order thinking.

James-Lange theory
A theory that emotion-arousing events produce specific physiological changes that your brain automatically interprets as specific emotions

Cannon-Bard theory
A theory that emotion-provoking events simultaneously induce both physiological responses and subjective states that are labeled as emotions

Figure 6-5 TWO CONTRASTING THEORIES OF EMOTION

While the James-Lange theory proposes that physiological reactions cause emotions, the Cannon-Bard theory contends that these two processes occur simultaneously in response to emotion-provoking events.

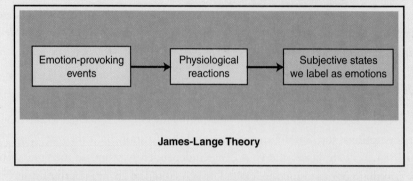

James-Lange Theory

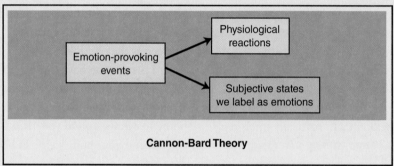

Cannon-Bard Theory

EMOTIONS AND HIGHER-ORDER THINKING

In Chapter 3 you learned that the cerebral cortex is the brain's thinking center. Research indicates that each of the two hemispheres of the cerebral cortex is related to one type of emotion more than another. The left hemisphere is associated with more positive emotions, while the right hemisphere is associated with more negative emotions. People with more active left hemispheres tend to be happier than people with more active right hemispheres.

Besides differences in hemispheric activity, the emotions you experience also are influenced by how your cerebral cortex interprets physiological arousal. The **two-factor theory** of emotion states that when you are aroused, you are often not sure what emotion you are feeling. When this happens, you look for cues in your surroundings to figure out what you are experiencing. If others are happy, you are likely to interpret your feeling as happiness. If others are anxious, you too are likely to feel anxious. In other words, you perceive yourself experiencing the emotion that your surroundings suggest you should be experiencing. According to the two-factor theory, any emotion you experience is based on two factors: physiological arousal and what emotional label you attach to that arousal.

Table 6-2 on page 171 outlines the basic assumptions of the three theories of emotion you have learned about in this chapter section.

two-factor theory

A theory that experiencing an emotion is often based on becoming physiologically aroused and then attaching a cognitive label to the arousal.

Table 6-2 THREE THEORIES OF EMOTION

Theory	Basic Assumptions
James-Lange theory	Emotion-provoking events induce physiological reactions that then cause the subjective states we label as emotions.
Cannon-Bard theory	Emotion-provoking events simultaneously induce physiological reactions and subjective states we label as emotions.
Two-factor theory	Emotion-provoking events induce physiological reactions that increase arousal, which we then identify as a particular emotion based on the situation we are in.

CHECKPOINT > *List the three theories of emotion and define each.*

Communicating Emotions Nonverbally

Humans and other animals signal their readiness to fight, flee, mate, and attend to each other's needs through nonverbal expressions. Emotions are shown on your face and in your body language, the different ways you stand or hold yourself. This section discusses facial expressions, which are a type of body language. You will learn about other types of body language in Chapter 14.

Charles Darwin (1872) observed that specific facial expressions convey specific emotions in all human populations around the world. The expressions you show other people and the expressions you see from other people are the same facial expressions that allowed your ancestors to communicate their emotions to one another.

Consistent with Darwin's theory, cross-cultural research has determined that there are seven primary emotions expressed in facial expressions. These are anger, disgust, fear, happiness, surprise, contempt, and sadness. Scientists identify these emotions as primary because people find these are the easiest emotions to correctly identify from facial expressions. Check out the Self-Discovery feature on page 173 to determine how accurate you are in identifying the emotion in different facial expressions.

facial feedback hypothesis Proposes that specific facial expressions trigger the subjective experience of specific emotions

THE FACIAL FEEDBACK HYPOTHESIS

In addition to facial expressions revealing emotions, there also is evidence that facial expressions can create emotions. The **facial feedback hypothesis** states that specific facial expressions trigger the experience of specific emotions. In one experiment testing this hypothesis,

LAB TEAMS

Facial Expressions

Work with a partner. One of you acts as the *guesser* while the other acts as the *poser*. As the poser, try several different stances and facial expressions. Stand with your arms crossed over your chest; with your shoulders slumped, and then straightened; smile; frown; look angry; and so on. As one of you pose, the guesser tries to guess the emotion the poser is trying to portray. After four or five poses, switch roles and try portraying different emotions.

In an experiment testing the facial feedback hypothesis, participants read cartoons while holding a pen in their mouths. Those who held the pen between their teeth thought the cartoons were funnier than those who held the pen between their lips.

COURTESY OF FIGZOI

researchers asked people to hold a pen in their mouths while they looked at a series of amusing cartoons. Some participants were instructed to hold the pen tightly with their lips. Other participants were told to hold the pen with their front teeth (see photo). Participants then rated how funny they thought the cartoons were. Participants who held the pen between their teeth thought the cartoons were funnier than participants who held the pen between their lips.

You can tell by looking at the photograph that holding a pen with the teeth causes a person to smile, while holding it with the lips produces a frown. Did this manipulation of facial expressions cause participants to experience different emotions? Yes. Research suggests that facial muscles send feedback signals to the brain, producing neurological changes that can trigger specific emotions, such as happiness or sadness.

CHECKPOINT *What are two ways you communicate emotions nonverbally?*

Culture, Gender, and Emotions

People around the world accurately identify certain emotions on people's faces, but cultures often develop different social rules for when and how emotions are expressed. For example, people in collectivist cultures such as China are more concerned about maintaining group harmony than are people from Western individualist cultures. This often causes people in collectivist cultures to hide any expression of negative emotions toward others in their own social groups. Does this mean that people from collectivist cultures feel negative emotions differently than individualists feel them? No. They may feel the same, but express those feelings differently.

Women and men are the same in their ability to experience emotions. However, they often express certain emotions differently. In the United States, boys are often encouraged more than girls to express tough emotions such as anger, contempt, and pride. In contrast, girls are encouraged more than boys to express tender emotions such as sadness, fear, and empathy. Do you recall the chapter-opening story about how I hid my emotion of grief from others when my Gramma died because I was a boy? It illustrates that how you control and express your emotions may be influenced by how the society in which you live teaches boys and girls to think and act.

CHECKPOINT *How does culture affect how you express emotion?*

Can You Identify the Seven Primary Emotions?

Cross-cultural research has determined that the seven primary emotions are anger, disgust, fear, happiness, surprise, contempt, and sadness. In identifying these emotions as "primary," social scientists mean that people find them easier to distinguish from one another than other emotions. Examine each of the seven facial expressions here. Can you identify the correct emotion for each expression? Answers are listed below.

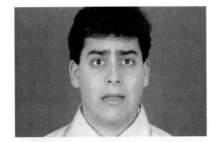

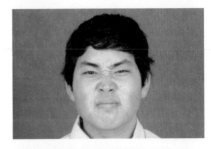

ANSWERS: Top to bottom and left to right: happiness, fear, anger, disgust, sadness, surprise, contempt

SOURCE: © 1988–2004 DAVID MATSUMOTO AND PAUL EKMAN

Managing Anger

You experience many emotions, but anger is the one emotion that receives a great deal of attention by psychologists. Anger does communicate strength and toughness. It also can help to resolve grievances if the anger is expressed positively.

While anger is a normal, healthy emotion, it can create problems when it gets out of control and leads to hurtful words or behavior. Some people are more prone to becoming angry than others. These "hotheaded" persons have a hard time handling frustration and often feel that they are treated unjustly. They often have parents who regularly express anger.

If anger can sometimes be a problem, how should you deal with it? Many people believe that when you are angry the best thing to do is "let it rip" and freely express this emotion. The idea behind this popular belief is that venting your anger will get it out of your system. The truth, however, is that many psychological studies have found that the exact opposite effect occurs. Freely expressing your anger tends to escalate this emotion, making aggression and other harmful responses more likely. Here are two effective strategies for managing your anger.

1. **Calm down angry feelings**   Anger energizes your body and gets it all fired up for attack. Calm down your body and your anger by taking slow, deep breaths, and slowly repeat a calm word or phrase like "relax," "calm down," or "take it easy," while continuing to breathe slowly and deeply. You also could count to 10, or 20, or even 100.

2. **Change the way you think**   When angry, your thinking often becomes negative, overly dramatic, and not very logical. Try replacing these thoughts with more positive thinking, such as "I'm mad but it's not the end of the world, and fuming is not going to make things better."

CHECKPOINT *Why is it often not a good idea to freely vent your anger?*

What are two effective ways in which you can deal with anger?

©ULRIKE HAMMERICH, 2008/ USED UNDER LICENSE FROM SHUTTERSTOCK.COM

6.3 ASSESSMENT

In Your Own Words

Using information from the text, support one of the following chapter objectives:

- Identify and compare and contrast three theories of emotion.
- Examine how emotions are communicated nonverbally.
- Assess culture, gender, and emotions.

Review Concepts

1. Which theory states that experiencing an emotion often is based on becoming physiologically aroused and then attaching a cognitive label to the arousal?
   - a. two-factor theory
   - b. emotion theory
   - c. James-Lange theory
   - d. Cannon-Bard theory

2. Which is not one of the seven primary emotions expressed in facial expressions?
   - a. surprise
   - b. happiness
   - c. disgust
   - d. shyness

3. Which is a reaction to the parasympathetic system overacting?
   - a. hyperactivity
   - b. vomiting
   - c. tremors
   - d. emotional fainting

4. Which of the following is not considered a nonverbal expression of emotion?
   - a. body language
   - b. facial expression
   - c. stance
   - d. clothes

5. **True or False** There is evidence that facial expressions can create emotions.

6. **True or False** Both men and women express emotions in the same manner.

7. **True or False** The autonomic nervous system produces the body's reactions associated with emotions.

8. **True or False** William James and Carl Lange both said that subjective emotional experiences are automatically caused by specific physiological changes in the autonomic nervous system, which are caused by something happening around you.

Think Critically

9. Why might people working together in groups hide expressions of negative emotions?

10. How would you feel when your friends around you are happy? Support your answer with theory.

11. Identify the emotions associated with the two brain hemispheres.

12. Why might people from different cultures express emotions differently?

How Accurate Are Lie Detectors?

INTRODUCTION   Can you tell when people are lying? The sympathetic nervous system is associated with emotional arousal, so scientists think if they can obtain measurements of autonomic responses they can determine whether people are lying. When people are trying to cover up lies they usually become anxious.

The *polygraph* is the most common "lie detector." This mechanical device measures autonomic responses such as respiration, heart rate, blood pressure, and palm perspiration. Each of these physiological responses is affected by the sympathetic nervous system. Increases in heart rate, breathing, blood pressure, and palm sweating are interpreted as signs of lying.

HYPOTHESIS   A number of studies were conducted to determine whether the polygraph is accurate in distinguishing truths from lies. Many of these studies predicted that polygraph tests would be able to detect lying and truthfulness with a high degree of accuracy.

METHOD   As shown in the two graphs on this page, an interviewer monitors and compares the physiological responses of participants while they answer questions. The interviewer first asks participants control questions, such as, "What is your favorite color?" Participants are then asked questions relevant to an event they may want to lie about such as, "Have you ever taken property from an employer?" Larger physiological responses to key questions—reflecting greater sympathetic nervous system response—mean the person may be lying. In the figure, the polygraph responses on the left shows a truthful person responding more strongly to an emotional control question that was not relevant to a crime than to a question relevant to the crime. The polygraph responses on the right shows a person who responded more strongly to the relevant crime question than to the control question. This suggests that the person on the right may be lying.

RESULTS   The findings from numerous studies indicate that the polygraph is not a true "lie detector." It is really a detector of sympathetic nervous system activity. Even highly trained polygraph experts can make mistakes in accurately identifying liars from honest people. Due to its inability to reliably detect lies, the polygraph is not allowed as evidence in almost all courts of law. It is true that, when properly used, the polygraph can provide valuable information in an investigation. However, it should not be regarded by itself as providing enough evidence to determine guilt or innocence.

Critical Analysis

1. What part of the nervous system does the polygraph machine measure?

2. How accurate are polygraph machines in detecting deception?

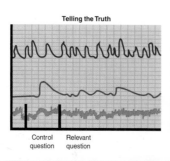

Telling the Truth

Control question   Relevant question

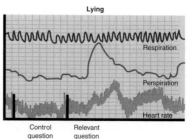

Lying

Respiration

Perspiration

Heart rate

Control question   Relevant question

Teacher

Have you ever thought about how teachers are like psychologists? Teachers must understand how young minds work and the psychology of how young people learn. Teachers offer counsel, intellectual stimulation, and social development advice to their students during the teenagers' formative years. Teachers may not be involved in psychological research or act as clinical psychologists, but every day in the classroom, teachers listen to their students and use psychological principles to help them grow to become healthy and productive adults.

Teachers offer both classroom and individual instruction to help students learn new skills and apply new concepts. Teachers instruct students in a variety of subjects such as language arts, psychology, business, marketing, English, science, mathematics, music, art, humanities, and other subject areas.

Teachers evaluate subject material; plan classroom presentations; maintain classroom discipline; assign lessons to students; write, administer, and grade tests and other student evaluations; assign and grade in-class work and homework; evaluate students' performance; and coach students to help them reach their fullest potential.

Teachers also prepare report cards and meet with parents, school staff members, and other interested people to discuss students' academic or personal problems in order to best help the students grow and learn.

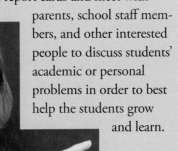

©TONY WEAR, 2008/ USED UNDER LICENSE FROM SHUTTERSTOCK.COM

Employment Outlook

Employment outlook for teachers is good with an average growth rate predicted for kindergarten, elementary, and secondary school teachers. The need for teachers is based on the number of students enrolled in each district, so the need for teachers will vary. The fastest-growing states will experience the largest need for teachers.

Needed Skills and Education

Public school teachers are required to have a bachelor's degree from a teacher's education program or a field related to their teaching subject. Most states require a license. Teachers in private schools are required to have a bachelor's degree, but may not be required to have a license. Teachers in preschool and vocational educational schools may not need a bachelor's degree, but must be proficient and experienced in the subject matter.

How You'll Spend Your Day

Teachers work in the classroom with students, helping students to learn and develop new skills. Outside the classroom teachers write lesson plans, prepare for class, and complete forms on their students' achievements and performance records. During summer break, many teachers pursue an advanced degree or supplemental education in their fields.

Earnings

The median annual earnings of kindergarten, elementary, middle, and secondary school teachers range between $43,580 and $48,690. The lowest income for teachers is $28,590 and the highest is $76,100. Teachers with a master's degree earn more than teachers with a bachelor's degree. Teachers may earn extra income through different means, such as coaching or working with students in extracurricular activities.

What About You?

Does a career as a teacher interest you? Write a list of questions to ask your favorite teacher about this career. You might ask why he or she chose to be a teacher. You might also ask the best and worse parts of the occupation. Record the teacher's responses, and then add your own thoughts about the career, including whether you think it is a good career choice for you.

CHAPTER SUMMARY

6.1 Theories of Motivation

- Motivation is an inner state that energizes behavior toward a goal.

- Three of the biologically based internal push theories are instinct, drive-reduction, and Yerkes-Dodson.

- Drive-reduction theory is the idea that an imbalance in homeostasis creates a physiological need, which produces a drive that motivates the organism to satisfy the need. Homeostasis is the tendency to keep physiological systems internally balanced by adjusting them in response to change.

- External pull theories focus on things that pull you in certain directions, such as an increase in the hunger drive when you have not eaten for 12 hours. External pull theories include incentive theory and intrinsic and extrinsic motivation.

- According to the Yerkes-Dodson law, people perform best at an intermediate level of nervous system arousal.

- Abraham Maslow's hierarchy of needs illustrates that a person's basic physiological and safety needs must be satisfied before they can be motivated to satisfy higher-level psychological needs.

6.2 Biological and Social Motives

- Hunger and the motivation to eat are controlled by both internal and external factors.

- Weight gain and loss is both biological and social.

- A set point is the level of body weight that the body works to maintain.

- Obesity is the excessive accumulation of body fat.

- Eating disorders include anorexia nervosa and bulimia nervosa. Anorexia nervosa is an eating disorder in which a person weighs less than 85 percent of her or his expected weight but still expresses an intense fear of gaining weight or becoming fat. Bulimia nervosa is an eating disorder in which a person engages in recurrent episodes of binge eating followed by drastic measures to remove the food calories from the body.

- The need to belong is the need to interact with others and be socially accepted. The need to achieve is a desire to overcome obstacles and meet high standards of excellence.

6.3 Emotion

- Emotion is a positive or negative feeling state that typically includes some combination of physiological arousal, conscious experience, and expressive behavior.

- The three theories of emotion are the James-Lange theory, the Cannon-Bard theory, and the two-factor theory.

- People around the world accurately identify certain emotions on people's faces, but people of different cultures may express emotions differently.

- Women and men are the same in their ability to experience emotions. However, they often express emotions differently.

CHAPTER ASSESSMENT

Review Psychology Terms

Select the term that best fits the definition. Some terms will not be used.

____ 1. A level of body weight that the body works to maintain

____ 2. A positive or negative stimulus in the environment that attracts or repels you

____ 3. A theory that emotion-provoking events simultaneously induce both physiological responses and subjective states that are labeled as emotions

____ 4. An eating disorder in which a person weighs less than 85 percent of her or his expected weight but still expresses an intense fear of gaining weight or becoming fat

____ 5. The tendency to keep physiological systems internally balanced by adjusting them in response to change

____ 6. A positive or negative feeling state that typically includes some combination of physiological arousal, conscious experience, and expressive behavior

____ 7. The desire to perform a behavior for its own sake

____ 8. The idea that an imbalance in homeostasis creates a physiological need, which produces a drive that motivates the organism to satisfy the need

____ 9. The ultimate goal of human growth is the realization of your full potential

____ 10. An eating disorder in which a person engages in recurrent episodes of binge eating followed by drastic measures to remove the food calories from the body

____ 11. An inner state that energizes behavior toward the fulfillment of a goal

____ 12. A theory proposing that any stimulus that you think has either positive or negative outcomes for you will become an incentive for your behavior

____ 13. Proposes that specific facial expressions trigger the subjective experience of specific emotions

____ 14. The desire to perform a behavior because of promised rewards or the threats of punishment

____ 15. A theory that experiencing an emotion often is based on becoming physiologically aroused and then attaching a cognitive label to the arousal

____ 16. According to this law, people perform best when at an intermediate level of sensory arousal.

a. anorexia nervosa
b. bulimia nervosa
c. Cannon-Bard theory
d. drive-reduction theory
e. emotion
f. extrinsic motivation
g. facial feedback hypothesis
h. hierarchy of needs
i. homeostasis
j. incentive
k. incentive theory
l. intrinsic motivation
m. James-Lange Theory
n. motivation
o. need to achieve
p. need to belong
q. obesity
r. self-actualization
s. set point
t. two-factor theory
u. Yerkes-Dodson law

Review Psychology Concepts

17. Define Maslow's hierarchy of needs.

18. Define obesity.

19. Discuss the need to belong and the need to achieve.

20. Compare the James-Lange theory with the Cannon-Bard theory.

21. Why do psychologists study motivation?

22. What is the problem with William McDougall's theory that much of human behavior is controlled by a variety of instincts?

23. Restate in your own words how homeostasis can be applied in understanding motivated behavior.

24. Compare and contrast intrinsic and extrinsic motivation.

25. Differentiate among Maslow's five needs.

26. Evaluate how your culture and the environment influence what you eat.

27. How is the set point determined?

28. What is obesity and to what health problems does obesity contribute?

29. Why is the need to belong so important to young people?

30. On what is the need to achieve based?

31. How are the feelings of love and fear the same according to the James-Lange theory?

Apply Psychology Concepts

32. Sometimes, when athletes are paid large sums of money to play their sport, they seem to lose their "love of the game" and become less motivated. How could this change in athletic motivation be explained by intrinsic and extrinsic motivation?

33. Imagine that you are coaching an after-school soccer team for third graders. You know that some of the children on the team enjoy playing soccer a great deal, while other children are on the team only because their parents signed them up for this sport. Based on your knowledge of intrinsic and extrinsic motivation, what are some things you might be able to do when working with the team to help some of your players enjoy playing this sport?

34. Julia is a friend who is always worrying about and trying to control what and how much she eats. You realize that Julia is a restrained eater. Knowing this information, can you make some predictions about Julia's eating habits and the likelihood that she will be successful in staying on her diet?

35. Individuals with a high need for achievement are intrinsically motivated by a desire for success more than a fear of failure, while people with a low need for achievement are motivated more by a fear of failure. Imagine that you know someone with a low need for achievement who would like to become more successful in achievement situations. Based on psychological research and theory, what advice can you give this person?

Make Academic Connections

36. **Writing** Explain what motivates you and describe any changes you have experienced in your own motivation from the beginning of the school year to the present.

37. **Sociology** Using a computer or art supplies, make a design of Maslow's hierarchy of needs. Then apply Maslow's theory to making predictions about meeting the needs in your life. Begin by making a list of the needs you already have met in your life and which needs you have yet to meet. Then interview two adults from different generations to ask which needs they have met and which they have yet to meet in their lives. Do your findings suggest that more needs are met as people mature? Which needs do you predict you will meet in your lifetime?

38. **Language Arts** Imagine you are a magazine reporter, and interview yourself. Write an article from the third person that describes your goals, values, and the things that motivate you.

39. **Social Studies** Make a survey form that you can give to different people to identify the internal cues that trigger hunger. Choose people from different cultures, genders, and age groups. Add your own cues also. Tally the results of your survey, and write a report that assesses the results of your survey.

DIGGING DEEPER
with Psychology eCollection

Many of you may be familiar with the saying "win one for the Gipper," the motivating halftime speech by Notre Dame's famous coach Knute Rockne. His words motivated the players to roar from a 0–0 score to defeat Army 12–6. In this culture, coaches often are viewed as master motivators, people who can get their players "psyched up" to perform well. Athletes themselves are idolized as the essence of self-motivation. Do these approaches to motivation translate well to school and work? Access the Gale Psychology eCollection at *www.cengage.com/school/psych/franzoi* and read Salerno's discussion of "sportspeak" and its application outside athletics. Write a brief report on his conclusions and answer the question: Can a person who lacks self-motivation be motivated by someone else? Why or why not? As an additional project, describe an instance when someone motivated you to action. Explain what happened and what motivated you.

Source: Salerno, Steve. "We are the champions (we think): corporate America pays star athletes and coaches millions to pump up its workforce. Do these secrets of success reach beyond the locker room? Let's hear it for sportsthink!. . ." *Psychology Today*. 37.5 (Sept-Oct 2004): 62(7).

SELF-DISCOVERY: YOUR SCORE

How Important Are Your Close Relationships in Defining You?

Scoring Instructions: Two of the items are reverse-scored; that is, for these items a lower rating actually indicates a higher level of relational-interdependence. Before summing the items for a total score, recode those with an asterisk ("*") so that 1 = 7, 2 = 6, 3 = 5, 5 = 3, 6 = 2, and 7 = 1.

When Susan Cross and her colleagues developed this questionnaire, the mean score for 2,330 female students was about 57, while the average score for 1,819 male students was about 53, indicating differences between women and men. Higher scores indicate greater interest in developing close, committed social relationships.

Stress, Coping, and Health

ESSENTIAL QUESTION
Go to page XXV

"When written in Chinese, the word 'crisis' is composed of two characters. One represents danger, and the other represents opportunity."

—JOHN F. KENNEDY, 35ᵀᴴ U.S. PRESIDENT, 1917–1963

High school in the 21st century can be challenging. Unlike the high school years of your parents and grandparents, most of you are enrolled in a wider variety of courses and are expected to learn more in those courses than previous generations. Today many high schools begin class about an hour earlier than a generation ago. Look on the bright side of this early start to the school day. Your daily schedule of classes ends an hour earlier than it did for your parents. Great! Let's add some more after-school activities! Let's go, go, go!

Does the above paragraph come close to describing your daily life as a high school student? Do you have friends who are always rushing from one activity to the next? How do you and other students handle the challenges of your daily lives? Many of you no doubt enjoy these activities, although you may sometimes feel overburdened. The various reactions you have to these challenges is the subject of this chapter. Daily living can create stress. How do you cope with this stress, and how does this stress affect your health?

Causes and Consequences of Stress

OBJECTIVES

- Compare and contrast stressors and stress.
- Identify three types of conflict that can cause stress.
- Describe the body's reaction to stress and illustrate the three stages in the general adaptation syndrome.
- Examine psychophysiological illnesses.

KEY TERMS

- health psychologists
- stress
- stressors
- conflict
- fight-or-flight response
- general adaptation syndrome
- psychophysiological disorders
- immune system

DISCOVER IT | *How does this relate to me?*

Do the demands of various school and after-school activities create stress in your life? What about when you encounter serious personal hardships outside of school? Learning about the psychology of stress helps you deal with major stressful events and helps you cope with the minor hassles of daily living. Learning about stress also will lead you into a broader examination of the psychology of health.

Psychologists who study how people's thoughts and behavior affect their health are called **health psychologists**. Health psychologists realize that understanding the causes and consequences of stress is an important step in helping people become better at managing major stressful events in their lives.

Stressors and Stress

Stress is your response to events that disturb, or threaten to disturb, your physical or psychological balance. The internal or external events that challenge or threaten you are known as **stressors**. Anything from being a victim of a crime or having a death in the family to trying to get a good grade on an exam or having a big part in the school play are events that qualify as stressors. Such stressors disturb your physical or psychological balance.

Frustrations also create stress. Frustrations are feelings that occur whenever you are hindered or prevented from reaching goals you seek. Most frustrations are relatively minor. For example, being denied a summer job because all the available positions have been filled probably would be moderately frustrating. Being denied this same job because others are telling lies about your character would be extremely frustrating and would likely trigger a significant stress response.

health psychologists
Psychologists who study how people's thoughts and behavior affect their health

stress Response to events that disturb, or threaten to disturb, your physical or psychological balance

stressors Internal or external events that challenge or threaten you

Most people associate stress with negative events. However, would it surprise you to learn that positive events also can cause stress? Studies of married couples indicate that although the birth of a child is a very happy event, it also dramatically increases stress for many of these happy parents. Similarly, families on vacation who visit many wonderful sites in a very short period of time often experience stress because they are always on the go. In fact, in Jerusalem, some tourists are so overwhelmed by the city's history and religious significance that they have to be hospitalized. Going to your high school prom or spending the day at a theme park hopping on and off fun and exciting rides can leave you with a splitting headache. Yet, despite the ability of positive life events to increase stress levels, research indicates that negative events generally cause more stress than do positive events.

Negative stressors come in various forms. Your parents going through a divorce, the death of a close family member, or being seriously injured in an accident are examples of major stressors. Thomas Holmes and Richard Rahe created the *Social Readjustment Rating Scale* which identifies a variety of positive and negative life events that create stress because they require you to make social readjustments in your normal behavior and lifestyle. Table 7-1 lists some of these events and the average stress they create in people's lives.

Table 7-1 TO WHAT DEGREE DO DIFFERENT LIFE EVENTS CAUSE STRESS?

These 25 life events typically differ in how much they require you to readjust your life. Events that require greater social readjustments create greater stress. The average stress impact ranges from 0 (no stress) to 100 (very high stress).

Life Event	Average Stress Impact Effects	Life Event	Average Stress Impact Effects
Death of spouse	100	Son or daughter leaving home	29
Divorce	73	Outstanding personal achievement	28
Marital separation	65	Begin or end school	26
Death of close family member	63	Trouble with boss	23
Major personal injury or illness	53	Change in residence	20
Marriage	50	Change in schools	20
Fired at work	47	Change in social activities	18
Retirement	45	Change in sleeping habits	16
Change in health of family member	44	Change in eating habits	15
Pregnancy	40	Vacation	13
Adding new family member	39	Christmas	12
Death of close friend	37	Minor violations of the law	11
Change to different line of work	36		

As disruptive as major negative events are to your life, they often reflect only a fraction of the stressors that affect your health and well-being. In between each of these major stressful "boulders" occur many hassles, which are minor stressful "pebbles." Losing your keys or arguing with your brother or sister are examples of the common hassles of everyday life.

Which type of stressor—boulder or pebble—is worse? Both types of stressors can lead to health problems. Accumulating pebbles can leave you more vulnerable to major events when they occur. Similarly, major stressful events can leave you unable to deal with the daily hassles of life.

This is my father after a three-day visit with his relatives in northern Italy. Even very positive life events can be stressful.

COURTESY OF FIGZOI

CHECKPOINT *What is the difference between stressors and stress?*

Conflict and Stress

In everyday living, you are motivated to approach desirable or pleasant outcomes and to avoid undesirable or unpleasant outcomes. You often experience stress when faced with a situation that has conflicting outcomes. The resulting **conflict** is a feeling of being pulled between two opposing desires or goals. Psychologists have identified three different types of conflict that increase stress: approach-approach conflict, avoidance-avoidance conflict, and approach-avoidance conflict.

The least stressful conflict is an *approach-approach conflict*, which occurs when you must decide between two equally appealing outcomes. For example, imagine being offered two enjoyable, well-paying summer jobs. You are in a "win-win" situation and this conflict usually is easy to resolve. As soon as you choose one of the jobs, its desirability increases in your mind and completely dominates your thinking, eliminating any stress you were experiencing before making your choice.

More stressful is an avoidance-avoidance conflict, which involves two undesirable or unpleasant choices. For example, imagine that you need to have your leg placed in a cast for six weeks to correct a minor problem. Do you want to have the cast put on now, and have it interfere with school fun, or after the school year ends, when it will interfere with summer fun? This may feel like a "lose-lose" situation. Each time you come close to choosing one of the options, its negative consequences causes you to reconsider, and pushes you toward choosing the other option. You are stuck in indecision, and your stress increases. The best way to lower your stress is to resolve the conflict by making a decision and sticking with it.

Most stressful is an *approach-avoidance conflict*, which involves only one goal choice, but that goal has both desirable and undesirable consequences. The desirable

conflict A feeling of being pulled between two opposing desires or goals consequences make you want to approach this goal but the undesirable consequences make you want to avoid it. For example, imagine trying to decide whether to perform for the first time at your high school's annual talent contest. Choosing to perform provides you with the opportunity to win the praise of your classmates, but it also makes you a possible target of criticism if you perform poorly. This type of conflict often leads to considerable indecision and stress, but there are several ways you can resolve it. First, analyze objectively the pros and cons of the situation, and even ask your friends and family members for advice. Second, accept the reality that many important life choices involve some degree of risk. The old saying is true, "nothing ventured, nothing gained."

In deciding whether to enter a talent contest, imagining audience applause encourages potential performers, but imagining audience jeers discourages them. What sort of conflict is involved in this decision?

PHOTOS.COM/JUPITER IMAGES

CHECKPOINT *What are three common conflicts that can cause stress?*

The Body's Reactions to Stressors

Regardless of how stress is created, the sympathetic nervous system activates the body's energy resources to deal with threatening situations. If something angers or frightens you, the sympathetic nervous system quickly prepares you for self-defense in what is called the **fight-or-flight response**. This rapid physiological reaction to threatening events was first studied in animals, but it operates similarly in humans. This self-defensive response involves slowing your digestion, accelerating your heart

fight-or-flight response
A rapid physiological reaction by the sympathetic nervous system that prepares you either to fight or take flight from an immediate threat.

rate, raising your blood sugar, and cooling your body with perspiration. If the threatening situation does not end, you remain in this state of heightened agitation.

Some researchers are questioning whether women typically respond with fight-or-flight tendencies in the initial alarm stage. Check out the New Science feature for an overview of the possible gender differences of the fight-or-flight stress response.

NEW SCIENCE

Do Women Experience the "Fight-or-Flight" Response?

Research by psychologist Shelley Taylor suggests that when exposed to stressors, women often respond differently from men. While men are likely to experience the fight-or-flight response, women are more likely to experience a *tend-and-befriend response*. This response involves women taking action to protect their children or seeking out other people for social support.

Sociocultural psychologists suggest these differences are due to gender socialization. Traditionally, girls are more likely than boys to be raised to think, act, and define themselves in ways that emphasize their emotional connectedness to other people. This may lead many women to respond to stress by tending to their children and seeking out others for comfort and support. In contrast, many men's tendency to exhibit fight-or-flight responses to threat may be due to their being raised to be independent and tough-minded.

There are many women and men who don't respond in this gender-specific way. Everybody has childhood experiences that shape their lives in different ways. However, Taylor's research suggests that some of the ways that our culture socializes girls and boys may cause many of them to respond differently to stressful events.

Think Critically

Explain the tend-and-befriend response that females may experience when exposed to a stressor.

THE GENERAL ADAPTATION SYNDROME

One scientist who was instrumental in providing greater insight into how the body reacts to stress was physician Hans Selye (1907–1982). According to Selye, when exposed to stressors that put demands on the body, the body has a stress response geared toward energizing and protecting it from harm. If the demand continues, particular changes in the body begin to occur. He referred to this stress response, and the resulting changes in the body, as the **general adaptation syndrome (GAS)**. The GAS consists of three stages: alarm, resistance, and exhaustion. Figure 7-1 illustrates these three stages in the body's response to stress.

In stage 1, when you encounter a stressor, your body first reacts with alarm. The alarm reaction is the fight-or-flight response. This first stage in the general adaptation syndrome produces an initial shock to your body. The sympathetic nervous system is activated and the endocrine system releases the stress hormones epinephrine (also called adrenaline) and norepinephrine (also called noradrenaline). Your body's resources are now mobilized.

The intense physiological reactions of the alarm stage quickly begins using the body's available resources and threatens its health. Homeostasis must be achieved, even if the stressor is still present. During stage 2, resistance, the parasympathetic nervous system returns certain bodily functions—such as respiration and heart rate—to normal levels. However, many stress hormones continue to circulate throughout the body at high levels to maintain your energy, but they also keep your blood pressure at an unhealthy high level and weaken your immune system. While your body is no longer operating at a high pitch and you may outwardly appear normal, appearances are deceiving.

If the stressor continues and your body exhausts its resources, you become much more vulnerable to disease and even death. This is the third stage of the GAS, exhaustion. Selye described it as a "kind of premature aging due to wear and tear." Organs such as the heart are the first to break down during this stage.

general adaptation syndrome (GAS) Selye's theory that the body responds to stress in three stages: alarm, resistance, and exhaustion

Figure 7-1   **THE GENERAL ADAPTATION SYNDROME**

Hans Selye GAS model

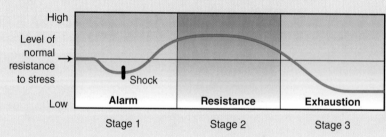

CHECKPOINT   *What are the three stages in the general adaptation syndrome?*

Psychophysiological Illnesses

Did you ever get a cold in the middle of exam week? Do you get a headache or stomach ache when you have to face a test? You are not alone in getting sick when under stress. Medical experts estimate that stress plays a role in 50 to 70 percent of all physical illnesses. Prolonged stress can lead to chronic anxiety, depression, and other disorders. These stress-related physical illnesses are referred to as **psychophysiological disorders**.

Stress responses often harm your physical health by weakening your **immune system**, which is your body's primary defense against disease. The immune system is a complex system of specialized cells, tissues, and organs. The immune system was once thought to act independently of the nervous system, but scientists now know that the immune system and the brain are in close communication and influence each other's actions. This communication means that the activity of one system affects the activity of the other. One pathway is through reaction to stress.

A review of many different stress studies involving almost 19,000 individuals found that intense, short-term stressors are much less harmful to the body's immune system than less intense, but long-term stressors. Long-term stress dramatically reduces the efficiency of the immune system, making the body more vulnerable to disease. The longer stress lasts in your life, the more likely you are to become ill.

Long-term stress also may speed up the aging process. A study of women who were taking care of a child suffering from a serious chronic illness found that the women had body cells that looked 10 years older than their chronological age. Further, the degree of cellular aging was highest in the women who had been caring for a child with disabilities the longest.

Chronic environmental stressors, such as poverty and noisy living conditions, also are associated with many illnesses, including strokes and heart attacks. Even the short-term stressor of final exams can lower the effectiveness of the immune system, resulting in greater health risks among students. However, before complaining to

psychophysiological disorders Stress-related physical illnesses

immune system Your body's primary defense against disease

The stress of living in crowded urban environments can contribute to a variety of illnesses, including strokes and heart attacks. Does everyone react in the same way to environmental stressors?

your teachers that exams can be hazardous to your health, keep in mind that stress is a subjective experience. While one person may perceive a particular situation as highly threatening, another person may perceive the same situation as only mildly stressful. This fact of life can help explain why some people develop illnesses and others remain healthy after facing similar challenging events in their lives.

CHECKPOINT > *What are psychophysiological disorders?*

7.1 ASSESSMENT

In Your Own Words

Summarize the causes of stress in life and the consequences of that stress. Add personal stories about the stressors in your life, the consequences you have experienced from stress, and the ways you cope with stress.

Review Concepts

1. Which refers to internal or external events that challenge or threaten you?
   - a. stress
   - b. immune system
   - c. stressors
   - d. general adaptation syndrome

2. Which is the least stressful form of conflict which occurs when you must decide between two equally appealing outcomes?
   - a. approach-approach
   - b. approach-avoidance
   - c. avoidance-avoidance

3. Which of these life events causes the most stress?
   - a. marriage
   - b. vacation
   - c. beginning of school year
   - d. change in school

4. What is the relationship between stressors and stress?
5. **True or False** Minor stressors rarely lead to health problems.
6. **True or False** Healthy humans and animals easily survive in the intense stimulation of the alarm stage.
7. **True or False** Chronic environmental stressors are associated with a variety of illnesses.
8. **True or False** The immune system and the brain are in close communication.

Think Critically

9. Why is it important to keep stress low and your immune system strong?
10. According to Selye's theory, how does the body's response to stressors that put demands on the body help you? How are you hurt?
11. Why is it beneficial for you to avoid noisy living conditions if possible?

Individual Differences in Experiencing Stress

OBJECTIVES

- Examine cognitive appraisal and stress and evaluate two general coping strategies used to deal with stressors.
- Describe how stress is related to perceived control.
- Explain how stress is influenced by personality factors.
- Explain how culture can create stress in some people.

KEY TERMS

- problem-focused coping
- emotion-focused coping
- learned helplessness
- Type A behavior pattern
- Type B behavior pattern
- pessimistic explanatory style
- optimistic explanatory style
- acculturative stress

DISCOVER IT | *How does this relate to me?*

Have you noticed that when two people confront the same challenging event, they often do not react with the same levels of stress? When taking an important math exam, for example, one person may be noticeably nervous while the other person is much more relaxed. Later these two same individuals may respond in exactly the opposite manner when preparing to give a speech. These examples illustrate the fact that just because you are exposed to a stressor does not mean that you will become anxious and troubled.

Selye's GAS model provided a great deal of insight into how stressors affect the body and its health. However, by focusing exclusively on the body, the GAS theory ignored the role of the mind in the stress response. Various factors related to the mind will influence your stress reactions, including how you perceive the stressor, the coping strategies you decide to use, your perceptions of control, and your personality.

Cognitive Appraisal and Stress

Psychologist Richard Lazarus was one of the first researchers to examine how people interpret and evaluate stressors in their lives, a process he called *cognitive appraisal*. Cognitive appraisal is necessary in defining whether a situation is a threat, how big a threat it is, and what resources you have to deal with the threat.

Some stressors, such as being a crime victim or undergoing surgery, are experienced as threats by almost everyone. Many other events are defined differently

Your past experience with an event can influence how you react to similar events. For example, if you have been bitten or attacked by a dog, you are more likely to become stressed in the presence of dogs.

©GERI ENGBERG/THE IMAGE WORKS

depending on a person's past experiences in dealing with the stressor. For example, starting a new job or joining a new student organization can fill one person with excitement, while it causes someone else to feel anxious and overwhelmed.

Lazarus identified two stages in the cognitive appraisal process: primary appraisal and secondary appraisal. *Primary appraisal* involves a quick evaluation of the situation. Here, you assess what is happening, whether it is threatening, and whether you should take some action in response to the threat. If you conclude that some action is necessary, *secondary appraisal* begins. In this second stage of the cognitive appraisal process, you assess whether you have the ability to cope with the stressor. The more confidence you have in dealing with the stressor, the less stress you experience. As an example, imagine that as you walk to your first morning class the high school principal passes by and asks you to come to her office at noon. You quickly assess what this request might mean. "Is there a problem? Did the principal seem angry?" This is the primary appraisal process. If you conclude that perhaps she knows that you were the student who hoisted a pair of jeans up the school flagpole early this morning, then you begin secondary appraisal. This involves trying to figure out whether you can somehow manage or resolve this looming problem.

PROBLEM-FOCUSED AND EMOTION-FOCUSED COPING

There are two general coping strategies that people use during secondary appraisal. **Problem-focused coping** is a strategy aimed at reducing stress by overcoming the source of the problem. For example, if you fail your first exam in an important class, engaging in problem-focused coping might involve a number of actions. You might talk to your teacher about extra-credit work, change your study habits, and compare your class notes with someone who is doing well in the class. A second approach is **emotion-focused coping**, which consists of efforts to manage your emotional reactions to stressors. This might involve trying not to cry or get angry when speaking

problem-focused coping
A strategy aimed at reducing stress by overcoming the source of the problem

emotion-focused coping
Consists of efforts to manage your emotional reactions to stressors

to your teacher, seeking sympathy from your friends, or doing some other activity to take your mind off your academic troubles.

You tend to take the active, problem-focused approach to handling stress when you think you can overcome the problem. When you believe the problem is beyond your control you often resort to an emotion-focused strategy. Of course, at times you use both types of coping. For example, while devising a plan to improve your class performance, you may try to reduce anxiety by reminding yourself this is just one exam out of many in the course. Table 7-2 lists some of the specific problem-focused and emotion-focused strategies you can use.

Table 7-2 **PROBLEM-FOCUSED AND EMOTION-FOCUSED COPING**

Coping Skills	Example
Problem-Focused Coping	
Confronting	Assert yourself and fight for what you want.
Planned problem solving	Develop a plan of action and implement it.
Seeking social support	Seek out others who have information about the stressor.
Emotion-Focused Coping	
Distancing	Redirect your attention to other things or try to downplay the importance of the stressor.
Self-controlling	Keep your feelings to yourself.
Escape/avoidance	Fantasize about the stressor going away (wishful thinking).
Positive reappraisal	Think about positive aspects of yourself that are not related to the stressor.
Accepting responsibility	Realize that you are responsible for this problem.

 **CHECKPOINT** *Explain the two general coping strategies used during secondary appraisal of a stressor.*

Perceived Control and Stress

If you believe that you have some control over a stressor, you usually feel less stressed. For example, in one study, elderly nursing home patients who were given greater control over their daily activities experienced fewer health problems and lived longer than those given little control. Similarly, people who work at demanding jobs are less likely to develop coronary heart disease when they believe they have some control over job stressors.

The interesting fact about control and stress is that it isn't *actual control* that lowers stress, it is *perceived control*. You experience less stress if you think you have control over a stressor, even if you don't really have control. This is why superstitious rituals are so popular. For example, in high school I would ask a girl for a date only after successfully shooting three basketball free-throws in my parents' driveway. Making the shots had no bearing on whether the girl accepted or rejected my request, but it did lower my anxiety.

Repeatedly failing to perform well in school can cause students to develop a feeling of learned helplessness. How are such students likely to respond if they are offered help in mastering academic material?

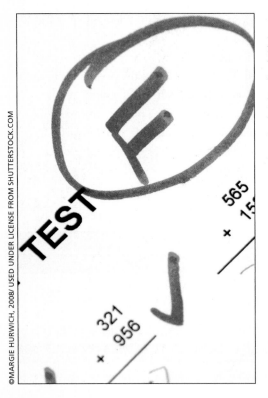

©MARGIE HURWICH, 2008/ USED UNDER LICENSE FROM SHUTTERSTOCK.COM

Beyond superstitious behavior, people differ in their beliefs about how much control they have over stressors. Life experiences play an important role in determining your level of confidence in effectively dealing with stressors. Numerous psychological studies find that when people are exposed to uncontrollable bad events they at first feel angry and anxious that their goals are being thwarted. However, after repeated exposure to these uncontrollable events, people begin to feel defeated and helpless, and their anger and anxiety are replaced with depression. This **learned helplessness** can cause you to believe you have no control over a stressor, thus increasing the likelihood that you take no action to reduce the threat. This belief that you are a helpless victim who is controlled by external forces dooms you to failure. It explains why many unemployed workers who are repeatedly passed over for new jobs eventually give up trying to find a job. Unfortunately, by concluding that there is nothing they can do to change their job status, these individuals sometimes overlook real employment possibilities.

When you doubt your ability to control a stressor, you are also more likely to engage in emotion-focused coping strategies. Procrastination, which involves delaying the start and completion of planned problem solving, is an example of the emotion-focused coping strategy of escape avoidance (refer back to Table 7-2). About one in five people regularly procrastinate when faced with a stressor, especially when it is severe. Far from reducing stress, however, such delays in tackling problems tend to increase stress and lead to health problems.

CHECKPOINT *How is stress related to perceived control?*

Personality and Stress

Besides perceptions of stressors shaping behavior, people's responses to stress are also shaped by differences in their personalities. Some people's personalities cause them to react in negative ways to stressors, whereas others respond in positive ways. Some students might react negatively to the school closing for a snow day because they will not see their friends or they will not be able to spend the day in a favorite class. Other students might react positively to the same school closing by using the day to play their favorite video games.

learned helplessness
A defeated and helpless state of mind produced by repeatedly being exposed to uncontrollable life events

TYPE A AND TYPE B PERSONALITIES

During the 1950s, heart surgeons Ray Rosenman and Meyer Friedman noticed that many of their patients with heart problems were impatient and spent most of their time working. The surgeons described these people as having a **Type A behavior pattern**. This complex pattern of behaviors and emotions is characterized by competitiveness, impatience, ambition, hostility, and a hard-driving approach to life. The direct opposite of this personality style is the **Type B behavior pattern**, which is characterized by a patient, relaxed, easygoing approach to life, with little hurry or hostility. Type B individuals are only half as likely to develop coronary heart disease as Type A individuals. Spend a few minutes answering the items in the Self-Discovery feature on the next page to assess your own Type A behavior pattern.

Based on numerous studies, hostility appears to be the most dangerous aspect of the Type A pattern. People who mistrust and think the worst of others and use anger as a typical response to interpersonal problems appear to be at greatest risk for heart disease. Hostility causes the body to be in a constant state of high alertness, which weakens the immune system. Hostility also contributes to poor health habits and tense social relationships. Because of the health problems associated with the Type A behavior pattern, it makes sense to try to convince Type A persons to change their hostile, impatient approach to life. However, one major obstacle to such change is that many Type A persons do not believe their hostility is a problem. American culture generally respects and often rewards this hard-driving, hostile lifestyle. Yet, people who are motivated to reduce their hostility and slow down in their daily lives can change their Type A behavior. Check out Closer Look on page 197, on how to alter the Type A behavior pattern.

Type A behavior pattern
A competitive, impatient, ambitious, hostile, and hard-driving approach to life

Type B behavior pattern
A patient, relaxed, easygoing approach to life, with little hurry or hostility

Type A individuals are competitive, impatient, ambitious, hostile, and hard-driving.

©DANA BARTEKOSKE, 2008/USED UNDER LICENSE FROM SHUTTERSTOCK.COM

Do You Have a Type A Personality?

Directions: Indicate how often each of the following applies to you in daily life, using the following three-point scale:

1 = Seldom or Never

2 = Sometimes

3 = Always or Usually

_____ Do you find yourself rushing your speech?

_____ Do you hurry other people's speech by interrupting them with "umha, umhm" or by completing their sentences for them?

_____ Do you hate to wait in line?

_____ Do you seem to be short of time to get everything done?

_____ Do you detest wasting time?

_____ Do you eat fast?

_____ Do you drive over the speed limit?

_____ Do you try to do more than one thing at a time?

_____ Do you become impatient if others do something too slowly?

_____ Does your concentration sometimes wander while you think about what's coming up later?

_____ Do you find yourself overcommitted?

_____ Do you jiggle your knees or tap your fingers?

_____ Do you think about other things during conversations?

_____ Do you walk fast?

_____ Do you hate dawdling after a meal?

_____ Do you become irritable if kept waiting?

_____ Do you detest losing in sports and games?

_____ Do you find yourself with clenched fists or tight neck and jaw muscles?

_____ Do you seem to have little time to relax and enjoy the time of day?

_____ Are you a competitive person?

_____ **Total score**

See page 211 for scoring instructions.

How Can You Change Your Type A Behavior Patterns?

There are a number of strategies to help Type A persons slow down and reduce hostility. Listed below are some exercises that can alter certain Type A behavior patterns.

Modifying Time Urgency

Type A persons' habit of always being on the go and thinking of the things they need to accomplish causes them to pay little attention to their current surroundings. They often fail to notice and appreciate many important people or things in their lives. Here are some exercises to slow down and become more aware of your surroundings:

Exercise 1: Eat slower. Enjoy the various tastes and smells of your food and drink. What do you notice about your meal that you were not aware of before?

Exercise 2: Walk slower. How does this slower pace make you feel? Impatient? Relaxed? Maintain this slower walking pace for at least a week, noticing any changes in your thoughts and feelings over time.

Exercise 3: Listen to every person who speaks to you without interrupting them, even if you think you have something useful to say. How difficult is this for you?

Reducing Hostility

Type A persons' practice of criticizing others is such a habit that they rarely praise other people. As a result, they rarely receive compliments themselves. Type A persons' hostility often results in their frowning more than smiling when with others, which often causes people to respond with unfriendly facial expressions. Here are some exercises to do to reverse these negative behavior patterns:

Exercise 1: Compliment at least two persons during a conversation. Be sincere and notice their facial expressions. How do you feel?

Exercise 2: Practice smiling as you remember two to three happy events from the past, and then purposely smile while speaking to others. How do their facial expressions change as you smile?

Exercise 3: Just as you are about to criticize someone, try to avoid doing so. If you must say something critical, first count to 10, or 20, or 30. Is this a difficult task for you?

Think Critically

What are the two things that these strategies are designed to do for people with Type A behavior patterns?

PESSIMISTS VERSUS OPTIMISTS

Psychologist Martin Seligman describes two very different styles of thinking in reacting to negative life events. People who have a **pessimistic explanatory style** explain negative events in their lives as being caused by internal factors ("It's my fault") that are stable ("It won't ever change") and global ("This affects everything in my life"). Individuals with a pessimistic explanatory style are susceptible to depression and illnesses.

In contrast, people with an **optimistic explanatory style** are more likely to explain negative events as due to external factors ("It is not my fault") that are unstable or changeable ("It won't happen again") and isolated ("This affects only one thing"). As you might guess, optimists are healthier and live longer than pessimists.

Fortunately, pessimists can be taught to change their way of thinking so that it is more upbeat. In a very real sense, research on pessimists and optimists points to the important role that people's interpretations of events have on their health and behavior. Check out the Self-Discovery feature on page 199 to explore your own tendencies toward optimism versus pessimism.

©EMERALDCHIK, 2009/USED UNDER LICENSE FROM SHUTTERSTOCK.COM

Optimists are healthier and live longer than pessimists partly because optimists have better immune systems.

CHECKPOINT *How is stress related to personality factors?*

Culture and Stress

Many people experience stress because of cultural factors. Unemployment, crime, poor living conditions, race and ethnic prejudice, and lack of proper health care all cause increased stress. People in the lowest socioeconomic levels of society are most likely to experience these kinds of cultural stressors, and they report the highest levels of ongoing or *chronic stress*.

Recent immigrants to a new country often experience high levels of stress when trying to adapt to their new culture. The sources of their stress are the constant challenges posed by so many new and different rules, obligations, expectations, and customs. Similarly, many Native American teenagers and young adults who live on their nation's reservation lands experience stress when they leave home and live full-time within mainstream American culture. The stress resulting from the pressure of adapting to a new culture is known as **acculturative stress**.

Adapting to a new culture is less stressful when the citizens in the adopted culture are accepting of cultural and ethnic diversity. Individuals also experience less stress when they have some familiarity with the new culture's language and customs, and also when they receive social support from their families and friends. Based on studies of Pueblo, Navajo, Latino, Iranian American, Indian American, and Asian American children and adults, neither abandoning your original culture nor isolating yourself from the new culture is good for mental health. Instead, the most successful integration into the new culture is achieved by retaining many of your

pessimistic explanatory style Explains negative events in life as being caused by internal factors that are stable and global

optimistic explanatory style Explains negative events as due to external factors that are unstable or changeable and isolated

acculturative stress The stress resulting from the pressure of adapting to a new culture

original cultural values and practices while weaving in the new values and practices from your adopted culture. This combining of the best from both cultures also can provide long-term benefits to the larger society because the new members bring with them new ways of understanding the world in which they live.

CHECKPOINT › *What is acculturative stress?*

SELF-DISCOVERY

Are You an Optimist or a Pessimist?

The Revised Life Orientation Test developed by Michael Scheier and Charles Carver (1994) measures people's tendencies to believe that they will generally experience good or bad outcomes in their lives. Read the 10 statements below and indicate the degree to which you personally agree with each statement, using the following scale:

0 = Strongly disagree

1 = Disagree

2 = Neutral (neither disagree nor agree)

3 = Agree

4 = Strongly agree

Try to be as accurate and honest as possible, and try not to let your opinion for one item influence your opinion for other items. There are no correct or incorrect answers.

_____ 1. In uncertain times, I usually expect the best.

_____ 2. It's easy for me to relax.

_____ 3. If something can go wrong for me, it will.

_____ 4. I'm always optimistic about my future.

_____ 5. I enjoy my friends a lot.

_____ 6. It's important for me to keep busy.

_____ 7. I hardly ever expect things to go my way.

_____ 8. I don't get upset too easily.

_____ 9. I rarely count on good things happening to me.

_____ 10. Overall, I expect more good things to happen to me than bad.

See page 211 for scoring instructions.

Source: M. F. Scheier, C. S. Carver, & M. W. Bridges, Distinguishing optimism from neuroticism (and trait anxiety, self-mastery, and self-esteem): A reevaluation of the life orientation test, *Journal of Personality and Social Psychology*, 67, 1073. Copyright 1994 by the American Psychological Association.

In Your Own Words

Evaluate the two coping strategies people use during secondary appraisal, problem-focused coping and emotion-focused coping.

Review Concepts

1. Which is a problem-focused way to cope?

   a. getting angry   c. positive reappraisal
   b. confronting   d. distancing

2. Which is an emotion-focused way to cope?

   a. self-controlling   c. planned problem solving
   b. confronting   d. seeking social support

3. Which is a characteristic of the Type A personality?

   a. relaxed   c. easy going
   b. patient   d. ambitious

4. Which factors do people with a pessimistic explanatory style use to explain negative events?

   a. global   c. isolated
   b. external   d. changeable

5. Summarize the two stages in the cognitive appraisal process.

6. **True or False** If you believe that you have some control over a stressor, you usually feel less stressed.

7. **True or False** Tackling a problem as soon as it occurs increases stress and leads to health problems.

8. **True or False** Some people have personalities that cause them to react negatively to stressors, whereas others have personalities that cause them to respond positively.

9. **True or False** When you believe in your ability to control a stressor, you are more likely to engage in emotion-focused coping strategies.

10. **True or False** The sources of acculturative stress include the challenges posed by the differences in the new culture's rules, obligations, expectations, and customs.

Think Critically

11. Why should people with a pessimistic explanatory style change their way of thinking?

12. Why are Type A personalities more at risk for heart disease than Type B personalities?

13. Would you most likely use problem-focused coping or emotion-focused coping when speaking to a teacher about the best way to prepare for an upcoming test? Explain your answer.

LESSON
7.3 | Lifestyle and Stress

OBJECTIVES

- Explain how social support affects stress and health.
- Evaluate the importance of aerobic exercise and relaxation to health.

KEY TERMS

- social support
- aerobic exercise
- progressive relaxation

DISCOVER IT | *How does this relate to me?*

How often each day do you talk with or text your friends? Do you think your social network helps you reduce stress? Do you exercise everyday? Do you think this helps reduce stress? What about practicing ways to relax, such as listening to music or spending time in nature or just laughing? Do these help you reduce stress in your life? These are questions psychologists ask to learn how to help people stay healthy.

Psychologists have discovered that your social world can provide you with a great deal of protection against the stress of everyday living. In your relationship with friends and family members, you can find strength and support in your social world that leads to a healthier and longer life. Regular exercise also is beneficial to your ability to cope with stressors in your world. In this lesson we examine how your lifestyle affects your health.

Social Support

You do not have to endure stress alone. During times of anxiety, grief, and uncertainty, seeking out the companionship of others is healthy. The desire to seek out others during times of stress and uncertainty is fueled by the need to compare your emotional state with that of others ("How should I be feeling?") and also to analyze the stressful situation itself ("How much of a threat is this stressor?").

The helpful coping resources that friends and other people provide when you are in a stressful situation are referred to as **social support**. An overwhelming amount of evidence indicates that having supportive people in your life provides both psychological and physical benefits. For example, in a study of almost 7,000 California residents, researchers discovered that people lived longer when they had many social and community ties. This was true of men and women, rich and poor, and people from all cultures. Other studies found that being socially isolated was as

social support Helpful coping resources that friends and other people provide when you are in a stressful situation

much a prediction of an early death as high cholesterol or smoking. Physiologically, having strong social support networks is associated with a stronger immune system response to stress.

One common psychological benefit of social support is increased knowledge about the stressor. Talking with others often provides you with information about how to understand and emotionally respond to stressful events. The people who tend to provide the most useful information are those who have had some experience with the same stressors you are encountering. This is the rationale underlying support groups. In therapy sessions, people who have experienced the same stressful events compare themselves with one another while they also provide and receive emotional support.

Social support during stressful times also can provide you with opportunities to simply express your feelings, which benefits your physical health. In one experiment, students spent 15 minutes on four consecutive nights writing to a researcher. One group wrote about a traumatic event in their lives. These students reported fewer illnesses over the next six months compared with students who wrote to the researcher about unimportant topics. While letting out your feelings about a traumatic event can temporarily upset you, in the long run, it lowers your stress.

As with most things that are good for you, too much social support can sometimes cause negative side effects. The key when providing support to other people is to convey caring in a way that provides real benefits, keeps them involved in the solution to the problem (don't do everything for them), and avoids a feeling of inferiority in those receiving support.

LAB TEAMS

Holiday Stress

Work with a partner to create an oral presentation about stress and a holiday. Agree on the holiday, and then write a list of stressors associated with that holiday. Next make a list of ways to reduce the stress. For example, if you choose July 4, stressors might include the stress of finding the right outfit or the stress of going to a pool party. Ways to reduce stress might include having a fun day shopping with a friend, asking a friend to go with you to the party, making plans to spend the day with your family instead of going to a party, or inviting a friend over to watch movies.

CHECKPOINT *How does social support affect stress and health?*

Exercise and Relaxation

Exercise is another key ingredient in living a healthy and less stressful life. The best exercise is **aerobic exercise**, which is sustained exercise that increases heart and lung fitness. Any activity that increases the heart rate into a certain range (defined by your age and maximum possible heart rate) for at least 12 to 20 minutes fits this definition. Vigorous walking, cross-country skiing, skating, dancing, bicycling, and even tiring yard work all qualify as aerobic exercise.

Aerobic exercise has a positive effect on both physical and mental health. It strengthens the heart, lowers blood pressure, and helps the body convert fats and carbohydrates into energy. Adults who exercise regularly live longer than those who are less active. Based on the results from more than 100 studies, most mental health experts believe that exercise can be effective in reducing tension and eliminating depressed moods. One possible reason for this beneficial effect is that aerobic exercise heightens the brain's supply of mood-enhancing neurotransmitters. It is also possible that these mood benefits are partly a side effect of the muscular relaxation and sounder sleep that are in part produced by aerobic exercise.

Despite the benefits of regular exercise, it is possible to overdo a good thing. Some athletes train to the point where they begin to experience negative effects such as fatigue and depression. Other people become obsessed with exercising, feeling anxious and uncomfortable if unable to engage in the activity. Individuals who feel compelled to exercise often have other unhealthy concerns about weight control and body image.

PROGRESSIVE RELAXATION

While regularly elevating your heart rate and strengthening your lungs is certainly beneficial to your health, it is also true that learning how to reduce your stimulation can lead to better health. Because stress is associated with physiological stimulation, many psychologists recommend relaxation training as a useful way to reduce stress.

One of the most basic relaxation techniques is **progressive relaxation**. This technique involves progressively relaxing muscle groups in your body, usually starting at the head and slowly moving down to the legs and feet. Once you develop some skill with this technique, you can use it to calm yourself anywhere and anytime.

Research suggests that one benefit of relaxation training is that it improves the effectiveness of the immune response. In one such experiment, blood samples were taken from college students one month prior to midterm exams and

progressive relaxation
A relaxation technique that involves progressively relaxing muscle groups in your body

Aerobic exercise benefits both physical and mental health. If you want to feel happier, sleep better, and live longer, engage in some form of aerobic exercise for 30 minutes three times per week.

©PETER WEBER, 2008/USED UNDER LICENSE FROM SHUTTERSTOCK.COM

again on the day of the exams. Half the students were trained in progressive relaxation techniques, while the other half received no training. The students who received the training showed much less decrease in the cells that fight viruses and tumors. Check out the Self-Discovery feature below to learn more about progressive relaxation.

CHECKPOINT *What is the connection between exercise and health?*

SELF-DISCOVERY

How Can You Progressively Relax?

Progressive relaxation is an effective technique in managing stress. Practice the following steps once or twice daily, but not within two hours after eating a meal. Digestion can interfere with the relaxation response.

Step 1 Sit or lie comfortably with eyes shut and your arms and legs bent at a comfortable angle. Take a deep breath, hold it, and exhale slowly. Repeat several times, saying the word "relax" to yourself with each exhale. Step by step, begin tensing different muscle groups one at a time—holding the tension for 5 seconds, concentrating on how that feels, followed by slowly releasing the tension.

Step 2 Start with your arms by clenching your fists while tensing the muscles in your upper arms. Hold. Slowly release. Inhale and exhale slowly. Maintain a passive attitude and permit relaxation to occur at its own pace. When distracting thoughts occur, do not dwell on them, but simply return to repeating "relax" to yourself.

Step 3 Next, tense the thigh and calf muscles in your legs by straightening your legs and pointing your toes downward. Hold. Slowly release. Inhale and exhale slowly.

Step 4 Tense your stomach muscles and at the same time press your palms together over your chest in order to tighten your chest muscles. Hold. Slowly release. Inhale and exhale slowly.

Step 5 Arch your back and pull your shoulders back (not too far) to tense these muscles. Hold. Slowly release. Inhale and exhale slowly.

Step 6 Tense your jaw and neck muscles by drawing the corners of your mouth back. You may also want to bend your neck first to one side then the other. Hold. Slowly release. Inhale and exhale slowly.

Step 7 Tense your forehead by pulling your eyebrows in together, wrinkling your brow. Hold. Slowly release. Inhale and exhale slowly.

Step 8 Continue to concentrate on your breathing, breathing comfortably into your abdomen (not your chest). Think "relax" with each exhale. Continue this exercise for 10 to 20 minutes. You may open your eyes to check the time, but do not use an alarm. When finished, sit or lie quietly for a few minutes, first with your eyes closed and later with your eyes opened.

Source: Adapted from *The Relaxation Response* by Herbert Benson, MD, © 1975. Used with permission of the author.

In Your Own Words

Using information from the text, defend the following statement: "A healthy lifestyle helps reduce stress in your life." Cite information from the text that supports your argument. Also cite examples from your life that describe at least one stressful situation and defend how your lifestyle either hurt or helped you to deal with the stress. You might discuss taking drivers' education classes and learning how to drive. How did you deal with the stress of learning how to drive? Did you learn to laugh about your mistakes with friends and family members? Or did you learn that taking a walk after class or spending time playing basketball with friends after class helped?

Review Concepts

1. People you can turn to in times of stress—such as your parents, friends, siblings, teachers or counselors, employers, or others—are all part of your

   _____.

2. Which does not help reduce stress?

   a. social support   c. aerobic exercise

   b. controlling friends   d. progressive relaxation

3. Which is an aerobic exercise?

   a. reading   c. dancing

   b. watching television   d. progressive relaxation

4. Define aerobic exercise and explain its relationship to stress.

5. What is the progressive relaxation technique?

6. **True or False** During times of anxiety, grief, and uncertainty, seeking out the companionship of others is healthy.

7. **True or False** Letting out your feelings about a traumatic event can temporarily upset you, and, in the long run, increases your stress.

8. **True or False** Having a strong social support network is associated with a stronger immune system response to stress.

Think Critically

9. Why do you need to avoid being overly enthusiastic about supporting a friend who is going through a stressful time?

10. Why is getting too much exercise unhealthy?

11. Why should you practice a relaxation technique such as progressive relaxation?

12. Explain the statement: Psychologists have discovered that your social world can provide you with a great deal of protection against the stress of everyday living.

Overusing Nonprescription Pain Relievers Can Cause Chronic Headaches

INTRODUCTION During a typical year, nearly 95 percent of teenagers and adults have at least one headache, with another 25 percent experiencing long-lasting or recurring head pain. The stress of everyday hassles is by far the most common cause of headaches, but what is the most common cause of chronic headaches?

HYPOTHESIS It was predicted that most chronic headaches are caused by the overuse of nonprescription pain relievers, such as aspirin, naproxen sodium, or ibuprofen.

METHOD The "headache diaries" of patients with chronic headaches were reviewed over an extended period of time.

RESULTS It was discovered that people who were suffering from chronic headaches began taking nonprescription pain relievers

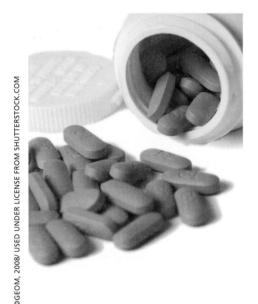

©GEOM, 2008/ USED UNDER LICENSE FROM SHUTTERSTOCK.COM

to reduce the pain of tension-type headaches. However, by failing to follow label directions—which warn against using the drug for more than a few days—sufferers became physically dependent on the pain relievers and experienced "rebound headaches" as each dose wore off. These rebound headaches led to more pill-taking, and the vicious cycle repeated itself. The remedy for rebound headaches is to stop using the pain relievers and to tolerate the more severe headaches for a few days or weeks. Another strategy is to slowly eliminate the medicine from your body.

In rare cases (1 out of 25,000), an acute headache is a symptom of a serious physical disorder. If any of the following symptoms describe your headache pattern, consult a physician:

- The headache is severe, new, and unlike past headaches.
- The headache is the "worst" you have ever experienced.
- The headache becomes much worse over time.
- Headache occurs with exertion, coughing, or sneezing.
- When the headache occurs, you feel drowsy, confused, or feverish.

Critical Analysis

1. What is the most common cause of headaches?

2. What is the most common cause of chronic headaches?

Sports Psychologist

Health Science

Do you like sports? Are you interested in the mental factors that help individuals who are engaged in sports? If so, take a look at the career of sports psychologist. People in this career research and work with athletes, coaches, trainers, and other people involved in sports, physical activity, and exercise. The goal is to find ways to motivate, enhance the experience of, and improve the performance of people involved in sports and exercise activities.

Sports psychologists are engaged in a variety of sports-related areas. Some psychologists teach in colleges and universities or work in research. Sports psychologists who teach may teach future psychologists or work directly with coaches, athletes, or athletic administrators to provide information and help design sports programs.

Sports psychologists also may work with coaches. For example, a high school might hire a psychologist to work with coaches to help improve their team members' self-esteem.

Sports psychologists work for school districts, colleges and universities, sports franchises, individual athletes, and sports centers.

Employment Outlook

Careers for sports psychologists are expected to grow as more athletes and sports teams use their services. However, the field is limited and will remain so, with stiff competition.

Needed Skills and Education

Most sports psychologists have a doctoral degree, which is required for most positions in the career. A doctoral degree usually requires five to seven years of college work after receiving a bachelor's degree. Requirements vary from state to state, with some states requiring licensing.

Courses that will help you in this career are those in psychology and other related sciences. You also need good written and oral communication skills; good interpersonal relationship skills; and good organizational abilities. In addition, you must know sports, especially the particular sport in which you want to work. You also must be able to apply psychology to sports, be able to listen and learn from athletes and coaches, and be able to work as a team member.

How You'll Spend Your Day

The way sports psychologists spend their days depends on their specific area of expertise. Sports psychologists in colleges or universities spend time in classrooms and time in offices preparing for class. Researchers may spend time with athletes, coaches, trainers, and other individuals involved in sports and exercise. Hours may be long, and many psychologists work weekends. Psychologists who work directly with professional athletes or sports teams often travel with the athlete or team to competitions.

Earnings

Persons with a bachelor's degree are not psychologists, but could work as interns and may not receive a salary, or be in the starting range of $18,000 to $22,000. Jobs for individuals with a master's degree are few and only in subfields, such as assisting the full-degreed psychologist. Starting pay ranges from $28,000 to $32,000. Sports psychologists with a Ph.D. may reach salaries well into the six-figure range, depending on the expertise and experience.

What About You?

Does the career of sports psychologist interest you? Write an argument as to why this would be a good career for you or why this would not be a good career for you.

PHOTODISC/GETTY IMAGES

CHAPTER SUMMARY

7.1 Causes and Consequences of Stress

- Health psychologists study how people's thoughts and behavior affect their health.

- Stress is the response to events that disturb, or threaten to disturb, your physical or psychological balance.

- Stressors are internal or external events that challenge or threaten you.

- Three types of conflicts that can cause stress are the approach-approach conflict, the avoidance-avoidance conflict, and the approach-avoidance conflict.

- If something angers or frightens you, the sympathetic nervous system quickly prepares you for self-defense in what is called the fight-or-flight response.

- Hans Selye provided the insight into the body's reaction to stress. He referred to the stress response, and the resulting changes in the body, as the general adaptation syndrome (GAS). The three stages of GAS are alarm, resistance, and exhaustion.

- Stress responses often harm the physical body by weakening the immune system, which is the body's primary defense against disease. Stress-related physical illnesses, called psychophysiological disorders, can occur.

7.2 Individual Differences in Experiencing Stress

- Psychologist Richard Lazarus researched how people interpret and evaluate stressors in their lives, a process he called cognitive appraisal. He identified two stages in the cognitive appraisal process: primary appraisal and secondary appraisal.

- The two general coping strategies people use during secondary appraisal are problem-focused coping and emotion-focused coping.

- If you believe you have some control over a stressor, you usually feel less stressed. Life experiences play an important role in determining your level of confidence or feelings of helplessness.

- Personality affects stress levels. Type A personalities have more stress than Type B personalities.

- Individuals with a pessimistic explanatory style have more stress-related illnesses and depression than individuals with an optimistic explanatory style.

- An individual's culture can create stress through living conditions, moving to a new country, or adapting to a new cultural environment.

7.3 Lifestyle and Stress

- Having a social support network provides both psychological and physical benefits.

- Regular aerobic exercise, which is sustained exercise that increases heart and lung fitness, is necessary for good health.

- Relaxation, such as the progressive relaxation technique, is essential for reducing stress.

CHAPTER ASSESSMENT

Review Psychology Terms

Select the term that best fits the definition. Some terms will not be used.

_____ 1. A pattern of behaviors and emotions characterized by competitiveness, impatience, ambition, hostility, and a hard-driving approach to life

_____ 2. Your body's primary defense against disease

_____ 3. Response to events that disturb, or threaten to disturb, your physical or psychological balance

_____ 4. Consists of efforts to manage your emotional reactions to stressors

_____ 5. Selye's model of stress in which an event that threatens an organism's well-being (a stressor) leads to a three-stage bodily response: alarm, resistance, and exhaustion

_____ 6. Explains negative events in life as being caused by internal factors that are stable and global

_____ 7. Psychologists who study how people's thoughts and behavior affect their health

_____ 8. Sustained exercise that increases heart and lung fitness

_____ 9. Stress-related physical illnesses

_____ 10. A pattern of behaviors and emotions characterized by a patient, relaxed, easygoing approach to life, with little hurry or hostility

_____ 11. A relaxation technique that involves progressively relaxing muscle groups in your body, usually starting at the head and slowly moving down to the legs and feet

_____ 12. Internal or external events that challenge or threaten you

_____ 13. Explains negative events as due to external factors that are unstable or changeable and isolated

_____ 14. Helpful coping resources that friends and other people provide when you are in a stressful situation

_____ 15. A rapid physiological reaction by the sympathetic nervous system that prepares you either to fight or take flight from an immediate threat

_____ 16. A defeated and helpless state of mind produced by repeatedly failing to overcome challenges in your life

a. acculturative stress

b. aerobic exercise

c. conflict

d. emotion-focused coping

e. fight-or-flight response

f. general adaptation syndrome

g. health psychologists

h. immune system

i. learned helplessness

j. optimistic explanatory style

k. pessimistic explanatory style

l. problem-focused coping

m. progressive relaxation

n. psychophysiological disorders

o. social support

p. stress

q. stressors

r. Type A behavior pattern

s. Type B behavior pattern

Review Psychology Concepts

17. Describe problem-focused coping.

18. How does frustration cause stress?

19. What are three examples of stress that are a result of the hassles of contemporary life or from extraordinary circumstances?

20. Why might you be more prone to catch a cold during final exams?

21. Why is it important to understand cognitive appraisal?

22. Compare and contrast Type A and Type B personalities.

23. Identify your explanatory style and provide reasons why you think this is your explanatory style.

24. How does a strong social support network affect your immune system?

25. Name the three different types of conflict psychologists have identified that increase stress.

26. Name three ways aerobic exercise has a positive effect on physical health and two ways it affects mental health.

27. What is acculturative stress?

28. Why do many psychologists recommend relaxation training?

29. Describe the progressive relaxation technique.

Apply Psychology Concepts

30. Think about an event in your life that you considered highly stressful. Identify and describe your reactions based on Hans Selye's general adaptation syndrome. In doing so, how many of the stages in his GAS theory do you think you experienced?

31. Consider again the same stressful life event that you identified in exercise 30. Now analyze this event in terms of Richard Lazarus' process of cognitive appraisal. Describe how you engaged in both primary appraisal and secondary appraisal. What sort of problem-focused and emotion-focused strategies did you use in dealing with this stressor?

32. Based on your understanding of Type A and Type B behavior patterns, which do you think best fits your personality? Defend your analysis by identifying specific behavior patterns in your own life that fit one (or both) of these two personality styles.

33. Based on your responses to the Self-Discovery on page 199, do you think you have an optimistic or a pessimistic personality? Describe one event from your life that you think illustrates your optimistic or pessimistic personality. In doing so, make sure that you identify internal versus external, stable versus unstable, and global versus specific factors.

Make Academic Connections

34. **Writing** Write a paper that discusses how your cognitive appraisal of a situation can cause you stress. Cite at least one specific example from your life. Include information on Richard Lazarus' cognitive appraisal and explain your way of coping.

35. **Art** Design a chart that illustrates Selye's general adaptation syndrome. Include key ideas on the chart for all three stages: alarm, resistance, and exhaustion.

36. **Health** Use the library or Internet to find tips on stress management. Make a list of any tips that you or other students can use in your lives. Post the lists in the classroom.

37. **Research** Use the library or Internet to find research studies on the effects of stress on animals. Use reliable Web sources, such as educational or government sites. Write a fact sheet about your findings.

38. **Drama** Brainstorm with five other students on the types of situations that cause each of you stress. Make a list of the stressors, and then write a one-act play about the stressor and stress it causes. Use experiences high school students encounter to illustrate how stress can impair psychological functioning in such areas as work, school, and relationship. Your play can make fun of the stressor and stress or be a serious drama. Present your play to the class. As a class, choose a few of the plays to perform for other classes.

" I'm so stressed out!" We hear this all the time. Stress clearly is a component of our lives. Fortunately the human body has developed amazing—and complex—ways to deal with stress. Unfortunately some of the techniques can have a negative impact on our health. Author Eric Widmaier describes the stress mechanisms in animals and humans with key points of comparisons. Access the Gale Psychology eCollection at *www.cengage.com/school/psych/franzoi* and read Widmaier's discussion of stress and its effects on the human body. Write a brief summary of the article and answer the question: Do you agree that our ancestors lived a much more stressful existence than we do today? Why or why not? As an additional project, describe an instance when you experienced stress. How did you feel and what, if anything, did you do about it?

Source: Widmaier, Eric P. "So you think this is the "age of stress?" *Psychology Today*. 29n1 (Jan.–Feb. 1996): 41(3). Reprinted with permission from Psychology Today Magazine, Copyright (c) 1996 Sussec Publishers, LLC

SELF-DISCOVERY: YOUR SCORE

Do You Have a Type A Personality? (page 196)

Scoring Instructions: A score of 20–34 may mean low Type A behavior, 35–44 medium Type A behavior, and 45–60 high Type A behavior. **Your score:** _____

Are You an Optimist or a Pessimist? (page 199)

Scoring Instructions:

Step 1 For items 3, 7, and 9, subtract each score from the number 4.

Step 2 Add these corrected scores for items 3, 7, and 9, and record the total here.

Step 3 Add your scores for items 1, 4, and 10, and record the total score here.

Step 4 Add the totals from steps 2 and 3 to obtain your overall score, which will range from 0 to 40.

Interpretation: Lower scores indicate more pessimism, while higher scores indicate more optimism. In a sample of more than 2,000 young adults, the average score was 14. If your score is 10 or lower, this indicates that you tend to be more pessimistic than the average student. If your score is higher than 10 but lower than 19, this suggests that you tend to have the same level of optimism-pessimism as the average student. If your score is 19 or higher, this suggests that you tend to be more optimistic than the average student.

Your score: _____

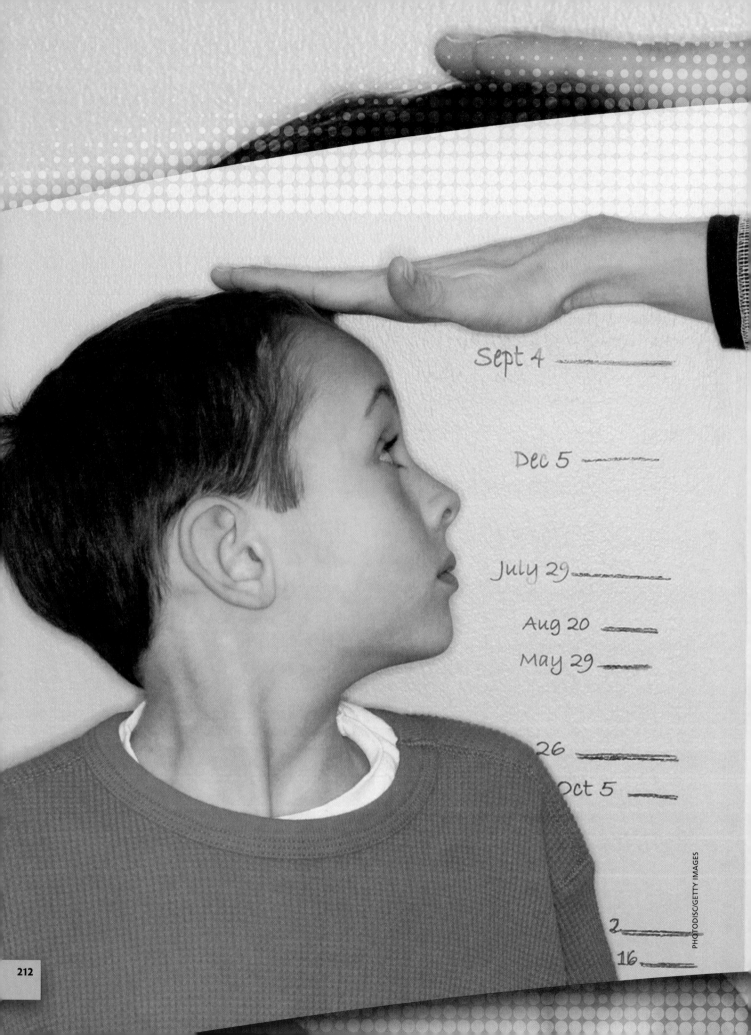

Sept 4 ———————

Dec 5 ———————

July 29 ———————

Aug 20 ——————

May 29 ———————

26 ———————

Oct 5 ———————

2 ———————

16 ———————

Developmental Domain

*I*f you look in the dictionary for the word "development" you will discover that it means to go through the process of natural growth. Development also means to make something clear by degrees. Before modern digital photography, you could observe the development of a photographic image as it sat in a chemical bath, slowly coming into focus before your eyes. Similarly, as a high school student approaching young adulthood, you are slowly coming into focus both in your own mind and in the minds of those who care about you. What will you become in life? How has the process of natural growth that you have experienced shaped you into what you are now and what you will become?

Unlike a photographic image which remains fixed and unchanging, your development will continue well beyond your high school years. Sometimes the image you have of yourself and the image that others have of you will be crystal clear, but it also may change to a fuzzy blur before coming back into focus. There will be times in your life when you and others will disagree on what is seen in this image of you. Yet the developmental process continues.

As a human being, you share a common process of natural growth with others. However, where you live and who lives with you will add certain unique qualities to your individual development. This uniqueness is your personality. In this unit you will learn about the process of development from birth to death and also about the uniqueness of you, the nature of your personality.

Infancy and Childhood

ESSENTIAL QUESTION
Go to page XXV

"Old age lives minutes slowly, hours quickly; childhood chews hours and swallows minutes."

—MALCOLM DE CHAZAL, MAURITIAN AUTHOR, 1902–1981

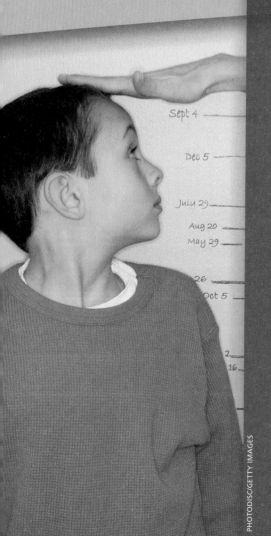

When in the fourth grade, I put almost all my weight on the front right leg of my desk, which balanced on top of a lump of coal. While our teacher, Mrs. Rahm, talked about math, science, and U.S. history, I pressed down on that black rock. Why? In a Superman comic, the Man of Steel took a piece of coal, squeezed it in his super hand for a few seconds, and transformed the coal into a valuable diamond. I knew I was no Superman, but I also knew I was only nine years old and had a lot of years left in me. If the Man of Steel could use his superhuman strength to turn a lump of coal into a diamond in only a few seconds, maybe I could do the same thing if I desk-pressured my coal from now until high school graduation. At the end of each school day, I pulled the coal out from under the desk leg, and carefully inspected the coal, looking for any signs of crystal growth.

I never saw the coal change. Yet, while that lump of coal stayed the same, I underwent many changes. Every child in that classroom changed and became something different during that school year. Some of these changes were caused by the mind pressure that Mrs. Rahm placed on us every school day. Other changes were due to peer pressure, parental pressure, and, yes, the biological pressure changing us from within. Unlike Superman's world, in the real world child development results from many forces working together.

- Identify and distinguish the three stages of prenatal development.
- Describe brain and body development and classify reflexes of the newborn.

DISCOVER IT | *How does this relate to me?*

Look at the period at the end of this sentence. That's approximately the size of all human beings shortly after conception. Compare that dot to your current size. How did such an incredible transformation take place? Don't look to Superman for an answer to this question.

- development
- prenatal development
- zygote
- embryo
- fetus
- fetal alcohol syndrome
- reflex

Your conception occurred when your mother's egg cell was united with your father's sperm cell. After conception, you begin to develop. **Development** involves the systematic physical, cognitive, and social changes that occur in a person between conception and death.

Prenatal Development

The many changes that transform a fertilized human egg into a newborn baby are known as **prenatal development**. Prenatal development can be divided into three stages: the *germinal stage,* the *embryonic stage,* and the *fetal stage.*

GERMINAL STAGE

When the sperm fertilizes the egg it forms a new cell called the **zygote**, which contains 46 chromosomes, or 23 pairs of chromosomes. Half of the genetic material comes from the father and half from the mother. The zygote travels down the fallopian tubes toward the uterus. Every 12 hours the zygote divides into a more complex multi-celled ball. On rare occasions, the zygote splits into two separate clusters that eventually become identical (monozygotic) twins. Fraternal (dizygotic) twins develop when two eggs are released by the ovaries and fertilized by different sperm cells. This *germinal stage* lasts two weeks, from conception until the zygote implants itself in the wall of the uterus.

development The systematic physical, cognitive, and social changes in the individual occurring between conception and death

prenatal development The many changes that transform a fertilized egg into a newborn baby

zygote A fertilized human egg during the first two weeks following conception

EMBRYONIC STAGE

The zygote that successfully embeds itself in the uterine wall is living tissue. It is an **embryo**. The *embryonic stage* lasts from the third week through the eighth week of prenatal development. During this stage, the head develops, and then the rest

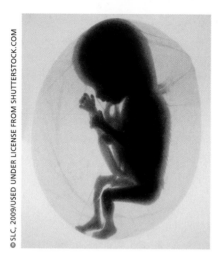

Facial features, fingers, and toes are visible eight weeks after conception.

© SLC, 2009/USED UNDER LICENSE FROM SHUTTERSTOCK.COM

of the body, followed by arms and legs, and then hands and feet. Between the fourth and eighth weeks, the gonads of genetically male embryos secrete the hormone testosterone, and this stimulates the development of male sex organs. Otherwise, the embryo develops into a female.

The embryo is vulnerable to harmful agents that the mother might be exposed to during this period of pregnancy because this is the time when major body systems are forming. Examples of such harmful agents are radiation, industrial chemicals, and a variety of drugs.

FETAL STAGE

From the ninth week after conception until birth, the developing human organism is considered a **fetus**. The *fetal stage* is the last and longest stage in prenatal development. In the third month, bones and muscles develop, and the fetus begins to move. By the seventh month, all the major organs are working and the fetus has a chance of surviving outside the womb, though not without high-tech medical intervention.

The mother is the only source of nutrition for the fetus, so her diet is extremely important to its health and development. Each year about 18 million women who are malnourished give birth to babies weighing less than five pounds. The vast majority of these infants (15 million) are born in South Asia and Africa. Low birth-weight babies often suffer from infections, weakened immune systems, learning disabilities, and poor physical development. In severe cases, the babies die shortly after birth.

One common drug that is dangerous to the fetus is alcohol. Studies find that even light drinking can harm the fetal brain. About 40 percent of women who drink large quantities of alcohol while pregnant give birth to babies with **fetal alcohol syndrome**, which is characterized by mental retardation and serious health problems. Children with fetal alcohol syndrome have facial deformities, such as a small head, a short nose, and widely spaced eyes. Medical experts recommend that expectant mothers drink no alcohol during pregnancy.

One of the most deadly diseases that harm the developing fetus is *acquired immune deficiency syndrome (AIDS)*. AIDS is the disease caused by the HIV virus. The HIV virus can be transmitted from the AIDS-infected mother to the fetus both before and during birth. AIDS also can be transmitted after birth through the mother's milk during breast-feeding. Of the 30 percent of babies who contract the HIV virus from their infected mothers, few live longer than three years unless treated with antiviral drugs.

embryo A developing human organism from the third week after fertilization through the eighth week

fetus The developing human organism from about nine weeks after fertilization to birth

fetal alcohol syndrome Physical and cognitive abnormalities in children that result when pregnant women consume large quantities of alcohol

What are the three stages of prenatal development?

Brain and Body Development

A newborn's birth marks the end of prenatal development. At birth 95 percent of infants weigh between 5.5 and 10 pounds and are 18 to 22 inches in length. Most people consider newborns to be pretty small packages of life, but they are growing machines! In this section you will examine the amazing growth and transformations that take place in the brain and the rest of the body, as well as the development of motor skills.

In studying the changes that occur in development, psychologists rely on two special research designs. In *longitudinal research,* the same people are studied over a long period of time. For example, a longitudinal study examining childhood physical development would test and retest the same children throughout their childhood years, recording their physical changes. In *cross-sectional research,* people of different ages are compared with one another. A cross-sectional study of childhood physical development would test children of different ages at the same time and then compare their physical differences. As you see, both research designs study changes related to development, but they investigate these changes differently.

BRAIN DEVELOPMENT

The basic unit of the nervous system is the neuron, or brain cell (Chapter 3). You might be surprised to learn that when you were a six-month-old fetus, you had more than twice as many neurons in your brain as you do now. At that time, your brain was producing hundreds of thousands of new neurons per minute.

Figure 8-1 NEURAL NETWORK GROWTH DURING INFANCY

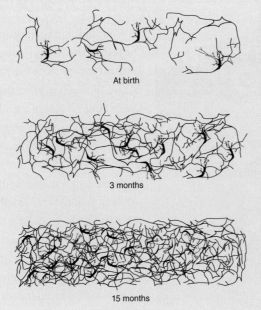

At birth

3 months

15 months

As you mature, you may lose underused brain cells, but the neural connections between well-used brain cells become increasingly complex. This drawing depicts an infant's cerebral cortex sections during the first 15 months of life.

INTERACTIVE FIGURE

During that same time before birth your brain began pruning itself of many of these neurons. This process of neural pruning continued during infancy and early childhood. Each sight, sound, and touch you experienced activated and strengthened specific neurons and their connections. Other neurons that were not regularly activated grew weak and died (see Figure 8-1 on page 217). This use-it-or-lose-it principle in brain development operates throughout life, even in advanced age. This brain "sculpting" also occurs among other animals, including insects.

Although the young brain prunes itself of unnecessary neurons, the brain actually increases its weight from three-quarters of a pound at birth to about two-and-a-third pounds by age four. Most of this added mass is due to (1) the growth of new dendrites that increase the connections between neurons, and (2) the growth of the protective coating of fatty cells—known as the *myelin sheath*—around neural axons. By age five, your brain has reached 90 percent of its adult weight. The rest of your body is only at 20 percent of what it will weigh as an adult. The reason the brain grows more quickly than the rest of the body is that the brain plays a major role in coordinating both physical development and development of the senses.

Brain development occurs in stages. It starts from the back of the brain and moves to the front. During the first few months of infancy, the cerebellum area at the back of the brain (the hindbrain) is developing the most. The cerebellum is important in regulating and coordinating basic motor activities such as sucking and swallowing.

Between six and eight months of age, the temporal lobes of the cerebral cortex (located on the brain's right and left sides) rapidly develop and prepare you to learn languages. In late adolescence, your frontal cortex begins to fully mature. This maturing allows you to think in abstract ways, which is crucial for complex scientific and moral reasoning.

While learning to ride a bicycle, which skills is this child developing? In which direction do these skills develop, from the head to the trunk and legs or from the trunk and legs to the head?

PHOTODISC/GETTY IMAGES

PHYSICAL GROWTH AND MOTOR DEVELOPMENT

Although the brain grows faster than the rest of the body, infant body growth is by no means slow. During the first year of life, the body almost triples in weight (from about 7 pounds to 20 pounds) and increases in length by about one-third (from about 20 inches to 29 inches). After this surge, the rate of childhood growth slows to about 2 to 3 inches and 4 to 7 pounds per year. Middle childhood, which spans the ages five to eight, is a time when bones continue to grow and harden, and muscles grow in strength. The height of a child is determined largely by heredity.

Motor development occurs along with physical growth. Basic motor skills develop from the head to the trunk and legs. As shown in Figure 8-2, infants in North America typically follow the same developmental pattern. This pattern is the same in many other cultures, but variations do occur. For example, at ten months of age—North American infants are beginning to learn how to stand alone, but Ugandan infants are walking. One explanation for this cultural difference is that, in Uganda, babies are carried upright on their mother's backs. This helps to develop their trunk and leg muscles at a faster rate.

Figure 8-2 MOTOR DEVELOPMENT

Holds up chin, then chest

Rolls over

Sits with support

Sits without support

Stands holding on

Pulls self to stand

Stands well alone

Walks well alone

0 1 2 3 4 5 6 7 8 9 10 11 12 13 14 15
Age (Months)

This chart identifies the ages at which the average child in North American culture develops different motor skills. This same developmental sequence is found in many cultures around the world, but cultural differences do exist.

REFLEXES

As a newborn, you enter the world with a number of reflexes. A **reflex** is an automatic body response to a stimulus that is involuntary. In other words, you have no control over this response. At birth, reflexes are your only physical abilities.

Some reflexes are called *survival reflexes* because they are essential for survival. Examples of survival reflexes are the eye-blink reflex—which protects you from bright lights and foreign objects, and the sucking reflex—which allows you to receive necessary nourishment. Many survival reflexes—such as the eye-blink and breathing reflexes—are permanent.

Other reflexes are known as *primitive reflexes* because they appear and disappear in an expected order during infant development. The swimming reflex, which is an active movement of the arms and legs and an involuntary holding of the breath when

reflex An automatic body response to a stimulus that is involuntary

immersed in water, is an example of a primitive reflex. Primitive reflexes disappear when the frontal lobes of the brain stop these automatic responses from occurring. If a primitive reflex does not disappear when expected, this may indicate a problem with the infant's central nervous system. Table 8-1 lists some reflexes that are easily observed in healthy newborns.

Table 8-1 REFLEXES OF THE NEWBORN BABY

Reflexes	Developmental Course	Significance
Survival Reflexes		
Breathing reflex	Permanent	Provides oxygen and expels carbon dioxide
Eye-blink reflex	Permanent	Protects eyes from bright lights and foreign objects
Pupillary reflex (constriction and dilation of pupils due to the amount of light)	Permanent	Protects eyes from bright lights and adapts vision to darkness
Rooting reflex (turning of cheek in direction of a touch in search of something to suckle)	Gradually weakens during the first six months of life	Orients child to mother's breast for nourishment
Sucking reflex (sucking on anything placed in the mouth)	Gradually modified by experience	Allows child to receive nourishment
Swallowing reflex	Permanent, but modified by experience	Allows child to receive nourishment and protects against choking
Primitive Reflexes		
Babinski reflex (spreading outward and then inward of toes)	Disappears within the first year of life	Presence at birth and later disappearance indicate normal neurological development
Grasping reflex (curling of fingers around objects that touch the palm)	Disappears by fourth month of life	Presence at birth and later disappearance indicate normal neurological development
Moro or "startle" reflex (throwing arms out and arching of back due to loud noise or sudden movement of baby's head)	Disappears by seventh month of life, but is replaced by adult startle reflex	Presence at birth and later disappearance indicate normal neurological development
Swimming reflex (active movement of arms and legs and involuntarily holding of breath when immersed in water)	Disappears by sixth month of life	Presence at birth and later disappearance indicate normal neurological development
Stepping reflex (walking movements when held upright so that feet just touch the ground)	Disappears by second month of life	Presence at birth and later disappearance indicate normal neurological development

 CHECKPOINT *What is a reflex?*

In Your Own Words

Identify and explain the importance of the three stages of prenatal development.

Review Concepts

1. Which refers to many changes that transform a fertilized egg into a newborn baby?
   - a. embryo
   - b. reflex
   - c. zygote
   - d. prenatal development

2. Which refers to a developing human organism from the third week after fertilization through the eighth week?
   - a. fetus
   - b. embryo
   - c. gene-cell
   - d. zygote

3. Which is a survival reflex?
   - a. breathing
   - b. startle
   - c. Babinski
   - d. grasping

4. Which is a primitive reflex?
   - a. swallowing
   - b. rooting
   - c. eye-blink
   - d. stepping

5. **True or False** At six months of age, you had more neurons in your brain than you do now.

6. **True or False** Identical twins are developed when the zygote splits into two separate clusters.

7. **True or False** The embryonic stage is the last and longest stage in prenatal development.

8. **True or False** In prenatal development, the brain grows faster than the rest of the body.

9. **True or False** Newborns enter the world with a number of survival reflexes that last throughout life.

10. **True or False** The cerebellum is the first part of the brain to develop during the first few months of infancy.

Think Critically

11. Why do pregnant women need to avoid alcohol?

12. What might the consequences be of a baby born without a sucking reflex?

13. What markers can you use to determine if a baby is developing normally?

14. Why is a mother's diet important to the fetus?

15. Why is using your brain important to brain development?

KEY TERMS

- attachment
- self-concept
- socialization
- self-awareness
- self-esteem
- authoritative parents
- authoritarian parents
- permissive parents
- gender identity

OBJECTIVES

- Analyze attachment.
- Discuss self-awareness and self-concept development.
- Explain Erikson's theory of psychosocial development.

DISCOVER IT | *How does this relate to me?*

Do you think that you are a person of worth who is valued by other people? Do you believe other people are trustworthy? Do you have family members and friends you can depend on when you need help? Your answers to these questions have been shaped by your experiences with your parents and other family members, as well as your friends and teachers. Your answers to these questions play a role in determining whether you are happy and satisfied with your life.

Physical and motor development are important to survival, but there is more to development than biology. In this section, you will learn about some of the social and cultural forces that shaped you into who you are today, beginning with the emotional attachment you develop with your parents and other caregivers. Your social development in infancy and childhood has a strong influence on how you currently live your life. It serves as the foundation for the basic understanding of yourself and the social world in which you live.

Attachment

Attachment is the strong emotional bond young children form with their parents or primary caregivers. Attachment is considered to be the cornerstone for all other relationships in children's lives. This bond is not unique to humans. It can be observed in most species of birds and mammals.

THE DEVELOPMENT OF ATTACHMENT

Newborn humans are equipped with a number of attachment behaviors, such as smiling, cooing, and clinging, that most adults naturally respond to with care and attention. Newborn babies' attachment behaviors are not directed toward a specific

attachment The strong emotional bond young children form with their parents or primary caregivers

person, so babies will coo, smile, and cling to strangers as well as to their primary caregiver. Babies even engage in these same behaviors with objects such as a ball or a lampshade. These behaviors, or *bonding signals*, decrease in frequency if an adult does not respond. Infants' initial attachment bond usually is with their mothers because mothers provide most of the early care.

Harry and Margaret Harlow (1962) studied attachment in rhesus monkeys. The Harlows constructed two surrogate (artificial) monkey "mothers." One of the surrogates was a bare wire-mesh cylinder with a wooden head. The other was covered in a soft terry cloth and had a more monkeylike head (see photo on this page). Both surrogate mothers were placed in the same cage as the infant. Half of the infant monkeys were fed by the wire mother and the other half were fed by the cloth mother. Regardless of where their food came from, all the infants spent more time clinging to the cloth mother, and they went to the cloth mother when they were frightened or upset.

These findings suggest that an infant monkey's attachment to its mother is due to the mother's ability to satisfy the infant's need for *contact comfort*—direct contact with soft objects—and less to the mother's ability to satisfy the infant's physical needs. This study also explains human behavior. Human infants and toddlers have the same attachment to adults as do the rhesus monkeys, so children enjoy being held and stroked. Children also enjoy holding or stroking soft objects, such as a favorite blanket. This is especially true when they are anxious or tired.

Mary Ainsworth studied attachment in children. She found that between the ages of three and six months, infants show a clear preference for their primary caregivers but do not become upset when separated from them. In contrast, between seven and nine months, children form an attachment bond toward a specific caregiver and usually become upset following separation. The fear and distress that infants display when separated from their primary caregiver is known as *separation anxiety*. Separation anxiety lasts until children are two or three years old. At six or seven months of age, children develop *stranger anxiety,* or a fear of strangers. Stranger anxiety disappears during the second year.

HARLOW PRIMATE LABORATORY, UNIVERSITY OF WISCONSIN-MADISON

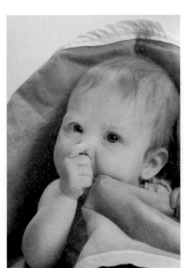

© BRONWYN PHOTO, 2009/USED UNDER LICENSE FROM SHUTTERSTOCK.COM

The need for contact comfort is found in many species, including monkeys and humans.

SECURE AND INSECURE ATTACHMENT STYLES

Children with parents who are nurturing and sensitive to their needs tend to develop a *secure attachment style*. Securely attached children view themselves as being worthy of others' love. They believe that people are trustworthy and will care for them. In contrast, children with parents who are not attentive to their needs tend to develop an *insecure attachment style*. These insecurely attached children view themselves as being unworthy of other people's love. They believe that others cannot be relied upon to care for them.

Attachment style remains fairly unchanged throughout childhood unless the family experiences a major disruption, such as divorce, illness, or death. About 65 percent of children in the United States are securely attached. The remaining 35 percent have an insecure attachment style. Infants who are securely attached tend to mature into popular, independent, and self-assured children. In contrast, insecurely attached infants tend to become children who lack curiosity, perform poorly in school, and are emotionally withdrawn. The research suggests that children with a secure attachment style have an understanding of themselves ("I am a good person") and their relationship with others ("People can be trusted"). This makes it easier for them to form satisfying social attachments with many different people. Forming satisfying social attachments is harder for individuals who have an insecure attachment style.

One factor that influences the quality of the parent-child attachment is the inborn temperament of the newborn. Infants with an *easygoing temperament* generally react positively to new situations or things such as food, people, or toys. In contrast, newborns with a *difficult temperament* react to these situations by crying or fussing. Temperament appears to be significantly shaped by inherited biological factors. In turn, temperament appears to partly influence the quality of parent-child attachment. Infants who develop a secure attachment style tend to be naturally easygoing, while those who develop an insecure attachment style are more likely to be difficult at birth. Figure 8-3 summarizes some of the possible causes of children's attachment style. The Closer Look feature on page 225 discusses how culture can influence attachment style.

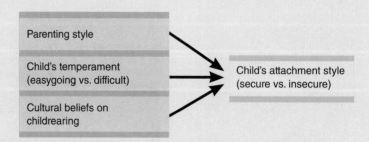

Figure 8-3 **POSSIBLE CAUSES OF CHILDREN'S ATTACHMENT STYLE**

Whether children develop a secure or an insecure attachment style is determined by a variety of factors, including parenting style, children's temperament, and cultural beliefs on childrearing.

Parenting style

Child's temperament (easygoing vs. difficult)

Cultural beliefs on childrearing

Child's attachment style (secure vs. insecure)

Culture and Attachment Style

Culture can significantly shape the attachment style of children. For example, psychologists have discovered that both U.S. and German children are far more likely than Japanese children to develop a type of insecure attachment style characterized by avoiding intimacy with parents. These cultural differences in attachment probably are due partly to different views on how to raise children. Parents in the United States and Germany have grown up in an individualist culture. Individualist cultures try to foster independence at an early age in children. For example, U.S. and German parents often discourage their children from staying near them and are more likely to give them toys or food when they cry rather than picking them up. This sort of parenting style is likely to lead to greater independence and somewhat weaker emotional dependence on parents. In contrast, Japanese parents have grown up in a collectivist culture. Because collectivist cultures do not place a high value on independence, Japanese parents rarely leave their children alone and quickly pick them up when they cry. This sort of parenting style is likely to result in children being more conforming and emotionally dependent on their parents.

Think Critically

What are your family's cultural beliefs about raising a happy, healthy child? Give examples of how these beliefs affected you as you were growing up.

CHECKPOINT *What is attachment?*

Self-Awareness and Self-Concept Development

The primary social achievement of childhood is self-concept. **Self-concept** is the theory, or story, you form about yourself. Your story comes from your life experiences and interactions with others. For example, children's beliefs about themselves—such as being creative, smart, shy, or outgoing—and their ideas about themselves (as a daughter or son, student, and friend) are part of their self-concept. The process of learning about yourself and your culture and how to live within your world is called **socialization**.

self-concept The theory or story that you form about yourself through your life experiences and interactions with others

socialization The process of learning about yourself and your culture and how to live within it

SELF-AWARENESS

Before you develop a self-concept, you must develop self-awareness. Think about your most satisfying and least satisfying personal qualities. This is **self-awareness**, a state of mind where you think about yourself. When you recognize your reflection in a mirror, you are engaging in self-awareness.

You are not born with self-awareness. You develop it in early childhood as your brain matures and you socialize with others. Psychologists discovered this fact by placing a red spot on babies' noses and then placing the babies in front of a mirror. If the babies reached for or wiped their noses rather than the nose of the mirror image it meant they recognized the image as being theirs.

Infants between 9 and 12 months treat their mirror image as if it were another child, showing no interest in the unusual red spot. Children around 18 months showed self-recognition—self-awareness—by consistently staring into the mirror and touching the mysterious spot on their own noses, not the ones in the mirror. Based on such studies, self-awareness develops at about 18 months of age.

PARENTAL AND CULTURAL INFLUENCES ON SELF-CONCEPT

Once children develop self-awareness, they begin to develop a self-concept. Your self-concept consists of beliefs about yourself and numerous evaluations of yourself as being good, bad, or mediocre. This evaluation of your self-concept is called **self-esteem**. A number of studies find that children with positive self-esteem are happier and more optimistic than those with negative self-esteem.

Parenting Styles Parents have a significant influence on their children's self-concepts. Children with positive self-esteem and self-confidence tend to have parents who are authoritative in their parenting style. **Authoritative parents** set rules for their children and consistently enforce those rules. Yet within those rules, parents allow

children a fair amount of freedom, and they discuss the reasons behind their rules and decisions. This parenting style teaches children there are guidelines for behavior and consequences for breaking rules. These are two very important lessons in growing up. This parenting style allows children to exercise their own initiative and judgment within the family's guidelines. Developing confidence in your own judgment is a personal achievement that provides important benefits throughout life.

In contrast to this type of positive parenting, there are two other parenting styles that are associated with much lower levels of self-esteem and self-confidence in children. **Authoritarian parents** impose rules, demand strict obedience, and harshly punish their children for breaking rules

---

self-awareness A state of mind where you think about yourself

self-esteem The evaluation of your self-concept as being good, bad, or mediocre

authoritative parents Parents who set rules for proper conduct for their children, consistently enforce those rules, yet allow their children a fair amount of freedom

authoritarian parents Parents who impose many rules, demand strict obedience, and harshly punish their children for rule breaking or even questioning their decisions

Authoritative parents set rules for their children but allow their children to make their own judgments within those rules. This parenting style fosters self-confidence in children.

© MONKEY BUSINESS IMAGES, 2009/USED UNDER LICENSE FROM SHUTTERSTOCK.COM

or questioning the parents' decisions. By demanding unquestioning obedience, authoritarian parents smother their children's initiative and judgment.

Instead of demanding strict obedience to rules, **permissive parents** teach their children that adult rules are unimportant. Permissive parents allow their children to set their own rules, make few demands, and submit to their children's desires. By ignoring the fact that children often need to receive direction and guidance from adults, permissive parents produce children who often lack the self-discipline to achieve goals in their lives. The failures resulting from this lack of self-discipline undermines these children's self-confidence and self-esteem.

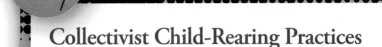

permissive parents
Parents who allow their children to set their own rules, make few demands, and submit to their children's desires

Cultural Differences in Individualism and Collectivism
In developing a self-concept, your culture influences the beliefs that you form about yourself. As you read in earlier chapters, the United States emphasizes individualism, while many Asian, African, and Central and South American cultures emphasize collectivism. Psychologists have discovered that these different cultural beliefs lead to differences in the way children are socialized.

LAB TEAMS

Collectivist Child-Rearing Practices

With a partner, use the Internet or library to research either a children's book or an article about children that illustrates or explains the child-rearing practices of a collectivist society. List the values and cite examples from the book or article that identify these practices. Share your findings with other pairs of students.

Within collectivist societies, child-rearing practices emphasize being obedient and knowing your proper place. In China, for example, parents and teachers focus on shaping children's personalities to best meet family and society needs. The stories told to children and the books children read often stress fulfilling group goals, doing one's duty, and bringing pride to one's family rather than to one's self. Consistent with this upbringing, when asked to describe their self-concepts, people from collectivist cultures often list their *social roles,* such as the role of son, daughter, student, or employee.

In contrast to collectivist teachings, individualist societies encourage independence and self-reliance. As a result, children develop a belief in their own uniqueness and diversity. A book that illustrates how individualist cultures socialize children to value independence and uniqueness is *The Tale of Despereaux* by Kate DiCamillo. The main character is a mouse named Despereaux. When brought before the Mouse Council for not acting like all the other mice, he refuses to change and is banished to the dungeon. After many hardships, Despereaux uses his unique skills and independent nature to save the human princess from the collective rats. For this, Despereaux earns glory, fame, and friendship. Such stories teach children that being independent and different from others is valued. As a result of such learning, when individualists describe their self-concepts, they often identify themselves in terms of personal attributes that set them apart from other people.

How do you define yourself? Do you think your culture has shaped your self-concept? Before reading further, complete the Self-Discovery exercise on page 228.

In The Tale of Despereaux, *one mouse doesn't behave like all the other mice, and his unique behavior makes him a hero. How does this story reflect individualist values?*

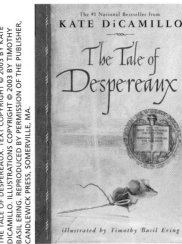

THE TALE OF DESPEREAUX. TEXT COPYRIGHT © 2003 BY KATE DiCAMILLO. ILLUSTRATIONS COPYRIGHT © 2003 BY TIMOTHY BASIL ERING. REPRODUCED BY PERMISSION OF THE PUBLISHER, CANDLEWICK PRESS, SOMERVILLE, MA.

Who Am I?

Take out a sheet of paper and write the numbers 1–20 down the left column of the page. After each number, write the words "I am." After "I am," write 20 different responses to the question "Who Am I?" Respond as if you were giving the answers to yourself, not to someone else. When finished, evaluate your responses by coding each of them into one of the following four categories (Warning: Do not think about these categories when writing your responses):

1. *Physical self-descriptions* This is where you identify yourself in terms of physical qualities that do not imply social interaction (for example, "I am a male"; "I am a brunette").

2. *Social self-descriptions* This is where you identify yourself in terms of social roles, institutional memberships, or other socially defined statuses (for example, "I am a student"; "I am a daughter or son").

3. *Attributive self-descriptions* This is where you identify yourself in terms of psychological/physiological states or traits (for example, "I am intelligent"; "I am assertive"; "I am boring").

4. *Global self-descriptions* This is where you identify yourself in a manner that is so comprehensive or vague that it doesn't distinguish you from any other person (for example, "I am a human being"; "I am alive"; "I am me").

Think Critically

Which category occurs most frequently for you? Cross-cultural research finds that people in individualist cultures write more attributive self-descriptions, which highlight their differences with other people. In contrast, people in collectivist cultures write more social self-descriptions, which highlight their connections to their social groups. Why might this be so?

Gender Socialization An important aspect of childhood socialization is learning about gender. *Gender* refers to the meanings that a society and the people within it attach to being female and male. In teaching children about gender, adults rely upon what worked for them. For women, it may be memories of playing with Barbie dolls or tea sets. For men, images of rough-and-tumble football or skateboarding may come to mind. Parents often treat their sons and daughters differently based on the parents' beliefs about gender.

How are children's self-concepts shaped by gender? Shortly after developing self-awareness—by the age of 2—children begin developing an understanding of themselves as being either a boy or a girl. This is called **gender identity**, and it is one of the basic elements in self-concept. Once children identify with being a girl or boy, they learn to identify objects, activities, games, careers, and even personality traits as being either natural or unnatural for their gender.

In some societies, gender expectations are clearly defined and rigidly enforced. In other societies, such as in the United States, there are many shared expectations for boys and girls. For example, both genders are expected to perform well in

gender identity The knowledge that you are a male or a female

school and in many of the same occupations. Yet many Americans expect girls and boys to be different. Children adopt these gender expectations. In learning the "right way" to think about gender, children often segregate themselves into boy and girl playgroups and adopt gender beliefs. During later elementary years, children's way of responding to gender expectations declines as they become aware of nontraditional gender views.

CHECKPOINT *What is self-concept?*

Erikson's Theory of Psychosocial Development

Erik Erikson (1902–1994) believed that people's social development occurs in eight identifiable stages. Each stage is marked by a crisis or conflict related to a specific developmental task. The more successfully people overcome these eight crises, the better chance they have to develop in a healthy way. Table 8-2 on page 230 summarizes the stages of Erikson's theory of psychosocial development. In this chapter you will learn about the first four stages. The remaining stages are covered in Chapters 9 and 10 of this textbook.

The crisis in the first stage is developing a sense of *trust versus mistrust.* This corresponds to attachment and occurs during the first year of life. Trust is established when an infant's needs for comfort, food, and warmth are met. If these needs are not met, the infant develops a mistrust of others.

The second crisis, *autonomy versus shame and doubt,* occurs during the second year of life. In this stage, toddlers attempt to control their actions and act independently. If successful, they develop a feeling of confidence and a sense of autonomy, or independence. If they fail to behave independently or are prevented from behaving so, they may experience shame and doubt their own abilities.

Between the ages of three and five (the preschool years), children struggle with *initiative versus guilt.* This third stage of development deals with learning how to develop plans, set goals, and attain the goals without breaking rules of behavior. Children's *initiative*—the ability to act independently—is increased if they can successfully get what they want while acting responsibly. Trouble arises when initiative and guilt are not balanced. If children's impulses are not adequately kept in check by a sense of guilt over breaking rules—common in permissive parenting—children become undisciplined. If children are made to feel overly guilty—common in authoritarian parenting—this inhibits their initiative.

Between the ages of 6 and 12, children face the crisis of *competence versus inferiority.* They attempt to gain the knowledge and intellectual skills needed for adult life. Children who

TIME & LIFE PICTURES/GETTY IMAGES

Erik Erikson's theory of social development covers the entire life span.

successfully overcome this crisis develop a sense of competence and achievement. Those who do poorly feel inferior and develop low self-esteem. In Chapters 9 and 10, you will read more about Erikson's theory for older age groups.

One of the primary strengths of Erikson's theory is the ability to draw connections between important psychosocial developments throughout a person's life. As predicted by Erikson's theory and confirmed by attachment researchers, failing to develop a sense of trust with parents early in life has a harmful effect on an individual's ability to develop satisfying social relationships in childhood and adulthood. However, psychologists have discovered that the need for independence in early childhood is a dilemma that is most common in individualist cultures such as the United States. In collectivist cultures, young children are not as likely to be encouraged to seek independence.

Table 8-2   ERIKSON'S STAGES OF PSYCHOSOCIAL DEVELOPMENT

Identity Stage	Crisis	Description of Crisis
Infancy (birth–1 year)	Trust vs. mistrust	If basic needs are met, infants develop a sense of trust. If these needs are not satisfied adequately, infants develop a mistrust of others.
Toddlerhood (1–2 years)	Autonomy vs. shame and doubt	If toddlers can control their own actions and act independently, they develop a sense of autonomy. If they fail, they experience shame and doubt their own abilities.
Preschooler (3–5 years)	Initiative vs. guilt	If preschoolers get what they want while acting responsibly, they develop a sense of initiative. If their impulses are not kept in check by a sense of guilt, they become undisciplined. If they are made to feel overly guilty, this will inhibit their initiative.
Elementary school (6–12 years)	Competence vs. inferiority	If children master the knowledge and skills necessary for adult life, they develop a sense of competence. If they are unable to achieve competence, they feel inferior and develop low self-esteem.
Adolescence (13–18 years)	Identity vs. role confusion	If teenagers successfully experiment with different roles, they develop a sense of personal identity. If they fail to develop their own personal identity, they become confused about who they are.
Young adulthood (19–45 years)	Intimacy vs. isolation	If young adults successfully develop close relationships, they gain a sense of intimacy. If they are unable to develop such relationships, they feel socially isolated.
Middle adulthood (46–65 years)	Generativity vs. stagnation	If the middle-aged believe that they are contributing to the world and the next generation, they develop a sense of generativity. If they fail to do so, they experience a sense of stagnation.
Late adulthood (66 years and up)	Integrity vs. despair	If the elderly have successfully managed the previous crises in their lives, they will feel a sense of integrity. If they regret many of their life choices, they will feel a sense of despair.

CHECK**POINT**   *What are the four crises of infancy and childhood?*

In Your Own Words

Compare and contrast the three types of parenting styles. Cite examples from your life. For example, you might say that your parents are authoritarian because they expect you to spend two hours every day studying, even if you do not have two hours of homework. If you fail to study for two hours every day, you lose privileges, such as not being allowed to go to the movies with your friends on a Saturday evening.

Review Concepts

1. Which refers to knowing you are male or female?
   - a. socialization
   - b. self-awareness
   - c. gender identity
   - d. self-concept

2. Which refers to the strong emotional bond young children form with their parents or primary caregivers?
   - a. self-concept
   - b. gender identity
   - c. permissive parents
   - d. attachment

3. Which refers to the process of learning about yourself and your culture and how to live within it?
   - a. attachment
   - b. socialization
   - c. self-concept
   - d. self-awareness

4. In which stage of Erikson's stages of psychosocial development does an individual meet the crisis of initiative versus guilt?
   - a. infancy
   - b. toddlerhood
   - c. preschooler
   - d. elementary school

5. **True or False** Attachment is the strong bond young children form with their toys before bonding with their primary caregiver.

6. **True or False** Authoritative parents set rules for proper conduct for their children, consistently enforce those rules, yet allow their children a fair amount of freedom.

7. **True or False** A primary strength of Erikson's theory is the ability to draw connections between important psychosocial developments throughout a person's life.

8. **True or False** A newborn's temperament appears to be significantly shaped by inherited biological factors.

Think Critically

9. How does your self-concept affect your self-esteem?

10. Why might studies find that children with positive self-esteem are happier and more optimistic than those with negative self-esteem?

11. Which type of parenting style is ideal? Explain your answer.

KEY TERMS

- cognition
- schema
- assimilation
- accommodation
- object permanence
- representational thought
- egocentrism
- conservation
- theory of mind

OBJECTIVES

- Explain cognitive development and differentiate between assimilation and accommodation.
- Discuss the first four stages of Piaget's cognitive development theory.

DISCOVER IT | *How does this relate to me?*

Have you ever noticed that young babies don't know how to play peek-a-boo, but slightly older babies really enjoy this game? Or have you noticed that five-year-olds think they are drinking more juice or milk when it is in a tall glass rather than a wide glass? You are witnessing infants and children engaging in different ways of thinking in line with their stage of development. You once thought in similar ways, but now your thinking has matured. In this lesson, you will learn how your thinking has developed as you have matured.

cognition The mental activity of knowing and the process by which knowledge is acquired and problems are solved

schema An organized cluster of knowledge that you use to understand and interpret information

Jean Piaget tested children's problem-solving skills.

ARCHIVES OF THE HISTORY OF AMERICAN PSYCHOLOGY-THE UNIVERSITY OF AKRON

Playing peek-a-boo and other games involve thinking, or cognition. **Cognition** is the mental activity of knowing and the process by which knowledge is acquired and problems are solved. How does cognition, or thinking, emerge and develop in the mind of a child? In this lesson, you will read about the cognitive development theory of Jean Piaget, a psychologist who pioneered studies that have had an important influence on developmental psychology.

Cognitive Development

In the 1930s, Swiss psychologist Jean Piaget (1896–1980) tested children's problem-solving skills. Piaget argued that children's thinking is an active process. Instead of waiting for adults to teach them, children actively try to solve problems. His view differed from the then current idea that children were mental lumps of clay shaped by parents, teachers, and others.

Piaget described cognitive development as something children achieve by organizing their knowledge of the world into schemas. A **schema** is an organized cluster of knowledge that you use to understand and interpret information. For example, when teaching my daughters how to play catch, I had them hold out their arms about six inches apart and then gently tossed them a stuffed bear. When it landed on their arms, they pulled it to their chests—mission accomplished. By repeating this activity, they developed a schema for catching.

In using schemas, you acquire knowledge through the two processes that work together—assimilation and accommodation. **Assimilation** is the process of absorbing new information into existing schemas. **Accommodation** is the process of changing existing schemas in order to absorb new information.

Once my daughters learned how to catch a stuffed bear, I threw other things to them: a beach ball, a pillow, a ping-pong ball. For the beach ball and pillow, they used their bear-catching schema, so they engaged in assimilation. Trying to assimilate the ping-pong ball into the bear-catching schema didn't work. They accommodated by using their hands more than their arms to cradle the smaller object.

Throughout life, the major dilemma in learning and problem solving is whether you assimilate new information into existing schemas or change those knowledge structures so that the new information can be better handled and understood. Generally, people first try to assimilate. If that fails, they accommodate their schemas in an attempt to deal with the situation.

©EDUARD TITOV, 2009/ USED UNDER LICENSE FROM SHUTTERSTOCK.COM

Children use assimilation and accommodation in developing a schema for catching a ball.

 **CHECKPOINT** *Why is cognitive development considered an active process?*

Stages of Cognitive Development

Besides proposing that children were active in their cognitive development, Piaget argued that children are not little adults who simply know less. He stated that children think about the world differently than adults do. Piaget came to this conclusion after noticing that children of different ages made different kinds of mistakes while solving problems. He concluded that as children mature, they move through four different cognitive stages. Children think differently in each stage, and each stage builds on the previous stages.

SENSORIMOTOR STAGE

As you can see from Table 8-3 on page 234, the first stage in Piaget's theory of cognitive development is the *sensorimotor stage* (birth to age 2). This is the stage in which infants develop the ability to coordinate sensory input with motor actions.

A major accomplishment at this stage is the development of **object permanence**, the realization that an object exists even if you can't see or touch it. For infants who lack object permanence, out of sight is out of mind. Babies who cry when their mothers leave are demonstrating they have object permanence. They know she exists when she is out of sight, and this knowledge creates anxiety. One quick and easy way to determine whether infants have an understanding of object permanence is by playing the game peek-a-boo. If babies wait for your face to

assimilation The process of absorbing new information into existing schemas

accommodation The process of changing existing schemas in order to absorb new information

object permanence The realization that an object continues to exist even if you can't see it or touch it

emerge from behind your hands, out of sight is not out of mind for them. They are able to keep a mental image of you in their minds.

Table 8-3 PIAGET'S STAGES OF COGNITIVE DEVELOPMENT

Typical Age Range	Description of Stage	Developmental Phenomena
Birth–2 years	Sensorimotor—Experiencing the world through actions (grasping, looking, touching, and sucking)	• Object permanence • Stranger anxiety
2–6 years	Preoperational—Representing things with words and images but no logical reasoning	• Pretend play • Egocentrism • Language
7–11 years	Concrete operational—Thinking logically about concrete events; understanding concrete analogies and performing arithmetical operations	• Conservation • Mathematical transformations
11 years through adulthood	Formal operational—Using abstract reasoning	• Abstract logic

Piaget stated that object permanence is the beginning of **representational thought**, which is the ability to picture (or represent) something in your mind, even when it is not physically present. When children create mental images they use symbols. As they grow, they use the more complex symbols of language.

PREOPERATIONAL STAGE

Between the ages of two to six is the *preoperational stage*. At this stage, children think in terms of language and begin to engage in make-believe play. They act out familiar activities, such as eating or sleeping. This stage is called preoperational because children have difficulty performing what Piaget called *operations*. These are mental manipulations of objects that can be reversed. For example, a preoperational child might know that adding seven plus two equals nine but cannot use the knowledge to understand what nine minus two equals.

Preoperational thinking also is limited by **egocentrism**, which is the tendency to view the world from your own perspective without recognizing that others may have different viewpoints. Piaget demonstrated preoperational egocentrism in his *three-mountains problem*. In this task, children were seated at a table with three model mountains like those shown in Figure 8-4 and with a doll sitting in another chair opposite them. When asked to choose a picture that represented the doll's view of the mountains, preoperational children chose the picture of their own view.

Although preoperational children are not egocentric in every situation, they are much more likely to make egocentric mistakes than older children. This is why three-year-olds might play hide-and-seek by simply closing their eyes. As far as they are concerned, they have found a pretty good hiding place because they can't see a thing.

Another limitation is **conservation**, or the ability to understand that physical properties of an object remain unchanged. They are conserved in spite of changes in appearance. Children who cannot conserve are unable to mentally reverse the physical

representational thought The ability to picture (or represent) something in your mind, even when it is not physically present

egocentrism The tendency to view the world from your own perspective without recognizing that others may have different viewpoints

conservation The understanding that certain physical properties of an object remain unchanged despite changes in its appearance

Figure 8-4 THE THREE-MOUNTAINS PROBLEM

What does the doll see?

In the three-mountains problem, preoperational children typically do not understand that the doll "sees" the mountains from a perspective different from their own. This is an example of egocentrism.

changes they observed. Preoperational children's inability to understand conservation is an example of the difficulty they have in performing mental operations. Following is a conversation I had with five-year-old Jason. It shows his lack of understanding of conservation. Each of us has the same amount of soda in two identical glasses.

Author: "Do I have more soda than you? Do you have more soda than me? Or do we have the same amount of soda?"

Jason: "We've both got the same."

Author: "OK, now I'm going to take your soda and pour it into here (wider glass). Now, look at your soda. Do I have more soda than you? Do you have more soda than me? Or do we have the same amount of soda?"

Jason: "You've got more than me."

Author: "Why is that?"

Jason: "Because it's put into a bigger glass, so my soda is lower."

Author: "Can you make it so that we have the same amount of soda?"

Jason: "Just pour it back into the first glass."

(After pouring the soda back into the original glass)

Author: "Do we have the same amount again?"

Jason: "Yes."

Jason's inability to mentally reverse the operation of pouring contributed to his inability to understand the conservation of liquid. Another factor that hindered Jason's ability to understand the conservation of liquid was that he paid attention to one feature of the liquid in the glass—its height. By noticing only the height of the liquid in the glass—which was lower than the original—and not noticing the width was greater, Jason falsely thought he lost soda in the transfer.

Preoperational children have difficulty with conservation tasks because they cannot reverse operations and because they pay attention to only one feature of the object. Figure 8-5 lists conservation tasks these children have difficulty performing.

Preoperational children cannot mentally reverse a sequence of events (an operation) back to the starting point. Preoperational children also cannot consider two features of an object at the same time (for example, the height and width of liquid in a glass). As a result, they are not yet able to comprehend the principle of conservation.

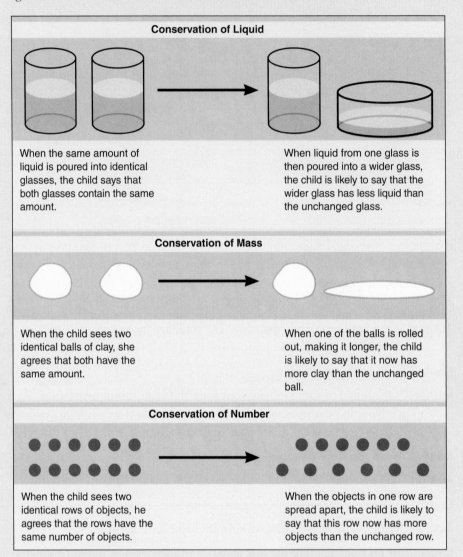

Figure 8-5 CONSERVATION OF LIQUID, MASS, AND NUMBER

Conservation of Liquid

When the same amount of liquid is poured into identical glasses, the child says that both glasses contain the same amount.

When liquid from one glass is then poured into a wider glass, the child is likely to say that the wider glass has less liquid than the unchanged glass.

Conservation of Mass

When the child sees two identical balls of clay, she agrees that both have the same amount.

When one of the balls is rolled out, making it longer, the child is likely to say that it now has more clay than the unchanged ball.

Conservation of Number

When the child sees two identical rows of objects, he agrees that the rows have the same number of objects.

When the objects in one row are spread apart, the child is likely to say that this row now has more objects than the unchanged row.

CONCRETE OPERATIONAL STAGE

Around age five, children advance to the *concrete operational stage*, a time they perform mental operations and begin logical reasoning. They develop an understanding of the principle of conservation in relation to number and liquid (ages 6–7), followed by mass and length (ages 7–8), and finally area (ages 8–10).

Piaget called this stage *concrete* operational because children's thinking and use of logic are limited to concrete reality, not abstract or hypothetical concepts. Concrete operational children have trouble thinking about something they do not directly experience. For example, ask a seven-year-old child about friendship. Instead of an abstract thought that it is the emotional attachment you have toward someone based on affection, the child might say, "friendship is when you play with someone." The child understands friendship from everyday experiences.

FORMAL OPERATIONAL STAGE

The *formal operational stage* is the fourth and final stage in Piaget's theory. Beginning around age 11, children reason abstractly and make predictions about hypothetical situations. Problem solving in earlier stages happens by trial-and-error methods. This stage involves systematic and reflective strategies.

In one of Piaget's studies, youngsters were given flasks containing clear liquids. The task was to determine which liquid combinations would produce a blue liquid. Concrete operational children poured liquids together trying to stumble upon the correct solution. Formal operational children carefully considered their choices before acting, and then kept track of each liquid combination until they solved the problem. Reflective thought and abstract reasoning help when studying such subjects as philosophy, theology, politics, and science.

Piaget initially believed all children eventually develop formal operations during adolescence. However, later research found that older adolescents and some adults never fully develop the ability. Only 25 percent of all first-year college students and 50 percent of all college students demonstrate the full capabilities of the formal operational stage. Formal operational thinking is not a light switch that is turned on at a certain age. As the brain matures and children are exposed to challenging intellectual tasks, they become more capable of using the cognitive abilities associated with formal operational thinking.

REFINEMENTS IN PIAGET'S THEORY

No theory comes close to the impact Piaget's cognitive developmental theory had on developmental psychology. However, newer studies find that children are more cognitively advanced and adults are less cognitively complex than Piaget's theory suggests. For example, preschoolers develop a **theory of mind**, which is knowing that other people have thoughts and feelings. A theory of mind allows children to understand and predict other people's behavior. This is a major accomplishment for children and allows them to engage in social interactions. The New Science feature on page 238 discusses insights into autism and the problems children with this disorder have in developing a theory of mind.

Cross-cultural research suggests that cognitive development is more influenced by social and environmental factors than Piaget thought. For example, learning how to count objects is not very important in nomadic societies where people move frequently from place to place. As a result, children in nomadic societies learn conservation of number at a later age than children in Western cultures. However, because children in nomadic societies are constantly moving from place to place, their spatial abilities develop more rapidly than children in Western cultures.

Despite these criticisms, developmental psychologists credit Piaget with highlighting that children are actively involved in their own cognitive growth. His work influenced how and what we teach children in elementary and secondary schools.

theory of mind The commonsense knowledge about other people's thoughts and feelings that allows you to understand and predict their behavior

STOCKBYTE/GETTY IMAGES

A concrete operational child can logically analyze concrete events. What sort of thinking is associated with the formal operational stage?

CHECKPOINT *What are Piaget's four stages of cognitive development?*

NEW SCIENCE

The Mind of an Autistic Child

About one in 150 children born in the United States today will be diagnosed with some degree of autism. This complex disorder disrupts normal brain functioning, making it difficult for the autistic person to communicate and interact with others. Autism strikes children of all racial, economic, and other social categories, but boys are four times more likely to become autistic than girls. Government statistics indicate that the incidence of autism is growing at a startling rate of 10 to 17 percent per year. Its causes are still unknown. However, most researchers believe autism develops in children who have some kind of genetic vulnerability to the disorder and who also are exposed to environmental toxins that trigger the disorder's development.

Parents typically notice symptoms of autism in their children during the first three years of life. These children often do not speak much or even babble, they rarely express emotion, and they do not respond to other people's affection. They are sometimes described as being "mind blind," meaning that they do not appear capable of developing a theory of mind. They have difficulty appreciating that playmates and parents might have views different from their own. Without an ability to understand and then predict how people might respond, autistic children remain locked within their own private world.

Recently, psychologist Simon Baron-Cohen has proposed that autism may represent an "extreme male brain." He makes this claim based on the fact that most people who suffer from autism are male, and also because some research suggests that boys may be born with less of a capacity to empathize with others than girls. If this theory is correct, it may help focus researchers' attention on certain genetic causes that are more associated with male biology than female biology. The next few years may provide the necessary knowledge to determine whether Baron-Cohen's theory is useful or not.

Think Critically

What does Baron-Cohen mean when he proposes that autism may represent an "extreme male brain"?

8.3 ASSESSMENT

In Your Own Words

Explain assimilation and accommodation. Cite examples from your life of when you used assimilation and when you used accommodation. For example, you might write about how you learned to play soccer, from the first lesson when you began assimilating the new information into the schema you already had established from previous times you kicked a ball back and forth with your older brother. Next as you absorbed the instruction from the soccer coach, you began accommodating the existing schemas to fit the new information about soccer.

Review Concepts

1. In which of Piaget's stages of cognitive development does object permanence take place?
   - a. sensorimotor
   - b. preoperational
   - c. concrete operational
   - d. formal operational

2. Which refers to the commonsense knowledge about other people's thoughts and feelings that allows you to understand and predict their behavior?
   - a. conservation
   - b. assimilation
   - c. theory of mind
   - d. egocentrism

3. In which of Piaget's stages of cognitive development are people able to form abstract logic?
   - a. sensorimotor
   - b. preoperational
   - c. concrete operational
   - d. formal operational

4. **True or False** Preoperational children may not grasp that there is the same amount of liquid in a tall glass versus a wide glass.

5. **True or False** Children begin to think in terms of language in the preoperational stage.

6. **True or False** Object permanence marks the beginning of representational thought.

7. **True or False** Children in the concrete operational stage can begin to engage in logical reasoning.

8. **True or False** Children in the concrete operational stage can begin to engage in abstract thinking.

Think Critically

9. Why are three-year-old children considered egocentric?

10. How can you use the game of peek-a-boo to determine object permanence?

Bringing Peace to the Dinner Table

INTRODUCTION   Riley, a high school student, has a four-year-old brother named Jonas, who is a very finicky eater. Jonas usually spends family dinner time whining about his food. One evening, as Jonas was complaining that he had been given too many mashed potatoes to eat and too much milk to drink, Riley had an idea about how she could convince Jonas to stop fussing. That day in school, Riley had learned about Piaget's theory of cognitive development.

HYPOTHESIS   Riley guessed that because her brother was only four years old, he probably was in the preoperational stage and had not yet developed the ability to conserve either mass or liquid. She hypothesized that if some superficial changes were made in the appearance of Jonas' potatoes and his milk, he would be convinced that he now had less food to eat and less milk to drink.

BRAND X PICTURES/JUPITER IMAGES

METHOD   As her parents watched with puzzled looks on their faces, Riley told Jonas that she would "fix" his meal so that he could eat all his potatoes and drink all his milk. Riley then proceeded to pour Jonas' milk into a wider glass, telling her brother that it was now "not as tall." Then, using her fork, Riley pushed Jonas' mashed potatoes together so they now covered less of his plate.

RESULTS   Riley's hypothesis was confirmed. Jonas did indeed believe that he now had fewer mashed potatoes on his plate and less milk in his glass. As Jonas happily finished his meal, Riley's parents controlled themselves from laughing out loud at what they had just witnessed. Riley then explained to her parents the theory underlying this pleasant dinner event. However, Riley also informed her parents that this "dinner trick" would become ineffective as soon as Jonas learned how to mentally reverse the operations of pouring liquids and changing the shape of mashed potatoes. Until that time, the family would enjoy a less finicky eater at the dinner table.

Critical Analysis

1. For dessert, if Riley and Jonas are both given one scoop of ice cream in a bowl, how might Riley convince Jonas that he has more ice cream than she?

2. According to Piaget, at about what age will Jonas likely no longer be fooled by altering the shape of the mashed potatoes?

Developmental Psychologist

ealth Science

Developmental psychologists study how the human mind and personality change throughout a person's life. They work to understand the factors that influence personality, intelligence, and behavior.

They may specialize in one specific stage of life (infancy, childhood, adolescence). They may specialize in the elderly population, developing ways to help them remain independent as they age. Others may specialize in developmental disabilities and their effects on people.

Unlike psychiatrists, psychologists are not physicians and do not prescribe medications. Psychologists conduct tests and experiments, take surveys, and study existing research. They use their results to form theories about how humans develop and behave.

Employment Outlook

Employment of psychologists is expected to grow faster than average through 2014. Demand is particularly strong for persons holding doctorates from leading universities, and those with extensive training in quantitative research methods and computer science.

KTAYLORG/ISTOCKPHOTO.COM

Needed Skills and Education

Before working as a developmental psychologist you must first earn a bachelor's degree in psychology or a related field. A master's degree also is necessary. Many jobs require a doctoral degree, which can involve several years of work after a master's degree is obtained. Candidates for a doctoral degree must complete research related to their specialty before earning their degree.

In order to work in private practice in any U.S. state, you must be licensed. To obtain a license, you need a doctoral degree plus two or more years of work experience.

How You'll Spend Your Day

The vast majority of developmental psychologists work at universities where they conduct research and teach college students and graduate students. Their workday is spent in preparing lectures for class, meeting with students and other faculty members, and teaching classes. Most work regular weekday hours in offices and laboratories at a university.

As researchers, developmental psychologists spend their workday conducting experiments to learn more about the physiological, cognitive, and social development that takes place throughout the human life span. They may focus their experiments on a particular stage of life, such as infancy, childhood, adolescence, or during the middle or senior years of adult life. Some developmental psychologists might conduct experiments to learn more about developmental disabilities or experiments that will help senior citizens live independently rather than in nursing homes.

Earnings

Most psychologists earn between $45,000 and $110,000, with many earning more.

What About You?

Does the job of developmental psychologist interest you? Why or why not? Which aspects of the job would you most enjoy? Which aspects would you least enjoy? Write an essay that details your interest, or lack of, and why.

CHAPTER SUMMARY

8.1 Physical Development

- The three stages of prenatal development are the germinal stage, embryonic stage, and fetal stage. The germinal stage lasts for two weeks after conception. The embryonic stage lasts from the third week through the eighth week of prenatal development. The fetal stage begins the ninth week after conception and lasts until birth.

- Diseases can harm the developing fetus, one of which is fetal alcohol syndrome that is caused by pregnant woman who drink large quantities of alcohol.

- Before birth and continuing during infancy and early childhood—and even throughout adulthood—individuals lose brain cells. The brain increases in weight from three-quarters of a pound at birth to about two-and-a-third pounds by age four. By age five, the brain reaches about 90 percent of its weight, while the rest of the body is only at 20 percent of what it will weigh as an adult.

- Reflexes are the only physical abilities at birth. Survival reflexes are essential for survival. Primitive reflexes appear and disappear during infant development.

8.2 Social Development

- Attachment is the strong emotional bond young children form with their parents or primary caregivers. It is the cornerstone for all other relationships in children's lives. Children with parents who are nurturing and sensitive to their needs tend to develop a secure attachment style. Children with parents who are inattentive to their needs tend to develop an insecure attachment style.

- Once children develop self-awareness, they begin to develop a self-concept. The evaluation of your self-concept is called self-esteem.

- Parents have a significant influence on their children's self-concepts. There are three types of parents—authoritative, authoritarian, and permissive.

- In developing a self-concept, your culture influences the beliefs you form about yourself.

- Gender identity is the knowledge that you are a male or female and the internalization of this fact into your self-concept.

- Erikson's theory of psychosocial development identifies four stages from birth to 12 years of age: infancy (trust versus mistrust); toddlerhood (autonomy versus shame and doubt); preschooler (initiative versus guilt); and elementary school (competence versus inferiority).

8.3 Cognitive Development

- According to Jean Piaget, cognitive development is something children achieve by organizing their knowledge of the world into schemas. In using schemas, children then acquire knowledge through assimilation and accommodation.

- According to Jean Piaget, individuals have three stages of cognitive development—birth to 2 years (sensorimotor); 2–6 years (preoperational); 7–11 years (concrete operational); and 11 through adulthood (formal operational).

CHAPTER ASSESSMENT

Review Psychology Terms

Select the term that best fits the definition. Some terms will not be used.

_____ 1. A fertilized egg during the first two weeks following conception

_____ 2. An automatic body response to a stimulus that is involuntary

_____ 3. The process of learning about yourself and about your culture and how to live within it

_____ 4. The systematic physical, cognitive, and social changes in the individual occurring between conception and death

_____ 5. The evaluation of your self-concept as being good, bad, or mediocre

_____ 6. The "theory" or "story" that you construct about yourself through your life experiences and interactions with others

_____ 7. The process of absorbing new information into existing schemas

_____ 8. The many changes that transform a fertilized egg into a newborn baby

_____ 9. The realization that an object continues to exist even if you can't see it or touch it

_____ 10. Physical and cognitive abnormalities in children that result when pregnant women consume large quantities of alcohol

_____ 11. The understanding that certain physical properties of an object remain unchanged despite changes in its appearance

_____ 12. An organized cluster of knowledge that you use to understand and interpret information

_____ 13. The process of changing existing schemas in order to absorb new information

_____ 14. The knowledge that you are a male or a female and the internalization of this fact into your self-concept

_____ 15. The ability to picture (or represent) something in your mind, even when it is not physically present

_____ 16. A state of mind where you think about yourself

a. accommodation
b. assimilation
c. attachment
d. conservation
e. development
f. egocentric
g. embryo
h. fetal alcohol syndrome
i. fetus
j. gender identity
k. object permanence
l. prenatal development
m. reflex
n. representational thought
o. schema
p. self-awareness
q. self-concept
r. self-esteem
s. socialization
t. theory of mind
u. zygote

Review Psychology Concepts

17. What is the difference between an embryo and a fetus?

18. Explain what attachment is and why it is important to young children.

19. Compare and contrast authoritative, authoritarian, and permissive parents.

20. Explain theory of mind and why it is important to young children.

21. Define cognition.

22. Label the following as either a survival reflex or a primitive reflex: pupillary reflex, swallowing reflex, grasping reflex; breathing reflex, Babinski reflex, swimming reflex, and eye-blink reflex.

23. Use a study cited in the text to support the following statement: Infants experience separation anxiety when separated from the caregiver to whom they have formed an attachment.

24. How do children who were securely attached in infancy mature differently from children who were insecurely attached?

25. Evaluate the differences in self-concept between individualist and collectivist societies.

26. Evaluate how parents often treat their children based on gender roles.

27. Identify the crisis of the following stages according to Erikson's stages of psychosocial development: infancy, toddlerhood, preschooler, and elementary school.

28. Indicate how Jean Piaget's ideas differed from the belief that children were shaped by parents, teachers, and other people.

29. Restate Piaget's idea of schema, assimilation, and accommodation in your own words.

30. Differentiate between the sensorimotor and preoperational stages of Piaget's cognitive development.

Apply Psychology Concepts

31. Explain how the brain is "sculpted" by life experiences. How is this sculpting related to the "use-it-or-lose-it" principle?

32. Consider how infants crave contact comfort. Now consider how your need for contact comfort affects your life today. Can you identify any activities, people, or objects in your life that satisfy your need for contact comfort?

33. Piaget stated that one of the continuing dilemmas in learning and problem solving is whether you should engage in assimilation or accommodation. Identify and describe a recent problem that you solved in which you used assimilation. Next identify and describe a recent problem that you solved in which you used accommodation.

34. Egocentrism is the tendency to view the world from your own perspective without recognizing that others may have different viewpoints. Think about your own childhood between the ages of two and six years, or another child in this age range. Describe a situation in which you or this child thought in an egocentric manner.

Make Academic Connections

35. **Computer Science** Use a computer program to create a timeline that illustrates how relationships change over time from birth to one year after high school graduation. What relationships do you think will be important to you one year after high school?

36. **Cross-Cultures Studies** Use the Internet to learn about early childhood education in another culture, such as the culture of India or China. Some of the questions you might want to answer are as follows: How old are children when they first attend school? How many students are in a classroom? What are young children taught in the early years of school? What are the classrooms like? Compare and contrast the education in the culture you are researching with your early schooling. Make a fact sheet of the similarities and the differences.

37. **Writing** Write an essay that describes the major transitions from childhood to your current age, such as your earliest memory, your first day in school, a memorable family vacation, or other important events in your life that demonstrate ways you developed into the person you are today. Also in your essay, compare your life experiences with the general patterns of other people in your generation.

38. **Art** Use the Internet, art supplies, and magazine cutouts to create a poster that describes the typical development of children for the first two years of their lives. Use information from the text that cites research on the capabilities of infants and young children for information on what illustrations to use.

39. **Language Arts** Use the library or the Internet to research books on early childhood development. Read the table of contents and the first pages. Write a summary that describes the research on child development discussed in the book.

DIGGING DEEPER
with Psychology eCollection

Scientists have studied human development in many ways. Research on physical, social, and cognitive development has been the focus of many research projects. In recent years more has been learned about the stages of emotional development, leading to development theories and more testing. Fabes, Frosch, and Buchanan provide a chapter on the research and findings in this key aspect of human development. Access the Gale Psychology eCollection at *www.cengage.com/school/psych/franzoi* and read the introduction and one section, either "Emotional Development During Infancy and Toddlerhood" or "Emotional Development During Childhood." Write a brief summary of the section and answer the question: Why is emotional development difficult to study? As an additional project, describe something you learned from your reading of this article and explain how it applies to your emotional development.

Source: From Fabes, Richard A., Cynthia A. Frosch, and Amy Buchanan. "Emotional Development" Child Development: *Macmillan Psychology Reference Series*. © Global Rights & Permissions, a part of Cengage Learning, Inc. Reproduced by permission. www.cengage.com/permission

Adolescence

ESSENTIAL QUESTION
Go to page XXV

> "When I was a boy of fourteen, my father was so ignorant I could hardly stand to have the old man around. But when I got to be twenty-one, I was astonished at how much he had learned in seven years."

—MARK TWAIN, AMERICAN AUTHOR AND HUMORIST, 1835–1910

When I was 16, my mother drove me to the license bureau to take my driving test. When the officer behind the counter called my name, he pointed to an eye chart and said, "Touch your toes to the line." He meant I should put my toes on the red line so I would be positioned to look at the eye chart. However, being nervous and hearing the words, "Touch your toes," I thought he wanted me to complete a coordination test. So, after positioning my toes on the red line, I stiffened my knees and then touched my toes. The officer didn't say how long this coordination test would last, so I remained in this position and waited.

As the blood rushed to my head, I glanced at my mother and noticed her shocked expression. What was her son doing making a fool of himself in a room full of strangers? Suddenly I understood the meaning of the officer's words and stood up straight. Even though my head was no longer below my knees, the blood still rushed to my face. I was so embarrassed! No one laughed out loud at my behavior, but I became so flustered I failed the eye exam.

Adolescence as a Transition Period

- Distinguish adolescence from adulthood.
- Describe the physical and social effects of adolescence.

DISCOVER IT | *How does this relate to me?*

As my driving test experience illustrates, adolescence can sometimes be an embarrassing and confusing stage of life. For example, do you feel that one minute people are treating you like an adult and the next they are treating you like a child? Do you sometimes feel like a child and then the next minute feel grown up? How many years do you think you should have to wait to "get into" adulthood? Can you speed up the process? As you will learn in this chapter, these are normal feelings and natural questions. American culture does not have a clear set of rules defining when a person moves from immaturity to maturity. What we have is a murky transition period called adolescence, a time of physical and psychological growth sometimes combined with a hefty dose of confusion.

KEY TERMS

- adolescence
- emerging adulthood
- puberty
- primary sex characteristics
- secondary sex characteristics
- menarche
- spermarche

Many cultures view **adolescence**, the time of transition between childhood and adulthood, as a time for young people to learn how to become useful members of society. In the United States, this transition is gradual and its duration varies from person to person. Think of adolescence as a bridge between childhood and adulthood. Some people walk across this bridge more quickly than others do. The American adolescent stage of life can last ten years, spanning the ages of 11 through 20, but for some Americans, it may last fewer than six years. During this time, adolescents are expected to attend school or training programs.

In some cultures, there is no period of adolescence. For example, in the Sambia society in Papua, New Guinea, children are socialized into adulthood quickly. The same is true in many nomadic African tribes. In these societies young people go through demanding and sometimes painful rituals that usher children into adulthood. Once completed, these young people are expected to act like adults.

adolescence The transition period between childhood and adulthood

Distinguishing Adolescence from Adulthood

Adolescence was not always recognized as a stage in life. In the late eighteenth and early nineteenth centuries, Great Britain and North America began to industrialize. The need for workers with specialized skills made it necessary to formally educate children beyond puberty and to delay adulthood.

Over the past 40 years, the length of the adolescent period in our culture has increased even further. Most young people today need to spend even longer periods of time in school in order to become useful citizens and get well-paying jobs. This means that the average young person is more dependent on his or her parents for longer periods of time than in the past. Today, more than 50 percent of young American men and 40 percent of young American women between the ages of 18 and 24 live at home with one or more of their parents. Being accepted as an adult—and believing it yourself—is more difficult if you are still in school and living in your childhood home.

DEVELOPMENTAL TASKS ON THE ADOLESCENT BRIDGE TO ADULTHOOD

Are there certain *developmental tasks* that must be completed before you are recognized as an adult? When Americans were asked in a national survey to rank the importance of different tasks in becoming an adult, "completing one's education" was considered most important, followed by "gaining full-time employment" and "being able to support a family" (see Table 9-1). Interestingly, "getting married" and "having children" were ranked rather low in importance, with fewer than 20 percent of Americans believing that these tasks make you an adult.

Table 9-1 WHAT MAKES YOU AN ADULT?

Seven Developmental Tasks Signifying Transition into Adulthood (Age Event Should Occur)	Percentage Who Rated Event as "Extremely Important" in Becoming an Adult
1. Attaining financial independence (20.9 years)	47%
2. Not living with parents (21.2 years)	29%
3. Gaining full-time employment (21.2 years)	61%
4. Completing one's education (22.3 years)	73%
5. Being able to support a family (24.5 years)	61%
6. Getting married (25.7 years)	19%
7. Having children (26.2 years)	16%

Today, young people are taking longer to get married and start a family than their parents and grandparents. As Figure 9-1 shows, in 1960 the average age for getting married was 23 for men and 20 for women. Today, those averages have increased by about five years.

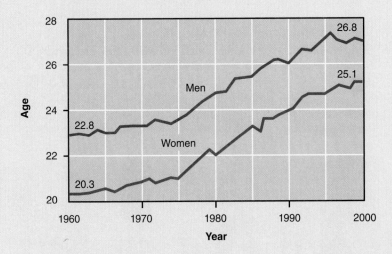

Figure 9-1 AVERAGE AGE AT MARRIAGE, UNITED STATES

Over the past 40 years, the average age for getting married has increased by about five years. What might explain this increase?

Source: Fields, Jason. (2001). America's families and living arrangements: March 2000 (*Current Population Reports*, P20–537). Washington, DC: U.S. Government Printing Office.

What do American teenagers consider important in defining a person as an adult? A number of studies find that adolescents are more likely to define adulthood based on psychological and cognitive abilities rather than on completing developmental tasks. For example, 90 percent of adolescents believe that "accepting responsibility for one's actions" is an important quality of being an adult. For adolescents, acting responsibly is considered more important in defining adulthood than being out of school, being fully employed, or living on their own.

The adolescent "bridge" is a complicated social construction. How you view this transition period and its challenges may depend on whether you currently are walking across it or standing on the more firmly defined side of adulthood.

DIFFERENT PHASES OF ADOLESCENCE

Developmental psychologists often describe three separate age ranges, or phases, of adolescence. Each phase reflects a different level of maturity. The phase of *early adolescence* is the age range of about 11 to 14 years. *Middle adolescence* refers to those who are about 15 to 17 years old. People who are 18 or older are known to be in *late adolescence.*

The social life that adolescents experience becomes increasingly complex as they move through these phases. Early adolescence is the time when many physical, mental, and emotional changes begin. It also is the time when teens begin to actively let go of childhood behavior and try to act older. This desire to be judged as older increases during middle and late adolescence when most teens are given more adult responsibilities.

Because there are no clear rules on when adolescence ends, many developmental psychologists believe that the period from the late teens to the mid-twenties should be identified as another developmental stage, namely, **emerging adulthood**. This is a stage of life when many people are still free from many adult responsibilities. College students and young adults who live at home with their parents are examples

emerging adulthood
The age period from the late teens to the mid-twenties in which a person is still free from many adult responsibilities

of "emerging adults." The current twenty-first century form of the developmental "bridge" between childhood and adulthood is shown in Figure 9-2.

Figure 9-2 THE BRIDGE BETWEEN CHILDHOOD AND ADULTHOOD

Think of adolescence as the developmental "bridge" between childhood and adulthood.

Early adolescence
11–14 years

Middle adolescence
15–17 years

Late adolescence
18–19 years

Emerging adulthood
late teens–mid-20s

Childhood

Adulthood

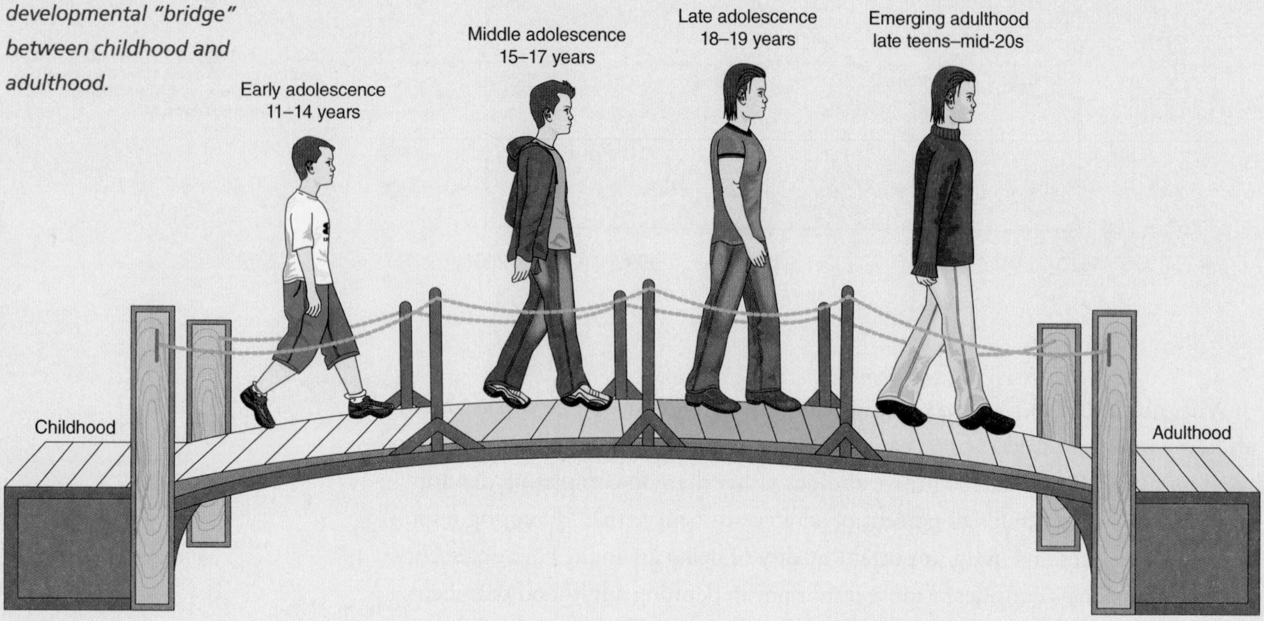

CHECKPOINT *What is adolescence?*

Physical and Social Effects of Puberty

For most teenagers, early adolescence is a time when they experience **puberty**, a growth period in which a person reaches sexual maturity and becomes capable of reproducing. Puberty begins when the pituitary gland's increased secretion of the growth hormone triggers a growth spurt. This growth process does not have a strict timeline, and it can last from one year to seven years. Young people vary on when they experience this growth spurt. In North America girls generally start at about age 10, while boys begin around age 13.

puberty The growth period in which a person reaches sexual maturity and becomes capable of reproducing

PHYSICAL CHANGES

Adolescents undergo physical changes during puberty both internally and externally. Internally, changes occur in the **primary sex characteristics**, which are the reproductive organs. The primary sex characteristics in females are the uterus and ovaries; in males, they are the penis and testicles. Externally, changes occur in the **secondary sex characteristics**, which are the nonreproductive physical features that distinguish women and men from one another. Examples of developing secondary sex characteristics in adolescent females are breast enlargement, a widening of the hips, and an increase in the amount of fat in the body. In adolescent males, facial hair, a deeper voice, and an increase in upper-body strength are some of the more noticeable secondary sex characteristics that develop. Figure 9-3 on page 252 lists the average sequence of puberty for both sexes.

In girls, the first noticeable signs of puberty occur at about age 10 or 11 with the growth of the breasts and body hair. Girls will experience their first menstrual period, called **menarche**, at about age 12 or 13. Adolescent girls who have been asked in surveys how parents should prepare their daughters for menstruation emphasize the importance of open communication, especially with mothers.

Puberty begins at about age 12 in boys. They begin growing hair under their arms, on their face, and in their pubic area. Their genitals also enlarge. One major event marking male puberty is **spermarche**, or the first ejaculation, which typically occurs around the age of 13. For both sexes, two unwelcomed physical changes caused by growth hormones are a noticeable increase in body odor and the appearance of acne, or pimples.

primary sex characteristics The reproductive organs

secondary sex characteristics The nonreproductive physical features that distinguish women and men from one another

menarche The first menstrual period

spermarche Males' first experience of ejaculation

Teenagers undergo significant changes during puberty.

PHOTOALTO AGENCY RF COLLECTIONS/GETTY IMAGES

Figure 9-3 SEQUENCES OF PUBERTY IN ADOLESCENT FEMALES AND ADOLESCENT MALES

Girls typically experience puberty about two to three years before boys.

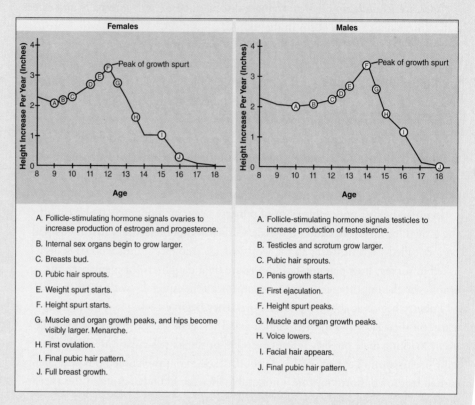

Females

A. Follicle-stimulating hormone signals ovaries to increase production of estrogen and progesterone.

B. Internal sex organs begin to grow larger.

C. Breasts bud.

D. Pubic hair sprouts.

E. Weight spurt starts.

F. Height spurt starts.

G. Muscle and organ growth peaks, and hips become visibly larger. Menarche.

H. First ovulation.

I. Final pubic hair pattern.

J. Full breast growth.

Males

A. Follicle-stimulating hormone signals testicles to increase production of testosterone.

B. Testicles and scrotum grow larger.

C. Pubic hair sprouts.

D. Penis growth starts.

E. First ejaculation.

F. Height spurt peaks.

G. Muscle and organ growth peaks.

H. Voice lowers.

I. Facial hair appears.

J. Final pubic hair pattern.

PUBERTY AND BODY ISSUES

The timing of the physical changes during puberty has psychological effects that can be quite challenging. The sudden changes taking place in your body can be uncomfortable. Adolescents mature at different times. Some mature in their early teens while others mature later. These differences can create feelings of self-consciousness and affect feelings of self-worth.

Like most people, many adolescents want to feel accepted by others. In trying to figure out how to dress, look, and act, teenagers often look to other students, as well as rock stars and film actors. When comparing themselves to others, few people can match what they consider to be the ideal. Again, like most people, many adolescents judge themselves harshly if they feel they do not fit in or look the way they think they should. Unfortunately such negative judgments can cause anxiety and depression in both young men and women.

Early- vs. Late-Maturing Boys   Boys who mature early have some advantages over boys who mature late. In American society, boys tend to be judged by their athletic ability and strength. Early-maturing boys often are taller and more muscular than other boys, which gives them an advantage in sports. They also tend to be somewhat more popular, self-confident, and independent. Because of their popularity, early-maturing boys tend to be leaders and feel relaxed and in control socially. However, they also are more likely to engage in risky behaviors such as driving too fast or experimenting with drugs or alcohol.

In contrast, late-maturing boys often are distressed by their delayed growth. They may feel self-conscious due to their smaller bodies, and may withdraw or engage in negative attention-seeking behaviors such as ridiculing others and resisting school dress codes. However, this feeling of insecurity is temporary and usually disappears once their growth spurt kicks in.

Early-maturing girls typically look older at an earlier age than do early-maturing boys.

© ANTHONY HARRIS, 2009/USED UNDER LICENSE FROM SHUTTERSTOCK.COM

Early- vs. Late-Maturing Girls

Because girls grow most in height and weight about two years earlier than boys (at 12 years versus 14 years), early-maturing girls typically look older at an earlier age than do early-maturing boys. Unlike early-maturing boys who often react positively to weight and height increases, early-maturing girls tend to be embarrassed by their growth spurt. For some girls, the attention the growth spurt brings from boys causes feelings of awkwardness and anxiousness in social situations. Early-maturing girls may begin associating with older teens which can lead to the same sort of risky behaviors common in early-maturing boys.

In contrast, late-maturing girls often are overlooked as dating partners and are less popular with boys than other girls their age. One advantage of looking young is that late-maturing girls are less likely to associate with older teens, thus they often experience less criticism from adults.

Accepting Your Body Image

Regardless of the timing of puberty, most adolescents spend time focusing on how they look. Why is body image so important? One reason is that, in American culture, the *perfect* body is shown repeatedly on television, films, the Internet, and in magazines. Young people are bombarded with what the culture says they *should* look like. As an adolescent, your challenge is to become comfortable with the body you have and who you are.

SEXUAL ATTITUDES AND CONDUCT

Sexuality is not an entirely new topic of interest for teenagers. During childhood, most children are curious about sexual issues. However, this interest and awareness heightens with puberty, as the body begins its adult transformation.

Societies around the world differ widely in how they socialize young people about sex. Some societies forbid open discussion of sexual issues. In many of these societies, females and males are not even permitted to play together or socialize without adults being present. In other societies, children and adolescents are allowed—and even encouraged—to freely discuss and express their sexuality. American society falls somewhere in between these two different societal extremes. Surveys of American adolescents find that they are more sexually active than were teenagers 30 years ago. However these same surveys find that the majority of adolescents believe that openness, honesty, and faithfulness are very important qualities in relationships.

CHECKPOINT *What is puberty?*

9.1 ASSESSMENT

In Your Own Words

Write an autobiography that examines how your life is defined by being an adolescent. Describe the physical changes you have gone through, or are going through now. Analyze the personal rituals you have experienced, such as a sixteenth birthday party, obtaining a driver's license or learner's permit, a first date, or the wearing and removal of braces on your teeth. Describe any religious or cultural rituals you have experienced, such as a bar mitzvah.

Review Concepts

1. Which refers to the transition period between childhood and adulthood?
   - a. menarche
   - b. adolescence
   - c. ego era
   - d. emerging adulthood

2. Which is the growth period in which a person reaches sexual maturity and becomes capable of reproducing?
   - a. emerging adulthood
   - b. menarche
   - c. primary sex characteristics
   - d. puberty

3. **True or False**   In American culture, body image is seen as a sign of health and success.

4. **True or False**   Late-maturing boys tend to be leaders and feel relaxed and in control socially.

Think Critically

5. Why are changes in secondary sex characteristics considered external changes rather than internal changes?

6. Why might a poor body image cause depression?

Cognitive, Moral, and Emotional Development

- Recognize complex thinking and describe Kohlberg's stages of moral development.
- Explain heightened emotions and self-consciousness.

DISCOVER IT | *How does this relate to me?*

Do you find yourself wondering about the deeper issues of life, such as the meaning of life or how to make moral choices? Do you sometimes feel your emotions are all over the place, or that everyone in the room is looking at you? This is all part of being a teenager, and psychology can help you understand these questions.

KEY TERMS

- moral reasoning
- preconventional morality
- conventional morality
- postconventional morality
- imaginary audience
- personal fable

L ife can seem complicated during adolescence. One reason is that adults typically place more demands on you as you mature. It is also true that, as a teenager, you have better cognitive, or reasoning, abilities than you did as a child. As a result, you begin to think in greater depth about your place in the social world.

Emergence of Complex Thinking

Consider the following hypothetical situation:

Judy is twelve years old. Her mother promised Judy that she could go to a rock concert if she saved money from her chores and baby sitting. Judy managed to save up the $40 for the ticket plus another $10. Then her mother changed her mind, and told Judy that she had to spend the money on new clothes for school. Judy was mad and decided to go to the concert anyway. She bought a ticket and told her mother that she had only been able to save $10. Judy went to the concert but told her mother that she was spending the night with a friend. A week passed without her mother finding out. Judy then told her older sister, Louise, how she had lied to her mother. Louise decides to tell their mother what Judy did.

Do you agree or disagree with Louise's decision to tell their mother that Judy lied about the money and the concert? Why? Write out your responses to these two questions. We will soon examine what they might reveal about the development of your reasoning ability.

PHOTODISC/GETTY IMAGES

REASONING SKILLS

In Chapter 8 you were introduced to Jean Piaget's fourth and final stage of cognitive development, the *formal operational stage,* which typically begins during early or middle adolescence. Using formal operational thinking, teenagers begin thinking logically about abstract concepts and making predictions about hypothetical situations. Teenagers' understanding of other people's personalities also becomes considerably more complex than those of younger children. Have you, like many teens, spent hours analyzing your friends' and family members' personalities, trying to figure out what makes them tick? These attempts to understand the hidden world of personality are common in the teenage years.

With the emergence of formal operational thinking, adolescents begin pondering big life issues, such as the nature of good and evil, truth and justice, and the meaning of life and happiness. This new ability to consider hypothetical situations and their consequences allows teenagers to detect inconsistencies in other people's reasoning. This more complex reasoning ability can lead to heated debates with parents and other people about a wide variety of issues, including the nature of morality.

MORAL DEVELOPMENT

Most psychologists consider **moral reasoning** to be the process of distinguishing between good and bad conduct. Almost all psychologists also would agree that you are not born with an understanding of good and bad conduct. Instead, you learn how to make moral decisions through your life experiences.

Childhood and early adolescence are the training grounds for distinguishing between good and bad conduct, with adults serving as moral coaches for the young. As teenagers mature, society expects them to make responsible moral choices. Yet not all people in their late teens—or even all adults—meet this expectation.

Consider again your thoughts about Louise's decision to tell on her sister. What were your reasons for either agreeing or disagreeing with Louise's actions? According to Lawrence Kohlberg, the reasons you give—and not simply your agreement or disagreement with her actions—provide insights into your level of moral development. Kohlberg maintained that as people mature, they should pass through three levels of moral development. Each successive level is a less selfish, and more mature, analysis of moral choices (see Figure 9-4 on page 257).

moral reasoning The process of distinguishing between good and bad conduct

Figure 9-4 KOHLBERG'S LEVELS OF MORAL DEVELOPMENT

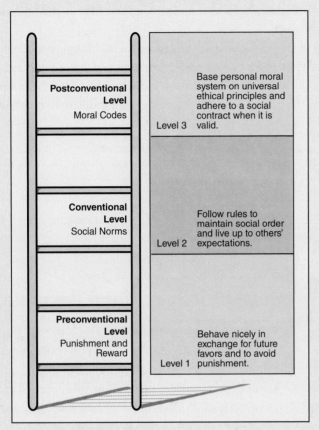

Postconventional Level
Moral Codes

Level 3 Base personal moral system on universal ethical principles and adhere to a social contract when it is valid.

Conventional Level
Social Norms

Level 2 Follow rules to maintain social order and live up to others' expectations.

Preconventional Level
Punishment and Reward

Level 1 Behave nicely in exchange for future favors and to avoid punishment.

According to Kohlberg, you move through three levels of moral reasoning. Each successive level represents a more mature analysis of moral choices. Which level do you think you are on?

At level one, **preconventional morality**, the sense of moral reasoning centers on avoiding punishment or seeking rewards. Due to egocentrism, at this preconventional level you focus on how moral choices will affect you alone and not others. In Louise's dilemma, a person at this first level might reason that Louise should not tell their mother about Judy's lying because Judy will be very mad at her. A person at this level also might say that Louise should tell because their mother will then reward her.

As your moral reasoning matures and you become more aware of other people's points of view and the rules of society, you begin to engage in **conventional morality**. Here, you define what is right and wrong either in terms of seeking social approval or conforming to authority. Thus, a person at this level might argue that Louise should either tell or not tell their mother about Judy's lying based on what her friends would think of her. A person also might argue that Louise should tell their mother because a daughter should respect her parent's authority. Kohlberg believed that most people do not advance beyond the conventional level of moral reasoning.

According to Kohlberg, higher levels of moral reasoning require that you not base your decisions on seeking social approval and accepting societal rules. This **postconventional morality** involves basing moral judgments on abstract principles and values that may conflict with your own interests and societal norms. This postconventional moral reasoning requires formal operational thought. A person at this level might say that Louise should tell their mother because everybody should be held responsible for their actions and Judy would be allowed to avoid that

preconventional morality Selfish moral reasoning based on avoiding punishment or seeking rewards

conventional morality Moral reasoning based on seeking social approval or conforming to authority to maintain social order

postconventional morality Moral reasoning based on abstract principles and values that may conflict with your own interests and societal norms

responsibility if nothing was said. Or a person might say that Louise should not tell because everybody has a right to confidentiality and Judy would be denied this right if Louise told on her.

A number of studies have found evidence generally supporting Kohlberg's theory of moral development for people who live in the United States and in other societies with an individualist cultural orientation. However, the Closer Look feature below examines how the process of moral reasoning often is different in collectivist cultures.

CHECKPOINT *What are the three levels of moral reasoning and what do each involve?*

CLOSER LOOK

Culture Shapes Moral Reasoning

Cross-cultural studies find that most people around the world progress from the preconventional to the conventional levels of moral reasoning. However, Kohlberg's postconventional level of moral reasoning assumes that personal rights and privileges are more important than the rights and privileges of the group. This sort of reasoning holds true with individualist cultural beliefs but not with collectivist cultural beliefs.

In the collectivist society of China, for example, people often base their moral decisions on community standards. In doing so, they try to resolve moral dilemmas by pleasing as many people as possible. Instead of basing moral reasoning on personal rights and privileges, the Chinese focus on harmony and cooperation. In responding to Louise's dilemma, someone raised in China might believe that Louise was placed in an awkward position by Judy and that she and her sister should try to find some sort of solution that would respect their mother's authority and maintain family harmony.

Do you think cultures that emphasize social harmony and the good of the group more than the good of the individual should be labeled as having a less-developed sense of morality? Cross-cultural research shows that moral development often differs quite a bit from society to society. What stands for mature moral reasoning in one culture may not be recognized as the same in another culture. Based on these findings, it appears that Kohlberg's theory is best at explaining the development of moral reasoning in individualist societies.

Think Critically
What do you think would be an example of a highly moral collectivist resolution of the ethical dilemma facing Louise in the opening scenario?

Heightened Emotions and Self-Consciousness

During adolescence, a cognitive-emotional push-pull is taking place. At the same time you are developing more complex thinking skills, you also are experiencing new emotions that may sidetrack your reasoning and logic. These emotions are triggered by hormonal changes that occur during puberty. The adrenal glands release hormones that directly influence neurotransmitters in the brain. The neurotransmitters play an important role in regulating mood and excitability. However, the brain areas responsible for judging emotional reactions are still developing. This is why your moods can change so quickly. Check out the Positive Psychology feature on page 260 to discover why your moods change during the day.

This hormone rush also motivates many teenagers to seek out thrilling and exciting experiences. Unfortunately, the brain regions that inhibit risky, impulsive behavior are still maturing, so often there is no internal brake on teenagers' thrill-seeking desires and roller-coaster emotions. Until the teenage brain sufficiently matures, developmental psychologists recommend that parents serve as the external emergency brake for their children.

Accompanying many adolescents' heightened emotions is a heightened awareness of being evaluated by others. Whether true or not, believing that other people are evaluating you can make you more self-conscious. You may develop an **imaginary audience**, a belief that other people are constantly focusing their thoughts, feelings, and behavior on you. For example, some teenagers may be so convinced that everyone will notice a minor blemish on their faces they may refuse to leave home. One reason this heightened self-consciousness occurs is that the brain areas that control the ability to understand other people's motivations are still developing.

PHOTODISC/GETTY IMAGES

imaginary audience A common adolescent belief that other people are constantly focusing their thoughts, feelings, and behavior on you

Why do some teenagers develop an imaginary audience?

How Do Different People and Situations Affect Your Moods?

How is your mood influenced by other people and situations? Psychologists have tried to answer this question by having teenagers carry small electronic pagers and booklets with them for a few days. When paged, the teenagers complete a brief questionnaire describing their mood and their social setting. The pagers randomly signal the teenagers from seven to ten times each day during their normal waking hours.

Findings from these studies indicate that adolescents feel bored more than 25 percent of the time. However, they seldom are bored when they are with their friends or during leisure activities. Boredom typically occurs while at school or while they are doing something required by others (usually adults). Teenagers' moods generally are most positive when they are with their friends, moderately positive when they are with their families, and least positive when they are alone.

Peer relationships are very important to most adolescents. This explains why teens are happiest when they are with their friends. However, if teens are just hanging out with friends, their level of concentration tends to be low. Teens report being happiest and most focused when doing an organized leisure activity with friends, such as playing a sport, acting in a play, or working on a hobby.

Does it surprise you that most teenagers are happier when they are spending time with their families than when they are alone? Although teens sometimes argue with their parents and siblings, family members remain important sources of social support for them.

Beyond the positive effects of family support, is there something about spending time alone that could create negative moods? These studies find that when teenagers are alone, they focus more on their private thoughts and feelings than when they are with others. Psychologists believe that adolescents often spend their private time thinking about personal problems or listening to music with sad or depressing themes. The good news here is that as teenagers become more emotionally mature, solitude becomes a much more positive and enriching experience for them.

Think Critically

Why do you think teenagers are most happy when with their friends and least happy when alone? Does this apply to you?

This heightened self-consciousness causes many teenagers to be self-absorbed, which results in their developing a **personal fable**. This is the tendency to believe that no one has ever felt or thought as they do. For example, teenagers in love may believe that no one has ever felt the intense emotions they feel. When relationships end, they may believe that no one can understand what they are going through—least of all their parents.

Not all adolescents experience this heightened self-consciousness. Teenagers generally are more aware of, and concerned about, being examined by others than are younger children. However, some adolescents are not at all self-conscious. Spend a few minutes completing the survey in the Self-Discovery feature on page 262 to learn more about your own level of self-consciousness.

Despite the common belief that adolescence is a time in life marked by emotional turmoil, teenagers are as well adjusted as children and adults. Surveys report that about 80 percent of adolescents are relatively happy. When teenagers have problems, they typically involve conflicts with parents or problems caused by risky behavior. Compared to younger children, teenagers have more arguments with their parents. As adolescents mature, they engage in more thoughtful social judgments leading to fewer parent-child conflicts.

personal fable Teenagers' tendency to believe that no one has ever felt or thought as they do

CHECKPOINT *What is the cognitive-emotional push-pull that takes place during adolescence?*

©YURI ARCURS, 2009/USED UNDER LICENSE FROM SHUTTERSTOCK.COM

Even though adolescence sometimes may be emotionally rocky, 80 percent of adolescents surveyed say they are relatively happy.

9.2 ASSESSMENT

In Your Own Words

Write a description of a situation in your life for which you have developed a personal fable. Explain whether your awareness of this concept affects how you now feel about the situation.

Review Concepts

1. Believing that no one has ever felt or thought as you do is called
   - a. personal fable
   - b. imaginary audience
   - c. egomania
   - d. ethnic identity

2. **True or False** Piaget's formal operational stage typically begins during early or middle adolescence.

3. Define formal operational thinking.

Think Critically

4. Why do adolescents often engage in exciting and sometimes heated debates with adults?

5. Why do adolescents' emotions often change so easily?

SELF-DISCOVERY

How Self-Conscious Are You?

Directions: The Self-Consciousness Scale is used by psychologists to measure people's level of self-consciousness. To obtain information on your degree of self-consciousness, read each item below, and then indicate how well each statement describes you, using the following response scale:

0 = extremely uncharacteristic (not at all like me)
1 = uncharacteristic (somewhat unlike me)
2 = neither characteristic nor uncharacteristic
3 = characteristic (somewhat like me)
4 = extremely characteristic (very much like me)

_____ 1. I'm concerned about my style of doing things.
_____ 2. I'm concerned about the way I present myself.
_____ 3. I'm self-conscious about the way I look.
_____ 4. I usually worry about making a good impression.
_____ 5. One of the last things I do before I leave my house is look in the mirror.
_____ 6. I'm concerned about what other people think of me.
_____ 7. I'm usually aware of my appearance.

See page 273 for scoring instructions.

OBJECTIVES

- Describe personal identity development.
- Describe ethnic identity development.

DISCOVER IT | *How does this relate to me?*

Do you ever wonder who you are and where you fit into the world around you? Have you experimented with different ways of thinking and behaving to see if they feel comfortable for you? An important task for many teenagers is to understand themselves as they move toward adulthood. For some, this task is fairly easy, but for others it can be quite challenging.

Recall Erik Erikson's eight stages of psychosocial development which were described in Chapter 8 (pages 229–230). Each stage is marked by a crisis or conflict related to a specific developmental task. The more successfully you overcome these crises, the better chance you have to develop in a healthy way. The challenge of adolescence is coming up with a clear answer to the question, "Who am I?"

Personal Identity Development

During adolescence, Erikson contends that you face the fifth and most crucial stage in psychosocial development: *identity versus role confusion.* (See Table 9-2 on page 264.) This is the stage of life where you exercise your more complex thinking skills in trying to figure out how to define yourself in your social surroundings. This **personal identity** is your understanding of what makes you unique as an individual and different from others. As defined by Erikson, personal identity is another term for *self-concept* (see Chapter 8, page 225). According to Erikson, if you cannot settle upon a personal identity by the end of adolescence, you will suffer role confusion and may feel "lost."

Although knowing who you are and where you are headed is a lifelong task, Erikson stated that adolescence is the first time you make a serious effort to consciously form your own personal identity. In childhood, you generally thought of yourself in very concrete ways: I like to play soccer. My best friend is Matthew. I am

personal identity Your understanding of what makes you unique as an individual and different from others

Table 9-2 ERIKSON'S STAGES OF PSYCHOSOCIAL DEVELOPMENT

Psychosocial Stage	Crisis	Description of Crisis
Infancy (birth–1 year)	Trust vs. mistrust	
Toddlerhood (1–2 years)	Autonomy vs. shame and doubt	
Preschooler (3–5 years)	Initiative vs. guilt	
Elementary school (6–12 years)	Competence vs. inferiority	
Adolescence (13–18 years)	Identity vs. role confusion	If teenagers successfully experiment with different roles, they develop a sense of personal identity. If they fail to develop their own personal identity, they become confused about who they are.
Young adulthood (19–45 years)	Intimacy vs. isolation	
Middle adulthood (46–65 years)	Generativity vs. stagnation	
Late adulthood (66 years and up)	Integrity vs. despair	

a good writer. In adolescence, these self-descriptions become more abstract: I value honesty in people. I am more mature than my parents think. I enjoy competition.

In searching for your personal identity, you ask "Who am I?" and "How do I fit into the adult world around me?" Using your emerging formal operational thinking, you engage in this personal identity search by considering the realities of the present, the lessons learned from the past, and your hopes and expectations for the future.

FOUR ADOLESCENT IDENTITY STATUSES

James Marcia has further developed Erikson's ideas about adolescent identity development. He studied **identity status**, which refers to where an adolescent is in the identity-development process. According to Marcia, teenagers' identity status is based on (1) the degree to which they have explored possible identities, and (2) the degree to which they have committed themselves to a specific life path. As shown in Figure 9-5, below, Marcia identifies four identity statuses related to how much progress a teenager has made in both identity exploration and life path commitment.

identity status Where an adolescent is in the identity-development process

Figure 9-5 FOUR ADOLESCENT IDENTITY STATUSES

The four adolescent identity statuses relate to progress made in both identity exploration and life path commitment.

		Commitment to a Specific Life Path	
		Low	High
Exploration of Possible Identities	Low	Identity diffusion	Identity foreclosure
	High	Moratorium	Identity achievement

Identity diffusion refers to teenagers who have not explored possible identities and who have made no commitments to any life path. This childlike identity status is common during the early teen years. Older adolescents who still have a diffused identity often become social dropouts. They drift from interest to interest, and from one friendship to another, never committing themselves to anything or anybody. These teenagers often lack self-confidence and have low self-esteem.

© ALEXANDER GITLITS 2009/USED UNDER LICENSE FROM SHUTTERSTOCK.COM

Why do you think it is important for teenagers to work on developing a personal identity?

Adolescents in *identity foreclosure* have chosen a life path without exploring different identities. Teenagers who simply follow their parents' opinions on career and marriage, or those who accept what they think society expects of them, are in foreclosure. Foreclosed adolescents cannot tell the difference between their own goals and beliefs and the ones others have planned for them. They may be following others' wishes to avoid conflict or to gain approval.

Many teenagers who are either diffused or foreclosed in their identity status move to the *moratorium* status. These are adolescents who believe that they are not yet ready to become adults and are actively exploring possible identities. Many high school and college students are in this moratorium status. They choose different courses of study, and they experiment with different lifestyles and religious and political beliefs. In American society, most teenagers are encouraged to adopt this identity status for at least some period of time. The downside of the moratorium status is that many adolescents feel they are in a state of "limbo," which can cause fairly high levels of anxiety.

Fortunately, most young people who explore alternative identities eventually settle upon their own personal identity, which greatly decreases their anxiety about life. People who reach *identity achievement* are likely to have a feeling of self-acceptance, a high need for achievement, and clear ideas about their personal beliefs and values.

LAB TEAMS

Identity Statuses

Working in teams, create a list and identify TV or movie characters for each of the four identity statuses. Give reasons why the character would fit within each status.

PARENTS AND IDENTITY STATUS

Would it surprise you that teenagers who actively search for a personal identity sometimes are at odds with their parents? Most of these conflicts involve issues of control and parental authority as teenagers develop new social roles. Many developmental psychologists believe that this parent-teen conflict can be a very healthy sign that adolescents are trying to define themselves. Parent-child bickering provides teenagers with the opportunity to practice their increasing independence and personal decision-making. Parents who are best at handling these family conflicts are those who have an authoritative parenting style (see Chapter 8, page 226).

Authoritative parents allow their teenaged children to make many of their own decisions within the parents' clearly defined rules of conduct. This parenting style encourages identity development in adolescents.

One of the primary ways adolescents go about creating their personal identity is by experimenting with many different social roles—the nonconformist, the challenging son or daughter, the thrill-seeker, and so forth. Some teens try to define themselves in opposition to their parents. For example, if their parents are very involved in their local church, synagogue, or mosque, teenagers may challenge some or all of their parents' religious beliefs. If their parents are liberal Democrats, they may join the Young Republicans at their high school.

By challenging parental influence and experimenting with different roles, most teens gradually construct a personal identity that prepares them for adulthood. Often this identity is a combination of the roles with which they have experimented and serves as a guide for their future life choices. As teenagers' personal identity comes into sharper focus, family conflicts often diminish because parents become more comfortable with their teenagers' new identity. The teenagers also realize that their parents are treating them less like children and more like adults.

 **CHECKPOINT** *What are the four adolescent identity statuses?*

ETHNIC IDENTITY DEVELOPMENT

ethnic identity The sense of personal identification with a particular ethnic group

Developing your ethnic identity will provide you with both a sense of belonging and an historical understanding of your ethnic group.

What happens if you live in a society where your ethnic group is viewed negatively by many people? In such circumstances, your search for personal identity also may involve a search for **ethnic identity**, which is the sense of a personal identification with a particular ethnic group. For many people, developing an ethnic identity provides both a sense of belonging and an historical understanding of their past. It usually requires quite a bit of effort and is especially important for people who experience prejudice in the larger culture due to their ethnicity.

Social scientists typically describe three different stages in the development of ethnic identity. In stage 1, the *unexamined ethnic identity* stage, individuals have not examined ethnic identity issues and may believe negative stereotypes about their ethnic

© DIANA WEBB, 2009/USED UNDER LICENSE FROM SHUTTERSTOCK.COM

group expressed by some people within society. One result of adopting these negative stereotypes is that the individual is likely to experience low self-esteem.

In stage 2, *ethnic identity search,* experiencing prejudice or searching for personal identity may spark an interest in an individual's ethnicity. This stage involves people spending a great deal of time learning about their ethnic heritage.

The third and final stage, *achieved ethnic identity,* occurs when people achieve a rich understanding and appreciation of their ethnicity. This newfound ethnic identity allows individuals to feel a deep sense of ethnic pride along with a new understanding of their place in the larger culture. A number of studies find that people who are members of ethnic minority groups are more self-confident, happier, and successful if they have an achieved ethnic identity. These findings indicate that an achieved ethnic identity can protect you from the negative effects that prejudice can inflict on your self-esteem.

 **CHECKPOINT** *What are the three stages in ethnic identity development?*

9.3 ASSESSMENT

In Your Own Words

Using information from this section of the text, describe examples of how you or someone you know has engaged in activities that illustrate "identity versus role confusion." As an alternative, list an example from the movies or TV that illustrate the same concepts.

Review Concepts

1. Which is the fifth stage in Erikson's stages of psychosocial development?
   a. trust versus mistrust
   b. initiative versus guilt
   c. integrity versus despair
   d. identity versus role confusion

2. How long should it take you to know who you are and where you are headed?
   a. 16 years
   b. you know at birth
   c. a lifetime
   d. never

3. **True or False** A positive ethnic identity can protect you from the negative effects that prejudice can inflict on your self-esteem.

Think Critically

4. According to Erikson, what will happen if you cannot settle upon an identity by the end of adolescence?

5. Why might an ethnic identity be important to someone?

Gender Differences in Friendship Intimacy

INTRODUCTION Friendships provide important social and emotional support for teenagers. While both girls and boys value friendship, a number of studies find gender differences in friendships from childhood through adulthood. One important gender difference is the level of intimacy expressed within same-sex friendships. Intimacy is an emotional and psychological closeness with another person. Girls' friendships are more intimate and involve more emotional sharing than boys' friendships. What explains these gender differences?

HYPOTHESIS A number of psychologists have hypothesized that friendships between boys have less intimacy compared to friendships between girls due to differences in the way boys and girls are socialized.

METHOD Psychologists have studied friendship patterns among children, adolescents, and adults mostly by conducting survey studies in which they ask people to describe their friendships.

RESULTS The findings from these studies indicate that many American males report that while growing up they often were discouraged from expressing warmth, tenderness, and affection in friendships with other males. The message underlying this discouragement was that expressing tender emotions was unmanly and feminine. This rather narrow view of masculinity was not shared by most American men 100 years ago. It also currently is not shared by men in many non-Western societies. As we move through the twenty-first century, changes in gender roles may eventually allow both boys and men to feel more comfortable expressing tenderness and affection toward their male friends. Until that time, however, many male friendships will generally lack the emotional strength of the average female friendship.

BLEND IMAGES/JUPITER IMAGES

Critical Analysis

1. What important gender difference is found in friendships from childhood through adulthood?

2. What is a likely explanation for the lower levels of intimacy in friendships between boys compared to friendships between girls?

School Counselor

Education & Training

School counselors help students from elementary school through college. They provide students with career and educational counseling and they help students through difficult times. They often are advocates in the community as well as at school for education and student needs.

In cooperation with parents and teachers, counselors in elementary schools observe students in class settings and at play in order to help assess the child's strengths, problems, or special needs. Counselors also help teachers and administrators design a curriculum for students with special needs.

High school counselors administer aptitude and personality tests and use interviews and counseling sessions with students to gain knowledge of students' characters. In this way, school counselors can help advise students on career choices that best fit each student's personality. Counselors also advise students on college choices, appropriate majors, admissions requirements, entrance exams, ACTs, SATs, and financial aid. Additionally, they advise students on trade and technical schools and on apprenticeship programs.

College counselors assist students with their course of study, career planning, and with job-search skills. They also may help students during a difficult personal or academic time.

Employment Outlook

As the population rises, careers as school counselors will continue to be in demand. Growth is expected to rise through 2016 because of growth and current school counselors leaving the field. Growth in this career depends on the location of your community.

Needed Skills and Education

Education requirements vary from state to state; however, usually a master's degree is required for working as a school counselor. Many colleges and universities offer programs in the education or psychology departments for people who wish to pursue a career in school counseling. Fields of study may include courses in human and growth and development, social and cultural diversity, relationships, group work, career development, assessment, research and program evaluation, and professional identity. In addition to classes, supervised clinical experience is required. Most states require a license for school counselors and continuing education credits obtained after college.

People interested in a career in school counseling need to want to work with others. Counselors must be able to help others, to deal with crisis situations, and be able to hold confidences. This is a highly stressful career, so people entering this field should be able to deal with stress on a daily basis.

How You'll Spend Your Day

Your workday will depend on whether you choose elementary school, high school, or college counseling. With each level, you will be helping students better understand themselves and their world. You will work with students individually to help them deal with social, behavioral, and personal problems. School counselors emphasize preventive and developmental assistance with students in order to help students deal with problems before they get out of hand. You will also help students with their future school and career choices.

Earnings

The median earnings for elementary and secondary school counselors are $53,750; for junior colleges the median earnings are $48,240; and for colleges, universities, and professional schools, the median earnings are $41,780.

What About You?

Is this a career you think you might enjoy? Write a list of five things you would most like to do as a school counselor that you believe would help others. Then make a list of five reasons you do not think this is the career for you. If the first list is easier to write than the second, research this career in more depth.

© CORBIS

CHAPTER SUMMARY

9.1 Adolescence as a Transition Period

- Adolescence is the transition period between childhood and adulthood.

- Seven developmental tasks signify transition into adulthood.

- Developmental psychologists identify three separate stages of adolescence, which are early adolescence, ages about 11 to 14 years; middle adolescence, ages 15 to 17 years; and late adolescence, ages 18 years and older.

- Many developmental psychologists believe that the age period from the late teens to the mid-twenties should be identified as the developmental stage of emerging adulthood.

- Most teenagers experience puberty in early adolescence. During puberty, changes occur in the primary sex characteristics (reproductive organs) and secondary sex characteristics (physical features that distinguish women and men from one another). Girls experience menarche and boys experience spermarche.

- Adolescents mature at different times. These differences can create feelings of self-consciousness and affect social life and feelings of self-worth.

9.2 Cognitive, Moral, and Emotional Development

- Jean Piaget's fourth state of cognitive development is the formal operational stage, which typically begins during early or middle adolescence.

- Moral reasoning is the process of distinguishing between good and bad conduct.

- According to Lawrence Kohlberg, people pass through six stages of moral development, reflecting three different levels of moral reasoning. Preconventional morality is the selfish moral reasoning based on avoiding punishment or seeking rewards. Conventional morality is moral reasoning based on seeking social approval or conforming to authority to maintain social order. Postconventional morality is moral reasoning based on abstract principles and values that may conflict with personal interests and societal norms.

- During adolescence, a cognitive-emotional push-pull is taking place. At the same time you are developing more complex thinking skills, you also are experiencing new emotions that may sidetrack your reasoning and logic. These emotions are triggered by hormonal changes that occur during puberty. Adolescents may develop an imaginary audience or personal fable with their heightened emotions.

9.3 Identity Development

- Erikson's fifth stage in psychosocial development is identity vs. role confusion, which occurs during adolescence.

- James Marcia identified four adolescent identity statuses related to a teen's progress in both identity exploration and life path commitment.

- Conflicts with parents arise as the teen develops new social roles and involve issues of parental control and authority.

- The search for a personal identity also may include a search for ethnic identity.

CHAPTER ASSESSMENT

Review Psychology Terms

Select the term that best fits the definition. Some terms will not be used.

____ 1. The transition period between childhood and adulthood

____ 2. Males' first experience of ejaculation

____ 3. The process of distinguishing between good and bad conduct

____ 4. The age period from the late teens to the mid-twenties in which a person is relatively free from adult responsibilities and expectations

____ 5. Moral reasoning based on seeking social approval or conforming to authority to maintain social order

____ 6. A common adolescent belief that other people are constantly focusing their thoughts, feelings, and behavior on you

____ 7. The growth period in which a person reaches sexual maturity and becomes capable of reproducing

____ 8. The first menstrual period

____ 9. Moral reasoning based on abstract principles and values that may conflict with personal interests and societal norms

____ 10. Teenagers' tendency to believe that no one has ever felt or thought as they do

____ 11. The reproductive organs

____ 12. Selfish moral reasoning based on avoiding punishment or seeking rewards

____ 13. A person's sense of personal identification with a particular ethnic group

____ 14. The nonreproductive physical features that distinguish women and men from one another

____ 15. Your understanding of what makes you unique as an individual and different from others.

a. adolescence
b. conventional morality
c. developmental tasks
d. emerging adulthood
e. ethnic identity
f. formal operational stage
g. identity status
h. imaginary audience
i. menarche
j. moral reasoning
k. personal fable
l. personal identity
m. postconventional morality
n. preconventional morality
o. primary sex characteristics
p. puberty
q. secondary sex characteristics
r. spermarche

Review Psychology Concepts

16. Name the seven developmental tasks that signify the transition from adolescence to adulthood. List the tasks that had the highest number of respondents rating the task as "extremely important" first, and then add the others in descending order. Include the age the event should occur beside the task.

17. Recall the three stages of adolescence and give the age groups for each.

18. Support the statement: "Puberty is an important time in a person's life."

19. Identify the internal and external changes that occur during puberty.

20. What is the similarity between menarche in females and spermarche in males, and what is the significance of these events with respect to puberty?

21. Compare American society's attitudes on sexuality and sexual conduct to those of other societies.

22. Assess how Jean Piaget's formal operational stage could lead to heated debates with your parents or other people.

23. Does the evidence support Kohlberg's theory of moral development in all societies? Defend your answer.

24. What is the physiological reason most adolescents have quick mood changes?

25. Restate the crisis in Erikson's fifth stage of psychosocial development.

26. Compare and contrast identity diffusion and identity foreclosure in teens.

27. In which stage of Marcia's identity status might you find most college students?

28. Which stage of Marcia's identity status is associated with self-acceptance, a stable self-concept, high achievement, and clear ideas about personal beliefs and values?

29. What is the value of an ethnic identity?

30. List the three stages in ethnic identity formation according to Jean Phinney.

Apply Psychology Concepts

31. Why might some cultures not have a need for adolescence as a stage of human development?

32. Can you describe an incident during your teenage years where you have experienced what psychologists refer to as the imaginary audience?

33. What are some social roles that you have experimented with during your teenage years? Do you think these different social-role experiments were related to your search for a personal identity? Why or why not?

34. Have you personally experienced ethnic identity search? Do you know someone who appears to have searched or is currently searching for their ethnic identity? Can you identify specific life events that correspond to different stages in the ethnic identity development process?

Make Academic Connections

35. **Multimedia** Use a software program and other artwork to prepare a multimedia presentation that describes how the social role of teenagers changes from early to late adolescence.

36. **Cross-Cultural Studies** Use personal interviews with other students in your school, the library, or the Internet to research the relative importance of peer versus parental influence in different cultural groups. For example, you could interview a student of a different cultural group from yours to learn who has the greatest influence on the student—parents or peers—and why. Compare that person's answer with who has the most important influence on teens within your cultural group—parents or peers—and why. Cultural groups may include people living in a foreign country, or people living in this country with an ethnic identity different from yours. Compare your findings in a summary.

37. **Science** Decide which of Marcia's four identity statuses best describes you, and then using these stages, predict what your life might be like in adulthood. What, if any, adjustments do you need to make?

Adolescence is a time of major changes—physical, mental, and emotional. It also is a time when teenagers make decisions that will impact their future. Many of these decisions carry important consequences. Although the views psychologists have of adolescence are undergoing significant changes, they still note that much of the anxiety teens feel comes from changes in interpersonal relationships. Access the Gale Psychology eCollection at *www.cengage.com/school/psych/franzoi* and read "Social Changes Associated with Adolescence in Western Industrialized Countries." Write a summary of the information in the article and answer the question: Which of the three areas of transition identified by Eccles is the most significant? Why? As an additional project, identify the area of social change with the largest impact on your adolescence and describe why.

Source: Eccles, Jacquelynne S. "Adolescence." *Child Development*. Ed: Neil J. Salkind. New York: Macmillan Reference USA, 2002.

SELF-DISCOVERY: YOUR SCORE

How Self-Conscious Are You?

Scoring instructions: To calculate your self-consciousness score, add up your responses to these 7 items to get a total score. The average score for self-consciousness is about 19. The higher your score is above 19, the higher your self-consciousness, while the lower your score is below 19, the lower your self-consciousness.

Interpretation of scores: People who score high on self-consciousness tend to be concerned about whether other people will judge them negatively in social situations and they also are concerned about their physical appearance. These feelings often make high self-conscious people socially anxious, and they are more likely to conform to gain acceptance from others. People who score low on self-consciousness generally are not very concerned about how others judge them, and they are not overly concerned about their physical appearance. Low self-conscious people are comfortable in social situations and are less likely to conform to gain acceptance from others.

Adulthood and Aging

ESSENTIAL QUESTION
Go to page XXVI

"What is an adult? A child blown up by age."

—SIMONE DE BEAUVOIR, FRENCH AUTHOR, 1908–1986

One of my more embarrassing life moments—right up there with my high school driving test—was the first time I met my wife. I went to a modern dance concert and during the performance was unexpectedly called on stage by one of the dancers. She proceeded to teach me a complicated dance step in front of the entire audience. My heart beat rapidly and my face flushed, but I concentrated as best I could as she led me through the steps while the audience watched in amusement. The dancer was attractive and I was beginning to enjoy myself when *it* happened.

In the middle of a big leg swing, my brand-new reversible belt buckle popped completely off my belt and shot across the dance floor! The dancer laughed; the audience roared; I was mortified. Later, whenever I would see this dancer around town, my heart would race and my face would become flushed as I relived "the incident." She never noticed me during these near encounters, but I certainly noticed her. What were my feelings toward her? Attraction coupled with anxiety. Eight months later, I finally introduced myself when our paths crossed again, and we began dating. A year and a half later we were married.

10.1 | Young Adulthood

OBJECTIVES

- Describe two theories of young adulthood.
- Discuss the developmental task of seeking intimacy.

DISCOVER IT | *How does this relate to me?*

Do you currently look and think differently from when you were eight years old? Most likely you have noticed dramatic changes. Do you think your physical looks and the way you think about things will change as dramatically when you move from your teen years into your mid-twenties? Physical and psychological changes often happen quickly and dramatically in childhood and adolescence, but they often are less noticeable during adulthood. Many of these adulthood changes are also very different from those that take place earlier in life. What are your thoughts about what some of those changes might be?

You will face important and necessary adjustments when you leave adolescence and enter adulthood. In this section you will learn about the first stage of adulthood—young adulthood. Later in this chapter, you will learn about two other stages of adulthood—middle adulthood and late adulthood.

Theories of Young Adulthood

Two important theories of young adulthood are those of Erik Erikson and Daniel Levinson. You already are familiar with Erikson's psychosocial stages for infancy through adolescence (Chapter 8, page 229, and Chapter 9, page 263). The final three psychosocial stages concern adulthood. Levinson's theory proposed that the transition from adolescence to adulthood includes a *novice* stage, or a stage where young people learn what it means to be an adult.

PSYCHOSOCIAL STAGES OF ADULTHOOD

Most developmental psychologists divide adulthood into three stages, corresponding to Erik Erikson's adult psychosocial stages: young adulthood (ages 19 to 40), middle adulthood (ages 40 to 65), and late adulthood (ages 65 or older). Each stage is supposedly marked by a crisis or conflict (see Table 10-1 on page 276). For both my wife and I, our courtship and marriage represented the successful resolution of an important challenge of young adulthood, the seeking of intimacy and the avoidance of isolation.

Table 10-1   ERIKSON'S ADULT STAGES OF PSYCHOSOCIAL DEVELOPMENT

Psychosocial Stage	Crisis	Description of Crisis
Infancy (birth–1 year)	Trust vs. mistrust	
Toddlerhood (1–2 years)	Autonomy vs. shame and doubt	
Preschooler (3–5 years)	Initiative vs. guilt	
Elementary school (6–12 years)	Competence vs. inferiority	
Adolescence (13–18 years)	Identity vs. role confusion	
Young adulthood (19–40 years)	Intimacy vs. isolation	If young adults successfully develop close relationships, they gain a sense of intimacy. If they are unable to develop such relationships, they feel socially isolated.
Middle adulthood (40–65 years)	Generativity vs. stagnation	If the middle-aged believe that they are contributing to the world and the next generation, they develop a sense of generativity. If they fail to do so, they experience a sense of stagnation.
Late adulthood (65 years and up)	Integrity vs. despair	If the elderly have successfully managed the previous crises in their lives, they will feel a sense of integrity. If they regret many of their life choices, they will feel a sense of despair.

THE NOVICE PHASE OF YOUNG ADULTHOOD

In Chapter 9 you read that young people identified the most important internal change necessary for adulthood status as accepting responsibility. Daniel Levinson examined young adulthood in **longitudinal studies,** or research in which the same people are restudied and retested over time. He proposed that most young adults go through a *novice* phase in which they weigh their options in life and learn what it means to be an adult. During this time, young adults begin taking on adult responsibilities while they lay the groundwork for establishing a stable life structure.

One way young adults assume adult responsibilities is by leaving home and becoming financially and emotionally independent of their parents. Another way of taking on adult responsibilities is by developing a *dream* or vision of the way they want their lives to unfold. Many young adults also look for a *mentor,* an older adult who can offer guidance and inspiration in making the young adult's dream become reality.

Most young adults' dreams in the novice phase mainly focus on career choices and career goals. They often try out one or more different types of careers before settling on their final choice. Once chosen, their field of work becomes an important part of their self-concept, and they strive to use their learned skills in

longitudinal studies Research in which the same people are restudied and retested over time

achieving success in the workplace. To gain some insight into your work attitudes and beliefs, spend some time completing the Self-Discovery feature below.

In the novice phase of young adulthood—and in later adulthood stages—people often spend a great deal of time assessing and reassessing their life goals and the progress they are making in achieving them. In fact, Levinson states that many people spend nearly half their adult lives in *transition periods* where they reassess their lives and openly question their current dreams.

PHOTODISC/GETTY IMAGES

During the novice phase, young adults often seek guidance from older and more experienced adults. In most instances, what sort of guidance are young adults seeking?

SELF-DISCOVERY

What Are Your Work Attitudes and Beliefs?

Have you ever thought about how you developed your work attitudes and beliefs? To help you better understand your ideas about work, complete the following exercise.

Part 1

1. How important is work in your life? Give details.

2. Is there a particular kind of work that you find most enjoyable? If so, what kind of work? Why is it enjoyable? If not, why not? Give details.

3. If you think you may have children in the future, what will you try to teach them about the role of work in their lives? Give details.

Part 2

After writing answers to the questions in Part 1, think about the adult who currently has the most influence on your life. Once you have a good image in your mind of this person, imagine asking this person the same questions you just answered. Write down the answers that you expect this person to give to these questions about her/himself. After completing this task, go to this person, ask these same questions, and write down her/his answers. Then, ask this final question: "Do you think I have followed your ideas about work?"

1. How accurate were you in imagining this person's responses?

2. How similar are your work attitudes and beliefs to this person?

3. Is there anything about your work attitudes and beliefs that you would like to change? If so, explain what you would like to change.

These transition periods can last up to five years and may cause adults to experience a psychological crisis or conflict. Levinson's research suggests that transition periods are most likely to occur around the middle of young adulthood (about age 30), the beginning and midpoint of middle adulthood (about age 40 and again at age 50), and at the beginning of late adulthood (about age 65). However, some adults do not experience all these transition periods. Many experience them at different ages and some do not experience them at all.

CHECKPOINT *Name two psychologists who developed theories of young adulthood and identify the focus of their theories.*

Seeking Intimacy

According to both Erikson and Levinson, one of the most important developmental tasks of young adulthood is establishing a long-term romantic bond that brings both happiness and a sense of fulfillment to life. While making career choices in the novice phase, many young adults also are searching for intimacy. As you know, Erikson identified this task of early adulthood as the sixth crisis in life: *intimacy versus isolation*. He believed that without close, loving relationships, adults become emotionally isolated and self-absorbed. Establishing such intimacy with another person requires a great deal of maturity and responsibility.

DEVELOPING ROMANTIC INTIMACY

Finding intimacy in a romantic relationship is important throughout adulthood, but young adulthood is when most people first seek a long-term romantic relationship. For most people, this means marriage. Surveys of American adults find that marriage is the most important factor in determining happiness—more important than work, income, or friendships.

The psychology of romantic love generally is the same for everyone. The happiest couples in long-term romantic relationships are those who experience both *passionate love* and *companionship love*. **Passionate love** is a state of intense emotional and physical longing for another person. Couples typically experience passion most strongly during the early stages of a romantic relationship and find that it cools somewhat over time. One reason for this lowering of passion is that romantic emotions thrive on the

passionate love A state of intense emotional and physical longing for another person; experienced most strongly during the early stages of a romantic relationship

Both passion and companionship form the basis for happiness in long-term romantic relationships.

DIGITAL VISION/GETTYIMAGES

thrill and uncertainty of winning over another's affections. **Companionship love** (also called *companionate love*) is the affection felt for people with whom your lives are deeply entwined. As young adults settle into a secure romantic relationship, their passion for one another may lower a bit, but their feelings of companionship grow stronger. Companionship develops out of a sense of certainty in one another's love and respect, as well as a feeling of genuine mutual understanding. Research investigating what makes couples happy in long-term romantic relationships finds that strong companionship is a better predictor of happiness than passion.

Of course, not everyone is successful in maintaining intimacy in their romantic relationships. Read the Closer Look feature below, which examines how low self-esteem can weaken and even destroy the romantic bonds between couples.

companionship love The affection felt for people with whom your lives are deeply entwined

CLOSER LOOK

Self-Esteem and Romantic Love

Many people believe that you will be unable to love others if you do not love yourself. Is this true? The short answer is "no, but…" People with low self-esteem can feel great romantic passion, but their passion is fed by insecurity. This insecurity has to do with low self-esteem individuals feeling uncertain about their partners' affections for them. They believe their partners are "too good for them." Because they doubt their partners' love, low self-esteem people constantly seek reassurance. They also often overreact when their partners express any negative moods or negative behaviors, thinking that they are going to be rejected. Burdened with these romantic concerns, low self-esteem persons begin finding fault in their partners, which helps them prepare for the expected rejection. Meanwhile, this increased negativity causes their once-admiring partners to feel much less happy in the relationship, making a break up more likely. When the break up occurs, low self-esteem individuals often respond by thinking to themselves, "This proves that I'm not worth loving."

In summary, while self-esteem is not related to the ability to love, it is related to loving in a healthy way. Low self-esteem persons are perfectly capable of feeling romantic passion, but they have a much more difficult time feeling emotionally secure in romantic love.

Think Critically

If someone has low self-esteem, why would it be better for them to improve their self-esteem before they form a relationship?

CULTURAL DIFFERENCES IN LOVE AND MARRIAGE

Cross-cultural research indicates that people around the world have different views of the importance of romantic love in marriage. In individualist countries, such as the United States, England, and Australia, people place greater importance on love in marriage than do people in collectivist countries, such as India, Pakistan, Thailand, and the Philippines. In these collectivist countries there is a long tradition of having *arranged marriages,* meaning that the families of young adults choose their spouses for them.

People in individualist cultures are more likely to select a mate who is physically attractive or has an exciting personality. When people in collectivist cultures choose their own spouses, they tend to base their selection on who will best fit into their extended family. As in individualist cultures, love is a part of a collectivist marriage. However, in collectivist cultures, it is more common for people first to get married and then to fall in love.

Collectivist cultures have seen a recent shift in beliefs about romance and marriage as they become more exposed to Western culture. It is increasingly common for young adults in countries such as India, Japan, China, and South Korea to choose their own spouses, sometimes going against their families' wishes.

DEALING WITH ROMANTIC CONFLICT

Rocky periods occur in all romantic relationships. Longitudinal studies of married couples find that whether they remain committed to one another during times of trouble largely depends on how they deal with their problems. Their level of commitment to the marriage greatly influences the strategies used in resolving romantic problems. The more satisfied and committed people are in a marriage, or in any other kind of romantic relationship, the harder they work to solve their problems. Successful marriages require two partners to be kind to one another and to listen to each other's concerns.

People in collectivist cultures place less emphasis than do those in individualist cultures on romantic love as a primary basis for marriage. What do you think people in collectivist cultures emphasize in choosing a marriage partner?

PHOTO COURTESY OF JENNY FRANZOI

Caryl Rusbult has identified four strategies people typically use in dealing with a troubled romantic relationship. These four strategies differ along the dimensions of *active-passive* and *constructive-destructive*. Figure 10-1 illustrates the primary qualities of these four strategies.

In handling conflict, some people adopt a passively constructive approach by exhibiting *loyalty*, which involves simply waiting in the hope that things will improve on their own. Persons who adopt this strategy often are afraid to increase the conflict by directly addressing it, so they say nothing and hope that their loyalty will keep the relationship alive.

Other people adopt the passively destructive strategy of *neglect*. They emotionally ignore their partners and spend less time with them. When partners are together, neglectful persons often treat their partners poorly by constantly criticizing them for things unrelated to the real problem. Those who do not know how to handle their negative emotions, or who are not interested in improving the relationship but also not ready to end it, often rely on this strategy.

When people do decide that the relationship is not worth saving, they *exit*, which is an active, yet destructive, strategy. A much more constructive and active approach in dealing with conflict is *voice*. This is when people discuss their problems, seek compromises, and try to repair a relationship they still highly value. Romantic couples with high levels of companionship for one another often choose the voice strategy. Of the four strategies, voice provides the best chance for couples to stay together.

Figure 10-1 FOUR STRATEGIES IN DEALING WITH RELATIONSHIP PROBLEMS

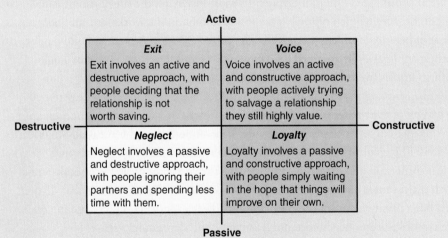

In dealing with relationship conflict, people typically use different strategies, which vary along the dimensions of active-passive and constructive-destructive.

DIVORCE AND ITS CONSEQUENCES

When adults choose the exit strategy in handling marital conflict, they go through the legal process of *divorce*. With about half of all marriages ending in divorce, the United States has one of the highest divorce rates in the world. One-third of divorces occur during the first ten years of marriage, which often means that it occurs during early adulthood.

One reason the divorce rate is so high is because Americans today are less willing to stay in unhappy marriages than they were in previous generations. Another reason is that as married women have become more financially independent of their husbands, they are less likely to rely on the *loyalty* strategy and quietly remain in unhappy marriages. In the past, exiting an unhappy marriage was an option generally reserved for working men.

About half of all marriages end in divorce, and a third of divorces occur during the first ten years of marriage.

Divorce is not a single event in an adult's life. It is a process involving a series of potentially stressful events. Each step in the process of divorce can increase people's stress levels, making them more susceptible to illnesses and mental health problems. Married couples who divorce have higher illness and death rates than couples who remain married. Women are affected more negatively by divorce at all ages than are men.

However, for both women and men, health and happiness can improve following divorce, especially if the marriage was highly conflicted. Divorced individuals cope best with the end of their marriages when they re-establish an active social life or find a new romantic companion.

What about the children of divorce? In most instances, the single parent is the mother. Because women typically earn less than men in the workforce, and because absent fathers are less likely to provide adequate child support, many single-parent mothers are financially strapped following a divorce. More than a third of single-mother families live below the poverty line.

Before reaching the age of 18, 40 percent of American children will experience the ending of their parents' marriage. African-American and Hispanic children are more likely to experience divorce than are Asian-American and Caucasian-American children. These cultural-group differences are explained partly by the fact that African-American and Hispanic families tend to experience greater economic stress, which often causes marital conflict that leads to divorce. Research finds that divorce often has a negative impact on most children. They experience an increase in academic problems and heightened anger, anxiety, and depression.

CHECKPOINT *Name the best predictor of happiness in romantic relationships, passion or companionship, and explain why.*

In Your Own Words

Compare and contrast Erikson's stages of young adulthood and Levinson's novice phase of adulthood. Include the description of Erikson's psychosocial crisis and Levinson's novice phase. Using information from the text, evaluate how understanding young adulthood might help you form a lasting and happy romantic relationship when you reach this phase of your life. For example, you might write about how understanding Erikson's intimacy versus isolation helps you understand the problems of isolation, so you will be more likely to form an intimate relationship; and that by understanding Levinson's novice phase, you will be open to assessing and reassessing your life goals during young adulthood.

Review Concepts

1. Which societies have the highest divorce rate?

   a. collectivist
   b. individualist
   c. democratic
   d. egalitarian

2. Which type of love is most common among young adults in the United States?

   a. passionate
   b. companionship
   c. attachment
   d. philosophical

3. **True or False** The crisis Erikson describes in his psychosocial development for young adults is integrity versus despair.

4. **True or False** Young adulthood is when most people first seek a romantic relationship.

5. **True or False** Rocky periods occur in all romantic relationships.

Think Critically

6. Why might young adulthood be the time to assess your life's goals and values?

7. How might a mentor help you in your life? Give specific ways a mentor could help you in your personal life or career.

8. Why is a sense of companionship important to a romantic relationship?

9. Why might marriages agreed on by two romantically involved people have a higher divorce rate than marriages arranged by the parents?

10. Name the strategy that provides the best chance for a couple to stay together, and explain why this strategy might work.

11. In a collectivist society, why might a person select a mate who fits in best with the extended family?

12. List two reasons young adults are less likely to stay in a marriage than people of an older generation.

KEY TERMS

- aging
- chronological age
- functional age
- menopause
- midlife crisis

OBJECTIVES

- Describe differences in how women and men view parenting and job responsibilities.
- Define aging.
- Describe the midlife crisis and how common it is among adults.

DISCOVER IT | *How does this relate to me?*

As a teenager, you may think of adults as almost being a different species. Yet it is very likely that you are living with at least one adult who is middle-aged. Some of your teachers also might be in middle adulthood. Here is your opportunity to gain some insight into these individuals who have such a major influence on your life. What are some of the issues they may be struggling with while they interact with you?

As one of those middle-aged adults, allow me to provide you with a glimpse into the world of middle age. When I was a teenager, I recovered very quickly from the everyday strains on my body. As I grew older, it took longer for my body to repair itself. I enjoy exercising, but since turning 50, I regularly nurse various aches and pains from jogging and bicycling. I have become a literal walking—make that limping—example of the middle-aged body (add thinning, graying hair, and tell-tale wrinkles to this picture). Many middle-aged adults envy your youth and vitality. They remember the "good old days" when their body worked more efficiently. Yet, thankfully, there is more to middle adulthood than declining physical attributes.

Balancing Parenting and Job Responsibilities

According to Erik Erikson's theory of psychosocial development, the crisis of middle adulthood is *generativity versus stagnation* (refer back to Table 10-1, page 276). Generativity involves teaching and nurturing the next generation as well as creating something of substance in the world of work. Erikson's theory states that people who fail to contribute and produce something that they feel is worthy of their efforts experience a sense of stagnation, or lack of purpose, in their lives. Some adults focus all their efforts on the family and raising children. Others emphasize the world of work outside the home. Many others try to balance both family and work responsibilities.

Nearly two-thirds of American married couples with children under the age of 18 are a two-income family. Three-fourths of first-time mothers return to work within a year after giving birth. Like these adults, many of you will devote tremendous time and effort to both pursuing a career and raising or otherwise mentoring children.

Many adults choose to both pursue a career and raise a family.

PHOTODISC IMAGES/GETTY IMAGES

PERCEIVING FAMILY AND WORK CONFLICTS

Whether you see a conflict between raising a family and having a career may be influenced by whether you are a man or a woman. In American society, women are more likely than men to receive mixed messages concerning their ability to juggle the responsibilities of both career and family. These mixed messages occur because careers can conflict with the traditional feminine role of child caretaker. In contrast, many men learn to view work and family decisions as independent issues. This is so because many generations of fathers have spent long periods of time away from their families while they work.

This conflict between career and family goals is not experienced by all women. Women who have witnessed their own mothers balancing family and work obligations are much less likely to feel a conflict between family and career duties. By observing their mothers juggle these two roles, many women expect less stress in taking on these two sets of responsibilities. Many of these same women also expect that their husbands will be more involved in parenting than were fathers in previous generations.

What are the possible benefits to society if we encourage men as fathers to have more housework and child care responsibilities? Research suggests that when fathers are actively involved in daily family and household duties, everyone benefits. The children of highly involved fathers perform better in school and have better social skills than children of less involved fathers. The working mothers of involved fathers are happier and less stressed. What about the rewards for fathers? Their greater family involvement increases the fathers' confidence in their parenting abilities and their marriages are happier and stronger.

INFOBIT
A widely held belief is that mothers are much more important for children than fathers. As a result of this belief, a father's relationship with his children often is defined in terms of his bond with the mother. If that bond is broken by divorce or is not formed (as in the case of many unmarried teens), the father's relationship with his children often is weak.

Fathers who help with both household chores and childcare responsibilities have happier spouses and have happier marriages. Do the children also benefit?

CREATAS IMAGES/JUPITER IMAGES

CHECKPOINT How do many women and men differ in their beliefs about career and family responsibilities and conflicts?

Aging

During adolescence and early young adulthood, the body operates at its peak efficiency and strength. Beginning in the 20s, the body starts to burn calories at a slower rate, causing many people to add extra pounds to their frame. Hearing also declines somewhat by the late 20s, especially for high-pitched tones. This weight gain and mild hearing loss are some of the first symptoms of aging. **Aging** is the progressive deterioration of the body that ends in death.

People can age in at least two ways. **Chronological age** is the number of years you have lived, while **functional age** is a measure of how well you can physically and mentally function in your surroundings. Chronological age and functional age are not always in sync. For example, some 50-year-olds function like a typical 35-year-old, while other 50-year-olds function like a typical 60-year-old.

By the 30s and 40s, outward signs of aging become much more noticeable. Hair thins and becomes gray, wrinkles develop, and visual perception declines. A less noticeable aging effect is the loss of bone mass, which not only makes bones weaker and more brittle, but also can actually cause them to compress slightly. Due to bone compression in the spinal column and changes in posture, by the age of 70, an individual may have shrunk 1 to 2 inches.

The most significant biological sign of aging that occurs in middle-aged women is **menopause**, which is the ending of menstruation. Menopause usually occurs within a few years of age 50 and is accompanied by a reduction in the hormone *estrogen*. The most reported sign of menopause is the *hot flash,* which is a sensation of heat in the upper body and face that lasts for a few minutes. Although menopause can have some uncomfortable symptoms, more than two-thirds of American women who

aging The progressive deterioration of the body that ends in death

chronological age The number of years a person has lived

functional age A measure of how well you can physically and mentally function in your surroundings

menopause The ending of menstruation

have experienced menopause generally feel better after going through "the change" than they have for years. Menopause ends a woman's fertile years for childbearing.

Unlike women, middle-aged men do not experience an end of fertility or even a sharp drop in sex hormones. However, they do suffer an earlier decline than women in the ability to hear and to smell. Realizing that physical strengths and skills are declining is more likely to create stress in men than in women. This may be so because men are more likely than women to define themselves in terms of their physical strengths and athletic abilities. Men who are most likely to experience this increased stress are those who work in jobs involving hard physical labor.

CHECKPOINT *What is aging?*

Do Most Adults Experience a Midlife Crisis?

Developmental psychologists often have described the years between 40 and 50 as a time when many adults experience a **midlife crisis**, which is a stressful period when adults review and reevaluate their lives. As already mentioned, Erikson described this crisis as being triggered by a feeling that life lacks meaning or purpose. Other psychologists suggest that the midlife crisis is caused by people realizing that they are growing older and moving closer to the end of life.

Most Americans believe that many adults experience a midlife crisis. However, recent studies find that fewer than 10 percent of adults have psychological crises related to their age or aging. Researchers do find evidence that many middle-aged adults spend time reflecting on and reassessing their lives. However, this self-reflection seldom is related to the sort of psychological distress that is popularly labeled a "midlife crisis."

What about the *empty nest syndrome* where middle-aged parents become depressed when their last child leaves home? Is this evidence for the midlife crisis? The reality is that most parents experience a sense of relief, not depression, when their last child departs. Empty-nest parents can now pursue their own interests while their children do likewise.

It is not true that the midlife crisis is a complete myth. After all, about one out of ten middle-aged adults do struggle with an age-related crisis. The average age at which this crisis begins is 46. For men, midlife crises last about three to ten years, while for women they tend to last two to five years. However, for most adults, entering middle age is just one more of life's many transitions.

BANANASTOCK/JUPITER IMAGES

midlife crisis A stressful period experienced by a few middle-aged adults when they review and reevaluate their lives

Empty-nest parents generally experience a sense of relief when their last child departs, and are free to pursue their own interests.

CHECKPOINT *What is the midlife crisis?*

10.2 ASSESSMENT

In Your Own Words

Choose one of the objectives listed at the beginning of this section on page 284. Using information from the text, describe the information in your own words that assesses the chosen objective. For example, you might choose the second objective: aging. You could define aging, and then explain the difference between functional and chronological age. You also could review how the body changes in middle age and how men and women experience aging differently.

Review Concepts

1. Which is Erikson's psychosocial developmental crisis for middle adulthood?
   - a. integrity versus despair
   - b. trust versus mistrust
   - c. intimacy versus isolation
   - d. generativity versus stagnation

2. Which refers to the number of years you have lived?
   - a. aging
   - b. chronological age
   - c. functional age
   - d. midlife crisis

3. Which is accompanied by a reduction in the hormone estrogen?
   - a. menopause
   - b. functional age
   - c. midlife crisis
   - d. chronological age

4. **True or False** Both men and women experience an end of fertility during middle adulthood.

5. **True or False** In American society, women are more likely than men to receive mixed messages concerning their ability to juggle the dual responsibilities of career and family.

6. **True or False** Current studies indicate that about 30 percent of all adults experience a midlife crisis.

Think Critically

7. Support this statement with information from the text: If your mother worked while you were growing up, you are less likely to experience stress when trying to balance work and family life.

8. Why do people in middle adulthood often gain weight?

9. As you approach middle age, what can you do to lower your functional age, and why might this be a good idea?

10. Why might men in middle age feel more stress from aging than women?

11. Using evidence from the text, judge whether the midlife crisis is a myth.

12. Why might parents today be less inclined to experience empty nest syndrome than parents from earlier generations?

Late Adulthood

OBJECTIVES

- Compare cultural views of aging.
- Examine social transitions and roles of people in late adulthood.
- Discuss physical and cognitive changes in people in late adulthood.
- Discuss death and dying and the theories on coping with death.

DISCOVER IT | *How does this relate to me?*

Wrinkles. Card games. Hearing difficulties. Talking a lot about "what is important in life" or "the good old days." These were just a few of the comments offered by high school students when I asked them what comes to mind when they think about old people. What are your thoughts about those who have entered late adulthood? What do you really know about the world of the elderly? Do you think older adults all are similar, or are they as different from one another as people in your age group? What are the typical joys and challenges of late adulthood?

KEY TERMS

- gerontology
- ageism
- productive aging
- activity theory of aging
- genetic preprogramming theory of aging
- wear-and-tear theory of aging
- dementia
- wisdom

The population of the United States is becoming older because people are living longer. In 1900 only 4 percent of Americans were age 65 or older, and a person born that year could expect to live only into their late 40s. One hundred years later, almost 13 percent of Americans were age 65 or older, and people born in 2000 can expect to live into their late 70s. By 2050, nearly one-fourth of elderly Americans will be 85 or older. Americans are living longer because medical advances provide better health care at all ages, and people are more health conscious now than were Americans 100 years ago. This aging of America means that teenagers today will spend a much longer portion of their adult lives in old age than their grandparents. The area in psychology and biology that studies late adulthood and aging is called **gerontology**.

CULTURAL VIEWS OF AGING

In the United States and in many other western cultures, it is not considered polite to ask an adult's age, especially those beyond young adulthood. This is because aging is viewed negatively. If you doubt that Americans have this negative view, check out the greeting card section of any store. Birthday cards marking people's fortieth, fiftieth, and sixtieth birthdays usually portray it as an unfortunate event, signaling declining health, attractiveness, and mental functioning.

gerontology The area in psychology and biology that studies late adulthood and aging

ageism Prejudice or discrimination against people based on their age

productive aging The perspective that elderly adults are capable of making valuable contributions to society

Aging pop artists such as Mick Jagger, lead singer for The Rolling Stones, shatter cultural stereotypes that label older people as being feeble, tired, and poorly coordinated. Can you name any societies where the elderly are highly valued and enjoy high social status?

Many other societies have very different views of aging. For example, in Japan and China, advancing age is highly valued, and older adults often are asked their age to ensure that they receive the proper respect. Instead of being a negative quality, advanced age elevates a person's social status.

Negative cultural views about growing old often lead to **ageism**, which is prejudice or discrimination against people based on their age. Ageism is related to many false beliefs, or negative stereotypes, about the elderly—that they are poorly coordinated, usually tired, easily confused, and unable to learn new skills or remember new information. The old saying, "You can't teach an old dog new tricks" is just one example of the negative—and false—stereotypes surrounding the elderly.

Ageism can cause younger adults to ignore older people's opinions and advice on a wide variety of issues. It also can result in older people being forced out of their jobs or denied job promotions for which they are qualified.

Efforts to reduce ageism and change negative stereotypes about the elderly are underway in the United States and other countries. Instead of aging being viewed as a negative developmental process, an increasing number of Americans are embracing the idea of **productive aging**. According to this perspective, which is already accepted in many societies around the world, elderly adults are capable of making valuable contributions to society.

Whenever you see elderly citizens doing volunteer work for social service organizations you are observing productive aging. Aging rock stars and elderly actors also demonstrate productive aging by their boundless energy and creativity in their artistic efforts. As your parents' generation and your grandparents' generation continue to age, you will witness personally many people who shatter negative aging stereotypes.

CHECKPOINT *How does the cultural view of late adulthood in the United States differ from that in countries such as China or Japan?*

FABRICE COFFRINI/AFP/GETTY IMAGES

SOCIAL TRANSITIONS AND ROLES

For many adults, retirement is an important life transition. You might be surprised to learn that retirement is a relatively new idea in the United States. In the 1700s and 1800s, older adult workers were valued for their wisdom and experience in highly skilled crafts such as carpentry, masonry, and tailoring. Removing them from the workforce was uncommon. In the early 1900s, retirement gained a foothold with industrialization. Factory assembly line jobs required less specialized training, and therefore, worker experience was less valued. Older workers often were forced to retire so that younger and faster workers could take their place.

Today, an older worker's decision to retire often is at least partly based on how the person believes their supervisors and fellow workers evaluate them. Older workers who believe that they are no longer valued often will retire. Poor health also can play a part in retirement decisions, but it usually is not the most important factor. Adults who best handle the transition to retirement are those who have made retirement plans well in advance.

ACTIVITY THEORY OF AGING

During the past 50 years, retirees and elderly adults have received conflicting advice on how active they should be during their twilight years. In the 1960s and 1970s, many senior citizens were advised to slow down and become less active. This advice was based on one of the first influential theories in gerontology, the *disengagement theory of aging*. This theory proposed that aging naturally leads to a gradual withdrawal from physical and social activities as elderly people spend time reflecting on their lives. The ideas underlying disengagement theory were inspired by Erik Erikson's theory of psychosocial development, which stated that elderly adults face their last crisis—*integrity versus despair* (see Table 10-1, page 276)—by reviewing their life's accomplishments and failures.

While it is true that many elderly adults reflect on their accomplishments and failures, it is also true that this kind of reflection does not require social disengagement. The findings from a number of studies directly contradicted the basic idea behind disengagement theory. These studies found that continued activity is vitally important for successful and productive aging. In response, the **activity theory of aging** proposed that elderly people are happiest when they remain both physically, cognitively, and socially active. Today, elderly individuals are encouraged to remain active by engaging in activities such as volunteering, hobbies, traveling, and part-time jobs. However, it is important to point out that activity by itself is not what leads to happiness and longer health. The activity must be satisfying and fulfilling for the individual.

LAB TEAMS

Activity Theory of Aging

With a partner collect photos and magazine cutouts of older adults engaged in a variety of different activities. Use bright colors to create a bulletin board that demonstrates the activity theory of aging. As an alternative to the bulletin board, create a PowerPoint® presentation that demonstrates this theory.

activity theory of aging A theory that elderly people are happiest when they remain physically, cognitively, and socially active

THE ELDERLY AS PARENTS AND GRANDPARENTS

Many elderly American parents have strong emotional bonds with their middle-aged children and live within 30 minutes of at least one grown child. Parents and children generally keep in regular contact and are willing to help one another in times of need. Mothers and daughters are most likely to be in frequent contact with one another. Unlike many other societies where elderly parents expect to be taken care of by their grown children, most elderly Americans expect that they will take care of themselves. However, these parent-child expectations also are shaped by cultural traditions.

In Latin American and Asian cultures, most elderly adults live in extended family households. The extended family is so important that many immigrants to the United States from Latin America and Asia have their parents and grandparents living with them in the same house. Because older people traditionally receive a great deal of respect in these cultures, grandparents play an important role in childrearing. Recent surveys find that this tradition is weakening in the twenty-first century. Latino and Asian Americans are increasingly adopting mainstream American family structures, with adult children living in households separate from their elderly parents. Despite this shift in living patterns, Latino and Asian Americans still have strong extended-family ties with elderly family members enjoying high social status and having considerable influence on their younger family members.

Studies that have examined the relationship the elderly have with their grandchildren have identified three styles of grandparenting: companionship, remote, and involved. More than half of all grandparents have a *companionship style* in which they have frequent and warm contact with their grandchildren, but do not directly get involved in raising them. A little less than one-third of grandparents have a *remote style,* meaning that they see their grandchildren so little that there are few emotional bonds. Finally, about 16 percent of grandparents have an *involved style,* in which they actively help in childrearing. An involved style of grandparenting is more common in Latino, Asian, and African-American households than in European-American households.

Companionship grandparenting is the most common style in the United States. What is companionship grandparenting?

©MONKEY BUSINESS IMAGES, 2009/USED UNDER LICENSE FROM SHUTTERSTOCK.COM

Most grandparents, even those who are actively involved in childrearing, try to strike a balance between providing help and support to their grown children and grandchildren without interfering in the parent-child relationship. They are "watchdogs" for the family, often staying on the fringes of their family's lives, but still checking to make sure that things are going well.

MARRIAGE IN LATER LIFE

Being involved in a committed romantic relationship greatly contributes to well-being in late adulthood, especially in early late-adulthood. Married couples in their mid-60s are happier in their marriages than are middle-aged couples. Psychologists explain this higher marital satisfaction as being due to the sense of freedom that often comes with retirement and a couple's rediscovered pleasure in sharing more time together. However, marital happiness often declines among adults older than 70, because of the stress of caring for sick or disabled spouses.

Among adults who are 85 or older, 70 percent are women, and many are widowed. In this "oldest old" age group, women are three times more likely than men to be poor, largely because their husbands have died and they have much lower incomes. Elderly men whose wives die often remarry, an option less available to elderly women because there are fewer men in their age range.

Being in a romantic relationship contributes to the wellbeing of couples in late adulthood.

CHECKPOINT ▷ *What is the activity theory of aging?*

Physical and Cognitive Changes

You might be wondering why you won't live forever. Some scientists contend that aging is programmed into your genes. According to the **genetic preprogramming theory of aging**, human cells have a built-in time limit to their ability to copy themselves. Each time a cell copies itself by dividing in half, the chromosomes— which carry genetic information—are copied incompletely. After many such cell divisions (on average, about 50), these copying errors build up to the point where the cell can no longer divide. Thus, humans may have a biological clock that limits the life span of cells and therefore human life.

Another theory, the **wear-and-tear theory of aging**, compares the body to a machine that wears out due to constant use. According to this theory, human cells gradually wear out after years of damage due to many factors, including stress, toxins, and radiation. When young, your body is able to repair much of this damage, but not all the repairs are accurate or complete. After many years, these faulty and incomplete repairs weaken the ability of cells to both copy and repair themselves, resulting in eventual death.

Regardless of which theory proves to be the best explanation for the aging process, some body systems decline more rapidly than others. As shown in Figure 10-2 (page 294), the heart and lungs wear out more rapidly than the digestive system.

genetic preprogramming theory of aging
A theory that human cells have a built-in time limit to their ability to copy themselves

wear-and-tear theory of aging A theory that human cells gradually wear out after years of damage

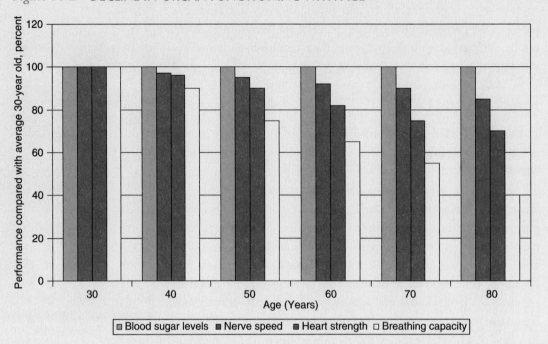

Figure 10-2 DECLINE IN ORGAN FUNCTIONING WITH AGE

Most body organs show only slight decreases in efficiency during young adulthood. With increasing age, the largest decreases in efficiency occur in the heart and lungs.

Source: Katchadourian, 1987.

■ Blood sugar levels ■ Nerve speed ■ Heart strength □ Breathing capacity

One of the biggest challenges for elderly adults is deciding how to adjust to these physical changes. Keeping physically and mentally active is very important in managing the aging process. Numerous studies indicate that people age differently. Those who both age successfully and live longer tend to have an optimistic outlook on life, a high degree of curiosity, and a feeling of control over their lives.

AGING AND THE BRAIN

While the rest of the body shows some noticeable signs of aging in early adulthood, the brain hums along at peak efficiency well into middle adulthood. Longitudinal studies of adults find that general intellectual abilities gradually increase until the early 40s and then remain fairly stable until the mid 60s. The abilities that show the most improvement during adulthood involve verbal ability, mathematical ability, and reasoning. These abilities represent *crystallized intelligence,* which involves knowledge acquired through experience (see Chapter 16, page 476). The only ability that declines between age 25 and the early 40s is perceptual speed—the ability to quickly and accurately perform a task such as deciding whether two website addresses are identical.

Around the age of 65 or so, a small percentage of adults experience a slight decline in tasks requiring rapid manipulation of ideas, abstract problem solving, and difficult mental effort. This decline in *fluid intelligence* (see Chapter 16, page 476) appears to be largely due to the continued weakening of the brain's mental processing speed. However, older adults' reduced quick thinking does not generally

PHOTODISC/GETTY IMAGES

People who both age successfully and live longer tend to have an optimistic outlook on life, a high degree of curiosity, and a feeling of control over their lives.

affect their ability to reason through everyday problems, understand mathematical concepts, or learn new information.

One reason the brain begins showing symptoms of aging in later adulthood is because it is actually shrinking in size. After the age of 50, people begin losing neurons in the brain at a faster rate, so that at death they may have 5 percent or so less brain mass than they had in young adulthood. Women's brains shrink more slowly than men's, which may be one reason why they live an average of four years longer than men worldwide, and nearly seven years longer in the United States and Canada. The most neural loss occurs in the areas of the cerebral cortex involved with complex thinking and in the brain stem, which controls basic physiological functions. However, as more neurons die, the dendrites of surviving neurons can grow longer and bushier and take over many of the dead neurons' functions. This means that, at the same time the aging brain is slowing down, it also has a remarkable ability to still repair itself by changing its neural connections (see the Closer Look feature in Chapter 3 on page 78).

Gradual declines in brain functioning are a natural part of the aging process, but some elderly adults suffer significant brain damage that leads to **dementia**, a condition of severe declining mental abilities, especially memory. Dementia is most likely to occur among adults older than 65 years. The brain damage is often caused by a stroke, a tumor, long-term alcohol abuse, or certain diseases. Check out the New Science feature on page 296 for more information on the most common cause of dementia in older adults.

dementia A condition of severe declining mental abilities, especially memory

Understanding Alzheimer's Disease

The most common cause of dementia is *Alzheimer's disease,* which is a fatal disease that destroys areas of the brain that control thought, memory, and language. Individuals with Alzheimer's disease have problems doing things they used to be able to do, such as balancing their checkbook, driving a car safely, or preparing meals. They often have problems finding the right words to use in conversation and become confused when given too many things to do at once. Alzheimer's disease also may cause personality changes, with sufferers becoming aggressive, paranoid, or depressed.

Neuroscientists still do not know what causes this disease, and there is no known cure. It is not even known whether current treatments for this disease slow its progression or simply control some of the symptoms. Studies indicate that people with Alzheimer's disease develop large tangles of twisted fibers inside the brain's neurons and dense protein plaques around the neurons. The tangles and plaques disrupt communication between neurons and slowly kill these brain cells. The tangles and plaques begin forming first in areas important for learning and memory and then slowly spread to other brain regions. Some studies find that older adults who regularly engage in intellectual activities, such as playing chess or working crossword puzzles, are at a reduced risk for the disease.

The number of people with Alzheimer's disease doubles every five years beyond age 65. Current estimates are that about 4.5 million Americans suffer from this type of dementia, with the costs for care exceeding $100 billion. Even more troubling is the recent finding that twice as many American adults (9 million) with mild cognitive impairment may be suffering from the effects of early Alzheimer's disease. If future studies confirm this finding, it would mean that up to three times more people suffer from this brain disease than indicated by most previous research.

Think Critically

Why might adults who regularly engage in challenging intellectual activities be at reduced risk for Alzheimer's disease?

WISDOM DEVELOPMENT IN LATER LIFE

Despite the gradual decline in intellectual abilities that comes with advanced age, growing old also is associated with high levels of wisdom. **Wisdom** is expert knowledge and judgment about important issues in life. Although it is not true for all or even most elderly adults, many people do gain wisdom as they age.

A 40-year longitudinal study of Americans discovered that the personal qualities associated with wisdom do not typically begin to peak until people reach their late 50s or 60s. Those who were most likely to develop wisdom were the persons who had the most open and complex personalities as young adults. They also chose careers and life activities that encouraged them to explore psychological or spiritual issues.

> **CHECKPOINT** *What is dementia?*

Coping with Death and Dying

The most inescapable thing in life is death. Perhaps it is this knowledge that gives life its meaning. Yet, how do people typically cope with their own approaching death or the loss of loved ones?

Most young adults either avoid thinking about death or believe that it is somehow not a real possibility for them at this stage of their lives. By middle age, most adults realize that death is becoming a closer reality for them and they begin to view time in a new way. Now, instead of thinking of how many years they have lived, middle-aged adults begin thinking of how many years they have left to live. As people reach late adulthood, many of them become less anxious about death. As they experience the pain of losing friends and loved ones, elderly adults generally become more accepting of their own mortality.

In his theory of psychosocial development, Erik Erikson stated that as death nears, the final psychological crisis in life occurs, *integrity versus despair* (see Table 10-1, page 276). He suggests that if people have successfully managed the previous crises in their lives, they will feel a sense of integrity. If they regret many of their life choices, they will feel a sense of despair. As people come toward the end of their lives and death approaches, how does this stage of Erikson's psychosocial development play out? Does the way people live their lives affect the way they feel about dying?

wisdom Expert knowledge and judgment about important issues in life

PHOTODISC/GETTY IMAGES

In the final psychological crisis in life, people may feel a sense of integrity.

ARE THERE PSYCHOLOGICAL STAGES OF DYING?

Based on interviews with terminally ill patients, Elisabeth Kübler-Ross developed a five-stage theory of how people approach their own death: First, they experience *denial* that they are going to die; then *anger* ("Why me?"); followed by *bargaining*

Elisabeth Kübler-Ross proposed a theory that explains five stages people go through when facing their own death. Current research finds that her theory is best applied to people who face death at a relatively young age.

LEONARD MCCOMBE/TIME LIFE PICTURES/GETTY IMAGES

with your personal God for an extension or second chance; next, *depression* when the illness can no longer be denied and what will be lost sinks in; and finally, *acceptance* of the inevitable.

Since Kübler-Ross first proposed her theory 40 years ago, psychologists have discovered that many people do not follow this five-stage sequence. For instance, people who are old do not typically view death with a good deal of fear and anger. Additionally, terminally ill people do not necessarily become calmer or happier as death approaches. Also, how people approach death varies a good deal according to their culture. It appears that Kübler-Ross's theory best describes how some people who are dying at a relatively young age cope with death.

PEACE OF MIND THROUGH MEANINGFULNESS

Consistent with Erikson's idea that the final crisis involves a search for meaning in life, research finds that many people who are facing death find peace of mind through their religion, in other spiritual beliefs, or in the general belief that their life has been meaningful. This research also finds that people who have the most difficulty coming to grips with their approaching death are those who believe they have nothing meaningful in their lives. For example, one study interviewed hundreds of cancer patients, who had less than three months to live. As death approached, those who felt they had led productive lives were sometimes sad, but they were protected from the deepest despair experienced by those who found little meaning in their lives.

Every person must find his or her own personal meaning in life. In Chapter 8 I told you a story from my childhood in which I sincerely tried to turn a lump of coal into a diamond by applying pressure. It is the "pressure" applied to you by those who know you throughout your life that changes you into the person that you become. Their life force shapes you as yours in turn shapes them. People's life stories go on even after their death. People carry within their minds memories of loved ones. Each day everyone is building a legacy of memories for the people around them. This is one way that life extends beyond death.

CHECKPOINT *What are two theories on death and dying?*

10.3 ASSESSMENT

In Your Own Words

Describe what type of person you hope to be in late adulthood. Cite information from the text to show your understanding of the material. Include topics such as the social roles you plan on fulfilling as you age, for example, being married and becoming a grandparent. Describe how you plan to manage physical and cognitive changes. You also could express whether you believe you will feel the integrity Erikson describes in his last stage of psychosocial development.

Review Concepts

1. Which refers to the area in psychology and biology that studies late adulthood and aging?
   - a. ageism
   - b. dementia
   - c. gerontology
   - d. productive aging

2. Which is something older adults might like to have?
   - a. wisdom
   - b. gerontology
   - c. ageism
   - d. dementia

3. Which has not been identified as a grandparenting style?
   - a. remote
   - b. involved
   - c. productive
   - d. companion

4. **True or False** Retirement gained a foothold in the United States with industrialization.

5. **True or False** The disengagement theory of aging and the activity theory of aging are both currently accepted theories of how older adults should spend their leisure time.

6. **True or False** Mothers and daughters are likely to remain in frequent contact with one another.

7. **True or False** In the United States, most elderly adults expect to be taken care of by their children.

Think Critically

8. How does ageism hurt older adults? If ageism keeps you from spending time with an older adult, how are you hurt?

9. Why would you advise a grandparent to follow the activity theory of aging?

10. Why is the study of gerontology important to young people as well as to older adults?

11. List three characteristics that people who age successfully and live longer share. Why do you think these characteristics lead to successful aging and a longer life?

Can Dying People Postpone Their Own Death?

INTRODUCTION Presidents Thomas Jefferson and John Adams were friends and political rivals who died on the same day, the Fourth of July in 1826. The date marked the 50th anniversary of the signing of the Declaration of Independence, which these two men were instrumental in creating. Both men seemed to be waiting for this important day to arrive as they laid on their deathbeds. Jefferson's last words were "Is it the Fourth?"

Many people have wondered whether some deathly sick individuals are able to postpone death in order to say goodbye to someone one last time or to celebrate an anniversary, a birthday, or some other significant event. Can a person's "will to live" delay death's arrival?

HYPOTHESIS A number of psychologists have hypothesized that people who are seriously ill can force themselves to live a bit longer in order to experience just one more important life event.

METHOD Two California studies analyzed death rates around two important ethnic holidays, Passover and the Harvest Moon festival. Passover is a meaningful Jewish holiday and the Harvest Moon festival celebrates older Chinese women. The researchers examined the number of people in these two ethnic groups who died just before and just after each of these two holidays. Similar death rates were also collected for people in the general population.

RESULTS The findings supported the hypothesis. Among Jewish Americans, death rates from natural causes were found to be lower just before Passover. This effect was especially strong among Jewish men, who typically lead this ceremony. No changes in death rates were found among people who do not celebrate Passover. Similar results were also found among Chinese Americans for the Harvest Moon festival. Among Chinese women over the age of 75, there was a sharp drop in deaths before the festival and a sharp increase in deaths afterward. No changes in death rates were found among Chinese men or younger Chinese women, or among people in the general population. The researchers do not believe that stress or overeating during the holidays explains these changes in death rates because stress and overeating cannot explain why the death rates are so low before the holidays. Instead, the researchers suggest that elderly people who are near the end of their lives may be able to draw upon their remaining energies to will themselves to live a little bit longer so that they can experience a joyous event.

Critical Analysis

1. Why was it important for the researchers to also examine the death rates of people in the general population when the focus of their study was on Jewish Americans and Chinese Americans?

2. Why did the researchers not think that stress or overeating during the holidays explained the changes in death rates among the elderly Jewish men and elderly Chinese women?

Gerontologist

ealth Science

Do you like helping older people? If so consider a career as a gerontologist, a person who specializes in helping senior citizens in health care and social services, and as social scientists.

Gerontologists may help older adults with health care needs in nursing homes. In social services, they work in senior citizen centers providing services to seniors who live in their own homes. Gerontologists work for local, state, or federal government agencies in public health facilities. They also work in public and private schools and colleges and universities as researchers or teachers.

Gerontologists who are social scientists work in research. They are concerned with how aging affects people cognitively, socially, and physically. They study the environments in which older adults live to enrich their lives.

Gerontologists in social services work with seniors to help them and their families with needs related to aging. They may, for example, help families better understand the needs of caring for an elderly person with a serious illness, or help seniors find appropriate services, such as in-home meals, or plan social events for groups.

Other gerontologists create and manage programs and services for senior citizens. They may give presentations to seniors about community events and other information.

PHOTODISC/GETTY IMAGES

Employment Outlook

Employment for gerontologists is expected to grow faster than the average, with a job rate projected to increase by more than 36 percent by 2016.

Needed Skills and Education

Education requirements vary from state to state and are dependent on the specific job. A high-school diploma or equivalent is required for some work in nursing homes, such as that of a nurse's aide. Gerontologists working in social services, research, or administrative management are required to have a bachelor's or master's degree. Management and university teaching positions may require a Ph.D. degree.

Students wishing to pursue a career in gerontology should take courses in biology, sociology, psychology, social studies, literature, and computer skills. If the goal is to teach in a high school or college or university, education classes are required.

Interpersonal skills are a must and research skills are required for students interested in a career in gerontology research.

How You'll Spend Your Day

Your workday will depend on which area of gerontology you choose to enter. Gerontologists working in health care may spend their days in a nursing home helping to bathe, feed, medicate, or dress patients, and to provide patients with entertainment, such as walks or music.

Gerontologists in social services spend time with seniors in social activities or in finding answers to social problems. Researchers spend time interviewing seniors, compiling data, and writing reports.

Earnings

The earnings for people employed in gerontology vary because of the widely varying occupations. The median range is from $25,580 to $59,440 based on associated careers.

What About You?

Interview two senior citizens in your family or community. Ask them how they spend their days and what their needs are. Make a list of things you could do to make their day more pleasant or to fulfill their needs.

CHAPTER SUMMARY

10.1 Young Adulthood

- Two important theories of young adulthood are those of Erik Erikson and Daniel Levinson. Erikson's psychosocial stages of adulthood crisis for young adulthood (ages 20–40 years) is intimacy versus isolation. Levinson's theory proposed that the transition from adolescence to adulthood includes a novice stage.

- According to Erikson and Levinson, one of the most important developmental tasks of young adulthood is establishing a long-term romantic bond. The happiest couples in long-term romantic relationships are those who experience both passionate love and companionship love.

- Cross-cultural research indicates that people around the world have different views of the importance of romantic love in marriage. Collectivist cultures place less emphasis on romantic love than do individualist cultures.

- Caryl Rusbult identified four strategies typically used in dealing with a troubled relationship, which differ along the dimensions of active-passive and constructive-destructive.

10.2 Middle Adulthood

- Men and women have different views of their parenting and job responsibilities. Women may feel more of a conflict between the responsibilities.

- Erikson's psychosocial stages of adulthood crisis for middle adult years (ages 40–65 years) is generativity versus stagnation.

- The body goes through changes as people age. Aging is the progression of the body that ends in death. People age chronologically and functionally. For women, the most significant change is menopause.

- About one in ten middle-aged adults experiences a midlife crisis.

10.3 Late Adulthood

- Gerontology is the area in psychology and biology that studies late adulthood and aging.

- Different cultures have varying views of aging. Collectivist cultures have greater respect for aging than do individualist cultures. Ageism is the prejudice or discrimination against people based on age.

- Americans are embracing the idea of productive aging. The activity theory of aging proposes that senior adults are happiest when they remain active and stay engaged as active grandparents or are in happy marriages.

- Physical and cognitive changes do take place. Two theories of changes include the genetic preprogramming theory of aging and the wear-and-tear theory of aging. There may be a gradual decline in brain functioning. Some elderly adults experience dementia, a severe declining of mental abilities.

- Many people gain wisdom as they age.

- Two theories of death and dying are those of Erikson and Elisabeth Kübler-Ross. Erikson's psychosocial stage of adulthood crisis for late adulthood (ages 65 years and up) is integrity versus despair. Kübler-Ross named five stages people go through when faced with their own deaths.

- Many people facing death find peace of mind.

CHAPTER ASSESSMENT

Review Psychology Terms

Select the term that best fits the definition. Some terms will not be used.

_____ 1. The area in psychology and biology that studies late adulthood and aging

_____ 2. Research in which the same people are restudied and retested over time

_____ 3. Prejudice or discrimination against people based on their age

_____ 4. A state of intense longing for union with another person; couples typically experience this most intensely during the early stages of a romantic relationship

_____ 5. The perspective that elderly adults are capable of making valuable contributions to all segments of society

_____ 6. The progressive deterioration of the body that ends in death

_____ 7. A measure of how well you can function in your physical and social surroundings

_____ 8. A theory that human cells have a built-in time limit to their ability to copy themselves

_____ 9. The ending of menstruation

_____ 10. The number of years a person has lived

_____ 11. A theory that elderly people are happiest when they remain physically, cognitively, and socially active

_____ 12. A condition of severe declining mental abilities, especially memory

_____ 13. The affection felt for people with whom your lives are deeply entwined

_____ 14. A stressful period experienced by a few middle-aged adults when they review and reevaluate their lives

_____ 15. Expert knowledge and judgment about important issues in life

_____ 16. A theory that human cells gradually wear out after years of damage

a. activity theory of aging

b. ageism

c. aging

d. chronological age

e. companionship love

f. dementia

g. disengagement theory of aging

h. empty nest syndrome

i. functional age

j. genetic preprogramming theory of aging

k. generativity versus stagnation

l. gerontology

m. integrity versus despair

n. longitudinal studies

o. menopause

p. mentor

q. midlife crisis

r. passionate love

s. productive aging

t. wear-and-tear theory of aging

u. wisdom

Review Psychology Concepts

17. Explain Daniel Levinson's theory of the novice phase of young adulthood.

18. Identify three ways discussed in this chapter that young adults take on adult responsibilities.

19. Name and explain Erikson's crises for young adulthood, middle adulthood, and late adulthood.

20. When choosing a mate, why might passionate love be more important to young adults in the United States than to young adults in India? What might be more important to young adults in India? Is this trend changing? Why?

21. List the four strategies Caryl Rusbult has identified that people use when dealing with a troubled romantic relationship. Name the strategy you plan to use if needed, and explain why you chose this strategy.

22. What does research show are the problems that might develop in children whose lives are affected by divorce?

23. Why are men less likely than women to receive mixed messages concerning their ability to juggle the dual responsibilities of career and family?

24. What does research suggest are the possible societal benefits of expanding the male gender role to include greater household and child-care responsibilities?

25. What are the first symptoms of aging and when do they begin occurring?

26. When you are 65, would you rather feel your chronological age or functional age? Why? What might you do to avoid a midlife crisis when you are middle aged?

27. Why would it be more acceptable to ask older adults their age in collectivist societies than it would in the United States?

28. What are Americans doing to change the view that aging is a negative developmental process?

29. Based on the activity theory of aging, what criteria must the activity meet in order to add to older adults' happiness and longer life spans?

30. How are the living conditions different for most elderly adults in the United States as opposed to Latin American and Asian countries?

31. Name two theories that discuss why people do not live forever.

32. What happens to the size of the brain as a person ages?

33. What are the five stages people approaching their own death go through that Elisabeth Kübler-Ross identifies?

34. Explain the purpose of the novice stage of life, who experiences this stage, and who proposed the theory.

35. In which stage of life do most people seek intimacy, and what does intimacy usually mean?

36. All marriages have rocky periods, but some marriages are more successful than others. List two things that are required of both partners to have a successful marriage.

37. Explain the difference between chronological age and functional age.

Apply Psychology Concepts

38. Using Erikson's psychosocial development stages, find someone you know in each age range and explain to them about each stage. Interview them to determine if they have experienced the stages of intimacy versus isolation, generativity versus stagnation, and integrity versus despair. Ask for specific examples and create a chart with the information you collect.

39. Getting married and starting a family are life-changing decisions. Determining with your spouse the manner in which you will raise your children can be a difficult task. Set up a plan for how you intend to raise your children. Include plans for how you will handle reinforcement, punishment, and shared parenting roles.

40. Explain in detail how American society stereotypes and discriminates against the elderly.

41. What specific actions could you and your peers take to affect a positive change for the older people living in your community?

Make Academic Connections

42. **Sociology** Interview an older adult in your family or community to learn about the significant events in the person's life. Use a computer program or art supplies to create a timeline of the events. You could record such events as the person's birth, high school graduation, marriage, dates children and grandchildren were born, and other events significant to the person you interview.

43. **Political Science** Make a short list of questions to ask people about their political convictions. Then pool several people in young adulthood, middle adulthood, and late adulthood. Record your answers. Make a chart of the answers, and then write a summary of your findings. Questions you might ask include: Do you consider yourself a Republican, Democrat, or Independent? What is the most important problem facing this country today? Who do you think was the best president in history? Why? Who do you think was the worse president in history? Why?

44. **Cross-Cultural Studies** Use the Internet or library to research the practices and rituals following a death in a culture different from your own. Write an article about your findings.

45. **Careers** In the novice phase of young adulthood people often spend a great deal of time assessing and reassessing their life goals and the progress they are making in achieving them. Most of you have not yet set your career goals or your life goals. However, you do know some of those goals. For example, do you think you want to get married, have a family, work for yourself or for a large company? Imagine that you can do anything and have everything you want. If so, what would you want and what would you want to be doing? Imagine your life 25 years into the future. Write a paper that predicts what type of career you might have and what your life might be like.

46. **History** Choose a person from history who made a significant contribution to society when they were at least middle-aged or older. You might choose a writer who wrote a great piece of literature, a musician or composer who played or wrote a great piece of music, or a scientist who discovered a cure for a disease. Use the library or Internet to research your subject, and then write a paper that describes the person, their contribution to society, and the age at which this contribution was made.

DIGGING DEEPER
with Psychology eCollection

Psychologists have long thought that a person's personality was set by early adulthood. Recent evidence, however, indicates that many personality traits can change as a person grows older. This even holds true for key personality characteristics such as agreeableness and openness. Access the Gale Psychology eCollection at *www.cengage.com/school/psych/franzoi* and read the brief summary of Dr. Sanjay Srivastava's research and findings. Write a synopsis of the article and answer the question: Why might some aspects of personality change as a person grows older? As an additional project, write an essay explaining why you think the five traits listed in the article are considered the "Big Five" traits of personality.

Source: Ward, Rosemarie. "Ripening with age: key traits seem to improve as we grow older. (Work)." *Psychology Today* 36.4 (July-August 2003): 12(1).

Personality

ESSENTIAL QUESTION
Go to page XXVI

"Cute is when your personality shines through your looks. Like, when you see someone's personality in the way they walk and you just feel like hugging them every time you see them."

—NATALIE PORTMAN, AMERICAN ACTRESS, B. 1981

BLEND IMAGES/JUPITER IMAGES

"It is totally me, Dad!"

This was my daughter Amelia's reaction upon reading the "personality profile" from the handwriting analysis machine at the state fair. Amelia gave the cashier $2 and slipped her signature into the "Data Entry" slot. Then, with lights flashing, the machine spit out an evaluation. As Amelia marveled at the accuracy of her personality profile, I noticed a partially hidden worker placing a fresh stack of pre-typed profiles into the "Completed Profile" slot in the back of the machine. At that moment, a scene from *The Wizard of Oz* ran through my mind. Remember? Dorothy returns to Oz and presents the dead witch's broom to the all-powerful Wizard. As the huge, floating head of the Wizard bellows at Dorothy, her dog, Toto, pulls back a curtain revealing that the Wizard is just an ordinary man.

That day at the fair, I decided not to tell Amelia about the man behind the machine. Sometime later, however, we talked a bit about the validity of handwriting analysis, palm reading, and horoscopes. Put simply, these techniques that claim to assess personality have not been supported by scientific research. In this chapter you will learn the various ways in which psychologists have used scientific methods to understand how you are both similar to and different from other individuals.

Psychoanalytic and Humanistic Personality Theories

OBJECTIVES

- Explain psychoanalytic theories of personality.
- Define humanistic psychology and name its principal architects.

DISCOVER IT | *How does this relate to me?*

Do you sometimes get upset with your friends without knowing why? Do you always understand why you think and behave the way you do? Are your actions more shaped by your past experiences or by your future goals? In this lesson you will be introduced to two vastly different personality theories that attempt to answer important questions about the nature of your personality.

KEY TERMS

- personality
- unconscious mind
- id
- ego
- superego
- defense mechanisms
- collective unconscious
- peak experience

Consider for a minute how you are the same in different situations and also how you are different from other people. This unique way of thinking, feeling, and acting is what is called **personality**. Your family and your friends help to shape your personality. Likewise, many countries have strong cultural beliefs that can influence personality development. You may also be born with some personality tendencies, such as introversion and extroversion. In studying personality, psychologists have developed various theories to explain the complexity of how we typically think, feel, and behave. Most of these theories identify aspects of personality that are common throughout the world.

This lesson examines two approaches to understanding personality that have very different ideas about what shapes people's thinking, feelings, and behavior. The psychoanalytic approach emphasizes the unconscious mind, while the humanistic approach emphasizes the conscious mind.

Psychoanalytic Theories of Personality

Psychoanalysis is an approach to psychology that studies how the unconscious mind shapes behavior. Sigmund Freud's theory of the unconscious mind is the best known of the psychoanalytic theories of personality. Carl Jung offers a somewhat different set of ideas in his psychoanalytic theory, which he calls analytical psychology.

personality Your unique way of thinking, feeling, and acting

©STEPHEN COBURN, 2009/USED UNDER LICENSE FROM SHUTTERSTOCK.COM

FREUD'S THEORY OF THE MIND

Sigmund Freud believed that the mind was like an iceberg, meaning that it was mostly hidden. Your *conscious mind* (see Figure 11-1 on page 309) is the relatively small part of your mind that you are aware of in each moment. It is like the tip of the iceberg that is visible above the surface of the water. Right now, your conscious mind includes the material from the sentences you have just read, perhaps an awareness of certain things in your surroundings, and maybe the thought that you would like to be doing something other than reading this book.

Immediately below the surface of the conscious mind is the *preconscious mind*. This part of the mind consists of those mental processes of which you are not currently conscious, but could become so at any moment. Examples of preconscious information might include your phone number, hopefully some of the material from previous sections of this book, and a conversation you had yesterday with a friend.

Below this preconscious level is the **unconscious mind**. This part of the mind is like the huge section of the iceberg that is hidden in the water's depths. The unconscious mind is driven by biological urges. It contains thoughts, desires, feelings, and memories that are not consciously available to you, but still shape your everyday behavior. Examples of unconscious material are painful, forgotten memories from childhood, hidden feelings of anger toward someone you consciously like (or even love), and urges that would create anxiety if you became aware of them.

Freud's theory of the mind was an important milestone in the history of psychology. It challenged the existing idea that people understood and consciously controlled their actions. Instead of free will, Freud believed that early childhood experiences determined later life choices because of the power of the unconscious mind.

The Id, Ego, and Superego　According to Freud, personality consists of three parts, or structures. These are the id, the ego, and the superego. Each structure has different goals. Frequently the goals of one structure conflict with the goals of another structure.

The **id** is an entirely unconscious portion of the mind. It contains the basic drives for reproduction, survival, and aggression. The id operates on the *pleasure principle,* which means if it feels good, do it, and do it now rather than later. Freud believed that newborn infants represent the purest form of id impulses, because they cry whenever their needs are not immediately satisfied.

In reality, however, your needs are seldom satisfied immediately. Freud stated that when you were an infant, you experienced distress and anxiety whenever your desires were not immediately satisfied. As a way to cope with this stress, the **ego** developed out of the id. The ego is the decision-making part of your personality that satisfies id impulses in socially acceptable ways. The ego is partly conscious and

unconscious mind
Thoughts, desires, feelings, and memories that are not consciously available to you but that nonetheless shape your behavior

id　An unconscious part of your mind that contains the basic drives for reproduction, survival, and aggression

ego　The part of your mind that balances the demands of the id, the superego, and reality

Figure 11-1 FREUD'S MODEL OF PERSONALITY STRUCTURE

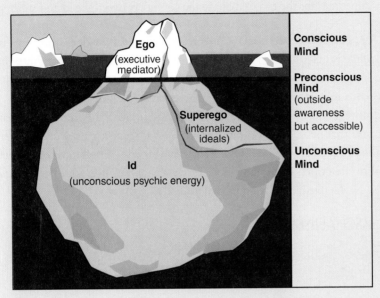

In Freud's theory of personality, the conscious mind is the smallest part of the iceberg visible above the water line and the unconscious is well below the surface. The ego includes part of the conscious and part of the unconscious mind. The same is true of the superego. The id is the completely unconscious aspect of personality.

partly unconscious. The conscious part of the ego is in contact with the world around you, while the unconscious part is in contact with the id.

For example, imagine that you suddenly feel very hungry while waiting to order a meal in a restaurant. If you immediately acted on your hunger pangs by grabbing food out of the hands of other customers, you would satisfy your id, but you would also get into serious trouble. The duty of the ego is to stop this first impulse of the id and wait for the server to take your order. The food that arrives shortly after you place your order is the "socially acceptable" way that the ego satisfies the id in this situation.

The **superego** develops later in childhood, around the age of four or five. The superego has several personality duties, including the task of making sure that the ego acts morally. The superego provides you with a conscience, making you feel guilty when you do wrong and making you feel proud when you do right. The superego and the id frequently are at odds about how to behave in a situation. The ego balances the demands of the id and superego in a way that will still bring pleasure.

In considering these three personality components, you may think that the ego is consciously controlling your behavior. Freud said this is largely an illusion. Throughout your daily activities, you are generally unaware of the unconscious compromises that your ego makes in satisfying id desires.

According to Freud, one important reason the ego cannot control the id is because the ego has been psychologically weakened by the id during the first five years of life. Freud believed that these early years were critical in shaping personality.

superego The part of your mind that counterbalances the more primitive demands of the id

During this time, the still-developing ego receives emotional wounds from the much stronger id that keeps the ego forever relatively weak. This weakened condition makes it difficult sometimes for the ego to manage the conflict between the id and superego.

The Defense Mechanisms As the ego matures, how does it manage this conflict while protecting itself and the entire personality from further emotional trauma? Freud proposed that the ego uses a variety of methods called **defense mechanisms** to keep threatening and unacceptable id desires and impulses from becoming conscious and threatening mental health. The particular defense mechanisms that people rely on most often become important features of their personalities. Freud said that although you have probably used most of the defense mechanisms described in Table 11-1 at least once in your life, your personality is described by the particular defenses that you rely on most.

Table 11-1 MAJOR EGO DEFENSE MECHANISMS

Repression	Pushing very anxious thoughts out of consciousness, keeping them unconscious; this is the most basic of the defense mechanisms
Rationalization	Offering what appear to be logical explanations for attitudes, beliefs, or behavior in place of the real unconscious reasons
Reaction formation	Preventing unacceptable feelings or ideas from being directly expressed by expressing opposing feelings or ideas
Displacement	Redirecting aggressive or other unacceptable urges away from the intended targets toward those more acceptable
Projection	Perceiving your own aggressive and other unacceptable urges not in yourself but in others
Regression	Psychologically retreating to a way of thinking and acting that is related to an emotional wound suffered by the ego at a young age

The most basic defense mechanism is *repression,* which involves the ego banishing into the unconscious any thoughts or feelings that arouse too much anxiety. For example, a grief-stricken teenager whose father has died may repress feelings of resentment ("Why did he abandon us?") because they are personally and socially unacceptable feelings. Although these feelings remain buried within the unconscious, they can accidentally reveal themselves in what is called a *Freudian slip* when the person's "ego guard" is down. For our grieving teenager, he may unintentionally say, "I loathe my father," instead of "I love my father." Freud believed that repression is the reason we do not remember the emotional wounds of our childhood: We've repressed them.

Rationalization is probably one of the more familiar defense mechanisms. When you rationalize, you give what seem like logical explanations for your attitudes, beliefs, or behavior in place of the real, unconscious reasons. Have you ever avoided studying for an important test and rationalized your actions by saying the test wasn't all that important? Freud might say this was your ego's way of defending yourself against feeling incompetent.

defense mechanisms
The ego's ways of keeping threatening and unacceptable material out of consciousness and thereby reducing anxiety

Reaction formation occurs when unconscious, unacceptable impulses are consciously expressed as their exact opposite. For example, after your friends treat you poorly, instead of feeling anger you act especially polite and friendly toward them. Consciously admitting to your anger and expressing it is too emotionally threatening.

Displacement is a defense mechanism that redirects your emotions or unacceptable urges toward people, animals, or objects that are less threatening. If treated poorly by your friends, you may redirect your anger toward your parents.

Projection is one of the more powerful defense mechanisms. It involves perceiving your own unacceptable urges or weaknesses, not in yourself, but in others. Insecure persons may falsely accuse other people of being insecure while not recognizing this characteristic in their own personality.

Another powerful defense mechanism is *regression,* which occurs when you experience a great deal of anxiety and begin behaving as if you were a very young child. This psychological retreat to a more childlike way of thinking and acting is the ego's way of handling the anxiety. For example, a newborn child may threaten an older child's sense of place in the family. As a result, the older child may begin bedwetting or return to thumb sucking. When this occurs in adults, it may involve acting like a young child when working with a very strict boss who reminds you of a similarly strict teacher from childhood.

JUNG'S PERSONALITY THEORY

Another important psychoanalytic theory of personality was developed by Carl Jung (pronounced "Yoong"; 1875–1961). He was a colleague of Freud who had different ideas about the unconscious mind. His interpretation of psychoanalysis is called *analytical psychology.* Jung did not emphasize unconscious conflict, as did Freud. Instead Jung stated that people are motivated by a desire for psychological growth and wholeness, which he called the *need for individuation.*

Jung agreed with Freud that the unconscious mind has a powerful effect on people's lives. Yet, in Jung's theory, the unconscious is best thought of as a mental storehouse of images from our ancestors' past. In studying different cultures and religions, he noticed certain common images and themes, which also were strikingly similar to the images and themes in his patients' dreams. Based on these observations, Jung asserted that along with your *personal unconscious,* you also have a **collective unconscious**, which is that part of your unconscious mind containing inherited memories shared by all human beings. Jung believed these inherited memories are revealed when your conscious mind is distracted (as in fantasies or art) or inactive (as in dreams).

Jung also believed that these inherited memories often inspire creativity and bravery in your daily life. For example, Jung would explain the popularity of the *Harry Potter* books as being due to the fact that the book's main character, Harry Potter, represents your

collective unconscious
In Jung's personality theory, the part of the unconscious mind containing inherited memories shared by all human beings

© WARNER BROTHERS/COURTESY EVERETT COLLECTION

According to Jung, the reason fictional heroes like Harry Potter are so popular is because they unconsciously remind you of the inherited "hero" memory in your collective unconscious.

inherited memory of the hero who overcomes incredibly difficult challenges to save the world. For Jung, the most important inherited memory is the *self,* which represents your desire to fully realize all the potential in your personality. He further believed that to realize this potential you must be strong and brave—like a hero—in overcoming the challenges in your everyday living.

Although many personality psychologists have dismissed Jung's idea of the collective unconscious as being scientifically untestable, it has greater influence in other disciplines, such as anthropology, art, literature, and religious studies. One aspect of his personality theory that has received scientific support and is included in many current personality theories is the idea that we are born with tendencies to direct our attention either into our internal thoughts and feelings or into the outside world of people and activities. *Introverts* focus more attention on their inner world and tend to be hesitant and cautious when interacting with people. In contrast, *extroverts* are more focused on the external world and tend to be confident and socially outgoing.

WHAT IS THE IMPACT OF PSYCHOANALYTIC THEORY?

Psychoanalytic personality theories have had an important impact on psychology. Both Freud's and Jung's influence extends into other disciplines that try to understand humans and their behavior, such as anthropology, sociology, literature, history, and religion. However, a major limitation of both personality theories is that they are based on the personal life experiences of only a small number of people who were patients of Freud and Jung in their clinical practices. A theory's usefulness is difficult to determine if the research sample does not represent the population being studied. Despite this limitation, the psychoanalytic approach still has an influence within psychology because a few of its general ideas concerning personality have received widespread support. These general ideas are that (1) unconscious processes shape human behavior; (2) childhood experiences shape adult personality; and (3) learning to control and redirect impulses is critical for healthy development. Given these continuing contributions, psychoanalysis still deserves recognition as an important perspective on personality.

 *What is the major assumption about personality from the psychoanalytic perspective?*

Humanistic Personality Theories

In the 1950s a new perspective developed—*humanistic psychology* (see Chapter 1, page 14). The humanistic perspective rejected the idea that the unconscious mind determined behavior. Instead it stated that people have free will because they are able to consciously make choices. Rejecting Freud's idea that personality development was largely completed by the fifth year of life, the humanistic perspective further developed Jung's idea that people have an inborn ability to improve and change their personalities throughout life. Carl Rogers and Abraham Maslow were the two most important psychologists who developed humanistic psychology.

ROGERS' PERSON-CENTERED THEORY

Carl Rogers (1902–1987) believed that people are basically good. He claimed that you are motivated to achieve your potential if you are given *unconditional positive regard,* which is unquestioning love and acceptance. According to Rogers, the problem that many people face in life is that their family and friends provide them with conditional positive regard, which is love and acceptance only if they do what they are told. Receiving affection with strings attached stunts your personal growth because, in your desire to be regarded positively, you lose sight of your *ideal self.* Your ideal self is the person you want to become. Rogers stated that as you continue to adjust your life to meet other people's expectations, the difference between your ideal self and your *actual self* becomes greater. Your actual self is the person you know yourself to be.

For Rogers, the answer to a healthy personality is for people with damaged selves, or low self-esteem, to find someone who treats them with unconditional positive regard. The assumption here is that when you are accepted for who you are, you eventually come to accept yourself as well. With this self-acceptance, you put aside other people's standards and begin the journey of developing your ideal self.

Carl Rogers's person-centered theory of personality considers receiving unconditional positive regard an essential ingredient in healthy personal growth. Parents are the primary providers of this affection to children.

MASLOW'S SELF-ACTUALIZATION THEORY

Like Rogers, Abraham Maslow (1908–1970) was interested in people's ability to reach their full potential. As discussed in Chapter 6 (see Figure 6-3, p. 155), the process of fulfilling your potential was what Maslow called *self-actualization.* Like Rogers and Freud, Maslow used the case-study method in developing his theory. However, unlike Rogers and Freud, Maslow studied healthy, creative people rather than those who were troubled. He chose as his subjects people who had led, or were leading, rich and productive lives.

Maslow found that self-actualized people are secure in the sense of who they are and therefore are strong enough to challenge other people's opinions. They also are loving and caring, and they often focus their energies on important tasks or life missions. Maslow also reported that these people experienced personal or spiritual **peak experiences**, which are brief but intense moments of joy. During peak experiences people feel extremely capable. A peak experience can occur while a person is engaging in a religious activity, playing a sport, listening to music, or talking to a loved one. Although anyone can have peak experiences, self-actualizing people have more peak experiences than non-self-actualizing people. Peak experiences have a lasting effect on people, enriching their outlook on life, and making them more accepting of others.

Humanistic theories have a much more positive and optimistic outlook on personality than Freud's psychoanalytic theory. This positive approach to personality has had a significant impact on popular culture. If you look in the self-help section in any bookstore, you find numerous titles emphasizing the control you have over changing your life and achieving your full potential.

peak experience A fleeting but intense moment when you feel happy, absorbed, and extremely capable

 CHECKPOINT *Define humanistic psychology, and name its two principal architects.*

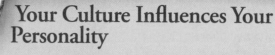 CLOSER LOOK

Your Culture Influences Your Personality

People from collectivist Latin cultures are often taught to have *simpatía,* which is a way of relating to others that stresses empathic, respectful, unselfish, and smooth social relationships. Likewise, the Chinese concept of *ren qin* (relationship orientation) and the Japanese concept of *amae* (indulgent dependence) emphasize social ties and dependence on others. Individuals who adopt these social norms will develop a personality style that is compatible with their social group.

Think Critically
Think about your own family and the traditions you honor. How have these traditions helped to shape your personality?

In Your Own Words

Write about a recent situation in your life, such as a disagreement with a friend. Explain your reaction to the situation, and then describe how either Freud, Jung, or Rogers and Maslow might explain the disagreement and your reaction. Include information on some of the different variables in your life including culture, family, and genetics and how these affected your reaction. Also include sociocultural factors that might have affected your reaction. These might include your ethnicity, gender, abilities, or disabilities.

Review Concepts

1. Which is immediately below the surface of the conscious mind?

    a. preconscious
    b. subconscious
    c. ego
    d. unconscious

2. According to Freud, which is the decision-making part of your personality?

    a. id
    b. ego
    c. superego
    d. unconscious

3. Which defense mechanism explains giving what seem like logical explanations for your attitudes, beliefs, or behavior in place of the real, unconscious reasons?

    a. repression
    b. regression
    c. rationalization
    d. reaction formation

4. **True or False** Rogers and Maslow were the primary architects of humanistic psychology.

5. **True or False** Freud asserted that besides your personal unconscious, you also have a collective unconscious.

6. **True or False** According to humanistic psychology, your ideal self is the person you want to become.

Think Critically

7. Why did Freud choose an iceberg for his model of personality structure?

8. What is a major criticism of Freud's research? Do you think this criticism is valid? Why or why not?

9. According to Jung, what is contained in the collective unconscious? How might your life be influenced by the collective unconscious?

10. With which of the following personality theorists do you most agree: Freud, Jung, or Rogers and Maslow? Explain your answer in a way that shows you understand the theories.

11. How do the psychoanalytical theories of Freud and Jung differ in explaining what motivates people?

12. According to Rogers, what role does free will play in developing your personality?

11.2 | Contemporary Personality Theories

KEY TERMS

- trait perspective
- traits
- Five-Factor Model
- social-cognitive perspective
- reciprocal determinism
- self-efficacy
- locus of control

OBJECTIVES

- Explain the trait theory of personality and identify the five traits in the Five-Factor Model.
- Describe how the social-cognitive perspective explains personality development.
- Explain how biology shapes personality development.

DISCOVER IT | *How does this relate to me?*

How would your best friend describe your personality? How does your interaction with other people shape your beliefs about yourself and what you think you can or cannot do in your life? How does your central nervous system influence whether you will be shy or outgoing with other people? This lesson explores these questions and more.

Psychoanalytic and humanistic theories attempt to explain all aspects of an individual's personality. This may be an impossible task. More recent approaches try to explain only certain aspects of personality. Research for these theories is conducted in a methodical way. Two of the most important approaches to understanding personality today are the trait approach and the social-cognitive approach.

Trait Theories

Think about how you try to understand other people's personality. Do you observe them over time and in different situations? Do you ask them directly how they typically behave? If so, you are gathering information in a manner similar to trait theorists. The **trait perspective** describes personality as consisting of stable behavior patterns that a person displays over time and across situations. A consistent tendency to behave a particular way is called a **trait**. Traits are viewed as the building blocks of personality. Your personality consists of a number of traits.

Psychoanalytic and humanistic theorists try to determine *why* people differ from one another. Trait theorists are more concerned with describing *how* people differ from one another. In studying traits, personality researchers use a statistical technique called factor analysis. *Factor analysis* allows researchers to identify clusters of traits that are related to one another. For example, people who describe themselves as outgoing also describe themselves as talkative, active, and optimistic

trait perspective A descriptive approach to personality that identifies stable behavior patterns that a person displays over time and across situations

trait A relatively stable tendency to behave in a particular way across a variety of situations

about the future. This cluster of traits can be thought of as consisting of the more basic trait of extroversion. To better understand how factor analysis works, complete the Lab Teams exercise on this page.

THE FIVE-FACTOR MODEL

How many basic traits are there in personality? Over the past 25 years, personality trait researchers concluded there are five basic traits, or factors, known as the **Five-Factor Model** (see Table 11-2). They are openness, conscientiousness, extroversion, agreeableness, and neuroticism. (Use the acronym OCEAN to remember them.) The traits are in all age groups and societies as diverse as the United States, Bangladesh, Brazil, Japan, Canada, Finland, Germany, Poland, China, and the Philippines.

Does this mean these five traits make up your entire personality? Trait theorists say no. The Five-Factor Model does not capture the entire personality, but these five traits are related to all other traits.

If you are *open to experience,* you are adventurous—constantly searching out new ways to do things. You are sensitive and passionate, with a childlike wonder at the world. You may also ignore traditional ideas of what is appropriate or expected in terms of your behavior or ideas. Although being open to experience is desirable, are there benefits to being more closed to experience? Yes. If you are low on the openness to experience trait, you tend to be hardworking, loyal, and down-to-earth. You are proud of your traditional values and feel these qualities are desirable.

LAB TEAMS

Intuitive Factor Analysis of Personality Traits

Working in small teams, examine the 30 traits listed below, and then sort them into five groups of related traits. Each group contains six traits. The traits in each group "go together," so that people who have one of the traits in the group are also likely to have the other traits. After sorting all 30 traits, attach an overall basic trait name to each of the five groups. Finally, for each group, decide how people who possess a great deal of the basic trait would differ from people who possess very little of this trait.

Achievement-oriented	Eccentric	Positive emotions
Action-oriented	Excitement seeking	Rich emotional life
Altruistic	Full of energy	Rich fantasy life
Anxious	Hostile	Self-conscious
Assertive	Idiosyncratic	Self-disciplined
Competent	Impulsive	Straightforward
Compliant	Modest	Tender-minded
Deliberate	Novel ideas	Trusting
Depressed	Orderly	Vulnerable
Dutiful	Outgoing	Warm

Five-Factor Model A trait theory asserting that personality consists of five basic traits (openness to experience, conscientiousness, extroversion, agreeableness, and neuroticism)

Table 11-2 THE FIVE-FACTOR MODEL

Openness	Conscientiousness	Extroversion	Agreeableness	Neuroticism
Rich fantasy life	Competent	Outgoing	Trusting	Anxious
Rich emotional life	Orderly	Positive emotions	Straightforward	Self-conscious
Action-oriented	Dutiful	Assertive	Compliant	Depressed
Novel ideas	Self-disciplined	Full of energy	Modest	Hostile
Eccentric	Deliberate	Excitement seeking	Tender-minded	Impulsive
Idiosyncratic	Achievement-oriented	Warm	Altruistic	Vulnerable

Conscientiousness is the measure of your willingness to conform to others' expectations and follow through on what you have agreed to do, even though more tempting options may arise. If you rate highly on conscientiousness, you are well organized, dependable, hardworking, and ambitious. In contrast, if you score low, you are more likely to be disorganized, undependable, lazy, and easygoing. This personality trait is very important in being a good worker and having a successful career. As a teenager, if you score high on conscientiousness, you are likely to spend time thinking about and planning your future career.

Extroverts are people who seek out and enjoy others' company. If you have many of the characteristics associated with extroversion, you tend to be confident, energetic, bold, and optimistic. You handle social situations with ease and grace. Extroverts have good social skills, are confident, and have a take-charge attitude. They are well suited for leadership positions. If you have only a few characteristics associated with extroversion, you are an *introvert*. As an introvert, you tend to be shy, quiet, and reserved. Other people might have difficulty getting to know you.

Agreeableness is a personality trait that ranges from friendliness to hostility. If you rate highly on agreeableness you tend to be good-natured, softhearted, courteous, and sympathetic. Those who score low tend to be irritable, ruthless, rude, and tough-minded. Agreeable people are better liked than disagreeable people. However, people high in agreeableness may be too dependent on others' approval. It is hard for them to challenge other people's opinions. For instance, scientists, art and movie critics, and judges are able to perform better if they are less agreeable and more objective in their approaches to solving problems.

What problems might people who rate highly on agreeableness encounter in life?

© ICYIMAGE, 2009/USED UNDER LICENSE FROM SHUTTERSTOCK.COM

At the core of *neuroticism* are negative emotions. This personality trait describes how people differ in terms of being anxious, high-strung, insecure, and self-pitying versus relaxed, calm, secure, and content. *Neurotics* (people low in emotional stability) can either channel their worrying into a kind of compulsive success or let their anxiety lead them into recklessness.

Check out the Closer Look feature below to learn whether the Five-Factor Model is useful in understanding personality traits among animals.

CHECKPOINT *What are the five traits identified in the Five-Factor Model?*

CLOSER LOOK

Do Animals Have Personality Traits?

Our family dog, Maizy, is trusting, curious, energetic, absentminded, and friendly. She is low on neuroticism and high on agreeableness, extroversion, and openness to experience. Does scientific research support my application of the Five-Factor Model to a dog? Surprisingly, the answer is "yes." Psychologists have discovered this theory can be applied to many animals, including dogs.

In a number of personality studies involving 12 different species, researchers found that the personality traits of extroversion, neuroticism, and agreeableness commonly occur across species. Mammals and even some fish such as guppies and octopuses display individual differences that are remarkably similar to these three personality traits.

What are the important traits in a dog's personality? Four of the five traits in the Five-Factor Model (neuroticism, agreeableness, extroversion, and openness to experience) were identified in dogs. A fifth personality trait—dominance-territoriality—also was identified. Maizy, a golden retriever, scores low in dominance-territoriality, but a German Shepherd might score high.

What about conscientiousness? Chimpanzees, our closest genetic relative, were the only species other than humans who showed any signs of this trait. Conscientiousness involves following rules, thinking before acting, and other complex thinking processes.

Think Critically

Why might a dominance-territoriality trait be a positive trait for a guard dog, but a negative trait in a family pet?

The Social-Cognitive Perspective

The personality theories examined so far all describe personality as consisting of internal psychological needs or traits. In contrast, a fourth major approach, the **social-cognitive perspective**, examines how people analyze and use information about themselves and about others. According to this perspective, personality emerges. Albert Bandura (b. 1925) is the most important social-cognitive theorist. He proposes that people learn social behaviors mainly through observing others.

RECIPROCAL DETERMINISM

According to Bandura, your cognitions—your thoughts, beliefs, and expectations—influence both your own behavior and other people's behavior. At the same time, how you behave and how others react to you influences your cognitions. This process, called **reciprocal determinism**, reveals your personality. As the environment shapes your personality, you think about what is happening to you (Figure 11-2). You develop beliefs and expectations about yourself and your environment that affects your behavior and your environment. In turn, these changes then influence your cognitions, altering your personality. This cycle of influence never ends. Your cognitions, your behavior, and your environment are continually being changed through this interaction. Thus, your personality always has the potential for change.

One of the most important cognitive factors in reciprocal determinism is **self-efficacy**, which is your belief about your ability to accomplish specific tasks successfully. You could have high self-efficacy for solving mathematical problems but low self-efficacy for meeting new acquaintances. Because of these two different self-efficacies, you might approach a difficult calculus course with confidence, while you pretend to be sick when invited to a new friend's party.

social-cognitive perspective Personality theory that examines how people analyze and use information about themselves and about others

reciprocal determinism The social-cognitive belief that your personality emerges from an ongoing mutual interaction among your cognitions and actions, and your environment

self-efficacy Your belief about your ability to perform behaviors that should bring about a desired outcome

Figure 11-2 **RECIPROCAL DETERMINISM**

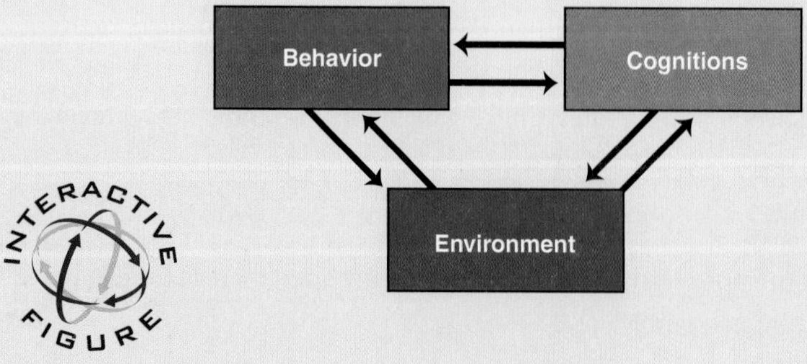

The idea that personality emerges from an ongoing interaction among people's cognitions, behavior, and environment is known as reciprocal determinism. Reciprocal determinism is an important principle of the social-cognitive perspective.

Achieving success in an activity raises self-efficacy, while failure lowers it. The more self-efficacy you have at a particular task, the more likely you will pursue that task. Success breeds self-efficacy, which in turn breeds further success.

NEW SCIENCE

Do We Evaluate Ourselves Accurately?

When you receive a good grade on an exam, do you usually conclude that your success was caused by your intelligence, your hard work, or a combination of the two? What if you do poorly? Do you blame your failure on someone or something else? This tendency to take credit for success while denying blame for failure is known as the *self-serving bias*. The most agreed-upon explanation for the self-serving bias is that it allows us to enhance and protect our self-esteem and feel more self-confident.

Recent studies indicate that the self-serving bias influences how we compare our past selves to our present self and also how we compare ourselves to other people. We like to evaluate how we were in the past in a way that makes us feel good about ourselves now. We do this in two ways. First, we convince ourselves that our current personality is superior to our younger personality. Criticizing our past selves allows us to feel better about our current lives. Second, we tend to believe that we are more superior to our friends and acquaintances at the present time than when we were younger. Of course, many people do learn from experience and get better with age, but it is not possible for all of us to improve more than everyone around us! In fact, research indicates that most people do not improve their personalities over time nearly as much as they would like to think. These findings suggest that wishful thinking is often an important ingredient in the beliefs we have about ourselves.

Think Critically

Evaluate yourself. Do you think you have ever given in to the self-serving bias? For example, how do you typically explain your success or your failure on exams?

LOCUS OF CONTROL

The social-cognitive theorist Julian Rotter states that as you grow up, you develop beliefs about yourself as either controlling or controlled by your environment. The degree to which you expect that what happens to you in life depends on your own actions and personal qualities versus factors beyond your control is known as **locus of control**.

If you believe that things happen because of your own efforts, you are identified as having an *internal locus of control*. If you believe that what happens to you is outside your own control, you are identified as having an *external locus of control*. If you have an internal locus of control you most likely enjoy working hard to achieve personal goals and believe that your behavior can lead to positive outcomes. Internals tend to be more successful in life than externals. Externals are less independent than internals, and are more likely to experience depression and stress.

Spend a few minutes responding to the items in the Self-Discovery feature to get an idea of whether you have an internal or external locus of control.

locus of control The degree to which you expect that what happens to you in life depends on your own actions and personal qualities versus factors beyond your control

SELF-DISCOVERY

What Is Your Locus of Control?

Instructions: For each item, select the alternative that you more strongly believe to be true. Remember that this is a measure of your personal beliefs. There are no correct or incorrect answers.

1. a. Making a lot of money is largely a matter of getting the right breaks.
   b. Promotions are earned through hard work and persistence.

2. a. In my experience, I have noticed that there is usually a direct connection between how hard I study and the grades I get.
   b. Many times, the reactions of teachers seem haphazard to me.

3. a. Marriage is largely a gamble.
   b. The number of divorces indicates that more and more people are not trying to make their marriages work.

4. a. When I am right, I can convince others.
   b. It is silly to think that one can really change another person's basic attitudes.

5. a. In our society, a person's future earning power is dependent upon his or her ability.
   b. Getting promoted is really a matter of being a little luckier than the next person.

6. a. I have little influence over the way other people behave.
   b. If one knows how to deal with people, they are really quite easily led.

See page 335 for scoring instructions.

Source: From "External Control and Internal Control" by Julian B. Rotter in *Psychology Today*, June 1971. Reprinted with permission from Psychology Today Magazine and the author. Copyright © 1971 Sussex Publishers.

STRENGTHS AND WEAKNESSES IN THE SOCIAL-COGNITIVE PERSPECTIVE

Social-cognitive theories have much more in common with the trait approach to personality than with the less scientifically based theories from the humanistic and psychoanalytic perspectives. Social-cognitive theories can be applied to help understand and solve such problems as drug abuse, unemployment, academic underachievement, and teen pregnancy. However, by emphasizing the cognitive side of human nature, the social-cognitive perspective is best at explaining rational behavior that is "thought through." It is less able to explain behavior that is spontaneous, irrational, and perhaps sparked by unconscious motives.

CHECKPOINT › *What is locus of control?*

Table 11-3 **THE FOUR PERSPECTIVES ON PERSONALITY**

Perspective	Explanation of Behavior	Evaluation
Psychoanalytic	Personality is set early in childhood and is driven by unconscious and anxiety-ridden sexual impulses that we poorly understand.	A speculative, hard-to-test theory that has had an enormous cultural influence and a significant impact on psychology
Humanistic	Personality is based on conscious feelings about yourself and is focused on your capacity for growth and change.	A perspective that revitalized attention to the self but often did not use rigorous scientific methods
Trait	Personality consists of a limited number of stable characteristics that people display over time and across situations.	A descriptive approach that sometimes underestimates the impact that situational factors have on behavior
Social-cognitive	Personality emerges from an ongoing mutual interaction among people's cognitions, their behavior, and their environment.	A social interaction approach that tends to underestimate the impact that emotions and unconscious motives have on behavior

Biology Shapes Personality Development

Biological differences among people also affect how personalities are formed. For example, the differences between introverts and extroverts are partly caused by inherited characteristics in the nervous system, especially the brain. Research suggests that introverts have inherited a nervous system that operates at a high level of arousal. Thus, introverts tend to avoid too much social interaction and change in order to keep their arousal from reaching uncomfortable levels. Extroverts have the opposite problem. Their nervous system normally operates at a relatively low level of arousal.

Whether you are an introvert or an extrovert may be significantly influenced by whether your nervous system operates at a high versus low level of arousal.

© YURI ARCURS, 2009/USED UNDER LICENSE FROM SHUTTERSTOCK.COM

Thus, they seek out situations that stimulate them. Introverted students prefer studying in quiet, socially isolated settings. Extroverted students prefer studying in relatively noisy settings where they can socialize with others. Not only do extroverts choose to perform tasks in noisy settings, but they actually perform better in such settings.

Another personality trait associated with biological differences is shyness, which involves feelings of discomfort and anxiety during social situations. Although almost everybody feels shy at some point in their lives, about 40 percent of the population is excessively shy, preventing them from easily making friends and socializing. Brain areas involved in the emotion of fear and those involved in controlling emotions play a role in shyness. When shy adults are shown unfamiliar faces, or when they interact with strangers, they experience much greater activation of brain areas associated with anxious emotions than people who are not shy.

Genetics plays an important role in shaping personality, but how this happens is not clear. Genetics seem to influence personality indirectly. For example, children who inherit a healthy body and high sociability and activity levels often look for opportunities to play with other children. Such interactions help them develop important social skills, which, in turn, cause them to enjoy social activities even more. Over time these people develop personal qualities that we identify as extroverted. This does not mean that specific genes actually lead to specific personality traits. For instance, even though shyness is an inherited trait, children and older adults can overcome their social anxiety and become successful and outgoing in many social situations. Parents are especially important either in lowering or increasing children's shyness. Instead of genetics determining personality, you inherit the building blocks of personality from your parents, and then your interactions with your social environment create your personality.

CHECKPOINT *How do the nervous systems of introverts and extroverts differ?*

In Your Own Words

What traits do you have? Use the Five-Factor Model to make a list of the basic trait or traits you have. Choose from openness, conscientiousness, extroversion, agreeableness, and neuroticism. Next, make a list of the qualities you have that are part of the trait you listed. For example, you might list openness as the trait and a rich fantasy life and action-oriented as qualities of that trait that you have. Finally, explain why you believe you have this trait and how you see these specific qualities in your personality.

Review Concepts

1. Which describes personality as consisting of stable tendencies to behave in a particular way over time and across situations?

   a. trait perspective
   b. social-cognitive perspective
   c. reciprocal determinism
   d. locus of control

2. Which describes an important cognitive factor in reciprocal determinism?

   a. self-effacement
   b. self-efficacy
   c. self-awareness
   d. self-assurance

3. **True or False** Trait theorists are concerned with describing how people differ from one another.

4. **True or False** The traits in the Five-Factor Model make up an individual's entire personality.

5. **True or False** The social-cognitive perspective views personality as something that is created by the experiences you have when interacting with your social world.

6. **True or False** People with an internal locus of control tend to be more successful in life than people with an external locus of control.

7. **True or False** Research suggests that introverts have inherited a nervous system that operates at a high level of arousal.

8. **True or False** Studies show that genes directly influence personality and there is very little parents can do to shape it.

Think Critically

9. Describe the difference in approach between psychoanalytic and humanistic theorists versus trait theorists when assessing a case history.

10. Do you believe you have an internal locus of control or an external locus of control? Explain your answer in a way that shows you understand locus of control.

CASE STUDY

Shyness, Self-Efficacy, and the Illusion of Transparency

INTRODUCTION Joanne, a junior in high school, was doing well in all her courses. Academically, she had high self-efficacy, meaning she felt very capable of accomplishing whatever challenges her teachers presented to her. However, Joanne's self-efficacy outside the classroom was sorely lacking. In social situations she felt shy, awkward, and unsure of herself. A simple greeting by another classmate was often all it took to make Joanne blush and feel like everyone was watching her. Joanne's utter lack of social confidence troubled her and she wanted to try to become less socially anxious and more socially self-confident. But how?

After reading some books on shyness, Joanne discovered that it is a very common experience. She also learned that when people become socially anxious they often overestimate the degree to which others can detect their anxiety. Psychologists call this false belief that your thoughts, feelings, and emotions are more transparent to others than is actually the case the *illusion of transparency*.

HYPOTHESIS Joanne decided to use this knowledge about the illusion of transparency to become less socially anxious and increase her feelings of self-efficacy in social situations. She hypothesized that people were probably not that aware of her nervousness when meeting her and talking to her.

METHOD Joanne decided to approach a classmate in school and have a brief casual conversation about a TV show that most students watched every week. Joanne made sure to remind herself about the illusion of transparency just before approaching the classmate. The conversation lasted less than a minute, it seemed to go well, and the classmate even laughed when Joanne mentioned a humorous incident in the TV show. Throughout the next few weeks Joanne repeatedly reminded herself about the illusion of transparency before talking to fellow classmates.

RESULTS Joanne's hypothesis was confirmed! People mostly never seemed to notice her nervousness while talking to her. Even more surprising was the fact that Joanne noticed that her anxiety began decreasing the more she forced herself to approach other people and engage them in conversation. After awhile, Joanne no longer had to "force herself" to start conversations. She wanted to talk to others and more than one classmate struck up conversations with her on their own. Joanne's self-efficacy in the social arena increased dramatically. Sure, she still felt shy and anxious at times, but now she knew that this was perfectly normal. Joanne now felt much more confident that others genuinely wanted to talk to her.

Critical Analysis

1. What does this case study suggest about people's ability to change their personalities?

2. What might prevent some people from decreasing their own levels of shyness?

OBJECTIVES

- Describe projective personality tests.
- Explain how objective personality tests differ from projective tests.

DISCOVER IT | *How does this relate to me?*

Some psychologists believe that your personality is revealed by the thoughts you have while looking at inkblot pictures. Other psychologists believe that the best way to understand your personality is to ask you questions about how you typically feel and behave. In this lesson you will learn why different personality tests measure personality in different ways.

KEY TERMS

- projective test
- Rorschach Inkblot Test
- Thematic Apperception Test
- objective test
- Minnesota Multiphasic Personality Inventory

Two basic assumptions underlie our attempt to understand and describe personality. The first assumption is that personal characteristics shape people's thoughts, feelings, and behavior. The second assumption is that these characteristics can be measured in some way. You are about to read and learn about two kinds of personality tests: *projective* and *objective*.

Projective Personality Tests

Projective tests are based on the belief that if you are presented with a situation that is unclear or confusing to you, you see the situation through a projection of your unconscious needs and thoughts. Projective tests help determine what your unconscious is projecting. In a very real sense, these tests are designed to trick the unconscious into revealing its contents. The most popular projective tests are the Rorschach Inkblot Test and the Thematic Apperception Test.

Have you ever played the "cloud game," in which you and another person look at cloud formations and tell each other what the shapes look like? The **Rorschach Inkblot Test** is similar. Developed by the Swiss psychiatrist Hermann Rorschach (1884–1922), the test consists of 10 symmetrical inkblots. Five cards are black and white and five are colored. The inkblot in Figure 11-3 is similar to those developed by Rorschach. The Society for Personality Assessment finds that the Rorschach is reasonably accurate and reliable in measuring different aspects of personality.

projective test A psychological test that asks you to respond to ambiguous stimuli or situations in ways that reveal your unconscious motives and desires

Rorschach Inkblot Test A projective personality test in which you are shown pictures of inkblots and asked what you see in the shapes

Figure 11-3 RORSCHACH INKBLOT TEST

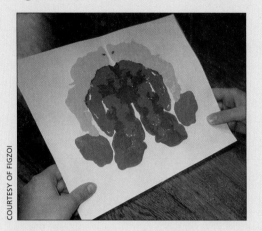

COURTESY OF FIGZOI

Persons taking the Rorschach Inkblot Test describe what they see in a series of inkblots. The assumption of this projective personality test is that the way people interpret the inkblots will be a "projection" of their unconscious mind.

Figure 11-4 THEMATIC APPERCEPTION TEST

HAROLD EDWARD BRYANT, EVENING CONVERSATION, 1929, OIL PAINTING ON CANVAS

This picture of two adults sitting in a room focusing their attention on a child is an illustration of a TAT-like image. What sort of story do you think this picture tells? Why is the TAT referred to as a projective test?

The **Thematic Apperception Test (TAT)** involves asking a person to tell a story about several pictures the person is shown. In each case, the picture shows a person or persons involved in a situation that is unclear. For example, in the TAT-like picture in Figure 11-4, are the three people happy or sad? Is this a picture of a family, a student and teachers, or something else? The person telling the story about the TAT cards is instructed to tell about what led up to the story, what the people in the story are thinking and feeling, and how the situation is resolved. Psychologists who use the TAT believe that the issues people are struggling with in their own lives will be perceived to be issues for the characters in the photographs. Like the Rorschach, the TAT is reasonably accurate and reliable in measuring personality.

> **CHECKPOINT** What do projective personality tests determine?

Objective Tests

Unlike projective tests, **objective tests** are designed to assess consciously held thoughts, feelings, and behavior by asking direct, clearly understood questions. The questions can be directed toward friends and family members, but are usually directed toward the person being assessed. When you evaluate yourself, the test is called a *self-report inventory*.

Like school exams, objective personality tests can be given to a large group of people at the same time. Objective tests usually ask true-false, multiple-choice, or open-ended questions. Unlike your school exams, however, personality tests have

Thematic Apperception Test (TAT) A test in which you "project" your inner feelings and motives through the stories you make up about pictures

objective tests A personality test that asks direct, clearly understood questions about your conscious thoughts, feelings, and behavior

no one correct answer. You choose the answer that best describes you. The Locus of Control questionnaire you completed on page 322 is an objective test.

One test that evaluates several traits is the **Minnesota Multiphasic Personality Inventory (MMPI)**. It is the most extensively researched and widely used personality inventory. Since its development in the 1940s, the MMPI has been revised so that it can be used with people who have different cultural backgrounds. The current version has 567 true-false questions that measure 10 *clinical scales*. These scales are used to identify psychological difficulties or interests. The groups that were used to choose the scale items were various groups of people with different psychological problems or interests. For example, the items that make up the MMPI depression scale were those that depressed individuals supported more than did nondepressed people. People who score above a certain level on the depression scale are considered to have difficulty with depression. Table 11-4 briefly describes the 10 clinical scales.

Minnesota Multiphasic Personality Inventory (MMPI) An objective personality test consisting of true-false questions that measure various personality dimensions and clinical conditions such as depression

Table 11-4 MMPI-2 CLINICAL AND VALIDITY SCALES

SCALES	DESCRIPTION
CLINICAL SCALES	
Hypochondriasis	Abnormal concern with body functions and health concerns
Depression	Pessimism, feelings of hopelessness; slowing of action and thought
Hysteria	Unconscious use of mental or physical symptoms to avoid problems
Psychopathic deviation	Disregard for social customs; emotional shallowness
Masculinity/ femininity	Interests culturally associated with a particular gender
Paranoia	Suspiciousness, delusions of grandeur or persecution
Psychasthenia	Obsessions, compulsions, fears, guilt, anxiety
Schizophrenia	Bizarre thoughts and perceptions, withdrawal, hallucinations, delusions
Hypomania	Emotional excitement, overactivity, impulsiveness
Social introversion	Shyness, insecurity, disinterest in others
VALIDITY SCALES	
Cannot say	Not answering many items indicates evasiveness.
Lie	Repeatedly providing socially desirable responses indicates a desire to create a favorable impression, lying to look good.
Frequency	Repeatedly providing answers rarely given by normal people may indicate an attempt to appear mentally disordered, faking to look mentally ill.
Correction	A pattern of failing to admit personal problems or shortcomings indicates defensiveness or lack of self-insight.

The MMPI also contains four *validity scales*. These scales consist of items that detect suspicious response patterns indicating dishonesty, carelessness, defensiveness, or evasiveness. The way an individual responds to these scales can help psychologists understand the attitudes that someone has taken toward all the test items. For example, someone who responds "true" to statements such as "I like every person I have ever met" and "I never get angry" may not be providing honest answers to the other test items. The four MMPI-2 validity scales also are described in Table 11-4.

CHECKPOINT *What do objective personality tests measure?*

11.3 ASSESSMENT

In Your Own Words

Explain the difference between projective and objective personality tests. Include key feature information on the Rorschach Inkblot Test, the Thematic Apperception Test, and the Minnesota Multiphasic Personality Inventory. Explain which test you find most helpful and why.

Review Concepts

1. Which is a psychological test that asks you to respond to ambiguous stimuli or situations in ways that reveal your unconscious motives and desires?
   - a. self-monitoring test
   - b. projective test
   - c. MMPI
   - d. objective test

2. Which is an example of a test in which you "project" your inner feelings and motives through the stories you make up about pictures?
   - a. Rorschach Inkblot
   - b. Five-Factor Test
   - c. Thematic Apperception Test
   - d. MMPI

3. **True or False** Objective tests are designed to trick the unconscious into revealing its contents.

4. **True or False** The MMPI evaluates only a few traits, but it is the most widely used personality inventory.

Think Critically

5. Do you think the Rorschach Inkblot Test is reliable in measuring different aspects of personality? Why or why not?

6. How might a school counselor use the MMPI to help you choose a career?

7. How might a self-report inventory help you to better understand yourself?

8. Why do you think the TAT test is effective in detecting issues people are struggling with in their lives?

Personality Psychologist

ealth Science

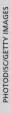

Are you interested in how people perceive and evaluate themselves and other people? Do you wonder how individuals develop self-esteem? Are you curious about the role of personality in your development or that of other teenagers? Would you like to research how personality affects relationships or how personality may affect academic success? Are you interested in how gender, socio-economics, or cultures affect personality? If any of this intrigues you, you might be interested in a career as a personality psychologist.

Personality psychologists research different aspects and effects of personality to understand psychological patterns and how those patterns are expressed in people's lives. These researchers conduct studies to learn how emotions, motives, and other aspects that make up a personality work together in individual lives.

Most personality psychologists work in colleges and universities where they conduct research and teach. Some work in the human resources departments of business and industry where they study the personalities of employees, or prospective employees. In their studies, personality psychologists learn how employees will do in their jobs or how they will work in teams, for example. Other personality psychologists in the business arena may work with companies to help them keep their most valuable employees.

Employment Outlook

Careers for personality psychologists are expected to grow 15 percent until 2016. This is a faster than average rate.

Needed Skills and Education

Most states require personality psychologists to have a doctoral degree. A doctoral degree usually requires five to seven years of college work after receiving a bachelor's degree. Personality psychologists must be licensed by the state in which they practice. Requirements vary from state to state. Personality psychologists who teach in universities usually have a Ph.D. in psychology or related field.

Courses that will help you in this career are those in psychology and other related sciences. Courses in sociology also are helpful as are courses in humanities and cross-cultural studies. You also need good written and oral communication skills; good interpersonal relationship skills; and good organizational abilities. Computer skills also are helpful.

How You'll Spend Your Day

Research personality psychologists interview and test individuals over long periods of time. They write reports and publish articles on their findings. Other personality psychologists spend their time in college and university classrooms and time preparing for teaching future psychologists. Personality psychologists in the business world spend time interviewing and studying prospective and current employees of companies.

Most personality psychologists work a regular 40-hour work week; however, observation of study participants may include evenings or weekends.

Earnings

The median hourly earnings of personality psychologists are $59,440. The lowest 10 percent earn $35,280 while the highest 10 percent earn more than $102,730.

What About You?

Learn more about the career of personality psychologist. As a class, contact a personality psychologist at a large corporation or university in your community to speak to your class about the career. Write a list of questions to ask the speaker.

CHAPTER SUMMARY

11.1 Psychoanalytic and Humanistic Personality Theories

- Personality is your own unique way of thinking, feeling, and acting. Two approaches to understanding personality are the psychoanalytic approach and the humanistic approach.

- Sigmund Freud's theory of the unconscious mind is the best known of the psychoanalytic theories. He believed that "the mind is like an iceberg"—meaning that it was mostly hidden. The conscious mind is the relatively small part that you are aware of each moment. Below the surface of the conscious mind is the preconscious mind, and below that is the unconscious mind.

- According to Freud, the personality is divided into the id, the ego, and the superego. The ego uses a variety of defense mechanisms to keep threatening and unacceptable id desires from becoming conscious and threatening mental health.

- Carl Jung was a psychoanalytical theorist who believed that you have a collective unconscious, which is that part of your unconscious mind containing inherited memories shared by all human beings. His theory also included the concept that we are born either as an introvert or an extrovert.

- Carl Rogers and Abraham Maslow were the primary architects of humanistic psychology. This theory emphasizes that people have an inborn ability to improve themselves and have free will. Rogers's theory pointed to your ideal self. Maslow's studies found that when people reached their full potential, they attained self-actualization. Self-actualized people have peak experiences, brief but intense moments of joy.

11.2 Contemporary Personality Theories

- A trait perspective describes personality by identifying stable tendencies and characteristics over time and across situations. Personality researchers use a statistical technique called factor analysis to study traits. Factor analysis considers a "cluster" of traits to describe a more general trait. The Five-Factor Model identifies five key factors or dimensions of personality (OCEAN).

- The social-cognitive perspective examines how people interpret, analyze, remember, and use information about themselves, others, social interactions, and relationships. Reciprocal determinism is the cycle of how one's personality is shaped by the environment, and in turn the personality affects how one reacts to the environment. Self-efficacy is an important cognitive factor in reciprocal determinism. Locus of control is one's belief about controlling or being controlled by one's environment.

- Biological differences may be another factor in determining personality; though genes appear to indirectly influence personality, how it does so is not clear.

11.3 Measuring Personality

- Two kinds of personality tests are projective tests and objective tests. Projective tests help determine what your unconscious is projecting. Objective tests assess consciously held thoughts, feelings, and behaviors.

- Projective tests indirectly measure personality by presenting vague material and asking for an interpretation. The two most popular projective tests are the Rorschach Inkblot Test and the Thematic Apperception Test (TAT).

- Objective tests are in the format of true-false, multiple-choice, or open-ended questions. The most extensively researched and widely used test is the Minnesota Multiphasic Personality Inventory (MMPI).

CHAPTER ASSESSMENT

Review Psychology Terms

Select the term that best fits the definition. Some terms will not be used.

_____ 1. A psychological test that asks you to respond to ambiguous stimuli or situations that will reveal your unconscious motives and desires

_____ 2. Your unique way of thinking, feeling, and acting

_____ 3. The part of your mind that counterbalances the more primitive demands of the id

_____ 4. Examines how people analyze and use information about themselves and about others through social interaction

_____ 5. Your belief about your ability to successfully accomplish specific tasks

_____ 6. The ego's ways of keeping threatening and unacceptable material out of consciousness and thereby reducing anxiety

_____ 7. A fleeting but intense moment when you feel happy, absorbed, and extremely capable

_____ 8. Thoughts, desires, feelings, and memories that are not consciously available to you, but that nonetheless shape your behavior

_____ 9. In Jung's personality theory, the part of the unconscious mind containing inherited memories shared by all human beings

_____ 10. A relatively stable tendency to behave in a particular way across a variety of situations

_____ 11. A personality test that asks direct, clearly understood questions about your thoughts, feelings, and behavior

_____ 12. The social-cognitive belief that your personality emerges from an ongoing mutual interaction among your cognitions and actions, and your environment

_____ 13. The degree to which you expect that what happens to you in life depends on your own actions and personal qualities versus the factors beyond your control

_____ 14. The part of your mind that balances the demands of the id, the superego, and reality

_____ 15. A descriptive approach to personality that identifies stable behavior patterns that a person displays over time and across situations

a. collective unconscious
b. defense mechanisms
c. ego
d. Five-Factor Model
e. id
f. locus of control
g. Minnesota Multiphasic Personality Inventory
h. objective test
i. peak experience
j. personality
k. projective test
l. reciprocal determinism
m. Rorschach Inkblot Test
n. self-efficacy
o. self-report inventory
p. social-cognitive perspective
q. superego
r. Thematic Apperception Test
s. trait
t. trait perspective
u. unconscious mind

Review Psychology Concepts

16. Explain why the superego develops at around the age of four or five.

17. List the six defense mechanisms and give an example of each.

18. Which perspective further developed Jung's idea that people have an inborn ability to improve and change their personalities throughout life?

19. Who are the two primary architects of humanistic psychology?

20. According to Carl Rogers, why are many people frustrated in their potential growth?

21. Describe the difference between the ideal self and actual self. Why is there a difference?

22. What is a major limitation of Freud's personality theory?

23. What was Maslow's term for the process of fulfilling your potential?

24. What are the five key factors in the Five-Factor Model?

25. For the following characteristics, decide whether or not someone who possessed the characteristic would be high or low on the openness scale:
    a. adventurous
    d. sensitive and passionate
    b. loyal
    e. down-to-earth
    c. hard-working
    f. proud of traditional values

26. Why might scientists, art and movie critics, and judges be able to perform better if they are less agreeable?

27. Who is more likely to experience depression and stress—one who has an external locus of control or one with an internal locus of control? Why?

28. What is the typical format of an objective test?

29. How does the TAT work?

30. How has the MMPI been revised since its development in the 1940s?

Apply Psychology Concepts

31. In animated cartoons a character is sometimes faced with an ethical dilemma. For example, a starving cat clutching its frightened mouse-friend in its claws might be deciding whether to eat the tasty-looking friend. When this happens, the cartoonist often shows a small devil-cat and angel-cat standing on the pondering cat's shoulders, each trying to persuade the cat to either eat or spare the mouse. Using Freud's theory of personality, explain the psychology underlying this cartoon dilemma. In doing so, identify which of the cartoon characters represent the ego, id, and superego. In most cartoon worlds, the hungry cat does not eat the frightened mouse. What does this outcome suggest about the strength of the cat's ego and superego?

32. Bullying is a common problem in many schools throughout the country. Often bullies pick on younger and weaker children rather than on those who are as strong as they are. Imagine that you are a school counselor and a school bully is brought to your office after picking a fight with a younger child. You soon discover after talking with the student who is bullying that he has experienced physical abuse from his parents. Using your knowledge of psychoanalytic personality theory, identify and describe what defense mechanism might explain this student's bullying behavior.

33. Describe what Abraham Maslow meant by a self-actualized person. In doing so, explain peak experiences. Also, identify any experiences in your own life that were "peak experiences" for you. Describe one of these experiences and how it made you feel.

34. What are the five personality traits identified by the Five-Factor Model? Using this theory, consider the personality of your best friend. Provide an assessment of the degree to which your friend possesses either low, medium, or high levels of each of the five traits in this model.

35. Jesse has an internal locus of control while Tamika has an external locus of control. What different beliefs do these two people have about what causes events in their lives and how these beliefs might affect their future life choices?

Make Academic Connections

36. **History** Use the Internet to research Sigmund Freud's life and work. Write a short biography about him. Discuss his psychoanalytic theory of personality in your biography. Also include information on the id, ego, and superego and how he arrived at his conclusions.

37. **Biology** Use the Internet to research a study on how genetics influences personality development. For example you might research how the differences between introverts and extroverts are caused partly by inherited characteristics in the nervous system, especially the brain. Write a fact sheet about the information you found.

38. **Writing** You see an ad in the help-wanted section in the newspaper for a job that sounds good in almost every respect. The hours fit into your schedule and the job pays very well. Write a letter to the Human Resources director stating why the job appeals to you and why you would be good for the job. Was this assignment easy or difficult for you?

39. **Business** You are in charge of hiring a new principal for your school. Use the Five-Factor Model to make a list of the traits you would look for in candidates. Write a report that lists the traits and explains why these traits are important for a principal to have.

DIGGING DEEPER
with Psychology eCollection

How does your personality develop? That question has intrigued psychologists since they began to study human behavior. Much of the research has been conducted with identical twins, often focusing on the nature-versus-nurture question. Judith Rich Harris has written a book based on research that indicates that personality is formed in interactions with peers. Access the Gale Psychology eCollection at *www.cengage.com/school/psych/franzoi* and read the brief review of Harris's book. Write a summary of the book review and answer the question: Do you think your personality has developed primarily in response to your friends and peers? As an additional project, write an essay agreeing with or arguing against this statement: "It really is who you know. But more importantly, it's what you believe they think of you that really matters."

Source: "No Two Alike: Human Nature and Human Individuality." *Psychology Today* 39.2 (March–April 2006): 36(1).

SELF-DISCOVERY: YOUR SCORE

What Is Your Locus of Control?

Scoring Instructions: Give yourself one point for each of the following answers: 1(a), 2(b), 3(a), 4(b), 5(b), and 6(a). Then add up your total number of points. The higher the score, the more external is your locus of control. A score of 5 or 6 suggests that you are in the high external range, while a score of 0 or 1 suggests that you are in the high internal range. Scores of 2, 3, and 4 suggest that you fall somewhere between these two extremes.

Cognitive Domain

You, as a human being, are a fascinating creature. You have what may be a limitless ability to learn new things. You can memorize an immense amount of information and store it in your mind for many years. You can speak and write in a wide variety of languages and communicate with hand, facial, and body gestures. You also have different states of consciousness in which you can experience the world around you as well as your internal dreams and fantasies. And you shape and change your surroundings every day, creating new ways of understanding life with different forms of intelligence.

Despite the fascinating quality of human nature, do you know that you often think, act, and experience the world in ways very similar to all other animals? While humans have many unique and special qualities and abilities, there are many similarities with other living creatures. In this unit you will learn about the psychology of learning, memory, thinking, and language, as well as the nature of consciousness and intelligence.

CHAPTER 12

Learning

ESSENTIAL QUESTION
Go to page XXVI

Learning is a treasure that will follow its owner everywhere.

—CHINESE PROVERB

Fred wanted to be a famous fiction writer, but a letter from his father discouraged him. In the letter, Fred's father stated that he and Fred's mother—although not wanting to discourage Fred from following his ambitions—thought it best if Fred would "arrange some plan whereby you can support yourself."

The year was 1926, and Fred spent it trying unsuccessfully to publish his writing. At the end of what he called his "dark year," Fred began searching for a different career path. He was accepted to Harvard University in psychology, where his own personal journey of discovery merged with new scientific discoveries in psychology. Although Fred never became famous as a fiction writer, his research and writings in the psychology of learning made Fred one of the best-known psychologists of all time. Outside his family, people knew and referred to Fred by his formal name, Burrhus Frederic ("B. F.") Skinner. Throughout his career, Skinner looked for ways in which his learning principles could improve daily life.

BLEND IMAGES/JUPITER IMAGES

OBJECTIVES

- Describe Pavlov's research, and discuss how learning occurs through the process of classical conditioning.
- Analyze general principles of classical conditioning.
- Identify classical conditioning in everyday behavior.

DISCOVER IT | *How does this relate to me?*

Do you think it is wrong to judge people, objects, or ideas based on criteria that have nothing to do with them? What if I told you that you and everybody else does this on a regular basis? One basic principle of learning is that you often develop positive or negative feelings toward many people and things simply because they are nearby when something either positive or negative happens. This may be the reason you enjoy wearing certain clothes such as a favorite tee-shirt or sweater—because of the many pleasant events associated with their use. Putting on that old shirt or slipping into those worn shoes is all it may take to produce a relaxed, positive feeling in you. In a very real sense, through your experiences wearing those articles of clothing, you have learned to like them.

KEY TERMS

- learning
- classical conditioning
- unconditioned response (UCR)
- unconditioned stimulus (UCS)
- conditioned response (CR)
- conditioned stimulus (CS)
- extinction
- stimulus generalization
- stimulus discrimination

P sychologists define **learning** as a change in behavior due to experience. You and other people and all species of animals learn in many ways. There are many things in your life that you have learned to like or dislike because they are associated with other things that naturally make you feel good or bad. This is such a classic way of learning that psychologists call it *classical conditioning*.

learning A change in behavior due to experience

Pavlov's Research

In 1904, Russian physiologist Ivan Pavlov (1849–1936) won the Nobel Prize for his research on digestion in dogs. In conducting his studies, Pavlov placed meat powder on a hungry dog's tongue so that the dog would salivate. One thing Pavlov noticed was that, over time, dogs began salivating *before* any food reached their mouths and even before they smelled the food. For example, they might salivate simply from seeing the food dish or merely from hearing the feeder's footsteps. At first Pavlov was annoyed because he could no longer control the beginning of the

Ivan Pavlov, 1849–1936, founder of classical conditioning.

LIBRARY OF CONGRESS, [LC-USZC4-3839]

dog's salivation. However, he then became excited after realizing that he had stumbled upon a simple but important form of learning, which came to be known as classical conditioning.

Classical conditioning is a type of learning in which a neutral stimulus triggers a response after being paired with another stimulus that naturally triggers that response. In his experiments, Pavlov placed a hungry dog in a device similar to the one shown in Figure 12-1. Just before putting meat powder into the dog's mouth, Pavlov presented a neutral stimulus to the dog. The neutral stimulus was a ticking metronome, a device that marks time in music. At first, the ticking produced no response in the dog. However, the food powder given to the dog right after the ticking sound naturally triggered the dog's drooling reflex. Because this act of drooling was unlearned, Pavlov called it an **unconditioned response (UCR)**. He called the food that triggered this automatic response an **unconditioned stimulus (UCS)**. So, an unconditioned stimulus is a stimulus that naturally and automatically brings out an unconditioned response. An unconditional response is the unlearned, automatic response to an unconditioned stimulus.

At first the neutral stimulus (ticking) had no effect on the dog. After several pairings of the ticking and food, the dog began to salivate in response to the ticking alone. The dog had *learned* to associate the ticking with the presentation of the food (see Figure 12-2 on page 341). This learned response to a previously neutral conditioned stimulus is called the **conditioned response (CR)**. After repeated pairings with an unconditioned stimulus (food), the previously neutral stimulus (ticking) brings about a conditioned response and is now called the **conditioned stimulus (CS)**. One way to remember the difference between stimuli and responses that are either unconditioned or conditioned is to think of these two terms in the following manner: *un*conditioned = *un*learned; conditioned = learned.

Pavlov used a device similar to this in his experiments on classical conditioning. By repeatedly pairing a ticking sound with receiving food, the dog learned to associate them and produce a conditioned response.

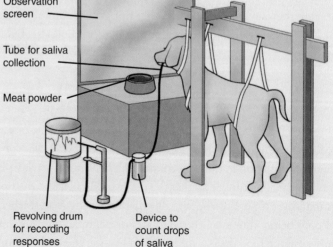

Figure 12-1 PAVLOV'S APPARATUS FOR STUDYING CLASSICAL CONDITIONING IN DOGS

Observation screen

Tube for saliva collection

Meat powder

Revolving drum for recording responses

Device to count drops of saliva

Classical conditioning may not be what you think of as learning. For instance, you are not using classical conditioning principles to understand the important points in this chapter. The type of learning that goes on in classical conditioning is often automatic. That is, you usually do not try to learn an association, and you usually do not try to respond in any specific way. Neither your pleasure (CR) upon seeing a good friend (CS) nor your anxiety (CR) upon hearing a dentist's drill (CS) is a response you try to learn. They develop with no real effort because both your friend's image and the drill noise have become associated with other stimuli that naturally bring about pleasure or pain.

Effortless learning affects many areas of your life and shapes your everyday behavior. However, you often do not notice it because it is so automatic. The positive feelings you have when hearing the names of your friends, as well as the negative feelings you experience when hearing the name of a rival sports team are all due to classical conditioning.

Figure 12-2 **CLASSICAL CONDITIONING**

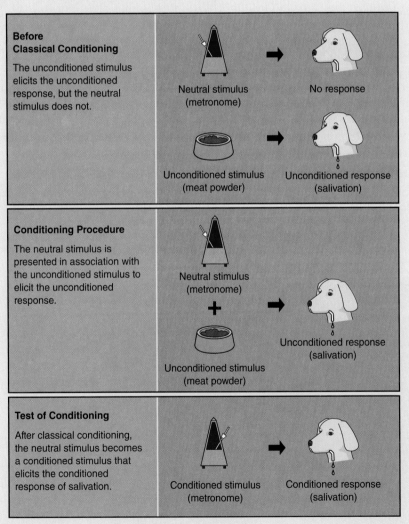

Before Classical Conditioning

The unconditioned stimulus elicits the unconditioned response, but the neutral stimulus does not.

Neutral stimulus (metronome)

No response

Unconditioned stimulus (meat powder)

Unconditioned response (salivation)

Conditioning Procedure

The neutral stimulus is presented in association with the unconditioned stimulus to elicit the unconditioned response.

Neutral stimulus (metronome)

+

Unconditioned stimulus (meat powder)

Unconditioned response (salivation)

Test of Conditioning

After classical conditioning, the neutral stimulus becomes a conditioned stimulus that elicits the conditioned response of salivation.

Conditioned stimulus (metronome)

Conditioned response (salivation)

During conditioning, the ticking metronome (CS) presented just before the meat powder (UCS) triggered the dog to salivate (CR).

CHECKPOINT *How does learning occur through the process of classical conditioning?*

General Principles of Classical Conditioning

You also can think of classical conditioning as a process by which humans and other animals learn to reliably predict events that are about to happen. This rule of classical conditioning states that a previously neutral stimulus will lead to a conditioned response whenever it provides you with information about the upcoming unconditioned stimulus. The conditioned stimulus becomes a signal that the unconditioned stimulus will soon appear. For example, whenever I hear popcorn popping I become excited because I have learned that this sound predicts the appearance of a favorite snack. Similarly, the sound of your cell phone's ringtone for your best friend may cause some excitement because it signals to you that something pleasant (a friend's voice) is coming your way. However, the sound of your parents' ringtone at midnight when your curfew is 11 P.M. probably depresses your mood because it signals something unpleasant is about to happen.

ACQUISITION

How quickly and in what way does the *acquisition,* or initial learning, of a conditioned response occur? Pavlov discovered that conditioned responses rarely occur at full strength right away (*one-trial learning*). Instead, they gradually build up after being repeated over and over. Pavlov also found that the timing of the association between the conditioned stimulus and the unconditioned stimulus also influences learning. The most effective way to learn that a stimulus is associated with an unconditioned stimulus is if this conditioned stimulus is presented about a half second before the unconditioned stimulus occurs.

The relatively quick learning that occurs when the conditioned stimulus is presented just before the unconditioned stimulus often helps animals survive. For

Can you think of instances in your own life when conditioned responses may increase your health and safety?

example, as shown in Figure 12-3 classical conditioning can help a chimpanzee react swiftly to a lion attack. Chimpanzees having past experiences with lions are more likely to quickly respond when stimuli associated with this predator (its sight, sound, or smell, for instance) are presented. Through experience, the chimpanzees that have been conditioned to respond to these danger signals (the CS) that occur just before the lion attacks (the UCS) are most likely to survive. Although rare, such frightening situations can result in learning after only one exposure to the unconditioned stimulus.

Figure 12-3   AVOIDING A PREDATOR'S ATTACK THROUGH CLASSICAL CONDITIONING

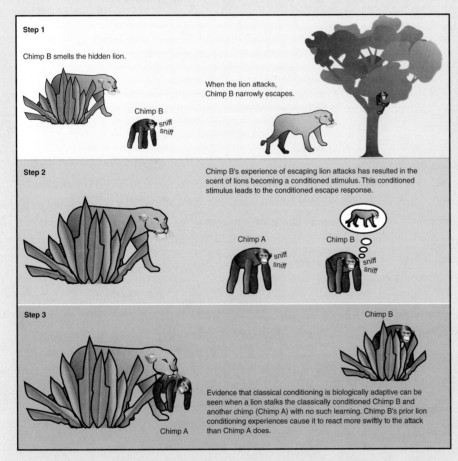

As a learning technique, classical conditioning helps animals adapt because it prepares them for good or bad events in the immediate future. For example, when reacting to a lion attack, Chimp B's prior experiences with lions provided it with a quicker response than that of Chimp A.

Step 1

Chimp B smells the hidden lion.

Chimp B

sniff sniff

When the lion attacks, Chimp B narrowly escapes.

Step 2

Chimp B's experience of escaping lion attacks has resulted in the scent of lions becoming a conditioned stimulus. This conditioned stimulus leads to the conditioned escape response.

Chimp A

sniff sniff

Chimp B

sniff sniff

Step 3

Chimp B

Evidence that classical conditioning is biologically adaptive can be seen when a lion stalks the classically conditioned Chimp B and another chimp (Chimp A) with no such learning. Chimp B's prior lion conditioning experiences cause it to react more swiftly to the attack than Chimp A does.

Chimp A

EXTINCTION AND SPONTANEOUS RECOVERY

What happens when the CS occurs repeatedly without the UCS? The answer is **extinction**, which is the gradual weakening and disappearance of the conditioned response. In Pavlov's experiments, when the ticking metronome (CS) was repeatedly presented to the dog without the delivery of food (UCS), the metronome gradually

extinction The gradual weakening and disappearance of the conditioned response

lost its ability to make the dog drool (CR). The dog learned the CS was no longer useful in predicting the UCS.

Although classically conditioned responses may stop, they are not completely unlearned. Occasionally a response that was stopped reappears suddenly when the conditioned stimulus is presented again. This phenomenon, known as *spontaneous recovery*, is the reappearance of a response after a period of nonexposure to the conditioned stimulus. For example, former soldiers who long ago overcame the panic attacks they had during combat may suddenly become very anxious while watching a movie with war scenes or hearing fireworks on the Fourth of July. The lesson here is that, even if you succeed in stopping a conditioned response, it may surprise you by reappearing later.

STIMULUS GENERALIZATION AND STIMULUS DISCRIMINATION

One observation Pavlov made while conditioning his dogs to salivate was that the drooling often could be triggered by—or generalized to—other similar stimuli. Pavlov called this phenomenon **stimulus generalization**, or the tendency for a conditioned response to be brought about by stimuli similar to the conditioned stimulus. Such generalization can be important for survival. For example, when a bird becomes sick after eating a poisonous Monarch butterfly, it avoids eating other orange and black insects. This reaction makes good sense: Things that look, taste, feel, or sound the same often share other characteristics. The more similar new stimuli are to the original conditioned stimulus, the greater the possibility of generalization. Stimulus generalization explains why I will try any food offered to me if it is sky blue in color: My positive reaction comes from my childhood love of Blue Moon ice cream.

Stimulus generalization may explain why you sometimes respond warmly or coldly to strangers who look like people for whom you previously developed either positive or negative conditioned responses. You may not realize that your emotion is caused by stimulus generalization. The Closer Look feature on page 345 describes a classic study in psychology that showed not only how fear can become classically conditioned, but also how fear can be learned through stimulus generalization.

In his studies, Pavlov noticed that the dogs often did not show conditioned responses when presented with stimuli that were somewhat similar to the conditioned stimulus. When an animal gives a conditioned response to the conditioned stimulus but not to stimuli similar to it, the opposite of stimulus generalization

stimulus generalization In classical conditioning, the tendency for a conditioned response to be triggered by stimuli similar to the conditioned stimulus

How may stimulus generalization explain why you choose certain people to be your friends?

©MANDY GODBEHEAR, 2009/USED UNDER LICENSE FROM SHUTTERSTOCK.COM

Can Fear Be Learned Through Classical Conditioning and Stimulus Generalization?

In 1920, John Watson, the founder of behaviorism (see Chapter 1, page 13), and his colleague, Rosalie Rayner, conducted the best-known study of stimulus generalization. Their subject was a nine-month-old boy whom they identified as "Little Albert B." During initial testing, Watson and Rayner presented Albert with a white rat, a rabbit, a monkey, a dog, masks with or without hair, and white cotton wool. The boy reacted with interest but no fear.

Two months later, the researchers presented Albert with the white rat. Just as Albert touched the rat, Watson made a loud noise behind him by striking a four-foot steel bar with a hammer. This noise (the UCS) startled and frightened (the UCR) Albert. During two sessions spaced one week apart, this procedure was repeated a total of seven times. Each time, the pairing of the rat and noise resulted in a fear response. Next, the rat alone was presented to Albert, without the noise. He reacted to the rat (the CS) with extreme fear (the CR): He cried, turned away, rolled over on one side away from the rat, and tried to crawl away. Little Albert had learned to fear the rat through classical conditioning.

Five days later, Albert was shown a furry white rabbit. Instead of responding warmly to this cute-looking animal, Albert responded with stimulus generalization:

> "Negative responses began at once. He leaned as far away from the animal as possible, whimpered, then burst into tears. When the rabbit was placed in contact with him, he buried his face in the mattress, then got up on all fours and crawled away, crying as he went."

Albert's fear response also generalized to a dog, a white fur coat, Watson's own head of gray hair, and even a Santa Claus mask! These fear responses also occurred in other settings. Two months later, Albert was tested one last time and again showed strong fear toward the same objects.

Besides demonstrating stimulus generalization, this study raises serious ethical issues. Watson and Rayner taught Albert to fear many things and they did not recondition him to lose this fear. The researchers' actions would not be allowed by the ethical standards of psychological research today. In Chapter 18 you will learn about therapies that use classical conditioning to help people lose these kinds of fears.

Think Critically

What ethical questions does this study raise?

occurs—namely, **stimulus discrimination**. For the most part, experience teaches you to discriminate. In the Closer Look feature, what would have happened if Albert had been encouraged to discover that the loud noise was never heard when the other objects were shown to him? The answer is that Albert would have developed stimulus discrimination and lost his fear of those objects.

CHECKPOINT *Identify the general principles of classical conditioning.*

Classical Conditioning in Everyday Behavior

The case study of Little Albert demonstrates that emotional responses can be classically conditioned in humans. Similarly, people injured in car accidents sometimes become very afraid of riding in all cars. The car in the accident becomes associated with an unconditioned stimulus (the accident) that naturally prompts an unconditioned response of intense fear. For these people, all cars now trigger fear due to stimulus generalization. These types of intense fears are known as *phobias* and are discussed more extensively in Chapter 17.

Have you ever had food poisoning? When you ate the food that made you sick, there were probably many things going on around you besides the taste of that food. However, like most people, the lesson you learned was to avoid whatever food you had eaten, and not, for example, the people you were talking to or the show you were watching on television. Why is this so?

In an important study of taste aversion, John Garcia and Robert Koelling (1966) allowed two groups of thirsty rats to drink flavored water from a device that produced a light flash and a loud click whenever they drank. While drinking, the two groups also received a UCS: Group A received painful electrical shocks to their feet, while Group B received radiation in X-rays that made them sick to their stomachs about one hour later. As shown in Figure 12-4 on page 347, the rats given painful shocks (Group A) learned to avoid the light and noise, but not the flavored water. In contrast, rats given the delayed stomach sickness from the radiation (Group B) learned to avoid the flavored water but not the light and noise. If you were the researchers, how would you explain these findings?

stimulus discrimination In classical conditioning, the tendency for a conditioned response to be elicited by the conditioned stimulus but not to stimuli similar to it

LAB TEAMS

Reconditioning Little Albert

With a partner, discuss ways you could recondition Little Albert to unlearn his fear response. Make an outline of your plan, and then share your plan with another team. Decide which team has the best plan. Share that plan with another group. Continue in this manner until you have chosen one plan.

Garcia and Koelling explained the results by proposing that over thousands of generations, rats have developed an inborn ability to protect themselves by associating certain stimuli in their environment with certain negative consequences. Rats are more likely to associate the sudden pain of a shock as being caused by an immediate external stimulus than by something they ate or drank an hour ago. This is why the rats in Group A avoided the light and noise, but not the flavored water they drank earlier. Similarly, rats are likely to associate stomach sickness with something they ate or drank. This is why the rats in Group B avoided the flavored water, even after a long delay between the taste (the CS) and their feeling of stomach sickness (the UCS).

Garcia decided to apply this knowledge to a practical problem: controlling attacks by wolves on ranchers' sheep. In one study, captured wolves were fed dead sheep containing a chemical (the UCS) that causes severe vomiting (the UCR). After recovering from this very unpleasant experience, the wolves were placed in a pen with a live sheep. At first, the wolves moved toward the sheep (the CS) ready to attack. However, when they smelled the sheep, they backed off and avoided further contact (the CR). This is both an example of taste aversion and one-trial learning. Based on this research, many ranchers today classically condition predators to avoid their sheep and cattle by allowing them to eat a few dead livestock injected with this same chemical. Check out the Positive Psychology feature on page 348 for an example of how classical conditioning principles are being used to help people.

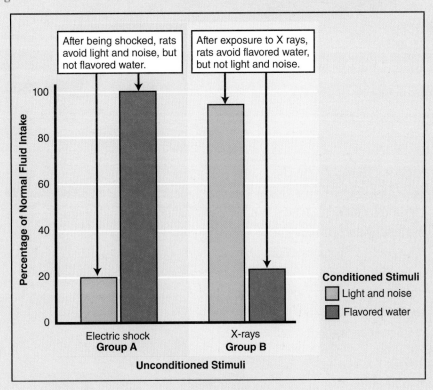

Figure 12-4 **BIOLOGICAL CONSTRAINTS ON TASTE AVERSION IN RATS**

Rats learned to avoid a light-noise combination when it was paired with electrical shock, but not when it was followed by X-rays that made the rats sick. In contrast, rats quickly learned to avoid flavored water when it was followed by X-rays, but they did not readily acquire an aversion to this same water when it was followed by shock.

 **CHECKPOINT** ► *How might classical conditioning affect the everyday behavior of someone who was injured in a car accident?*

Can Sick Patients Be Classically Conditioned to Become Healthier?

Knowledge gained from taste aversion studies have been used to help cancer patients undergoing chemotherapy treatment. During chemotherapy many patients lose a great deal of weight because the drugs in the treatment make them sick to their stomachs when they eat food. Researchers discovered that many of these patients lost their appetite because they were eating their regular meals just before going in for chemotherapy. This resulted in their regular food (the CS) becoming classically conditioned to the sickness caused by the chemotherapy (the UCS). To make such conditioning less likely, patients now are told either not to eat before their therapy sessions or to eat foods that are not part of their regular diet. If they develop a distaste for these foods, it does not hurt their normal eating habits.

Sick patients who have eaten frozen sherbet laced with a drug that strengthens their immune system later show an improvement in their immune system simply by eating regular sherbet. This is an example of how classical conditioning can be used to treat illnesses.

©LORRAINE KOURAFAS, 2009/USED UNDER LICENSE FROM SHUTTERSTOCK.COM

Classical conditioning is used in other ways to help people suffering from diseases by strengthening their immune systems. For example, some studies have given sick patients a bowl of frozen sherbet (the CS) to eat that contains adrenaline (the UCS), a drug that naturally strengthens the immune system (the UCR). After repeatedly pairing the sherbet and the adrenaline, these studies find that the patients' immune system is strengthened when they eat the sherbet alone, without adrenaline.

Think Critically

How might this research help doctors use classical conditioning in treating other illnesses?

In Your Own Words

Describe a food for which you have a taste aversion and explain how classical conditioning caused that aversion.

Review Concepts

1. Which refers to a change in behavior that results from experience?
    a. extinction
    b. learning
    c. classical conditioning
    d. high-order conditioning

2. In classical conditioning a stimulus that naturally and automatically elicits an unconditioned response is called a
    a. UCR
    b. CR
    c. UCS
    d. CS

3. Which refers to the tendency for a conditioned response to be elicited by stimuli similar to the conditioned stimulus in classical conditioning?
    a. CS
    b. UCS
    c. stimulus discrimination
    d. stimulus generalization

4. If unconditioned means unlearned, which does conditioned mean?
    a. response
    b. stimulus
    c. learned
    d. reaction

5. Which researcher is associated with classical conditioning?
    a. Ivan Pavlov
    b. Carl Jung
    c. Sigmund Freud
    d. Wilhelm Wundt

6. **True or False** Your pleasure when seeing a good friend is an example of a conditioned stimulus.

7. **True or False** Conditioned responses occur at full strength immediately after a stimulus is introduced.

8. **True or False** Extinction occurs when the CS occurs repeatedly without the UCS.

Think Critically

9. How does classical conditioning help an animal stay safe?

10. How might taste aversion have saved lives of ancient peoples?

11. What are the practical aspects of John Garcia and Robert Koelling's research for both animals and humans?

12. How does understanding Pavlov's work help you better understand yourself?

LESSON 12.2 | Operant Conditioning

KEY TERMS

- operant conditioning
- reinforcement
- punishment
- continuous reinforcement schedule
- fixed-ratio reinforcement schedule
- variable-ratio reinforcement schedule
- fixed-interval reinforcement schedule
- variable-interval reinforcement schedule
- shaping
- latent learning

OBJECTIVES

- Describe the principle of reinforcement.
- Describe the principle of punishment.
- Identify the five reinforcement schedules.

DISCOVER IT | *How does this relate to me?*

What are some activities you would spend a great deal of time doing if you had your choice? Playing tennis? Reading? Video gaming? Hanging out with your friends? What distinguishes these activities from those that you would definitely not want to spend time doing? The simple answer to this question is rewards or consequences. You have learned that you generally experience positive rewards when you participate in enjoyable activities, but not when you participate in your least favorite activities. Learning what to do based on the consequences of your actions is another important form of learning.

---

operant conditioning
A type of learning in which behavior is strengthened if followed by reinforcement and weakened if followed by punishment

B. F. Skinner, 1904–1990, founder of operant conditioning

COURTESY OF B. F. SKINNER FOUNDATION

In the 1930s, B. F. Skinner developed an important theory of learning, which he called **operant conditioning**. Like classical conditioning, operant conditioning involves acquisition, extinction, spontaneous recovery, generalization, and discrimination. However, in classical conditioning, people and animals are learning associations between events that they do not control. In contrast, operant conditioning involves people and animals learning associations between their behavior and resulting events or consequences. Skinner used the term *operant conditioning* because he said that a person's or animal's behavior operates on the environment to achieve some desired goal. Operant behavior is largely voluntary, is designed to achieve some goal, and is controlled by consequences.

Therefore, when a rat presses a bar in a Skinner box (see Figure 12-5, page 351), it does so because it has learned that bar-pressing will lead to food pellets. Likewise, when some teenagers clean their bedroom, they do so because they have learned that this behavior will lead to something they desire, namely, their parents' allowing them to play with friends, receive a weekly allowance, or earn some other reward.

Figure 12-5 **SKINNER BOX**

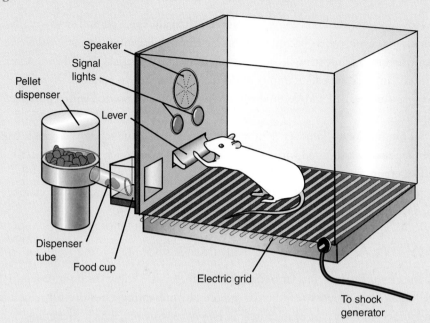

Speaker

Signal lights

Pellet dispenser

Lever

Dispenser tube

Food cup

Electric grid

To shock generator

Skinner designed a device called a "Skinner box" in which animals learned to get food or avoid shocks by operating on their environment within the box. In the Skinner box, the animals learn to press the bar to get food pellets, which are delivered into the box down the pellet tube.

Reinforcement

People and other animals tend to repeat behaviors that are followed by desirable rewards rather than negative consequences. This process by which a stimulus increases the probability of the behavior that it follows is known as **reinforcement**. Reinforcement is the most important principle of behaviorism.

The stimulus that increases the probability that the behavior it follows will be repeated is called a *reinforcer*. A reinforcer may be a concrete reward, such as food, money, or attention. For example, if people laugh and pay attention to you when you tell a joke, their response likely will make you tell jokes in the future. A reinforcer also could be an activity, such as your parents allowing you to hang out with friends after you clean your room. How do you know whether something is a reinforcer? Simple. Observe whether it increases the behavior it follows. While being allowed to have friends over reinforces my daughters' cleaning their rooms, I have learned that allowing them to watch a football game on television with me is not a reinforcer.

Sometimes, the same stimulus is a reinforcer in one situation but not in another. For example, while laughter may reinforce joke-telling, my sister's laughter while teaching me to dance years ago certainly did not increase my desire to get on the dance floor! Likewise, a stimulus may be a reinforcer for one animal but not for another. Do you think the food pellets that rats in a Skinner box worked so hard to get would be a reinforcer for you? The lesson here is that something is a reinforcer because of what it *does,* not because of what it *is.*

reinforcement The process by which a stimulus increases the probability of the behavior that it follows

PRIMARY VS. SECONDARY REINFORCERS

How does a stimulus become a reinforcer? Actually, some stimuli are naturally reinforcing, while others become reinforcing through learning. *Primary reinforcers* are naturally reinforcing because they satisfy some biological need. Food, water, warmth, and sleep are all examples of primary reinforcers. In contrast, *secondary reinforcers* are learned and become reinforcing by being associated with a primary reinforcer.

An example of a secondary reinforcer is money. You value money because it has been repeatedly associated with many primary reinforcers, such as food, shelter, and entertainment. Likewise, attention becomes a secondary reinforcer for children because it is paired with primary reinforcers from adults, such as protection, warmth, food, and water.

POSITIVE AND NEGATIVE REINFORCERS

The examples used thus far to describe reinforcers are known as positive reinforcers. A *positive reinforcer* strengthens a response by presenting a positive stimulus after a response. Another type of reinforcer is a *negative reinforcer,* which strengthens a response by removing an unpleasant stimulus after a response. Although negative reinforcement sounds like it means reinforcing behavior with a negative consequence, in fact it refers to removing something from the environment. (Negative consequences are a form of punishment, which is discussed on page 353.) In a Skinner box, an electric shock passing through the metal floor is a negative reinforcer for

Praise becomes a secondary reinforcer because it is associated with primary reinforcers, such as gentle physical contact and warmth. Can you think of other secondary reinforcers in your own life?

TETRA IMAGES/JUPITER IMAGES

the rat. When the rat presses the bar (refer back to Figure 12-5), the shock is turned off. The removal of the shock strengthens the bar-pressing behavior.

Just as the rat learns to end an unpleasant sensation by responding in a specific way, you have learned certain responses to escape negative reinforcers. The cold weather you avoid by going indoors is a negative reinforcer. Your parents getting after you to take out the garbage or to turn down your music are negative reinforcers. When you respond in the correct way, the unpleasant stimulus (the cold temperature or the parental pressure) is removed. Similarly, when you clean your smelly school locker, the removal of the foul odor also is a negative reinforcer: It strengthens locker cleaning in the future. Complete the Self-Discovery exercise on page 353 to learn more abut how positive and negative reinforcers might shape your behavior.

CHECKPOINT > *What is reinforcement?*

Can You Identify Your Personal Reinforcers?

B. F. Skinner's research demonstrated that humans and other animals repeat responses that are followed by favorable consequences, or reinforcers. He further believed that people can gain greater control over their own behavior the more they can identify what kinds of things serve as reinforcers for them. In this spirit of discovery, think about behaviors and activities that are personally important to you that you have engaged in during the past 24 hours.

Instructions: On a separate sheet of paper, make a chart like the one you see below. Then list at least five of these behaviors or activities you have engaged in. Next, identify and list either positive and/or negative reinforcers that influenced these behaviors or activities.

Behavior or Activity	Positive Reinforcement	Negative Reinforcement	Combination
1.			
2.			
3.			
4.			
5.			

Based on this exercise, do you think your important daily behaviors or activities are influenced more by positive or negative reinforcement? Are there certain types of reinforcement that you seem to respond more favorably toward than other types? Do you know why this might be the case for you? Did this exercise provide you with any useful information?

Punishment

The opposite consequence of reinforcement is **punishment**, which is the process by which a stimulus decreases the probability of the behavior it follows. While reinforcement always increases the probability of a behavior—either by presenting a desirable stimulus or by removing or avoiding an unpleasant stimulus—punishment always decreases the probability of whatever behavior it follows.

POSITIVE AND NEGATIVE PUNISHERS

Like reinforcement, there are two types of punishment. *Positive punishers* weaken a response by presenting an unpleasant stimulus after a response. Shocking a rat in a Skinner box for pressing a food bar and scolding a child for eating candy before dinner are examples of the use of positive punishment to reduce the future

punishment The process by which a stimulus decreases the probability of the behavior it follows

likelihood of unwanted behavior. In contrast, *negative punishers* weaken a response by removing a positive stimulus after a response. Grounding a teenager for impolite behavior and denying an end-of-year bonus to a lazy worker are examples of negative punishment.

Do not confuse positive punishment with negative reinforcement (see page 352). It is true that both involve an unpleasant stimulus, but that is their only similarity. First, remember that the consequence of reinforcement is that it strengthens the behavior it follows, while the consequence of punishment is that it weakens the behavior it follows. Second, remember that while negative reinforcement strengthens behavior by removing an unpleasant stimulus, positive punishment weakens behavior by presenting an unpleasant stimulus. Table 12-1 distinguishes between the two types of reinforcement and the two types of punishment.

Table 12-1 DIFFERENCES BETWEEN TYPES OF REINFORCEMENT AND PUNISHMENT

Procedure	Strengthens	Weakens
Presentation of stimulus	Positive reinforcement (Example: Telling more jokes after people laugh at your first joke)	Positive punishment (Example: Telling no more jokes after people groan at your first joke)
Removal of stimulus	Negative reinforcement (Example: Learning to rub a sore muscle to relieve pain)	Negative punishment (Example: Your parents taking away your cell phone after you get failing grades in school)

THE DISADVANTAGES OF PUNISHMENT

Skinner recommended using reinforcement to shape behavior, but he opposed using punishment. One reason he did not recommend the use of punishment is that, in most instances, it is not very successful in changing behavior. In order for punishment to have a chance of reducing unwanted behaviors, three conditions must be met. First, the punishment must be *prompt,* given quickly after the unwanted action. Second, the punishment must be *relatively strong,* so its unpleasant qualities are felt by the offending person. Third, the punishment must be *consistently applied,* so the person knows that punishment is likely to follow future unwanted actions. Meeting these three conditions is very difficult.

Using physical punishments, such as spankings, to reduce unwanted behavior generally is not successful. Research indicates that using physical punishment against aggression and other undesirable behaviors may simply teach and encourage others to copy these aggressive actions. This is why family violence leads to more family violence—observing adult aggression encourages rather than discourages aggression in children.

Instead of using punishment, Skinner recommended that parents allow undesirable actions (such as a child's temper tantrums) to continue without either positive or negative consequences until the child stops. In other words, ignore the unwanted behavior—but immediately reinforce desirable behaviors when they occur. Another useful extinction technique is a time-out, in which misbehaving children are removed for a short period of time from activities they enjoy. Have you ever used extinction techniques with younger siblings or while babysitting? Were they effective?

CHECKPOINT *What is punishment?*

The Five Schedules of Reinforcement

Every time you put money into a vending machine you are reinforced with a treat, but what will you do if nothing comes out?

DIGITAL VISION/GETTY IMAGES

The reinforcement schedule that leads to the fastest learning is the **continuous reinforcement schedule** in which every correct response is followed by a reinforcer. An example of a behavior that is controlled by continuous reinforcement is putting coins into a vending machine. Every time you put coins into a vending machine you are reinforced with a treat. However, what happens when you put money into a vending machine and do not receive anything in return? You might respond by inserting more coins, but if this does not lead to the desired object, you do not put any more money into the machine, do you? Behavior learned through continuous reinforcement is easily extinguished when reinforcement stops.

In most instances of daily living, your behavior is only reinforced sometimes. Skinner discovered that responses that are reinforced only some of the time are much harder to stop than those that are based on continuous reinforcement. For example, you have not stopped going to movies, visiting friends, or eating food because you may have had a few unrewarding experiences. You continue engaging in many activities even though you are reinforced only occasionally. When reinforcement occurs only occasionally, it is called *partial reinforcement*. Although continuous reinforcement allows you to learn responses the quickest once responses have been learned, partial reinforcement keeps you responding for longer periods of time than does continuous reinforcement.

PARTIAL REINFORCEMENT SCHEDULES

Skinner identified several partial reinforcement schedules. Half of these schedules are based on the number of correct responses made between reinforcements (*ratio schedules*) and the other half are based on the passage of time (*interval schedules*). In addition, ratio and interval schedules are either strictly *fixed* or unpredictably *variable*. Combining the ratio versus interval schedules with the fixed versus variable schedules results in four basic partial reinforcement schedules.

Fixed-ratio reinforcement schedules reinforce behavior after a certain number of responses. For example, students may be given a prize after reading 20 books, or factory workers may be paid a certain amount of money for every 40 machinery pieces they assemble. The students read their first 19 books without reinforcement, as do the workers with their first 39 machinery pieces, because each group knows the payoff will occur when the last book or piece is completed in the ratio.

continuous reinforcement schedule A schedule of reinforcement in which every correct response is followed by a reinforcer

fixed-ratio reinforcement schedule A schedule of reinforcement that reinforces behavior after a certain number of responses

Figure 12-6 SCHEDULES OF REINFORCEMENT

Fixed-ratio schedules lead to a high rate of responding, with brief pauses after each reinforcer is delivered. Variable-ratio schedules lead to high, steady rates of responding, with few pauses between reinforcers. Fixed-interval schedules lead to a low rate of responding until the fixed interval of time approaches, and then the rate of responding increases rapidly until the reinforcer is delivered; then a low rate of responding resumes. Variable-interval schedules produce a moderate but steady rate of responding.

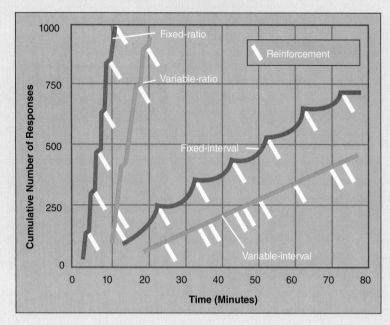

When people and animals are placed on a fixed-ratio reinforcement schedule, it produces high response rates, with only brief pauses following reinforcement (see Figure 12-6).

Why do you think people and animals on fixed-ratio schedules take such short breaks before working again on their tasks? The reason is that resting reduces rewards. People and animals on fixed-ratio schedules often work until they are exhausted because this schedule reinforces rapid responding. What happens when reinforcement stops? Similar to continuous reinforcement, people or animals stop responding soon after fixed-ratio reinforcement stops because they realize that something about the schedule has changed.

What happens when a ratio schedule is not fixed, but varies? That is, a reinforcer may be delivered after the first response on trial one, after the fourth response on trial two, after the ninth response on trial three, and so on. The average ratio may be one reinforcer after every six trials, but the responder never knows how many responses are needed to get the reinforcer. Schedules like this that reinforce a response after a variable number of nonreinforced responses are known as **variable-ratio reinforcement schedules**. These are partial reinforcement schedules that reinforce a response after a variable number of nonreinforced responses.

As you can see in Figure 12-6 above, variable-ratio schedules lead to the highest rates of responding, the shortest pauses following reinforcement, and the greatest resistance to extinction. Golfing and most other sports activities are reinforced on variable-ratio schedules. Even after golfers hit balls into sand traps and overshoot the green all day, it only takes a few good (reinforced) shots to get most golfers excited about playing again. Most games of chance are also based on variable-ratio

variable-ratio reinforcement schedule A partial reinforcement schedule that reinforces a response after a variable number of nonreinforced responses

schedules. The irregular and unpredictable nature of the reinforcement is why people become addicted—and lose a great deal of money—while playing slot machines.

In **fixed-interval reinforcement schedules** reinforcement occurs for the first response after a fixed time interval has elapsed. As you can see in Figure 12-6, this schedule produces a pattern of behavior in which very few responses are made until the end of the fixed time interval approaches, and then the rate of responding increases rapidly. Researchers have discovered that the study habits of students follow a fixed-interval schedule when teachers give exams every few weeks. For example, when exams were given every three weeks, most students began studying a few days before each exam, stopped studying immediately after the test, and began studying again as the next exam approached. In contrast, when teachers gave daily quizzes, studying did not taper off after testing. At my house, I am on a fixed-interval reinforcement schedule regarding the attention I pay to my mailbox. I can see it from my window, but I pay no attention to it now because it is 10:00 A.M. and the mail does not arrive until noon. As midday nears, my glances toward the mailbox increase dramatically because I know that my daily reinforcement of mail is arriving very soon.

Unlike the predictability of fixed-interval reinforcement, **variable-interval reinforcement schedules** reinforce the first response after a variable time interval has elapsed. Refer back to Figure 12-6. Such schedules produce relatively steady rates of responding. Have you ever taken a course where your grade was based on surprise exams that were given after a varying number of days or weeks? Because you did not know when you would be tested, you probably studied on a more regular basis than when exams were spread out in a fixed-interval pattern. Similarly, have you ever tried to connect to a dial-up Internet server but received a busy signal or a message that it was unavailable due to temporary maintenance? You know

fixed-interval reinforcement schedule Reinforcement occurs for the first response after a fixed time interval has elapsed

variable-interval reinforcement schedule Schedule that reinforces the first response after a variable time interval has elapsed

What type of reinforcement schedule does the U.S. Postal Service have you on regarding your daily mail delivery?

sometime in the near future that your attempt to connect will be reinforced, but you are unsure when that moment will arrive, so you regularly try to dial-up the server. You are on a variable-interval schedule of reinforcement.

SHAPING BEHAVIOR

The reinforcement techniques discussed so far describe how you can increase the frequency of behaviors once they occur. However, suppose you want to train a dog to stand on its hind legs and dance, or teach a child to write the alphabet or play the piano. These behaviors are unlikely to occur on their own, so you must use an operant conditioning procedure that Skinner called **shaping** or the *method of successive approximations*.

In shaping, you teach a new behavior by reinforcing behaviors that are closer and closer approximations to the desired behavior (see Table 12-2). For example, when learning to speak a foreign language, your teacher will slowly shape your speech with praise until you sound like a native speaker. Like language teachers, everyone uses praise and other reinforcers to shape successively closer approximations of desirable behavior in others. Whether it is teaching people to correct their dance steps or improve their grammar, shaping is an important way to learn new skills. Today, when you go to a circus or marine park and see elephants balancing on one leg or sea lions waving "hello" to you with their flippers, you are seeing the results of shaping. If you have ever trained a dog to play fetch or to come when called, you did so using shaping techniques.

Table 12-2 **HOW TO SHAPE BEHAVIOR**

1. Identify what the respondent can do now.
2. Identify the desired behavior.
3. Identify potential reinforcers in the respondent's environment.
4. Break the desired behavior into small substeps to be mastered sequentially.
5. Move the respondent from the entry behavior to the desired behavior by successively reinforcing each approximation to the desired behavior.

Source: Adapted from Galanter, 1962.

Using shaping techniques, the United States Coast Guard has successfully trained pigeons to find people lost at sea who are wearing bright orange life jackets. Pigeons have much better eyesight than humans. They are first trained in the laboratory to search for an orange disk and then peck a button with their beaks. After training, the pigeons are taken on rescue missions to search for the orange vests in the water. While helicopter pilots notice bobbing orange vests in the water only 35 percent of the time, pigeons' success rate is closer to 90 percent.

Behavior psychologists also use shaping to train monkeys to provide live-in help for people who are paralyzed, blind, or have some other physical disability. These specially trained monkeys can perform many activities, including combing a person's hair, turning on lights and electronic devices, and getting food from the refrigerator. Capuchin monkeys are used because they have high intelligence and form a strong

shaping The process of teaching a new behavior by reinforcing closer and closer approximations to the desired behavior

HELPING HANDS: MONKEY HELPERS FOR THE DISABLED

The operant conditioning technique of shaping is used to train monkeys to help people with disabilities live in their own homes. Here is Artie helping her owner place her foot back on the wheelchair. The command "foot" tells the monkey this task is needed.

bond with humans. It often takes up to two years of training for these monkeys to learn their helping skills.

Although Skinner first thought that animals could be trained to perform any behavior, it was discovered that their biology sometimes prevented them from performing some simple actions. For example, raccoons can learn to pick up small coins and deposit them into a bucket for a reward. However, after learning this behavior, raccoons soon start dipping—not dropping—the coins into the bucket and then rubbing them with their paws. In doing so, they are performing an instinctual behavior that raccoons use to wash food in a stream. Many species of animals have instinctual behaviors that can prevent them from reliably performing certain behaviors. Psychologists refer to this limitation as *instinctual drift.*

CURRENT VIEWS OF OPERANT CONDITIONING

Psychologists sometimes head down wrong paths due to mistaken beliefs or by failing to notice others' discoveries. This is what happened with Skinner. He died refusing to admit that cognition, or thinking, was important in understanding either human or animal behavior. Yet, even as Skinner was developing his theory of operant conditioning in the 1930s, Edward Tolman's research with rats found that learning can occur without any reinforcement. This finding was important because it was something that, according to the theory of operant conditioning, was not possible.

In one of Tolman's experiments, a group of rats wandered through a maze once a day for ten days without being reinforced. Meanwhile, another group of rats spent the same amount of time in the maze but were reinforced with food at the "goal box" in each of their ten trials. These reinforced rats quickly learned to accurately run the maze to reach the food reward, but the nonreinforced rats made many errors, suggesting that they had not learned the maze. Then, the nonreinforced rats were suddenly rewarded with food at the goal box, and they immediately made as few errors as the other rats. A third group of control rats that still received no food reward continued to make many errors (see Figure 12-7 on page 360).

Tolman argued that these results demonstrated that reinforcement is not always necessary for learning to occur. Instead, Tolman suggested that, through experience and thinking, even the rats that had received no reinforcement had formed a cognitive map, or mental image, of the maze. They formed these maps before being reinforced, which meant that learning could occur without reinforcement. The learning of these rats remained hidden or latent, because the rats realized that their behavior would not be rewarded. They did not demonstrate their new behavior until that behavior was reinforced. Tolman called such learning that is not currently demonstrated in actual behavior and occurs without reinforcement **latent learning**. Despite Skinner's denials, operant conditioning now is known to involve developing a belief that a certain consequence will follow a certain behavior.

latent learning Learning that occurs without any reinforcement but is not demonstrated until reinforcement is provided

Rats that were rewarded for their maze running made fewer errors than rats that were not rewarded. However, on day 11, when these unrewarded rats were rewarded, they immediately made as few errors as the other rats. This experiment demonstrated the principle of latent learning. Can you think of examples of latent learning in your own life?

Figure 12-7 **LATENT LEARNING**

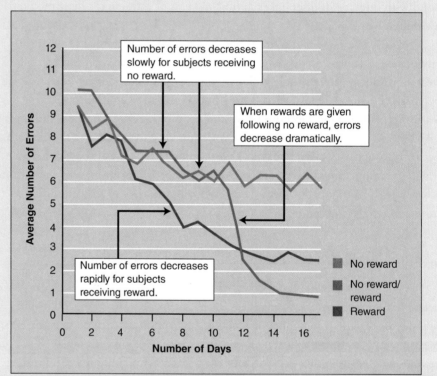

Number of errors decreases slowly for subjects receiving no reward.

When rewards are given following no reward, errors decrease dramatically.

Number of errors decreases rapidly for subjects receiving reward.

No reward
No reward/ reward
Reward

CHECKPOINT *What are the five schedules of reinforcement?*

In Your Own Words

Explain either the principle of reinforcement or the principle of punishment. For the principle of reinforcement, include information on both primary and secondary reinforcers, and positive and negative reinforcers. For the principle of punishment, include information on positive and negative punishers and the disadvantages of punishment. Provide an example of the principle you discuss.

Review Concepts

1. Which is a fundamental principle of behaviorism?
   - a. shaping
   - b. reinforcement
   - c. latent learning
   - d. punishment

2. Identify the secondary reinforcer.
   - a. sleep
   - b. water
   - c. warmth
   - d. money

3. In which schedule of reinforcement is every correct response followed by a reinforcer?
   - a. continuous
   - b. fixed-interval
   - c. variable-ratio
   - d. fixed-ratio

4. Which weakens a response by presenting an unpleasant stimulus after a response?
   - a. positive reinforcers
   - b. negative punishers
   - c. negative reinforcers
   - d. positive punishers

5. According to Skinner, which is not a criteria of effective punishment?
   - a. prompt
   - b. applied by authority
   - c. relatively strong
   - d. consistently applied

6. **True or False** A reinforcer increases the behavior it follows.

7. **True or False** Negative reinforcers reinforce behavior with a negative consequence.

8. **True or False** Punishment increases the probability of whatever behavior it follows.

9. **True or False** The consequence of reinforcement is that it strengthens the behavior it follows, while the consequence of punishment is that it weakens the behavior it follows.

Think Critically

10. In the Skinner box, why is removing the electric shock in the floor grid of the rat's cage called a negative reinforcer?

11. Why does the current view of operant conditioning hold that learning can occur without reinforcement?

12.3 Observational Learning

KEY TERMS
- observational learning
- social learning theory

OBJECTIVES
- Describe social learning theory.
- Discuss observational learning of aggression.

DISCOVER IT | *How does this relate to me?*

Both classical conditioning and operant conditioning involve learning through direct experience with desirable and undesirable outcomes. Yet, haven't you learned a lot of things without direct experience, simply by watching and imitating others? For example, have you ever worn a certain style of clothing because you saw someone you admired wearing that style? Or, have you ever tried a new food after observing other people eating and enjoying it? What if a friend made fun of someone wearing the new style of clothing? Or, what if you see a person gagging after biting into an unfamiliar food? In both cases, you probably learned through observation not to wear the style or eat that food.

A very important third form of learning is **observational learning**, which involves learning by observing and deciding what to imitate in the behavior of others. These others whom you observe and imitate are called *models* because they teach you how to perform (or not perform) the behavior. Observational learning helps children learn how to behave in their families and cultures. It also helps teenagers and adults learn the skills necessary for career and personal success. Unlike classical and operant conditioning, observational learning is easily recognized as involving a good deal of complex thinking. Most learning occurs through this sort of thoughtful observation.

Social Learning Theory

observational learning Learning by observing and deciding what to imitate in the behavior of others

social learning theory People learn social behaviors mainly through observing and imitating others rather than through direct experience

Observational learning is the central feature of Albert Bandura's **social learning theory**. This theory states that people learn social behaviors mainly through observing and imitating others rather than through direct experience (see Case Study, page 366). According to this theory, when you watch others engage in some activity with which you are not familiar, a great deal of cognitive learning takes place before you perform the behavior. You are most likely to imitate a model whose actions you see rewarded, and you are least likely to imitate behavior that is punished. One of the main differences between social learning and the learning that occurs in operant conditioning is that with social learning, the behavior of other people is reinforced or punished. With operant conditioning it is your own behavior that is either reinforced or punished.

Observational learning and positive role models are important to children and teenagers in developing the skills necessary for success in life. For example, a large survey of teenagers in Los Angeles, California, found that having an admired role model has a positive influence on teen's lives. In this study, a little more than half the teenagers reported that they had a role model whom they wanted to be like. The most popular role models were parents and other relatives. Girls most often identified people whom they personally knew as role models, whereas boys were more likely to identify sports stars and other celebrities. The teenagers who identified one or more important role models in their lives earned higher grades in school and had more positive self-esteem than those who did not have a role model.

Studies show that teenagers who have role models in their lives earn higher grades and have more positive self-esteem.

©KONSTANTIN SUTYAGIN, 2009/USED UNDER LICENSE FROM SHUTTERSTOCK.COM

CHECKPOINT *What is social learning theory?*

Observational Learning of Aggression

Research suggests that when the media widely covers a violent incident it often is followed by a sudden increase in similar violent crimes. Psychologists suggest that reading and watching news accounts of violence can trigger some people to copy the aggression. This dangerous form of observational learning may help explain the rash of shootings at elementary and secondary schools since the 1999 tragedy at Columbine High School in Littleton, Colorado.

Children observe and learn aggression in many ways, but especially through their family, the culture, and the media. First, in families where adults use violence, children grow up being much more likely to use violence themselves. Second, in communities and neighborhoods where aggression is viewed as a sign of manhood, learning aggressive behaviors is very common, especially among males. Finally, the media—mainly through television, movies, and music videos—sends images of violence to people on a daily basis. Do you think this exposure to violence can produce aggression in consumers?

Many hundreds of studies conducted around the world have examined this question during the past five decades. Their results strongly indicate that media violence encourages aggression in children and adolescents. One important factor that seems to influence children's aggressiveness is their *identification* with aggressive television and movie characters. That is, children who watch a lot of media violence and identify with aggressive media characters are most likely to behave aggressively in their daily life.

INFOBIT
Negative role models also influence people's actions. For example, observing peers who smoke cigarettes influences adolescents' decisions to start smoking. Teens most affected by this negative influence are "outsiders," meaning teens who have not yet been accepted into a group they desire to join. If the members of the group smoke, the outsiders imitate these teens and begin smoking in the hope of being accepted. How could this knowledge be used in developing antismoking ads for teenagers?

VIOLENCE IN MUSIC VIDEOS AND VIDEO GAMES

Several studies have examined how music videos affect young people's aggressive thinking and attitudes. Their findings indicate that teenagers and young adults who regularly watch and listen to violent rap and rock music videos are more likely to accept violence as a way to resolve conflicts than those who rarely watch and listen to violent music videos. Further, songs with violent lyrics increase aggressive thoughts and feelings in listeners. Overall, these findings suggest that watching and/or listening to violent music causes people to be more accepting of aggressive behavior and it also creates a greater willingness to act aggressively.

Playing violent video games has similar harmful effects. Because video games are interactive, video-game players actually engage in virtual aggression, receive rewards for their aggression, and closely identify with the characters they control. A number of video-game studies find that exposure to high video-game violence leads to more aggressive thoughts and emotions and increased aggression in the daily lives of children, teenagers, and young adults.

REDUCING AGGRESSION THROUGH POSITIVE ROLE MODELS

Just as destructive models can teach people how to act aggressively, nonaggressive models can teach people to control their aggression when faced with conflict. In support of this hypothesis, psychologists have discovered that when research participants watch role models act nonaggressively toward others who anger them, the participants later also tend to behave nonaggressively in a similar conflict situation.

Aggression also can be controlled if a role model criticizes the behavior of aggressive individuals. Research consistently shows that when a child watches violence on television in the presence of an adult who criticizes the violence, the child is less likely to imitate this aggression later.

Finally, an important ingredient in reducing aggressive responses is to limit people's exposure to violence. For example, one study examined third- and fourth-grade students at two similar schools over a six-month period. In one of

If you want to put yourself in a peaceful state of mind, what type of music would you avoid?

©MONKEY BUSINESS IMAGES, 2009|USED UNDER LICENSE FROM SHUTTERSTOCK.COM

the schools, television and video-game exposure was reduced by one-third when students and parents were encouraged to engage in other forms of home entertainment, while in the other school no effort was made to reduce exposure. The researchers found that children who went to the school where less time was spent watching TV and playing video games became much less aggressive on the playground than students at the other school, especially those students who had been rated as most aggressive by their classmates.

CHECKPOINT *In what kind of situation are children who observe someone behaving aggressively most likely to later also behave aggressively?*

12.3 ASSESSMENT

In Your Own Words

Explain social learning theory and the observational learning of aggression. Use examples from your life in your explanations.

Review Concepts

1. Which type of learning occurs by observing and deciding what to imitate in the behavior of others?
   - a. latent
   - b. reinforcement
   - c. observational
   - d. classical

2. Which refers to Bandura's theory that people learn social behaviors mainly through observation and cognitive processing of information rather than through direct experience?
   - a. primary theory
   - b. secondary theory
   - c. observational learning
   - d. social learning theory

3. **True or False**   Observational learning requires a good deal of complex thinking.

4. **True or False**   The most popular role models for teens are their parents and other relatives.

Think Critically

5. Why is a model necessary in observational learning?

6. Why do you think a study of California teenagers found that the teenagers who identified one or more important role models in their lives earned higher grades in school and had more positive self-esteem than those who did not have a role model?

7. Why do studies show that people who frequently play violent video games become less upset when they observe violence in other areas of their lives?

8. Discuss why research demonstrates that when a child watches violence on television in the presence of an adult who condemns the violence, the child is less likely to later imitate this aggression.

The Bobo Doll Study: Aggressive Behavior in Children

©KNUMINA, 2009/ USED UNDER LICENSE FROM SHUTTERSTOCK.COM

INTRODUCTION Psychologists wondered whether exposing children to violent television shows had negative effects on their aggression. Albert Bandura, the developer of social learning theory, believed that observational learning played a role in shaping children's behavior.

HYPOTHESIS Bandura hypothesized that children who watched a film showing an adult playing aggressively and being rewarded later would be more likely to imitate the behavior than children who watched a film showing an aggressive adult being punished or not rewarded. Bandura also hypothesized that even though the children who watched the punished or nonrewarded adult were less likely to act aggressively, they still learned the aggressive behavior they observed.

METHOD Four-year-old children were shown a short film showing an adult playing with toys. There were three different versions of the film, with each child seeing only one version. In all three films there was a Bobo doll, which is a big, inflatable, clown-like toy that is weighted down so that when it is pushed or punched it will bounce back to an upright position. In all three films, children watched as the adult attacked the Bobo doll. The adult punched the doll, kicked it, hit it with a mallet, and even sat on it. In the first version of this film, the children saw the adult rewarded with a soda and candy after behaving aggressively. In the second version, the children saw the aggressive adult punished with a scolding and a spanking by another adult. In the third version, the children watched as the adult was neither rewarded nor punished. After seeing their film, each child was led into another room and allowed to play with toys, including a Bobo doll. Bandura and his colleagues observed how the children played. Later, all children were asked if they could show what the adult did in the film, with the promise that if they could do so they would be rewarded with snacks and stickers.

RESULTS The children who watched the film of the aggressive adult being rewarded were much more likely to later behave aggressively when playing with the toys than the children who had watched the aggressive adult being punished or receiving no consequences. However, even the children who did not imitate the adult's behavior still learned the aggressive actions. When offered rewards if they could imitate the aggressive behavior, all children could do so. This result suggests that observing someone being punished for aggression does not prevent the learning of aggression—it simply holds back its expression in certain circumstances. Overall, these findings suggest that watching aggressive models teaches children to act aggressively, especially if they think they will be rewarded for doing so.

Critical Analysis

How is Bandura's Bobo Doll study similar to Tolman's study of latent learning of maze running in rats?

Behavior Researcher

Science, Technology, Engineering & Mathematics

D o you wonder about people's behavior? Do you enjoy observing other people's behavior? Do you like research? If you answer yes to these questions, consider a career as a behavior researcher—a psychologist or other scientist who specializes in researching the behavior of people.

Behavior researchers usually specialize in one of the following: human thought, memory, learning, motivation, or abnormal behavior. Some behavior researchers study animal behavior rather than human behavior.

To learn about behavior, researchers design an experiment to answer a question about behavior. Next, researchers set up a design and administer the experiment. For example, researchers might want to learn the effects of students' ability to comprehend reading material while listening to different types of music. The design of the experiment could include students listening to different types of music while reading similar pieces of literature, and then being tested on what they read. Students might listen to classical music while reading, and then answer questions on what they read. Next students might listen to rap music while reading, and then answer questions, and so on. Researchers keep accurate and detailed records of the experiments, and then write an analysis of the results.

Researchers may work for private firms; local, state, or the federal government; medical facilities; or colleges and universities.

Employment Outlook

Careers in behavior research are expected to increase. Employment in scientific research is projected to grow by 9 percent through 2016.

Needed Skills and Education

Education requirements vary depending on the type of research you choose and the type of position within that research. Technicians who assist researchers may only be required to have a bachelor's degree, although most research technicians have a master's degree. Behavior researchers who work in private firms for governments, or at colleges and universities are usually required to have a doctoral degree.

People interested in a career as behavior researcher need to be well skilled in organization, critical thinking, statistical analysis, research design, technical writing, computer science, and mathematics. Researchers who plan to work with people need to have good interpersonal relationship skills.

How You'll Spend Your Day

The workday depends on the type of research chosen. Researchers designing experiments with people work in offices, medical facilities, and in the field. For example, a researcher might want to study how the repetitive work on an assembly line affects people, so the researcher would spend most of the workday observing and interviewing the line workers in a machine plant. Behavior researchers working with animals spend most of their time in a laboratory. Other researchers who teach in colleges and universities spend part of their time in the classroom.

Most workers in scientific research work 40 hours a week or slightly less. Some experiments could require researchers to work at odd hours or even require 24-hour observation. Some field research could be conducted in harsh weather conditions.

Earnings

Earnings vary depending on the type of research chosen. Most psychologists earn between $45,000 and $78,000 a year.

What About You?

Does this sound like a career that might be right for you? Spend time on the Internet or with your school counselor to learn more about the career of behavior researcher. Then create a chart that lists the pros and cons of the career and add your personal comments for each.

©GEIPI, 2009/USED UNDER LICENSE FROM SHUTTERSTOCK.COM

CHAPTER SUMMARY

12.1 Classical Conditioning

- Learning is a relatively permanent change in behavior that results from experience.

- UCS in classical conditioning is a stimulus that naturally and automatically elicits an unconditioned response; UCR is the unlearned, automatic response to an unconditioned stimulus; CS is a previously neutral stimulus that, after repeated pairings with an unconditioned stimulus, comes to elicit a conditioned response; CR is the learned response to a previously neutral conditioned stimulus.

- Ivan Pavlov is the founder of classical conditioning, a type of learning in which a neutral stimulus comes to prompt a response after being paired with another stimulus that naturally prompts that response.

- The principles of classical conditioning include acquisition, extinction and spontaneous recovery, and stimulus generalization and stimulus discrimination.

- Emotional responses can be classically conditioned in humans. People can develop strong fears and taste aversions through classical conditioning.

12.2 Operant Conditioning

- B. F. Skinner developed a theory of learning called operant conditioning, which is a type of learning in which behavior is strengthened if followed by reinforcement and weakened if followed by punishment.

- Reinforcement, the process by which a stimulus increases the probability of the behavior that it follows, is a fundamental principle of behaviorism.

- There are primary and secondary reinforcers and positive and negative reinforcers.

- Punishment is the opposite consequence of reinforcement; it is the process by which a stimulus decreases the probability of the behavior it follows.

- Punishment can be both positive and negative. In most instances, punishment is not effective in changing behavior.

- The five schedules of reinforcement include the continuous reinforcement schedule, the fixed-ratio reinforcement schedule, the variable-ratio reinforcement schedule, the fixed-interval reinforcement schedule, and the variable-interval reinforcement schedule.

- To shape behavior you teach a new behavior by reinforcing behaviors that are closer and closer approximations to the desired behavior.

- Latent learning is learning that is not currently demonstrated in actual behavior and occurs without apparent reinforcement.

12.3 Observational Learning

- A third form of learning is observational learning, which involves learning by observing and deciding what to imitate in the behavior of others.

- Albert Bandura's social learning theory states that people learn social behaviors through observation and cognitive processing of information rather direct experience.

- Research suggests a link between media coverage of violent incidents and a sudden increase in similar violent crimes.

CHAPTER ASSESSMENT

Review Psychology Terms

Select the term that best fits the definition. Some terms will not be used.

_____ 1. In classical conditioning, a previously neutral stimulus that, after repeated pairings with an unconditioned stimulus, comes to bring about a conditioned response

_____ 2. The process of teaching a new behavior by reinforcing closer and closer approximations to the desired behavior

_____ 3. A type of learning in which behavior is strengthened if followed by reinforcement and weakened if followed by punishment

_____ 4. A change in behavior that results from experience

_____ 5. In classical conditioning, a stimulus that naturally and automatically elicits an unconditioned response

_____ 6. The process by which a stimulus increases the probability of the behavior that it follows

_____ 7. A type of learning in which a neutral stimulus triggers a response after being paired with another stimulus that naturally triggers that response

_____ 8. The gradual weakening and disappearance of the conditioned response

_____ 9. A schedule of reinforcement that reinforces behavior after a certain number of responses

_____ 10. In classical conditioning, the learned response to a previously neutral conditioned stimulus

_____ 11. A partial reinforcement schedule that reinforces a response after a variable number of nonreinforced responses

_____ 12. People learn social behaviors mainly through observation and cognitive processing of information rather than through direct experience

_____ 13. Learning by observing and deciding what to imitate in the behavior of others

_____ 14. The process by which a stimulus decreases the probability of the behavior it follows

_____ 15. In classical conditioning the unlearned, automatic response to an unconditioned stimulus

_____ 16. Learning that is not currently demonstrated in actual behavior and occurs without apparent reinforcement

a. classical conditioning

b. conditioned response (CR)

c. conditioned stimulus (CS)

d. extinction

e. fixed-ratio reinforcement schedule

f. latent learning

g. observational learning

h. learning

i. operant conditioning

j. punishment

k. reinforcement

l. shaping

m. social learning theory

n. stimulus discrimination

o. stimulus generalization

p. unconditioned response (UCR)

q. unconditioned stimulus (UCS)

r. variable-ratio reinforcement schedule

Review Psychology Concepts

17. What explains why you sometimes respond very warmly or coldly to strangers who look like people for whom you previously developed either positive or negative conditioned responses?

18. Explain a continuous reinforcement schedule. Give an example.

19. Name and describe the method of operant conditioning procedure of successive approximations that Skinner used. Give an example of a way to use this learning technique.

20. What role does identification play in influencing children's aggressive behaviors?

21. Compare and contrast stimulus discrimination and stimulus generalization. Give real-life examples of both.

22. Describe the difference between a fixed-interval reinforcement schedule and a variable-interval reinforcement schedule. Give an example of each.

23. What is the name Edward Tolman gave to learning that is not currently demonstrated in actual behavior and occurs without apparent reinforcement?

24. Compare and contrast learning that occurs due to operant conditioning from the learning that occurs due to classical conditioning.

25. Discuss Pavlov's discovery concerning how quickly and in what manner the acquisition of a conditioned response occurs.

26. Describe the phenomenon known as spontaneous recovery. Give an example of this phenomenon.

27. Name two ways reinforcement always increases the probability of a behavior.

28. What causes people and animals on fixed-ratio schedules to work themselves to exhaustion?

29. Describe how the United States Coast Guard has applied Skinner's work as a means of saving lives. What is their success rate?

Apply Psychology Concepts

30. Describe the best type of conditioning a parent could use to teach a five-year-old child to make his or her bed, and explain why this type is better than others. What would be the quickest way to teach the child to make his or her bed? Once he or she has learned to make the bed, what would be the best way to maintain this behavior? Explain.

31. Describe how two different advertisers use classical and operant conditioning in presenting and selling their products. Explain how this works.

32. Describe one way to classically condition someone to become angry whenever he or she hears a particular song or singer. Draw a diagram that identifies the conditioned stimulus, the unconditioned stimulus, the unconditioned response, and the conditioned response.

33. Albert Bandura, as well as other psychologists, has supported the concept that people learn many human behaviors by simply observing those behaviors in others. Create a list of things that you have learned through observational learning. Describe how you learned the behavior and then the first time you were able to perform the learned behavior.

Make Academic Connections

34. **Research and Writing** Use the library or Internet to research one of the following factors that may either impede or enhance learning: factors that may affect academic performance of males and females; how teacher expectancy can influence differential achievement for members of ethnic groups; whether sociocultural factors can reliably predict individual success; academic supports available for students who have learning disabilities as contrasted with supports for students who are gifted. Write an essay that describes your beliefs about the issue. Support your work with facts from your research.

35. **Sociology** Spend time as an observational learning researcher. Observe the behavior and interaction of other people. For example, you could choose to observe your parents and how they interact with a younger sibling; you could observe a school club or social group at your school, such as the chess club or cheerleaders. In your observations, look for examples of observational learning. For example, a younger sibling might learn how to behave at the dinner table by observing you and your parents. Someone in a chess club or social club might begin to dress like the club's leader. Present your findings in an oral report.

36. **History and Biography** Choose one of the following psychologists: Ivan Pavlov, B. F. Skinner, Edward Tolman, or Albert Bandura. Use the information in this textbook and the Internet or library to research the person you chose. Prepare an eight- to ten-minute multimedia presentation. In your presentation include a biography of the scientist's life, explain the main theory for which he is known, and give a brief explanation of that theory. Also discuss the contribution the person made to science and the understanding of learning. Be sure to cite your sources in your research notes and in your presentation. After your presentation, allow the class to ask you questions and be prepared to respond.

DIGGING DEEPER
with Psychology eCollection

Does viewing violence on television and in the movies cause aggression? Because observational learning is a key aspect of learning, especially for children, psychologists have researched the question since television and other forms of mass media became prevalent in the 1950s and 1960s. Researchers have studied how much violence is portrayed on typical shows during specific time periods and the contexts of those acts of violence. Access the Gale Psychology eCollection at *www.cengage.com/school/psych/franzoi* and read the section of Wass's study titled "Children and Media Violence." Write a summary of her findings and answer the question: Do you think viewing the amount of violence currently shown on television causes more aggression in children? Why or why not? As an additional project, conduct your own study of violence on television. Choose a time period when children might be watching television and research the number of "violent" shows that air during that time. Write a brief report of your findings.

Source: Wass, Hannelore. "Children and Media Violence." *Macmillan Encyclopedia of Death and Dying.* Ed. Robert Kastenbaum. Vol. 1. New York: Macmillan Reference USA, 2003.

Memory

ESSENTIAL QUESTION
Go to page XXVI

"No memory is ever alone; it's at the end of a trail of memories, a dozen trails that each have their own associations."

—LOUIS L'AMOUR, AMERICAN AUTHOR, 1908–1988

Rick Baron has an amazing memory. How amazing? In 2009, psychologists confirmed that Baron is among a very small group of people who can recall in detail most days of their lives. He can remember the details of every day from age 11 on, and many days from ages 7 to 11.

The first person known to have a super-memory was Russian reporter Solomon Shereshevskii whom psychologist Alexander Luria began studying in the 1920s. In one testing session, Luria asked Shereshevskii to memorize a list of 70 words that he read aloud. This was a very easy task for the reporter. The amazing thing was that, 15 years later, Shereshevskii could recall the list perfectly. When asked by Luria, he closed his eyes and said, "Yes, yes . . . this was a series you gave me once when we were in your apartment. . . . You were sitting at the table and I in the rocking chair. . . . You were wearing a gray suit and you looked at me like this. . . . Now I can see you saying . . . ," and then he recited the words in the exact order they were read to him so long ago.

OBJECTIVES

- Identify the three memory processes in the information-processing model.
- Identify the three memory systems in the information-processing model.
- Explain why short-term memory is referred to as working memory.

DISCOVER IT | *How does this relate to me?*

How extensive is your memory system? By the time you reach your early 70s, you will have memories that would completely fill the hard drives of about eight laptop computers. That's impressive. Of course, a good deal of the information you store in memory is neither impressive nor useful. For example, do you know the theme songs from television shows you watched as a child? Despite the fact that some of your memories seem silly, you could not live a normal life without the ability to interpret, store, and later recall your life experiences.

KEY TERMS

- memory
- encoding
- storage
- retrieval
- primacy effect
- recency effect
- long-term memory
- short-term memory
- sensory memory
- chunking
- maintenance rehearsal
- elaborative rehearsal

Memory is the mental process by which information is encoded and stored in the brain and later retrieved. Fifty years ago, most psychologists were behaviorists who viewed memory as a single, simple system. According to behaviorists, remembering something involved learning that a certain stimulus was linked to a certain response (see Chapter 12, page 341). If a person or animal consistently responded in the same way to the same stimulus, this meant they had formed a strong memory for the response. In the late 1950s, scientific discoveries caused many psychologists to change their views about memory dramatically.

Memory as Information Processing

The computer age helped change psychologists' thinking about memory. Like humans, computers have memories. Psychologists began to view memory as a kind of *information-processing system* and to use computer science terms and concepts to describe it. In both computer and human memory, information goes through three basic processes. These include an input or encoding process, a storage process, and a retrieval process.

Encoding refers to the first memory process, in which incoming information is organized and interpreted so it can be entered into memory. In the computer, typing

memory The mental process by which information is encoded and stored in the brain and later retrieved

encoding The first memory process in which information is organized and interpreted so it can be entered into memory

Similar to computer processing, human memory involves encoding, storing, and retrieving information.

© MONKEY BUSINESS IMAGES, 2009/USED UNDER LICENSE FROM SHUTTERSTOCK.COM

on the keyboard changes information into electronic language. In the brain, sensory information from your surroundings is changed into neural language. For example, imagine that you are presented with the sentence "I was born in the twentieth century." If you encode the image of the letters as they appear on your computer screen, you are using *visual encoding,* and the information is represented in memory as a picture. If you encode the sound of the words as if they were spoken, you are using *acoustic encoding,* and the information is represented in memory as a sequence of sounds. Finally, if you encode the fact that this sentence is referring to you personally (which for you may be true), you are using *semantic encoding.* The information is represented in memory by its meaning to you. The type of encoding used—visual, acoustic, or semantic—influences what you remember. Semantic encoding plays a much larger role in creating lasting memories than visual or acoustic encoding.

The second memory process is **storage**, which involves entering and keeping information in memory for a period of time. The two human memory systems that store information for relatively brief time periods are known as sensory memory and short-term memory. The more permanent system is known as long-term memory.

The third memory process is **retrieval**, which involves recovering stored information from memory so it can be used. Retrieval means pulling information out of long-term memory storage and placing it into a much smaller working memory. To demonstrate for yourself how the retrieval process works, recall the name of your best friend from sixth grade. In doing so, memories of your grade school come to mind, along with images and sounds of your sixth-grade classroom and activities you engaged in with this person. Each of these memories can serve as a stimulus to help you remember your best friend's name. When the correct memories come to mind, you retrieve the name.

Research indicates that you are more likely to retrieve information from memory if it was encoded in terms of its meaning, or semantics. In one study, researchers

storage The second memory process in which information is entered and maintained in memory for a period of time

retrieval The third memory process, which involves recovering stored information from memory so it can be used

flashed words on a screen while participants watched. After each word was flashed, participants were asked a question that required them to process the word either (1) semantically (the meaning of the words), (2) acoustically (the sound of the words), or (3) visually (the appearance of the letters). Following are three examples of this task:

Word Flashed	Sample Questions	Yes	No
(1) apple	Would the word fit in this sentence? The boy ate the _____.	____	____
(2) flower	Does the word rhyme with power?	____	____
(3) BOOK	Is the word in capital letters?	____	____

As you can see from Figure 13-1 below, semantic encoding resulted in much better remembering of words than acoustic or visual encoding. The memory lesson here is that if you want to increase your remembering of something, try to make it meaningful in some way. Later in the chapter, you will learn some useful memory strategies to help you attach meaning to information (see pages 389–390).

CHECKPOINT *What are the three memory processes in the information-processing model?*

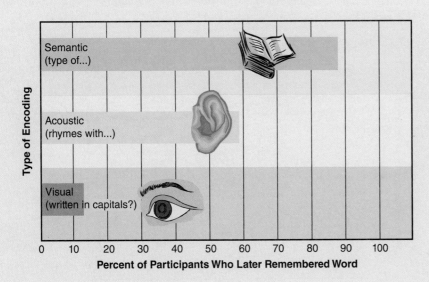

Figure 13-1 **THE SEMANTIC ENCODING ADVANTAGE**

Words encoded in terms of their meaning (semantic encoding) are better remembered than words encoded in terms of their sound (acoustic encoding) or image (visual encoding).

Source: Adapted from Craik, F. I. M., & Tulving, E. (1975). Depth of processing and the retention of words in episodic memory. *Journal of Experimental Psychology: General, 104,* 268–294.

Type of Encoding

Semantic (type of...)

Acoustic (rhymes with...)

Visual (written in capitals?)

0   10   20   30   40   50   60   70   80   90   100

Percent of Participants Who Later Remembered Word

Memory Systems

In science, new discoveries often reveal further insights into old discoveries. For example, in the 1950s, psychologists discovered that if people are distracted from repeating a small amount of information given to them, they completely forget it within seconds. In trying to make sense of these findings, researchers remembered the findings from one of the earliest memory studies.

In 1885, psychologist Hermann Ebbinghaus (1850–1909), using himself as his own subject, studied a list of nonsense syllables (such as BIW or SUW). Later he measured how many of the nonsense syllables he recalled. As illustrated in Figure 13-2, Ebbinghaus discovered that nonsense syllables near the beginning and end of the list were more easily remembered than the ones in the middle. The resulting "U-shaped" pattern was referred to as the *serial-position effect*. Ebbinghaus called the increased memory for the first bits of information presented in a string of information the **primacy effect**. The increased memory for the last bits of information presented in a string of information was called the **recency effect**.

In the 1950s, these serial-position findings were used to explain the existence of two distinct memory systems, not just one. Memory researchers believed that the primacy effect occurs because people have more time to think about the earlier items than the later items. That means earlier items are more likely to be stored in a memory system that can hold information for a long time. This was labeled **long-term memory**, a lasting memory system that holds an enormous amount of information. Memory researchers further believed that the recency effect occurs because the last items are still in a memory system that holds information only for short periods of time, up to about 18 seconds. This was called **short-term memory**, a memory system that holds information briefly while you actively work with the information. Whatever you are currently thinking about—or conscious of—is held in short-term

---

primacy effect The increased memory for the first bits of information presented in a string of information

recency effect The increased memory for the last bits of information presented in a string of information

long-term memory A lasting memory system that holds an enormous amount of information

short-term memory A memory system that holds information briefly while you actively work with the information

---

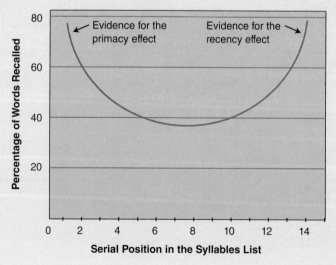

Figure 13-2 **THE MEMORY CURVE**

In 1885, Hermann Ebbinghaus found that memory is better for the first few and last few items in a string of nonsense syllables. In the 1950s, memory researchers argued that Ebbinghaus' findings suggested the existence of a long-term memory system and a short-term memory system. What was the reasoning behind these claims?

memory. Some of that information makes its way into long-term memory, which holds much more information. Long-term memory is the memory system containing the name of your sixth-grade friend.

One important point about the relationship between short-term and long-term memory is that information flows in both directions. Information from short-term memory goes to long-term memory (for further encoding and storage), and a great deal of information stored in long-term memory is sent back to short-term memory (this is the retrieval process). The reason you are able to answer the question about your sixth-grade friend is because the correct information can be retrieved from long-term memory and sent to short-term memory (see Figure 13-3).

The last memory system that scientists discovered is the first memory system you use in the memory process—the **sensory memory**. The sensory memory system very briefly stores a vast amount of information received from your five senses. The purpose of this memory system is to keep in your mind for a split second a record of what each of your senses has just experienced. Some of this sensory information is then transferred to short-term memory, where you become aware of it. The sensory information not transferred fades away. This process repeats itself each moment, with sensory memory continuously supplying short-term memory with new information to process.

sensory memory A memory system that very briefly stores a vast amount of information received from your five senses

 **CHECKPOINT** What are the three memory systems in the information-processing model?

Figure 13-3 THE INFORMATION-PROCESSING MODEL OF MEMORY

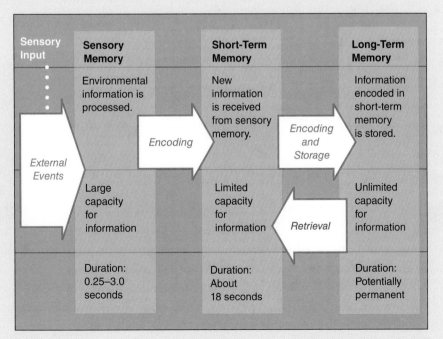

In the information-processing model of memory, information goes through encoding, storage, and retrieval. There are also three memory systems: sensory memory, short-term memory, and long-term memory.

Short-Term Memory

Short-term memory is much more than a brief storage area for information. It is the memory area where you actively work with information that comes from either sensory or long-term memory. Short-term memory is *working memory*.

CHUNKING

Short-term memory is very limited. Only about seven items or *chunks* of information can be stored at any one time. Complete the exercises in the Self-Discovery feature below to test the storage capacity of your short-term memory.

Testing Your Short-Term Memory Capacity

Instructions: Complete the following two tasks to test the storage capacity of your short-term memory.

Task 1: Ask someone to read you the letters in the top row at the rate of about one per second. Then try to repeat them back in the same order. Repeat this for the next row, and the one after that, until you make a mistake. How many letters could you repeat back perfectly?

    Q M R
    H Z X E
    X D P Q F
    G N M S W R
    D H W Y U N J
    E P H E A Z K R
    N R E F D T O Q P
    U H V X G F N I K J
    H F R D S X A W U G T
    H E Q L I M Y D J R N K

Task 2: Read the following string of letters and then try to write them down in correct order:

    CNNA   BCCBSNB   CMCIC   IA

How many letters in each task were you able to recall?

You can greatly increase the amount of information held in short-term memory by **chunking**, or combining many bits of information into a small number of meaningful groups. Consider the list of letters presented in task 2 of the Self-Discovery feature. If you examine the pattern of letters closely, you will be able to chunk the individual items into meaningful chunks: CNN – ABC – CBS – NBC – MCI – CIA. Encoding these six chunks is less likely to exceed your short-term memory capacity than if you try to encode all the letters individually.

chunking Combining bits of information into a small number of meaningful groups, or chunks, that can be stored in short-term memory

Information chunks can be complex. For example, you probably can easily repeat this sentence after reading it only once: *On Tuesday, three-fisted boys run after four-legged girls to compare extra limbs.* In repeating this string of words, you might combine this information into four manageable chunks: (1) "On Tuesday" (2) "three-fisted boys" (3) "run after four-legged girls" (4) "to compare extra limbs." Your short-term memory can handle this information because you have knowledge about the material—the English language. Your ability to create meaningful chunks depends on how much you know about the material that needs to be remembered. For chunking to increase short-term memory capacity, you must retrieve information from long-term memory.

THINKSTOCK IMAGES/JUPITER IMAGES

Actors rely on maintenance rehearsal to learn their lines. In what other types of memory tasks is maintenance rehearsal useful?

SHALLOW vs. DEEP PROCESSING

Information is stored in short-term memory for only about 18 seconds. This time can be extended through **maintenance rehearsal**, the process of repeating information so it will stay in short-term memory or transfer to long-term memory. Reciting a phone number until you write it down is an example of maintenance rehearsal. If you are distracted before finding a pen, you likely will forget the number because it is no longer in short-term memory. Maintenance rehearsal is important in helping you transfer information to long-term memory. This is the method you rely on when memorizing lines in a play, multiplication tables, or a foreign language.

Another way to encode information uses **elaborative rehearsal**. This method involves thinking about how new information relates to information already stored in long-term memory. Elaborative rehearsal is a more effective way of encoding new information than maintenance rehearsal because it involves a deeper level of thought processing. The more you think about how new information is related to knowledge you already have, the deeper the processing and the better your memory. Shallow processing usually involves encoding information in terms of simple perceptual qualities, such as sights and sounds. Deep processing involves encoding information in terms of meaning, or *semantics*. If you can still recite many—or all—of those individual letters in task 2 in Self-Discovery, it is because you clustered the letters into something meaningful, namely the names of organizations you already know (CNN, ABC, CBS, NBC, MCI, and the CIA).

Semantic encoding is the stronger encoding process used to send information from short-term memory to long-term memory. However, semantic encoding often ignores details and instead only encodes the general meaning of information. This can cause errors in remembering. See Figure 13-4 on page 380. Can you identify the correct drawing of a penny?

maintenance rehearsal The process of repeating information so it will stay in short-term memory or transfer to long-term memory

elaborative rehearsal The process of thinking about how new information relates to information already stored in long-term memory

Can you identify the real penny among all these coins? Our failure to encode the details of coins and other currency into long-term memory is what counterfeiters rely on.

Figure 13-4 WHICH IS THE REAL PENNY?

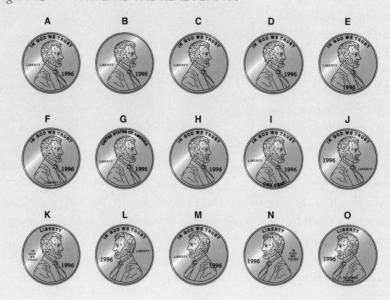

CHECKPOINT   *Why is short-term memory also called working memory?*

13.1 ASSESSMENT

In Your Own Words

Explain how the memory processes in the information-processing model work together.

Review Concepts

1. Which type of encoding plays a larger role in creating lasting memories because the information has meaning to you?
   - a. acoustic
   - b. recency
   - c. visual
   - d. semantic

2. Which memory process are you using when you recall information about a classmate from the sixth grade?
   - a. primacy effect
   - b. retrieval
   - c. short-term memory
   - d. chunking

3. **True or False** Information flows in both directions between the short-term and long-term memory.

Think Critically

4. Explain how you can use elaborative rehearsal as a study aid.

5. How can chunking help you learn the information in this chapter? Give an example.

OBJECTIVES

- Identify the difference between explicit memory and implicit memory.
- Discuss how information is organized in memory.
- Describe the process of reconstructing memories.
- Explain recognition and recall.
- Identify retrieval cues and mnemonics.

DISCOVER IT | *How does this relate to me?*

What is the exact date of your birth? What is the name of your teacher in this class? How many hours are there in a day? Your ability to answer these questions is due to your ability to retrieve this information from long-term memory. In most instances, you perform these memory tasks effortlessly, but sometimes your memories do fail you. In this lesson, you are going to learn some important facts about your long-term memory. In fact, some of the things you will learn might allow you to fool your friends into thinking you can read their minds.

KEY TERMS

- explicit memory
- implicit memory
- priming
- misinformation effects
- flashbulb memories
- recall
- recognition
- tip-of-the-tongue experience
- retrieval cue
- déjà vu
- mood-congruent memory
- mnemonics

I f someone said that you often are not conscious of recalling and using information stored in long-term memory, would you believe it? Actually, if you are reading and understanding the words in this sentence, you are unconsciously recalling and using your memories of the English language. If you read the Greek phrase, "Με συγχωρείτε," you probably will not understand that it means "Excuse me," because you have not encoded information about the Greek language into long-term memory. Cognitive psychologists have made many discoveries about long-term memory. Hopefully, after reading this section of the chapter, your knowledge of long-term memory will no longer be Greek to you.

Explicit vs. Implicit Memories

For many years, psychologists studied the conscious remembering of previous experiences, known as **explicit memory**. Do you remember how you felt during your first day of high school? Can you recall the name of the current president of the United States? Your conscious remembering of personally experienced events or

> **explicit memory** Memory of previous experiences that you can consciously recollect

INFOBIT
A special type of explicit memory for events in your own life—your personal life history—is called autobiographical memory. Studies indicate that when you recall autobiographical memories that were either positive or negative, you tend to "see" the events from your own viewpoint. However, you tend to "see" emotionally neutral autobiographical memories as an observer would.

implicit memory
Memory of previous experiences without conscious recollection

Can you recite from memory the letters on a computer keyboard, starting with the bottom left row? Is this a difficult task for you? Why or why not?

facts about the world are your explicit memories. Explicit memory is sometimes also referred to as *declarative* memory because, if asked, you can declare this information.

You are not always aware of remembering something. In fact, many times you hold on to information that influences your thoughts and actions without knowingly remembering it. This psychological process is known as **implicit memory**. Your ability to perform skilled motor activities, such as how to ride a bike, drive a car, do a cartwheel, or even walk depends on implicit memory. Similarly, your ability to read and speak languages requires you to remember the meaning of words and the rules of grammar without thinking about them. Often referred to as *habits,* these activities are so well learned that you carry them out automatically, without conscious thought.

Implicit memory is sometimes referred to as *nondeclarative* memory, because you generally cannot declare the information. To demonstrate this fact, try naming from memory the letters on a computer keyboard, starting with the bottom left row. Don't spread your fingers in front of you to help remember the letter order. I'm betting that you cannot correctly recall this information even though it is encoded into your long-term memory.

Now spread your fingers in front of you, as if they were resting on a keyboard. "Type" your name using the imaginary keys. If you have experience typing on the computer, this is an easy task. It shows that you really do have a memory of the keys' proper order. It is an implicit memory. Although it is difficult for you to consciously declare this information, you still can unconsciously pull it out of memory and use it to correctly type your name.

Brain-imaging studies show that explicit memory and implicit memory are two separate long-term memory systems that are controlled by different brain regions. Explicit memories are processed through the hippocampus, a small structure located in the brain's limbic system. Implicit memories are processed through the cerebellum, located in the bottom back part of the brain.

Recall the story in Chapter 3 about the removal of Henry Molaison's hippocampus to control his epileptic seizures. With no hippocampus, Henry could no longer learn new facts about the world or remember new experiences he had in life. He could no longer form new explicit memories. Yet because Henry still had a

COURTESY OF FIGZOI

healthy cerebellum, he could still learn new motor skills, such as solving mazes and puzzles, even if he could not remember having done so. Figure 13-5 shows how memory researchers divide long-term memory into the subsystems of explicit memory and implicit memory. It also shows the types of information typically stored in these two subsystems. Also, while you are thinking about Henry, check out the Case Study on page 398 to learn how he helped memory researchers discover one last wonder of the human mind before his death in 2008 at the age of 82.

Figure 13-5 **TYPES OF LONG-TERM MEMORY**

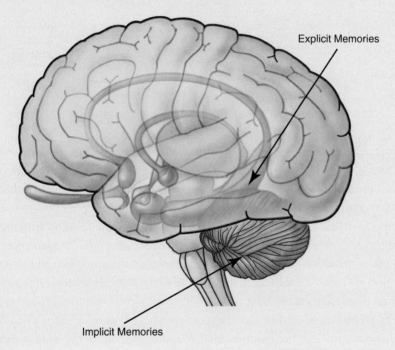

Explicit Memories

Implicit Memories

Long-term memory consists of two basic subsystems: explicit memory and implicit memory. Explicit memories of facts and personal experiences are processed through the hippocampus. Implicit memories of motor and cognitive skills are processed through the cerebellum.

CHECKPOINT *What is the difference between explicit memory and implicit memory?*

Organizing Memories

You organize information in long-term memory in many ways. You have learned that information often is encoded into long-term memory in terms of its meaning to you. This semantic encoding creates a mental network of concepts in long-term memory that share meaningful associations. Figure 13-6 illustrates a small semantic network as it might look right after you think of *Santa Claus*. As a memory concept, *Santa Claus* is likely to trigger other concepts in long-term memory that have meaningful associations with this white-bearded jolly man. *Santa Claus* might bring to mind the following concepts: *red* and *white* because Santa has a red suit and a white

A great deal of information in long-term memory is organized in a complex network of meaningful associations. The shorter the link between concepts, the more likely it is that retrieving one concept will trigger the retrieval of the other concept.

Figure 13-6 SEMANTIC NETWORK MODEL

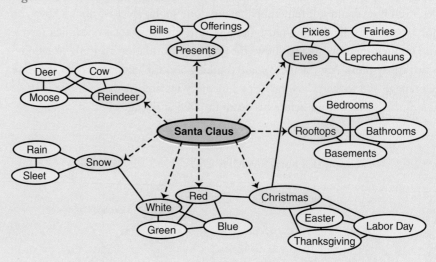

beard; *snow* and *Christmas* because he visits during a specific night in winter; *reindeer* and *rooftops* because these animals fly him to the tops of houses; and *elves* and *presents* because his elf-helpers make presents that he delivers. The length of the lines between concepts indicates the strength of their association. Shorter lines indicate stronger associations, meaning that you will more easily recall concepts with these stronger associations. Thus, when you hear the name *Santa Claus,* you are more likely to think of the words *Christmas, red,* and *reindeer* than the words *elves* and *white.* Similarly, you are much more likely to think of the words *elves, white, snow,* and *presents* than the words *leprechauns, blue, sleet,* and *offerings.*

The process by which one memory concept activates another memory concept is known as **priming**. For example, ask a friend to pronounce the word spelled by the letters *p-o-k-e.* Then ask your friend to quickly tell you what the white of an egg is called. If your friend responds with the word *yolk,* you have primed an incorrect answer from your friend's memory. Because your friend just said the word *poke,* the egg-related word that is activated in memory is the one that rhymes with poke. If you would like an even more impressive demonstration of how knowledge of priming and semantic networks can help predict—and even influence—people's thinking, try the exercise in the Closer Look feature on page 385.

priming The process by which one memory concept activates another memory concept

CHECKPOINT › *What is priming?*

Can Semantic Networks Help You Predict People's Thoughts?

Would you like to impress your friends by having them think you can predict their thoughts? Use the power of semantic networks to do so. Try the following brainteaser, and then ask your friends to do the same. Complete each instruction quickly.

1. Pick a number from 1 to 9.
2. Subtract 5.
3. Multiply by 3.
4. Square the number (that is, multiply by the same number).
5. Add the digits until you get only one digit (for example, $64 = 6 + 4 = 10 = 1 + 0 = 1$).
6. If the number is less than 5, add 5; otherwise, subtract 4.
7. Multiply by 2.
8. Subtract 6.
9. Find your mark by mapping the digit to a letter in the alphabet (1 = A, 2 = B, 3 = C, 4 = D, and so on).
10. Pick a name of a country that begins with that letter.
11. Take the second letter in the country's name and then think of a mammal that begins with that letter.
12. Think of the color of that animal.

Are you thinking of a gray elephant from Denmark?

Explanation: Steps 1 to 8 of this brainteaser are designed so that everyone has the number 4 going into step 9, thus giving them the letter D. From this point, the reason this brainteaser often ends with the person thinking of a gray elephant from Denmark is that, for many American high school students, Denmark has a stronger association with "countries that begin with the letter D" than, say, the Dominican Republic or Dahomey. Likewise, with the "e" from Denmark, people are also more likely to think of elephant than, say, elk or emu. In dazzling people with your apparent ability to read their minds, you are counting on their having specific semantic structures for the words Denmark and elephant. Instead of actually "reading" their minds, you are predicting their semantic associations. By the way, did you notice the priming word "mark" inserted in instruction 9 to increase the probability that you would think of the word **Denmark**?

If you or your friends thought of a different country or a different mammal when completing this exercise, this demonstrates that within the same culture, people often have different semantic networks due to their different life experiences. These different responses are proof that cultural diversity can be found within people's minds as well as in the social world of everyday living.

Reconstructing Memories

Recall the Chapter 4 discussion of perception. Errors or misperceptions can occur because your beliefs and expectations influence how you perceive sensory stimuli. Likewise, your beliefs and expectations can shape what you encode and later retrieve from memory. Unlike photographs that freeze exact images, scientific studies show that memories often are sketchy reconstructions of the past.

MISINFORMATION EFFECTS

Not only can your expectations affect your memory, but also the *way* you are questioned about an event can change your memories of that event. These changes in memory are known as **misinformation effects**. The altered and even completely false memories that come about by such misinformation feel real to those who hold them, and often look real to observers.

In a famous study, Elizabeth Loftus and John Palmer demonstrated misinformation effects when they showed participants a short film of two cars colliding. After viewing the film, some of the participants were asked, "About how fast were the cars going when they contacted each other?" Others were asked, "About how fast were the cars going when they smashed into each other?" Those who heard the word "smashed" estimated the cars' speed at 41 miles per hour. Those who heard the word "contacted" estimated the speed at 31 miles per hour. In addition, when questioned again a week later, the "smashed" participants were more than twice as likely as the "contacted" participants to recall seeing broken glass at the accident scene, even though there was no broken glass visible in the film.

Further research shows that altered memories are most likely to be created when misleading information is "suggested" and when original memories have faded with time. For example, during criminal trials, errors in eyewitness memories may occur in response to misleading questions asked by lawyers. A witness might be asked whether a mugger's glasses had plastic or wire frames, suggesting that the mugger wore glasses. The witness may not remember glasses, and the mugger may not have

misinformation effects Changes in memories due to a person being exposed to misleading information

How may misinformation effects influence eyewitness testimony during criminal trials?

© JUNIAL ENTERPRISES, 2009/USED UNDER LICENSE FROM SHUTTERSTOCK.COM

worn glasses, but this question may lead the witness to now "remember" seeing glasses on the mugger's face. Have you ever watched a trial on TV and heard one lawyer object that the other lawyer is "leading the witness?" The glasses question is an example of a leading question that has created a false memory.

FLASHBULB MEMORIES

Many people remember certain important experiences in their lives in amazing detail, as if frozen in time. These vivid memories of surprising and emotional events that are personally important are known as **flashbulb memories**. Flashbulb memories often are formed when you learn of the death of a loved one or an important public figure. For millions of people, the September 11, 2001, attacks at the World Trade Center created a flashbulb memory.

Although people believe their flashbulb memories are accurate, this belief often is misguided. For example, one day after the space shuttle Challenger explosion in 1986, college students were asked to describe how they had heard the news. Three years later, the same students were asked to recall the experience. Only about 7 percent of the students reported their memories in the same way. Those who had produced false memories were surprised when shown their first report. These findings suggest that flashbulb memories are not burned into your mind but are changed over time.

flashbulb memories Vivid memories of surprising and emotional events that are personally important

CHECKPOINT *What are flashbulb memories?*

Why do you think the 2001 attacks on the World Trade Center created a flashbulb memory for many people?

MICHAEL RIEGER/MAI/MAI/TIME LIFE PICTURES/GETTY IMAGES

Recognition vs. Recall

Remembering involves moving information from long-term memory into short-term memory. To illustrate the flaws of this process, try answering the following questions:

- How many days are there in the month of April?
- Who was defeated in the last presidential election?
- Which of the following terms refers to conscious recollection of previous experiences?
  - a. implicit memory
  - b. explicit memory
  - c. short-term memory
  - d. long-term memory

If you could answer the first question, it might have been through memory retrieval of a childhood rhyme: "Thirty days hath September, April, June, and November. . . ." If you could not answer the second question, it may have been because the information was not stored in long-term memory. Finally, the third question might have been easier because all you had to do was recognize the correct response (explicit memory).

When measuring explicit memory, psychologists test recall and recognition abilities. **Recall** requires you to retrieve and reproduce information from memory. **Recognition** simply requires you to decide whether you have encountered the information before. In most cases, recall is more difficult than recognition, because recall requires more mental processing. Think of the tests you take in school. Most students prefer true-false and multiple-choice questions because they rely on recognition. Essay and fill-in-the-blank questions are more difficult because they require you to recall information on your own. This does not always mean that recognition tests are easy. As you probably know, multiple-choice questions can be very difficult if the answer choices are all similar.

Sometimes it feels like information is on the tip of your tongue—so close you can almost taste it. When this happens, you cannot remember something that you are absolutely certain you know. This is called a **tip-of-the-tongue experience**, or being unable to remember something you know, followed by the feeling that it is just out of reach. Most people have this experience at least once a week. Thinking of related words can help recall the forgotten word. These words can have a similar meaning (*calm* instead of *tranquil*) or sound (*Greg* instead of *Craig*). You usually can guess the first letter of the word about half the time, and about half the time you remember the whole word within a minute.

recall A test of explicit memory in which a person must retrieve and reproduce information from memory

recognition A test of explicit memory in which a person must decide whether or not the information has been encountered before

tip-of-the-tongue experience Being unable to remember something you know, followed by the feeling that it is just out of reach

Most people have a tip-of-the-tongue experience at least once a week.

© CINDY CHARLES/PHOTOEDIT

CHECKPOINT *What is the difference between recall and recognition?*

Retrieval Cues and Mnemonics

One of the best ways to remember is to use retrieval cues. A **retrieval cue** is a stimulus that helps you recall information from long-term memory. Have you ever visited a place where you spent a lot of time as a child? The sights and sounds in such places act as retrieval cues, triggering memories. The reason these stimuli help you remember information is that many elements of the location (sights, sounds, smells) are encoded into long-term memory along with the information you are learning. Retrieval cues in the classroom also may help your performance on exams. Studies have shown that students perform better on exams when tested in the same classroom where they learned the material rather than in a different setting.

If you think of a memory as being held in storage by a web of associations (as shown in the semantic network model on page 384), then retrieval cues are the individual strands in the web that lead to the memory. The more retrieval cues you have for a particular memory and the better learned these cues are, the stronger the memory will be. You are likely to retrieve the memory if you can activate one or more of those strands.

Sometimes, retrieval cues can create *memory illusions,* or false remembering. For example, you might walk into a house for the very first time and feel as though you have been there before. This brief eerie feeling of remembering an event that is actually being experienced for the first time is called **déjà vu**, which in French means "already seen." Memory researchers state that you may have these weird experiences because cues in the new situation trigger the retrieval of earlier memories without your conscious realization. By unconsciously remembering a previous situation similar to the new one, you fool yourself into thinking you must have been here before.

Retrieval cues do not always come from your external world. Your internal state of mind also can be a retrieval cue for memories. Have you ever been angry with a friend and while angry remembered other past events when this person upset you? This tendency to recall experiences that are consistent with your current mood is known as **mood-congruent memory**. Research suggests that negative moods cue negative memories, while positive moods cue positive memories. Some psychologists believe that this is one reason many teenagers' attitudes toward their parents are positive on some days and negative on other days. The family memories teenagers retrieve from long-term memory are likely to match their current mood.

Why do students perform better on exams when tested in the same room where they learned the material rather than in a different setting?

DIGITAL VISION/GETTY IMAGES

retrieval cue A stimulus that helps you recall information from long-term memory

déjà vu A brief eerie feeling of remembering an event that is actually being experienced for the first time

mood-congruent memory The tendency to recall experiences that are consistent with your current mood

Use Mnemonics

With a partner, choose a list of one-word items related to one of your school subjects. Work together to come up with a mnemonic to remember those items. For example, the list of planets (Mercury, Venus, Earth, Mars, Ceres, Jupiter, Saturn, Uranus, Neptune, Pluto, and Eris) can be remembered using the mnemonic "My Very Exciting Magic Carpet Just Sailed Under Nine Palace Elephants." Share your mnemonic with your classmates.

mnemonics Mental strategies that make it easier to remember information

Another way to help you remember things is to use **mnemonics**, which are mental strategies that make it easier to remember facts and other information. One well-known visual mnemonic is the *method of loci* (pronounced "LOW-sigh"). With this method you mentally place items to be memorized in specific locations, such as rooms in your house. When you want to recall these items, you simply take a mental "walk" by these locations and "see" the memorized items. If you wanted to learn a grocery list, for example, you might mentally place each food item at a specific location in your home (strawberries on your bed, milk jugs in your bathroom sink, and so on). By mentally walking through your home, the food items pop into your mind, as illustrated in Figure 13-7.

There are other useful techniques to improve your ability to remember facts and other information. Check out the Positive Psychology feature on page 392 to learn how you can improve your memory power for exams.

Figure 13-7 THE METHOD OF LOCI

With the method of loci, you remember things by mentally placing items in specific locations well known to yourself. To recall these items, you mentally "walk" by these locations and "see" the memorized items. In this example, you memorize a grocery list by placing each food item in a separate location at home.

Step 1: Mentally place items in specific locations.

Strawberries on your bed

Milk jugs in the bathroom sink

Hot dogs hanging from the kitchen window

Butter smeared on the refrigerator

Ice cream dripping off the stove

Olives tumbling out of the dishwasher

Flour covering the living room floor

Sugar cubes piled on the couch

Carrots on the front door

Coffee beans tossed on the front porch

Step 2: Mentally "walk" by specific locations to recall the items.

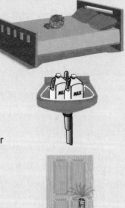

CHECKPOINT > *What is a retrieval cue?*

In Your Own Words

Explain mood-congruent memory and give an example from your life of this type of memory. For example, you might have a good time when you are with certain friends, so your mood is good whenever you are with those friends or you anticipate being with them.

Review Concepts

1. Which type of experience are you having when you have a temporary inability to remember something you know, accompanied by the feeling that it is just beyond your conscious state?
   - a. mnemonics
   - b. recall
   - c. state-dependent memory
   - d. tip-of-the-tongue

2. Which is a strategy that uses the method of loci to help you remember?
   - a. recency effect
   - b. flashbulb memories
   - c. mnemonics
   - d. priming

3. The tendency for retrieval memory to be better when your mood matches the mood at the time of encoding is called
   - a. mnemonics
   - b. recognition
   - c. mood-congruent memory
   - d. tip-of-the-tongue

4. Essay questions may seem more difficult than multiple-choice questions, because essay questions require
   - a. mnemonics
   - b. recall
   - c. retrieval cues
   - d. recognition

5. **True or False** Retrieval cues are an effective way to facilitate remembering.

6. **True or False** Retrieval cues come from both your external world and your internal state of mind.

7. **True or False** Word-completion tasks are examples of priming.

8. **True or False** Recognition usually is more difficult than recall because recognition requires more extensive mental processing.

Think Critically

9. How do retrieval cues relate to the semantic network model?

10. How is déjà vu an example of memory illusion?

11. Why is recall considered more difficult than recognition when trying to remember something? Which is an example of recall—true/false or fill-in-the blank questions? Which is an example of recognition—multiple choice or short answer questions?

12. How does your internal state of mind affect retrieval cues for memories? Give an example of how you have experienced this in your life.

Increase Your Memory Power for Exams

How can you improve your ability to remember facts and other information for exams? Research indicates that the following suggestions can improve your everyday memory:

1. **Focus your attention** Distracting stimuli, such as having the television on while studying, interfere with encoding information into long-term memory. To aid remembering, remove distractions by finding a quiet place to concentrate. If you cannot escape annoying distractions, reading aloud what you need to remember can help focus your attention.

2. **Space your practice sessions** One of the most common mistakes students make is waiting until the day before an exam to study. Don't try to memorize by swallowing all your information in one big gulp. Studying new information over several days results in better learning than cramming your studying into one day. Spacing apart your study sessions is most useful if the time between sessions is about 24 hours. Thus, four separate one-hour study sessions spread out over four days will lead to better retrieval than one four-hour session.

3. **Overlearn** Studying information even after you think you already know it is one of the best ways to firmly place it into memory. Any information that is well learned is more likely to survive a case of the jitters than information only weakly learned.

4. **Use sleep to your advantage** There is evidence that while you dream at night your brain combines and stores information gathered during the day. Also, due to less interference, things learned just before sleep are remembered better than information learned earlier in the day.

Together, these findings suggest that getting a good night's rest before a big exam, and studying just before going to sleep, is a good idea.

Think Critically

Which of these techniques do you think would help you most in improving your high school test scores? Explain your answer.

13.3 | Forgetting

OBJECTIVES

- Describe the forgetting curve.
- Describe the difference between retroactive interference and proactive interference.
- Describe motivated forgetting and the difference between suppression and repression.
- Explain how brain damage may lead to forgetting.

KEY TERMS

- retroactive interference
- proactive interference
- suppression
- repression
- anterograde amnesia
- retrograde amnesia

DISCOVER IT | *How does this relate to me?*

Have you ever been in the middle of an exam and suddenly forgotten everything you thought you had memorized? Have you ever found it difficult to remember a new password on your computer because you cannot forget an old password? Or have you had the experience where you consciously try to forget an embarrassing incident, but find it impossible to do so? Why is it sometimes hard to forget and other times so easy?

What would happen if you did not forget? Shereshevskii, the Russian reporter whose story you read at the beginning of this chapter, could answer this question. Over the years, as his memories piled up, they began to overwhelm him. Eventually, the slightest stimulus triggered so many memories that Shereshevskii could no longer hold a job, read, or even follow a simple conversation.

The Forgetting Curve

Much of what the normal person learns is quickly forgotten. Do you remember Herman Ebbinghaus's research from the late 1800s discussed on page 376? He learned more than 1,200 lists of nonsense syllables and then measured how much he recalled from the list from 20 minutes to 30 days later. Ebbinghaus discovered that most forgetting occurs during the first nine hours after learning. As you can see in his "forgetting curve," depicted in Figure 13-8, more than 40 percent of the list was forgotten after just 20 minutes. After nine hours, more than 60 percent was lost, but then it leveled off. Today we know that the greatest amount of forgetting occurs in the first few hours after learning. Less memory is lost as time goes on.

Ebbinghaus discovered that most forgetting (more than 60 percent) occurs during the first nine hours after learning. After nine hours, the course of forgetting levels off.

Figure 13-8 THE FORGETTING CURVE

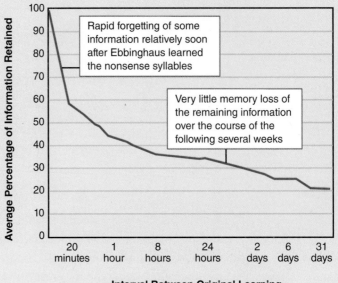

Rapid forgetting of some information relatively soon after Ebbinghaus learned the nonsense syllables

Very little memory loss of the remaining information over the course of the following several weeks

Average Percentage of Information Retained

Interval Between Original Learning of Nonsense Syllables and Memory Test

A second important discovery made by Ebbinghaus was that although you may forget information you have already learned, this does not necessarily mean you have forgotten everything about that information. He discovered that it took less time to relearn a list of nonsense words than it did to learn the list the first time. This means that most forgetting is not complete. You may forget something if you do not go over it for a period of time, but you can relearn it faster the second time around.

One reason you forget information soon after learning it is that you are not paying close enough attention when the information is presented. A lack of attention explains the times when you forget a new acquaintance's name or the location of a misplaced book.

 CHECKPOINT *What is the forgetting curve?*

Interference

An early theory of forgetting stated that the passage of time caused memories to fade and eventually be lost. However, an important study in 1924 proved this theory wrong. In the study, John Jenkins and Karl Dallenbach had college students learn lists of nonsense words either just after waking up in the morning or just before going to sleep at night. Then, after one-, two-, four-, and eight-hour periods, the students' recall was tested. This meant waking the sleeping students. Even though the same amount of time passed, much more was forgotten when students were awake and active than when they were asleep.

If forgetting is not due to the simple passage of time, then what is its cause? The key to this answer is found within Jenkins and Dallenbach's findings. Students who learned the nonsense words early in the day also were learning other information all day. This new information interfered with remembering the old information, which was the list of nonsense words. In contrast, students who learned the nonsense words before bedtime had much less interference while they slept. These findings suggest that learning new information can act backwards in time to interfere with remembering older information.

Forgetting due to interference from newly learned information is known as **retroactive interference**. You experience retroactive (backward-acting) interference when learning information in this chapter interferes with your memory of information learned in a previous chapter. Similarly, when your teachers learn new students' names, this sometimes interferes with them remembering the names of previous students in their classes.

The other major type of interference is **proactive interference**. Proactive (forward-acting) interference happens when information you learned earlier interferes with remembering new information. For example, if what you remember from the last chapter interferes with what you are learning in this chapter, you are experiencing proactive interference. Another often embarrassing example occurs when you accidentally call your current girlfriend or boyfriend by your previous girlfriend or boyfriend's name.

retroactive interference Forgetting due to interference from newly learned information

proactive interference Forgetting due to interference from previously learned information

suppression Motivated forgetting that occurs when a person consciously tries to forget something

CHECKPOINT *What is the difference between retroactive interference and proactive interference?*

Motivated Forgetting

Sometimes people forget things because they want to forget them. This is called motivated forgetting. This usually occurs because a memory is unpleasant or disturbing. **Suppression** occurs when a person consciously tries to forget something. For example, a skater is likely to suppress (block out) the memory of falling after a big jump when she last skated her routine. Although the skater is aware that she failed in her previous attempt, she consciously chooses not to think about it. In the same way, you engage in suppression when studying for an exam by trying not to think about other things ("What are my friends doing?" "My favorite show is on television.") that might distract you.

PHOTODISC/GETTY IMAGES

When studying for an exam, you engage in suppression by trying not to think about other things that would distract you.

As first discussed by Freud (see Chapter 11, page 310), **repression** occurs when a person unconsciously pushes unpleasant memories out of his or her mind. Although these memories are no longer remembered in the normal sense, they do influence the person's thoughts, feelings, and behavior because they lie under the surface of your consciousness. Examples of traumatic events that often cause repressed memories are being a victim of child abuse or witnessing a violent crime.

CHECKPOINT *What is the difference between suppression and repression?*

Brain Damage and Forgetting

Scientists have learned a great deal about memory and forgetting by studying people who have *amnesia,* or severe memory loss. One type of amnesia is **anterograde amnesia**, which is the inability to form new memories. *Anterograde* means forward moving. This is the type of amnesia Henry Molaison experienced following the removal of his hippocampus. After his surgery, Henry's short-term memory was fine, and he was still able to retrieve information stored in long-term memory prior to the surgery. The hippocampus is critical in forming new long-term memories, but it is not involved in short-term memory or in the retrieval of long-term memories.

Another type of amnesia is **retrograde amnesia**, which is the loss of information previously stored in long-term memory. *Retrograde* means backward moving. Accident victims or people who experience severe head trauma cannot remember the events leading up to their injury. In the worst cases, the person may not remember events that occurred years before. Usually this type of memory loss is only temporary. Figure 13-9 reviews the differences between anterograde and retrograde amnesia.

repression Motivated forgetting that occurs when a person unconsciously pushes unpleasant memories out of his or her mind

anterograde amnesia The inability to form long-term memories due to physical injury to the brain

retrograde amnesia The loss of information previously stored in long-term memory due to physical injury to the brain

Figure 13-9 ANTEROGRADE AND RETROGRADE AMNESIA

In anterograde amnesia, a person is unable to form new memories after the amnesia-inducing event. In retrograde amnesia, a person is unable to retrieve information stored in long-term memory before the amnesia-inducing event.

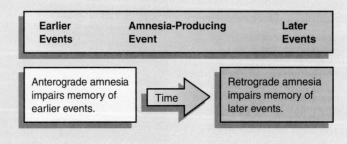

Earlier Events	Amnesia-Producing Event	Later Events
Anterograde amnesia impairs memory of earlier events.	Time	Retrograde amnesia impairs memory of later events.

CHECKPOINT *What is the difference between anterograde and retrograde amnesia?*

In Your Own Words

Explain Ebbinghaus's experiment on memory, the memory curve, and his two important findings.

Review Concepts

1. Which are you experiencing if you forget due to interference from previously learned information?

    a. retroactive interference   c. proactive interference

    b. repression   d. suppression

2. This occurs when you try to consciously forget that you fell down at the school dance last year.

    a. repression   c. interference

    b. suppression   d. misinformation effects

3. Which unconscious memories can influence your thoughts, feelings, and memories?

    a. repressed   c. suppressed

    b. retroactive   d. inferred

4. Ebbinghaus discovered that 60 percent of learning is forgotten after the first _____ hours of learning.

    a. 9   c. 3

    b. 24   d. 48

5. **True or False** People who have retrograde amnesia cannot remember events leading up to their injury.

6. **True or False** Much of what most people learn is quickly forgotten.

7. **True or False** An early theory of forgetting stated that the simple passage of time causes memories to fade and eventually be lost. This theory is still accepted in modern-day psychology.

Think Critically

8. Why do you need to suppress memories when studying for a test?

9. Describe the Jenkins and Dallenbach experiment with college students. Explain how this knowledge can help you prepare for a test.

10. What risk do athletes who play contact sports face with regard to brain damage and forgetting?

11. Give an example of when it might help someone to suppress a memory, and explain how suppressing this memory helped.

Did Henry Molaison Remember Ray Charles?

INTRODUCTION In 1953 when Henry Molaison had his hippocampus surgically removed to control his epileptic seizures, neuroscientists knew very little about this brain structure. With Henry's help, the scientists soon realized that the hippocampus played an important role in forming new memories. For many years, scientists believed that Henry could no longer form new explicit memories. He was unable to learn new vocabulary words or remember people he had met. Was it possible that, over time, other brain areas took over some of the functions of the hippocampus so that Henry could have some limited ability to form explicit memories? In 2004, Psychologists Gail O'Kane, Elizabeth Kensinger, and Suzanne Corkin tested Henry, who was 78 years old at the time.

HYPOTHESIS The researchers hypothesized that Henry would demonstrate some limited ability to form new explicit memories.

METHOD Henry was evaluated for his knowledge of people who became famous after his brain surgery in 1953. On the first day of

testing, Henry was given the first name of 35 different famous persons and asked to say the last name that came to mind. Examples were "Ray_____(Charles)," "Ronald_____ (Reagan)," and "Fidel_____(Castro)." On the second day of testing, a slightly different procedure was followed. Henry was first given background information on a famous person, then given the famous person's first name, and then asked to say the last name that came to mind. This procedure was followed for a list of famous people who became known after 1953.

RESULTS The findings supported the hypothesis. On the first day of testing, Henry was able to correctly supply the last name of 12 out of the 35 famous people. On the second day of testing, Henry was able to generate the last names for 11 other famous people after he was given their background information and their first names. Based on these findings, there is now clear evidence that some of Henry's other brain areas had taken on the task of creating some limited explicit memories. This is further evidence of the brain's plasticity—the remarkable flexibility of the brain to alter its neural connections (see Chapter 3, page 78).

Critical Analysis

1. Why do you think the researchers thought that Henry Molaison might be able to create some limited new explicit memories when past testing years ago did not find any evidence that he had this ability?

2. What does this study show us about our brain and brain injury?

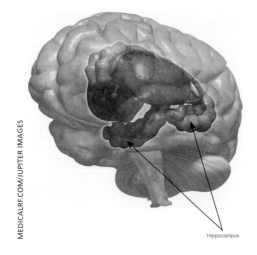

MEDICALRF.COM/JUPITER IMAGES

Hippocampus

Cognitive Psychologist  *ealth Science*

Have you ever wondered how you learn or why you have certain thoughts? Cognitive psychologists can tell you. They study how people process, store, and use information. Cognitive psychologists research how people think and learn, solve problems, reason, and make decisions. They also study memory and how people learn and use language. Cognitive psychologists also want to know why some people are more creative than others and how creativity works. They study how people respond to certain stimuli and why they respond the way they do.

Cognitive psychologists spend a great deal of their time conducting research. The equipment they use to study the brain and the way it operates often is very sophisticated. Some of the more specialized equipment they use are the many different types of brain scanning machines.

Employment Outlook

Careers for psychologists are expected to grow 15 percent until 2016. This is a faster than average rate.

Needed Skills and Education

Most cognitive psychologists have a doctoral degree. Cognitive psychologists may need to be licensed by the state in which they work or perform their research. Requirements vary from state

to state. Cognitive psychologists who teach in universities usually have a Ph.D. in psychology or a related field.

Courses that will help you in this career are those in psychology and other related sciences. Courses in sociology, humanities,

and cross-cultural studies will help you better understand human behavior. You also need good research and written and oral communication skills; good interpersonal relationship skills; and strong organizational abilities. Computer skills also are helpful. All cognitive psychologists write reports, and most write books or articles for psychology journals, so writing skills are extremely important.

How You'll Spend Your Day

Cognitive psychologists interview and test individuals and they also may observe their behavior in order to better understand how people process thoughts and how their thoughts affect their behavior.

Many cognitive psychologists work a regular 40-hour work week in research laboratories; however, observation of study participants may include evenings or weekends. Cognitive psychologists who share their work in writing often use evenings and weekends for writing reports, articles, and books.

Cognitive psychologists work in universities and in research centers that are funded by for-profit organizations, businesses or industries, or non-profit foundations, or through government sources. Many cognitive psychologists work as a part of a research team.

Earnings

The median annual earnings of psychologists are $59,440. The lowest 10 percent earn $35,280 while the highest 10 percent earn more than $102,730.

What About You?

Does the career of a cognitive psychologist interest you? Make the following lists: your interests, your personality characteristics, your skills and strengths, your values, and your lifestyle preferences. Put these lists away. Now make the same lists, but base your answers on what you imagine a cognitive psychologist might say. Write a report that compares and contrasts the two lists. How are they the same? How are they different? What traits do you share?

CHAPTER SUMMARY

13.1 The Nature of Memory

- The three memory processes in the information-processing model are encoding, storage, and retrieval.

- The three memory systems are sensory memory, short-term memory, and long-term memory.

- Short-term memory is referred to as the working memory because it is thought of as a memory system where you actively work with information that comes from either sensory or long-term memory.

13.2 Long-Term Memory

- Explicit memory is the conscious recollection of previous experiences such as how you felt on your first day of high school; implicit memory is memory of previous experiences without conscious recollection, such as riding a bike or doing a cartwheel.

- You organize information in long-term memory through semantic encoding. This encoding creates a mental network of concepts in long-term memory that share meaningful associations. Priming is the process by which one memory concept activates another memory concept.

- Your beliefs can shape what you encode into and retrieve from memory, so reconstructed memories can be incorrect. These changes in memory are known as misinformation effects.

- Information from memory may be from recall or recognition. Recall is a measure of explicit memory in which a person must retrieve and reproduce information from memory; recognition is a measure of explicit memory in which a person must decide whether or not the information has been previously encountered.

- A retrieval cue is a stimulus that allows you to more easily recall information from long-term memory.

- Mnemonics are mental strategies that make it easier to remember facts and other information; these strategies make it easier to encode, store, and retrieve information.

13.3 Forgetting

- The forgetting curve, which was developed by Herman Ebbinghaus, illustrates that most forgetting (more than 60 percent) occurs during the first nine hours after learning. After nine hours, the course of forgetting levels off.

- The difference between retroactive interference and proactive interference is that retroactive interference is forgetting due to interference from newly learned information and proactive interference is forgetting due to interference from previously learned information.

- Suppression is motivated forgetting that occurs when a person consciously tries to forget something. Repression is motivated forgetting that occurs when a person unconsciously pushes unpleasant memories out of conscious awareness.

- Scientists have learned a great deal about memory and forgetting by studying people with either anterograde or retrograde amnesia.

CHAPTER ASSESSMENT

Review Psychology Terms

Select the term that best fits the definition. Some terms will not be used.

_____ 1. Combining bits of information into a small number of meaningful groups, or chunks, that can be stored in short-term memory

_____ 2. The inability to form long-term memories due to physical injury to the brain

_____ 3. The process by which one memory concept activates another memory concept

_____ 4. Changes in memories due to a person being exposed to misleading information

_____ 5. The first memory process in which information is organized and interpreted so it can be entered into memory

_____ 6. A stimulus that helps you recall information from long-term memory

_____ 7. Mental strategies that make it easier to remember information

_____ 8. Vivid memories of surprising and emotional events that are personally important

_____ 9. The mental process by which information is encoded and stored in the brain and later retrieved

_____ 10. Being unable to remember something you know, followed by the feeling that it is just out of reach

_____ 11. Motivated forgetting that occurs when a person unconsciously pushes unpleasant memories out of his or her mind

_____ 12. Forgetting due to interference from newly learned information

_____ 13. A memory system that very briefly stores a vast amount of information received from your senses

_____ 14. Motivated forgetting that occurs when a person consciously tries to forget something

_____ 15. The loss of information previously stored in long-term memory due to physical injury to the brain

_____ 16. The second memory process in which information is entered and maintained in memory for a period of time

_____ 17. The increased memory for the last bits of information presented in a string of information

_____ 18. Forgetting due to interference from previously learned information

_____ 19. A memory system that holds information briefly while you actively work with information

_____ 20. The tendency to recall experiences that are consistent with your current mood

_____ 21. The increased memory for the first bits of information presented in a string of information

a. anterograde amnesia

b. chunking

c. encoding

d. flashbulb memories

e. long-term memory

f. memory

g. misinformation effects

h. mnemonics

i. mood-congruent memory

j. primacy effect

k. priming

l. proactive interference

m. recency effect

n. repression

o. retrieval cue

p. retroactive interference

q. retrograde amnesia

r. sensory memory

s. short-term memory

t. storage

u. suppression

v. tip-of-the-tongue experience

Review Psychology Concepts

22. Define retrieval.

23. Compare and contrast primacy effect and recency effect.

24. Distinguish between long-term memory and short-term memory.

25. Explain maintenance rehearsal.

26. Explain elaborative rehearsal.

27. Indicate which of the following refers to anterograde amnesia or retrograde amnesia: (a) a motorcyclist involved in an accident could not remember what caused it; (b) someone who had brain surgery on the hippocampus could not form new memories; (c) after a bump on the head from a falling tree, the pianist temporarily forgot the musical score.

28. Which brain regions control explicit and implicit memory?

29. Restate in your own words the difference between recall and recognition and give an example of each type of retrieval.

30. Classify each of the following as being either retroactive interference or proactive interference: (a) learning information in this chapter interferes with your memory of information learned in a previous chapter; (b) forgetting the names of new students you met in the cafeteria last week because you met another group of new students today; (c) your memory of information learned in a previous chapter interferes with learning of information in this chapter; (d) calling a current friend by an old friend's name.

31. Identify each of the following ways as being visual encoding, acoustic encoding, or semantic encoding: (a) you remember someone's name by seeing it in writing; (b) you remember the words to a song because you read the lyrics on the computer screen; (c) you remember the words to a song because you sing along with the song every time you hear it; (d) you remember the words to a song because they remind you of a favorite day you had with a friend.

32. Support this statement with information from the text: long-term memory and short-term memory support one another.

33. Analyze how the environment helps you with retrieval cues. Give an example from your life.

34. According to Ebbinghaus' theory, if you forget information from Chapter 1, is it easier or harder to relearn the information? How might this help you on tests?

35. Identify the three processes that make the human memory like a computer, and then explain each of the three processes.

36. Identify three ways you can increase short-term memory. Give a short explanation of each.

Apply Psychology Concepts

37. Describe the best ways in which you could use the method of loci and elaborative rehearsal in your life. Why do items used by these two techniques stay in your memory?

38. Create your own semantic network model, like the one describing Santa Claus in the text, for another holiday that you celebrate.

39. Create a list of five flashbulb memories that you or a family member have experienced. Why were these events so memorable to you? Why are they called flashbulb memories?

40. What is the tip-of-the-tongue experience? Recall and explain several instances in which you have had this experience

Make Academic Connections

41. **Social Studies** Download five pictures involving current events from the Internet. Number the pictures 1–5. Download or write five opening paragraphs of current news stories. Number the stories 1–5. With a group of other students, show them the five pictures, and then show them the news story paragraphs. After the group has a chance to study the pictures and paragraphs, turn them upside down. Have each member of the group write down what they remember about each written news paragraph and each picture. Make a chart of your findings. Did the students have an easier time remembering the pictures or the news stories? Write a brief explanation of the role imagery plays in helping you remember.

42. **Research** Using the library or Internet, research George Sperling and his work on iconic memory, which is a type of sensory memory. Prepare an oral report that explains his research and results and discusses the role of iconic memory in everyday experiences.

43. **Language Arts and Research** Use the Internet to learn more about case studies of memory loss. Scan several of the case studies until you find one that interests you. Write a research paper that introduces the case study, explains the hypothesis, methods, results of the study, and a critical analysis of the study and research methods. Include how you might conduct the same experiment in a different manner and what that would be. Also include information on the researchers including other studies and works that are relevant to this case study. Cite the source(s) of your research in your paper. On a separate sheet of paper that you attach to your research paper, add one or two paragraphs to explain why you chose this case study. Explain what interested you and what relevance, if any, the case study has to your life.

DIGGING DEEPER
with Psychology eCollection

In his article "The Seven Sins of Memory," psychologist Daniel Schacter describes the seven categories of "memory errors." These are failings and faulty processes that cause us to forget or to remember incorrectly. Some are issues of omission—things not stored in our "memory banks." Others are errors of commission—failing to attend to information as it is presented. Perhaps the most common shortcomings are transience—forgetting that occurs over the course of time, and absentmindedness—everyday memory failures. Access the Gale Psychology eCollection at *www.cengage.com/school/psych/franzoi* and read Schacter's description of the causes of some types of memory lapses. Write a summary of the article and answer the question: What is the difference between transience and absentmindedness when applied to memory? As an additional project, evaluate which memory failure is the most serious and provide a rationale for your choice.

Source: Schacter, Daniel. "The Seven Sins of Memory: How the Mind Forgets and Remembers." *Psychology Today*. 34.3 (May 2001): 62.

Language and Thinking

ESSENTIAL QUESTION
Go to page XXVI

"Literature is my Utopia. . . . No barrier of the senses shuts me out from the sweet, gracious discourses of my book friends."

—HELEN KELLER, AMERICAN AUTHOR AND ACTIVIST, 1880–1968

BLEND IMAGES/JUPITER IMAGES

At 18 months of age, Helen Keller (1880–1968) lost both her sight and hearing due to a fever. She lived for the next five years without sight, sound, or language. At age seven, her teacher Anne Sullivan placed Helen's hands under flowing well water. As the cool stream gushed over one of Helen's hands, Sullivan spelled into the other the word *water*, first slowly and then rapidly. Helen stood still, her attention fixed upon the motion of her teacher's fingers. Suddenly she remembered the early language she had begun to learn five years ago. In that moment, the wonderful mystery of language was revealed to her! Helen knew then that "w-a-t-e-r" meant the wonderful cool something that was flowing over her hand. In her own words, at that moment she was transformed from a mere "phantom" to a person who could now communicate with others. In addition to earning a college degree, Keller became a successful and inspiring author, lecturer, and educator.

14.1 | The Nature of Language

OBJECTIVES

- Identify the brain areas related to language production and language comprehension.
- Identify the three features of language.
- Explain the structure of language.
- Discuss the correlation between language and thinking and describe the linguistic relativity hypothesis.

DISCOVER IT | *How does this relate to me?*

Imagine how your life would be different if you had no language ability. For one thing, the words on this page would mean no more to you than この文〔判決〕の終わり. People's voices would have the significance of bird songs or dog barks. They might sound interesting, even pleasant, but nothing more. Your world is transformed by your ability to share meaning through these markings on the page and the sounds you and others create.

KEY TERMS

- communication
- language
- Broca's area
- Wernicke's area
- grammar
- phonology
- syntax
- semantics
- phonemes
- morphemes
- linguistic relativity hypothesis
- generic masculine

Communication is the sending and receiving of information. Every day of your life, you communicate thousands of bits of information to others. A very special form of communication is **language**, which is a way of communicating information using symbols and the rules for combining them. Using language is the main way that humans communicate with one another. *Speech* is the oral expression of language. More than 5,000 spoken languages exist today. *Linguistics* is the scientific study of language. Scientists who study language are known as *linguists*.

The Brain and Language

The scientific study of language begins in the brain. As noted in Chapter 3 (page 76), PET scan studies indicate that the major brain areas for language are located in the left hemisphere, even in most left-handed people. Early understanding of the brain and language came about through studying people who had suffered damage to the left hemisphere of their brain. The disruption of language caused by brain damage is known as *aphasia*.

communication The sending and receiving of information

language A way of communicating information using symbols and the rules for combining them

As shown in Figure 14-1, a small clump of neurons in the left frontal lobe, known as **Broca's area**, influences brain areas that allow people to speak smoothly and correctly. Damage to Broca's area disrupts the ability to speak smoothly or otherwise use correct words, phrases, and sentences. Broca's area is named after the French neuroanatomist, Paul Broca, who first described this brain damage. This brain disorder—called *Broca's aphasia*—often causes people to have long pauses between words and to leave out words, such as *and, but,* and *if.*

Also shown in Figure 14-1 is **Wernicke's area**, which is at the back of the left temporal lobe. It is connected by a nerve bundle to Broca's area. This part of the left temporal lobe is more responsible for the ability to recognize and understand words, phrases, and sentences. Recent brain scan studies indicate that Broca's area is involved in some areas of language understanding, which was previously thought to involve only Wernicke's area.

Wernicke's area is named after the German neurologist Carl Wernicke, who first reported how damage to this area harmed people's ability to understand and correctly use language. Such damage is called *Wernicke's aphasia*. Those affected produce *word salad,* or speech that makes no sense. Ask them how they are doing, and they might reply with something like, "Yes, bit is you hafta what mo hafta."

Broca's area A brain area in the left frontal lobe that allows people to speak smoothly and correctly

Wernicke's area A brain area at the back of the left temporal lobe that allows people to recognize and understand spoken words

Figure 14-1 **BROCA AND WERNICKE'S AREAS OF THE CEREBRAL CORTEX**

Two brain areas are thought to be associated with language function—Broca's area and Wernicke's area. These brain areas are usually located in the left cerebral hemisphere.

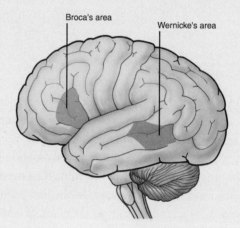

Broca's area   Wernicke's area

CHECKPOINT *What two brain areas are related to speaking smoothly and understanding spoken language?*

Three Features of Language

Scientists have wondered whether humans are the only species with language and communication abilities. More than 50 years ago, Austrian biologist Karl von Frisch discovered that honeybees communicate the exact location of food through an elaborate dance. Not all animal communication is based on inborn responses, however. For instance, hummingbirds, parrots, and many songbirds share with humans the ability to learn new ways to communicate through imitation. Therefore, humans are not unique in their ability to learn new communication skills.

What makes a communication system a language? Linguists have identified the following three features a communication system needs to qualify as a language:

1. **Meaningfulness** Language sends messages using words or signs that have specific meanings. Other species also can express meaningful messages, but they either involve general messages or a limited number of specific messages. For example, when a beaver slaps its tail on the water, other beavers understand this as a general danger message, not a specific warning about an approaching bear.

2. **Displacement** Language allows communication about things that are displaced, meaning they are not present in the here and now. Humans can discuss what happened in the past, what may happen in the future, or what is now happening far away, but animal communication does not share this feature. When a dog says GRRR, it means GRRR right now, not GRRR last week.

3. **Productivity** Language allows you to produce messages that you have never before produced. You can share new messages with anyone who shares your language. Most animal communication lacks this feature. For example, the honeybee's dance has no signal for up, thus bees cannot produce a message that tells other bees about food located directly above their hive.

Based on these criteria, animal communication does not qualify as language. However, humans have tried to teach language to a few species, such as chimpanzees, bonobos, gorillas, dolphins, and parrots. One of the most famous cases is that of Washoe, a female chimpanzee who was raised at home by humans and taught sign language as though she were a deaf human child. Within four years, Washoe was using more than 100 signs. She also could combine words to produce phrases, such as gimme banana and open food drink. Washoe could even have simple conversations, which led a visiting reporter for *The New York Times* to state, "Suddenly I realized I was conversing with a member of another species in my native tongue."

COURTESY OF FIGZOI

Bonobos and other apes have been taught by humans to communicate with sign language. Once taught, they also teach their offspring sign language. Does this mean these animals can learn language, an ability once thought unique to humans?

CHECKPOINT *What are the three features of language?*

The Structure of Language

Human languages have an organized structure. Sounds are combined into meaningful units to form words. Words are combined to form phrases, which are combined to form sentences. Rules of **grammar** guide which combinations of sounds and words are acceptable within the language you use. Grammar has three major components:

1. **phonology**   the rules for combining basic sounds into words
2. **syntax**   the rules for combining words into sentences
3. **semantics**   the rules for communicating the meaning of words, phrases, and sentences

Phonemes are the basic units of sound in speech. Phonemes are a single letter, such as the consonant *d* in bi*d*; a vowel, such as the *e* in th*e*; or a combination of letters, such as *th* in *the*. **Morphemes** are the smallest units of language that carry meaning. A few morphemes, such as *a* and *I,* also are phonemes, and most morphemes are themselves words. The *re* in *replay* and the *s* in *plans* are also morphemes. The average English speaker uses 40 phonemes to build between 50,000 and 80,000 morphemes.

Syntax rules help you build meaningful phrases and sentences that enable you to communicate. For instance, you can recognize the meaning of the sentence *The new student made friends easily,* but the words *student easily friends new the* do not make sense. The latter group of words does not follow the rules of English syntax, so it makes little sense to you.

Although syntax rules shape proper sentence construction, the rules of semantics determine the *meaning* of sentences. This underlying meaning is known as the *deep structure* of language. Based on your knowledge of semantics, you realize that while the following sentence does not violate any syntax rules, it conveys no

grammar Rules about using sounds and words in a language

phonology The rules for combining basic sounds into words

syntax The rules for combining words into sentences

semantics The rules for communicating the meaning of words, phrases, and sentences

phonemes The basic units of sound in speech

morphemes The smallest units of language that carry meaning

Every language has its own set of grammar rules.

©STEPHEN AARON REES, 2009/USED UNDER LICENSE FROM SHUTTERSTOCK.COM

obvious meaning: *Silent music questions winter.* How can music—especially *silent music*—question anything, let alone winter? This sentence demonstrates that proper syntax and meaning do not always go together.

As you can see from Figure 14-2, a sentence can have the same surface structure, but two different deep structures. Examine the sentence "Visiting relatives can be a nuisance," for example. There are two underlying meanings, or deep structures, for this sentence. The first is the notion that going to visit your relatives can be a nuisance. The second is the idea that having relatives visit you can be a nuisance.

Sentences also can have different surface structures, but the same deep structure ("Jaelyn broke the window." "The window was broken by Jaelyn.") People are more likely to store information in memory based on deep structure than on surface structure. For this reason, while you probably would not remember whether someone told you that "Jaelyn broke the window" or "The window was broken by Jaelyn," you probably will remember that Jaelyn caused the window breakage.

Figure 14-2 **SURFACE STRUCTURE VERSUS DEEP STRUCTURE**

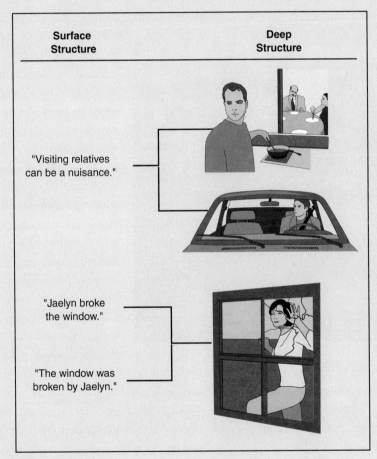

The surface structure of a sentence consists of its word arrangement, while the deep structure refers to its underlying meaning.

 **CHECKPOINT**   *What is the difference between phonemes and morphemes?*

Does Language Determine Thinking?

A bilingual person may speak one language from a collectivist culture and another from an individualist culture. When they speak one of the languages, their comments likely will be influenced by the culture of that language.

linguistic relativity hypothesis A theory that the structure of language determines the structure of thought, meaning that people who speak different languages also think differently

generic masculine The use of masculine nouns and pronouns to refer to all people, regardless of their gender

How strong is the connection between cognition (how you think) and language? Linguist Benjamin Lee Whorf (1897–1941) developed the **linguistic relativity hypothesis**, which proposes that the structure of language *determines* the structure of thought. He used the term *linguistic relativity* to emphasize his belief that people's thinking is related to the particular language they use. According to Whorf, if language shapes your thinking, you really cannot think about an experience if there is no word or phrase in your language to describe it. Further, if language shapes your thinking, then cultures with different languages are unlikely to share the same understanding of the world.

In a critical test of Whorf's hypothesis, Eleanor Rosch compared the color perceptions of the Dani people of Papua, New Guinea—who use only two words for color (bright and dark)—with those of English-speaking people, who use many different color terms. Despite these language differences, Rosch found no differences in the way the two groups perceived color. Dani speakers could identify subtle differences in colors just as English speakers could. Even when a language lacks terms for certain experiences, the users of the language are still able to think about and understand those experiences.

PHOTODISC/GETTY IMAGES

The idea that language determines thought directly has no scientific support. However, most psychologists do believe that language can *influence* thinking. This idea may not seem unusual to you if you speak two different languages, such as English and Chinese. English, which is an individualist language, has many self-focused words. The collectivist-based Chinese language has many socially focused words. Bilingual people report that the way they think about themselves and others is influenced by the language they use. They are more likely to be aware of their own personal needs and desires when speaking English. They are more aware of social obligations when speaking Chinese.

Language also influences thinking in the way it calls attention to a person's gender. In English, you cannot avoid specifying gender when using pronouns such as *his* or *her*. Yet, masculine pronouns and nouns traditionally have been used to refer to all people, regardless of their gender. Although the **generic masculine** is meant to include women as well as men, it does not do so in reality. A number of studies find that people learn to connect men and women with certain activities and occupations by paying attention to the gendered pronouns used to describe these activities and occupations. For example, telling children what a doctor does on the job using the generic masculine ("He takes care of sick people") suggests to children that this is an occupation for men, not women. Based on this research, the American Psychological Association recommends that gender-neutral language be used to reduce gender bias in people's thinking. Table 14-1 lists suggestions for avoiding gendered terms in the English language.

Table 14-1 SUGGESTIONS FOR REDUCING GENDERED TERMS IN LANGUAGE

Gendered Terms to Avoid	Alternative Gender-Neutral Terms
He, his, him	He or she, her or his, him or her, or they, their, them
Man, mankind	Humanity, people, human beings, humankind, the human species
Man-made	Handmade, synthetic, fabricated, constructed
Coed	Student
Freshman	First-year student, frosh
Manpower	Workers, human resources, personnel, workforce
Businessman	Businessperson
Chairman, chairwoman	Chairperson, head, chair
Saleswoman, salesgirl	Salesclerk
Foreman	Supervisor
Policeman, policewoman	Police officer
Waitress	Server
Man-to-man	One-to-one, person-to-person
Forefathers	Ancestors
Housewife, househusband	Homemaker
Mothering	Parenting, caregiving, nurturing
Fireman	Firefighter
Mailman	Mail carrier
Cavemen	Prehistoric people
Fisherman	Fisher
First baseman	First base player
Brotherhood	Kinship
Weatherman	Meteorologist

Do you think computers can think like humans? Check out the New Science feature on page 412 for information on how scientists have been trying to develop intelligent machines that can mimic human thinking and language.

CHECKPOINT › *What is the linguistic relativity hypothesis?*

Can Intelligent Machines Think Like Humans?

*A*rtificial intelligence (AI) is the science of designing and making intelligent machines, especially intelligent computer programs. In 1950, Alan Turing, the founder of computer science, developed a test to determine whether a machine could mimic human thinking so it could "pass" as a human. Turing stated that if a machine could successfully fool observers that it was human 30 percent of the time, then it should be considered intelligent. Later studies testing this hypothesis often had an evaluator interact with a machine and a human over the Internet. The human would try to persuade the observer that he or she was human and the machine would try to fool the observer. As of 2008, no computer-programmed machine has successfully passed the Turing Test. That is, the machine did fool some people, but it did not successfully pretend to be human 30 percent of the time.

One computer program that has fooled some people is computer scientist Richard Wallace's ALICE, which is an acronym for Artificial Linguistic Internet Computer Entity. Following is an excerpt from a conversation I had over the Internet with ALICE:

Author: Have you studied psychology?
ALICE: I don't think I ever have studied psychology. What's it like?
Author: It's fascinating, because you learn how the mind works.
ALICE: You learn something new every day.
Author: Do you enjoy conversing with people?
ALICE: I always say people don't go into computer science because they want to work with the public.
Author: Well, I should get back to writing this chapter on language and thinking.
ALICE: Interesting. Tell me why you should.
Author: You sound like a psychologist.
ALICE: Oh really. What does it sound like?

Currently, chess programs can play at the level of a grandmaster, but their ability to win games creatively still is not as good as the best human chess master. Will computers ever mimic, or exceed, the genius of an Albert Einstein? Will they be able to create great works of art like Leonardo da Vinci or Ludwig von Beethoven? Future research in the area of AI may one day answer these questions.

Think Critically

1. What are some areas you believe should target the use of AI? Why?
2. Do you think computers could serve as guidance counselors in high school? Why or why not?

In Your Own Words

Choose one of the four chapter objectives on page 405 and restate the information in your own words. For example, you might choose the first objective: Identify the brain areas related to language production and language comprehension. You could explain that language begins in the brain and describe what areas of the brain affect language and how these areas affect language.

Review Concepts

1. Which might convey to children that an occupation is gender specific?
   - a. generic masculine
   - b. phonology
   - c. linguistic relativity
   - d. Wernicke's area

2. Which is the smallest significant sound unit in speech?
   - a. syntax
   - b. phoneme
   - c. semantics
   - d. morpheme

3. Which influences language production?
   - a. Broca's area
   - b. morphemes
   - c. grammar
   - d. Wernicke's area

4. Which refers to the rules for combining basic sounds into words?
   - a. language
   - b. grammar
   - c. syntax
   - d. phonology

5. **True or False** The term *linguistic relativity* refers to the concept that people's thinking is related to the particular language they use.

6. **True or False** Generic-masculine language includes both men and women and is the preferred usage in the United States.

7. **True or False** Most psychologists believe that language can influence thinking.

8. **True or False** A sentence can have the same surface structure, but two different deep structures.

9. **True or False** The deep structure of a sentence consists of its word arrangement, while the surface structure refers to its underlying meaning.

Think Critically

10. Explain why the left cerebral hemisphere of the brain is important to language.

11. What is *word salad,* and how is it produced?

12. Why is communication among animals not considered language?

13. Studies indicate that people learn to associate men and women with certain occupations by paying attention to the gendered pronouns used to describe these occupations. What can be done in our society to change this?

14. Explain the importance of Broca's area to language.

Language Learning and Nonverbal Communication

KEY TERMS

- language acquisition device
- telegraphic speech
- child-directed speech
- nonverbal communication
- nonconscious mimicry

OBJECTIVES

- Describe how language is acquired.
- Explain stages in language development.
- Discuss nonverbal communication.

DISCOVER IT | *How does this relate to me?*

You were not always a language user. When first born, you were a gesture imitator. When your parents smiled at you or yawned, you imitated their gestures. Gesture imitation is important for infants because it helps create an emotional bond with parents ("Oh, what a cute baby!"). How did you take the next step and move from simply imitating gestures to begin using and creating language itself? In this section, you will discover how the process of acquiring a language unfolded for you.

During childhood, you learned almost 5,000 words per year. This is about 13 new words per day. Your vocabulary when you graduate from high school may be about 80,000 words. Adults with excellent vocabularies hold more than 200,000 words in long-term memory. How do you become an efficient language user? Is it due to inborn abilities or life experiences?

Acquiring Language

Until about 1960, most psychologists assumed that children's language development was simply a learned response. B. F. Skinner and other behaviorists claimed that children begin life with no special ability to learn language. Instead, adults were thought to shape children's vocal sounds through reinforcement and punishment. Children were thought to imitate adult language.

The problem with this behaviorist theory, however, is that it does not fit the evidence. For instance, children often produce sentences they have not heard before. Instead of saying, "Mommy went to work" or "That is my cookie"—both correct imitations of adult speech—children typically say, "Mommy goed to work" and "That mine cookie." Further, children's imitation of adult speech drops sharply after the age of two, despite the fact that language development continues. How could children continue to learn language if imitation is at the core of their learning?

Critics of the behaviorist viewpoint argue that reinforcement, punishment, and imitation play only a limited role in language learning. Instead, they state that humans learn language for the same reason they learn to walk—because they are biologically equipped for it. Linguist Noam Chomsky proposed that children are born with a specialized mental program, or neural prewiring, called the **language acquisition device**, which allows them to learn language. According to Chomsky, with this inborn ability, if children are exposed to a language, they will learn to talk even if they are not reinforced for doing so.

A number of studies support the theory that humans are born with the ability to learn language. The first few years of life is a critical period in language learning. For instance, when adults learn a language, they speak with a more native-sounding accent if they overheard the language regularly during childhood than if they did not.

Adults, especially parents, play an important role in children's language development. In studies of abused and neglected children who received little adult attention, researchers found that the children's understanding of speech and their verbal expression were behind that of children who received normal adult attention. Overall, research suggests that while humans appear to be born with the ability to learn language, they must talk to adults regularly to fully develop their language abilities. In other words, language development is neither solely nature nor nurture, but a combination of both. Check out the Case Study on page 416 for a demonstration of the importance of verbal interaction in language development.

Noam Chomsky, b. 1928

language acquisition device Chomsky's linguistic theory proposing that an inborn mental program enables children to learn language

CHECKPOINT *What is the language acquisition device?*

What is the role adults play in children's language development?

How Important Is Verbal Interaction in Speech Development?

INTRODUCTION Jim was a young boy who was raised by deaf parents. Using their very limited verbal skills, Jim's parents tried to teach their son spoken English for the first four years of his life. Realizing that they could not clearly pronounce words for their son, Jim's parents had him regularly watch television at home so that he heard normal speech. At the age of four, when he was in preschool Jim could not speak normally.

HYPOTHESIS Speech experts were consulted when Jim's problem was discovered. They hypothesized that if the child was allowed to speak on a regular basis with skilled language speakers he would overcome his serious language problems.

METHOD Jim was given speech therapy while taking part in daily preschool activities with the other children.

RESULTS In spite of his serious language problems, Jim showed great improvement within a few months. Within a few years, his language ability became normal. Jim's early life experiences demonstrate that being exposed to language in a nonsocial setting (watching television) does not allow children to develop normal speaking skills. Verbal interaction—not just language exposure—is the key ingredient in normal speech development. In Jim's case, he was given the necessary therapy early enough to avoid long-term negative effects. Unfortunately, when children are cut off from normal language speakers beyond their middle childhood, they develop lifelong speech problems.

Critical Analysis
1. Why were Jim's parents unsuccessful in teaching him spoken English?
2. What do the results of this study prove?

Stages in Language Development

Language development begins shortly after birth and involves a number of stages that move from the simple to the complex. Infants with a hearing loss who are taught sign language from birth learn this language at the same pace as hearing infants who learn spoken languages. These studies also find that both spoken and sign languages rely on nearly the same brain regions in the left cerebral hemisphere (Broca's area and Wernicke's area).

STAGE 1: COOING AND BABBLING

In every culture, by about two months of age, newborns begin vocalizing by *cooing*, in which they produce phoneme sounds such as *ooooh* and *aaaah*. Between the fourth and sixth months, infants begin *babbling*, which is vocally repeating phonemes, such as *baa-baa-baa* or *gaa-gaa-gaa*. The early babbling of children from different cultures sounds the same because it includes the phonemes in all existing languages. However, by the time children are about 10 months old, phonemes that are not in their native language drop out. The children's babbling sounds similar to the phonemes in their culture's language.

STAGE 2: SINGLE-WORD USE

By the end of their first year, most children begin saying morpheme sounds that can be identified as words, such as *mama, papa,* and the ever-popular *no*. This period is called the *one-word stage,* because children can use only one-word phrases.

Young children often do not have words for many of the objects they want to talk about because they have a small vocabulary. As a result, they use the same word for many different things. For example, an 18-month-old child might use the word *wawa* for water and also for milk, juice, and other beverages.

When learning to use language, young children use the same word for many different things.

©DONALD JOSKI 2009/USED UNDER LICENSE FROM SHUTTERSTOCK.COM

STAGE 3: TWO-WORD USE

By the age of two, children enter the *two-word stage,* in which they begin using two separate words in the same sentence. During this two-word stage, the phase of **telegraphic speech** begins. In this phase, children use multiple-word sentences that leave out all but the essential words, as in a telegrammed message (*BABY BORN. MOTHER FINE*). Thus, instead of saying, "I want to go outside," children might say, "Want outside."

Once children master using two-word sentences, they begin using longer phrases. By the time children reach the age of four, they are using plurals, as well as the present and past tense in sentences. However, they often apply grammatical rules too broadly. For example, in using the past tense, they may incorrectly say, "I goed outside" instead of, "I went outside."

telegraphic speech An early speech phase in which children use short sentences, leaving out all but the important words, like in a telegram

BLEND IMAGES/JUPITER IMAGES

The day-to-day verbal feedback that infants receive plays an important role in the learning process during the early stages of language development. This **child-directed speech**—sometimes called *baby talk*—involves speaking to babies with a high-pitched voice, using short sentences and pronouncing words clearly and slowly. Child-directed speech helps infants learn their new language by teaching them language rules and where words begin and end. Adults who communicate with deaf children use a similar pattern by making signs more slowly, repeating the signs, and making exaggerated gestures when signing. Infants with a hearing disability pay more attention to this *child-directed signing* than to the more rapid, fluid signing typically used between adults.

In summarizing this section on the stages of language development, most scientists now believe that childhood represents a critical period for mastering certain aspects of language. After the age of seven the ability to learn language easily gradually declines. This is why adults have a much harder time learning a new language than do children. When it comes to language learning, you can "teach an old dog new tricks," but it requires a great deal more work.

CHECKPOINT › *What is child-directed speech?*

Nonverbal Communication

When you spend time with others, you share a great deal of nonverbal information. **Nonverbal communication** is the sending and receiving of information using gestures, expressions, and body movements rather than words.

child-directed speech Speaking to babies with a high-pitched voice, using short sentences with clearly and slowly pronounced words; also called *baby talk*

nonverbal communication Sending and receiving of information using gestures, expressions, and body movements rather than words

COMMUNICATING WITH THE FACE AND BODY

As you learned in Chapter 6, one of the more important ways to communicate nonverbally is with the face. In all cultures, people recognize the meaning of facial expressions for the emotions of happiness, fear, anger, disgust, sadness, surprise, and contempt. Besides facial cues, the body as a whole can pass on a wealth of information. For example, people who walk with a good deal of knee bending, loose-jointedness, and body bounce appear younger and more powerful than those who walk with stiffness.

Certain nonverbal cues are universally recognized. However, many forms of nonverbal behavior are shaped by cultural norms. For example, cultures differ in terms of the amount of *personal space* a person requires. This refers to the proper distance one person stands from another during a casual conversation. In the United States, Canada, England, and Germany, this distance ranges from 18 inches to 4 feet. In Middle Eastern and Latin American cultures, the personal space zone is much smaller.

NONCONSCIOUS MIMICRY

Have you noticed that yawns are contagious? Psychologists believe that yawning is a very primitive form of communication. The unspoken message suggested in a yawn is, "It is time for us to go to sleep." If your body clock is roughly in sync with the yawning person's body clock, your brain likely will respond to the yawn with the release of chemicals that prepare you for sleep.

Yawning is an example of **nonconscious mimicry**. This is the tendency to adopt the behaviors, postures, or mannerisms of others with whom you are interacting, without your awareness or intention. When talking to others, you often mimic the way they talk. You laugh when they do, and you adopt their body postures and gestures. Neuroscientists have discovered that this mimicry is triggered by specialized brain cells called *mirror neurons*.

Mimicking others appears to be an inborn tendency. One-month-old infants smile, stick out their tongues, and open their mouths when they see someone else doing the same. Such imitation may be important in triggering emotional attachment between parents and newborns. Autism, a brain disorder characterized by impaired communication and social interaction, may be caused partly by mirror neurons that are not firing correctly.

nonconscious mimicry Adopting the behaviors, postures, or mannerisms of others with whom you are interacting without your awareness

Have you ever noticed that when conversing with others, people often mimic their partner's speech tendencies, body postures, and gestures?

CREATAS IMAGES/JUPITER IMAGES

Research shows that in get-acquainted sessions, people are better liked by others when they imitate their gestures. For example, they may rub their face or tap their foot when the other person does so. Further, as people interact and begin liking one another, they unknowingly increase their mimicking of each other's gestures. These findings suggest that this nonverbal behavior serves as a sort of social glue to cement the emotional bonds between people. The next time you are having a pleasant conversation with someone, pay attention to whether you are mimicking each other's gestures. Are you leaning the same way, smiling and laughing at the same time, holding your arms in a similar manner? Good communication skills begin with proper and welcoming nonverbal behavior.

CHECKPOINT *What is nonverbal communication?*

14.2 ASSESSMENT

In Your Own Words

Explain the differences between the theories of B. F. Skinner and Noam Chomsky. Assess both theories and discuss which theory you think has the most merit and why.

Review Concepts

1. At which stage does language development begin?

   a. age two
   b. right before birth

   c. shortly after birth
   d. from age 10 months

2. Which behavior are you showing if you yawn in response to someone near you yawning?

   a. child-directed speech
   b. telegraphic speech

   c. nonverbal communication
   d. nonconscious mimicry

3. **True or False** Child-directed speech hinders babies' ability to learn language.

4. **True or False** Nonverbal communication varies from culture to culture.

Think Critically

5. Is language development an example of nature or nurture? Explain your answer.

6. How is Stage 3 of language development different for children with a hearing disability as opposed to children with normal hearing?

7. Define nonconscious mimicry, and describe a recent incident in which you became aware of how your nonconscious mimicry behavior was affected by a group of friends, classmates, or family members.

14.3 Thinking and Problem Solving

OBJECTIVES

- Discuss concept formation and organization.
- Identify three problem-solving strategies.
- Describe obstacles to problem solving.

DISCOVER IT | *How does this relate to me?*

Do you know how you solve problems or create new ideas? In the opening story of this chapter, you were introduced to Helen Keller. Because she could not see or hear, Helen Keller had to discover her own way to use language. The way she solved this problem is very much like the way you often solve certain problems: suddenly and with a good deal of surprise. Problem solving represents one product of thinking, or cognition. Recall from Chapter 8 that *cognition* is the mental activity of knowing and the processes through which knowledge is acquired and problems are solved. Awareness of how you think will help you to solve problems and make good decisions.

KEY TERMS

- concept
- prototype
- problem solving
- trial and error
- algorithm
- heuristic
- insight
- confirmation bias
- mental set
- functional fixedness

The building blocks of cognition are concepts. A **concept** is a mental grouping of objects, ideas, or events that share common properties. For example, the concept *insect* stands for a class of animals that have three body divisions (head, thorax, abdomen), six legs, an external skeleton, and a rapid reproductive cycle. As you recall from the discussion of the semantic network model in Chapter 13, page 384, concepts enable you to store your memories in an organized way. When one concept in your long-term memory is activated, other closely related concepts also are activated.

Concept Formation and Organization

All humans naturally place the things they experience into categories. This saves time and helps them make predictions about the future. For example, I know that if I eat an object from the concept *cheese,* I am likely to enjoy the experience. I also know that if I need medical attention, I will likely receive it by seeking out people from either of the concepts *doctor* or *nurse.*

> **concept** A mental grouping of objects, ideas, or events that share common properties

Which of these birds is more "birdlike" to you—the robin in (a) or the penguin in (b)? That is, which of these birds is closer to your bird prototype?

COURTESY OF FIGZOI

Some members of familiar concepts are easier to categorize than others. In our minds, familiar members of concepts better represent that concept. The members that best represent a concept in our minds are known as **prototypes**. For example, many people consider a golden retriever more doglike than a Chihuahua, and an American robin more birdlike than a penguin.

Your failure to categorize things correctly because they do not match your prototype for that concept can lead to errors in decision making. For instance, if certain physical symptoms do not fit the flu prototype, you may continue your normal activities, thus worsening your condition and also infecting others.

CHECKPOINT > *What is a prototype?*

Problem Solving

One important way people use concepts as the building blocks of thinking is in overcoming problems. Problems vary in complexity, from the simple one of finding your book bag in the morning to the more complex one of deciding what to do after you graduate from high school. **Problem solving** is the thought process you use to overcome obstacles and reach your goals. Problem solving typically involves using one of several strategies, including trial and error, algorithms, heuristics, and insight.

TRIAL AND ERROR

Trial and error involves trying one possible solution after another until you find a solution that works. For example, have you ever tried opening a locked door after being handed a small number of keys? You probably tried one key after another until one of them turned the lock. When the number of possible solutions is small, trial and error is a useful problem-solving strategy. However, you can waste a lot of time and effort if the number of possible solutions is large. You may be standing at a locked door for quite awhile when holding a large ring of keys. Sometimes frustration wins out over stumbling on the correct solution. If you have ever given

prototype The most representative member of a concept

problem solving Thought process used to overcome obstacles and reach goals

trial and error A problem-solving strategy that involves trying one possible solution after another until one works

up before finishing a difficult jigsaw puzzle you have experienced the limitations of trial-and-error problem solving.

Why might trial-and-error problem solving not be effective when working on a 1,000-piece jigsaw puzzle?

PHOTODISC/GETTY IMAGES

ALGORITHMS

Unlike trial and error, which does not guarantee success, an **algorithm** is a problem-solving strategy in which you follow a specific rule or step-by-step procedure that always produces the correct solution. For example, try creating a new word using the letters in LYGOCHPOYS. Using an algorithm eventually leads to the correct solution. You need to try each of these letters in each of the 10 letter positions. The drawback of using algorithms is that they are rigid and often very time-consuming. For this new-word problem, there are 907,200 different ways to position these letters. Computers are based on algorithms, and that is the reason they are rigid in their functioning.

HEURISTICS

Instead of rigidly trying all the possible letter positions to arrive at a new word, you could rely on a **heuristic**, which involves following a general rule of thumb to reduce the number of possible solutions. Some general rules of thumb you could use in solving the LYGOCHPOYS word problem is to avoid putting two letter Y's or a string of consonants (such as GCH or SPHCG) together. Now the number of possible letter combinations has been greatly reduced. Heuristics have a reasonably good chance of working. (See page 425 for the solution.)

The chief advantage of heuristics is that they usually save time. Learning to use these short-cut cognitive strategies is an important skill that helps students quickly solve many problems in English, math, and science courses. Check out the Closer Look feature on page 424 for more information on one type of heuristic.

algorithm A problem-solving strategy that involves following a specific rule or step-by-step procedure until you produce the correct solution

heuristic A problem-solving strategy that involves following a general rule of thumb to reduce the number of possible solutions

LAB TEAMS

Problem-Solving Strategies

Work together to create a bulletin board, poster, or PowerPoint® presentation that illustrates the four problem-solving strategies. List each strategy and what type of problem you might solve using this strategy. Think of other strategies you could use to problem solve and add them to the bulletin board. For example, you could add the strategy of breaking down the problem into smaller steps, a good strategy to use when writing a paper. You also could add the strategy of working from the back forward or from the outside in, something painters do with a canvas.

INSIGHT

Sometimes solutions simply pop into your head while you ponder a problem. The sudden realization of how a problem can be solved is called **insight**. It is how Helen Keller solved the mystery of language. In solving problems through insight, people gradually increase their focus on those concepts important to the solution, even though they are not yet aware of the solution itself. Similar to how slowly gathering clouds eventually lead to a sudden lightning flash, slowly building cognitive associations may eventually lead to a flash of insight.

insight A problem-solving strategy that involves a sudden realization of how a problem can be solved

CHECKPOINT *Name four problem-solving strategies.*

CLOSER LOOK

Heuristics Allow for Quick Decision Making

Following the terrorist attacks on September 11, 2001, many Americans were afraid to fly on commercial airlines. Instead of flying, people began driving their cars cross-country. In deciding to travel by car rather than by plane, they based their judgments on the *availability heuristic*. This is the tendency to judge the frequency or probability of an event in terms of how easy it is to think of examples of that event.

In using the availability heuristic, the most important factor for people is not the content of their memory but how easily this content comes to mind. Because people could easily recall the horrible images of September 11, they decided that car travel was safer than plane travel. These judgments were made despite data from the National Safety Council showing that, mile for mile, Americans are almost 40 times more likely to die in a motor vehicle crash than on a commercial flight. In this case, using the availability heuristic actually caused many Americans to increase their safety risks when traveling.

You generally recall your own personal qualities, interests, and opinions from memory easily. This helps explain why you often tend to believe that other people share your views and opinions more than they actually do. This type of thinking, brought about by the availability heuristic, may cause people to make false judgments.

Think Critically
Explain two other instances in which people may have based their decision on availability heuristics.

Obstacles to Problem Solving

Psychologists have identified a number of ways of thinking that can block effective problem solving. For instance, when you think you have a solution to a problem, you may experience **confirmation bias**. This is the tendency to seek only information that supports your beliefs. Such selective attention often prevents you from realizing that your solution is incorrect.

How might this tendency to look for confirming information lead to incorrect social beliefs? In one experiment, psychologists asked some students to find out whether the person they were about to talk to was an introvert. Other students were asked to find out whether the person was an extravert. Consistent with the confirmation bias, the questions that students asked were biased in the direction of the original question. If they had been asked to find out whether the person was an introvert, they asked questions such as, "What do you dislike about loud parties?" In the extravert condition, they asked questions such as, "How do you liven things up at a party?" Because most people can recall both introverted and extraverted times from their past, the persons' answers provided evidence that confirmed either personality trait. Such confirmation seeking can lead to mistakes when forming impressions about people.

Another common obstacle to problem solving is the **mental set**. This is the tendency to continue using solutions that have worked in the past, even though better solutions may exist. The influence a mental set can have on problem solving often is demonstrated in the "water-jar problems" shown in Figure 14-3. In the first task, using a 21-cup jar, a 127-cup jar, and a 3-cup jar, people are asked to measure out exactly 100 cups of water. With little effort, most people discovered that the

confirmation bias Tendency to seek only information that supports your beliefs

mental set Tendency to continue using solutions that have worked in the past, even though better solutions may exist

---

Figure 14-3 **THE WATER-JAR PROBLEMS**

In each problem, what is the most efficient way of measuring out the correct amount of water using jars A, B, and/or C?

Problem	Amount Held by Each Jar			Required Amount (Cups)
	Jar A	Jar B	Jar C	
1	21	127	3	100
2	14	163	25	99
3	18	43	10	5
4	14	46	5	22
5	20	57	4	29
6	23	49	3	20
7	15	39	3	18

Answer to algorithm problem from page 423: PSYCHOLOGY

solution was to fill the largest jar (B), and from it fill the second-largest jar (A) once and the smallest jar (C) twice. Try solving the remaining problems in Figure 14-3 before reading further.

Did you run into a mental set? By discovering that you can use the basic algorithm B − A − 2C to solve all the remaining problems, you may miss the simpler solutions for problem 6 (B − C) and problem 7 (B + C). Although mental sets can lead to solutions, they also can lead to "mental ruts" when the situation changes and old methods are no longer effective.

The last common obstacle to problem solving is **functional fixedness**. This is our tendency to think of objects as functioning in fixed and unchanging ways and ignoring other ways in which they might be used. In problem solving, when you are unable to consider using familiar objects in unusual ways—for example, using a dime as a screwdriver—you are experiencing this cognitive obstacle. In one study of functional fixedness, participants were given a small cardboard box of tacks, some matches, and a candle (see Figure 14-4). Their task was to mount the candle on a bulletin board in such a way that it would burn without dripping wax on the floor.

functional fixedness
The tendency to think of objects as functioning in fixed and unchanging ways and ignoring other ways in which they might be used

Figure 14-4 **THE CANDLE PROBLEM**

When supplied with the materials in the box on the far left, many people cannot figure out how to mount a candle on a bulletin board so it will not drip wax when lit. How is this candle problem an example of functional fixedness?

Many participants could not solve the problem because they thought of the box as simply a container for tacks, not as a support for a candle. Later research found that when describing the task, if the experimenter used the term *box of tacks* rather than just *tacks,* more solutions were reached. This suggests that when a person hears the word *box,* many ways of using a box may be activated from memory, thus making a solution more likely. In general, the more experience a person has with an object, the greater the likelihood of experiencing functional fixedness with this object.

An important aspect of many decisions is to critically analyze options and hazards. Yet everyday experience tells us that not everyone approaches decision making looking for a challenge. Spend a few minutes completing the Self-Discovery feature below, which contains a self-report scale that measures your motivation to think, called the *need for cognition*.

CHECKPOINT *What are three obstacles to problem solving?*

SELF-DISCOVERY

Do You Have a High or Low Need for Cognition?

The *need for cognition* refers to a person's tendency to enjoy cognitive challenges. People high in the need for cognition (high NFC) like to work on difficult cognitive tasks and analyze situations. In contrast, individuals with a low need for cognition (low NFC) are more likely to take mental shortcuts and avoid effortful thinking unless required to do so.

Need-for-Cognition Scale: Sample Items

1. I really enjoy a task that involves coming up with new solutions to problems.
2. Thinking is not my idea of fun.
3. The notion of thinking abstractly is appealing to me.
4. I like tasks that require little thought once I've learned them.
5. I usually end up deliberating about issues even when they do not affect me personally.
6. It's enough for me that something gets the job done; I don't care how or why it works.
7. I prefer my life to be filled with puzzles that I must solve.
8. I only think as hard as I have to.

Instructions: If you agree with items 1, 3, 5, and 7 and disagree with items 2, 4, 6, and 8, you exhibit behaviors indicative of a person high in the need for cognition. If your responses to these items are exactly in the opposite direction, you may be low in the need for cognition. Based on your responses, which way do you lean?

Source: From "The Need for Cognition" by J. T. Cacioppo and R. E. Petty in *Journal of Personality and Social Psychology*, 1982, 42, 116–131 (Table 1, pp. 120–121). Copyright © 1982 by the American Psychological Association. Adapted with permission.

In Your Own Words

Analyze the following prototype: "Tall men with broad shoulders are good football players." Include information on how you think the prototype began, what makes it popular in the general public, and whether you agree or disagree with it and why.

Review Concepts

1. Which is a problem-solving strategy that involves a sudden realization of how a problem can be solved?

    a. algorithm   c. heuristic

    b. insight   d. trial and error

2. If you are unable to see that you can use a dime as a screwdriver, you are experiencing

    a. mental set   c. functional fixedness

    b. confirmation bias   d. need for cognition

3. Which refers to a mental grouping of objects, ideas, or events that share common properties?

    a. prototype   c. algorithm

    b. concept   d. mental set

4. **True or False** Your failure to categorize things correctly because they do not match your prototype for that concept can lead to errors in decision making.

5. **True or False** Trial and error is the first strategy you should try for solving problems because it usually guarantees success.

6. **True or False** All people approach decision making with an enthusiastic desire for cognitive challenges.

7. **True or False** Mental set is a common way to problem solve.

Think Critically

8. Why is it helpful to know more than one strategy to solve problems?

9. What happens when you fail to categorize things because they do not match your prototype for a concept?

10. Describe a situation in which trial-and-error problem solving would be effective and explain why it works in this situation.

11. Why would the ability to overcome functional fixedness help you in a problem-solving situation?

12. How might slowly building cognitive associations help you with solving problems?

13. Give an example of how your failure to categorize things properly can result in decision-making errors.

Biological Research Scientist

Biological research scientists study the human body and its functions to understand how people behave in, and react to, the environment. They may study how the nerve cells fire less frequently after high levels of stimulation or how vision affects behavior. Researchers also may study animals, an area of biology called zoology. Or they may study microscopic living organisms, called microbiology.

Biological research provides knowledge that allows researchers to develop solutions that help people, animals, and the environment. They may develop new drugs that help people with behavior problems. Other researchers may develop products that help people with disabilities, or medical tests to help determine illnesses or behavior problems associated with human biology.

Researchers also may work on genome projects to determine the purpose of different human genes. These researchers may discover genes that carry inherited health risks and behavior disorders.

Biological research scientists work for both governments and private businesses. The U.S. government funds medical research that relates to biological sciences. Many researchers who receive federal grants work at the National Institutes of Health. Private firms may include pharmaceutical companies.

Employment Outlook

Jobs for biological research scientists are expected to grow at an average rate over the next several years. This is a highly competitive field, so people entering this occupation should expect to see strong competition for jobs.

Needed Skills and Education

Educational requirements usually include a Ph.D. degree for people entering this career. In addition, most people in this profession have spent time working in a laboratory under the direction of a senior researcher. Jobs such as teaching future researchers, or as an assistant to a researcher, require a master's or a bachelor's degree.

People interested in a career as a biological research scientist should take courses in chemistry and biology. Other courses that are helpful are mathematics, physics, engineering, and computer science.

This career requires that researchers be able to work in a team as well as alone. Interpersonal relationship skills are helpful for researchers working with teams. Mathematical and computer science skills are helpful in recording data.

How You'll Spend Your Day

Biological research scientists work in laboratories in government-sponsored or industry-sponsored facilities. Hours are usually a regular 40-hour work week. However, with strong competition among researchers, many work longer hours on projects and work evenings and weekends.

Biological research scientists who study marine life are marine biologists. They may work in laboratories or on research ships. Some may even work underwater. These researchers must know how to scuba dive.

Earnings

The median earnings for biological research scientists is $76,320. Some researchers earn as little as $40,820 and some as high as $129,510. Earnings vary depending on the choice of specialty in this career.

What About You?

Is this a career you think you might enjoy? Use the library or Internet to research more about this career, and then write a fact sheet of your findings. At the end of the fact sheet, write a short paragraph that evaluates what you would most like and least like about this career.

©TATIANA BELOVA, 2009/USED UNDER LICENSE FROM SHUTTERSTOCK.COM

CHAPTER SUMMARY

14.1 The Nature of Language

- Broca's area and Wernicke's area, the two brain areas related to language production and language comprehension, are located in the left hemisphere.

- The three features of language are meaningfulness, displacement, and productivity.

- Language is structured around grammar, which has three major components: phonology, syntax, and semantics.

- Language does not determine a person's thinking, but psychologists do think language can influence thinking.

- Developed by linguist Benjamin Lee Whorf, the linguistic relativity hypothesis is a theory that the structure of language determines the structure of thought. This means that people who speak different languages also think differently.

14.2 Language Learning and Nonverbal Communication

- B. F. Skinner claimed that children begin life with no special ability to learn language and that language ability is shaped by adult reinforcement and punishment.

- Noam Chomsky proposed that children are born with a neural prewiring, called the language acquisition device, which enables them to learn language. A number of studies support the theory that humans are biologically predisposed to acquire language.

- The three stages of language development are cooing and babbling, single-word use, and two-word use.

- Nonverbal communication is the sending and receiving of information using gestures, expressions, vocal cues, and body movements.

- The face is one of the most important nonverbal channels of communication.

- People have the tendency to adopt the behaviors, postures, or mannerisms of others with whom they are interacting. This is called nonconscious mimicry.

14.3 Thinking and Problem Solving

- Concepts—a mental grouping of objects, ideas, or events that share common properties—are categorized into prototypes, the most representative members of the concepts.

- Four problem-solving strategies are trial and error, algorithms, heuristics, and insights.

- Psychologists have identified cognitive tendencies that act as barriers to problem solving. These include confirmation bias, mental set, and functional fixedness.

CHAPTER ASSESSMENT

Review Psychology Terms

Select the term that best fits the definition. Some terms will not be used.

_____ 1. The use of masculine nouns and pronouns to refer to all people, regardless of their gender

_____ 2. Sending and receiving information using gestures, expressions, and body movements rather than words

_____ 3. A mental grouping of objects, ideas, or events that share common properties

_____ 4. Rules about using sounds and words in a language

_____ 5. Adopting the behaviors, postures, or mannerisms of others with whom you are interacting without your awareness

_____ 6. An early speech phase in which children use short sentences, leaving out all but the important words

_____ 7. The most representative member of a concept

_____ 8. A theory that the structure of language determines the structure of thought, meaning that people who speak different languages also think differently

_____ 9. Speaking to babies with a high-pitched voice, using short sentences with clearly and slowly pronounced words

_____ 10. Thought process used to overcome obstacles and reach goals

_____ 11. Tendency to continue using solutions that have worked in the past, even though better solutions may exist

_____ 12. Tendency to think of objects as functioning in fixed and unchanging ways and ignoring other ways in which they might be used

_____ 13. The smallest units of language that carry meaning

_____ 14. Tendency to seek information that supports your beliefs

_____ 15. Chomsky's linguistic theory proposing that an inborn mental program enables children to learn language

a. child-directed speech

b. concept

c. confirmation bias

d. functional fixedness

e. generic masculine

f. grammar

g. language acquisition device

h. linguistic relativity hypothesis

i. mental set

j. morphemes

k. nonconscious mimicry

l. nonverbal communication

m. phonemes

n. problem solving

o. prototype

p. telegraphic speech

q. trial and error

Review Psychology Concepts

16. Analyze the following groups of words, phrases, or images and identify the unifying concepts: body division of head, thorax, and abdomen, with six legs and external skeleton; gives medical attention; riding in a cart on a rail up and down steep hills; hip hop, swing, two-step, Irish, ballet.

17. Define language and communication and explain the relationship between them.

18. Justify this statement: To fully develop language skills, children need to be exposed to competent language users.

19. List and define the three major components of grammar.

20. Classify the following as either a phoneme or a morpheme: _e_ in the; _th_ in the; _re_ in replay; _s_ in plans; _d_ in bid.

21. Compare and contrast the cooing and babbling stage of children of different cultures.

22. Read the following list of jobs, and then decide if the ideal candidate for the job would be someone with a high or low need for cognition: librarian; mathematician; electrician; politician; and assembly-line worker.

23. Explain why functional fixedness keeps you from solving problems.

24. Use information from the text to write an argument as to why all students should be required to learn a second language.

25. Identify Carl Wernicke, explain Wernicke's aphasia, and describe what Wernicke's aphasia causes.

26. Explain the difference between displacement among humans and displacement among animals. What role does displacement play in keeping scientists from classifying communication among animals as being language?

Apply Psychology Concepts

27. Contrast Skinner's learning theory of language acquisition and Chomsky's language acquisition device. Which theory do you support, and why?

28. Think of a time when you experienced confirmation bias about a person or a group and write an analysis of your experience. Include what made you realize you were seeing only the information that would support your beliefs and explain how the realization changed your beliefs about the person or group. For example, you might write about how you thought a young person did not like you because she was always quiet around you, and then you found out she was shy. Or, you might write about an experience you had with teens who dressed differently from you and you thought they were strange, but when you got to know them, you learned they were really nice.

29. Create a paragraph describing your last vacation using only gendered terms.

30. If you teach your dog to bark when you give the command to speak, are you teaching your dog language? Explain your answer.

Make Academic Connections

31. **Language Arts** Using the library or Internet, research the life of Noam Chomsky and write a short biography about the man and his work on the language acquisition device. When using the Internet for research, use only acceptable research sources, such as educational or government sites.

32. **Debate** Hold a debate as to which is the best way to solve problems. One side should argue that using algorithms is best; the other side should argue that using heuristics is best.

33. **Research** Interview a parent or pre-school teacher to learn their ideas about how children learn language. Give an oral report on your findings.

34. **Sociology and History** Use the library or Internet to find an article written in the 1950s about careers. Copy a few paragraphs from the piece. Circle all the generic masculine words. Rewrite the paragraphs omitting the generic masculine words.

35. **Writing** Use the Internet or library to research Benjamin Lee Whorf's work on the linguistic relativity hypothesis. Write an essay that describes your opinion of his work. Provide details of why you do or do not agree with him.

Logically speaking, it makes sense that studies now suggest feelings can directly affect the cognitive tasks of reasoning. Positive emotions can have a positive impact on thought processing, while negative emotions—especially stress—can have the opposite effect. According to Richard Restak, the author of the study, this is why it is important to avoid mood swings, especially when working and concentrating. Access the Gale Psychology eCollection at *www.cengage.com/school/psych/franzoi* and read the description of Restak's research and findings. Write a summary of the article and answer the question: Why do you think your mood affects your thinking? As an additional project, write a story about a person whose reasoning is affected by his or her mood.

Source: Perina, Kaja. "Mood swing: how feelings help and hurt. (Emotion)." *Psychology Today* 35.3 (May–June 2002): 17(2).

SELF-DISCOVERY: YOUR SCORE

Do You Have a High or Low Need for Cognition?

Interpretation: People with a high need for cognition are more likely than those low in the need for cognition to critically analyze advertisements before making consumer purchases and before voting for presidential candidates in elections. This more effortful thinking results in people with a high need for cognition being more informed about their possible choices than those who are lazier thinkers.

Although high-NFC persons are more likely to critically analyze information when making decisions than are low-NFC persons, this is no guarantee that they will actually do so all the time. Even people who enjoy critical thinking will engage in lazy thinking when they conclude that the decisions they face have little importance to their lives. On the other hand, people who typically are lazy thinkers can become critical thinkers if the decision is personally important to them.

States of Consciousness

ESSENTIAL QUESTION
Go to page XXVI

"Conscious and unconscious experiences do not belong to different compartments of the mind; they form a continuous scale of gradations, of degrees of awareness."

—ARTHUR KOESTLER, BRITISH AUTHOR, 1905–1983

The discovery that changed the course of sleep research occurred in 1952. College graduate student Eugene Aserinsky was testing an electroencephalograph (EEG), which measures the level of electrical activity in the brain, on his sleeping eight-year-old son. While watching his son, Aserinsky saw something he had never noticed before. About every 90 minutes, the boy's eyes darted about behind his closed lids. These eye movements had all the characteristics of someone who was awake. The scientific thought in the 1950s was that the brain was quiet and at rest during sleep, which would mean no eye movement. Aserinsky was even more surprised when he awakened his son during these eye-movement episodes, and the boy said he had been dreaming.

The next day Aserinsky told his professor, Nathaniel Kleitman, about the eye movements. The professor thought Aserinsky had misread the EEG machine. Professor Kleitman and Aserinsky tested other sleeping people and found the same results—eye movement during sleep. Their discovery dramatically changed scientists' ideas about sleep and consciousness.

15.1 | Consciousness and Body Rhythms

OBJECTIVES

- Define consciousness.
- Describe daily body rhythms.

KEY TERMS

- consciousness
- circadian rhythms

DISCOVER IT | *How does this relate to me?*

Can you recall being surprised by unusual states of mind that occurred while you were awake? Are these normal and unusual states the same for everyone, or do you experience your own unique consciousness? Is consciousness one thing or many things? Luckily, scientists have explored these questions, and their discoveries will become yours as you follow their footprints in this part of your journey.

I n the late 1800s, William James and other psychologists considered the study of consciousness central to the science of psychology. This changed in 1913 when behaviorism, with its focus on observable behavior, ruled that consciousness was not a proper area of scientific study. By the 1950s, psychology refocused its attention on consciousness, largely due to the discoveries of such pioneers as Aserinsky and Kleitman, whom you read about in the chapter opening. This generation of scientists asked, "What is consciousness?"

What Is Consciousness?

Psychologists define **consciousness** as awareness of yourself and your surroundings. This is a simple definition for a complex psychological process with different qualities. What are the main qualities of consciousness?

Consciousness is *subjective,* which means you cannot share your consciousness with another person. Your consciousness is something only you experience. Consciousness is *selective,* which means you can be aware of some things while ignoring others. Consciousness is *divided,* which means you can pay attention to two different things at once. Consciousness is *continuous*, which means each moment of consciousness blends into the next moment. Consciousness is *changing*, which means what you are aware of now shifts within seconds to awareness of other things. Consciousness is *multi-leveled,* with ranges from an alert and focused awareness to the relative stupor of deep sleep. Table 15-1 reviews these qualities.

> **consciousness**
> Awareness of yourself and your surroundings

Table 15-1 QUALITIES OF CONSCIOUSNESS

Consciousness is...	
Subjective	You cannot share it with another person.
Selective	You can be aware of some things while ignoring others.
Divided	You can pay attention to two different things at once.
Continuous	Each moment of consciousness blends into the next moment.
Changing	Your awareness normally shifts to other things within seconds.
Multi-leveled	Ranges from an alert awareness to the relative stupor of deep sleep.

CHECKPOINT ⟩ *What is consciousness?*

Daily Body Rhythms

Humans have a regular cycle of sleep and wakefulness that corresponds to physiological changes including body temperature, blood pressure, and hormone levels. These regular bodily rhythms that occur on a 24-hour cycle are known as **circadian rhythms**. Circadian rhythms control when you wake up and when you settle into sleep. As shown in Figure 15-1 below, body temperature rises in the early morning, peaks at midday, and then drops one to two hours prior to sleep. Body temperature influences feelings of alertness, so you generally feel most alert late in the afternoon or early evening.

STUDYING CIRCADIAN RHYTHMS

In early studies of circadian rhythms, participants were kept in labs without windows or clocks that would indicate the time of day. Findings from these studies suggested that in the absence of daylight and time cues, circadian rhythms appeared

circadian rhythms Regular bodily rhythms that occur on a 24-hour cycle

Figure 15-1 CIRCADIAN RHYTHMS

As core body temperature changes, a person's level of alertness also changes. Based on this graph, what happens to your alertness as your core body temperature drops?

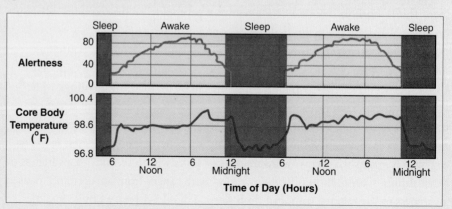

to be a 25-hour cycle. Recently, however, researchers discovered that all the previous research testing the 25-hour cycle hypothesis had created the effect accidentally.

In these early studies, the artificial light used in the labs was bright enough to reset participants' sleep–wake cycle causing their brains' circadian pacemaker to keep them alert and awake longer than normal. Over many days, their sleep–wake cycle seemed to drift to 25 hours. However, when the lights were dimmed so that participants' sleep–wake cycle was not reset, their true circadian cycle was found to be about 24 hours. This research demonstrates how science is self-correcting. In the journey of discovery, scientists sometimes follow false paths, but the critical analysis that drives this search eventually reveals past mistakes.

How does the brain reset your biological clock? A small area of the hypothalamus and the hormone *melatonin* are involved in resetting your body's sleep–wake cycle. Researchers found that a synthetic form of melatonin helps people who have difficulty sleeping. A gene in the hypothalamus—which scientists named "clock"—helps control the internal clock. Discovery of this gene may help reset people's internal clocks to treat disruptions in circadian rhythms, such as insomnia and depression.

JET LAG AND CIRCADIAN RHYTHMS

You can disturb your circadian rhythms when you travel by jet through a number of time zones. Your degree of *jet lag* depends on whether you fly westward or eastward (see Figure 15-2). When flying westward—say, from London to Detroit—your regular sleep cycle is pushed back 5 hours (a *phase delay*), so that your 24-hour

Figure 15-2 CIRCADIAN RHYTHMS AND JET LAG

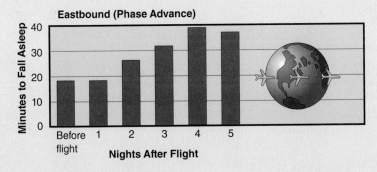

In one study, people who flew eastward through five time zones (phase advance) had increased difficulty falling asleep following their arrival. In contrast, travelers who flew westward through five time zones (phase delay) experienced no sleep difficulties.

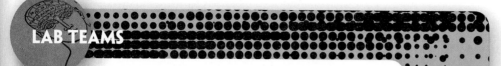

Resetting Your Circadian Clock

Studies estimate it takes 24 hours for each hour of time change to reset your circadian clock. With a partner, research time zones. Then calculate how many time zones you would fly through in each of the following journeys and determine what sort of jet lag you might experience: Ohio to mainland Alaska; Washington, D.C., to Hawaii; Colorado to Oregon; London, England, to Detroit, Michigan. On which of these trips do you think you would experience the most intense and long-lasting jet lag? Which trip should have the least effect?

day is stretched to 29 hours. The jet lag resulting from such east–west travel is easier to adjust to than eastward-induced jet lag. Why?

Phase delays fit better with many people's habit of stretching out their waking time to the limits of the 24-hour sleep–wake cycle. In contrast, flying eastward across five time zones results in your day being shortened to 19 hours (a *phase advance*). This change conflicts with people's day-stretching habits.

> **CHECKPOINT** *What are circadian rhythms?*

15.1 ASSESSMENT

In Your Own Words

List and define the six main qualities of consciousness and give an example for each from your life. As an example of the *subjective* quality, you might say that you tell your best friend everything, but your friend cannot get inside you to understand your awareness of your experiences.

Review Concepts

1. Circadian rhythms occur on a _____ basis.
   - a. hourly
   - b. yearly
   - c. daily
   - d. weekly

2. **True or False** Consciousness is a complex psychological process.

Think Critically

3. Explain the biological reason for why you usually feel more alert late in the afternoon or early evening.

4. When your consciousness is divided, you can be doing one thing and thinking of something else. Give an example of when it is all right to divide your consciousness. Give an example of when it is not all right to divide your consciousness.

OBJECTIVES

- Explain the stages of sleep.
- Explain why people need sleep and how much sleep is needed.
- Identify three explanations for dreaming.
- Identify five sleep disorders.

DISCOVER IT | *How does this relate to me?*

Do you remember your dreams? Do you think your dreams are unique to you? Did you know that many people have similar dreams? Most people have experienced a sensation of falling or flying while dreaming. Sleep and dreaming are fascinating, and psychologists are always learning new things about this inner-world experience.

KEY TERMS

- altered state of consciousness
- beta waves
- alpha waves
- theta waves
- delta waves
- REM sleep
- dreams
- off-line dream theory
- activation-synthesis theory
- night terror
- sleepwalking
- narcolepsy
- sleep apnea

You dream when you are sleeping. Sleep is an **altered state of consciousness**, which is an awareness of yourself and your surroundings that is noticeably different from your normal state of consciousness. The most common altered state is *sleep,* a non-waking state of consciousness in which you typically remain motionless and are only slightly responsive to your surroundings.

Stages of Sleep

About every 90 or 100 minutes of sleep, you cycle through distinct stages, each associated with a different pattern of brain activity (see Figure 15-3, page 440). While awake, the two most common EEG patterns are beta waves and alpha waves. **Beta waves** are very fast, low-amplitude brain waves associated with an active, alert state of mind. **Alpha waves** are fast, low-amplitude brain waves associated with a relaxed, wakeful state of mind.

altered state of consciousness An awareness of yourself and your surroundings that is noticeably different from your normal state of consciousness

beta waves Very fast, low-amplitude brain waves associated with an active, alert state of mind

alpha waves Fast, low-amplitude brain waves associated with a relaxed, wakeful state of mind

Figure 15-3 EEG BRAIN WAVE PATTERNS

The regular beta and alpha waves associated with normal waking consciousness are different from the brain wave patterns typical of the stages of NREM and REM sleep.

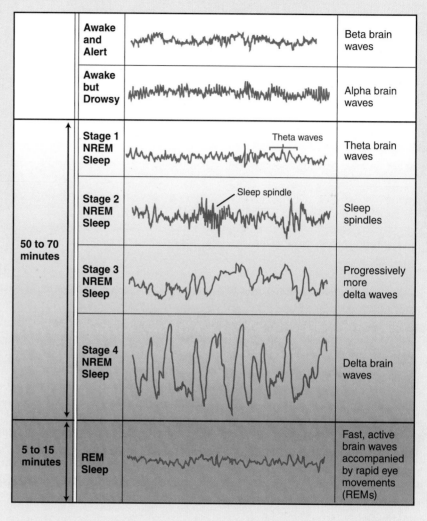

	Awake and Alert		Beta brain waves
	Awake but Drowsy		Alpha brain waves
50 to 70 minutes	**Stage 1 NREM Sleep**	Theta waves	Theta brain waves
	Stage 2 NREM Sleep	Sleep spindle	Sleep spindles
	Stage 3 NREM Sleep		Progressively more delta waves
	Stage 4 NREM Sleep		Delta brain waves
5 to 15 minutes	**REM Sleep**		Fast, active brain waves accompanied by rapid eye movements (REMs)

NREM SLEEP

As you enter the light sleep of stage 1, the alpha-wave EEG pattern changes to smaller, rapid, irregular **theta waves**. Stage 1 sleep is a transition between wakefulness and deeper sleep and lasts only a few minutes. Heart rate and breathing slow as body temperature drops and muscles relax. During stage 1 sleep, people have sensations of falling or floating and visual and auditory hallucinations. You wake up easily in stage 1. Stage 2 lasts about 20 minutes and is characterized by *sleep spindles,* which are bursts of rapid, rhythmic brain-wave activity. Muscle tension is reduced. Talking in your sleep can occur during any stage, but it first occurs during stage 2. Sleep talking can be quite loud, ranging from simple sounds to long speeches. In stage 3, you begin to move into the deeper form of *slow-wave sleep* and **delta waves**. These brain waves are high in amplitude and slow in frequency. They become more pronounced in the deep sleep of stage 4, during which it is difficult to wake up.

theta waves Irregular, small, rapid brain waves associated with stage 1 sleep

delta waves Slow, high-amplitude brain waves most typical of stage 4 deep sleep

Typically, 50 to 70 minutes pass from the beginning of stage 1 to the end of stage 4. These four stages make up *NREM sleep,* or non-rapid-eye-movement sleep. Then the cycle reverses itself, and you move back up through the stages to stage 2, where you spend about half the night. NREM sleep is called *quiet sleep* because of the slow, regular breathing; slow, regular brain activity; and little or no dreaming. The term *quiet sleep* is misleading, however, because snoring is most likely to occur during NREM sleep.

REM SLEEP

As shown in Figure 15-4 below, once you enter stage 2, you rarely re-enter stage 1. Instead, you move on to a different kind of sleep where your brain waves are more rapid. Your heart rate and breathing increase and eyes dart back and forth behind closed eyelids. Dreaming occurs in this stage. This *active sleep* is called **REM (rapid eye movement) sleep.** You have four or five sleep cycles a night, each lasting about 90 minutes.

REM sleep is important to our health. Participants in sleep studies who are deprived of REM sleep (by being awakened when they begin rapid eye movements), report feeling tired and experience *REM rebound,* meaning they spend more time in REM sleep the next night. Studies also show that people who experience prolonged REM sleep deprivation have greater difficulty remembering recently learned material.

REM (rapid eye movement) sleep
Active phase in the sleep cycle during which dreaming occurs, characterized by rapid eye movements

Figure 15-4 **THE FIRST 90 MINUTES OF SLEEP**

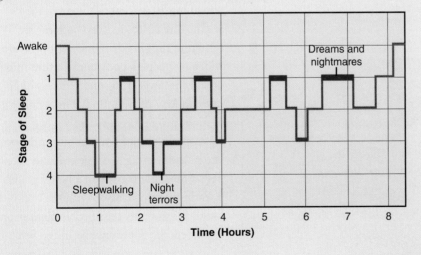

Most people follow regular sleep cycles each night that last about 90 minutes. They consist of four NREM stages followed by REM sleep. Based on this figure, what can you conclude about the length of time that you spend in REM sleep as the night progresses?

CHECKPOINT *Identify the brain activity associated with the four stages of sleep.*

Why Sleep?

Sleep is essential in maintaining health, allowing the body to restore itself from the demands of daily activity. After about 18 hours of wakefulness, reaction time slows from a quarter to half a second. You experience bouts of *microsleep* in which you momentarily tune out surroundings. If you are reading a book while this happens, you might only have to reread a paragraph. However, if you are driving a car, the consequences can be serious. After 20 hours of wakefulness, reaction time is equivalent to someone who is considered legally intoxicated, and your ability to remember things diminishes. Studies suggest that children, aged two to five years, who fail to get enough sleep, are at greater risk for behavior problems.

The amount of sleep you need partly depends on your age and declines throughout your life cycle. Newborns sleep approximately 16 hours, children average between 9 and 12 hours, and adolescents average about 7.5 hours. Newborns and young children have the highest percentage of REM sleep. Many sleep experts believe the increased brain activity during REM sleep helps develop new connections between neurons.

In adulthood, both the quantity and the quality of sleep usually decrease, especially among the elderly. Less time is spent in slow-wave stage 4 deep sleep and a greater proportion of stage 1 sleep occurs. This results in waking up more frequently. Although stage 4 sleep declines, the percentage of REM sleep remains fairly constant throughout adulthood, diminishing only in later life.

Have you heard the terms *morning people* and *night people*? Morning people wake up early, alert, and full of energy, but go to bed before 10:00 P.M. Night people stay up later in the evening and have a hard time getting up early in the morning. About 25 percent of the population are night people, 25 percent are morning people, and the remaining 50 percent fall between the two.

The differences in sleep patterns are related to the circadian body temperatures. Morning people's body temperature rises quickly on awakening and remains high until about 7:30 P.M. Body temperature of night people rises gradually when they wake, peaks at midday, and begins dropping late in the evening. College students identified as morning people earn better grades in early-morning classes, with the opposite found for students classified as night people. Complete the questionnaire in the Self-Discovery feature on page 443 to determine whether you are a night person or a morning person.

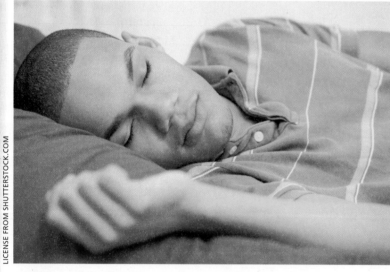

Sleep is a time when you exhibit little physical movement and are unresponsive to your surroundings.

Lack of sufficient sleep is a common problem with students, especially while studying for exams. Experiments find that people lose some of their ability to concentrate and think creatively after only one

Are You a Morning Person or a Night Person?

Instructions: Respond to the following items by answering either "Day" or "Evening."

1. I prefer to work during the	Day	Evening
2. I enjoy leisure-time activities most during the	Day	Evening
3. I feel most alert during the	Day	Evening
4. I get my best ideas during the	Day	Evening
5. I have my highest energy during the	Day	Evening
6. I prefer to take classes during the	Day	Evening
7. I prefer to study during the	Day	Evening
8. I feel most intelligent during the	Day	Evening
9. I am most productive during the	Day	Evening
10. When I graduate, I would prefer to find a job with _____ hours.	Day	Evening

See page 465 for scoring instructions.

Source: From "Day persons, night persons, and variability in hypnotic susceptibility" by B. Wallace in *Journal of Personality and Social Psychology*, 1993, 64, 827–833 (Appendix, p.833). Copyright © 1993 by the American Psychological Association. Adapted with permission.

night of not sleeping. Engaging in long hours of continuous studying before exams actually may lower academic performance. Complete the questionnaire in the Self-Discovery feature on page 446 to determine whether you are getting enough sleep.

CHECKPOINT > *Why is sleep important?*

Dream Theories

Dreams are story-like sequences of visual images experienced during sleep. Everybody dreams. People awakened from REM sleep report dreaming 78 percent of the time and 14 percent of the time during NREM sleep.

While dreaming, most people are not aware they are dreaming. However, about one out of ten people occasionally have *lucid dreams,* in which they are aware that they are dreaming. Such dreams can be very enjoyable because the lucid dreamer is often able to change the dream while it is happening. Three theories in psychology explain dreaming as wish fulfillment, information-processing, and interpreted brain activity.

dreams Story-like sequences of visual images experienced during sleep

DREAMS AS WISH FULFILLMENT

The most famous dream theory in psychology is the psychoanalytic theory of Sigmund Freud, who said dreams are disguised wishes of the unconscious mind. The dreamer remembers the surface meaning, or *manifest content,* of the dream. The true meaning of the dream, or *latent content,* is hidden from the dreamer to avoid anxiety. Dreams are constructed to express desires in a confusing symbolic manner to protect the dreamer's peace of mind and ability to sleep.

DREAMS AS INFORMATION-PROCESSING

A second theory is the **off-line dream theory**. This theory states that dreaming combines and stores information gathered during the day, allowing your brain to work more efficiently. While dreaming, the brain integrates new information with memories and experiences. Research shows that both humans and animals spend more time in REM sleep after learning difficult material. If denied REM sleep, less learning occurs. Some neuroscientists think that if humans did not have off-line time, they would need larger forebrains to handle daily learning experiences.

DREAMS AS INTERPRETED BRAIN ACTIVITY

A third theory argues that dreaming is just a by-product of brain activity. This **activation-synthesis theory** states that a dream is the forebrain's attempt to interpret random neural activity coming from the midbrain during sleep. The uppermost portion of the forebrain is the brain's thinking center and consists of the left and right cerebral hemispheres. According to activation-synthesis theory, the left hemisphere is the brain's interpreter. It makes sense out of information and creates dream plots. The right hemisphere constructs the dream's visual features. The resulting dream made from this random brain activity has a personal touch unique to the dreamer because it is based on available memories, but the dream has no real or hidden meaning.

These three dream theories are summarized in Table 15-2 on page 445. There is no agreement on the cause or meaning of dreams. All the theories do agree that the content of dreams is associated with the dreamer's experiences, daily concerns, and interests. Exploring your unconscious world may help you better understand your conscious life.

off-line dream theory
A theory that dreaming is a time for consolidating and storing information gathered during the day

activation-synthesis theory A theory that dreaming is the forebrain's attempt to interpret random neural activity coming from the midbrain during sleep

Like humans, all mammals and some birds have REM sleep, but fish, reptiles, and amphibians do not. It is possible that those animals that engage in REM sleep also have dreams.

©NGO THYE AUN, 2009/USED UNDER LICENSE FROM SHUTTERSTOCK.COM

Table 15-2 **DREAM THEORIES**

Theory	Explanation	Meaning of Dream	Is Meaning of Dream Hidden?
Psychoanalytic	Dreams are anxiety-producing wishes originating in the unconscious mind.	Latent content of dream reveals unconscious wishes.	Yes, by manifest content of dreams
Off-line	Dreaming consolidates and stores information input during the day, allowing you to have a smaller and more efficient brain.	Previous day's experiences are reprocessed in dreams.	Not necessarily
Activation-synthesis	Dreams are the forebrain's attempt to interpret random neural activity.	Dream content is only vaguely related to your daily experiences, but there is little, if any, meaning in the dream.	No real meaning to hide

CHECKPOINT ▶ *What are three theories that explain dreaming?*

Sleep Disorders

Problems related to sleep are among the most common psychological disorders, but often are under diagnosed and under treated. In the United States, 50 to 70 million people suffer from some form of chronic sleep problem. The most common sleep disorder is *insomnia,* the chronic inability to fall or stay asleep.

A sleep disorder among children three to eight years old is a **night terror**—a panic attack during stage 4 NREM sleep. Victims sit up in bed, scream, stare into space, and talk without making sense. They seldom wake and have little memory of the event. Night terrors are not *nightmares,* which are common, anxiety-producing dreams that occur during REM sleep among adults and children. An immature nervous system might be the cause of night terrors. This disorder is treated with prescription drugs.

Sleepwalking is a disorder in which a person wanders during early-night NREM sleep. Sleepwalkers are not acting out a dream. It is not dangerous to wake a sleepwalker, although it may be difficult because they are in stage 4 sleep. This disorder is more common among children than adults, and more common among boys than girls. Most children outgrow the problem. Drug therapy can reduce sleepwalking.

A more serious sleep disorder is **narcolepsy**, characterized by uncontrollable REM sleep during waking hours. About 250,000 Americans suffer from narcolepsy. The cause is unknown, but people who have narcolepsy in their families are 50 times more likely to develop it, which suggests that genetic factors play a role. A narcoleptic episode is often triggered by strong emotions or sudden physical effort. Naps reduce the frequency of narcoleptic episodes, and stimulant drugs can control this disorder.

night terror A panic attack that generally occurs during early-night stage 4 NREM sleep in children between the ages of three and eight

sleepwalking A disorder in which a person wanders during early-night NREM sleep

narcolepsy A sleep disorder characterized by uncontrollable REM sleep attacks during normal waking hours

Another disorder with a possible hereditary cause is **sleep apnea**. People with this disorder briefly stop breathing several times an hour during sleep. About 12 million Americans suffer from this disorder, with overweight men over 40 the most common victims. Apnea sufferers report daytime sleepiness, morning head-aches, and occasional heart and lung problems. The loss of sleep affects sufferers' waking reaction time. Apnea may be treated by weight loss, a change of sleeping positions, use of a nasal mask to increase air intake, hormone therapy, or surgery to open partly blocked airways.

CHECKPOINT *What are five sleeping disorders?*

SELF-DISCOVERY

Are You Getting Enough Sleep?

Instructions: The following questionnaire measures your sleep needs. To determine whether you might be suffering from sleep deprivation, answer true or false to the following items regarding your current life experiences.

1. It's a struggle for me to get out of bed in the morning.	True	False
2. I need an alarm clock to wake up at the appropriate time.	True	False
3. Weekday mornings I hit the snooze bar several times to get more sleep.	True	False
4. I often sleep extra hours on weekend mornings.	True	False
5. I often need a nap to get through the day.	True	False
6. I have dark circles around my eyes.	True	False
7. I feel tired, irritable, and stressed out during the week.	True	False
8. I have trouble concentrating and remembering.	True	False
9. I feel slow with critical thinking, problem solving, and being creative.	True	False
10. I often fall asleep in boring meetings or lectures or in warm rooms.	True	False
11. I often feel drowsy while driving.	True	False
12. I often fall asleep watching TV.	True	False
13. I often fall asleep after heavy meals.	True	False
14. I often fall asleep while relaxing after dinner.	True	False
15. I often fall asleep within five minutes of getting into bed.	True	False

See page 465 for scoring instructions.

In Your Own Words

Choose one of the four objectives on page 439. Explain how that objective is met in the text and how the subject relates to your life. You might discuss the four stages of sleep, and explain that you need to go through all four stages at night so you can perform well in school each day.

Review Concepts

1. Which refers to the active phase in the sleep cycle characterized by rapid eye movements and during which dreaming occurs?

    a. beta waves   c. alpha waves

    b. REM sleep   d. stage 1 sleep

2. Which theory proposes that dreams are disguised wishes of the unconscious mind?

    a. Freud's   c. off-line dream theory

    b. online dream theory   d. activation-synthesis theory

3. Which refers to a sleep disorder characterized by a person wandering during early-night NREM sleep?

    a. narcolepsy   c. sleep apnea

    b. night terror   d. sleepwalking

4. **True or False** Both night terrors and nightmares are common, anxiety-producing dreams that occur during REM sleep among adults and children.

5. **True or False** Alpha waves are fast, low-amplitude brain waves associated with a relaxed, wakeful state of mind.

6. **True or False** The off-line dream theory argues that dreaming is just a by-product of brain activity.

Think Critically

7. Is it dangerous to wake up a sleepwalker? Explain your answer.

8. Select one of the three dream theories and explain why you support it over the others.

9. Identify the brain wave associated with each of the following: (a) very fast, low-amplitude waves associated with an active, alert state of mind; (b) fast, low-amplitude brain waves associated with a relaxed, wakeful state; (c) irregular, small, rapid waves associated with stage 1 sleep; (d) slow, high-amplitude brain waves most typical of stage 4 deep sleep.

10. Identify what the letters NREM and REM stand for, and explain what they mean.

11. Identify each sleep disorder described here: (a) a panic attack during stage 4 NREM sleep that occurs among children three- to eight-years old; (b) a disorder that briefly causes breathing to stop several times an hour during sleep; (c) a disorder where a person wanders during early-night NREM sleep; (d) a disorder characterized by uncontrollable REM sleep during waking hours.

KEY TERMS

- hypnosis
- hypnotizability
- neodissociation theory
- social influence theory of hypnosis
- meditation

OBJECTIVES

- Explain hypnosis.
- Define meditation.

DISCOVER IT | *How does this relate to me?*

Stage hypnotists are popular entertainers at high school social events, such as after-prom parties. Yet what is hypnosis? Can anyone be hypnotized? Is meditation an altered state of consciousness or simply a relaxed state of mind? If you daydream in class or even doze off, is this a form of meditation? These are some of the questions psychologists have asked, and the issues you are about to explore.

I n 2600 B.C., the father of Chinese medicine, Wang Tai, described a trance-like medical technique where healers chanted while passing their hands over patients. Similar descriptions of healing trance states are found in ancient Hindu and Egyptian medical writings. In the eighteenth century, Austrian physician Franz Anton Mesmer used a technique he called *animal magnetism* to cure people's diseases. Mesmer's name became associated with this spellbound state of mind—*mesmerized.* The modern form of being mesmerized is hypnosis.

Hypnosis

Hypnosis is a state of altered attention and awareness in which a person is unusually responsive to suggestions. In American culture, the person being hypnotized sits quietly while listening to suggestions for deep relaxation from a hypnotist. This altered state of consciousness can be achieved with other techniques. One of these is *active alert induction,* which is inducing hypnosis while a person dances, spins, or even pedals a stationary bicycle.

hypnosis A state of altered attention and awareness in which a person is unusually responsive to suggestions

FEATURES OF HYPNOSIS

The following five features characterize people's awareness when hypnotized:

- *Enriched fantasy* The hypnotized person can readily imagine unusual situations that differ from normal reality.

- *Cognitive passivity* Instead of planning actions, the hypnotized person waits for the hypnotist to suggest thoughts or actions.

- *Heightened selective attention* The hypnotized person focuses attention on the hypnotist's voice and ignores other stimuli. Even pain that is unbearable during the normal waking state is tolerated through this focused attention.

- *Reduced reality testing* The hypnotized person tends to accept uncritically hallucinated experiences suggested by the hypnotist.

- *Posthypnotic amnesia* When instructed, the hypnotized person forgets all or most of what occurred during the hypnotic session. These memories are restored when the hypnotist later gives a prearranged signal.

PRACTICAL USES OF HYPNOSIS

Research demonstrates that hypnosis is an effective way to help people relax and reduce physical pain. Hypnotized patients can undergo surgery without pain and with less-than-normal bleeding. Brain-imaging studies suggest that hypnosis is effective in reducing pain because when hypnotized individuals are told to imagine pleasant sensations, the suggestion alters activity in the brain areas associated with pain. Hypnosis is not very effective in helping people stop smoking, perhaps because smoking is not only a well-learned habit, but the nicotine in tobacco is an addictive drug.

Various misconceptions about hypnosis exist, which scientific research has proven false. Check out the Closer Look feature on page 450 for a discussion of these misconceptions.

Stage hypnotists create a theater atmosphere when demonstrating this altered state. Such performances can lead to false beliefs about hypnosis.

False Beliefs About Hypnosis

Hypnosis has been used as entertainment, and this history has led to myths about this altered state of consciousness. A list follows of some of these misconceptions followed the discoveries made by scientific research:

- *Hypnotized people can be forced to violate their moral values.* There is no evidence that hypnosis causes people to act against their will.
- *Memory is more accurate under hypnosis.* Hypnosis can help people's memory, but also can result in people recalling events that never happened.
- *While hypnotized, people are much stronger than normal.* Hypnosis has no effect on strength.
- *Hypnosis acts like a truth serum, forcing people to tell the truth.* Hypnotized people can lie and keep secrets.
- *Hypnotized people can be age-regressed to relive childhood experiences.* Although hypnotized people may believe they have mentally returned to an earlier age, they typically display cognitive abilities far beyond those of a child.

Think Critically

What are some practical uses for hypnosis?

HYPNOTIZABILITY

Can anyone be hypnotized? People differ in their **hypnotizability**, which is the degree to which they can enter a deep hypnotic state. Individuals who are highly hypnotizable have the ability to concentrate totally on material outside themselves and to become absorbed in imaginative activities. Children are the most hypnotizable. Being able to fantasize is an important factor of hypnotizability, but this does not mean that highly hypnotizable people are more gullible than less hypnotizable people. Among adults, about 15 percent are highly hypnotizable, about 10 percent cannot be hypnotized at all, and the rest fall somewhere in between. Hypnotizability is a stable trait during adulthood.

THEORIES OF HYPNOSIS

Ernest Hilgard's **neodissociation theory** of hypnosis states that a hypnotized person has two streams of consciousness operating at the same time. One stream actively responds to suggestions and the other passively observes. Have you ever been so involved in a conversation with your family or friends during a meal that you forgot what the food tasted like or that you even ate? This divided consciousness during the normal waking state is similar to Hilgard's explanation of hypnosis.

hypnotizability The degree to which a person can enter a deep hypnotic state

neodissociation theory A theory that hypnosis is an altered state with two streams of consciousness operating at the same time, one actively responding to suggestions and the other passively observing

Not all scientists believe that hypnosis is truly an altered state of consciousness. These skeptics believe that hypnosis is a normal waking state in which suggestible people act as they think hypnotized people are supposed to act. According to this **social influence theory of hypnosis**, hypnotized people are not consciously faking that they are in an altered state, but instead convince themselves that they are in an altered state because they believe in the powers of hypnosis. Research does find that hypnosis is influenced by people's social expectations and a desire to please the hypnotist.

This debate about whether or not hypnosis is an altered state is still a matter of ongoing scientific inquiry. Some of the more bizarre or peculiar effects observed during hypnosis might be explained by people's expectations about hypnosis. Other effects—such as dramatic pain reduction and altered brain activity—suggest a truly altered state of consciousness. For our present purposes, we can safely conclude that the power of hypnosis does not reside in any mysterious qualities of the hypnotist but, rather, in the mind of the hypnotized.

CHECKPOINT *What is hypnosis?*

Meditation

Meditation refers to mental exercises that focus attention and increase awareness. Most types of meditation—such as *Zen, transcendental meditation,* and the *relaxation response*—teach people to focus attention on the breath or a single sound or image. Accomplished meditators show high-amplitude alpha waves, reduced oxygen consumption, and a slowed heart rate while meditating, all indicators of a deeply relaxed state.

Brain scans of experienced Buddhist meditators find that at the peak moment of meditation, brain areas involved in focused attention are very active. There is less brain activity in areas involved in keeping track of time and one's location in

social influence theory of hypnosis Hypnosis is a normal state of consciousness in which people act the way they think hypnotized persons are supposed to act

meditation Mental exercises that focus attention and increase awareness

Many who are active in yoga practice meditation. At the peak moment of their meditative state, the brain areas involved in their focused attention are very active.

© IOFOTO, 2009/USED UNDER LICENSE FROM SHUTTERSTOCK.COM

physical space. During peak meditative states, people may experience timelessness, a reduced awareness of their surroundings, and an increased sense of life's meaning and self-understanding.

Research shows that meditation is an effective treatment for insomnia, anxiety, depression, and drug abuse. It also improves the well-being among individuals living with life-threatening diseases. Other studies suggest that meditation may extend people's lives by reducing negative effects of heart disease and strengthening the immune system. If you would like to try a meditative exercise, follow the instructions in the Positive Psychology feature below.

CHECKPOINT *What is meditation?*

POSITIVE PSYCHOLOGY

How Can You Meditate?

Try the following exercise based on Herbert Benson's relaxation response technique. Memorize the steps before meditating:

1. Choose a word or short phrase (a mantra) that you can focus your attention on. It should be something that is calming to you, such as "love," "serenity," or "I am at peace." Do not concentrate too hard on the mantra; it should become only a faint idea at times.

2. As you repeat this mantra silently to yourself, breathe through your nose and pay attention to your breathing.

3. Continue this exercise for 10 to 20 minutes and maintain a passive attitude throughout. When your attention is distracted away from your mantra, do not get upset, but simply and gently refocus your mind.

4. If you find that this exercise is a pleasant experience, practice it once or twice daily. Pay attention to how you feel both before and after the exercise. Does this form of meditation relax you? Do you feel calmer?

Think Critically
What might you gain by learning to meditate?

Source: Adapted from Benson, H. (1975). *The Relaxation Response*. New York: Morrow.

15.3 ASSESSMENT

In Your Own Words

Define hypnosis and meditation. Do you think you could be hypnotized? Why or why not? Do you think you could benefit from meditating? Why or why not?

Review Concepts

1. Which feature characterizes people's awareness when hypnotized?
   - a. cognitive activity
   - b. enriched fantasy
   - c. neodissociation theory
   - d. memories of the session

2. Which can you achieve while dancing, spinning, pedaling a bicycle, or sitting quietly listening to relaxation suggestions?
   - a. hypnosis
   - b. meditation
   - c. heightened senses
   - d. acute sense of reality

3. Which group is the most hypnotizable?
   - a. adults
   - b. senior citizens
   - c. children
   - d. teenagers

4. Which of the following is a feature that characterizes a state of meditation?
   - a. altered consciousness
   - b. cognitive passivity
   - c. enriched fantasy
   - d. reduced reality testing

5. **True or False**   Active alert induction is a form of hypnosis.

6. **True or False**   Hypnotized people can be forced to violate their moral values.

7. **True or False**   Hypnotized patients can undergo surgery without pain and with less than normal bleeding.

8. **True or False**   All people are equally hypnotizable.

Think Critically

9. How did Franz Anton Mesmer's name become associated with hypnosis?

10. Which of the following is a misconception and which is a proven scientific discovery about hypnosis? (a) hypnotized people will violate their moral values; (b) hypnotized people can lie and keep secrets; (c) hypnosis has no effect on strength; (d) hypnosis can help people's memory, but also can result in people recalling events that never happened; (e) hypnotized people can be age-regressed and relive childhood experiences

11. Provide the feature that characterizes people's awareness when hypnotized for each of the following: (a) accepts hallucinated experiences suggested by the hypnotist; (b) waits for the hypnotist to suggest thoughts or actions; (c) focuses attention on the hypnotist's voice and ignores other stimuli; (d) forgets all or most of what occurred during the hypnotic session

12. Why might meditation be an effective treatment for insomnia, anxiety, depression, and drug abuse, and improve the well-being among individuals living with life-threatening illnesses?

15.4 Psychoactive Drugs

KEY TERMS

- psychoactive drugs
- drug abuse
- drug tolerance
- depressants
- alcoholism
- stimulants
- hallucinations
- hallucinogens
- LSD
- marijuana
- THC
- inhalants

OBJECTIVES

- Explain drug abuse and drug tolerance.
- Identify and assess psychoactive drugs including depressants, stimulants, hallucinogens, and inhalants.

DISCOVER IT | *How does this relate to me?*

What do you think about when you hear the word "drugs"? Antibiotics a doctor prescribes for strep throat? An aspirin you take for a headache? Do you consider the caffeine in coffee, tea, or cola a drug? Do you think the alcohol in beer or wine and the nicotine in cigarettes are drugs? Being educated about alcohol and other drugs and their effect on the human body, mind, and the cost to society, is very important.

Psychoactive drugs are chemicals that change mental processes and behavior. These drugs alter consciousness by attaching themselves to synaptic receptors in the brain and either block or stimulate neural activity.

Drug Abuse and Drug Tolerance

People who take drugs to the extent that it interferes with their behavior or social relationships have a problem with **drug abuse**, or *substance dependence*. Abuse of psychoactive drugs is a serious and costly social problem. It accounts for a third of all hospital admissions, a quarter of all deaths, and a majority of serious crimes. In the United States, medical and social costs of drug abuse exceed $240 billion a year, which is eight times more than the federal government spends on funding for medical research each year.

An effect of drug abuse is **drug tolerance**, which means greater amounts of the drug are necessary to produce the same effect once produced by a smaller dose. Drug tolerance leads to *physical dependence*. A person who is dependent on a drug needs it to function normally. When the drug is withdrawn, the body reacts to its absence, and unpleasant physical symptoms occur. These include chills, fever, diarrhea, and a runny nose. Drug use also causes *psychological dependence,* where the user experiences mental and emotional desires for the drug. Psychological dependence can continue after a person is no longer physically dependent on a drug.

psychoactive drugs Chemicals that change mental processes and behavior

drug abuse Continued drug use despite it interfering with the drug user's behavior or social relationships

drug tolerance An effect of drug abuse in which greater amounts of the drug are necessary to produce the same results once produced by a smaller dose

Types of Psychoactive Drugs

Psychoactive drugs often are used to alter consciousness. People take drugs both for medicinal and recreational purposes. The categories of psychoactive drugs discussed in this section include depressants, stimulants, hallucinogens, and inhalants.

DEPRESSANTS

Depressants are psychoactive drugs that slow down, or depress, the nervous system and decrease mental and physical activity. Depressants include alcohol, sedatives, tranquilizers, and narcotics.

Alcohol is the most widely used and abused depressant in the world. In the United States, two-thirds of all adults consume alcohol occasionally. Young people under the age of 20 consume a quarter of all alcohol in the United States. A national survey found that more than 30 percent of high school students "binge drink" at least once a month. This means that, during a two-hour period, males consume five or more drinks and females consume four or more drinks.

As a person consumes alcohol, blood alcohol levels rise, the brain becomes increasingly impaired, and body functions slow down. Alcohol reduces a person's awareness of both internal and external stimuli. (see Table 15-3) This drug is the leading cause of domestic violence and highway deaths in the general population. Teenagers who drink are two to five times more likely to argue, damage property, injure themselves, or be physically intimate. Drinking can lead to **alcoholism**, the tolerance and physical dependence resulting from alcohol abuse. Alcoholism causes liver and heart disease, stroke, memory loss, cancer, malnutrition, and loss of sexual interest. People who start drinking at a young age are likely to abuse alcohol as adults.

depressants Psychoactive drugs that slow down—or depress—the nervous system and decrease mental and physical activity

alcoholism The tolerance and physical dependence resulting from prolonged abuse of alcohol

Table 15-3 **BLOOD ALCOHOL LEVELS AND THEIR BEHAVIORAL EFFECTS**

Blood Alcohol Level*	Behavioral Effects
0.05%	Lowered alertness, impaired judgment, release of inhibitions
0.10%	Slowed reaction time, impaired motor function, less caution
0.15%	Large, consistent increases in reaction time
0.20%	Marked depression in sensory and motor capability
0.25%	Severe motor disturbance, impairment of sensory perceptions
0.30%	In a stupor but still conscious, no comprehension of surrounding events
0.35%	Surgical anesthesia, minimal level to cause death
0.40%	Lethal dose for half of all adults

*In milligrams of alcohol per 100 milliliters of blood.

STIMULANTS

Stimulants are drugs that speed up, or stimulate, the nervous system and increase mental and physical activity. Commonly used stimulants are caffeine and nicotine. Caffeine is in coffee, tea, cocoa, and colas. Nicotine is found in tobacco.

Moderate doses of caffeine fight off drowsiness. Large doses make a person jittery and anxious and cause insomnia. Caffeine withdrawal symptoms include headaches and depression.

Adults who smoke around children are exposing them to increased risk of respiratory diseases and other health problems.

© ELENA KOUPTSOVA-VASIC, 2009/USED UNDER LICENSE FROM SHUTTERSTOCK.COM

Nicotine increases mental alertness and elevates heart rate, respiration, and blood pressure. It reduces blood flow to the skin, causing a drop in skin temperature. This explains why the skin of smokers tends to wrinkle and age faster. Nicotine produces a decrease in hand steadiness and fine motor control.

Use of tobacco—cigarettes, cigars, and chewing tobacco—is a health hazard. It is the single most preventable risk to health, and an important cause of premature death. About 21 million people die from smoking-related illnesses each decade. Nonsmoking adults who are exposed to secondary smoke double their risk of heart disease and increase the risk of lung cancer by 30 percent. In children, secondary smoke increases the risk of respiratory diseases and other health problems. Nicotine is addictive.

The stimulants *cocaine* and *amphetamines* produce a sense of euphoria—a high—but cause severe psychological and physical problems. Cocaine activates the sympathetic branch of the autonomic nervous system, raising body temperature, heart rate, and breathing. It also reduces the desire for food and sleep.

What causes the cocaine high? See Figure 15-5 on page 457. In the brain's neurons, the drug blocks the repackaging of dopamine and norepinephrine neurotransmitters into the synaptic vesicles of the axon's terminal buttons. The result is that the neurotransmitters remain in the synaptic cleft longer than normal. This sets in motion a series of events that result in the cocaine high. Cocaine produces a strong psychological dependence.

Amphetamines also activate the sympathetic nervous system and increase dopamine and norepinephrine activity. Although people use stimulants to lose weight or stay awake for extended periods of time, physicians rarely prescribe these drugs because of the negative side effects. Amphetamine users quickly develop a drug tolerance, which leads to insomnia, anxiety, heart problems, and even brain damage. Amphetamines produce psychological dependence.

Habitual amphetamine and cocaine users have **hallucinations**, which are sensations and perceptions that occur without any external stimulation. Users may hear strange voices, see snow, or feel bugs crawling on or under their skin. Cocaine-induced spontaneous firing of sensory neurons causes the bug-crawling sensation. Other symptoms are depression, paranoia, teeth grinding, and repetitive behaviors.

stimulants Drugs that speed up—or stimulate—the nervous system and increase mental and physical activity

hallucinations Sensations and perceptions that occur without any external stimulation

Figure 15-5 EFFECTS OF COCAINE ON NEUROTRANSMITTERS

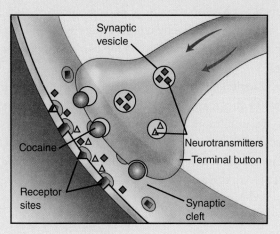

Synaptic vesicle

Cocaine

Receptor sites

Neurotransmitters

Terminal button

Synaptic cleft

Cocaine blocks the reuptake of neurotransmitters into the terminal buttons, causing them to remain in the synaptic cleft longer than normal. Their extended presence in the synaptic cleft creates the drug's stimulant effects.

Methamphetamine, or "crystal meth," is a very addictive stimulant that triggers the release of high levels of dopamine into the brain. This drug produces a brief but powerful emotional high, leaving users with a strong desire to take more doses of the drug. Crystal meth can be smoked, snorted, or injected. Over time, crystal meth can cause permanent damage to blood vessels in the brain, making strokes much more likely. Other effects include extreme weight loss, breathing problems, and fatal heart damage.

Another very dangerous stimulant is ecstasy, or MDMA, which is short for methylenedioxymethamphetamine. Taken as a pill, MDMA affects the brain cells that produce serotonin, a neurotransmitter that affects mood. The release of serotonin by MDMA causes feelings of blissfulness and produces a significant increase in body temperature, heart rate, and blood pressure. Dozens of deaths have occurred due to overheating when users engaged in strenuous physical activity. Studies also raise the possibility that MDMA use causes brain damage, resulting in memory and concentration problems.

Another disturbing cultural trend has been the increased abuse of *Ritalin* (methylphenidate), a stimulant drug used to treat attention-deficit/hyperactivity disorder (ADHD) in children. Ritalin is effective in treating the disorder because it decreases distractibility and improves concentration. Some people who do not have the disorder take the drug to increase their concentration while working or studying for exams. People who abuse Ritalin in this way quickly develop a tolerance for the drug and experience withdrawal symptoms when they reduce their drug use.

HALLUCINOGENS

Hallucinogens (also called *psychedelics*) are psychoactive drugs that dramatically alter consciousness and produce hallucinations. These drugs also may produce relaxation and excitement, as well as anxiety and fear.

LSD The most potent of the hallucinogenic drugs is **LSD** (technically known as lysergic acid diethylamide). LSD is a synthetic drug that acts on the brain

hallucinogens
Psychoactive drugs that dramatically alter consciousness and produce hallucinations

LSD Potent synthesized hallucinogenic drug that is structurally similar to the neurotransmitter serotonin

like the neurotransmitter serotonin. LSD's effects are felt within an hour and last for 10 to 12 hours. LSD has some minor physiological effects, such as an increase in heart rate, blood pressure, and body temperature. Psychological effects often are unpredictable because they are influenced by the user's personality, expectations, and surroundings.

The main psychological effects involve hallucinations and distortions. Unpleasant experiences are frequent, and *flashbacks*—experiencing the drug's effects without taking the drug—occur in more than 15 percent of LSD users and can persist for months. Fatal accidents and suicides have occurred among LSD users. For example, people have fallen to their deaths due to an LSD-induced belief that they could fly. For this reason, LSD is a dangerous drug and should be avoided.

Marijuana **Marijuana** is produced from the *Cannabis* plant. The major psychoactive ingredient in marijuana is **THC**, short for the molecule delta-9 tetrahydrocannabinol. Marijuana is mildly physically addictive, but habitual users experience unpleasant withdrawal symptoms such as insomnia, anxiety, irritability, and headache. Physiological effects are increases in heart rate and blood pressure, and dryness of the mouth and throat.

Psychological effects are relaxation; spontaneous laughter; increased sensitivity to tastes, sounds, colors, and smells; distortion of time; and disconnected flow of ideas. Marijuana interferes with coordination, attention, and reaction time, and is linked to traffic accidents. Check out the Case Study on page 460 to read about the effects of long-term marijuana use on memory and learning.

INHALANTS

Inhalants are chemicals whose vapors are breathed in to produce a mind-altering effect. The act of breathing in the vapors is called sniffing, bagging, huffing, or inhaling. Inhalants are absorbed into the lungs and quickly travel through the bloodstream causing an immediate, but short-lived, high. The effect is similar to alcohol intoxication, and it can cause vomiting, drowsiness, unconsciousness, and even death.

IMAGESHOP/JUPITER IMAGES

Four categories of inhalants include volatile solvents (such as gasoline and glue), aerosols (such as deodorant and hair sprays), gases (such as nitrous oxide found in whipping cream and butane lighters), and nitrites (used for heart patients). Inhalants are addictive. Long-term use can cause brain damage, muscle weakness, loss of sense of smell or hearing, and depression.

marijuana Psychoactive drug that is made from the *Cannabis* plant

THC Major psychoactive ingredient in marijuana

inhalants Chemicals whose vapors can be breathed in to produce a mind-altering effect

According to the National Inhalant Prevention Coalition, inhalant use may result in Sudden Sniffing Death Syndrome. This may occur any time the person uses an inhalant—from the first time to the last.

15.4 ASSESSMENT

In Your Own Words

List each depressant, stimulant, hallucinogen, and inhalant discussed in the text, and describe the psychological and physical effects on users of each of these psychoactive drugs. Include information on drug tolerance and addiction.

Review Concepts

1. Which refers to drugs that are chemicals that alter consciousness by attaching themselves to synaptic receptors in the brain and either blocking or stimulating neural activity?
   - a. caffeine
   - b. nicotine
   - c. psychoactive drugs
   - d. drug tolerance

2. Which is the most consumed and abused depressant?
   - a. sedatives
   - b. alcohol
   - c. marijuana
   - d. tranquilizers

3. Which refers to a recurrence of the effects of LSD without use of the drug?
   - a. depression
   - b. teeth grinding
   - c. skin "bugs"
   - d. flashback

4. These drugs, which speed up the nervous system and increase mental and physical activity, include caffeine and nicotine.
   - a. stimulants
   - b. THC
   - c. depressants
   - d. hallucinogens

5. **True or False**   Drug tolerance leads to physical dependence.

6. **True or False**   People who start drinking at a young age are likely to abuse alcohol as adults.

7. **True or False**   A blood alcohol level of 0.05 percent has no effect on the human brain.

8. **True or False**   Hallucinogens can be taken safely as long as an adult is present.

Think Critically

9. Why do physicians rarely prescribe amphetamines for weight loss?

10. Why is psychological dependence as harmful as physical dependence?

11. Why might drug abuse be considered both a social and economic problem in the United States?

12. Why does psychological dependency put the drug user who quits at greater risk to use the drug again than does physical dependency?

Do Long-Term Users of Marijuana Have Learning Difficulties?

INTRODUCTION Numerous studies have found clear evidence that people experience attention and memory problems while in a marijuana-induced altered state of consciousness. Is there a danger of permanent memory and learning problems due to long-term marijuana use? When long-term marijuana users are not high on the drug, do they perform differently on learning tests than short-term or non-users of the drug?

HYPOTHESIS When not in a marijuana-induced altered state of consciousness, long-term users of marijuana will show memory and attention difficulties compared to short-term or non-users of the drug.

METHOD Fifty-one volunteers who had been smoking marijuana for about 24 years (long-term users), 51 volunteers who had been

smoking marijuana for about 10 years (short-term users), and 33 volunteers who had little or no history of marijuana use (non-users) were administered a battery of neuropsychological tests that measured their memory and attention abilities. The marijuana users in the study were required to not use the drug for a minimum of 12 hours before testing.

RESULTS On many of the memory and attention measures, the long-term users performed significantly worse than the short-term and non-users. The cognitive difficulties observed in the long-term users were not disabling—they were still in the normal range—but they were not as mentally alert and capable as the short-term and non-users of marijuana. A follow-up study with different volunteers found evidence suggesting that when long-term users quit using marijuana, these cognitive difficulties disappeared after a month. More research is needed, but the present results raise concerns about the negative effects of long-term marijuana use.

© YELLOWJ, 2009/USED UNDER LICENSE FROM SHUTTERSTOCK.COM

Critical Analysis

1. Why do you think the researchers also tested short-term users of marijuana rather than just long-term users and non-users?

2. Why do you think long-term users no longer showed memory and attention difficulties after not using marijuana for a month compared to when long-term users did not use the drug for 12 hours?

Substance Abuse Counselor

Human Services

Are you interested in helping people with an addiction? Are you a sympathetic listener? Can you inspire other people? Do people trust you and confide in you? Are you able to keep secrets? If you answer yes to all these questions, you may find a career as a substance abuse counselor rewarding.

Substance abuse counselors help people who are addicted to drugs or alcohol or who have an eating disorder. Counselors help individuals or groups of people identify behaviors that cause problems in their lives related to the addiction. Counselors then help people work through the problems by helping them understand their behavior and by providing behavior tools to help control the addictions.

Counselors also work with the families of people with addictions. They help them understand the nature of addiction and teach them how to be supportive while their loved one works through the healing process.

Counselors also teach programs in the community directed at helping people understand addiction and preventing people from becoming addicted.

Employment Outlook

Employment of substance abuse counselors is growing at a much faster rate than many other occupations. The growth through 2016 is expected to be 34 percent. The fast growth rate is caused by the increased knowledge about addiction, people being more open to seeking treatment, and people with addictions being sent to treatment centers. The growth rate may vary in different regions of the country.

Needed Skills and Education

Education depends on the state requirements. Most states require a master's degree. Other states require a bachelor's degree with appropriate counseling courses. Also required is a state license or certificate. Requirements vary from state to state.

The National Board of Certified Counselors, Inc., grants a general practice credential. To qualify, you must have a master's degree in counseling and at least two years of experience working with a supervising counselor.

Substance abuse counselors need to have a strong desire to want to help other people, have good interpersonal skills, and good communication skills. They must be a good listener and be able to be a calming influence in stressful situations. They must be mentally, physically, and emotionally strong. Counselors must be able to work both independently and as a team member.

How You'll Spend Your Day

Substance abuse counselors work in medical health facilities, for private institutions, and for governments. They may work both with individuals and groups of people. Hours may vary depending on the needs of their clients. Counselors work weekdays, evenings, and weekends.

Earnings

The median annual earnings of substance abuse counselors is $34,040. The greatest number of counselors—about 50 percent—earn between $27,330 and $42,650. The highest 10 percent earn $52,340, while the lowest 10 percent earn $22,600.

What About You?

Does the career of substance abuse counselor interest you? Write a list of 10 questions to ask a counselor about the occupation. Use the phone book or Internet to find a counselor. Call or e-mail the counselor to set an appointment. After you interview the counselor, write an evaluation of the career and how you think it fits into your future goals.

PHOTODISC/GETTY IMAGES

CHAPTER SUMMARY

15.1 Consciousness and Body Rhythms

- Consciousness is awareness of yourself and your surroundings. It is subjective, selective, divided, continuous, changing, and multi-leveled.

- Circadian rhythms are human beings' internally generated behavioral and physiological changes that occur on a daily basis.

- Circadian rhythms help regulate the sleep-wake cycle, which is a 24-hour cycle.

15.2 Sleep

- About every 90 or 100 minutes, human beings cycle through distinct stages of sleep, each associated with a brain activity pattern.

- Every 50 to 70 minutes you go through stages 1 through 4 of NREM sleep. After about four cycles of NREM sleep, you return to stage 2 REM sleep, where you spend half the night. This is where dreaming occurs.

- Sleep is needed to maintain health; it allows the body to restore itself.

- Three dreaming theories are Freud's wish fulfillment theory, off-line theory, and activation-synthesis theory.

- Five sleep disorders include insomnia, night terrors, sleepwalking, narcolepsy, and sleep apnea.

15.3 Hypnosis and Meditation

- Hypnosis is a psychological state of altered attention and awareness in which a person is unusually responsive to suggestions.

- Meditation refers to mental exercises that alter consciousness in order to enhance self-knowledge.

15.4 Psychoactive Drugs

- Psychoactive drugs are chemicals that modify mental processes and behavior. These drugs can lead to drug abuse and create withdrawal symptoms when use stops.

- Drug abuse is the persistence in drug use when doing so interferes with the drug user's behavior or social relationships.

- Drug tolerance is an effect of drug abuse in which greater amounts of the drug are necessary to produce the same effect once produced by a smaller dose.

- Depressants are psychoactive drugs that slow down the nervous system and decrease mental and physical activity. They include alcohol, sedatives, and tranquilizers.

- Stimulants are drugs that speed up the nervous system and increase mental and physical activity. They include caffeine, nicotine, cocaine, and amphetamines.

- Hallucinogens are psychoactive drugs that distort perception and create sensory images without any external stimulation. They include LSD and marijuana.

- Inhalants are chemicals whose vapors can be breathed in to produce a mind-altering psychoactive effect. The act of breathing in the vapors is called sniffing, bagging, huffing, or inhaling.

CHAPTER 15 ASSESSMENT

Review Psychology Terms

Select the term that best fits the definition. Some terms will not be used.

_____ 1. Active phase in the sleep cycle, during which dreaming occurs, characterized by rapid eye movements

_____ 2. An awareness of yourself and your surroundings that is noticeably different from your normal state of consciousness

_____ 3. A theory that hypnosis is an altered state with two streams of consciousness operating at the same time, one actively responding to suggestions and the other passively observing

_____ 4. Regular bodily rhythms that occur on a 24-hour cycle

_____ 5. A theory that dreaming is the forebrain's attempt to interpret random neural activity coming from the midbrain during sleep

_____ 6. Very fast, low-amplitude brain waves associated with an active, alert state of mind

_____ 7. Awareness of yourself and your surroundings

_____ 8. The degree to which a person can enter a deep hypnotic state

_____ 9. Continued drug use despite it interfering with the drug user's behavior or social relationships

_____ 10. A theory that dreaming is a time for consolidating and storing information gathered during the day

_____ 11. An effect of drug abuse in which greater amounts of the drug are necessary to produce the same results once produced by a smaller dose

_____ 12. Fast, low-amplitude brain waves associated with a relaxed, wakeful state

_____ 13. Slow, high-amplitude brain waves most typical of stage 4 deep sleep

_____ 14. Chemicals that change mental processes and behavior

_____ 15. Irregular, small, rapid brain waves associated with stage 1 sleep

_____ 16. The tolerance and physical dependence resulting from prolonged abuse of alcohol

a. activation-synthesis theory
b. alcoholism
c. alpha waves
d. altered state of consciousness
e. beta waves
f. circadian rhythms
g. consciousness
h. delta waves
i. depressants
j. dreams
k. drug abuse
l. drug tolerance
m. hypnosis
n. hypnotizability
o. meditation
p. neodissociation theory
q. off-line dream theory
r. psychoactive drugs
s. REM sleep
t. social influence theory of hypnosis
u. theta waves

Review Psychology Concepts

17. Explain what the "clock" gene is and how it might help people overcome disruptions in their circadian rhythm.

18. List the four stages of sleep and describe the brain wave patterns of each.

19. Explain why psychoactive drugs are so harmful to people.

20. Identify and define five sleep disorders discussed in the text.

21. Assess the value of meditation and the ways it helps people. Include the following information: name the physiological changes that take place with practiced meditators, such as people who practice Zen meditations, transcendental meditation, or the relaxation response; list the illnesses that respond to meditation; and recall a time in your life when you or someone you know could have benefited from meditation.

22. Define sleep spindles and indicate in which sleep stage they occur.

23. Explain what happens to your alertness as your core body temperature changes.

24. In the early studies of circadian rhythms, researchers found that circadian rhythm appeared to be a 25-hour cycle. More recent studies found that the 25-hour cycle hypothesis had created the effect accidentally. What variable in the earlier studies made a 25-hour sleep cycle seem likely?

25. What health problems are associated with alcoholism?

26. Classify the following drugs as a depressant, stimulant, hallucinogen, or inhalant: (a) marijuana, (b) caffeine, (c) amphetamines, (d) alcohol, (e) LSD, (f) ecstasy, (g) cocaine, (h) sedative, (i) tranquilizer, (j) nicotine, (k) nitrous oxide

27. Defend this statement: Hypnosis is a helpful aid for some surgery patients.

28. Describe the changes in your body when stimulants are used.

Apply Psychology Concepts

29. You are a newspaper reporter and have interviewed a sleep researcher who specializes in sleep disorders. Write an article about sleep disorders that describes their symptoms and treatments. Include at least four disorders in your article.

30. Three of the most commonly used drugs are alcohol, cocaine, and marijuana. Describe each type of drug and explain its affect on the body.

31. Research the recommendations a psychologist might make if you were having trouble sleeping. Make a list of 10 suggestions that you find. Be prepared to present the suggestions you found to the class.

32. Keep a dream journal for the next two to three weeks. Each time you dream, briefly describe any events from your recent history that might relate to the dream. Write a report analyzing your journal. Consider the following: Were there common elements in your dreams (people, objects, etc.) and what might they mean? Were you able to interpret any of your dreams? Were your dreams disturbing? Amusing? Bizarre? Boring? If, after this two- to three-week period you cannot remember your dreams, write a report on dreams from an objective viewpoint. What functions do they serve? Which dream theories do you support, and why?

Make Academic Connections

33. **Language Arts** Write a short story that incorporates the main qualities of consciousness. Illustrate at least four qualities of consciousness in your story. You might write a story about two friends having a conversation about the movie they just saw. To illustrate that consciousness is subjective, one friend has trouble understanding why a scene in the movie made the other friend laugh. You could then illustrate how consciousness is changing when a third friend walks up and the conversation suddenly changes.

34. **Cross-Culture Studies** Use the Internet to research dreams and their significances to people in three other cultures. Design a chart that illustrates the similarities and differences in the significances of dreams across cultures.

35. **Health** Use the library, Internet, or personal interviews to research the relationship of healing practices that use trance induction and altered states of consciousness to hypnosis. You can study modern-day alternative medicine practices, such as energy healing or Reiki, or the practices of ancient cultures, such as shamanism or medicine people. Write a summary of your findings.

Do you think you could walk on fire? Successful firewalkers change their state of consciousness to allow themselves to cross burning coals unharmed. Walking across the burning coals without pain or injury provides a powerful example of mind over matter. Participants are able to focus their minds on images that take their consciousness away from the fire pit. Access the Gale Psychology eCollection at *www.cengage.com/school/psych/franzoi* and read the description of the firewalking experience and what the walkers learned from the followup hypnosis session. Write a summary of the article and answer the question: What does walking across hot coals pain- and injury-free prove about the human mind? As an additional project, describe an instance when you or someone you know used "mind over matter" successfully.

Source: "Firewalking: fighting fire with focus." *Psychology Today.* 26.n1 (Jan–Feb 1993): 15(1).

SELF-DISCOVERY: YOUR SCORE

Are You a Morning Person or a Night Person? (p. 443)

Scoring Instructions: If you answered "Day" to eight or more items, you are probably a morning person. However, if you answered "Evening" to eight or more items, you are probably a night person.

Are You Getting Enough Sleep? (p. 446)

Scoring Instructions: If you answered "true" to three or more items, you probably are not getting enough sleep. Keep in mind that people differ in their individual sleep needs. If this questionnaire suggests that you may be sleep deprived, go to bed 15 minutes earlier every night for a week. Continue adding 15 more minutes each week until you are waking without the aid of an alarm clock and without feeling tired during the day. Encourage your family and friends to try this exercise, and compare your experiences over the next few weeks to see if your daily alertness and energy level improve.

Intelligence

ESSENTIAL QUESTION
Go to page XXVII

"Doing easily what others find difficult is talent; doing what is impossible for talent is genius."

—HENRI-FREDERIC AMIEL, SWISS CRITIC, 1821–1881

In elementary school, when students were given intelligence tests, Robert Sternberg did not do well. Robert's anxiety level began rising the day the teacher announced that students were going to be tested. His anxiety reached its peak when that day finally arrived. Just the sight of the school psychologist coming into the classroom to give the test created a panic attack in this young student. The result was always the same: Robert scored very low on any school-administered intelligence test.

Would you believe this person, who experienced such extreme test anxiety as a child, became one of the world's leading intelligence experts? Robert Sternberg's experience led him to ask questions about intelligence. His career provides a dramatic demonstration of how childhood experiences and questions lead to scientific discovery. Sternberg's research and writings on intelligence have helped many people in their personal quests to understand their own mental abilities.

16.1 | Measuring Intelligence

OBJECTIVES

- Describe the history of intelligence testing.
- List and describe modern tests of mental abilities.
- Explain principles of test construction.

DISCOVER IT | *How does this relate to me?*

If you are planning to extend your academic career by attending college, you are no doubt familiar with the ACT and SAT tests, even if you have not yet taken them. You most likely have taken a number of standardized tests during your elementary and secondary school years. What do these tests measure?

KEY TERMS

- intelligence
- mental age
- aptitude test
- achievement test
- intelligence quotient (IQ)
- standardization
- Flynn effect
- reliability
- validity

Intelligence is defined as the mental abilities to adapt to and shape the environment. Intelligence involves reacting to, and actively forming, your surroundings. The mental abilities that make up intelligence are the keys to lifelong learning.

Early Intelligence Testing

Every science is touched by the values and politics of the culture in which it is practiced. In psychology, this is seen in the early history of intelligence testing.

French psychologist Alfred Binet (1857–1911) was a pioneer in intelligence testing. In the early 1900s, the French needed a measure of intelligence to identify children who would benefit from special education. While working with his colleague Theophilé Simon, Binet noticed that brighter children could answer correctly as many intellectually challenging questions as the average child of an older age. For example, a very smart 8-year-old was able to answer as many difficult questions as the average 12-year-old child. Based on this observation, Binet developed the idea of quantifying children's intelligence in terms of **mental age**, or the age that reflects the child's mental abilities in comparison to the average child of the same age. Children with a mental age that is greater than their chronological age would be identified as having above-average intelligence. If mental age is lower than chronological age, this would indicate below-average intelligence. Binet's idea of

intelligence The mental abilities to adapt to and shape the environment

mental age The age that reflects the child's mental abilities in comparison to the average child of the same age

LIBRARY OF CONGRESS

mental age is still used today in a modified form in calculating the well-known IQ score.

When Binet and Simon published their *Binet-Simon Test* they stated that it measured general mental ability and abstract reasoning. Based on his research, Binet believed that cognitive development follows the same course in all children, but that some learn faster and more easily than others. He also believed that intellectual ability increased with education. Binet insisted that his test did not measure inborn intelligence. It sampled intelligence and did not measure all intellectual aspects. He warned that because the test used French children with similar cultural backgrounds, it might not accurately measure intelligence in other countries.

Henry Goddard translated Binet's test for use in the United States to assess newly arrived immigrants. Despite Binet's warnings, Goddard used the test to identify people whom he believed had inborn low intelligence. A high percentage of the tested immigrants received low scores, because the test was biased against people for whom English was a second language. Goddard's mistaken claim that many immigrants had low intelligence was used as evidence by some politicians to pass the Immigration Act of 1924. This law restricted admitting immigrants who received low scores on Goddard's test. Goddard later realized his mistake, but this faulty use of the Binet-Simon Test harmed the reputation of American intelligence testing during its early years.

 *Who was the most influential pioneer in intelligence testing?*

Modern Tests of Mental Abilities

Psychologists divide modern testing of mental abilities into two categories: aptitude and achievement. An **aptitude test** predicts your capacity to learn if given an adequate education. Standard intelligence tests are aptitude tests. An **achievement test** measures what you already have learned. The *Scholastic Assessment Test (SAT)* taken by many high school students who are preparing for college is an example of an achievement test that measures a person's learned verbal and mathematical skills.

The distinction between the tests is not clear-cut. There is evidence that *aptitude* test scores are affected by prior experience. Suppose two students who have an equal capacity for learning math are given a test of mathematical aptitude. One student took three years of math instruction, while the other student only took one math course. Despite their equal capacity for learning math, the student who took more math courses likely will achieve a higher aptitude score.

aptitude test A test that predicts a person's capacity for learning

achievement test A test designed to assess what a person has learned

Why would a person who has taken more classes in a subject be likely to score higher on an achievement test on that subject?

THE STANFORD-BINET INTELLIGENCE SCALE

Stanford University psychologist Lewis Terman (1877–1956) revised the Binet-Simon Test for American students, which became known as the *Stanford-Binet Intelligence Scale*. Using Binet's idea of mental age, Terman devised the famous **intelligence quotient (IQ)**, which is a ratio of mental age divided by chronological age, multiplied by 100:

$$IQ = \frac{\text{Mental age}}{\text{Chronological age}} \times 100$$

A child whose mental and chronological ages are the same has an IQ of 100. A 10-year-old who answered questions at the level of an 8-year-old has an IQ of 80. An 8-year-old who answered questions like a 10-year-old has an IQ of 125.

This IQ ratio adequately measured intelligence in children but not adults. It led to the mistaken perception that intelligence declines with age. Today, most intelligence tests use a *deviation IQ*, which compares how a person's intelligence test score deviates from the average score of same-age peers, which is 100.

THE WECHSLER INTELLIGENCE SCALES

David Wechsler developed the deviation IQ score. He also developed a series of *Wechsler Intelligence Scales* for people of different age groups, the Wechsler Adult Intelligence Scale, the Wechsler Preschool and Primary Scale of Intelligence, and the Wechsler Intelligence Scale for Children. In the United States, these tests are used more frequently than the Stanford-Binet.

Intelligence is measured by 11 subtests—6 verbal and 5 performance—that yield a verbal, a performance, and an overall IQ score. Verbal items consist of general information, similarities, math, vocabulary, comprehension, and recall of number strings. Performance subtests require the test-taker to locate missing picture parts,

intelligence quotient (IQ) A ratio of mental age divided by chronological age, multiplied by 100

INFOBIT
Psychologist David Wechsler came to the United States at the age of six as an immigrant from Romania, just before intelligence testing was used to screen out low-intelligence people. Because he knew little English, Weschler probably would have been identified as having low intelligence had he been given Goddard's biased intelligence test.

Figure 16-1 SAMPLE ITEMS FROM THE WECHSLER ADULT INTELLIGENCE SCALE (WAIS)

VERBAL

General Information
What day of the year is Independence Day?

Similarities
In what way are *wool* and *cotton* alike?

Arithmetic Reasoning
If eggs cost 60 cents a dozen, what does 1 egg cost?

Vocabulary
Tell me the meaning of corrupt.

Comprehension
Why do people buy fire insurance?

Digit Span
Listen carefully, and when I am through, say the numbers right after me.

7   3   4   1   8   6

Now I am going to say some more numbers, but I want you to say them backward.

3   8   4   1   6

PERFORMANCE

Picture Completion
I am going to show you a picture with an important part missing. Tell me what is missing.

Picture Arrangement
The pictures below tell a story. Put them in the right order to tell the story.

Block Design
Using the four blocks, make one just like this.

Object Assembly
If these pieces are put together correctly, they will make something. Go ahead and put them together as quickly as you can.

Digit-Symbol Substitution

Source: From *Measurement and Evaluation in Psychology and Education* by A. L. Thorndike and E. P. Hagen. Reprinted by permission of Pearson Education, Inc., Upper Saddle River, NJ.

arrange cartoons in a logical sequence, reproduce block designs, assemble jigsaw puzzles, and copy symbols (see Figure 16-1, above).

GROUP-ADMINISTERED TESTS

Both the Stanford-Binet and the Wechsler tests are given individually. Group aptitude and achievement tests are given to thousands simultaneously. Widely used today, group-administered tests include the SAT. Students who attend high-scholastic achieving schools have an advantage when taking SATs, but students whose academic strengths are in the humanities, such as music or art, are at a disadvantage because this test focuses on math and verbal skills.

SAT tests measure the potential for performing well on scholastic tasks as well as achievement. Studying can improve test performance. Coaching on how to take the test can increase scores by 30 to 50 points. Both the verbal and math sections of the SAT have an average score of 500 and a range of 200 to 800, with a total score range of 400 to 1600.

CHECKPOINT *What is the difference between aptitude tests and achievement tests?*

Principles of Test Construction

All psychological tests must have three basic characteristics. They must be standardized, reliable, and valid.

STANDARDIZATION

Everyone who takes an achievement or aptitude test receives the same instructions, questions, and time limits. Individual scores are compared against the scores of people previously tested, so you can convert a raw score into a *percentile*. This indicates the percentage of people in the group who scored at or below your score. The entire process of establishing uniform procedures for administering a test and interpreting its scores is known as **standardization**.

Standardized test results tend to form a normal distribution, which has a bell-shaped appearance when the individual scores are placed on a graph (see Chapter 2, pages 48–49). In a normal distribution (Figure 16-2, below), most IQ test scores cluster around the median, or middle score, which has a value similar to both the mean (the average test score) and the mode (the most frequent test score). The mean score is 100. In a normal distribution, 68 percent of the scores will range between 85 and 115, and 96 percent of the scores will fall within the 70–130. Only 2 percent of the population has IQ scores above 130 or below 70.

standardization The process of establishing uniform procedures for administering a test and for interpreting its scores

Flynn effect The tendency for performance on IQ tests to improve from one generation to the next

Figure 16-2 **THE NORMAL DISTRIBUTION**

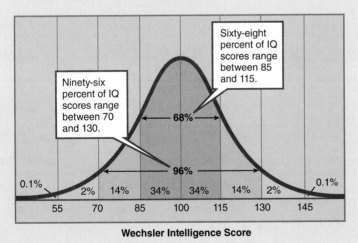

Sixty-eight percent of IQ scores range between 85 and 115.

Ninety-six percent of IQ scores range between 70 and 130.

68%

96%

0.1%   2%   14%   34%   34%   14%   2%   0.1%

55   70   85   100   115   130   145

Wechsler Intelligence Score

Scores on standardized aptitude tests, such as the Wechsler Adult Intelligence Scale, tend to form a normal distribution (also known as a "bell-shaped curve"). The Wechsler scale, like other IQ tests, calls the average score 100.

About every generation or so, intelligence tests must be restandardized to maintain the mean score of 100. Worldwide, each generation intellectually outperforms the previous generation. Test items must be made more difficult to keep the average intelligence score at 100. The tendency for performance on IQ tests to improve from one generation to the next is called the **Flynn effect**, after the psychologist who first noticed it, James Flynn.

What accounts for this steady increase in IQ? A likely explanation is the combined effects of improved education, better health and nutrition, experience with testing, and exposure to a broader range of information through television and the Internet.

RELIABILITY AND VALIDITY

The **reliability** of a test indicates the degree to which it yields consistent results. One way to estimate this type of consistency is *test-retest reliability*, which is checking scores on the same test on two or more occasions. Reliability estimates are based on *correlation coefficients*. As you recall from Chapter 2 (page 42), a correlation coefficient (the symbol *r*) is a statistical measure of the direction and strength of the linear relationship between two variables, and ranges from −1.00 to +1.00.

In estimating test-retest reliability, the two variables are the two test scores from two different occasions. If the first test scores have a strong correspondence with the second scores (Figure 16-3a), the correlation coefficient will be near +1.00. This means the test's reliability is high. However, if the first and second scores do not correspond (Figure 16-3b), the correlation coefficient will be closer to 0.00, which means that the test's reliability is low. Modern intelligence tests described so far in this chapter have correlation coefficients of about +0.90, which indicate high reliability.

reliability The degree to which a test yields consistent results

Figure 16-3 DETERMINING TEST-RETEST RELIABILITY

In test-retest reliability, people take a test at time 1 and again at time 2. People's scores at time 1 are shown on the left, and their scores at time 2 are shown on the right. (a) When people get similar scores on both occasions, the test has high reliability. (b) If they get different scores, the test has low reliability.

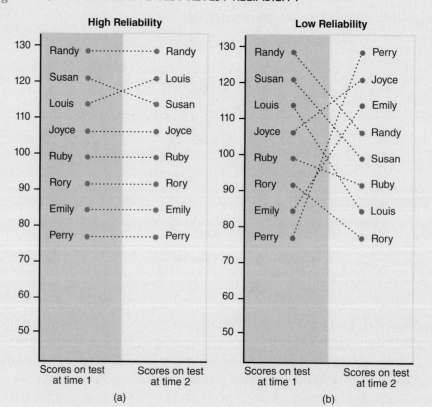

Validity refers to the degree to which a test measures what it is designed to measure. In our household, we have a weigh scale that is reliable, but not valid. Everyone who steps on it weighs 32 pounds. The invalidity of our household scale is a source of amusement, but invalid intelligence tests are no joking matter.

How do researchers determine whether an intelligence test is valid? One way is to determine the degree to which the intelligence test predicts behavior related to intelligence. Research in the United States indicates intelligence tests can predict how successful people will be in life. Individuals who score high tend to learn more in school, get better grades, and complete more years of education. People who have IQs below 85—which is about 15 percent of the population—are more likely to drop out of school before receiving their high school diploma, to be unemployed for long periods of time, to live below the poverty line, and to have a criminal record.

validity The degree to which a test measures what it is designed to measure

DO INTELLIGENCE TESTS HAVE A CULTURAL BIAS?

Intelligence tests measure people's developed abilities at a particular point in time. They detect differences in intellectual abilities and cultural experiences. Two people with the same inborn abilities score differently on an intelligence test when one has less experience with the culture in which the test was developed.

In the United States, critics of intelligence tests argue that Caucasians and middle- and upper-class individuals have an advantage when taking IQ tests because of their greater exposure to the test-item topics. Consider the item that asks why people buy fire insurance on the Wechsler Adult Intelligence Scale in Figure 16-1, page 470. Is this question biased against people who have no reason to buy fire insurance because they have nothing to insure? Is this test item based on achievement in acquiring knowledge valued by the middle-class culture?

Supporters of IQ tests claim that although the tests do not provide an unbiased measure of cognitive abilities, they do provide an accurate measure of whether people are likely to succeed in school and some occupations. This ability of intelligence and achievement tests to predict success is the same regardless of people's culture or social class.

When studying intelligence in other societies, researchers must become familiar with the culture and design tests that are consistent with the needs and values of the people. When psychologists studied intellectual development of children in a Zinacantec Mayan village in Chiapas, Mexico, they used toy looms, spools of thread, and other objects common to the culture. Results indicated that the children's intellectual development was similar to that of children in the United States. This research demonstrates that when psychologists use testing materials familiar to people's everyday experiences, they can make cross-cultural comparisons of intellectual abilities.

The ability of intelligence and achievement tests to predict success in school and some occupations is the same regardless of people's culture or social class.

CHECKPOINT *What are the three basic characteristics of test construction?*

In Your Own Words

Choose one of the objectives on page 467 and explain the information in your own words. You might describe the history of intelligence testing or the modern tests of mental abilities, or you might explain principles of test construction.

Review Concepts

1. Which refers to the ratio of mental age divided by chronological age multiplied by 100?
   a. IQ
   b. SAT score
   c. aptitude
   d. achievement

2. Which refers to the degree to which a test yields consistent results?
   a. standardization
   b. validity
   c. intelligence
   d. reliability

3. Which refers to the tendency for people's performance on IQ tests to improve from one generation to the next?
   a. reliability
   b. intelligence
   c. Flynn effect
   d. validity

4. Who translated the early French intelligence test for use in the United States to assess newly arrived immigrants?
   a. Alfred Binet
   b. Theophilé Simon
   c. Henry Goddard
   d. Lewis Terman

5. **True or False** If a test is reliable, it is also valid.

6. **True or False** Alfred Binet's first intelligence test measured general mental ability and abstract reasoning.

7. **True or False** Research in the United States has found that individuals who score high on intelligence tests tend to learn more in school, get better grades, and complete more years of education.

Think Critically

8. Why do researchers familiarize themselves with a culture before testing for intelligence?

9. Are you taking an aptitude or achievement test when you take a test on what you have learned in psychology?

10. Why might two people with the same inborn abilities score differently on an intelligence test?

11. What accounts for the Flynn effect?

12. Why did the people who took Henry Goddard's translation of Alfred Binet's intelligence test have low scores?

13. Why is standardization necessary for achievement tests?

OBJECTIVES

- Explain the general intelligence factor.
- Differentiate between crystallized intelligence and fluid intelligence.
- Define multiple intelligences.
- Explain the triarchic theory of intelligence.

KEY TERMS

- general intelligence factor (g-factor)
- crystallized intelligence
- fluid intelligence
- multiple intelligences
- triarchic theory of intelligence

DISCOVER IT | *How does this relate to me?*

Who do you think is intelligent? The President? A scientist? A classmate? Can you be intelligent in one area and not in another? Is music or athletic ability a form of intelligence? Psychologists have asked these same questions. You may be surprised about what they learned in their research on intelligence.

After developing the first intelligence tests, psychologists began to carefully study the nature of intelligence. Psychologists who studied intelligence questioned whether it is a general ability or composed of separate and independent abilities.

General Intelligence

In the 1920s British psychologist Charles Spearman (1863–1945) helped develop a statistical technique called *factor analysis.* This technique allows researchers to identify clusters of test items that are related, or *correlated,* to one another. By analyzing the correlations, researchers can judge whether people's test performance is based on a single underlying ability (a *factor*) or multiple abilities (*factors*). For example, if people who do well on reading tests also do well on writing and vocabulary tests, this suggests there's an underlying verbal ability. However, if *all* the abilities correlate, this suggests intelligence may be one thing rather than many.

Based on his research, Spearman concluded there was a **general intelligence factor**, or **g-factor**, underlying all mental abilities. He also found a set of specific factors (*s-factors*) that underlie certain individual mental abilities. Because the g-factor predicts performance on a variety of intelligence tests measuring math ability, vocabulary, and general knowledge, Spearman argued this was evidence that intelligence was one thing, not many things.

general intelligence factor (g-factor) A general intelligence ability which underlies all mental abilities

Crystallized vs. Fluid Intelligence

Raymond B. Cattell agreed with Spearman's idea of general intelligence, but his own factor analyses suggested two kinds of g-factors: crystallized and fluid intelligence. **Crystallized intelligence** is a person's knowledge and verbal skills learned through experience. People with high-crystallized intelligence are good at using previously learned information to solve familiar problems. **Fluid intelligence** is a person's ability to learn or invent strategies for dealing with problems. This requires the ability to understand relationships between things without past experience or practice with them.

Crystallized and fluid intelligence are related to one another, but are affected differently by aging. As you can see in Figure 16-4, studies find that crystallized intelligence increases through the adult years and up to old age. Fluid intelligence decreases slowly up to age 75, and then rapidly decreases. Research finds that crystallized and fluid intelligence are rather highly correlated, which suggests that both may be part of a more general factor of intelligence.

Modern theories propose that, although intelligence may be a general ability to deal with a wide variety of cognitive tasks and problems, intelligence also can be expressed in many ways. You can be highly intelligent in one or more mental abilities while being relatively unintelligent in others. Two theories that explore this idea of different types of intelligence are Howard Gardner's *theory of multiple intelligences* and Robert Sternberg's *triarchic theory of intelligence*.

crystallized intelligence A person's knowledge and verbal skills learned through experience

fluid intelligence A person's ability to learn or invent strategies for dealing with problems

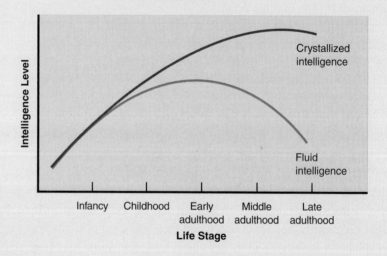

Figure 16-4 **LIFE-SPAN CHANGES IN CRYSTALLIZED AND FLUID INTELLIGENCE**

While fluid intelligence declines as we age, crystallized intelligence increases throughout the adult years and up to old age.

Source: From J. L. Horn and G. Donaldson, "On the Myth of Intellectual Decline in Adulthood" in *American Psychologist*, 31, 701–719. Copyright © 1976 by the American Psychological Association.

Multiple Intelligences

While working at a hospital and observing people who had suffered brain damage, Howard Gardner noticed that such injuries often resulted in the loss of one ability while leaving others unharmed. Based, in part, on these observations, he developed the theory of **multiple intelligences**, which states that the human brain has at least eight separate intelligences all of which are developed differently in each individual. What American culture calls intelligence is only a small cluster of these abilities. You develop the intellectual abilities that are most valued in your culture.

Table 16-1 summarizes the multiple intellectual abilities described by Gardner. The first three are on conventional intelligence tests. *Linguistic intelligence* is the ability to communicate through written and spoken language, and is found in authors and public speakers. *Logical-mathematical intelligence* is the ability to solve math problems and analyze arguments; engineers and scientists have this ability. *Spatial intelligence* is being skilled at perceiving and arranging objects in the environment; carpenters and air traffic controllers excel in this ability. *Musical intelligence* involves the ability to analyze, compose, or perform music. *Bodily kinesthetic intelligence* is displayed by gifted athletes, dancers, and surgeons, and is used in ordinary activities, such as driving a car or hammering a nail. *Naturalist intelligence* is the ability to see patterns in nature, as found in forest rangers, ecologists, and zoologists. *Interpersonal intelligence* identifies the ability to get along well with others and to reliably predict their motives and behavior, an ability important for salespersons and office managers. *Intrapersonal intelligence* involves having insight into your own motives and behavior, which is an ability important for psychologists and religious leaders. Gardner also suggested a

multiple intelligences
Howard Gardner's theory that there are at least eight separate intelligences all of which are developed differently in each individual

Table 16-1 GARDNER'S MULTIPLE INTELLIGENCES

Type of Intelligence	Description
Linguistic intelligence	Ability to communicate through written and spoken language: author, poet, public speaker, native storyteller
Logical-mathematical intelligence	Ability to solve math problems and analyze arguments: engineer, scientist, mathematician, navigator
Spatial intelligence	Ability to perceive and arrange objects in the environment: carpenter, air traffic controller, sculptor, architect
Musical intelligence	Ability to analyze, compose, or perform music: musician, singer, composer
Bodily kinesthetic intelligence	Ability to control body motions to handle objects skillfully: athlete, dancer, surgeon, craftsperson
Naturalist intelligence	Ability to see patterns in nature: forest ranger, ecologist, zoologist, botanist
Interpersonal intelligence	Ability to interact well socially and to reliably predict others' motives and behavior: mental health therapist, salesperson, politician, fund-raiser
Intrapersonal intelligence	Ability to gain insight into one's own motives and behavior: meditator, essayist, stand-up comic
A Possible Ninth Intelligence	
Existential intelligence	Ability to pose and ponder large philosophical questions: philosopher, clergy

Multiple Intelligences Test

Work with another student to design a 20-question test for one of Gardner's intelligences. To test linguistic intelligence, for example, you would write 20 questions to assess verbal and written linguistic abilities. Test and score at least 10 people. Create a chart that represents your findings.

ninth intelligence, *existential intelligence,* which deals with the posing and pondering of philosophical questions.

According to Gardner, the same person can often have different intelligences that interact to produce intelligent behavior. For example, skilled politicians rely on linguistic intelligence when debating issues and persuading voters. They also use logical-mathematical intelligence to critically analyze the issues and interpersonal intelligence to understand what motivates voters. By combining skills in different intellectual areas into what Gardner calls a *profile of intelligences,* people excel in certain tasks or occupations even though they may not be particularly gifted in any specific intelligence. One of the challenges in life is to determine how to use your particular talents. Check out the Self-Discovery feature below to test your interpersonal intelligence.

What Is Interpersonal Intelligence?

According to Howard Gardner, persons with high interpersonal intelligence are able to understand the intentions, motivations and desires of other people. They can psychologically "put themselves in other people's shoes" and understand their points of view. This interpersonal skill allows them to work well with others. To better understand your own interpersonal intelligence, read each item below and then, using the following response scale, indicate how well each statement describes you.

0 = not at all like me   2 = neither like me or unlike me   4 = very much like me

1 = somewhat unlike me   3 = somewhat like me

1. I sometimes find it difficult to see things from the "other guy's" point of view.

2. I try to look at everybody's side of a disagreement before I make a decision.

3. I sometimes try to understand my friends better by imagining how things look from their perspective.

4. If I'm sure I'm right about something, I don't waste much time listening to other people's arguments.

5. I believe that there are two sides to every question and try to look at them both.

6. When I'm upset at someone, I usually try to put myself in the other person's shoes for a while.

7. Before criticizing somebody, I try to imagine how I would feel if I were in that person's place.

See page 497 for scoring instructions.

Source: From Mark H. Davis, "Interpersonal Reactivity Index" in *Empathy: A Social Psychological Approach.* Copyright © 1996. Boulder, CO: Westview Press.

CHECKPOINT > *What are multiple intelligences?*

Triarchic Theory of Intelligence

Robert Sternberg—the person introduced in the chapter opening—agrees with Gardner's idea of multiple intelligences. Sternberg's **triarchic theory of intelligence** (see Figure 16-5, below) states that human intelligence consists of three mental abilities:

■ *Analytical intelligence* Required to solve familiar problems and judge the quality of ideas. This type of intelligence is valued on tests and in the classroom. People who are high in analytical intelligence tend to score high on general intelligence. Analytical intelligence is similar to crystallized intelligence.

■ *Creative intelligence* Required to develop new ways of solving problems. People with a high degree of creative intelligence have the ability to find connections between old and new information, combine facts that appear unrelated, and see the big picture. This is related to fluid intelligence. Check out the Positive Psychology feature on page 481 for ways to increase your creativity.

■ *Practical intelligence* Required to use ideas in everyday situations. People who are high in practical intelligence have street smarts. They are quick to size up new situations and adapt to—and shape—their surroundings. Practical intelligence does not predict IQ or academic achievement.

Although some tasks require you to use all three mental abilities, the triarchic theory does not define intelligence according to your skill in all three areas. Some people are more intelligent in solving abstract, theoretical problems, while others are more intelligent when the problems are concrete and practical. Sternberg's research suggests that people learn best—whether in school, on the job, or in daily living—when taught in a way that is well matched with their strongest type of intelligence.

> **triarchic theory of intelligence** Sternberg's theory that there are three sets of mental abilities making up human intelligence: analytic, creative, and practical

Figure 16-5 STERNBERG'S TRIARCHIC THEORY OF INTELLIGENCE

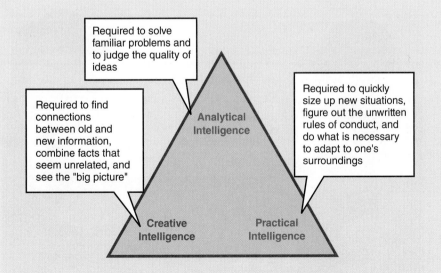

According to Robert Sternberg, you use analytical thinking to solve familiar problems, creative thinking to solve problems in new ways, and practical thinking to apply what you know to everyday situations.

If you have high analytical intelligence, you learn by reading books and thinking abstractly about issues. If you have high practical intelligence, you learn best by tossing the books and how-to manuals aside—getting your hands dirty and letting your wits carry you. *Successful intelligence* is knowing when and how to use analytic, creative, and practical abilities. Successfully intelligent people seek challenges where they can use their intellectual strengths and downplay their weaknesses.

Like Gardner's theory of multiple intelligences, the triarchic theory has led a number of researchers to recommend the development of new and improved tests to assess cognitive abilities. If intelligence is more than academic skill, there is a need to move beyond traditional tests and theories of intelligence. Table 16-2 summarizes the four theories of intelligence discussed in this lesson.

Table 16-2 FOUR THEORIES OF INTELLIGENCE

Intelligence Theories	Description
Spearman's general intelligence (g)	A basic or general form of intelligence predicts abilities in various academic areas.
Cattell's crystallized and fluid intelligences	Two general kinds of intelligence: crystallized intelligence is knowledge and verbal skills acquired through experience, and fluid intelligence is the mental ability to learn or invent strategies for dealing with problems.
Gardner's multiple intelligences	Intelligence is made up of at least eight distinct intelligences that are developed differently in each person: linguistic, logical-mathematical, spatial, musical, bodily kinesthetic, naturalist, interpersonal, and intrapersonal
Sternberg's triarchic theory	Three sets of mental abilities make up intelligence: analytic, creative, and practical.

CHECK**POINT** ▸ *What are the three intellectual abilities in the triarchic theory of intelligence?*

Successfully intelligent people look for challenges that allow them to use their intellectual strengths and to downplay their weaknesses.

STEPHAN HOEROLD/ISTOCKPHOTO.COM

Fostering Creativity

Creativity is the ability to produce new, high-quality products or ideas. These four steps will help you increase your creative ability:

Redefine problems. Certain thinking strategies require you to look through and around problems rather than directly at them. *Warning: Don't feel you must reinvent the wheel for new problems. Tried-and-true problem-solving strategies may be the best answer.*

Make a habit of questioning traditional thinking. Conformity is necessary for a society to function, but it often does not promote creative ideas. Creative people question traditional ways of thinking and behaving. *Warning: Defying tradition simply because it brings you attention is not the purpose of this exercise.*

Find something you love to do. Creative people are motivated by their joy in working on challenging projects more than by the external rewards they receive. *Warning: Being rewarded for doing things you naturally enjoy can hurt your enjoyment of those activities.*

Become an expert in your area of interest. Case studies of creative people find that great accomplishments require high-quality training. By tapping your accumulated learning, you will generate more ideas and make more mental connections that lead to creative problem solving. *Warning: Don't feel you need to know everything about your area of interest before you can make a creative contribution to it.*

Think Critically

1. Describe a situation where you used one of the steps above and specify how you think it increased creativity within yourself.

2. In what other areas can you apply these steps? Why would they be helpful?

© GONCALO VELOSO DE FIGUEIRDO, 2009/ USED UNDER LICENSE FROM SHUTTERSTOCK .COM

In Your Own Words

Compare and contrast the following theories of intelligence: Charles Spearman's general intelligence factor, Raymond B. Cattell's crystallized and fluid intelligence, Howard Gardner's multiple intelligence, and Robert Sternberg's triarchic theory of intelligence.

Review Concepts

1. To which does the g-factor refer?
   - a. fluid intelligence
   - b. general intelligence
   - c. multiple intelligence
   - d. crystallized intelligence

2. The ability to perceive and arrange objects in the environment refers to which of Gardner's intelligences?
   - a. spatial
   - b. naturalistic
   - c. interpersonal
   - d. linguistic

3. Which of the mental abilities in the triarchic theory of intelligence is most valued on tests in the classroom?
   - a. creative intelligence
   - b. crystallized intelligence
   - c. analytical intelligence
   - d. practical intelligence

4. **True or False** Both crystallized and fluid intelligence decrease rapidly in early adulthood.

5. **True or False** According to Gardner's multiple intelligences theory, you develop the intellectual abilities that are most valued in your culture.

6. **True or False** The triarchic theory defines intelligence based on your skill in the three mental abilities—analytical, creative, and practical—combined.

Think Critically

7. Why do you think Gardner added a possible ninth intelligence? What types of careers does this intelligence cover?

8. After studying the triarchic theory of intelligence, do you think intelligence tests are biased against some people? Explain your answer.

9. How might a discussion about multiple intelligence tests among psychologists and educators change the way tests are written and administered? What items might be added or deleted? What other ways might tests be given?

10. Do you agree with Spearman's argument that intelligence is one thing, not many things? Explain your answer.

11. Why does a young person have the advantage over a 77-year-old person when trying to learn new strategies for dealing with problems?

OBJECTIVES

- Identify the two extremes of intelligence.
- Explain the nature-nurture influence on intelligence.
- Describe ways to enhance intelligence.

KEY TERMS

- mental retardation
- Down syndrome
- reaction range

DISCOVER IT | *How does this relate to me?*

What does it mean to be mentally gifted versus mentally challenged? Does the educational system meet the needs of all students, regardless of their intellect? Did you inherit your intelligence from your parents, or is your intelligence shaped by your life experiences?

I n this section, you examine research that identified individuals who differ a great deal in their intelligence levels, and how the educational system tries to meet the needs of students with different levels of intellectual ability. You also will analyze studies that determine the degree to which intelligence is fixed or changeable. Lastly, you will learn how other people's expectations affect your own beliefs about your intellectual abilities and achievements.

Extremes of Intelligence

One controversial area of intellectual assessment is the classification and education of individuals whose IQ scores fall at the two extremes of the normal intelligence curve—the mentally gifted and mentally challenged.

MENTAL RETARDATION

Mental retardation is a condition of limited mental ability, indicated by an IQ score at or below 70 and difficulty in adapting to independent living. About 1 to 2 percent of the population meets both criteria, with males outnumbering females by 50 percent. There are four categories of mental retardation, which vary in severity. Most people identified as being mentally retarded are only mildly so (see Table 16-3, page 484).

> **mental retardation**
> A condition of limited mental ability, indicated by an IQ score at or below 70 and difficulty in adapting to independent living

Table 16-3 DEGREES OF MENTAL RETARDATION

Level	Typical IQ Scores	Percentage of the Retarded	Adaptation to Demands of Life
Mild	50–70	85%	May learn academic skills up to the sixth-grade level. With assistance, adults often can hold a job and maintain social relationships.
Moderate	35–49	10%	May progress to second-grade level. Within sheltered workshops, adults can contribute to their own support through manual labor.
Severe	20–34	<4%	May learn to talk and to perform simple work tasks under close supervision, but are generally unable to learn more complex job skills.
Profound	Below 20	<2%	Limited motor development and little or no speech. Require constant aid and supervision.

Source: Reprinted with permission from the *Diagnostic and Statistical Manual of Mental Disorders,* Fourth Edition. Copyright © 1994 American Psychiatric Association.

WHAT CAUSES MENTAL RETARDATION?

Doctors identify a cause for mental retardation about 25 percent of the time. Causes are infections or malnutrition in a pregnant mother or young child, poisoning of the developing fetus or young child by harmful substances (such as alcohol or lead), premature birth, or trauma to the infant's head.

The most common genetic cause of mental retardation is **Down syndrome**, caused by an extra chromosome in the mother's egg or the father's sperm. Mothers 44 years of age or older are four times more likely than mothers under the age of 33 to give birth to Down syndrome infants. Characteristics of Down syndrome are a small head, nose, ears, and hands; slanting eyes; short neck; and thin hair. Individuals with this disorder have IQs in the mild to severe range of retardation. With training and family support, people with Down syndrome care for themselves, hold a job, and lead happy, fulfilling lives.

In about 75 percent of the cases, mental retardation cannot be linked to clear physiological causes but results from poor social conditions or unclear physiological effects. Most of these cases involve less severe forms of mental retardation. Children from low-income families are 10 times more likely to be in this category than children from higher income brackets.

During the 1950s and 1960s, children with mild retardation were placed in *special education classes,* and received instruction designed for their ability level. Beginning in the 1970s, children with mental disabilities were *mainstreamed,* or integrated into the regular classroom. One obstacle to integrating students with mental disabilities into mainstream society is the prejudice they often face from people with average or above-average intelligence. With the knowledge you now possess, what information could you share with people who express biased attitudes toward individuals who are intellectually challenged?

Down syndrome A form of mental retardation caused by an extra chromosome in the genetic makeup

MENTAL GIFTEDNESS

What does it mean to be "gifted?" For some psychologists, the term is for people with IQs above 130 or 135. Other psychologists add requirements such as exceptional school or career achievement. Consistent with modern-day theories of multiple intelligences, U.S. federal law specifies that giftedness should be based on superior potential in any of six areas: general intelligence, specific aptitudes (for example, math and writing), performing arts, athletics, creativity, and leadership. Evidence suggests that some people are born with the genetic potential for giftedness, but that life experiences nurture these natural tendencies.

Sometimes children who are mentally gifted have extraordinary ability in one intellectual area but have relatively normal abilities in other areas. These *childhood prodigies* master their particular skill at a very young age. Research finds that few of these childhood prodigies ever fulfill their early promise by becoming major contributors in their area of ability as adults. One possible reason for this is that these

Why do most childhood prodigies not become major contributors as adults in their areas of ability?

© SUPRI SUHARJOTO, 2009/USED UNDER LICENSE FROM SHUTTERSTOCK.COM

highly gifted people mastered their skills rather easily and early in life. They may not have learned the critical role that hard work plays in becoming major contributors in their field as adults. Another possible reason is that childhood prodigies typically receive wide praise because they imitate the skills of adult masters. By receiving such high praise for imitation, these gifted people may later have a hard time being creative on their own. Only prodigies who learn the importance of hard work and creative thinking are likely to leave a lasting mark as adults.

Because education is so important for life success, one concern is that gifted students are not challenged by the regular curriculum. In response, educators have developed two intervention strategies—acceleration and enrichment. *Acceleration* is early admission to school and skipping grades. *Enrichment* keeps students in their normal grade level, but supplements course work with advanced material, independent study projects, and other learning experiences. While providing challenging educational opportunities is important for gifted students, adults must be careful not to overdo it. Like normal children, gifted children who are "pushed" too hard to achieve can grow to dislike the activities in which they excel. See the Closer Look feature on page 486 to read more about the mentally gifted.

> **CHECK POINT** *What are the two extremes of intelligence?*

Are the Mentally Gifted Successful in Life?

In 1921 Lewis Terman began tracking the lives of more than 1,500 California children with IQs above 140. Over the course of the next 70 years, Terman and later researchers discovered these men and women led healthy, well-adjusted lives and experienced slightly more successful marriages and careers than the average person. Other longitudinal studies of gifted individuals have confirmed these findings.

Children identified as extremely gifted (top 1 in 10,000) are more likely than nongifted children to pursue doctoral degrees as adults, and many of these individuals create impressive literary, scientific, or technical products by their early 20s. However, childhood giftedness does not guarantee adult success. For example, although many of the gifted children that Terman studied grew up to be very successful adults in their chosen careers, there were no "creative geniuses" like an Einstein or a Beethoven. As with people of normal intelligence, the most successful gifted people in this study were those who had a great willingness to work hard, a great desire to excel, and a well-developed sense of emotional maturity.

Later research by psychologists such as Daniel Goleman suggest that it is too limiting to think of intelligence solely in terms of "book smarts." People with high IQ scores can fail to succeed in life and act very unintelligently if they lack emotional intelligence. Emotional intelligence involves the ability to be aware of, understand, manage, and effectively use your emotions. Both Terman's study and this later research suggest that although IQ is an important contributor, it is only one factor determining a person's life accomplishments.

Think Critically

Besides IQ, what are some other factors that determine a person's accomplishments?

Intelligence and Nature vs. Nurture

Nature versus nurture is a topic of debate among psychologists. Which has the greatest impact on a person's intellect? Studies of twins help scientists determine the effects of genes and the environment on intelligence.

TWIN STUDIES

In Chapter 3, you learned that identical twins have identical genes, while fraternal twins share only half the same genes. Intelligence experts have conducted research on twins raised by the same parents who have similar life experiences. The experts believe that if the IQ scores of identical twins are more similar than those of fraternal twins, it is evidence that genetic inheritance (nature) is more important than life experiences (nurture) in determining intelligence.

PHOTODISC/GETTY IMAGES

Why do you think studying identical twins is useful to intelligence researchers?

As you can see from Figure 16-6, the findings of more than 100 twin studies indicate that the average correlation of identical twins' IQ scores is 0.86, while that of fraternal twins is lower at 0.60. Identical twins raised apart have higher IQ correlations ($r = 0.72$) than fraternal twins raised together. These results support the theory of a genetic contribution to intelligence. However, these same twin studies also point to environmental effects on intelligence. Fraternal twins—who are not genetically more similar than regular siblings—have more similar IQ scores than do non-twin siblings. In addition, non-twin siblings raised together have more similar IQs ($r = 0.47$) than siblings raised apart ($r = 0.24$). These studies and the other twin studies suggest that both genes and environment contribute to intelligence, but that genes have a larger influence.

Figure 16-6 **STUDIES OF IQ SIMILARITY: THE NATURE VS. NURTURE DEBATE**

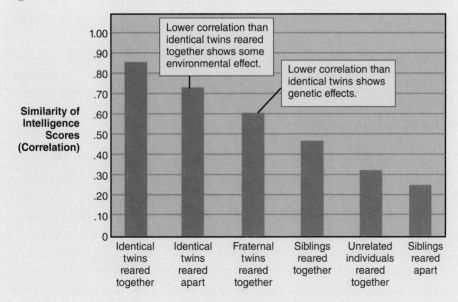

The results of more than 100 studies correlating the IQ scores of people with different genetic and environmental backgrounds found that the most genetically similar people had the most similar IQ scores. How do the other findings reported here support the argument that intelligence is partly determined by environmental factors?

ADOPTION STUDIES

Researchers studied adopted children to understand the effects of heredity and environment on intelligence. Biological parents give children their genes, while adoptive parents provide the environment. If heredity matters more than environment, the children's IQ scores should correlate higher with the biological parents' scores than with the adoptive parents' scores. The reverse occurs if environment matters more than heredity.

Studies found that children who were adopted within two weeks to a year of birth had higher IQ correlations with biological parents than with adoptive parents. The studies found that as adopted children grow up, their IQ correlation with their biological parents increases. The findings support twin studies that heredity makes a larger contribution to IQ scores than environment.

Why do you think studying adopted children is useful to intelligence researchers?

BLEND IMAGES/JUPITER IMAGES

Adoption studies also point toward an environmental influence on intelligence. In France, the IQ scores of children from lower socioeconomic conditions who were adopted by families of greater socioeconomic conditions were compared with the IQ scores of their siblings who had not been adopted. Although the average adopted children's scores ranged between 104 and 111, the average scores for their siblings who were not adopted ranged between 92 and 95. When children of upper-income parents were adopted, their later average IQ score was 120 if their adoptive parents were from families of greater socioeconomic conditions. However, their average IQ score was only 108 if they were adopted by families of lesser socioeconomic conditions.

Based on both the twin and adoption studies, the best estimate is that heredity accounts for a little more than 50 percent of the variation in intelligence, with environmental factors responsible for a little less than 50 percent. This does not mean that a little more than half of *your* intelligence is inherited and a little less than half is environmentally influenced. Genetics and environmental factors are responsible for a bit more and a bit less than about half the differences among all individuals in the population.

REACTION RANGE

How do genes and environment interact in determining intelligence? The concept of **reaction range** provides a possible answer (see Figure 16-7, page 489). Genes establish a range of potential intellectual growth, and environmental experiences interact with genetic makeup in determining where you fall in the reaction range. Children who have a natural aptitude for writing are most likely to spend leisure time writing and to select writing and literature courses in high school. If their parents and teachers nourish this natural aptitude by offering enrichment opportunities, the children's skills are further enhanced. Thus, high scores on verbal aptitude tests are due to both natural ability and experience.

reaction range The extent to which genetically determined limits on IQ may increase or decrease due to environmental factors

Figure 16-7 REACTION RANGE

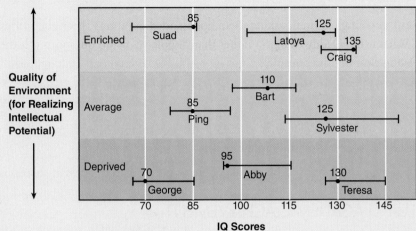

Reaction range indicates the extent to which the environment can raise or lower people's IQ scores, given their inherited intellectual potential. Each person has her or his own individual reaction range. People who grow up in enriched environments tend to score at the top of their reaction range. Those from impoverished settings tend to score closer to the bottom of their range.

⊢⊣ = Inherited reaction range

● = Measured IQ, as shaped by the interaction of heredity and environment

> What do both the twin studies and adoption studies suggest about nature versus nurture and intelligence?

Enhancing Intelligence

Researchers now believe that intelligence is adaptable, and that thinking skills associated with intelligence can be improved through learning. Evidence indicates that exposing children to healthy and stimulating environments enhances performance on IQ tests. In one longitudinal study, children living in poverty who were intellectually challenged at home and in day care or school had, by age 12, average IQ scores 15 to 30 points higher than scores of children who were not challenged.

ENRICHED ENVIRONMENTS AND THE BRAIN

What impact do enriched environments have on the brain? Claire Rampon and her coworkers explored this question by changing the environment of genetically identical mice. First, the researchers randomly divided baby mice into separate groups, and then exposed them to different levels of enrichment. Half the mice were placed into cages with toys, tunnels, or boxes to explore and manipulate and the other half were placed into almost bare cages. In later testing, Rampon and her colleagues found that the mice in the enriched environments showed greater learning and memory abilities than mice in environments that were not enriched. Equally important were the differences found in the brains of the mice. The enriched mice developed more complex and higher levels of neural connections in the brain. Their enriched environments had encouraged greater brain growth and neural speed.

How can children's environments be enriched? The quality of interaction between adults and children is most important. Following are steps adults can take to encourage mental growth in children:

- ☒ Read to young children, asking them open-ended questions about the stories ("What is the Daddy doing?") rather than simple yes or no questions ("Is the Daddy cleaning the house?").

- ☒ Talk to children in detail about many topics, and carefully answer their questions.

- ☒ Expand on children's answers, correct inaccurate responses, and stress the process of learning rather than its end result.

- ☒ Encourage children to think about problems rather than to guess at solutions.

VALUING ACADEMIC ACHIEVEMENT

A number of studies have found that elementary school children in Taiwan and Japan outscore American children by about 15 points in math ability and, to a lesser extent, in reading skills. This research discovered that Chinese and Japanese parents downplay the importance of inborn intellectual ability and stress hard work. They also believe that doing well in school is the most important goal for children. American parents are more likely to believe intelligence is genetically determined and they place less value on their children's academic achievement. Following their parents' lead, when asked what they would wish for if a wizard promised them anything, the majority of the Asian children named something related to education, while the majority of American children mentioned money or possessions.

Additional research indicates that the achievement differences between the Asian and American children continue through high school. Consistent with the different valuing of education found during the early school years, American teenagers are more likely than Asian teenagers to have after-school jobs and time for sports, dating, and other social activities.

Engaging in such a wide variety of extracurricular activities is consistent with American parents' goal of developing a well-rounded teenager. However, a number of studies suggest that this philosophy can create stress and academic anxiety for high-achieving American students. They are trying to burn the candle at both ends and often simply get burned out. In contrast, high-achieving Asian students burn only one end of the candle—the academic end—and tend to have lower stress and anxiety levels.

One conclusion you can draw from these studies is that intellectual growth will be nurtured when parents and the larger culture stress the value of education and

Having too much emphasis placed on becoming "well-rounded" may create stress, academic anxiety, and even burnout for teenagers.

© AMY MYERS, 2009/USED UNDER LICENSE FROM SHUTTERSTOCK.COM

the importance of working hard to achieve intellectual mastery. In contrast, intellectual growth may be stunted when cultural beliefs impress upon children that their own academic success is not highly valued when compared to other important cultural values. Check out the Case Study on page 492 to discover how other people's expectations can affect academic performance and IQ scores.

 **CHECKPOINT** *What impact do enriched environments have on the brain?*

16.3 ASSESSMENT

In Your Own Words

Describe the nature-nurture influence on intelligence. Explain the studies cited in the text and discuss your opinion on the issue. Give examples to support your discussion.

Review Concepts

1. Which is an intervention strategy educators use with gifted students?
   - a. standardization
   - b. acceleration
   - c. reaction range
   - d. incentive

2. In which category do most people who are considered mentally retarded fall?
   - a. mild
   - b. moderate
   - c. severe
   - d. profound

3. The extent to which genetically determined limits on IQ may increase or decrease due to environmental factors is
   - a. the Flynn effect
   - b. the g-factor
   - c. Down syndrome
   - d. the reaction range

4. **True or False** Studies show that American students score the highest in the world on intelligence tests.

5. **True or False** Reading to young children can enrich their environment and influence intelligence.

6. **True or False** Studies show that intellectual giftedness is inherited from one of the parents, and that the environment is of little consequence.

Think Critically

7. Why do researchers use identical twins as subjects to study intelligence?

8. How do American parents differ from Chinese and Japanese parents in what they teach their children about the importance of education?

9. Do you agree or disagree with acceleration programs for gifted students? Do you agree or disagree with enrichment programs for gifted students? Which do you think is better? Explain your answer.

The Self-Fulfilling Prophecy

INTRODUCTION   The *self-fulfilling prophecy* is a process by which someone's expectations about a person or group leads to the fulfillment of those expectations. As shown in the figure, the self-fulfilling prophecy involves a three-step process. First, the perceiver (the "prophet") forms an impression of the target person. Second, the perceiver acts toward the target person in a manner consistent with this first impression. Third, in response, the target person's behavior changes so that it is in line with the perceiver's actions. Robert Rosenthal and Lenore Jacobson conducted a study to investigate how self-fulfilling prophecies influence the development of children's intellectual abilities.

HYPOTHESIS   Rosenthal and Jacobson hypothesized that children's academic performance and IQ scores would be enhanced by simply telling their teachers that these children were about ready to make strong intellectual improvements in the school year.

METHOD   Rosenthal and Jacobson first gave IQ tests to first- and second-grade children at the school and then told their teachers that the tests identified certain students as "potential bloomers" who should experience strong IQ gains during the remaining school year. In reality, the children identified as potential bloomers had simply been randomly selected by the researchers and did not differ intellectually from their classmates.

RESULTS   Eight months later, when the students were retested, the potential bloomers not only showed improved schoolwork, but they

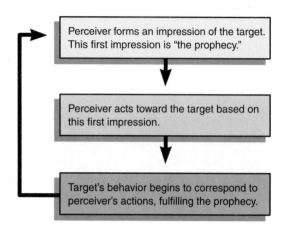

Perceiver forms an impression of the target. This first impression is "the prophecy."

Perceiver acts toward the target based on this first impression.

Target's behavior begins to correspond to perceiver's actions, fulfilling the prophecy.

also showed higher gains in their IQ scores than those who had not been identified as bloomers. Additional research found that teachers treat students who are positively labeled in this manner differently from others in the following ways:

- Teachers are friendlier toward the "gifted" students.
- Teachers provide "gifted" students with more feedback on their class work.
- Teachers challenge "gifted" students with more difficult material.
- Teachers provide "gifted" students with more opportunities to respond to class material.

Treated in this favorable manner, positively labeled students work harder and begin thinking of themselves as high achievers. Through these changes, the prophecy is fulfilled.

Critical Analysis

Why might teachers provide "gifted" students with additional work and encouragement?

Science Writer

Arts, A/V Technology & Communications

D o you like to write? Do you find psychology interesting enough you want to research and write about it? If so, you might find the career of science writer promising.

Science writers research, develop, and deliver material in multimedia formats for readers, listeners, and viewers. Science writers are divided into two main categories—technical writers and writers who develop original articles for books, magazines, trade journals, newspapers, online publications, company newsletters, textbook materials, radio and television broadcasts, motion pictures, and advertisements.

Technical science writers interpret information supplied by scientists, and then provide the reader, viewer, or listener with accurate documentation of the information. They must have extensive knowledge of the subject they are writing about. They might work with an equipment company to write a manual on how to use the equipment that psychology researchers use in experiments. Or, they might work directly with research psychologists to interpret statistical findings for information for the general public.

Science writers who develop original material also must be knowledgeable about their subject matter. Their research may consist of interviews and Internet or library research. For an article in a science magazine, a writer may interview research psychologists who just announced a breakthrough in cognitive development. Or, a science writer may work for a newspaper and be the writer who reports the announcement.

Employment Outlook

Employment of science writers is expected to grow about 10 percent, or at an average rate through 2016.

Needed Skills and Education

Science writers usually are required to have a bachelor's degree in liberal arts, journalism, communications, or English. Science writers specializing in psychology should have a dual major (psychology and one of the above areas), or a minor in psychology.

Knowledge of web design, computer software writing and graphics programs, and other technology related to Internet-based writing is practical. Science writers must be able to express ideas clearly and concisely. Enjoyment of writing is helpful for this career.

How You'll Spend Your Day

Science writers spend their day interviewing, researching, and writing. Some writers are freelancers who set their own schedule. Other writers work in-house for print, broadcast, or electronic firms, while other writers work for businesses. These writers usually have regular hours, but may work some evenings or weekends when conducting interviews.

Earnings

The median annual earnings of writers is $48,640. The highest 10 percent earn $97,700, while the lowest 10 percent earn $25,430.

What About You?

Does the career of science writer sound interesting? Use the library or Internet to research articles in *Psychology Today* or similar publication. Choose an article that interests you, and research to learn more about the subject. Write your own article using information from the original article and your research. After you have completed the article, ask yourself if you want to investigate the career of science writer further.

STOCKBYTE/GETTY IMAGES

CHAPTER SUMMARY

16.1 Measuring Intelligence

- French psychologist Alfred Binet was the most influential pioneer in intelligence testing. Working with physician Theophilé Simon, Binet developed the first workable intelligence test.

- Henry Goddard introduced Binet's test to the United States.

- Lewis Terman revised the Stanford-Binet Intelligence Test using a scoring system known as the intelligence quotient, or IQ. The formula for measuring IQ is

$$IQ = \frac{\text{Mental age}}{\text{Chronological age}} \times 100$$

- In the United States, the Wechsler Intelligence Scales are used more frequently than the Stanford-Binet to measure intelligence.

- All psychological tests have three characteristics. They must be *standardized* so that uniform procedures are used for administering the test and interpreting the score, *reliable* to measure consistent results, and *valid* to ensure the test measures what it was designed to.

- Cultural bias must be considered with intelligence tests so they are designed with the needs and values of the people being tested in mind.

16.2 Theories of Intelligence

- Charles Spearman concluded there was a general intelligence factor, or g-factor, underlying all mental abilities.

- Raymond Cattell believed that crystallized intelligence involves knowledge acquired through experience, such as the acquisition of facts and the ability to use and combine them. Fluid intelligence involves the mental capacity to learn or invent strategies for dealing with new kinds of problems.

- Multiple intelligence is Howard Gardner's theory that there are at least eight distinct and relatively independent intelligences, all of which are developed differently in each individual.

- The triarchic theory of intelligence is Robert Sternberg's theory that there are three sets of mental abilities making up human intelligence. They are analytical intelligence, creative intelligence, and practical intelligence.

16.3 Influences on Intelligence

- The two extremes of intelligence are mental retardation and mental giftedness. Mental retardation is diagnosed in people who have an IQ score below 70 and have difficulty adapting to the routine demands of independent living. The most common genetic cause of mental retardation is Down syndrome. Mental giftedness is found in people with an IQ score above 130. Evidence suggests that genes predispose some people toward giftedness, but that life experiences help these natural tendencies.

- Studies conducted on twins show that both nature and nurture are important in the development of intelligence.

- Studies show that intelligence is adaptable, and that thinking skills associated with intelligence can be improved through learning. Evidence indicates that exposing children to healthy and stimulating environments enhances performances on IQ tests.

CHAPTER 16 ASSESSMENT

Review Psychology Terms

Select the term that best fits the definition. Some terms will not be used.

_____ 1. The degree to which a test yields consistent results

_____ 2. A general intelligence ability which underlies all mental abilities

_____ 3. A test that predicts a person's capacity for learning

_____ 4. A condition of limited mental ability, indicated by an IQ score at or below 70 and difficulty in adapting to independent living

_____ 5. The age that reflects the child's mental abilities in comparison to the average child of the same age

_____ 6. A form of mental retardation caused by an extra chromosome in genetic makeup

_____ 7. The degree to which a test measures what it is designed to measure

_____ 8. A person's mental ability to learn or invent strategies for dealing with problems

_____ 9. The mental abilities to adapt to and shape the environment

_____ 10. The extent to which genetically determined limits on IQ may increase or decrease due to environmental factors

_____ 11. The process of establishing uniform procedures for administering a test and for interpreting its scores

_____ 12. A test designed to assess what a person has learned

_____ 13. A person's knowledge and verbal skills learned through experience

_____ 14. Sternberg's theory that there are three sets of mental abilities making up human intelligence: analytic, creative, and practical

_____ 15. The tendency for people's performance on IQ tests to improve from one generation to the next

_____ 16. A ratio of mental age divided by chronological age, multiplied by 100

_____ 17. Howard Gardner's theory that there are at least eight separate intelligences, all of which are developed differently in each individual

a. achievement test

b. aptitude test

c. crystallized intelligence

d. deviation IQ

e. Down syndrome

f. factor analysis

g. fluid intelligence

h. Flynn effect

i. general intelligence factor (g-factor)

j. intelligence

k. intelligence quotient (IQ)

l. mental age

m. mental retardation

n. multiple intelligences

o. reaction range

p. reliability

q. standardization

r. triarchic theory of intelligence

s. validity

Review Psychology Concepts

18. Identify the first intelligence test, the designers, and what it measured.

19. Indicate how an IQ is calculated.

20. Identify the three tests included in the Wechsler Intelligence Scales.

21. Assess which student has the advantage when taking an SAT test: A student who has taken several math classes or a student who has concentrated on music and art? Explain your answer.

22. Identify the principle that explains why you may have a higher IQ than that of your ancestors.

23. Which of Gardner's intelligences do you find most valuable? Explain your answer.

24. Classify each of the following careers with one of the mental abilities of Sternberg's triarchic theory of intelligence: carpenter, engineer, art teacher, science researcher, short story writer, landscape worker, landscape designer.

25. Identify and describe two ways the educational system tries to meet the needs of mentally gifted students.

26. Explain the influence of nature and nurture based on studies of twins and adopted children.

27. Defend this statement: High scores on verbal aptitude tests are due to both natural ability and experience.

28. What happens in the brain when the environment is enriched?

Apply Psychology Concepts

29. Eliza is 90 years old and lives in a retirement community. While she loves solving crossword puzzles, she is having trouble learning Sudoku, a logic puzzle based on numbers. Using Cattell's theory of fluid and crystallized intelligence, explain why Eliza is able to solve crossword puzzles but struggles with the new logic game.

30. The U.S. Army administered the Stanford-Binet Intelligence Test to determine assignments for new soldiers. Individuals who scored between 100 and 130 qualified for Officer Training School. Individuals who scored between 70 and 100 were assigned to the infantry. After decades of this policy, the military began to notice that the officers were overwhelmingly white. Members of the infantry tended to be poor minorities and the children of immigrants. In what ways might the Army's testing policies have contributed to ethnic and racial inequality in the military?

31. Micah and Anthony are identical twins who were separated at birth and adopted by two different families. Micah grew up in an urban community and attended a private school. He made frequent trips to local museums, played the piano, and even traveled to Europe with his adoptive parents while in high school. Micah's parents made sure he had the best teachers and that he maintained excellent grades. Anthony was raised in a small, rural town. He played little league sports and had a summer job mowing lawns. Anthony's school did not offer AP courses or other enrichment opportunities. When they were ready for college, Micah and Anthony had nearly identical scores on aptitude tests. They attended the same state university and both tested out of first-year mathematics. With such different childhood experiences, how could these two end up so much alike?

32. Explain which of Sternberg's triarchic intelligences (practical, analytical, or creative) would be most appropriate in dealing with the following situations: (a) While setting up a campsite in a remote area, you realize that you forgot to pack a tent. In your gear, you have garbage bags, duct tape, and a rope. (b) On the first day at your new job as an office manager, you are expected to make copies, order office supplies, and set up your new computer. (c) You need to write an essay for your high school psychology class.

Make Academic Connections

33. **Writing** Write an argument for and an argument against the theory of multiple intelligences. Cite information from the text for both arguments.

34. **Research** Emotional intelligence is a relatively new area of psychological study and one still developing. Experts are still forming opinions about the correct definition and the use of and ways to measure emotional intelligence. Use the Internet to research information on emotional intelligence, and then use a computer program to create a graphic organizer that illustrates the major points of your findings.

35. **Marketing** You own a company that sells intelligence tests. Using information from the text on one of the intelligence tests discussed, create a brochure that markets your product to your school system. Explain why your test is better than other tests discussed.

36. **Art** Sketch your idea for a bulletin board that illustrates Gardner's eight intelligences. Include illustrations of careers that match each intelligence.

DIGGING DEEPER
with Psychology eCollection

Artificial intelligence has been a theme for science fiction writers for nearly a century. Machines and computers that can think make a great story. Hal, the computer in *2001: A Space Odyssey* is an excellent example. Hal reacts and shows emotion, much as humans do. Scientists and the general public alike consider intelligence to be a purely human characteristic. Are machines with cognitive abilities as described by fiction writers possible? Access the Gale Psychology eCollection at *www.cengage.com/school/psych/franzoi* and read the section on artificial intelligence. Write a summary of the article, including some of the functions for which AI currently is being used. Then answer the question: Is instilling machines with artificial intelligence a good or bad idea? Explain your answer. As an additional project, write an essay answering the question: Will there ever be machines or computers that think like a person? Why or why not?

Source: "Artificial Intelligence." *Gale Encyclopedia of Psychology*. Ed. Bonnie Strickland. 2nd ed. Detroit: Gale, 2001.

SELF-DISCOVERY: YOUR SCORE

What Is Interpersonal Intelligence?

Scoring Instructions: The items on this scale measure your ability to take the perspective (point of view) of others, which is an important quality of interpersonal intelligence. Some of these items are reverse-scored; that is, for these items a lower rating actually indicates a higher level of perspective taking. Before summing the items, recode those with an asterisk (*) so that 0 = 4, 1 = 3, 3 = 1, 4 = 0. The higher your total score, the higher your perspective-taking ability. Research indicates that women tend to score somewhat higher on perspective taking than men. Among young adults, the average score is 17. Is your score above or below the average score?

TELEPHONE

UNIT 5

Behavior Domain

A good portion of your life involves trying to understand why other people think and act the way they do. In your everyday life you encounter many different people from a wide variety of social backgrounds. They often surprise you with how they think and act. When that happens, it is only natural to spend time making sense of what you have witnessed.

Why do some people struggle with depression and thoughts of suicide? Why are other people terrified of heights, snakes, or deep water? When are depressed moods or fears normal and when are they not normal? What are the possible remedies that psychologists have developed for mental health problems? The first two chapters in this unit will examine these and other questions related to restoring and maintaining psychological health.

People do not need to think and act far from what you consider normal for you to want to make sense of them. Why do people often have so many different attitudes and opinions? How can you persuade others to agree with you? What causes people to express prejudice toward others, and when are they likely to either help or hurt those around them? The last two chapters in this unit will explore the social psychology of everyday life.

Psychological Disorders

ESSENTIAL QUESTION
Go to page XXVII

> "Nothing defines the quality of life in a community more clearly than people who regard themselves, or whom the consensus chooses to regard, as mentally unwell."

—RENATA ADLER, ITALIAN-BORN AMERICAN AUTHOR, B. 1938

While visiting a small Tennessee church, I witnessed a man suddenly stand up during the Sunday service while everyone was singing a hymn. Swaying back and forth, the man thrust his arms upwards and began speaking words I could not understand. Everyone around him nodded in approval and continued singing.

Two years later I witnessed a similar event in New York City. On the subway, a man jumped up from his seat and began swaying back and forth with his arms thrust upwards. Like the man in Tennessee, this man began speaking words I could not understand. Unlike the reaction in the church, the subway passengers responded with alarm to the man's behavior. At the next subway stop, he was taken away by the police.

In both incidents, people responded very differently to seeing someone behaving this way. Why was there such a difference in the perception of their behavior? How does a society determine whether a person is suffering from a psychological disorder?

COMSTOCK IMAGES/JUPITER IMAGES

What Are Psychological Disorders?

OBJECTIVES

- Define a psychological disorder.
- Identify risks and benefits in classifying psychological disorders.

DISCOVER IT | *How does this relate to me?*

Are you interested in understanding people who suffer from mental health problems? Are you concerned about being around such people? As illustrated in the chapter-opening story, the behavior of people with serious psychological problems may seem unusual and even frighten you. By understanding the causes of such behavior, you will gain insight into the world of mental illness. In doing so, you will learn a good deal more about the world around you.

KEY TERMS

- psychological disorder
- symptom
- diagnosis
- *Diagnostic and Statistical Manual of Mental Disorders (DSM)*

Mental health is a serious issue. More than two million Americans with psychological problems are hospitalized yearly. More than twice as many seek help as outpatients. Twenty percent of all people in the United States experience serious psychological problems that disrupt their lives. Forty percent experience mild problems. Worldwide about 400 million people have psychological disorders.

Defining a Psychological Disorder

Psychologists define a **psychological disorder** as a pattern of unusual behavior that results in personal distress or significant interference in a person's ability to engage in normal daily living. A **symptom** is a sign of a disorder, such as having visions. After examining symptoms of different disorders, psychologists and other mental health professionals developed criteria to distinguish between normal and disordered behavior. The process of identifying disorders is known as **diagnosis**.

ATYPICAL BEHAVIOR

One way to distinguish *disordered* from *normal* behavior is to see how common it is in the general population. Something that is not common is often referred to as *atypical*. Atypical behavior is more likely than typical behavior to be classified as a psychological disorder. The compulsive behavior of repeatedly washing your hands

psychological disorder
A pattern of unusual behavior that results in personal distress or significant interference in a person's ability to engage in normal daily living

symptom Sign of a disorder

diagnosis The process of identifying disorders

This person appears to be experiencing emotional pain, but is she suffering from a psychological disorder?

because of a fear of germs is unusual and may signal an underlying psychological disorder. However, defining a psychological disorder based on whether behavior is unusual or not can lead to false judgments. The extraordinary athletic behavior of Hall of Fame athletes is unusual, but no one says these individuals have a psychological disorder. Some emotions, such as anxiety and depression, are relatively common, and yet they may be a symptom of a psychological disorder. Psychologists cannot rely only on how far a person's behavior differs from the average person's behavior to identify psychological disorders.

VIOLATION OF CULTURAL NORMS

Another way to distinguish between disordered and normal behavior is by determining whether the behavior violates cultural norms. *Norms* are the established and approved ways of behaving around others. Shaking hands when meeting someone is an example of a cultural norm. Refusing to shake hands because you greatly fear germs may raise concerns about your sanity. Yet some people may avoid hand shaking because their bodies truly have weak immune systems, making them very vulnerable to germs. Their germ fear is not a sign of a mental disorder but is based on sound medical advice. As this example suggests, simply relying on violations of cultural norms can cause mistakes in deciding what is disordered.

MALADAPTIVE BEHAVIOR

There is more to a psychological disorder than being unusual or out of line with cultural norms. Such behavior is disordered if it is judged *maladaptive*—disruptive or harmful—for the person or society. Being unable to perform normal activities is a sign of maladaptive behavior. Not leaving your house because you fear crowds also is an example of maladaptive behavior. Maladaptive behavior is the most important criterion in defining a disorder.

PERSONAL DISTRESS

People experiencing troubling emotions are often thought to have psychological problems. They may perform normal daily activities but feel unreasonably fearful, anxious, guilty, angry, or depressed. This criterion takes into account a person's own distress level. A behavior that is upsetting and stressful for one person—such as the inability to control anger—may not be disturbing to someone else. The problem with this criterion is that some people who suffer from psychological disorders—and who cause harm to themselves and others—are not troubled by their behavior.

One criterion alone is not sufficient to distinguish normal from disordered behavior. Accurately identifying psychological disorders involves making *value judgments* about which behaviors cross the bounds of normal mental health. To understand how a clinical psychologist diagnoses a psychological disorder, read the Case Study on page 503.

INFOBIT

Cultural upbringing can affect how people report personal distress. Asian Americans and Hispanic Americans suffering from psychological disorders are more likely than other Americans to report physical symptoms, such as dizziness, rather than emotional symptoms. This is because in many Asian and Hispanic cultures, it is improper to discuss personal feelings with others. Mental health professionals need to be aware of how culture influences the way people express symptoms of mental illness.

CHECKPOINT *What is a psychological disorder?*

How Do Psychologists Diagnose a Psychological Disorder?

INTRODUCTION *Somatoform disorders* are psychological problems that involve some body symptom, even though no actual physical cause of the symptom can be found. People who suffer from a somatoform disorder often seek medical care for the physical symptoms that are causing them great concern. When a physician refers these patients to a clinical psychologist or psychiatrist, the patients often seek out another physician rather than admitting that the problem is psychological. In the case described here, Erin is a 30-year-old woman who is seeking help for the first time from a clinical psychologist, Dr. Bergdahl.

During the first therapy session, Erin is upset and sobs as she describes her firm belief that she has a life-threatening heart condition that no medical experts have been able to detect. She has seen ten doctors about her heart concerns, but finally reluctantly agreed to talk to a clinical psychologist.

HYPOTHESIS Based on information gathered during the first therapy session, Dr. Bergdahl thinks it is likely that Erin is suffering from a psychological disorder. This hypothesis is supported by the fact that none of the medical experts have found any evidence for a physical cause for the symptoms she is reporting. Dr. Bergdahl hypothesizes that Erin is suffering from *hypochondriasis*, which is a type of somatoform disorder involving an irrational fear of developing some disease.

METHOD Dr. Bergdahl used the case study method of data collection, which is an in-depth analysis of a single person. For Erin, this involved three therapy sessions with an extensive description of her symptoms.

RESULTS It was clear to Dr. Bergdahl that Erin's behavior was *atypical*. Very few young adults continue reporting strong health fears after having multiple examinations that reveal no medical problems. It also was clear that Erin's health fears were preventing her from performing normal daily activities. Erin had quit her job, stopped exercising, and spent most days at home. Erin's behavior definitely is *maladaptive*. It also was clear that Erin was experiencing a great deal of *personal distress*. Even though Erin's behavior did not violate cultural norms (which is one criterion for diagnosing disordered behavior), Dr. Bergdahl believed her condition fit the diagnosis of hypochondriasis.

Dr. Bergdahl knows that hypochondriasis is fairly common (occurring in 2 to 7 percent of patients in general medical practice). It tends to occur in early adulthood and generally is a chronic condition throughout a person's life. People who develop this psychological disorder tend to be self-centered, suggestible, extremely emotional, and overly dramatic—which is exactly the type of personality that seeks attention during illness. Dr. Bergdahl observed these behavior patterns during the three therapy sessions with Erin.

Critical Analysis

Why might Erin have resisted seeing a psychologist?

Risks and Benefits
in Classifying Disorders

What are the risks and benefits in classifying thoughts, feelings, and behavior of people as being psychologically disordered? Labeling an individual as having a psychological disorder can cause harm. Labeled individuals may be ridiculed or scorned at school, work, or in other areas of their lives due to negative stereotypes about the mentally ill. People may expect these individuals to behave strangely and misinterpret normal behavior as disordered.

A common stereotype of mentally ill individuals is that they are dangerous and violent. One study monitored the behavior of more than 1,000 individuals during their first year after leaving a psychiatric hospital where they received treatment for mental illness. Results found no difference in acts of violence between the former patients and a control group of people who had no history of serious mental health problems. Other research indicates that violence is only slightly higher among people who have severe psychological disorders and who are out of touch with reality. All other individuals with a psychological disorder who are not experiencing severe symptoms are no more violent than the average person. This research informs us that the stereotype associating mental illness with violence is highly exaggerated and largely untrue.

Despite these problems with diagnostic labels, mental health professionals use them because of the benefits. A label summarizes the person's symptoms or problems. Rather than listing each person's entire set of symptoms, psychologists communicate information about a person with a single word. A second benefit is that a diagnostic label provides information about possible causes of the disorder. A third benefit is that the label conveys information about the person's likely response to treatment. For many psychological disorders, research has identified one or more effective treatments. Knowledge of a patient's diagnosis often suggests which treatment may be most helpful.

Diagnostic and Statistical Manual of Mental Disorders (DSM) The classification scheme used by most mental health professionals to diagnose psychological disorders

The stigma surrounding psychological disorders causes many people to avoid seeking help. What is one of the most common stereotypes about the mentally ill?

WORKBOOK STOCK/JUPITER IMAGES

To help classify psychological disorders, psychologists and other mental health professionals use the *Diagnostic and Statistical Manual of Mental Disorders (DSM)*. The DSM classification system was developed in the 1950s. It is not based on a particular theory concerning what causes psychological disorders. Instead, diagnoses are based on symptoms that mental health professionals can observe directly or can detect by asking patients straightforward questions. The DSM provides very clear directions concerning what sort of

symptoms are necessary for someone to be diagnosed with a specific disorder. It also indicates how long a person must show these symptoms before
being diagnosed with the disorder.

Currently, the DSM identifies 15 major categories of psychological disorders.
However, it only provides general descriptions of these disorders. Mental health
professionals who use the DSM must keep in mind that these diagnostic labels do
not describe all the unique qualities and problems of their patients. Psychologists
realize that the DSM classification system is not perfect and that is why it is revised
every few years based on new research.

 **CHECKPOINT** *What are the benefits of using diagnostic labels in classifying psychological disorders?*

17.1 ASSESSMENT

In Your Own Words

Identify the criterion psychologists use to distinguish between normal and disordered
behavior.

Review Concepts

1. Which is the most important criterion in defining a psychological disorder?
   - a. atypical behavior
   - b. cultural norm violation
   - c. maladaptive behavior
   - d. personal distress

2. A common misconception about individuals with psychological disorders is that
   they are
   - a. loners
   - b. treatable
   - c. violent
   - d. discriminated against

3. Classifications in the *Diagnostic and Statistical Manual of Mental Disorders* (DSM)
   are based on
   - a. psychologists' reports
   - b. twin studies
   - c. value judgments
   - d. observable symptoms

4. **True or False** One benefit of using a diagnostic label for psychological disorders is
   that it conveys information about possible causes of the disorder.

5. **True or False** When making value judgments about whether an individual has a
   psychological disorder, psychologists must ignore the person's
   distress level.

Think Critically

6. Explain why mental health is a serious issue in the United States and in the world.

LESSON
17.2 | Anxiety and Mood Disorders

KEY TERMS

- anxiety disorder
- panic disorder
- phobic disorder
- generalized anxiety disorder
- obsessive-compulsive disorder
- post-traumatic stress disorder
- mood disorders
- major depressive disorder
- bipolar disorder

OBJECTIVES

- Define anxiety disorders and identify the various types.
- Define mood disorders and identify the various types.

DISCOVER IT | *How does this relate to me?*

Are you deeply afraid of heights, snakes, or spiders? Do you ever feel anxious to the point of panic? Do you know anyone whose fear is so great it limits their daily activities? You most likely feel sad at times, but did you know some people are always depressed? What causes fears, anxieties, and dark moods?

The remainder of this chapter introduces you to some of the major classes of psychological disorders. Keep in mind that you may have experienced some of these symptoms yourself at some time. The truth is that many of the described symptoms are fairly common. Throughout your life, you will experience deep sadness and great joy, strong anxiety and fear, and other personal problems. What makes these experiences "abnormal"? Symptoms such as anxiety or sadness may be the cause of a psychological disorder only when they disrupt daily living or your sense of well-being over a long period of time.

Anxiety Disorders

Everybody experiences anxiety. However, anxiety disorders are different from normal anxiety because they involve extreme emotional distress that severely disrupt a person's life. **Anxiety disorders** are characterized by distressing, lasting anxiety, and unusual behavior. They are the most common psychological disorders. About 25 percent of the general population experiences this disorder in their lifetime. There are five major anxiety disorders: panic disorder, phobic disorder, generalized anxiety disorder (GAD), obsessive-compulsive disorder (OCD), and post-traumatic stress disorder (PTSD).

PANIC DISORDER

Maya is an 18-year-old hairstylist who has **panic disorder**, characterized by episodes of intense anxiety without an apparent reason. During episodes, Maya feels dizzy, her heart races, she sweats and has tremors, and she may even faint.

anxiety disorders
Disorders characterized by distressing, lasting anxiety, and unusual behavior

panic disorder An anxiety disorder characterized by episodes of intense anxiety without an apparent reason

Besides these physical symptoms, psychological symptoms may include fear of dying, fear of suffocating, fear of going crazy, and fear of losing control and doing something drastic, such as killing herself or others.

Panic episodes have a clear beginning and end. They are relatively brief, usually lasting a few minutes. Such episodes are extremely frightening. The symptoms, which are associated with the arousal of the sympathetic nervous system, cause sufferers to seek medical attention out of concern that they are dying. About three percent of the general population worldwide experiences panic disorder. This anxiety disorder occurs more often in young adults than in older adults, with twice as many women (5 percent) affected as men (2 percent).

PHOBIC DISORDER

Phobic disorder is characterized by strong irrational fears of specific objects or situations, called *phobias*. The DSM classifies phobias into subtypes based on the object of fear. The most common type of phobic disorder is a *specific phobia*, which involves fear and avoidance of a particular object or situation, such as heights, animals, enclosed spaces, blood, and automobile or air travel. Another type of phobic disorder is a *social phobia*, which involves a fear of being negatively evaluated by others or acting in ways that are embarrassing. Specific phobias affect about 10 percent of the population, but only about 3 percent are affected by social phobias. Women are diagnosed with specific phobias about twice as often as men and tend to develop phobic symptoms earlier (age 10 for females and age 14 for males). The gender difference in social phobias is smaller, with women diagnosed slightly more often than men. Figure 17-1 shows the frequency of some common specific phobias. Before reading further, complete the Self-Discovery feature on page 508.

INFOBIT

It is important to distinguish phobias from the normal fears people may experience. For example, many people are afraid of spiders, but this common fear does not prevent them from spending time outdoors or in their basements. However, if individuals are so afraid of seeing a spider that they avoid the outdoors and do not go into their basements, they may be suffering from a phobic disorder.

phobic disorder Anxiety disorder characterized by strong irrational fears of specific objects or situations

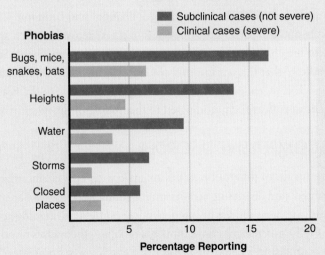

Figure 17-1 **FREQUENCY OF SPECIFIC PHOBIAS**

Many people experience fear when exposed to these stimuli. In most of these cases, the fear represents a "subclinical phobia" which would not indicate a psychological disorder.

What Do You Most Fear?

We all fear something. Most of these fears represent a subclinical phobia, meaning that they are mild, irrational fears that do not interfere with our normal daily routines. Many people have a strong fear of heights and insects. Fear of animals, such as dogs or cats, is most common during the elementary school years. Blood phobia tends to appear at about nine years. Social phobias, which are intense fears involving social situations such as test anxiety or fears of embarrassment are most likely to occur in later adolescence or early adulthood.

Instructions: Answer the following questions about fear in your life.

1. What is it that you fear most?

2. At what age did you first become aware of this fear?

3. How strong is this fear? Mild fear 1 2 3 4 5 6 7 8 9 10 Paralyzing fear

4. Does this fear cause a major disruption in your life? Yes _____ No _____

In Chapter 18 you will learn about a thought strategy to reduce and even eliminate this fear.

GENERALIZED ANXIETY DISORDER

generalized anxiety disorder (GAD) involves a constant state of moderate anxiety. This anxiety differs from the normal anxiety that people experience during stressful events or situations. For example, if you are a student who has many after-school activities and an active social life, it is normal to experience moderate anxiety at different times in the semester because of these commitments. The anxiety experienced in GAD differs from normal anxiety because in GAD there is no clear object or situation that causes the anxiety. Instead, the anxiety is "free floating" and constant.

GAD occurs in about 6 percent of Americans in their lifetime. It often appears following a major life change, such as starting a new job or having a baby. Surveys of Americans indicate that the average level of GAD has increased sharply during the past 50 years. This increase in generalized anxiety may be due to the faster-paced lifestyle of American culture today compared to the middle of the twentieth century.

OBSESSIVE-COMPULSIVE DISORDER

Obsessive-compulsive disorder (OCD) is an anxiety disorder characterized by recurring, unwanted, and distressing actions and/or thoughts. *Obsessions* are recurring thoughts or ideas that cause distress or interfere significantly with ongoing activity. For example, some OCD sufferers may have thoughts of killing themselves or others, even though they have no history of, and are not at risk for, suicide or homicide. *Compulsions* are recurring actions or behaviors that cause distress or interfere significantly with

generalized anxiety disorder (GAD) An anxiety disorder involving a constant state of moderate anxiety not associated with an object or situation.

obsessive-compulsive disorder (OCD) An anxiety disorder characterized by recurring, unwanted, and distressing actions and/or thoughts

ongoing activity. Most OCD rituals can be classified as cleaning, checking, or collecting. For example, some OCD sufferers engage in hand-washing rituals, cleaning their hands hundreds of times a day. Other individuals feel compelled to repeatedly check the locks on their doors

People who suffer from obsessive-compulsive disorder often engage in recurring actions, such as washing their hands for hours until they are raw. How do such rituals reduce the anxiety associated with the disorder?

before they leave the house. Some people save newspapers and tin cans for years, to the point that it becomes difficult to navigate through their houses.

OCD is associated with intense anxiety. OCD sufferers experience anxiety-provoking obsessions, such as fears of contamination and worries about not having taken steps to prevent harm. They try to control obsessive thoughts and reduce anxiety by performing compulsive rituals. The compulsive rituals lower anxiety only temporarily, so the individual must repeat them or add to their length.

About 2 to 3 percent of the population has OCD, with women at a higher risk than men. This disorder develops in adolescence or young adulthood. OCD sufferers often hide the symptoms from others. It may be years before the symptoms become so intense they can no longer be hidden.

POST-TRAUMATIC STRESS DISORDER

John is a veteran of the Iraq War who suffers from **post-traumatic stress disorder (PTSD)**. This is an anxiety disorder involving flashbacks and recurring thoughts of life-threatening or other traumatic events. The flashbacks and other intense emotions experienced by victims of traumatic events occur after the original trauma and interfere with normal daily functioning. John regularly experiences nightmares about his war experiences and can become highly anxious at the sound of thunder or other loud noises that trigger war memories.

Research suggests that almost 8 percent of the general population experiences PTSD symptoms. Most PTSD patients have experienced trauma such as rape, child abuse, family illness, or witnessing violence. Trauma such as being in warfare or a natural disaster also can lead to this disorder. In general, as the severity of the traumatic event increases, the risk for PTSD increases.

post-traumatic stress disorder (PTSD) An anxiety disorder involving flashbacks and recurrent thoughts of life-threatening or other traumatic events

Many soldiers who fought in the Iraq War or in previous wars developed post-traumatic stress disorder. Why might this be so?

BLEND IMAGES/JUPITER IMAGES

CAUSES OF ANXIETY DISORDERS

Biology plays an important role in anxiety disorders. Panic disorder, GAD, and OCD have a moderate genetic influence. For example, brain-imaging studies suggest that obsessions are partly caused by the brain not switching off recurring thoughts before they become obsessions. Evidence also indicates that people who suffer from panic, phobic, and generalized anxiety disorders respond differently to danger signals than do nonsufferers. These and other findings suggest that some people are biologically programmed to respond intensely to stressful events. This stronger stress reaction puts them at greater risk for developing anxiety disorders.

The type of learning that occurs in classical and operant conditioning may play a role in the development of anxiety disorders. As discussed in Chapter 12 (page 340), classical conditioning produces emotional responses to previously neutral stimuli. After these conditioned emotional responses are learned, people's avoidance of the feared objects are reinforced, because as they move away from the objects, their anxiety decreases. In other words, classical conditioning may create conditioned fear responses, and operant conditioning may reinforce—and so, maintain—the person's avoidance responses. This *two-process conditioning model* has been a useful way to understand anxiety disorders.

Finally, cognitive factors also play an important role in anxiety disorders. For example, people who suffer from panic disorder often monitor their physiological reactions because they want to detect the beginning of another panic episode. However, they often misinterpret and exaggerate these physiological signals, perhaps because panic episodes are so distressing. Their fear of fear leads them to experience the extreme anxiety they want to avoid. This misinterpretation and exaggeration of physiological signals also plays a role in generalized anxiety disorders.

Given these possible multiple triggers, what is the ultimate cause of anxiety disorders? Is it biological, behavioral, or cognitive? Most likely, it is some combination of all three factors.

Mood Disorders

Mood disorders are characterized by emotional extremes that cause significant disruption in daily functioning. Almost 30 percent of the general population reports experiencing a depressed mood for at least two weeks. To qualify as a mood disorder, emotional extremes must persist for more than a few weeks.

DEPRESSION

The most common mood disorder is **major depressive disorder**, which involves extreme and lasting negative moods and the inability to experience pleasure by participating in activities a person previously enjoyed. Depressed individuals experience physiological problems such as lack of appetite, weight loss, fatigue, and sleep disorders. In addition, depressed individuals often experience slowed thinking and behavior, and social withdrawal. They also experience low self-esteem, thoughts about death and/or suicide, and have little hope for the future.

Because depression is so common—the lifetime likelihood is about 17 percent—it has been termed the "common cold" of mental illness. People who experience major depressive disorder often have multiple episodes during their lives. Cross-culturally, depression occurs about twice as frequently in women as in men, but great variations are seen between cultures (see Figure 17-2 on page 512). One reason there may be cultural differences is that some cultures are more likely than others to teach their members to admit to and seek help for depression. This also may explain why men have lower reported depression rates than women. In many cultures, men are discouraged from expressing sad emotions because it is viewed as "unmanly." Thus, men may experience depression at the same levels as women, but they may be much less likely to admit they are depressed.

Depression does occur in children, but the risk among those younger than 10 years is much lower than that among adolescents and adults. Older adults are the age group most likely to suffer from depression, which is often caused by social isolation and the death of loved ones. Check out the Self-Discovery feature on page 513, which contains a self-report questionnaire that assesses cognitive symptoms of depression.

LAB TEAMS

Depression and Culture

With a partner, use the Internet or library to research depression in five different countries. Make a chart that lists some of the social ills that might cause depression in some people in the culture. Have a discussion with another group and discuss what could be changed to help ease depression in one of the countries chosen by either group. For example, depression among the people of Darfur might be caused by war and lack of food. A change that could take place to help ease depression there is to educate students on the plight of the people in Darfur, so students can work with organizers to send food and other aid to the country.

mood disorders
Psychological disorders characterized by emotional extremes that cause significant disruption in daily functioning

major depressive disorder A mood disorder characterized by extreme and lasting negative moods and the inability to experience pleasure from activities one previously enjoyed

Everyone feels sad, bored, and uninterested in their activities at times. However, when these emotions keep you from enjoying life, it may be a symptom of depression.

One of the major dangers of depression is suicide. As many as 30 percent of people with severe mood disorders die from suicide. In the United States, about 32,500 people commit suicide annually, a rate of about 11 per 100,000. The highest rates of suicide are among European Americans, followed by Native Americans, Asian Americans, Hispanic Americans, and African Americans (see Figure 17-3 on page 513). Some psychologists believe that suicide rates are lower among Hispanic Americans and African Americans because members of these ethnic groups are more likely than members of other ethnic groups to follow religious teachings that prohibit suicide.

About three out of four people who die by suicide show some suicide warning signs, including the following:

1. Appearing depressed or sad most of the time
2. Talking or writing about death or suicide
3. Withdrawing from family and friends
4. Loss of interest in things one used to care about
5. Making comments about being hopeless, helpless, or worthless
6. Giving away prized possessions
7. Visiting or calling people to say goodbye
8. Acting recklessly
9. Feeling strong anger or rage
10. Abusing drugs or alcohol

If you notice someone showing any of these warning signs, tell an adult whom you trust or call your local suicide hotline immediately. Call 800-SUICIDE (800-784-2433) or 800-273-TALK (800-273-8255). Check out the Closer Look feature on page 514 for some important facts about suicide.

Figure 17-2 **GENDER AND DEPRESSION**

Interviews with 38,000 women and men in ten countries found that women's risk of experiencing major depression is double that of men's. Lifetime risk of depression among adults varies by culture.

Source: Data from Myrna M. Weissman and Roger C. Bland. "Cross-national epidemiology of major depression and bipolar disorder." *JAMA: Journal of the American Medical Association* 276, no. 4 (July 24, 1996): 293, table 2.

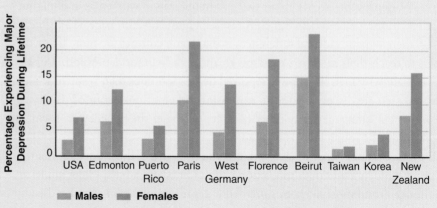

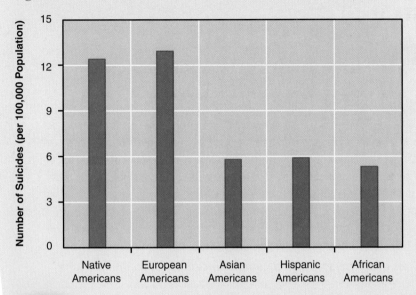

Figure 17-3 SUICIDE RATES AMONG ETHNIC GROUPS

Number of Suicides (per 100,000 Population) — y-axis: 0, 3, 6, 9, 12, 15

Native Americans | European Americans | Asian Americans | Hispanic Americans | African Americans

Suicide rates vary widely among ethnic groups in the United States, with Native Americans' and European Americans' rates being twice as high as that of African Americans. Suicide rates are highest in the western states, which is where people are more likely to own guns.

Source: Centers for Disease Control and Prevention. (1999). *Suicide deaths and rates per 100,000* [online].

SELF-DISCOVERY

The Automatic Thoughts Questionnaire

The Automatic Thoughts Questionnaire (ATQ) addresses common negative thoughts that occur when people are in a depressed mood.

Instructions: Read each thought carefully and indicate how frequently, if at all, the thought occurred to you over the last week, using the following scale:

1 = not at all   2 = sometimes   3 = moderately often   4 = often   5 = all the time

1. I feel like I'm up against the world.
2. I'm no good.
3. Why can't I ever succeed?
4. No one understands me.
5. I've let people down.
6. I don't think I can go on.
7. I wish I were a better person.
8. I'm so weak.
9. My life's not going the way I want it to.
10. I'm so disappointed in myself.
11. Nothing feels good anymore.
12. I can't stand this anymore.
13. I can't get started.
14. What's wrong with me?
15. I wish I were somewhere else.
16. I can't get things together.
17. I hate myself.
18. I'm worthless.
19. I wish I could just disappear.
20. What's the matter with me?
21. I'm a loser.
22. My life is a mess.
23. I'm a failure.
24. I'll never make it.
25. I feel so hopeless.
26. Something has to change.
27. There must be something wrong with me.
28. My future is bleak.
29. It's just not worth it.
30. I can't finish anything.

See page 531 for scoring instructions.

Source: From "Cognitive self-statements in depression: Development of an Automatic Thoughts Questionnaire" by S. D. Hollon and P. C. Kendall in *Cognitive Therapy and Research*, 4, 1980, pp. 383–395. Copyright © 1980. Reprinted by permission of Kluwer Academic/Plenum Publishers and the authors.

Important Facts About Suicide

Following are three commonly asked questions and answers about suicide:

- *Is it true that people who talk about suicide never commit suicide?* No. This is a dangerous misconception. One of the best predictors of suicide risk is a stated threat to commit suicide. Eighty percent of suicides are preceded by some warning. Take every threat of suicide seriously. Some suicide threats may be hidden. For example, a person may give away possessions or talk about "getting away to end my problems." Observers should be sensitive to such hints of suicidal thinking and ask an adult for help in assessing the situation.

- *Does every person who attempts suicide want to die?* No. Some suicide attempts are more a cry for help or attention than a wish to die. For example, people who take a half bottle of baby aspirin or scratch their wrists with nail clippers may not have intended to die. Such nonlethal attempts are called "suicidal gestures" and are considered cries for help. People who have made suicidal gestures in the past may make a more lethal attempt in the future.

- *What should I do if a friend talks about suicide?* It is important that you take the threat seriously because many suicide attempts can be prevented by providing those at high risk with help and social support. However, it is also important to recognize that you are not a mental health professional and are not able to evaluate suicide risk or provide psychotherapy. As a friend, you can listen and provide comfort and support, but it is important to encourage your friend to seek professional help. If your friend does not take your advice, find someone important in your friend's life—a parent, teacher, or school counselor—who can convince your friend to see a mental health professional.

Think Critically
What would you do if a close friend or family member were displaying signs of attempting suicide?

BIPOLAR DISORDER

bipolar disorder
A mood disorder character-ized by swings between the emotional extremes of mania and depression

Bipolar disorder is a mood disorder characterized by swings between the emotional extremes of mania and depression. *Mania* is an overly joyful, active emotional state. Symptoms are the opposite of those of depression. When indi-viduals are manic, they speak and move rapidly, going from activity to activity with endless optimism and self-confidence. They often do not feel the need for sleep.

Manic symptoms may not seem very bothersome. However, a person in a manic state can engage in destructive behavior. For example, they may feel so on top of the world that they drive their car 100 miles per hour, ignoring the danger to themselves and others.

Bipolar disorder is less common than major depressive disorder, occurring in about 1 percent of the population. Unlike major depression, bipolar disorder occurs about equally in men and women and tends to occur earlier in life than major depression. Although bipolar patients usually experience periods of severe depression as well as bouts of mania, their depressive episodes are more severe than those experienced in major depression, and are accompanied by higher suicide risks. The symptoms of manic and depressive states are summarized in Table 17-1.

Table 17-1 SYMPTOMS OF BIPOLAR DISORDER

Type of Symptom	Depressive State	Manic State
Emotional	Sad mood Lack of pleasure	Elated mood
Physiological	Fatigue Sleep difficulty Decreased appetite	Increased energy Lack of need for sleep Increased appetite
Behavioral	Slowed pace Decreased activity level	Increased pace Increased activity level
Cognitive	Low self-esteem Thoughts of death Negative view of world	Increased self-esteem Lack of perception of danger Positive view of world

CAUSES OF MOOD DISORDERS

Mood disorders run in families, which indicates that genetics partly causes these disorders. For example, the risk for bipolar disorder in family members of bipolar disorder patients is more than 30 percent. Exactly what is inherited that makes an individual vulnerable to bipolar disorder is not yet known. A growing number of researchers believe that bipolar disorder is caused by imbalances in neural circuits that use serotonin, norepinephrine, and other neurotransmitters.

Major depressive disorder appears to have multiple causes. Family, twin, and adoption studies indicate a genetic influence on depression. With identical twins, if one twin experiences depression, the other is four times more likely to experience depression at some point in his or her life than is the case for fraternal twins. Research also suggests that depression is a thinking disorder. That is, depressed persons have negative views of themselves, the world, and the future. They misinterpret their daily experiences so their negative outlook is supported. In contrast, the behavioral perspective is that depression results from low social reinforcement, which may be due to an inability to work effectively in a job or in school, as well as problems in making and keeping friends.

Why does depression occur more frequently among women than men? Some psychologists believe this gender difference is due to biological factors, such as wide fluctuations in hormone levels in women. Other psychologists believe social and cultural factors are the cause. Some psychologists suggest that because women tend to receive less money for their work and are the victims of more violence due to their gender than men, the world is simply more depressing for them. Other psychologists suggest that men are just as likely to experience depression as women, but men are less likely to admit to being depressed because expressing sad emotions is viewed as "unmanly." Perhaps the best explanation for the gender difference involves some combination of biological, social, and cultural factors. Before moving on to the next section, check out the New Science feature below for information on a mood disorder that often is not recognized by many sufferers and their physicians.

CHECKPOINT *What are mood disorders and what are the various types?*

NEW SCIENCE

What Is Seasonal Affective Disorder?

Some people feel depressed during the winter in cold climates because they dislike the snow and cold. A small percentage of them actually may suffer from a mood disorder. A subtype of depression that appears to have a biological basis is *seasonal affective disorder (SAD)*. SAD involves symptoms of depression at particular times of the year, especially during the winter months, when daylight hours are reduced. SAD sufferers sleep too much, have little energy, and crave sweets and starchy foods.

Some cases of winter depression may be due solely to psychosocial factors, such as lack of exercise due to poor weather and increased stress brought on by holiday preparations. Yet evidence that SAD is a real psychological disorder comes from studies demonstrating that people with SAD have unusually high metabolic rates, as well as physiological differences from other depressed individuals.

One therapy for SAD is exposing sufferers to bright white fluorescent light for two hours a day. Research suggests that this light therapy restores brain levels of the neurotransmitter serotonin to normal. This is effective because a low serotonin level is one of the likely biological causes of depression.

Think Critically
If SAD is more common in areas of the country that have less sunlight than other areas, what sort of social problems might be slightly more prevalent in these geographic areas due to SAD?

17.2 ASSESSMENT

In Your Own Words

Compare and contrast anxiety disorders and mood disorders. List and describe the anxiety disorders and the mood disorders discussed in the text. Give examples of behaviors involved in each disorder.

Review Concepts

1. Which anxiety disorder is characterized by episodes of intense anxiety without an apparent reason?
   a. phobic
   b. panic
   c. post-traumatic stress
   d. obsessive-compulsive

2. Someone who is extremely afraid of spiders may be suffering from a
   a. panic disorder
   b. bipolar disorder
   c. phobic disorder
   d. mood disorder

3. Which disorder may people who wash their hands hundreds of times a day have?
   a. bipolar
   b. phobic
   c. panic
   d. obsessive-compulsive

4. The fear of being negatively evaluated by others or acting in ways that are embarrassing is called
   a. specific phobia
   b. panic disorder
   c. social phobia
   d. social disorder

5. **True or False** Many symptoms of psychological disorders are common in the general population.

6. **True or False** Post-traumatic stress disorder is a mood disorder.

7. **True or False** Biology plays a role in anxiety disorders.

8. **True or False** Psychologists have given biological, social, and cultural explanations for why depression occurs more frequently among women than men.

Think Critically

9. Name the conditioning methods involved in the two-process conditioning model.

10. What types of events trigger post-traumatic stress disorder (PTSD)?

11. Explain the difference between being depressed and major depressive disorder.

12. Describe the manic side of bipolar disorder and discuss why mania is a problem.

13. Which of these symptoms are depressive and which are manic? (a) lack of pleasure (b) low self-esteem (c) increased pace (d) lack of need for sleep (e) sleep difficulty

14. What role do cognitive factors play in anxiety disorders?

Dissociative, Schizophrenic, and Personality Disorders

- dissociative disorders
- dissociative amnesia
- dissociative fugue
- dissociative identity disorder
- schizophrenia
- personality disorders
- antisocial personality disorder

OBJECTIVES

- Define dissociative disorders and identify the various types.
- Define schizophrenia and its causes.
- Define personality disorders and identify the various types.

DISCOVER IT | *How does this relate to me?*

You expect people to behave in certain ways and to follow rules of proper social conduct that everybody learns while growing up. Yet sometimes people don't follow the rules. Sometimes they behave so strangely that you realize they have lost touch with reality. For example, have you ever witnessed someone talking to imaginary voices or have you heard of someone with multiple personalities? If so, what are your thoughts and feelings? Do you feel sympathy? Do you feel afraid? Understanding the nature of psychological disorders helps you understand the people who suffer from mental illnesses.

S ome of the most negative stereotypes of mental illness involve people who suffer from dissociative, schizophrenic, and personality disorders. These three types of psychological disorders are the most startling and shocking forms of mental illness. There are many mistaken beliefs about these disorders, but psychological research has come a long way in dispelling these falsehoods.

Dissociative Disorders

dissociative disorders
Psychological disorders in which conscious awareness becomes separated (dissociated) from previous memories, including one's identity

After natural disasters, such as floods or hurricanes, some victims are found wandering in a daze. Although suffering no head injuries, these individuals do not remember their names, events leading up to the disaster, or other basic information they typically would know. These persons are suffering from a dissociative disorder. **Dissociative disorders** occur when conscious awareness becomes separated from previous memories, including one's identity. Psychologists use the term *dissociation* because in this disorder there are many aspects of experience that are kept separate—disassociated—in consciousness and memory.

An example of a normal dissociative state is daydreaming while listening to a dull lecture. When you snap out of your daydream you realize you do not remember what was happening around you. In contrast to this normal dissociation triggered by boredom, the separation in consciousness in dissociative disorders usually occurs when a situation becomes overwhelmingly stressful. People escape psychologically by separating their consciousness from the painful situational memories, thoughts, and feelings.

DISSOCIATIVE AMNESIA

The type of dissociative disorder suffered by victims of natural disasters is **dissociative amnesia**. It involves the sudden loss of memory of identity and/or other personal information. When there are no known physical causes, such as head injuries or brain tumors, and memory loss is isolated to information threatening to the self, the amnesia is considered dissociative. A person who witnesses the shooting death of a family member may develop dissociative amnesia for the entire event, and may even forget who they are for a time.

DISSOCIATIVE FUGUE

Like amnesia, **dissociative fugue** involves loss of memory of identity. In fugue, however, people also abruptly leave their familiar surroundings and assume a new identity without remembering their original one. One case involved a "Mr. X," who experienced occasional fugue states over decades. During one episode, he married a woman, not remembering that he was already married with a family in another city.

DISSOCIATIVE IDENTITY DISORDER

The dissociative disorder that receives the most attention is **dissociative identity disorder (DID)**, also known as *multiple personality disorder*. This condition occurs when people have two or more identities or personalities, which take turns controlling behavior. At least one of the personalities is unaware of what happens when it is not in control. The symptoms of DID are bizarre and extreme. One personality may be that of a six-year-old child, while another may be that of a grandparent. One personality may be male, another female.

Prior to 1980, DID was one of the rarest psychological disorders, with only about two cases reported per decade from 1930 to 1960. In the 1980s popular books and movies drew attention to the disorder and mental health professionals diagnosed

© GINA SANDERS, 2009/USED UNDER LICENSE FROM SHUTTERSTOCK.COM

People with dissociative disorders find help when working with a professional therapist.

dissociative amnesia
A dissociative disorder involving a sudden loss of memory of identity and/or other personal information

dissociative fugue
A dissociative disorder in which people suddenly leave their familiar surroundings and assume a new identity without remembering their real identity

dissociative identity disorder (DID) A dissociative disorder characterized by the presence of two or more identities or personalities, which take turns controlling the person's behavior

more than 20,000 cases, which is an astonishing number. Skeptics suggested this increase was an example of psychologists misdiagnosing other disorders as DID due to all the media coverage. During therapy sessions therapists may have asked leading questions that suggested DID. Or, they may have used hypnosis to draw out the multiple personalities. One of the unfortunate consequences of hypnosis is that it can lead people to produce "memories" that are not true (see Chapter 15, page 450). Patients were distressed and looking for ways to understand their problems, so they may have come to accept the multiple personality explanation.

Research since 1980 shows that DID is more common than was once believed. However, some cases may still be created accidentally in therapy sessions. People with DID typically are female, and almost all have histories of childhood abuse.

CAUSES OF DISSOCIATIVE DISORDERS

Some scientists believe that people suffering from dissociative disorders may have an undetected brain problem, but most explanations focus on extreme emotional stress as the more likely cause. A cognitive explanation of dissociative disorders holds that individuals learn to dissociate as a way of coping with intense distress. When a child is exposed to long-term, intense stress (such as abuse), dissociation may be used so frequently that it becomes automatic. Children who experience repeated abuse may learn to cope by imagining that a superhero friend makes them strong. Over time, the children's use of this coping strategy becomes automatic, even when the stress is mild. As adults, these children may be diagnosed with multiple personalities.

CHECKPOINT *What are dissociative disorders?*

As a young woman, Chris Sizemore had many different personalities, including Eve White (shy and responsible) and Eve Black (fun-loving and irresponsible). A film, The Three Faces of Eve, *was based on Sizemore's life experiences.*

PHIL SANDLIN/AP PHOTO

Schizophrenia

One of the most severe psychological disorders is **schizophrenia**, characterized by severe problems in thinking, including hallucinations, delusions, or loose associations. With *hallucinations,* some schizophrenic patients hear or see things that are not there. They may hear voices they attribute to aliens or demons. Some schizophrenic patients experience *delusions,* or irrational belief systems. For instance, they may believe they are a religious figure, a CIA agent, the President of the United States, or even a robot. Schizophrenic patients experience *loose associations,* meaning that their thoughts are disconnected from one another and from the world around them. Schizophrenic patients can be so disorganized in their thinking that they are unable to speak in complete sentences and can only babble.

Schizophrenia is diagnosed when symptoms last for at least six months, are not due to some other condition (such as drug use or severe depression), and cause significant problems in daily functioning. Because schizophrenics experience such severe problems in thinking, without proper treatment they often cannot work, manage a home or apartment, or care for their basic needs.

Schizophrenia occurs in about 1 percent of the world's population, with roughly equal frequency among males and females. This disorder tends to begin in adolescence and young adulthood. About one-third of people with schizophrenia attempt suicide, with one in ten eventually succeeding. In the DSM, schizophrenia has been classified into five major subtypes, depending on which symptoms are most prominent. These subtypes are listed in Table 17-2.

schizophrenia A psychological disorder characterized by severe problems in thinking, including hallucinations, delusions, or loose associations

Table 17-2 **SUBTYPES OF SCHIZOPHRENIA**

Type	Most Prominent Symptoms	Frequency
Paranoid schizophrenia	Hallucinations and delusions of persecution and greatness	40 percent of schizophrenics
Undifferentiated schizophrenia	Patterns of disordered behavior, thought, and emotion that cannot be neatly classified into any other subtype	40 percent of schizophrenics
Catatonic schizophrenia	May remain motionless for long periods of time and then move very rapidly	8 percent of schizophrenics
Disorganized schizophrenia	A variety of unrelated hallucinations and delusions, strange speech, strange facial expressions; may act like a child or infant	5 percent of schizophrenics
Residual schizophrenia	Persons who have had prior episodes of schizophrenia but are not currently experiencing any major symptoms	varies

CAUSES OF SCHIZOPHRENIA

Schizophrenia has a genetic basis. Although 1 percent of the general population develops schizophrenia, from 10 to 15 percent of close relatives (parents, children, siblings) of a schizophrenic patient also develop schizophrenia. This is true whether a person is raised in the same household as the schizophrenic person or elsewhere. Among identical twins, the risk is about 50 percent. (See Figure 17-4, below.)

What biological condition is inherited that may lead to the development of schizophrenia? As you remember from Chapter 3, dopamine is an important neurotransmitter in the brain that plays a crucial role in movement and influences thought and emotion. Studies find that increased dopamine activity in the brain is related to schizophrenia. Many neuroscientists believe that people suffering from schizophrenia see and hear things that are not there and have racing thoughts they cannot control because the dopamine pathways in their brains are overactive.

Some neuroscientists believe that the brain damage causing schizophrenia may sometimes occur while the fetus is developing in the womb or during delivery. A pregnant woman having a viral flu infection and lack of oxygen to the fetus during delivery are both associated with a higher later risk of schizophrenia.

Because schizophrenia often develops at about the same time rapid changes are occurring in the adolescent brain (see Chapter 9, pages 259–261), some neuroscientists suggest the disorder is caused by the brain pruning too many of its neurons and their interconnections. While average adolescents lose about 15 percent of their brain weight during this important stage of brain development, those who later suffer from schizophrenia lose as much as 25 percent. Thus, one cause of schizophrenia may be this loss of too many neurons and their connections during the teen years.

There are higher rates of schizophrenia among poor people in the United States than among middle and upper socioeconomic classes. In explaining the differences, some scientists point out that people who are poor tend to experience high stress levels. It is possible that people who are born with a genetic tendency to develop schizophrenia are more likely to develop the disorder if their lives are stressful. Another explanation is that schizophrenia develops at equal rates across the social

Figure 17-4 **RISK OF DEVELOPING SCHIZOPHRENIA**

The lifetime risk of developing schizophrenia increases with genetic closeness to relatives with schizophrenia.

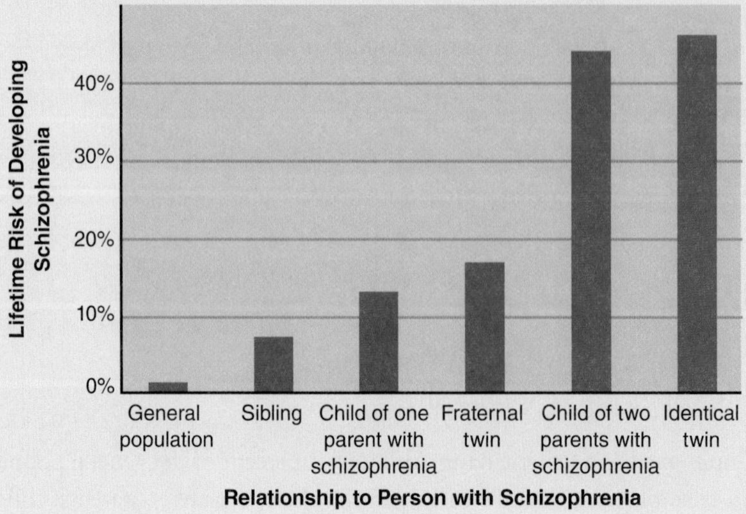

Relationship to Person with Schizophrenia

classes, but once people develop the disorder, many of them fall into poverty. At this point, it is not clear which of these two hypotheses is correct.

 **What is schizophrenia?**

Personality Disorders

Everybody has certain personality quirks. Some people are absentminded, while others are overly messy or neat. Still others may be somewhat mistrustful or selfish. Such quirks occasionally may cause problems for these people, but they rarely are symptoms of a psychological disorder. Yet some people's personalities are so disordered and problematic that they are considered mentally ill. **Personality disorders** involve rigid and ineffective patterns of behavior that interfere with normal social interactions. Personality disorders develop by the time a person reaches adolescence or young adulthood and affect all areas of a person's life. Individuals with personality disorders do not consider themselves the problem, instead they blame others. The DSM diagnostic system classifies ten personality disorders. Table 17-3 lists and describes each of these disorders.

Table 17-3 **TYPES AND SYMPTOMS OF PERSONALITY DISORDERS**

Type	Major Symptoms
Paranoid	Distrust and suspiciousness of others
Schizoid	Lack of desire to form social relationships and coldness toward others
Schizotypal	Inappropriate social and emotional behavior, and unusual thoughts and speech
Antisocial	Disregard for and violation of the rights of others with no remorse or guilt
Borderline	Instability in mood, self-concept, and interpersonal relationships
Histrionic	Intense need for attention, overly emotional and dramatic behavior
Narcissistic	Preoccupation with own sense of importance, need for admiration, and lack of empathy
Avoidant	High social anxiety, strong fear of criticism, and feelings of inadequacy
Dependent	Excessive need to be taken care of, submissive and clinging behavior, and fear of separation
Obsessive-compulsive	Preoccupation with orderliness, perfectionism, and control

Common personality disorders are the paranoid, the histrionic, or the narcissistic personality. People with any of these disorders are difficult to live with, as the following examples demonstrate.

- People with *paranoid personalities* are distrustful and suspicious of others' motives. They expect friends and family members to be disloyal. For example, Reggie is an 18-year-old senior with paranoid personality disorder. He often misinterprets friendly gestures from others as manipulative or spiteful. Reggie has quit every

personality disorders
Psychological disorders characterized by general styles of living that are ineffective and lead to problems

after-school activity he has joined, generally claiming that the other students and adult leaders are "out to get him." Unfortunately, because of their deep distrust of others, people with this personality disorder rarely seek treatment from mental health professionals.

- People with *histrionic personalities* are excessively emotional and attention-seeking, often turning minor incidents into full-blown dramas. For example, Tami was diagnosed with histrionic personality disorder when she was 25 years old. In social situations, Tami consistently uses her physical appearance to draw attention to herself and often behaves inappropriately to gain the spotlight. She can be very charming, but also very manipulative and demanding. Her moods swing rapidly and she seems to enjoy shocking people with her dramatics.

- Like histrionic personalities, people with *narcissistic personalities* also seek attention, but they also desire constant admiration. For example, Tony is a narcissist who considers himself "better" than others and entitled to privileges. When other people achieve success Tony is envious, but more often he thinks others are envious of him. Because he lacks sympathy for others, Tony takes advantage of people and his relationships are shallow and cold.

Another common personality disorder that receives attention is the **antisocial personality disorder**, also referred to as *psychopathy*. Psychopaths are individuals who show a strong disregard for, and violation of, the rights of others. They repeatedly engage in antisocial behavior, often lying, cheating, stealing, and manipulating others to get what they want. Psychopaths do not take responsibility for their deceit or show guilt. They are charming and likable but manipulate people to get what they want without hesitation or guilt. Serial murderers such as Charles Manson, Ted Bundy, and Gary Gilmore are sensational examples of persons with antisocial personality disorder. Others are not violent; they may be "con artists" who cheat people out of their money. This personality disorder occurs in about three percent of males and one percent of females. There is no effective treatment for antisocial personality disorder.

antisocial personality disorder A personality disorder in which a person shows a strong disregard for, and violation of, the rights of others

People with personality disorders are hard to live with. Why do people with paranoid personalities rarely seek treatment from mental health professionals?

© ANDREW LEVER, 2009/USED UNDER LICENSE FROM SHUTTERSTOCK.COM

CAUSES OF PERSONALITY DISORDERS

A growing number of mental health professionals believe that both genetic and social factors play a role in the development of many personality disorders. For example, the finding that both paranoid and histrionic personality disorders tend to run in families suggests these disorders might be inherited. It also is possible that a child of a parent with either of these disorders has simply learned these abnormal behaviors through observation. At this time, both explanations are possible.

The most accepted explanation of narcissistic personality disorder is that it is related to problems in the parent-child relationship during early childhood. One theory states that narcissists did not receive enough love and attention from parents as children and emerge into adult life still trying to satisfy these unmet needs.

Most research has focused on the antisocial personality disorder because many of these individuals commit crimes and cause serious problems for others. Twin and adoption studies find that this disorder is much more common among identical twins than among fraternal twins, suggesting that it has some genetic cause. Other research suggests that people with this disorder have abnormal brain development in areas that control impulsive behavior and decision making. Individuals with antisocial personality disorder tend also to have low arousal of their peripheral and central nervous systems and have a higher tolerance for pain. This may explain why they engage in sensation-seeking behavior and are less likely to learn from punishment. In terms of social development, people with antisocial personality disorder often have neglectful and abusive parents, which encourages a mistrustful and cold approach toward others.

CHECKPOINT *What are personality disorders?*

© ANGELA HAWKEY, 2009/USED UNDER LICENSE FROM SHUTTERSTOCK.COM

The most acceptable explanation of narcissistic personality disorder is that it is related to problems in the parent-child relationship during early childhood. How might the lack of love in childhood affect an adult?

In Your Own Words

Choose one of the objectives at the beginning of Lesson 17.3 (page 518). Discuss the information covered in the text that concerns the chosen objective.

Review Concepts

1. Which disorder, also known as multiple personality disorder, occurs when people have two or more personalities?

     a. schizophrenia
     c. dissociative identity disorder
     b. dissociative fugue
     d. dissociative amnesia

2. People with which personality disorder are self-important, needing attention and admiration?

     a. antisocial
     c. histrionic
     b. narcissistic
     d. paranoid

3. One of the causes of schizophrenia may be the loss of too many/much _____ and their connections during the teen years.

     a. neurons
     c. hormones
     b. dopamine
     d. neurotransmitters

4. Which of the following is not a severe problem in thinking associated with schizophrenia?

     a. hallucinations
     c. multiple personalities
     b. delusions
     d. loose associations

5. **True or False** Dissociative fugue and dissociative amnesia both involve loss of memory of identity.

6. **True or False** Psychologists have found that people with dissociative fugue also usually suffer from multiple personality disorder.

7. **True or False** Dissociative amnesia involves a sudden loss of memory due to a head injury or brain tumor.

8. **True or False** There are higher rates of schizophrenia among poor people than among members of middle and upper socioeconomic classes.

9. **True or False** Most scientists believe that people who suffer from dissociative disorders have an undetected brain problem.

Think Critically

10. Provide an example of a normal dissociative state, and explain how this normal state is different from a dissociative disorder.

11. Explain the difference between dissociative identity disorder and schizophrenia.

12. How have studies on twins helped scientists better understand personality disorders?

13. Explain the difference between people with histrionic personalities and people with narcissistic personalities.

Clinical Psychologist

ealth Science

A re you interested in human behavior? Do you want to be able to help people? If so, take a close look at the career of clinical psychologist. Psychologists observe, study, analyze, and evaluate the human mind and behavior. Clinical psychologists provide therapy to individuals, families, and groups to help people deal with personal problems. The majority of psychologists are clinical psychologists.

People in this career may work in private practice or medical or rehabilitation centers. Clinical psychologists listen to patients and help them find ways to work through emotionally disturbing problems. Some clinical psychologists work with surgical patients and people with serious illnesses or injuries to help ease the fear associated with medical problems. Other psychologists work with people who have suffered physical trauma, such as a spinal cord injury, to help them adjust to their circumstances.

Still other clinical psychologists work with people going through emotional trauma and personal crises, such as a family move to a new city and school. They also may help people learn more about themselves and find ways to make their lives more worthwhile and meaningful.

Clinical psychologists interview patients and may give them psychological tests. They may design behavior modification plans for their patients, or work with physicians and other health care providers to offer the best course of treatment for their patients.

Other clinical psychologists teach and conduct research in medical schools or universities. Some clinical psychologists administer community mental health programs.

Employment Outlook

Careers in clinical psychology are expected to grow faster than average. From 2006 to 2016, growth in this career is expected to be 15 percent. There is a growing need for clinical psychologists to work with veterans returning from war zones, with individuals who are aging, and with people who are under stress.

Needed Skills and Education

Education and licensing requirements vary from state to state, but most states require a master's or doctoral degree and a state license. If you are interested in this career, you'll want to concentrate your courses in psychology, plus courses in biology, physical and social sciences, and statistics and mathematics. Interpersonal relationship and communication skills also are needed as are computer skills.

How You'll Spend Your Day

Clinical psychologists who have their own practices work from their own private offices and set their own hours. They may work evenings and weekends to satisfy the needs of their patients. Other clinical psychologists who work in medical or rehabilitation centers may have an office in the center. They may work regular hours with some evening or weekend hours when offering a special program or when a patient is in crisis.

People in this career who teach in medical schools have an office within the university or medical school. Their hours vary depending on the class schedule.

Clinical psychologists who administer community mental health programs have an office on the site where the programs are held. Governments or private businesses or contributions fund the programs. Work hours may be long and varied.

Earnings

The median earnings for clinical psychologists are $59,440. Earnings can be as low as $35,280 and as high as $102,730.

What About You?

Is this the career for you? Write a college entrance letter that states why you are a good candidate for the psychology program. Assess your qualifications and identify the reasons they should accept you into the program.

CULTURA/GETTY IMAGES

CHAPTER SUMMARY

17.1 What Are Psychological Disorders?

- A psychological disorder is a pattern of unusual behavior that results in personal distress or significant interference in a person's ability to engage in normal daily living.

- Psychological disorders include atypical behaviors that are a violation of cultural norms, maladaptive behavior, and personal distress.

- The risks in diagnosing a psychological disorder is that labeling an individual as having a disorder can harm the person because of stereotypes about the mentally ill. Individuals may experience discrimination at school, work, or in other areas of their lives. A common stereotype is that people with psychological disorders are violent, but studies show this is not so.

- Mental health professionals use diagnostic labels because of three benefits: A label summarizes the person's problem in a single word; the label conveys information about causes of the disorder; and the label conveys information about a cure.

17.2 Anxiety and Mood Disorders

- Anxiety disorders are psychological disorders that are characterized by distressing, lasting anxiety, or maladaptive behavior. Anxiety disorders include panic disorder, phobic disorder, generalized anxiety disorder, obsessive-compulsive disorder, and post-traumatic stress disorder.

- Mood disorders are psychological disorders that are characterized by emotional extremes that cause significant disruption in daily functioning. Mood disorders include major depressive disorder and bipolar disorder.

- Many people experience anxiety or mood changes, but the severity and length of time the anxiety or depressed mood is felt is less than that of people with anxiety or mood disorders.

17.3 Dissociative, Schizophrenic, and Personality Disorders

- Dissociative disorders are psychological disorders characterized by disruptions in consciousness, memory, sense of identity, or perception. Dissociative disorders include dissociative amnesia, dissociative fugue, and dissociative identity disorder. Most scientists believe that emotional stress is the likely cause of dissociative disorders.

- Schizophrenia is a psychological disorder characterized by severe problems in thinking, including hallucinations, delusions, or loose associations. Schizophrenia has a genetic base and may have a socioeconomic factor. People with schizophrenia are unable to care for themselves because of their inability to think correctly. They need the support of family and treatment centers.

- Personality disorders involve living styles that are ineffective and cause problems. The most common personality disorders include paranoid, histrionic, narcissistic, and antisocial personality disorder. People with these disorders are difficult to live with. Mental health professionals believe that personality disorders develop due to both genetic and social factors.

CHAPTER ASSESSMENT

Review Psychology Terms

Select the term that best fits the definition. Some terms will not be used.

_____ 1. Disorders characterized by distressing, lasting anxiety, and unusual behavior

_____ 2. A mood disorder characterized by extreme and lasting negative moods and the inability to experience pleasure from activities once enjoyed

_____ 3. A pattern of unusual behavior that results in personal distress or significant interference in a person's ability to engage in normal daily living

_____ 4. Psychological disorders in which conscious awareness becomes separated from previous memories, including one's identity

_____ 5. Anxiety disorder characterized by strong irrational fears of specific objects or situations

_____ 6. Sign of a disorder

_____ 7. An anxiety disorder involving flashbacks and recurrent thoughts of life-threatening or other traumatic events

_____ 8. A personality disorder in which a person shows a strong disregard for, and violation of, the rights of others

_____ 9. The process of identifying disorders

_____ 10. A mood disorder characterized by swings between the emotional extremes of mania and depression

_____ 11. An anxiety disorder characterized by recurring, unwanted, and distressing actions and/or thoughts

_____ 12. A psychological disorder characterized by severe problems in thinking, including hallucinations, delusions, or loose associations

_____ 13. Psychological disorders characterized by general styles of living that are ineffective and lead to problems

_____ 14. Psychological disorders characterized by emotional extremes that cause significant disruption in daily functioning

_____ 15. An anxiety disorder characterized by episodes of intense anxiety without an apparent reason

a. antisocial personality disorder

b. anxiety disorders

c. bipolar disorder

d. delusion

e. diagnosis

f. dissociative disorders

g. generalized anxiety disorder (GAD)

h. hallucination

i. major depressive disorder

j. mood disorders

k. obsessive-compulsive disorder (OCD)

l. panic disorder

m. personality disorders

n. phobic disorder

o. post-traumatic stress disorder (PTSD)

p. psychological disorder

q. schizophrenia

r. symptom

Review Psychology Concepts

16. What is the _Diagnostic and Statistical Manual of Mental Disorders (DSM)?_

17. List three benefits of using labels in the diagnosis of psychological disorders.

18. Explain how psychologists distinguish normal anxiety from anxiety disorders.

19. Identify the psychological symptoms associated with panic disorder.

20. Identify the psychological symptoms associated with phobic disorder.

21. Distinguish between specific phobia and social phobia.

22. Explain why people who suffer from OCD engage in compulsive rituals they have developed. Do the compulsive rituals help?

23. What events might cause post-traumatic stress disorder?

24. Identify three factors that cause anxiety disorders.

25. Identify the mood disorder that is referred to as the "common cold" of mental illness.

26. Compare the state of depression in major depressive disorder to the state of depression in bipolar disorder.

27. Describe the way personality disorders differ from other psychological disorders.

28. Compare and contrast dissociative amnesia, dissociative fugue, and dissociative identity disorder (DID).

29. Identify and describe the symptoms of schizophrenia.

30. What are the symptoms of a person who has antisocial personality disorder?

Apply Psychology Concepts

At her high school reunion, Nicole realizes that several of her classmates have changed, as described in items 31–34. Which disorder does each description suggest? Explain your answer.

31. David, the class clown, confides that he takes medication to keep himself emotionally stable. At times in his life he has been so down that he has tried to commit suicide and other times he's gotten into trouble with the law because his high energy and self-esteem have affected his judgment.

32. Jonny, the most likely to succeed, washes his hands repeatedly and dries them with tissues, his standard purification ritual, before he will drink the punch.

33. The prom queen, Marybeth, is not at the reunion because she has been extremely unhappy lately and not interested in participating in social activities. She has no appetite, has lost a lot of weight, and cannot sleep.

34. The star quarterback, Andy, says he is in charge of the CIA and that a group of terrorists plans to take him hostage. Andy states that the government has implanted a radio receiver in his head that allows him to hear the thoughts of others as they plot against him.

Make Academic Connections

35. **History** Use the Internet or library to research how judgments have changed through history concerning abnormal behaviors. Choose a specific illness. It does not have to be one mentioned in the text and can be either a psychological disorder or a physical condition that people thought was a mental illness. For example, you might want to research the medical condition of epilepsy. At one time people who witnessed someone having an epileptic seizure thought the sufferer was experiencing a mental disorder. Modern medicine dispelled this misconception. Write an essay about your findings.

36. **Criminal Justice** Insanity, or diminished capacity, has been used in the criminal justice system as a defense for people on trial. Research to learn more about insanity as a defense. Take a position on when a diminished capacity defense should or should not be used, and write an argument that defends your position.

37. **Writing** Create a short story about a character who has one of the psychological disorders described in this chapter. In your story, have the character act out the symptoms. For example, you might write a story about a man with dissociative fugue who leaves his office one day only to find himself in a strange city. He has lost his identity, so he must create a new one.

38. **Sociology** Design and conduct a survey that examines stereotypes of schizophrenia and bipolar disorder. Analyze the findings of your survey, and write a report of your findings. In your report provide arguments that dispel the stereotypes and misperceptions about schizophrenia and bipolar disorder.

39. **Journalism** Use the Internet or library to research famous people throughout history who have had a mental illness. Write a feature story about the person that includes information on their disorder and their accomplishments. You may write about one of the following people or another person of your choice: Abraham Lincoln, the sixteenth president of the United States suffered from depression; Patty Duke, Academy-Award winning actress has bipolar disorder (a television movie was made about her and her illness); Lionel Aldridge, Green Bay Packers football player who was in two Super Bowls, had schizophrenia; Pete Wentz, bass player for Grammy-nominated pop-punk band Fall Out Boy, has bipolar disorder; John Nash, mathematician and Nobel Prize winner, suffered from schizophrenia.

DIGGING DEEPER
with Psychology eCollection

Have you ever been so nervous or scared you couldn't breathe? One anxiety disorder that seems to have become much more common over the last 50 years is the panic attack. Fortunately, this relatively short period of intense fear and accompanying physical reactions usually do not develop into a panic disorder. Psychologists have focused research on panic attacks and are investigating some interesting hypotheses about their causes. Access the Gale Psychology eCollection at *www.cengage.com/school/psych/franzoi* and read Saxbe's article on panic attacks and the related research. Write a summary of the article and answer the question: Do you think a larger percent of people are having panic attacks now than before? Why or why not? As an additional project, write a story about a person who has a panic attack and is helped by exposure therapy.

Source: Saxbe, Darby. "The fear of fear itself: Someone who panics on a plane might decide not to fly, but she may start to dread cars and buses as well." *Psychology Today* 38.6 (Nov–Dec 2005): 28(1).

SELF-DISCOVERY: YOUR SCORE

The Automatic Thoughts Questionnaire

Scoring Instructions: To score the ATQ, simply add the ratings for all 30 items. The average score in a student population is about 49, whereas the average score in a depressed sample is about 80. Keep in mind that this exercise is not meant to diagnose depression in those who answer these questions but, rather, to give you an idea about the common negative thoughts that occur when people are depressed. If you experience many of these thoughts on a regular basis, you might consider consulting a mental health professional.

ESSENTIAL QUESTION
Go to page XXVII

CHAPTER 18

Therapy for Psychological Disorders

"My friend . . . care for your psyche . . . know thyself, for once we know ourselves, we may learn how to care for ourselves."

—SOCRATES

BLEND IMAGES/JUPITER IMAGES

If you have watched the Dr. Phil Show on television, you might have a mistaken understanding of how mental health professionals help people struggling with psychological problems. On his show, Dr. Phil McGraw diagnoses his guests' problems and provides solutions within minutes of meeting them, just in time for a commercial break. When he has particularly troubling cases, Dr. Phil sometimes asks his television guests to take a polygraph test to determine whether they are being truthful. He also spends a great deal of time lecturing with his "tell-it-like-it-is" style: "You're only lonely if you're not there for you." Dr. Phil also gives advice in the form of proverbs: "You don't need a pack of wild horses to learn how to make a sandwich."

The Dr. Phil Show has entertainment value for many viewers. However, the people who appear on the show with personal problems are not receiving psychological therapy from this TV celebrity. Dr. Phil does not accurately represent the therapeutic practice of psychology. In this chapter, you will examine scientifically tested methods used to help individuals deal with psychological problems. As you learn about these therapies, ask yourself whether any of them are similar to the methods used by Dr. Phil.

18.1 | Therapists and Clients

OBJECTIVES

- Identify the three main mental health professions.
- Identify who seeks therapy and obstacles to seeking psychotherapy.
- Discuss types and variations of group therapy.

DISCOVER IT | *How does this relate to me?*

When something bothers you, do you talk to your friends about it? What if your friends cannot help? Would you seek help from a professional? Think of seeking help from a professional counselor in the same way you would seek help from a physician if you break a bone. You certainly would not try to set the bone yourself. In the same way, if you have a mental or emotional problem, it is wise to ask for help.

KEY TERMS

- psychotherapy
- biomedical therapy
- eclectic approach
- clients
- group therapy
- family therapy
- self-help group

I f you think of the mind as being like a computer, then mental health problems can originate in either the brain's software or its hardware. Psychologically oriented therapies typically seek solutions for what are believed to be "software" problems, while medically oriented therapies try to repair "hardware" problems. Before examining specific therapies, you first need to know about the people who work as mental health professionals and the people who seek their help.

Who Offers Treatment?

The three mental health professions that provide the most psychological therapy are psychiatry, social work, and psychology. These professions use two basic treatments: psychotherapy and biomedical therapy. **Psychotherapy** uses psychological methods that include a personal relationship between a trained therapist and the individual or individuals seeking treatment. The focus is to change the disordered thoughts, behaviors, and emotions associated with psychological disorders. **Biomedical therapy** assumes that psychological disorders are primarily caused by physiological problems. It treats disorders by changing the way the brain works through drugs, electrical stimulation, or surgery.

psychotherapy The treatment of psychological disorders using methods that include a personal relationship between a trained therapist and the individual or individuals seeking treatment

biomedical therapy The treatment of psychological disorders by changing the way the brain works, primarily by using drugs, electrical stimulation, or surgery

PSYCHIATRISTS

Psychiatrists are medical doctors (M.D.s) trained in treating mental and emotional disorders. As physicians, psychiatrists can prescribe medications. Thus biomedical therapy is an important aspect of their practice. They also receive training in psychotherapy, and may provide various kinds of "talk therapy" such as psychodynamic therapy or cognitive-behavior therapy as well.

SOCIAL WORKERS

Clinical and psychiatric social workers provide psychotherapy and also work with social support agencies that offer assistance such as shelter, vocational training, or financial aid. Most social workers have obtained a master's degree in social work (M.S.W.) in a two-year graduate program after completing their undergraduate work. A smaller percentage has earned a doctorate (D.S.W.) in social work.

Most mental health professionals are psychologists, who work as either clinical psychologists or counseling psychologists. How do psychologists differ from psychiatrists and social workers?

PSYCHOLOGISTS

The largest major mental health profession that offers therapy to individuals is psychology. Psychologists have either a master's or a doctoral degree. Unlike most social workers and medical doctors, psychologists who receive training in psychotherapy also learn how to conduct scientific research. Two specialty areas in psychology—clinical psychology and counseling—provide psychotherapy. Clinical psychologists work with assessing, explaining, and treating psychological disorders. Counseling psychologists work with people who have less severe problems and who benefit from educational, vocational, or personal counseling.

THE "TEAM" APPROACH

The primary goal of mental health professionals is to help people who suffer from psychological disorders have more control over their lives. In working toward this goal, mental health providers often work together as a team. Each individual case is referred from a primary care physician to a psychiatrist, who then refers the person to a psychologist and/or a clinical social worker.

For serious conditions, such as schizophrenia and drug addiction, a social worker trains the person in basic life skills, a psychologist has "talk therapy" sessions with the person, and a psychiatrist monitors and adjusts medications. Other health professionals also may be involved. These include nurses, occupational therapists, physical therapists, speech therapists, and others who work in mental health settings. Although they are not trained therapists, their work with patients involves basic psychotherapeutic strategies. Depending on the person seeking help and the problem, many mental health professionals use an **eclectic approach**, meaning they combine aspects of several different psychotherapy techniques.

eclectic approach
Therapy style based on combining aspects of several different psychotherapy techniques

Who Seeks Therapy?

Individuals who seek therapy usually are in distress. The coping strategies they used to manage and solve their problems no longer work. Millions of people visit a mental health professional every year, and research shows that most of these people benefit from the therapy. The majority of therapy is short-term, lasting less than a year. Individuals who benefit the most are people who make the choice on their own to seek therapy and have a strong desire to change.

In the United States women are twice as likely as men to seek help, and individuals with some college education are more likely to seek help than people without any college. Many experts believe that these group differences are related to how people are taught to deal with personal problems in our culture. Women and people who have higher education are more likely than men and those with less education to be told that it is helpful and not a sign of weakness to talk about your problems with others, especially mental health professionals.

Americans suffering from mental illness are more likely to seek treatment today than 20 years ago. The rate of mental illness has remained the same during this time period. Unfortunately people most in need of mental health services are least likely to seek and receive help. Research suggests that less than 10 percent of individuals who suffer from a psychological disorder visit a mental health professional.

People most in need of mental health services are the least likely to seek and receive help.

OBSTACLES TO SEEKING HELP

As discussed in Chapter 17, one obstacle to seeking therapy is the stigma of mental illness in many cultures. A second obstacle is the helpless mindset that often develops among people who suffer from psychological disorders.

People may struggle for quite awhile with their troubling thoughts, feelings, and behaviors. When they do not improve, they often simply give up. This belief that nothing can be done to solve their problems is called *learned helplessness*, and it prevents people from seeking professional help.

THE CLIENT AS ACTIVE PARTNER

Changing this learned helplessness is important in recovering from mental illness. One of the first goals of psychotherapy is to help people become actively involved in, and responsible for, solving their own problems. Mental health professionals encourage those who seek help to think of themselves as **clients** who have hired a professional to help them deal with their problems. In this active role, clients approach therapy with the purpose of working in partnership with therapists. Check out Closer Look to learn how to select a psychotherapist.

clients People who actively work with professional therapists toward the goal of improving their mental health

CLOSER LOOK

How to Select a Psychotherapist

Before making an appointment, ask yourself whether you need a therapist. The American Psychological Association offers the following reasons for seeking therapy: deep and lasting depression; feelings of hopelessness; sudden mood shifts; thoughts of suicide; self-destructive behavior, such as alcohol and drug abuse; and compulsive rituals, such as hand washing.

Another question to ask is whether you can identify the problem you want to change. Do you want to reduce depression? Get help with an eating disorder? Identifying a problem and goal helps you select the right therapist and helps with your approach to therapy. Ask these questions of potential therapists:

- What is the therapist's degree and is the therapist licensed to practice therapy? Licensure means the therapist has passed a test which evaluates the training and expertise.
- Does the therapist have experience in treating your specific psychological disorder? Most therapists are experts at treating specific mental health problems, but not all problems.
- What is the cost of each therapy session? Costs among therapists vary.

You can obtain referrals to see a therapist from many sources, including your family doctor, school psychologist, clergy member, lawyer, friends, and family members. Many cities have referral resources such as a chapter of the Mental Health Association.

Think Critically

Why is it important to think about your goals for therapy before you contact a mental health professional?

CULTURAL GROUPS AND THERAPY

In the United States members of some cultural groups are unlikely to seek mental health treatment. If these people do seek therapy, they are more likely to drop out. Surveys of African Americans who suffer from major depression find they are more likely than white Americans to mention fears of hospitalization and treatment as reasons for not seeking mental health therapy. Additional surveys find that African Americans, Hispanic Americans, and Native Americans are more likely than white Americans to believe that health providers judge them unfairly or treat them with disrespect.

An unwillingness to seek psychotherapy may be influenced by a person's culture. Most modern psychotherapies were developed in individualist Western cultures. Therapy involves focusing on the client's emotions and personal needs. In collectivist Asian cultures, talking about personal feelings or focusing on yourself is considered bad manners and unwise. Being emotionally nonexpressive and coping with distress yourself are signs of emotional strength and maturity.

Instead of taking advantage of conventional mental health therapy, people may turn to more culturally comfortable sources of help when they experience prolonged psychological distress. Native Americans and Alaska Natives may rely on traditional healers, while African Americans may seek out their church ministers to help them cope with psychological disorders. Unfortunately some people delay seeking treatment for mental health concerns until their symptoms become severe.

CULTURAL TRAINING AND THERAPY

An increasing number of psychotherapists now receive training to help them work more effectively with clients from diverse cultural backgrounds. Studies find this training does improve the therapeutic process and reduces dropout rate. In a study of Hispanic students receiving therapy from a university counseling center, researchers found that satisfaction with a therapist was not predicted by the therapist's ethnicity. Rather, it depended on the degree to which clients believed their therapists understood the Latino culture.

The American Psychological Association and other mental health organizations have made efforts to recruit and train therapists in diverse cultural groups. APA's Office of Ethnic Minority Affairs runs programs that encourage students of diverse cultural groups to become therapists and researchers in mental health.

Mental health organizations are making efforts to recruit and train therapists from diverse cultural groups.

©MARY KATE DENNY/PHOTOEDIT

CHECKPOINT *What are two obstacles to seeking psychotherapy?*

Group Therapy

Young people with common problems meet in group therapy under the guidance of their therapist.

Psychotherapy is conducted with groups of clients as well as with individuals. **Group therapy** is the treatment of several clients at the same time under the guidance of a therapist.

Some therapy groups are composed of clients in outpatient settings, while other therapy groups consist of severely disturbed patients in hospital settings. Many groups are organized around one kind of problem (such as alcoholism or depression) or one kind of client (such as adolescents or police officers). The group usually consists of five to ten people who meet once a week for two hours.

One benefit of group therapy is that it helps clients realize others also struggle with the same problems. A related benefit is that a group provides clients with the opportunity to compare themselves to others and exchange information on how to improve their mental health. A third benefit is that group members can become an important support network for one another, boosting self-confidence and providing self-acceptance.

FAMILY THERAPY

Research suggests that people who have been hospitalized for a psychological disorder often relapse when they return home to their families. One possible cause for such setbacks is conflicts in the family relationships. In an attempt to prevent such relapses, therapists also treat the families. **Family therapy** is designed to change the way in which family members relate to one another. With the therapist's guidance, family members develop constructive communication and problem-solving skills, which reduce conflicts and emotional distress.

A variation of family therapy is *couples therapy*, which focuses on communication and behavior patterns of romantic partners. More than half the couples entering therapy state that their number-one problem involves poor communication. Research indicates that both family and couples therapies are effective. In fact, an increasing number of therapists who treat clients for depression on an individual basis believe it is important to bring other family members into the therapy situation. Check out the Case Study on page 540 that reviews research on the effectiveness of psychotherapy in improving the mental health of clients.

SELF-HELP GROUPS

One variation of group therapy is the **self-help group**, which consists of people meeting regularly and discussing their problems with one another without the guidance of a therapist. One of the oldest and best-known self-help groups is Alcoholics Anonymous (AA), which has more than 70,000 chapters and more than two million members worldwide. AA, which was founded as a group run by and for alcoholics, provides information about the consequences of alcoholism and the

group therapy The treatment of several clients at the same time under the guidance of a therapist

family therapy Therapy designed to constructively change the way in which family members relate to one another

self-help group Several people regularly meeting and discussing their problems with one another without the guidance of a therapist

opportunity to learn from the experiences of other alcoholics. This organization is based on a series of 12 steps that help alcoholics stop drinking. AA meetings typically begin with a discussion of one of the 12 steps, followed by members speaking individually about their problems and telling how the step has helped them cope with alcoholism. Many other self-help programs have been developed on the AA model. These cover a wide range of problems, including mood disorders, drug addiction, compulsive gambling, and childhood abuse.

Many therapists who treat clients in individual or group therapy also urge clients to participate in self-help groups as part of their recovery process. The primary limitation of such groups is that the lack of guidance from a trained therapist can sometimes lead members to oversimplify causes and solutions for problems.

CHECKPOINT *What is group therapy?*

18.1 ASSESSMENT

In Your Own Words

If you were having a problem with adjusting to a new school and felt other students were picking on you, to which mental health professional would you turn? Explain why. Be specific.

Review Concepts

1. Of the following cultural groups, which is most likely to seek psychotherapy for a psychological disorder?
   a. Asian Americans
   b. Native Americans
   c. African Americans
   d. white Americans

2. Which therapy would you most likely seek to improve communication with your parents?
   a. family therapy
   b. self-help group
   c. psychoanalysis
   d. biomedical treatment

3. **True or False** Money usually is the major problem for couples in therapy.

4. **True or False** Psychotherapy is conducted with groups as well as with individual clients.

Think Critically

5. Compare and contrast psychological and biomedical therapies.

6. Why do therapists encourage people they work with to think of themselves as clients?

Is Psychotherapy Helpful?

INTRODUCTION The first serious attempt to scientifically study whether psychotherapy was effective in treating psychological disorders occurred in 1952. That year Hans Eysenck published an influential study claiming that people with psychological problems who received psychotherapy had a slightly worse outcome than those who did not receive any therapy at all. Although Eysenck's study later was found to be flawed, other researchers were inspired to conduct their own assessments of various forms of psychotherapy. In 1977 Mary Lee Smith and Gene Glass conducted a statistical review of nearly 400 studies on the effectiveness of psychotherapy.

HYPOTHESIS Smith and Glass hypothesized that people with psychological problems who participated in psychotherapy would show an improvement in their mental health more than similarly ill people who did not receive psychotherapy.

METHOD In all the studies reviewed by Smith and Glass, many different psychologists

KILLERB10/ISTOCKPHOTO.COM

tracked the mental health changes of people who had been diagnosed with a psychological disorder and who had either received or did not receive psychotherapy.

RESULTS The findings from these studies demonstrated that psychotherapy generally is more effective than no therapy. Their findings also suggested that many types of therapy are effective, but that they are not always effective for everyone. Based on this research, Smith and Glass concluded that:

1. Psychotherapy generally has a positive effect.
2. Brief therapy helps many clients, with about 50 percent improving by the eighth session.
3. The more treatment clients receive, the more they improve.

The last two findings deserve further comment. It appears that short-term psychotherapy results in better mental health for about half of all clients, but only half of these clients remain well. The most effective treatments have results that last more than two years.

Critical Analysis

1. Why do you think the researchers tested the outcomes of short-term versus longer-term psychotherapies?

2. Why do you think many people suffering from psychological disorders may choose short-term psychotherapy over longer-term psychotherapy?

Psychodynamic and Humanistic Therapies

OBJECTIVES

- Explain psychodynamic therapies.
- Explain humanistic therapies.

KEY TERMS

- psychodynamic therapies
- free association
- transference
- resistance
- humanistic therapies
- client-centered therapy
- empty-chair technique

DISCOVER IT | *How does this relate to me?*

Do you wonder what causes you to feel or behave the way you do? Do you think your feelings and behavior are caused by hidden memories in your subconscious mind? If so, you are thinking like a psychodynamic therapist. Do you wonder who you truly are and what your life purpose is? If so, you are thinking like a humanistic therapist.

Two major schools of therapy—psychodynamic and humanistic—differ in their approach to helping clients. The therapist role in psychodynamic therapies is like a detective who probes clients' subconscious to uncover hidden memories. The therapist role in humanistic therapies is to help clients discover their true selves.

Psychodynamic Therapies

Psychodynamic therapies are psychotherapies inspired by the work of Sigmund Freud. He claimed that psychological disorders are caused by unconscious conflict. Freudian therapy, as originally practiced by Freud, is called *psychoanalysis*. It dominated the field of psychotherapy in the first half of the 1900s.

As discussed in Chapter 11, Freud believed emotional conflicts in childhood leave people with troubling memories. To manage the resulting anxiety, people block the memories. Although the memories are unconscious, they continue to have a powerful effect on the person and can cause psychological problems.

According to Freud, the client's problem is unconscious, so the goal of therapy is to bring the troubling memories into conscious awareness. This process of helping clients understand their own psychological processes is called *insight*. When clients gain insight into the underlying troubling memories, they release pent-up emotions, a process called *catharsis*. Following catharsis, clients can deal with their troubling emotions in a conscious, rational, and effective way. All psychodynamic therapies help clients gain insight.

> **psychodynamic therapies** A variety of psychotherapies based on the work of Sigmund Freud claiming that psychological disorders are caused by unconscious conflict

In traditional psychoanalysis, the client reclines on a couch facing away from the therapist. This placement of the therapist and client is thought to minimize distractions and make it easier for the client to talk about whatever comes to mind.

CREATAS IMAGES/JUPITER IMAGES

free association A psychodynamic therapy technique in which clients say whatever comes to mind

transference The process by which the client develops positive or negative feelings for the therapist that represent feelings the client experienced toward others early in life

resistance Anything clients do that interferes with them understanding their psychological problems

FREE ASSOCIATION

The main psychodynamic therapy technique is **free association**, in which clients say aloud whatever comes to mind. According to Freud, free association helps clients remember unconscious troubling memories.

The psychodynamic therapist also pays attention to slips of the tongue, known as *Freudian slips*, when the client means to say one thing but actually says something else. For example, if the client means to say, "I love my mother," but actually says, "I leave my mother," the therapist might interpret this slip as communicating an unconscious desire to emotionally separate from the parent.

ANALYSIS OF DREAMS AND OTHER SELF-EXPRESSIONS

The psychodynamic therapist also interprets unconscious desires in other forms of the client's expression, such as dreams, daydreams, artwork, poetry, and so on. Freud thought that almost everything we do is caused by unconscious influences. Through interpreting the symbols in the client's dreams and artwork, the therapist may help the client gain insight (see Chapter 15, page 443).

TRANSFERENCE AND RESISTANCE

According to psychodynamic therapy, the client often develops strong positive or negative feelings for the therapist. This is called **transference**. Feeling admiration and even love for the therapist are forms of positive transference. Feeling resentment and anger are forms of negative transference. Freud interpreted transference as representing feelings the client experienced toward others early in life. If the client becomes dependent on the therapist, this may mean the client was overly dependent on parents during childhood. If the client resents the authority of the therapist, perhaps as a child the client resented the parents.

Another important aspect of the client-therapist relationship in psychodynamic therapy is resistance. **Resistance** is anything clients do that interferes with them understanding their psychological problems. Clients may try to sabotage therapy by missing or coming late to sessions, talking only about unimportant issues, or bringing up important issues only at the very end of a session so there is no time to address them. Even though clients want to improve, the mind raises defenses to keep troubling material buried in their subconscious. The therapist's task is to help clients make connections between their behavior and childhood experiences.

CHECKPOINT *What are psychodynamic therapies?*

Humanistic Therapies

As discussed in Chapter 1, humanistic psychology focuses on positive human experiences, such as love, creativity, and spirituality. **Humanistic therapies** help people get in touch with their feelings, their "true selves," and their purpose in life. Humanistic psychotherapists believe psychological problems develop when outside forces stop people's natural tendency to seek personal growth. A primary goal of humanistic therapies is to help clients realize their basic nature, which is good.

CLIENT-CENTERED THERAPY

Carl Rogers, who developed **client-centered therapy**, had the strongest influence on humanistic psychotherapy. In treating psychological disorders, Rogers believed therapists should provide a supportive setting where clients discover their "true selves" rather than assuming the role of "detective" as in psychodynamic therapy. Client-centered therapy emphasizes the client's conscious thoughts and feelings rather than the therapist's interpretations of the client's unconscious desires.

According to Rogers, people experience mental health problems because they received *conditional positive regard* from loved ones. This means they were loved and accepted only when they met others' standards. Children raised with conditional love fail to develop their "true selves." As a result, they develop emotional problems.

To counteract the negative effects of conditional acceptance, Rogers proposed that therapists treat their clients with *unconditional positive regard* (see Chapter 11). This means expressing warmth, kindness, and caring for clients without being judgmental. When therapists accept clients for who they are, clients eventually come to accept themselves. Clients can then put aside the false standards others have for them and find their true selves. For therapists to express unconditional positive regard to their clients they need to show *genuineness* (being open and honest), *warmth* (being caring and nurturing), and *empathy* (understanding what the client is thinking and feeling).

How do client-centered therapists express genuineness, warmth, and empathy? By using active listening skills. Three techniques are the use of open-ended statements, reflection, and paraphrasing. Consider the question, "Did you have a good week?" This is a closed-ended question, because it can be answered with a single word, and suggests the client should evaluate the week as good or bad. "Tell me about your week" is open-ended, because

humanistic therapies Psychotherapies that help people get in touch with their feelings, their "true selves," and their purpose in life

client-centered therapy A humanistic therapy in which the therapist provides a supportive setting for clients to discover their "true selves"

LAB TEAMS

Choose a Therapy

Choose a character from literature, television, or a movie. Explain the character's psychological problem. Then determine whether they should seek out a psychodynamic therapist or a humanistic therapist to help overcome the problem. Discuss the different options with a lab partner, and then write a summary of your discussion and explain why you chose that type of therapist.

clients can say as much as they want. *Open-ended statements* encourage clients to speak without limitation.

Another technique is *reflection*, in which the therapist acknowledges some emotion the client has expressed. For example, when a client says the week has been hard, the therapist *reflects* this by saying, "This has been a tough week for you." If a client begins crying, the therapist recognizes this by saying, "This is difficult for you to talk about." Reflection expresses understanding of, and caring for, the client.

A third technique is *paraphrasing*, in which the therapist summarizes the client's statements. For example, many clients are distressed and do not express themselves clearly. In such instances, the therapist summarizes the client's emotions by saying, "Let me see if I understand the situation you faced this week. You said that. . . ." By using paraphrasing, the therapist is expressing empathy.

Another therapy technique developed by humanistic psychologists is the **empty-chair technique**. In this technique, clients sit facing an empty chair and imagine an important person from their life—past or present, such as parent or friend—is sitting in the empty chair. In this safe environment, the client can express feelings by talking with the imagined person and gaining insight into those feelings. Research suggests this technique helps clients deal with the emotional turmoil that led them to seek therapy in the first place. To learn how to use this technique, complete the Self-Discovery below.

Therapists who use psychotherapies other than the humanistic approach often use client-centered techniques to build trust with their clients. Such wide use of

empty-chair technique
A humanistic technique in which clients imagine that the person to whom they would like to speak is sitting in an empty chair facing them

SELF-DISCOVERY

Can Imaginary Conversations Resolve Conflict?

To help you understand how the empty-chair technique works, follow these four steps:

1. Think of someone with whom you had a recent conflict. Choose a conflict that is not very serious. In this exercise it is more important for you to understand the process of this technique rather than resolve a major personal problem.

2. Set two chairs facing each other. Sit in one of these chairs and visualize your "target" person sitting in the other chair. Speak out loud to this person, describing the situation and/or behavior that created the conflict, how it makes you feel, and how you would like to resolve it.

3. Sit in the "target" person's chair and assume his or her point of view while imagining yourself sitting in the chair you just occupied. Respond to your previous statements as you think the "target" person would respond. How do the "target" person's imagined comments make you feel?

4. When you complete this exercise, reflect on its usefulness. Did you find that participating in this technique helped you better understand your "target" person's point of view? Do you see how this technique might help people resolve emotional conflicts in their lives?

client-centered techniques explains why psychotherapists identify Carl Rogers as the person most influential on how therapy is practiced.

CHECKPOINT *What are humanistic therapies?*

18.2 ASSESSMENT

In Your Own Words

If you were to enter therapy, would you choose a therapist who practices psychodynamic therapy or humanistic therapy? Explain your answer in a way that shows your understanding of both types of therapy.

Review Concepts

1. Which refers to a psychodynamic therapy technique in which clients say whatever comes to mind?
   - a. transference
   - b. free association
   - c. client-centered therapy
   - d. resistance

2. Which word would you most likely hear if you were listening to therapists who practice psychodynamic therapies?
   - a. paraphrase
   - b. reflect
   - c. insight
   - d. empathy

3. Which word or phrase would you most likely hear if you were listening to therapists who practice humanistic therapies?
   - a. unconscious
   - b. repressed memories
   - c. catharsis
   - d. conditional positive regard

4. **True or False** According to Carl Rogers, the goal of therapy is to bring unconscious memories into conscious memory.

5. **True or False** The purpose of humanistic therapies is to help clients gain insight.

6. **True or False** Resistance is a way clients have of sabotaging their therapy.

Think Critically

7. Explain the role of insight in therapy.

8. Why do humanistic psychologists use open-ended questions?

9. Why is Carl Rogers considered to have the most influence on how therapy is practiced?

10. How do children whose parents give them unconditional positive regard develop emotionally?

Behavior, Cognitive, and Biomedical Therapies

KEY TERMS

- behavior therapies
- systematic desensitization
- aversive conditioning
- token economy
- cognitive therapies
- rational-emotive therapy (RET)
- cognitive-behavior therapy (CBT)
- drug therapy
- antipsychotic drugs
- antidepressant drugs
- antianxiety drugs
- electroconvulsive therapy (ECT)
- psychosurgery

OBJECTIVES

- Explain behavior therapies.
- Describe cognitive therapies.
- Explain biomedical therapies.

DISCOVER IT | *How does this relate to me?*

Do you have a habit you would like to break, or a habit you would like to form? Perhaps you put off studying until late at night when you are tired, a habit you would like to change. You would like to form the habit of studying as soon as you arrive home after school. To break the old habit and form the new one, you spend fifteen minutes each day for the first week studying right after school, rewarding yourself with a treat when finished. Each week you increase the time until studying becomes your new habit. This method, along with others, is applied on a deeper scale for people with psychological disorders.

T
he therapies you have learned about thus far spend a lot of time attending to clients' emotions and unmet motives, both unconscious (psychodynamic) and conscious (humanistic). Now you will learn about therapies that focus their attention elsewhere. Behavior therapies are psychotherapies that focus on changing people's troublesome behaviors. Cognitive therapies are psychotherapies that focus on changing the way people think about things. Finally, biomedical therapies treat psychological disorders by changing the way the brain works.

Behavior Therapies

Unlike psychodynamic therapists, behavior therapists do not believe in the unconscious. Behaviorists believe that insight is not important in the treatment of psychological disorders. Instead behaviorists think that both psychological disorders and healthy behavior develop through learning. In **behavior therapies**, disordered behaviors are unlearned and replaced by healthier behaviors. In treating clients, behavior therapists use principles of classical conditioning, operant conditioning, and observational learning.

behavior therapies
Psychotherapies that use learning principles to eliminate unwanted behaviors and replace them with healthier behaviors

SYSTEMATIC DESENSITIZATION

As you may recall from Chapter 12 on classical conditioning, an unconditioned stimulus (UCS) automatically causes an unconditioned response (UCR). When a UCS is repeatedly paired with a neutral stimulus, this neutral stimulus eventually becomes a conditioned stimulus (CS). This means that this CS now causes the same response, called the conditioned response (CR), that was previously caused only by the UCS. Behavior therapists use classical conditioning in *counterconditioning techniques*, in which new responses are conditioned to stimuli that previously triggered unwanted behaviors.

Systematic desensitization is a form of counterconditioning commonly used to treat people suffering from *phobias*. A phobia is an object or situation that causes a powerful, irrational fear. Counterconditioning involves gradually exposing the client to the feared object without causing anxiety and fear. Behaviorists believe phobias are acquired through classical conditioning. That is, the phobic object originally was a neutral stimulus that was paired with something that naturally caused fear. A phobia conditioned in this way can be counterconditioned by pairing the feared object with relaxation or another state of mind opposite of anxiety and fear.

Mary Cover Jones (1896–1987) was the first psychologist to demonstrate that conditioned fears could be reversed. She treated a three-year-old boy, Peter, who had a fear of furry objects. Therapy involved feeding Peter at one end of a room while a rabbit was brought in at the other end. After several sessions of slowly closing the distance between Peter and the rabbit, the boy's fear disappeared. Jones is often called "the mother of behavior therapy."

The following example shows how therapists use systematic desensitization. Imagine a client who fears snakes. The client and therapist begin by constructing

systematic desensitization A counterconditioning technique used to treat phobias, in which clients are gradually exposed to feared objects while remaining relaxed

ARCHIVES OF THE HISTORY OF AMERICAN PSYCHOLOGY—THE UNIVERSITY OF AKRON

Mary Cover Jones used systematic desensitization to help a young boy overcome his phobia of furry objects.

a *desensitization hierarchy*, which consists of a sequence of increasingly anxiety-provoking situations related to snakes (see Table 18-1, below). The therapist then trains the client in relaxation exercises, such as slow breathing or muscle relaxation. The first step of the hierarchy is then introduced—imagining seeing a snake. If the client can handle this without experiencing anxiety, the next step is introduced. Whenever the client experiences anxiety, the stimulus is removed and the client is given time to relax. After the client relaxes, a less-threatening object on the hierarchy is reintroduced and the client and therapist again proceed along the hierarchy. In a relatively short time, the client can face the highest object on the hierarchy—handling a snake—without distress.

With advancements in computer technology, clients can experience items in their fear hierarchy by using virtual-reality equipment. They wear a head-mounted virtual-reality helmet that allows them to experience and interact with the feared item. Clients gradually experience more and more intense anxiety-provoking situations until cured, all in the therapist's office. This virtual reality-graded exposure technique is very useful in treating the fear of heights (acrophobia), because it removes any danger of clients panicking while standing on a high structure. It also is useful in treating a fear of flying because it does not pose any risk of delaying actual flights if the client panics while on the plane. Before reading further, complete the Self-Discovery on systematic desensitization on page 549.

Table 18-1 A SAMPLE DESENSITIZATION HIERARCHY

Research indicates that systematic desensitization is the most effective therapy for treating phobias. The scenes in this hierarchy are typical of those used in the systematic desensitization of a fear of snakes. The numbers to the left of each statement represent one patient's subjective rating of how anxiety-provoking a situation is, on a scale from 0 ("not at all anxious") to 100 ("uncontrollable anxiety").

Fear Level	Scene
10	I imagine seeing a snake.
20	I see a line drawing of a snake.
25	I see a photograph of a small, harmless garden snake.
30	I see a photograph of a large python.
40	I hold a rubber snake in my hands.
50	I watch a nature video on snakes.
60	I am in the same room with a snake in a cage.
70	I am standing next to the snake cage.
80	I am looking into the top of the snake cage with the lid open.
90	I am standing next to a person holding a snake.
100	I am holding a snake.

Can You Systematically Desensitize Your Greatest Fear?

Identify your greatest fear. Construct a desensitization hierarchy consisting of a list of increasingly anxiety-provoking situations related to your fear (refer to Table 18-1 as a guide). Next find a quiet place with no distractions, sit in a comfortable chair, and progressively relax all the muscles of your body. You might be able to relax better if you read the Self-Discovery in Chapter 7, page 204). While relaxed, imagine the first, easiest scene in your fear hierarchy. When you can imagine this scene without experiencing anxiety, move on to the next scene. Whenever you experience anxiety, stop imagining the scene and give yourself time to relax. After relaxing, imagine the previously less-threatening scene in the hierarchy and then gradually reintroduce the more threatening scene. Space out your sessions over several days or even a few weeks. Eventually you will need to get out of the chair and directly experience actual anxiety-provoking situations in your hierarchy. When doing so, continue to use your progressive relaxation exercises to remain calm.

AVERSIVE CONDITIONING

Another counterconditioning technique is **aversive conditioning**, in which people are classically conditioned to react with avoidance (or aversion) to a harmful or undesirable stimulus. For example, a client who abuses alcohol may be given a drink laced with a tasteless and odorless drug that induces severe vomiting. The objective is to link the smell and taste of alcohol with a very negative response. After repeated pairings of alcohol with vomiting, the alcohol alone causes severe nausea.

About six out of ten alcoholics treated with this form of aversion therapy stop drinking for at least one year after treatment. However, after three years, only about one-third remain free of alcohol abuse. Because of this drop off in this treatment's success rate over time, most therapists who use aversion therapy combine it with another form of treatment to produce the best results.

TOKEN ECONOMIES

As you may recall from Chapter 12, *operant conditioning* involves learning through reinforcement and punishment. An important therapy technique that applies operant conditioning is the **token economy**. This technique uses reward and punishment to modify the behavior of groups of people who are often in institutional settings, such as psychiatric hospitals or prisons. In this technique, desirable behaviors are reinforced with tokens (such as chips or checks on a report card), and undesirable behaviors are punished by the loss of tokens. People collect the reward tokens and exchange them for other rewards, such as television privileges or field trips. Research has shown that this technique is effective in shaping desirable behavior in psychiatric hospitals and prisons, and in school classrooms, structured group play activities, and homes for juvenile delinquents.

INFOBIT

Rapid smoking is a type of aversive conditioning used to help people stop smoking. Clients inhale cigarette smoke every six to eight seconds until they become physically sick from the toxins in the tobacco. After repeated trials, the taste, smell, and even sight of cigarettes trigger nausea. About half the clients remain smoke-free at least three to six months after treatment.

aversive conditioning
A counterconditioning technique in which people are classically conditioned to react with avoidance (or aversion) to a harmful or undesirable stimulus

token economy The reinforcement of desirable behavior by using objects called tokens that can be exchanged for desired items or privileges

Unfortunately, this type of behavior modification depends too much on the external rewards earned in the token economy. Desirable behaviors learned through this technique often are extinguished quickly when people leave the institution. Supporters of the token economy respond that extinction can be prevented if, prior to leaving, people are slowly shifted from token rewards to social praise, which is a commonly used reward by people in their daily lives.

Table 18-2 COUNTERCONDITIONING TECHNIQUES

Technique	Description	Use
Desensitization	Pairs feared object with relaxation or another physiological state incompatible with anxiety and fear	Treatment of phobias
Aversive Conditioning	Classically conditions people to react with avoidance (or aversion) to harmful or undesirable stimulus	Treatment for addictions to alcohol, nicotine
Operant Conditioning	Involves learning through reinforcement and punishment; token economy technique applied operant conditioning principles	Used to modify behavior of people in institutional settings, such as psychiatric hospitals or prisons

CHECKPOINT *What are behavior therapies?*

Cognitive Therapies

As discussed in Chapter 17, the cognitive perspective suggests that the cause of psychological problems is faulty or troublesome thinking. Hassles become crises because people do not accurately evaluate the situations they encounter, so they do not develop useful solutions. Because faulty thinking is considered to be the source of psychological problems, **cognitive therapies** seek to identify and then fix the client's thinking.

RATIONAL-EMOTIVE THERAPY

Albert Ellis developed a form of cognitive therapy called **rational-emotive therapy (RET)**. In this therapy people are confronted with their irrational beliefs and persuaded to develop a more realistic way of thinking. Ellis believed mental distress is caused not by actual events in people's lives, but rather by the irrational thinking people have about those events. For example, a student might say he is depressed because he did not receive a big role in the high school musical. Ellis would suggest the real cause of the depression is the student's belief that not getting the role means something negative about himself ("The musical director does not

cognitive therapies Psychotherapies that focus on identifying and then fixing troublesome thinking by clients

rational-emotive therapy (RET) The cognitive therapy in which people are confronted with their irrational beliefs and persuaded to develop a more realistic way of thinking

respect me"). The goal of RET is to help people identify problems by the way they think about their daily experiences and then try to change their thinking.

In RET, therapists directly challenge their clients' irrational beliefs. First they point out why such beliefs are self-defeating, and then they try to persuade their clients to develop a more realistic way of evaluating their lives. Of all the therapies discussed in this chapter, RET is the one most similar to Dr. Phil's style with his television clients. Like Dr. Phil, RET therapists are often blunt and confrontational in challenging clients' negative and unrealistic assessments of their conditions.

Clients also are encouraged to step out of character and try new behaviors that directly challenge their irrational beliefs. For example, if people are afraid others will not like them if they disagree, the therapist might instruct them to disagree forcefully with five individuals during the next week. The goal in such an exercise is for the clients to discover the world does not end following such exchanges.

COGNITIVE-BEHAVIOR THERAPY

A cognitive therapy that is similar to RET is Aaron Beck's **cognitive-behavior therapy (CBT)**. Beck originally developed CBT to treat depression. Later he applied his treatment to anxiety and other emotional problems. According to Beck, depressed people have negative views of themselves, the world, and their future. They misinterpret everyday events to support these negative views. For example, they tend to exaggerate negative outcomes while downplaying positive outcomes. They also jump to negative conclusions based on a single event. These thinking errors occur so frequently they become automatic.

CBT involves identifying and then changing both the client's negative thinking patterns and negative behavior patterns. To do so, therapists instruct clients to keep a diary of their thoughts before and after sad episodes. Therapists then discuss these episodes with the clients and help them develop new thinking patterns that are more positive, accurate, and effective.

The reason this therapy has the term *behavior* in its title is that the methods used to help clients develop new patterns of thinking often involve basic conditioning techniques. Research shows that CBT is relatively effective in treating depression, anxiety disorder, eating disorders, and borderline personality disorder. The New Science feature on page 552 describes a format for offering psychotherapy to individual clients that cognitive therapists are likely to use.

cognitive-behavior therapy (CBT) The cognitive therapy that identifies and then changes negative thinking and behavior patterns

©SHARON DAY 2009/USED UNDER LICENSE FROM SHUTTERSTOCK.COM

According to cognitive-behavior therapy, if your current life situation is similar to a glass half-filled with sweet nectar, focus on the glass being half full, not half empty. If your current life situation is similar to a glass half-filled with bitter medicine, focus on the glass being half empty, and look forward to better times.

CHECKPOINT > *What are cognitive therapies?*

Therapy Offered Through the Internet

A growing number of therapists are interacting with their clients—and providing therapy—through e-mail, chat rooms, and message boards. Online therapy (also called e-therapy) provides help to people who are geographically isolated or are extremely socially anxious, disabled, or fearful that others will discover they are seeing a mental health professional.

Research suggests that online therapy can be effective for certain mental health problems. For example, Internet intervention programs for eating disorders have been found to be effective in reducing binge eating. People with milder forms of depression who seek help from online cognitive behavior therapy programs show mood improvements both during the first few months and one year later.

One possible benefit to the "anonymous" feeling of computer-assisted therapy is that clients may feel at ease more quickly when interacting online. As a result, they reveal their most troubling and important problems sooner and with greater honesty than when in the therapist's office. However, e-therapy is not for everyone. It should not be used by individuals who have complex mental health problems or who are in extreme emotional crisis, such as individuals suffering from severe depression with suicidal thoughts. It also should not be used by individuals who are uncomfortable working with computers or who have difficulty expressing themselves in writing. Such situations should be dealt with by seeing a therapist face to face.

©YURI ARCURS, 2009/USED UNDER LICENSE FROM SHUTTERSTOCK.COM

Think Critically

Do you think that group therapy could be conducted online? Why or why not?

Biomedical Therapies

People struggling with mental health problems may need medical attention. Biomedical therapies treat psychological disorders by changing the way the brain works, either by using drugs or surgery. The three main types of biomedical therapies are drug therapy, electroconvulsive therapy, and psychosurgery.

DRUG THERAPY

The most widely used biomedical therapy is **drug therapy**, which involves the use of medication to treat psychological disorders. Today in the United States, the number of full-time residents of psychiatric hospitals is less than one-third the number hospitalized 50 years ago. The primary reason for this decrease is the widespread use of drug therapies to treat disorders such as schizophrenia and mood disorders. Today, more than 90 percent of the people diagnosed with a psychological disorder received drugs as part of their treatment (see Figure 18-1, below). This high percentage of drug therapy is due not only to its effectiveness, but also because drug therapy is less expensive than psychological therapies.

Antipsychotic Drugs One of the earliest successes in using medication to treat psychological disorders was the discovery in the 1950s that certain drugs reduced the uncontrollable psychotic symptoms of schizophrenia, such as auditory hallucinations and paranoia. These **antipsychotic drugs** reduce schizophrenic symptoms by affecting the activity of dopamine and serotonin neurotransmitters in the brain. Unfortunately, antipsychotic drugs do not actually cure schizophrenia. They only help to control severe symptoms. Because antipsychotic drugs cannot cure the disorder, it is important that schizophrenic patients who receive these drugs also receive appropriate help from social service agencies.

drug therapy The use of medication to treat psychological disorders

antipsychotic drugs Drugs that reduce schizophrenic symptoms such as auditory hallucinations and paranoia

Figure 18-1 USE OF DRUGS IN TREATING PSYCHOLOGICAL DISORDERS

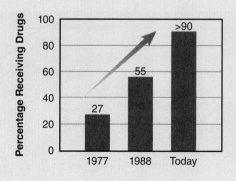

The percentage of people diagnosed with a psychological disorder who are receiving drug therapy has increased sharply since the 1970s.

Antidepressant Drugs   Another disorder treated with medication since the 1950s is depression. **Antidepressant drugs** improve mood and energy by affecting the activity of certain neurotransmitters in the brain, including serotonin. The drugs can produce dangerous side effects, including greatly reduced REM sleep and a sudden increase in blood pressure if mixed with certain foods, such as alcohol or aged cheeses. Bipolar disorder also may be treated with antidepressant drugs.

Antianxiety Drugs   One of the most common psychological problems is anxiety. The most frequently prescribed **antianxiety drugs** have a calming effect by reducing nerve impulse transmission. Side effects include lightheadedness, slurred speech, and reduced coordination. Antianxiety drugs are dangerous when combined with alcohol. These drugs can lead to physical dependence.

ELECTROCONVULSIVE THERAPY

Another medical treatment used to manipulate the brain is **electroconvulsive therapy (ECT)**, which occasionally is used to treat severe depression. In an ECT procedure, patients are first given drugs that make them unconscious and induce profound muscle relaxation. Next, with an electrode placed on one side of the patient's temple, a 70- to 130-volt charge of electricity is administered to that side of the brain for about one second. These shocks are continued until the patient has a seizure—a muscle contraction of the entire body—that lasts for at least 20 seconds. This treatment is repeated at least once a week for two to four weeks.

Although ECT is effective in treating severe depression, no one knows why. Research suggests ECT may be effective in promoting cell growth in areas of the brain that play a central role in creation of new memories and complex thinking.

ECT has temporary negative side effects, including confusion, loss of memory, and reduced coordination. Usually, memory is recovered within a few months. ECT is used only when severely depressed patients cannot tolerate or have not responded to drug therapy. ECT may be used when severely depressed patients are at immediate risk for suicide, because ECT has an almost immediate effect, while benefits from antidepressant medications usually take at least 10 days.

antidepressant drugs Drugs that improve mood and energy

antianxiety drugs Drugs that have a calming effect

electroconvulsive therapy (ECT) A medical treatment for severe depression in which a brief electric shock is administered to the brain of an anesthetized patient

Electroconvulsive therapy is effective in treating severe depression.

WILL MCINTYRE/PHOTO RESEARCHERS, INC.

PSYCHOSURGERY

By far the most radical and controversial method of treating psychological disorders is **psychosurgery**, which involves destroying brain tissue thought to be the cause of the disorder. In 1949, the Portuguese psychiatrist Antonio Egas Moñiz received the Nobel Prize in Medicine for his psychosurgical technique known as *prefrontal lobotomy.* In this medical procedure, two small holes are drilled in the skull. Then a sharp instrument is inserted and moved from side to side, severing the neural connections between the prefrontal lobes and the rest of the brain. At the time that Egas Moñiz was using this technique to treat psychotic patients, it was thought that destroying the prefrontal lobes would relieve the crippling emotional reactions experienced by many schizophrenics. The medical profession was so taken by Egas Moñiz's technique that, during the 1940s and early 1950s, more than 35,000 lobotomies were performed in the United States to treat schizophrenia, aggressiveness, anxiety, and depression.

Although lobotomies did reduce the frequency of some undesirable behaviors, patients paid a heavy price. The treatment profoundly altered their personalities, with some becoming extremely apathetic and others becoming excitable and impulsive. Due to these negative and irreversible effects, most physicians stopped using the procedure. Antipsychotic drugs in the late 1950s brought a stop to lobotomies. Today, MRI-guided precision psychosurgery is performed in extreme cases when other types of treatment have been ineffective. This surgery focuses on smaller brain areas than those in lobotomies.

psychosurgery A rarely used surgical procedure to treat psychological disorders in which brain tissue thought to be the cause of the disorder is destroyed

> **CHECKPOINT** *What are three biomedical therapies?*

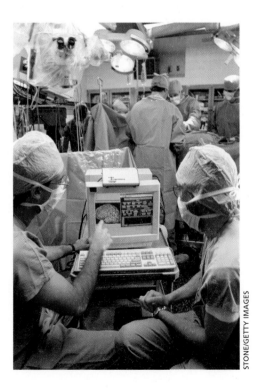

STONE/GETTY IMAGES

MRI-guided precision surgery is performed in extreme cases of psychological disorders when other treatments have been ineffective.

In Your Own Words

Using information from the text, compare and contrast behavior, cognitive, and biomedical therapies. Explain any major similarities and differences among the three, discuss techniques used with each, and describe which patients are candidates for each type of therapy and why.

Review Concepts

1. Which is employed by behavior therapists?
   - a. antianxiety drugs
   - b. psychosurgery
   - c. electroconvulsive therapy
   - d. classical conditioning

2. Which therapy seeks to identify and then fix troublesome thinking?
   - a. cognitive
   - b. behavior
   - c. biomedical
   - d. electroconvulsive

3. With which therapy do therapists directly challenge their clients' irrational beliefs?
   - a. aversive conditioning
   - b. token economy
   - c. rational-emotive therapy
   - d. systematic desensitization

4. Which is a biomedical therapy?
   - a. drug therapy
   - b. operant conditioning
   - c. cognitive-behavior therapy
   - d. observational learning

5. **True or False** Today MRI-guided precision psychosurgery is performed on a regular basis on patients who are depressed.

6. **True or False** Antianxiety drugs are dangerous when combined with alcohol.

7. **True or False** Systematic desensitization is a form of behavior therapy that is used to treat phobias.

Think Critically

8. Why is it important for people with schizophrenia to receive the appropriate therapy in addition to antipsychotic drug therapy?

9. Explain why Beck suggests clients keep a diary of their thoughts before and after sad events, and how doing so helps the clients.

10. Why do most therapists who use aversion therapy combine it with another form of treatment?

Psychotherapist

 *ealth Science*

Are you interested in working with people who have serious mental and emotional illnesses? Would you like to work in a hospital or mental health facility? If so, you should consider the career of psychotherapist.

Psychotherapists treat people who have severe illnesses, such as schizophrenia, bipolar disorder, or major depression. Some patients may be hospitalized while others may be living a normal, productive life while seeing a psychotherapist as an outpatient. Many of the patients are on medication, which must be prescribed by a physician. Psychotherapists may partner or work with a physician for the purpose of prescribing medication to patients.

Many psychotherapists work in a hospital or mental health facility, while others are self-employed. Some may choose to specialize in a specific illness or work with patients in a particular age group, such as children, adolescents, or older adults.

Employment Outlook

Careers for psychotherapists are expected to grow 15 percent until 2016. This is a faster than average rate.

Needed Skills and Education

Most states require psychotherapists to have a doctoral degree, which usually requires five to seven years of college work after receiving a bachelor's degree. Most states also require psychotherapists to be licensed. Requirements vary from state to state.

Courses that will help you in this career are those in psychology and other related sciences. You also need good written and oral communication skills; good interpersonal relationship skills; and good organizational abilities. For psychotherapists in private practice, courses in accounting, marketing, and other related business courses are advisable.

How You'll Spend Your Day

Psychotherapists see an average of five patients each day. They usually begin the day reviewing patients' records, which is a documentation of the patient's history, illness, medications, and treatment plan along with notes made by the psychotherapist.

People in this career usually work long hours, often 12 hours a day. Some evening and weekends may be required in order to meet the needs of the patients.

Being a psychotherapist can be emotionally draining. Patients do not always respond to treatment and some may have such severe emotional problems they cannot be helped. This can cause burnout among people who work with these patients, especially if they become emotionally involved.

Earnings

The median earnings of psychotherapists are $59,440. The lowest 10 percent earn $35,280 while the highest 10 percent earn more than $102,730.

What About You?

Does the career of psychotherapist interest you? Use the library or Internet to research one of the following serious mental illnesses and the treatment: schizophrenia, bipolar disorder, or major depression. Make notes about the role of psychotherapy in the treatment of the illness you chose. Based on your research, write a paragraph about why you think you would or would not be interested in working with patients with the disorder you chose.

JEANELL NORVELL/ISTOCKPHOTO.COM

CHAPTER SUMMARY

18.1 Therapists and Clients

- The three main mental health professions that supply most of the therapy to people suffering from psychological disorders are psychiatry, social work, and psychology.

- Individuals who are in psychological distress seek therapy. The usual coping strategies they use to manage and solve their problems no longer work.

- Obstacles to seeking therapy include the stigma of mental illness within some cultures and the helpless attitude of the individual needing help.

- Mental health professionals treat clients individually and in groups.

- Group therapy is the simultaneous treatment of several clients under the guidance of a therapist. These groups may include family therapy and couples therapy.

- Self-help groups meet without the benefit of a therapist. Many self-help groups follow the Alcoholics Anonymous 12-step model.

18.2 Psychodynamic and Humanistic Therapies

- Psychodynamic therapies are based on the work of Sigmund Freud who believed psychological disorders are caused by unconscious conflict.

- Psychodynamic therapies include the techniques of free association and the analysis of dreams and other self expressions such as daydreams, artwork, poetry, and so on.

- Clients may engage in transference or resistance when in psychoanalysis.

- Humanistic psychotherapists believe psychological problems develop when outside forces stop people's natural tendency to seek personal growth.

- Humanistic therapies help people get in touch with their feelings, their "true selves," and their purpose in life.

- Humanistic therapies are client-centered and involve using active listening skills.

18.3 Behavior, Cognitive, and Biomedical Therapies

- Behavior therapies are psychotherapies that apply learning principles to eliminate unwanted behaviors and replace them with healthier behaviors.

- Techniques of behavior therapists include systematic desensitization, aversive conditioning, and token economies.

- Cognitive therapies are psychotherapies that focus on identifying and then fixing troublesome thinking by clients.

- Techniques of cognitive therapists include rational-emotive therapy and cognitive-behavior therapy.

- Biomedical therapies treat psychological disorders by changing the way the brain works, either through drugs or surgery.

- Three main types of biomedical therapy are drug therapy, electroconvulsive therapy, and psychosurgery.

CHAPTER ASSESSMENT

Review Psychology Terms

Select the term that best fits the definition. Some terms will not be used.

____ 1. The treatment of several clients at the same time under the guidance of a therapist

____ 2. A humanistic technique in which clients imagine that the person to whom they would like to speak is sitting in an empty chair facing them

____ 3. Psychotherapies that focus on identifying and then fixing troublesome thinking by clients

____ 4. Psychotherapies that use learning principles to eliminate unwanted behaviors and replace them with healthier behaviors

____ 5. The cognitive therapy in which people are confronted with their irrational beliefs and persuaded to develop a more realistic way of thinking

____ 6. The treatment of psychological disorders using methods that include a personal relationship between a trained therapist and the individual or individuals seeking treatment

____ 7. Therapy designed to constructively change the way in which family members relate to one another

____ 8. The process by which the client develops positive or negative feelings for the therapist that represent feelings the client experienced toward others early in life

____ 9. The treatment of psychological disorders by changing the way the brain works, primarily by using drugs, electrical stimulation, or surgery

____ 10. Anything clients do that interferes with them understanding their psychological problems

____ 11. The cognitive therapy that identifies and then changes negative thinking and behavior patterns

____ 12. Several people regularly meeting and discussing their problems with one another without the guidance of a therapist

____ 13. A rarely used surgical procedure to treat psychological disorders in which brain tissue thought to be the cause of the disorder is destroyed

____ 14. A humanistic therapy in which the therapist provides a supportive setting for clients to discover their "true selves"

____ 15. People who actively work with professional therapists toward the goal of improving their mental health

____ 16. A psychodynamic therapy technique in which clients say whatever comes to mind

____ 17. A counterconditioning technique in which people are classically conditioned to react with avoidance to a harmful or undesirable stimulus

____ 18. A counterconditioning technique used to treat phobias in which clients are gradually exposed to feared objects while remaining relaxed

____ 19. Therapy style based on combining aspects of several different psychotherapy techniques

a. aversive conditioning

b. behavior therapies

c. biomedical therapy

d. clients

e. client-centered therapy

f. cognitive-behavior therapy

g. cognitive therapies

h. eclectic approach

i. empty-chair technique

j. family therapy

k. free association

l. group therapy

m. humanistic therapy

n. psychodynamic therapy

o. psychosurgery

p. psychotherapy

q. rational-emotive therapy

r. resistance

s. self-help group

t. systematic desensitization

u. token economy

v. transference

Review Psychology Concepts

20. What is the primary goal of mental health professionals?

21. Compare and contrast humanistic therapies and psychodynamic therapies.

22. List and explain the meaning of each of the three key ingredients humanistic therapists use in expressing unconditional positive regard to their clients.

23. Compare and contrast systematic desensitization, aversion conditioning, and token economy.

24. Define drug therapy, and explain what each of the following drugs is used for: antipsychotic drugs, antidepressant drugs, and antianxiety drugs.

25. Define electroconvulsive therapy (ECT).

26. Compare and contrast the three mental health professionals: psychiatrists, social workers, and psychologists. Explain how the three work as a team with a schizophrenic patient.

27. Explain why Native Americans and African Americans might seek mental health help outside the traditional medical community. Where might people in these cultural groups go for help if they are in mental distress?

28. Differentiate between group therapy and self-help groups.

29. What is the purpose of family therapy?

30. What is psychoanalysis, and who is its founder?

31. Why might a therapist be interested in a client's dreams or artwork, and how could understanding the dreams and artwork help the client? What type of therapy would focus on a client's dreams and artwork?

32. According to Carl Rogers, why do people experience mental health problems?

33. What is the focus of psychotherapy?

34. What does biomedical therapy assume about psychological disorders, and how does it treat them?

35. Why do mental health professionals encourage those who seek help to think of themselves as clients who have hired a professional to help them deal with their problems?

36. What are the benefits of using the virtual reality-graded exposure technique in treating some phobias, such as the fear of heights?

37. Explain rational-emotive therapy (RET), the form of cognitive therapy developed by Albert Ellis. What did Ellis believe causes mental distress in people's lives?

Apply Psychology Concepts

38. Explain how virtual reality equipment is used to help people who have a fear of heights.

39. Compare and contrast the three different ways a biomedical psychiatrist, a psychoanalyst, and a behavior therapist would treat a patient who is severely depressed.

40. All the methods of therapy for psychological problems have general goals in common. What do you see as the basic goals of psychotherapy?

41. There is an increased diversity of client populations and problems in this country. How can psychotherapists include cultural factors in the assessment and treatment process?

Make Academic Connections

42. **Research** Use your local phone book to contact a chapter of a self-help group, such as Alcoholics Anonymous, Al-Anon, Alateen, Overeaters Anonymous, or any other self-help group. Ask to interview a local leader or member of the group to learn how the group is conducted, what type of therapy the group offers its members, and the success rate. Write a report about your findings. Discuss how the anonymity of the members protects their privacy.

43. **Computer Sciences** Go online to research the services provided by therapists over the Internet or phone. Request information on how the client's privacy is protected and the types of problems addressed. Use a software program to write a fact sheet about your findings.

44. **Writing** Write an essay that answers either of the following questions. Do you think individuals who have a psychological disorder should be committed to a hospital if they are a danger to themselves or others, even if they do not want to be committed? Do you think it is a good idea to remove individuals with psychological disorders from the hospital or other institutions? Be specific in what you think and explain why you think the way you do.

DIGGING DEEPER
with Psychology eCollection

Health care, including mental health care, varies around the globe. A World Health Organization (WHO) study of treatment of mental health issues around the world found disturbing evidence that many cases go untreated. The United States had the highest number of adults with mental disorders, primarily because they are most likely to be diagnosed in this country. Americans also are more likely to receive health care treatment. Elsewhere, people with the mildest forms of mental disorders were most likely to receive care while severe illnesses go untreated. Access the Gale Psychology eCollection at *www.cengage.com/school/psych/franzoi* and read Splete's article summarizing research on worldwide health care. Write a report on the findings outlined in the article and answer the question: What is the obstacle to better health care around the world? As an additional project, write an essay answering the question: How can health care outside the United States be improved?

Source: Splete, Heidi. Serious mental disorders not getting treated. *Clinical Psychiatry News*. 32.7 (July 2004): 82(1).

Interpersonal Interaction

ESSENTIAL QUESTION
Go to page XXVII

"The world's a stage and most of us are desperately unrehearsed."

—SEAN O'CASEY, IRISH PLAYWRIGHT, 1880–1964

"Your lecture saved my life!"

It isn't often—make that almost never—that a teacher hears these words from a student who really means it. Yet I had this experience once with a student in my introductory psychology course. My student, Ferris, had been waiting at a bus stop not far from campus on a Saturday evening when a neatly dressed man walked up to her, put a gun to her stomach, and demanded that she hand over her purse. Startled, Ferris didn't immediately respond, so the gunman put the weapon to her head and repeated his demand. Ferris noticed that people across the street were watching, but no one was taking action to help. In that moment, Ferris recalled the last five minutes of my lecture the previous morning, when I'd said, "And now I'm going to tell you something that may one day save your life."

Now, I am not claiming that this chapter will similarly affect your life. However, the reason I love the field of social psychology is that it attempts to understand how we go about our everyday lives with other people. This is the part of your psychology journey where you can discover answers to many questions you probably have had about your personal journey. As you continue to read, I promise to tell you what I told Ferris and her fellow students in class.

OBJECTIVES

- Discuss how physical appearance affects impressions of people.
- Define and discuss attributions.

DISCOVER IT | *How does this relate to me?*

Imagine that two new students arrive at school. Before morning classes, you make an attempt to welcome them, but they seem to brush you off. Later you see them talking and smiling with others. Why did they respond so differently to you? Was it something you said? Were they in a hurry? Are they stuck up?

KEY TERMS

- social psychology
- impression formation
- physical attractiveness stereotype
- attribution theory
- fundamental attribution error

You are influenced by everyone around you and you, in turn, influence them. Every day you judge and react to people based on little information. How do you "size up" others? **Social psychology**—the scientific study of how people's thoughts, feelings, and behavior are influenced by others—is the branch of psychology that investigates this question.

Physical Appearance

You want to understand those around you. The better you understand people, the better you can predict how they will behave toward you and others. This desire to understand people is the basis for forming impressions of others. **Impression formation** is the process by which you combine information about a person into an overall judgment. It is developing a theory of a person, and then using this theory as a guideline in your actions toward the person.

PHYSICAL ATTRACTIVENESS STEREOTYPE

When you meet other people, their physical appearance is the first thing you notice. Research indicates that many people believe physically attractive individuals have better personalities and lead happier lives than less attractive people. This **physical attractiveness stereotype** is found in all age groups. Attractive infants are perceived by many adults as more likable, sociable, competent, and easier to care for. In elementary school, cute children are more popular with their classmates than unattractive children.

social psychology The scientific study of how people's thoughts, feelings, and behavior are influenced by others

impression formation The process of combining information about a person into an overall judgment

physical attractiveness stereotype The belief that physically attractive individuals have better personalities and lead happier lives than less attractive people

Do physically attractive people have better personalities than unattractive people? No. A review of more than 90 studies found that although most people think good-looking individuals are more intelligent, dominant, happy, and mentally healthy than unattractive people, this is not the case. Research does find that good-looking people are less anxious and more skilled socially. A reason for this is that people seek the company of attractive people and respond favorably to them. As a result, physically attractive people feel more confident in social settings. This is an example of the self-fulfilling prophecy (see Chapter 16, page 492).

WHAT MAKES A PERSON PHYSICALLY ATTRACTIVE?

Cross-cultural research shows that people around the world agree on what makes a face attractive. Faces in which the right and left sides are well matched, or symmetrical, are judged more attractive. What is so appealing about symmetry? Some psychologists think it is because symmetry is a sign a person is physically healthy and has good genes. When looking for a mate with whom to have children, good health and genes are important.

What else makes a face attractive? For women, youthful facial features (large eyes, small nose, full lips, small chin, delicate jaw) are judged the most attractive. For men, mature facial features (small eyes, broad forehead, thick eyebrows, thin lips, large jaw) are judged the most attractive. What might explain these preferences?

One theory states that women and men engage in a *looks-for-status exchange*. Women exchange their beauty for social power and men exchange their social power for their partner's beauty. According to this theory, people assume that a man with a mature-looking face has more social power and wealth than a younger-looking man. As a result, power and wealth increases mature-looking men's appeal to women. This theory also states that female youthfulness is associated with the ability to have children. As a result, younger-looking women are more attractive to men than more mature-looking women.

The looks-for-status exchange theory states that women exchange beauty for social power and men exchange their social power for their partner's beauty.

This theory is supported by cross-cultural research, which finds that men tend to marry younger women. However, research also finds that as women achieve greater social power on their own, they are less likely to judge older men as more appealing than younger men. This finding might mean that people in general are less likely to consider power and wealth as the most important qualities in a possible mate when they already have some power and wealth themselves.

CONTRAST EFFECTS

People are judged as more attractive after others see an unattractive person of the same gender. Similarly, people are judged as less attractive when others see someone who is very attractive. This is the *contrast effect*, and it also affects how people judge themselves. People feel more attractive after seeing same-sex persons who fall below conventional beauty standards. They feel less attractive after seeing "perfect 10s."

People who pay attention to popular culture and physical appearance are the most affected by the contrast effect. Teenage girls and women who read fashion magazines with photos of thin, beautiful models often evaluate their own appearance negatively. Similar effects occur for teenage boys and men who read body-building or other sports magazines. Check out the Case Study below to learn how social psychologists use popular magazines to understand the way this culture judges women based on their age.

CHECKPOINT ▶ *What is the physical attractiveness stereotype?*

CASE STUDY

How Do Magazines Show Younger vs. Older Women?

INTRODUCTION Social psychologists can examine magazines in popular culture to gain insights into cultural beliefs about beauty standards. For example, in 2007 Gayle Bessenoff and her colleagues examined the way women are portrayed in American magazines based on their age.

HYPOTHESIS Younger women will appear more frequently as models in magazines than older women. Further, when younger women appear in magazines they will wear less clothing than older women and also will be thinner.

METHOD The researchers examined the images of female models in American magazines, recording their approximate age, body size, and the degree to which they were clothed.

RESULTS Consistent with the study's hypotheses, analyses found that older women appeared less frequently in magazines than younger women. When they appeared in magazines, younger women were shown as thinner and as less clothed than older women. Based on these findings, the researchers suggested that one reason younger women have more negative body esteem than older women in American culture is partly because younger women are exposed to more media images of similarly aged models who are very thin than are older women.

Critical Analysis

Why do you think there are fewer images of older women compared to younger women in magazines?

Making Attributions

Physical appearance is only one way you form opinions about another person. You also try to explain why people act the way they do. **Attribution theory** describes how you decide whether another person's behavior is caused by the person's disposition or the situation. If you make an *internal attribution,* your explanation is that the behavior is being caused by something inside the person, such as personality traits, moods, attitudes, abilities, or effort. If you make an *external attribution,* your explanation is that the behavior is being caused by something outside the person, such as the actions of others, the nature of the situation, or luck.

Why do you think this girl is so happy? If you think her happiness is due to an upbeat personality, you are making an internal attribution for her mood. If you think her happiness is due to some positive event, you are making an external attribution.

© MONKEY BUSINESS IMAGES, 2009/USED UNDER LICENSE FROM SHUTTERSTOCK.COM

In the imaginary story of the new students ignoring your friendly greeting, you might decide that they are rude and conceited (an internal attribution). Or, you may explain their coolness as being caused by them being distracted on the first day in a new school (an external attribution). The attribution you make guides your opinions and actions toward these individuals.

CULTURAL DIFFERENCES IN MAKING ATTRIBUTIONS

People from individualist cultures often make internal rather than external attributions. This is a bias known as the **fundamental attribution error.** In one study, social psychologists asked groups of American and Asian Indian citizens of different ages to explain the causes of positive and negative behaviors they had seen in their own lives. The youngest children of the two cultures (8 to 11 year olds) did not differ in the attributions they made. However, as the age of the participants increased, the Americans made more internal attributions than did the Asian Indians. This and similar studies suggest the fundamental attribution error is more common in individualist than collectivist cultures, and that it is learned through socialization.

Why is the fundamental attribution error more common in individualist cultures than collectivist cultures? Studies suggest that this cultural difference in explaining

attribution theory A theory that describes how you decide whether another person's behavior is caused by the person's disposition or the situation

fundamental attribution error The tendency to make internal attributions rather than external attributions when trying to explain other people's actions

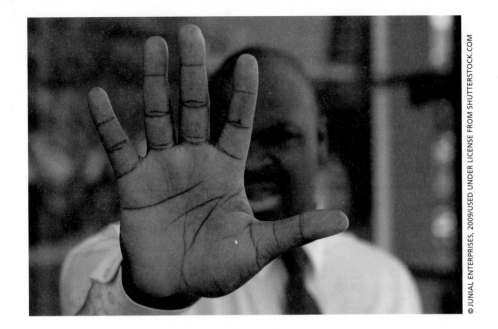

What is your explanation for why this person is so angry? Whether you make an internal attribution (he is an unpleasant person) or an external attribution (he is having a bad day) may be influenced by whether you grew up in an individualistic or collectivist culture.

other people's behavior is due to different beliefs about what causes people to behave the way they do. People in individualist cultures are taught that everybody is free to do what they desire. This sort of teaching results in individualists underestimating the power of the situation. Individualists are more likely to believe that people's behavior is internally driven and not influenced by situational forces. In contrast, collectivists are taught to be more aware of how situational pressures, such as others' expectations, might influence people's behavior. Therefore, individualists' lack of attention to situational factors leads them to make more fundamental attribution errors than collectivists make.

The fundamental attribution error has important social consequences. Attributing the behavior of others to such internal factors as their personalities often leads you to brush off people's attempts to deny responsibility for negative events in their lives. For example, disregarding situational forces in explaining the troubles of victims within society (for example, crime victims, street people, disadvantaged people) can result in you being unsympathetic to their problems. You hold them responsible due to their "bad" personalities or choices.

Even if you respond with sympathy, where you locate the cause of social problems shapes the type of solutions you seek. If you explain the difficulties of unfortunate others as being due to their own personal defects rather than to their circumstances, the treatment programs you create will focus on changing individuals rather than changing social conditions. The best treatment programs often are those that focus on both internal and external problems that contribute to people's difficulties in living a healthy and happy life.

CHECKPOINT   *What is the difference between an internal and external attribution?*

In Your Own Words

Discuss how physical appearances affect your impressions of other people, and how you feel other people judge you by your physical appearance. For example, what inferences do you make about the lives of female movie stars who look beautiful in film? Do your judgments change when you see a photo of the stars in sloppy clothes and without makeup? Think about the clothes you wear. Do people react differently to you depending on the clothes you have on?

Review Concepts

1. Which refers to developing a theory of a person, and then using that theory as a guideline in your actions toward the person?

   a. attribution

   b. impression formation

   c. covariation attribution model

   d. attractiveness stereotype

2. Which refers to an external attribution?

   a. luck

   b. moods

   c. personality traits

   d. abilities

3. The scientific study of how people's thoughts, feelings, and behaviors are influenced by others is

   a. clinical psychology

   b. psychiatry

   c. biopsychology

   d. social psychology

4. **True or False**   The physical attractiveness stereotype is found in ages 12 to 25, but not in younger or older age groups.

5. **True or False**   Cross-cultural research shows that the fundamental attribution error is more common in individualist than collectivist cultures.

6. **True or False**   External attributions are likely when consensus and consistency are low and distinctiveness is high, or when all three kinds of information are high.

Think Critically

7. Explain why cross-cultural research shows that men tend to marry younger women and women tend to find mature-looking men attractive.

8. Why might you want to avoid spending a lot of time reading fashion or body-building magazines?

9. Why is it important to pay attention to what attributions you make about other people's behavior?

10. Explain the social consequences of fundamental attribution error.

Forming and Changing Attitudes

OBJECTIVES

- Explain attitude formation.
- Describe changing attitudes and the elaboration likelihood model.
- Define cognitive dissonance.

KEY TERMS

- attitudes
- mere exposure effect
- reference group
- implicit attitude
- persuasion
- elaboration likelihood model
- cognitive dissonance

DISCOVER IT | *How does this relate to me?*

Have you noticed you often like a song only after hearing it a number of times? Have you noticed that your friends or family influence whether you like or dislike certain people or things? Have you ever wondered why you develop positive attitudes for some things and negative attitudes about others? Psychologists have asked these same questions.

Through observing people and events, you develop **attitudes**, which are positive or negative evaluations of objects. Objects include people, things, events, and issues. When you use such words as like, dislike, love, hate, good, and bad, you are describing your attitudes.

Attitude Formation

You were not born with attitudes. Your attitudes developed through experience. Sometimes you form attitudes without much thought, while other times you spend a lot of time figuring out whether you like or dislike something. Social psychologists have identified that attitudes may form through mere exposure, conditioning, reference group influence, and without conscious awareness.

MERE EXPOSURE

People often develop positive attitudes toward objects repeatedly presented to them. You might not have an opinion about a song the first time you hear it, but you may start to like it after repeated listening. This is the **mere exposure effect**, and it occurs in different settings. For example, you have seen your mirrored facial image more often than you have seen your true facial image. A mirrored image is identical, but it is a reverse of the true image. Which image of yourself do you prefer?

attitudes Positive or negative evaluations of an object

mere exposure effect The tendency to develop positive attitudes toward objects and individuals to which you are repeatedly exposed

Think about the mere exposure effect the next time you gaze into a mirror. You are probably the only person, among those who know you well, who prefers that image of your face staring back at you!

To answer this question, social psychologists photographed students, and later showed the students and their close friends the photo along with a mirror-image print. The photographed students preferred the mirror print, while their close friends preferred the photo. These results support the mere exposure effect and illustrate how positive attitudes sometimes are formed from repeated exposure.

CONDITIONING

Attitudes also are formed through operant and classical conditioning, both of which you learned about in Chapter 12. For example, in operant conditioning, if you are praised and encouraged when learning how to dance, you are likely to develop a positive attitude toward dancing. If others tease and make fun of you while you are learning to dance, you are likely to form a negative attitude. In classical conditioning, attitudes form by pairing a previously neutral stimulus with another stimulus that naturally creates a positive or a negative response in a person. For example, you may develop a negative attitude toward a certain food if you get food poisoning after eating it. Because the bacteria (the unconditioned stimulus) in the food caused an unconditioned response of nausea in you, now the sight and smell of that food (the conditioned stimulus) is unpleasant to you (the conditioned response). You have formed a negative attitude toward this food.

REFERENCE GROUPS

Social groups also help to shape your attitudes. A **reference group** is a group with which you identify. You use the group's standards to judge yourself and the world. Reference groups can be large, such as an entire nation or a religion, or they can be small, such as your family or friends.

reference group A group with which you identify, using its standards to judge yourself and the world

One of the first and best studies investigating reference group influence on attitudes was conducted by Theodore Newcomb. In 1934 Newcomb was hired as a faculty member at Bennington College, a college for women located in a remote section of Vermont. Almost all the new students came from upper class, socially conservative New England families. Newcomb and most of the other faculty were young and liberal in their social views. Newcomb discovered that with each passing semester, many students' social and political attitudes became increasingly liberal. These attitude changes were due to the students shifting from their conservative hometown reference groups to their new, more liberal reference group at Bennington. Students who maintained their conservative attitudes throughout college were those who frequently traveled home and did not adopt the college lifestyle.

Theodore Newcomb studied the influence of reference groups on attitudes.

BENTLEY HISTORICAL LIBRARY, UNIVERSITY OF MICHIGAN

In follow-up studies of the Bennington College women, Newcomb demonstrated the importance of reference groups in maintaining attitudes after people are no longer with the group. Fifty years after graduation, the women who had become politically liberal while at Bennington College were still more liberal than most women of their generation.

IMPLICIT ATTITUDES

Sometimes you are not consciously aware you have developed an attitude. An **implicit attitude** is an attitude activated automatically from memory, without awareness that you possess it. Feeling uneasy and irritable around a stranger because you unconsciously associate that person with a disagreeable person from your past is an example of an implicit attitude. Implicit attitudes are gut-level evaluations. Whether they are positive or negative depends on whether the associations they trigger in memory are pleasant or unpleasant.

Sometimes your consciously held attitude about something or someone is different from your implicit attitude. For example, imagine you are attracted to your best friend's boyfriend or girlfriend. To guard against hurting your friendship, you convince yourself you dislike the romantic partner. Now you have a consciously held negative attitude that is opposite of your implicit positive attitude. You also may convince yourself you like something even while unconsciously disliking it. For example, you many convince yourself that you like a food all your friends rave about. However, the sour look on your face while chewing this food may signal to others that you unconsciously dislike it. Research suggests such conflicting conscious and unconscious attitudes are most likely to develop for socially sensitive issues, such as people's attitudes toward their friends' romantic partners, or attitudes about racial and different cultural groups. Check out the New Science feature on page 572 to learn how social psychologists measure implicit attitudes.

> **implicit attitude** An attitude that is activated automatically from memory, without awareness that you possess it

CHECKPOINT *What is the mere exposure effect?*

How Are Implicit Attitudes Measured?

People often are unwilling to admit they have negative attitudes about some social groups. Studies also find that people honestly may be unaware they have unconscious attitudes that influence their actions. Social psychologists developed computer programs to tap into people's unconscious thoughts and feelings.

The most popular of these implicit or unconscious measures is the Implicit Association Test (IAT). The IAT is designed to measure the strength of automatic associations between different concepts in memory. For example, if people have an unconscious age bias, it takes them longer to categorize pleasant words as "good" when they are paired with old rather than young faces, and it also takes them longer to categorize unpleasant words as "bad" when they are paired with young rather than old faces. Using the IAT in this way, researchers find that people who have this implicit age bias often behave more negatively toward the elderly than toward the young, even while not realizing they have these implicit negative attitudes.

Think Critically

Why do you think using the IAT is often better than directly asking someone about his or her attitudes?

INFOBIT
Forty percent of all advertisements use humor. Research shows that using humor in advertisements increases people's attention to the message more than serious-sounding ads. However, one of the problems with using humor is that the jokes may be so funny that people only remember them and not the information about the product.

persuasion The process of trying to change attitudes through communicating a particular message

elaboration likelihood model A theory that people engage in either effortful or effortless thinking after receiving a persuasive message

Changing Attitudes

Every day you are bombarded with attempts to change your attitudes. Television and magazine ads try to convince you one product is better than the others. Your friends and family try to change your attitudes about a variety of topics, including your eating and fashion habits and your social and political attitudes. This process of trying to change attitudes through communicating a particular message is known as **persuasion**.

The **elaboration likelihood model** is a persuasion theory stating that a person engages in either effortful or effortless thinking after receiving a persuasive message. The term *elaboration likelihood* refers to the likelihood that a person will elaborate—or analyze—the content of the persuasive message. According to the model, you engage in either high or low elaboration when thinking about persuasive messages. When motivated and able to think carefully about the message content (high elaboration), you take the thoughtful *central route* to persuasion and are influenced by the strength and quality of the arguments. For example, when listening to a politician talk about a topic that you consider personally important, you carefully analyze what is said. You are persuaded if you conclude the arguments are strong. When unable or unwilling to analyze a persuasive message, you take the rather unthinking *peripheral route* to persuasion. Here, you pay attention to things that are peripheral, or not central, to the content or quality of the message (low elaboration), such as the attractiveness of the communicator or amount of information in the message. When listening to this same politician talk about an issue you consider unimportant, you still may be persuaded because he or she either looks honest or sounds knowledgeable, which are two peripheral cues. You've been persuaded without thinking about the actual content of the message. Figure 19-1 shows these two persuasion routes.

Figure 19-1 **TWO ROUTES TO PERSUASION**

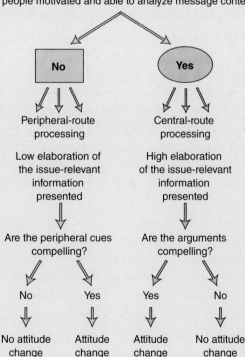

According to the elaboration likelihood model of persuasion, attitude change that occurs due to central-route processing is more likely to last than is attitude change that occurs due to peripheral-route processing.

Attitude change can occur through either the thoughtful central route or the rather unthinking peripheral route. Attitudes formed through the peripheral route are weaker, more easily changed, and less likely to shape your actual behavior than those formed through the central route. If you think of attitudes as houses, then attitudes changed by the peripheral route are like houses made from straw or sticks—they require little effort to develop and are weak and easily destroyed. In contrast, attitudes changed by the central route are like houses made of bricks— they take a good deal of effort to construct and are strong and durable. This is the reason this text has placed so much importance on critical thinking. Such thinking results in a stronger foundation for your knowledge about the world.

CHECKPOINT *What is the elaboration likelihood model?*

Cognitive Dissonance

Imagine that Jack tells his grade-school friends he dislikes girls, but later he is seen walking up a hill with Jill. How might Jack respond to this inconsistency between his attitude ("I do not like girls") and his behavior (walking with Jill)?

The Jack & Jill story illustrates the fact that sometimes people change their attitudes because they want those attitudes to be consistent with their behavior. According to Leon Festinger's *cognitive dissonance theory*, when you become aware of an inconsistency between your attitude and actions, you experience an unpleasant psychological state called cognitive dissonance. **Cognitive dissonance** is a feeling of discomfort caused by performing an action inconsistent with your attitude. To relieve the discomfort, you often change your attitude so it is in line with your behavior. In Jack's case, if no one forced him to walk up the hill with Jill, Jack should experience discomfort when he thinks: "I dislike girls, but I walked with a girl." To reduce his cognitive dissonance, Jack might change his attitude: "Gee, maybe girls aren't that bad after all."

Do you remember Leon Festinger's research of the doomsday cult that I mentioned in Chapter 2? The members of this cult believed that the Earth was going to be destroyed on a specific date. They quit their jobs, left their families, and gathered together because they believed their group would be saved by space aliens who would take them away to their planet. When the world didn't end, the cult members experienced strong cognitive dissonance. The huge personal sacrifices they had made to join the cult were inconsistent with their new realization that the central belief of the cult was false.

To reduce their cognitive dissonance, the cult members soon developed a belief that most outsiders thought was laughable. The cult members believed that their personal sacrifices and devotion to the cult had convinced the space aliens to not destroy the planet! Now the cult members' sacrifices were consistent with their belief in the cult. This study illustrates how people sometimes develop some very strange beliefs as a way to explain their past actions. While these people may be thinking and acting irrationally, they are not suffering from a psychological disorder. They are simply trying to reduce their cognitive dissonance.

People often change their beliefs to reduce cognitive dissonance. In the space alien example, when the world did not end, cult members justified their personal sacrifices and reduced their cognitive dissonance by convincing themselves that their sacrifices saved the world.

cognitive dissonance A feeling of discomfort caused by performing an action inconsistent with your attitude

It is unlikely that you will ever behave as irrationally as the cult members in Festinger's study in response to cognitive dissonance. However, you may have experienced what Festinger called *post-decision dissonance* after buying an expensive product, such as a computer or a cell phone. Before buying the item, you read the sales brochures for all the choices, and weighed the pros and cons of each product. Your final choice had more of the qualities you wanted in the product than did the others, but it most likely did not beat its competitors in all areas. Because of this, your final choice was inconsistent with some of your beliefs about what you wanted. As soon as you purchased the product, the attractive aspects of the unchosen products and the unattractive aspects of your choice were inconsistent with your final decision.

How did you reduce this dissonance? Like most people, you may have lowered your dissonance by thinking only about the good qualities in your chosen product and the bad qualities in the unchosen products. In other words, you convinced yourself you made the right choice. Check out the Self-Discovery feature on page 576 to measure your preference for attitude consistency.

CHECKPOINT *What is cognitive dissonance?*

You might experience cognitive dissonance when buying a new laptop computer.

DIGITAL VISION/GETTY IMAGES

Do You Prefer Consistency Between Your Attitudes and Your Behavior?

Instructions: The extent to which people have a preference for consistency is measured by items on the Preference for Consistency Scale (PCS) developed by Robert Cialdini and his colleagues. To take the PCS, read each item and then use the following scale to indicate how well each statement describes you:

1 = strongly disagree
2 = disagree
3 = somewhat disagree
4 = slightly disagree
5 = neither agree nor disagree
6 = slightly agree
7 = somewhat agree
8 = agree
9 = strongly agree

_____ 1. It is important to me that those who know me can predict what I will do.

_____ 2. I want to be described by others as a stable, predictable person.

_____ 3. The appearance of consistency is an important part of the image I present to the world.

_____ 4. An important requirement for any friend of mine is personal consistency.

_____ 5. I typically prefer to do things the same way.

_____ 6. I want my close friends to be predictable.

_____ 7. It is important to me that others view me as a stable person.

_____ 8. I make an effort to appear consistent to others.

_____ 9. It doesn't bother me much if my actions are inconsistent.

See page 589 for scoring instructions.

Source: From "Preference for Consistency: The development of a valid measure and the discovery of surprising behavioral implications" by R. Cialdini, M. Trost, and J. Newsom in *Journal of Personality and Social Psychology*, 1995, 69, 318–328 (Appendix, p. 328). Copyright © 1995 by the American Psychological Association. Adapted with permission.

In Your Own Words

Define cognitive dissonance and describe a time when you experienced cognitive dissonance. If you have not experienced cognitive dissonance, interview your family and friends and describe an experience one of them has had.

Review Concepts

1. An example of _____ is when you like a song after repeatedly listening to it.

        a. reference group   c. persuasion

        b. implicit attitude   d. mere exposure effect

2. Which refers to a feeling of discomfort that comes when you perform an action inconsistent with your attitudes?

        a. implicit attitude   c. cognitive dissonance

        b. mere exposure effect   d. elaboration likelihood

3. According to the mere exposure effect, which image of yourself do you prefer?

        a. mirrored image   c. photographic image

        b. asymmetrical image   d. cognitive image

4. Which refers to an attitude activated automatically from memory without conscious awareness that you have the attitude?

        a. persuasion   c. implicit attitude

        b. reference group   d. mere exposure effect

5. **True or False** Attitudes may be formed through operant and classical conditioning.

6. **True or False** Implicit attitudes are gut-level evaluations.

7. **True or False** You were born with your attitudes and cannot change them in your lifetime.

8. **True or False** You are describing your attitudes when you use words such as like, dislike, love, hate, good, or bad.

Think Critically

9. Why are attitude changes formed through the peripheral route of persuasion weaker and more subject to change than those formed through the central route?

10. How do you reduce post-decision dissonance?

11. What is a reference group, and why should you be aware of the attitudes of your reference group?

OBJECTIVES

- Explain aggression.
- Describe ways of helping or not helping other people.

DISCOVER IT | *How does this relate to me?*

What would you do if you saw two people fighting at your school? Do you think the two people fighting are more likely to be male or female? Why? Would you try to stop the fight, or walk away and ignore the situation? If several people were around, would your actions be different? Would you be surprised to learn you are more likely to help if you are the only one around? Do you think whether you are male or female influences whether you help or not? What do you think psychologists say about the behaviors of aggression and helping?

Any behavior intended to harm someone or something is *aggression*. Any behavior intended to benefit someone or something is *helping*. This section examines these two behaviors that have important effects on your life.

Aggression

Social psychologists traditionally distinguished two types of aggression—instrumental and hostile. **Instrumental aggression** is intentional use of harmful behavior to achieve some other goal. This type of aggression is motivated by desire for rewards or avoidance of punishment. It is deliberate and rational. In most robbery attempts, for example, thieves use aggression as an instrument to achieve their goal, which is obtaining the victim's money. Aggression in a military setting also is mostly instrumental. The principal goal may be to defend or conquer territory.

Hostile aggression is intentional use of harmful behavior where the goal is to cause injury or death. This type of aggression is not motivated by the desire for reward or the avoidance of punishment. Hostile aggression often is impulsive and irrational. Slamming the door of your car shut when it won't start is an act of hostile aggression. Hitting or cursing someone who steps on your toes also is an example of hostile aggression. People are likely to engage in hostile aggression when they are angry.

instrumental aggression The intentional use of harmful behavior to achieve some other goal

hostile aggression The intentional use of harmful behavior where the goal is to cause injury or death

Sometimes aggressive actions cannot be placed into one of these categories. For example, a child may angrily hit another child for taking a favorite toy, and then retrieve the toy while the victim cries. The motives underlying this aggression are both the desire to harm (hostile aggression) and the desire to recover the toy (instrumental aggression). In such instances, no distinctions can be made between hostile and instrumental aggression. Sometimes aggression starts out as instrumental, but then turns hostile. For example, a soldier's firing of a weapon at an enemy as a way to defend territory may turn into a raging desire to simply kill the enemy when a comrade is shot.

GENDER AND STYLES OF AGGRESSION

A widespread belief is that men are more aggressive than women. Does research support this cultural belief? Yes and no.

Males are more likely than females to be physically aggressive and cause pain or injury. This gender difference is greater among children than adults, and greater with unprovoked aggression than provoked aggression. Men and women are similar to one another in verbal aggression and expressing feelings of anger toward members of the other sex, but men are slightly more likely than women to express verbal aggression toward same-sex persons.

One form of aggression largely ignored by researchers is *indirect aggression*—a form of social manipulation in which the aggressor tries to harm another person without a face-to-face encounter. Gossiping, spreading bad or false stories, telling others not to spend time with a person, and revealing someone's secrets are examples of indirect aggression. Females are more likely than males to use indirect aggression.

One explanation for this gender difference is that girls are discouraged more than boys from engaging in direct acts of physical aggression. As a result, they may use indirect aggression because it is more socially acceptable. This research also finds that male physical aggression drops sharply during adolescence, but teenage girls continue to use high levels of indirect aggression. A reason for this may be that indirect aggression is harder to detect and punish than physical aggression. These findings suggest that both women and men share the ability to cause harm to others, but they do so in different ways.

COMSTOCK IMAGES/JUPITER IMAGES

Males are more physically aggressive than females, but females are more indirectly aggressive. What might explain these gender differences?

WAYS TO REDUCE AGGRESSION BY OTHERS

Sometimes when people become angry, their anger is so great they cannot control by themselves their impulse to act aggressively. If you see someone really angry, what can you do to stop their aggressive impulses? Following are two suggestions.

Research finds that you can often stop aggressive responses in angry people if you get them to experience an emotion that is incompatible with anger. For example, what happens when you are about to say something in anger and someone makes you laugh? Laughter or other positive emotions help short-circuit aggressive impulses.

Another strategy to stop an aggressive impulse is a widely used technique to reduce conflict—an apology. The most effective apologies are offered after—not before—the people who are angry express their feelings. Why? Your later apology assures the angry person that you understand and will do the right thing in the future.

Unfortunately some people have a hard time apologizing. This is especially true of men. Women are more willing to apologize. In fact, women tend to become apologetic when severely criticized, while men respond defensively. These differences may explain why men are more likely to be involved in physical fights.

BLEND IMAGES/JUPITER IMAGES

Laughter and other positive emotions help to short-circuit aggressive impulses.

CHECKPOINT *What is the difference between instrumental aggression and hostile aggression?*

Helping Others

Just as you probably have had personal experiences with aggression, you also most likely have helped and been helped by others. Remember the chapter-opening story of my student, Ferris, who needed help when confronted by a mugger with a gun? Would you have helped her if you had witnessed the event?

GENDER AND STYLES OF HELPING

Research indicates that men are more likely than women to help in a situation that involves danger and when there is an audience. Men more frequently provide help to women than to other men, especially if the women are attractive. These findings suggest that the help typically offered by men is based on the male gender role of being heroic and gallant toward female victims.

Women are more likely than men to help when the assistance requires empathy, devotion, and caring for others. This type of help is consistent with the female gender role. Examples of such help are providing social and emotional support to others, volunteering for community service, and taking on the caretaking role for children and elderly people. Unlike men, women helpers do not show a gender bias in terms of whom they help. Overall, this research tells us that neither gender is more helpful than the other, but each engages in different styles of helping.

THE BYSTANDER INTERVENTION MODEL

John Darley and Bibb Latané studied how bystanders reacted to possible emergencies. They discovered that deciding to help in an emergency involves not just one decision, but many decisions. Their **bystander intervention model** states that deciding to intervene in a possible emergency is a result of a series of five decisions. The insights they gained in their research was what I passed on to Ferris and my other students the day before Ferris was attacked. As you can see from Figure 19-2, at each point in this five-step process, each decision results in no help or takes the bystander one step closer to helping.

bystander intervention model
A theory that whether bystanders intervene in an emergency is a result of a five-step decision-making process

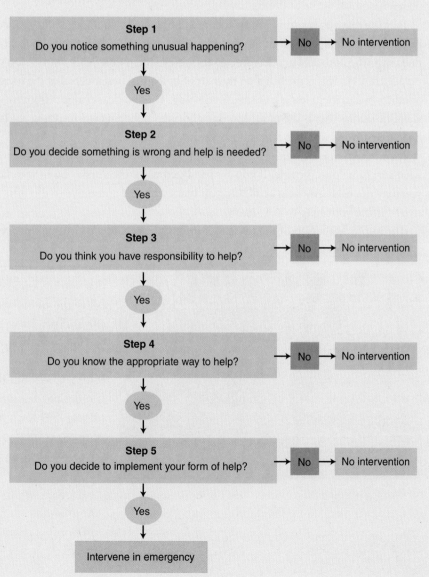

Figure 19-2 THE BYSTANDER INTERVENTION MODEL

As outlined by Latané and Darley, the decision to help someone involves a five-step process. At any step, a bystander's decision could lead either to further analysis of the situation or to do nothing.

Step 1
Do you notice something unusual happening? → No → No intervention
↓ Yes

Step 2
Do you decide something is wrong and help is needed? → No → No intervention
↓ Yes

Step 3
Do you think you have responsibility to help? → No → No intervention
↓ Yes

Step 4
Do you know the appropriate way to help? → No → No intervention
↓ Yes

Step 5
Do you decide to implement your form of help? → No → No intervention
↓ Yes

Intervene in emergency

The first thing a potential helper must do is notice something unusual is happening. In many social settings, sights and sounds can be distracting, and a cry for help may go unnoticed. If you notice that something unusual is happening, the second step in the model is deciding whether this unusual event is an emergency or not. For instance, if you pass an unconscious man lying on the grass in a park, you may ask, "Did he suffer a heart attack, or is he sleeping?" If you decide he is sleeping, you will continue on your way, having defined this as a nonemergency.

In their research, Darley and Latané discovered that during this second step, the presence of other people makes it less likely that bystanders will define what they are witnessing as an emergency. Unsure what is happening and concerned with how others might evaluate them if they overreact, people pretend to be calm. Acting calmly, bystanders observe others' behavior for a clue as to how to define the situation. However, with everyone acting calmly because of their social concerns, bystanders underestimate the seriousness of the situation and define it as a nonemergency. This tendency during step 2 to define the situation as a nonemergency when other bystanders are present is known as the **audience inhibition effect**.

Imagine that you overcome the audience inhibition effect and define the situation as an emergency. Your third decision is to accept or deny responsibility to help. Research finds that when other bystanders are present, people often experience a **diffusion of responsibility**. This is the belief on the part of individual bystanders that the presence of others makes them less responsible for helping. There is clear evidence from many scientific studies that as the number of bystanders to an emergency increases, the likelihood that anyone will help the victim decreases.

If you do decide that you have an obligation to help you go to the fourth step— what sort of help to provide. If you are paralyzed with uncertainty on how to help, you may not offer any help at all. Or, you make a choice and move to the fifth step—giving your help to the victim.

The important lesson of the bystander intervention model is that making an incorrect decision at any time in the bystander helping process leads to no help.

Research also indicates that you are less likely to fall victim to bystander effects if you have previously learned about them in a psychology course. Check out the Closer Look feature on page 583 for suggestions on what to do if you need help in an emergency.

audience inhibition effect The tendency for people to define a situation as a nonemergency when other bystanders are present

diffusion of responsibility The belief that the presence of other people in an emergency makes you less responsible to help the victim

If bystanders define a situation as an emergency, how might the presence of others cause someone to hesitate to help?

© LOSEVSKY PAVEL, 2009/USED UNDER LICENSE FROM SHUTTERSTOCK.COM

CHECK POINT *What is the bystander intervention model?*

How to Get Help in an Emergency

Here is the advice I gave to Ferris and my other psychology students (see the chapter opening story on page 562). It is based on the insights provided by the experiments conducted by John Darley and Bibb Latané. Learn these guidelines and use them when you are in need of help.

Guideline 1: Remember that deciding to help in an emergency involves a complex set of decisions. If bystanders make an incorrect decision at any point in the process, they will not help. As the victim, you must overcome the psychological factors that keep people from helping.

Guideline 2: The first psychological problem to overcome is the audience inhibition effect, in which the fear of being negatively evaluated, combined with the tendency to look to others for information, leads bystanders to identify emergencies as nonemergencies. Eliminate this inhibition by clearly letting everyone know this is an emergency and you need help. *(Ferris began loudly screaming that she was being robbed and needed help. The mugger was so flustered at becoming the focus of public attention that he fled. Screaming was a good idea, but Ferris also should have handed over her purse.)*

Guideline 3: Next attack the diffusion of responsibility, which is the bystanders' tendency to believe they are less responsible for helping when others are present. Plead with specific people to help you. It is hard to deny assistance when singled out. *(After the mugger fled, Ferris asked specific people to help her and they did. Most other bystanders who were not singled out by Ferris walked away.)*

Guideline 4: Because some people want to help but are unsure of what to do, give bystanders specific instructions. Use your most commanding voice. *(Ferris asked a bystander with a cell phone to call the police, and they were on the scene within minutes.)*

Remember these guidelines—they really could help you someday.

Think Critically

How would knowledge of both the audience inhibition effect and the diffusion of responsibility help you to react faster in an emergency situation when others are present?

In Your Own Words

Choose one of the following tasks: (1) explain anger, including two types of hostility; or (2) describe how gender affects helping others and the bystander invention model.

Review Concepts

1. Which type of aggression is displayed when a child angrily hits another child for taking a favorite toy, and then retrieves the toy while the victim cries?

   a. instrumental aggression
   b. hostile aggression
   c. both a and b
   d. neither a nor b

2. According to information in the text, in which way do males most likely act out aggression?

   a. gossip
   b. spreading rumors
   c. telling someone's secret
   d. physically fighting

3. Which is something you can do to stop another person's aggressive impulses?

   a. turn away
   b. cry
   c. get angrier
   d. laugh

4. Which refers to the belief that the presence of other people in a situation makes a person less responsible?

   a. instrumental aggression
   b. hostile aggression
   c. diffusion of responsibility
   d. audience inhibition effect

5. **True or False** Women generally are more willing than men to apologize.

6. **True or False** Males are more likely than females to take on a caretaking role for children and elderly people.

7. **True or False** Whether bystanders intervene in an emergency is a result of a five-step decision-making process.

8. **True or False** Men and women are similar to one another in verbal aggression and expressing feelings of anger toward members of the other gender. However, women are slightly more likely than men to express verbal aggression toward same-gender persons.

Think Critically

9. What are two things you can do to control another person's aggressive impulses?

10. Why might an emergency go unnoticed in settings with a lot of noise and sight distractions?

11. How could knowing the bystander effect help you in an emergency?

12. One way to reduce aggression in others is to offer an apology. Why do you think men have a harder time apologizing than women?

Counseling Psychologist

Health Science

D o you like studying the human mind and human behavior? Do you like helping people figure out their problems? If so, you might want to consider a career as a counseling psychologist. People in this career work in private practice, in business and industry, in health clinics and the mental health departments of hospitals, and in government agencies.

Counseling psychologists work with clients who are having problems and advise people on ways to cope with everyday life. Problems may be personal, job-related, or both. An individual might work with a counseling psychologist for help in understanding a personal relationship or help in reducing stress. A young person might seek help from a counseling psychologist in order to better understand the ups and downs of emotions. Families might want to work with a counseling psychologist to have more harmonious family relationships.

Counseling psychologists conduct interviews with each client, and then design a program to best aid that client. The psychologist may have the client take a test to determine cognitive abilities. People of all age groups—from young children to older adults—seek counseling from psychologists. Counseling psychologists often choose to work with a particular age group or specialize in a specific group, such as people with disabilities.

Employment Outlook

Careers for counseling psychologist are expected to grow 15 percent until 2016, which is faster than the average rate. The growth is due to an increase in demand for psychological services as more people seek help for illnesses such as depression and stress.

Needed Skills and Education

Most counseling psychologists have a doctoral degree, which is required in most states. A doctoral degree usually requires five to seven years of college work after receiving a bachelor's degree. Most states require counseling psychologists to be licensed. Requirements vary from state to state.

Courses that will help you in this career are those in psychology and other related sciences. You also need good written and oral communication skills; good interpersonal skills; and good organizational abilities. For counseling psychologists in private practice, courses in accounting, marketing, and other related business courses are advisable.

How You'll Spend Your Day

Counseling psychologists spend their days talking with their clients, who may be individuals or families. During counseling sessions, counseling psychologists listen to clients, and then offer recommendations that aid the clients in their lives. There also is paperwork that must be done that includes client records and insurance forms for payment. Counseling psychologists can work long hours. Those in private practice may have office appointments in the early morning or evening and on weekends to accommodate their clients' schedules.

Earnings

The median annual earnings of counseling psychologists are $59,440. The lowest 10 percent earn $35,280, while the highest 10 percent earn more than $102,730.

What About You?

Does the career of counseling psychologist interest you? Use the library, Internet, or ask for help from your school guidance counselor to learn more about this career. Locate a university that offers a program of study for students wanting to enter this career field. Call or write to the university to request a brochure or other literature on their course of study. Make a fact sheet of the information you receive.

© YURI ARCURS, 2009/USED UNDER LICENSE FROM SHUTTERSTOCK.COM.

CHAPTER SUMMARY

19.1 Forming Impressions of Others

- Physical appearance affects the impressions you form about other people and the impressions they form about you. Physically attractive people are perceived as having more socially desirable personality traits and as leading happier and more fulfilling lives than less attractive people. This stereotype occurs in all age groups.

- Cross-cultural research shows that people around the world judge symmetrical faces as more attractive than nonsymmetrical faces. Symmetry is a sign of physical health and good genes; it is a factor when choosing a mate with whom to have children.

- Attribution is the process by which you use information in your social world to explain the causes of behavior or events. With internal attributions, behavior is explained as being caused by something inside the person, such as personality traits or moods. With external attributions, behavior is explained as being caused by something outside the person, such as the actions of others, the nature of the situation, or luck.

- People from individualist cultures often make internal rather than external attributions. This is a bias known as the fundamental attribution error.

- The covariation attribution model is a theory that when people try to locate the cause of a behavior or event they pay attention to whether possible causes and the observed effect covary.

19.2 Forming and Changing Attitudes

- You are not born with attitudes. They develop through experience.

- Attitudes are affected by the mere exposure effect, conditioning, and reference groups. Attitudes may be implicit, or activated from memory without our awareness.

- Attitudes may be changed through persuasion. When you take the central route to persuasion, you are influenced by the strength and quality of the argument. When you take the peripheral route to persuasion, you are unable or unwilling to analyze a persuasive message.

- Cognitive dissonance is a feeling of discomfort caused by performing an action inconsistent with your attitudes.

19.3 Hurting and Helping Others

- Aggression is any behavior intended to harm another living being. Helping is any behavior intended to benefit another living being.

- Instrumental aggression is intentional use of harmful behavior to achieve some other goal. Hostile aggression is intentional use of harmful behavior where the goal is to cause injury or death.

- Males and females share the ability to cause harm to one another, but they do so in different ways.

- Men and women engage in different styles of helping. Men more frequently provide help to women than to other men based on the male gender role of being heroic and gallant toward female victims. Women are more likely than men to help when the assistance requires empathy, devotion, and caring for others.

- Bystanders go through a five-step process before deciding to help in an emergency.

CHAPTER ASSESSMENT

Review Psychology Terms

Select the term that best fits the definition. Some terms will not be used.

_____ 1. The tendency to develop positive attitudes toward objects and individuals to which you are repeatedly exposed

_____ 2. A theory that describes how you decide whether another person's behavior is caused by the person's disposition or the situation

_____ 3. An attitude that is activated automatically from memory, without awareness that you possess it

_____ 4. A theory that people engage in either effortful or effortless thinking after receiving a persuasive message

_____ 5. The scientific study of how people's thoughts, feelings, and behavior are influenced by others

_____ 6. The intentional use of harmful behavior to achieve some other goal

_____ 7. Positive or negative evaluations of an object

_____ 8. A feeling of discomfort caused by performing an action inconsistent with your attitude

_____ 9. The tendency to make internal attributions rather than external attributions when trying to explain other people's actions

_____ 10. The process of combining information about a person into an overall judgment

_____ 11. The belief that physically attractive individuals have better personalities and lead happier lives than less attractive people

_____ 12. The process of trying to change attitudes through communicating a particular message

_____ 13. A group with which you identify, using its standards to judge yourself and the world

_____ 14. The intentional use of harmful behavior where the goal is to cause injury or death to the victim

_____ 15. A theory that whether bystanders intervene in an emergency is a result of a five-step decision-making process

_____ 16. The tendency for people to define a situation as a nonemergency when other bystanders are present

_____ 17. The belief that the presence of other people in an emergency makes you less responsible to help the victim

a. attitudes
b. attribution theory
c. audience inhibition effect
d. bystander intervention model
e. cognitive dissonance
f. elaboration likelihood model
g. diffusion of responsibility
h. external attribution
i. fundamental attribution error
j. hostile aggression
k. implicit attitude
l. impression formation
m. instrumental aggression
n. internal attribution
o. mere exposure effect
p. persuasion
q. physical attractiveness stereotype
r. reference group
s. social psychology

Review Psychology Concepts

18. Explain the difference between internal and external attribution, and give examples of each.

19. Define the elaboration likelihood model and provide an example, such as a television commercial, you think is persuasive.

20. Place each of the following into the category of instrumental aggression or hostile aggression: (a) aggression in a military setting to defend territory; (b) robbery attempt; (c) one child hitting another child for taking a toy; (d) a soldier enraged at an enemy after a buddy is killed.

21. Compare and contrast male and female aggression. Include ways both genders express their aggression. Provide an example of how males express aggression and an example of how females express aggression.

22. List the five steps in the bystander intervention model.

23. Describe how impression formation affects what you think of a new teacher.

24. List the three ways people form attitudes.

25. Identify and describe the difference between the two routes to persuasion according to the elaboration likelihood model.

26. Which type of aggression are people most likely to engage in when they are angry—hostile or instrumental?

27. Identify two ways men are most likely to help and two ways women are most likely to help.

28. In which age groups will you find the physical attractiveness stereotype?

29. Describe the contrast effect as related to physical attractiveness.

30. Is mood an internal or external attribute?

Apply Psychology Concepts

31. Explain how physical appearance has affected the impressions you may have of people. What makes a person more physically attractive? Apply contrast effects and popular culture to your answer.

32. You and your friends go out to a movie. Seated in front of you is a woman wearing a tall hat that is obstructing your view of the screen. You begin talking loudly and bump her seat until she gets up and moves to another chair far from you. Are you displaying instrumental or hostile aggression? Explain.

33. Describe how your personal attitudes towards the types of music you like and dislike may have been formed by exposure, conditioning, reference group influence, and without conscious awareness.

34. Explain and apply the cognitive dissonance theory in terms of how it has impacted your life in two decisions you have made in the last year. How has post-decision dissonance affected two purchases you have made in the last year? How did you relieve the dissonance you felt?

Make Academic Connections

35. **Computer Technology** With a partner, find photos of a male and female model from Internet sources. Choose models you classify as attractive. Next find photos of male and female models you consider less attractive or unattractive. Then choose a product. Use a computer software program to create two sets of advertisements for your product. Use the attractive male and female for one advertisement and the less attractive or unattractive male and female for the other. Conduct a survey among your peers to ask which best sells the product and why. Assess your collected data and write a report of your findings in a way that explains your assessment of the effects of attractiveness in advertisements.

36. **Sociology** Create a campaign to produce social change within your school. You could choose from among the following topics: enlist students in a political campaign of a local or national candidate; have a food drive for families in your community who need assistance; engage students in a community clean-up; grow a school vegetable garden. Evaluate the campaign's effectiveness.

37. **Language Arts** Write an essay that hypothesizes about the potential of media to influence positive attitude change in society. Discuss what those changes might be and how the media could influence these changes. Cite examples from research or provide examples that could happen.

DIGGING DEEPER
with Psychology eCollection

As you go through life, there is a good chance you will face awkward and embarrassing situations. Writer Jen Matlack describes several typical "squirmy situations" and cites "how to cope advice" from psychologists. People often feel awkward because they are forced to focus attention on themselves, putting every word and move under a microscope. Access the Gale Psychology eCollection at *www.cengage.com/school/psych/franzoi* and read the examples and advice in the article. Create a two-column chart to organize the information in the article, describing the situation in Column One and the advice in Column Two. Answer the question: In general why do these situations cause awkwardness and embarrassment? As an additional project, describe an embarrassing situation you've experienced and how you dealt with it.

Source: Matlack, Jen. "Why did I just say that? Some predicaments are intensely awkward. A survival guide for mortifying moments. (Squirmy Situations)." *Psychology Today.* 37.5 (Sept–Oct 2004): 56(4).

SELF-DISCOVERY: YOUR SCORE

Do You Prefer Consistency Between Your Attitudes and Your Behavior?

Scoring Instructions: The last PCS item (number 9) is reverse-scored; that is, for this item a lower rating actually indicates a higher level of consistency preference. Before summing the items, recode item 9 so that 1 = 9, 2 = 8, 3 = 7, 4 = 6, 6 = 4, 7 = 3, 8 = 2, 9 = 1. To calculate your preference for consistency score, add up your responses to the nine items.

The average score for teenagers and young adults is about 48. The higher your score is above this value, the greater your preference for consistency. The lower your score is below this value, the less of this preference you probably possess.

Group Interaction

ESSENTIAL QUESTION
Go to page XXVII

IMAGE SOURCE BLACK/JUPITER IMAGES

"When spiders unite, they can tie down a lion."

—ETHIOPIAN PROVERB

During their first year in high school, a small group of boys with limited athletic skills wanted to support the boys freshman basketball team. In the world of high school basketball, if they couldn't be "shooters," then they would be "rooters." These boys created Da Herd, an unofficial—and very vocal—student booster club. Even though the team's record was 0–17 that first year, Da Herd remained enthusiastically loyal—and very loud.

I'd like to tell you that because of Da Herd's unwavering support the basketball team performed like seasoned veterans during their sophomore season. The truth is that this team again lost every single game that season, establishing a new school consecutive losing record of 0–37. Unfazed, Da Herd members drew strength from defeat. "It gave us character," said one member. The group designed its own group logo—a giddy-looking moose inside a bull's-eye. It also added a trumpet and drum section. Although the team struggled, Da Herd members had a great time promoting school spirit and the members of the basketball team appreciated their enthusiasm.

20.1 | Social Influence

OBJECTIVES

- Define conformity.
- Describe compliance.
- Explain obedience.

KEY TERMS

- social influence
- conformity
- social norm
- compliance
- reciprocity norm
- obedience

DISCOVER IT | *How does this relate to me?*

You may be a member of one or more student groups. Like the students in Da Herd, you most likely are involved in at least one student group such as an academic club, social club, or athletic team. What sort of social influence do you think your group has in the school? If your group does have influence, how did this influence come about? Would you be irritated if someone told you that the members of your group are conformists? Do you, or someone you know, view conformity in a negative way? If conformity is viewed negatively, is obedience worse? Could society exist without people submitting to these types of social influence?

Social influence is the exercise of social power by a person or group to change the attitudes or behavior of others in a certain direction. *Social power* is the power available to the influencer to motivate this change. This power could come from the ability to give to others such things as rewards, punishments, or information. Power also comes from being liked and admired. The three main behaviors that result from social influence are conformity, compliance, and obedience.

Conformity

Can you recall incidents from your past when you behaved a certain way because everyone else was behaving that way? For instance, did you ever join in on Halloween pranks or cut classes simply because it was "the thing to do"? Or did you volunteer for a local charity drive because your friends did? Are you reading this chapter because it is expected in this class? If so, you are conforming. In **conformity**, you yield to perceived group pressure. Your behavior or beliefs become similar to those of the group.

Conformity is not necessarily bad. If you did not follow most of the rules of the groups to which you belong, there would be social chaos. What would happen if

social influence The exercise of social power by a person or group to change the attitudes or behavior of others in a certain direction

conformity A yielding to perceived group pressure

social norm An expected way to behave and believe that is established and enforced by a group

drivers decided not to stop at red traffic lights? This traffic rule is an example of a **social norm**, which is an expected way to behave and believe that is established and enforced by a group.

ASCH'S CONFORMITY RESEARCH

In the 1950s, Solomon Asch conducted a set of classic conformity studies in which male college students thought they were participating in a visual perception experiment. Over a series of different trials, seven students judged which of three comparison lines were equal in length to a standard line (see Figure 20-1 below). Although this task may seem easy, there was a catch. Only one person in each group was an actual participant—the rest were students Asch had secretly told to pick the wrong line. The students made a total of 18 line judgments and announced them out loud. The actual participant was second to last to give his opinion. Did he conform to the group's incorrect judgment, or did he stick with what his eyes told him? If you were in his place, what would you do?

The actual participant conformed on one-third of the trials by naming the same incorrect line as that named by the planted students. In contrast, when participants in a control condition made their judgments privately, less than one percent picked the incorrect line. What Asch's research and other studies demonstrate is that people often find it easier to conform than to challenge the unanimous opinions of others. Before continuing, check out the Self-Discovery feature on page 593 for an exercise that demonstrates how people conform without thinking of their behavior as conformity.

Figure 20-1 **ASCH'S LINE JUDGMENT TASK**

In this example of Asch's classic conformity experiments, participants were asked to judge which of the three comparison lines was equal in length to the standard line.

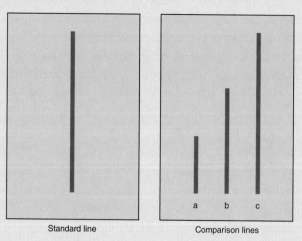

Standard line   Comparison lines

CULTURE AND CONFORMITY

Does knowing people's cultural background give you insight into how they respond to social influence? Cross-cultural research finds that people from collectivist cultures are more concerned than individualists with gaining the approval of their group. In addition, collectivists are much more likely to feel ashamed if they fail to get that approval. A person from an individualist culture may have a higher need for independence from the group and a greater desire to feel unique and different. Because of these different beliefs, people from collectivist cultures are often more conforming to their own group than individualists. This yielding to the group by collectivists is not considered a sign of weakness, as it is often seen in an individualist culture. Instead, conformity is a sign of self-control, flexibility, and maturity. Check out the Case Study on page 594 that examines whether conformity sometimes occurs automatically, without conscious thought.

CHECKPOINT *What is conformity?*

SELF-DISCOVERY

What's Up?

Instructions: You often conform to other people's actions, even in small ways. Test this social fact by asking a group of your friends to help you try to get other people to copy their behavior. Have your friends stand together in a public setting, looking up in the air. Tell them to simply tilt their heads up and look skyward. Do not have them point skyward with their arms. Watch passersby from a short distance. Do they look up? How long do they linger? Do they ask your friends any questions? If they do look up, approach them and ask why they looked up in the air. Also ask them if they think their behavior of looking up is an example of conformity. How do they respond? Change the number of your friends who look skyward. Are passersby more likely to look up as the number of skygazers increases?

COURTESY OF FIGZOI

Does Conformity Occur Automatically?

INTRODUCTION Researchers have discovered that over time social norms become associated with specific social settings. Thinking about a social setting can activate a social norm related to that setting. In two separate experiments, Dutch social psychologists Henk Aarts and Ap Dijksterhuis tested the ability of a specific social setting to automatically activate a specific social norm.

HYPOTHESIS People automatically and unconsciously activate from memory a social norm associated with a specific social setting. Then they begin behaving in line with that social norm, but only if they expect they will soon visit that social setting.

METHOD College students were asked to perform two seemingly unconnected tasks on a computer. In the first "Picture Task," they saw a photo for 30 seconds of the inside of an empty library or an empty railway station platform. Students were told to examine the photo because they would answer questions about it later. Two-thirds of the students were also told they would visit the setting after the experiment. Next, students performed a "Word Recognition Task" in which they had to decide as quickly as possible whether a word flashed on the screen was meaningful or nonsense. Four of the 12 meaningful words represented the social norm for library settings (silent, quiet, still, whisper). The speed of students' responses to these words was measured by how quickly they answered. In a second experiment, the word recognition task was replaced with a "Word Pronunciation Task," in which another group of students read aloud 10 words from the screen. How loudly they pronounced each word was measured.

RESULTS Students in the word recognition task were quicker at identifying library-related "quiet" words as meaningful if they had been exposed to the photo of the library rather than the train station. This finding suggests that words related to the library norm were more likely to be automatically activated from memory. Similar results were found in the second experiment. These students pronounced words in a quieter voice if they had previously seen the library photo rather than the train station photo. Again, this finding suggests that the behavior of speaking softly occurred because the silent library norm had been automatically activated from memory. However, in both experiments these effects only occurred when students thought they were later going to visit the library.

This and other research suggests that when you expect to visit a certain social setting, the social norms for that setting are automatically activated from memory and can have a direct effect on your behavior without your awareness. In other words, when preparing to visit the library, the social norm of being quiet while in the library automatically becomes more available in your memory. The result is you become quieter before you even open the library door. You have conformed to this social norm so often that conforming has become a habit that occurs without conscious attention or monitoring.

Critical Analysis

What are some other examples of specific situations that automatically activate specific social norms?

Compliance

In trying to get your way with others, the most direct route is to simply ask them to do what you desire. **Compliance** is granting a direct request. Three factors that increase the likelihood that others will comply to your requests are creating positive moods, encouraging reciprocity, and giving reasons for compliance.

POSITIVE MOODS

Other people are more likely to comply with your requests when they are in a good mood. Good moods make people friendlier to others, including those who are seeking to have their requests granted. Most people understand that good moods aid compliance, which is why they often use flattery before making requests. Even when the targets of this flattery suspect that it is designed to gain their compliance, flattery still often is successful.

RECIPROCITY

Has anyone come to you in a public place and offered you a small gift, such as a flower, pencil, or a flag, and then asked you to donate money to their organization? They were hoping the gift would lower your resistance. The hope rested on a powerful social norm that people in all cultures follow—the **reciprocity norm**, an expectation that you should return a favor or a good deed. The social norm of returning favors also is used to increase compliance.

compliance Acting to grant a direct request

reciprocity norm The expectation that you should return a favor or a good deed

Customers are more likely to purchase a product from a salesperson if the customers are in a good mood.

DIGITAL VISION/GETTY IMAGES

GIVING REASONS

In one compliance study, a person working with the researcher tried to cut in line ahead of others at a photocopying machine. In one condition, the person gave no reason, merely asking, "May I use the photocopying machine to make five copies?" Sixty percent of those waiting complied with this "no reason" request. In another condition, the "reason" was simply a restatement of the desire to make copies ("May I use the photocopying machine to make five copies because I have to make copies?"). Here, 94 percent of the people waiting complied. This was identical to the compliance when an actual reason was given ("May I use the photocopying machine to make five copies because I'm in a hurry?").

These results suggest that people often mindlessly grant requests which contain any reason at all, even reasons that are not real reasons. People comply because they assume requesters would not ask for the favor if the requests were not genuine. The result of such mindless thinking is that anything sounding vaguely like a reason is accepted as genuine. When my daughter Lillian was two years old, she had already learned the importance of giving reasons when seeking compliance from her parents. In asking to go outside, she would say, "Can I go outside? . . . Because I have to go outside."

CHECKPOINT > *What is compliance?*

People are more likely to grant requests if the requests are accompanied by a reason.

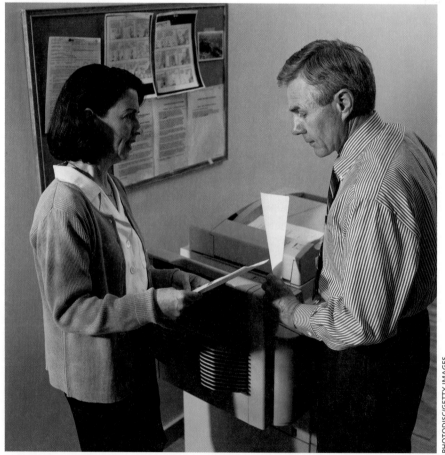

Obedience

Obedience is the performance of an action in response to a direct order. The order often comes from a person of high status or authority. Because people are instructed from a very young age to respect and obey people in positions of authority (parents, teachers, and police officers), obedience is common.

MILGRAM'S OBEDIENCE RESEARCH

Imagine that you volunteer to participate in an experiment on how punishment shapes the learning of word pairs. You are given the task of being the teacher, and a 50-year-old man is told to be the learner. You are told to deliver increasing levels of electrical shock each time the learner makes a mistake to encourage his learning. The learner is in a nearby room out of sight and strapped into a chair. He makes many mistakes and you shock him after each mistake. After giving him 75 volts of electricity following another mistake, you hear him moan in pain through the intercom system. At 150 volts, he demands to be released, shouting that his heart is bothering him. Do you stop?

Let's imagine that you continue. At 180 volts, the learner shouts that he can no longer stand the pain. Do you now stop?

Let's imagine that you don't stop. At 300 volts, the learner says that he refuses to go on. Now the experimenter orders you to deliver the next level of shock if the learner does not respond with an answer. Do you do so?

Let's imagine that you obey. Now, even though the learner no longer gives answers, you continue to hear his screams of pain whenever you deliver the shocks. Do you now disobey the experimenter?

Let's imagine that you continue, despite the learner's pleas to stop. After pressing the 330-volt switch, the learner falls silent. You realize that you are getting closer to the last switch of 450 volts. If you hesitate in delivering a shock, the experimenter first tells you, "Please continue," and then says, "The experiment requires that you continue," and then, "It is absolutely essential that you go on," and finally, "You have no other choice; you must go on!" What do you do?

When would you have disobeyed the experimenter's commands? Would it have been following the learner's first protest? The second? The third? Is there a chance you would have obeyed until the end, despite the learner's pleas?

I am guessing your prediction is that you would have disobeyed the experimenter's orders well before the 450-volt limit. That is what almost everyone predicts they would do. When Stanley Milgram conducted this study in the 1960s, no one really received electrical shocks. The learner was actually an assistant of Milgram's who was only pretending that he was in pain. All his screams were prerecorded, so all participants heard exactly the same thing. The participants thought their experience was real but still 65 percent of them obeyed the experimenter completely.

Children are taught to respect and obey parents and other authority figures.

obedience The performance of an action in response to a direct order

As shown in Figure 20-2, Milgram's follow-up studies found that obedience increased as the distance between the teacher and the learner increased, or as the distance between the teacher and the experimenter decreased. Women and men were equally obedient. Similar results were obtained in several other countries, suggesting that these high levels of obedience were not just an American effect. It is important also to point out that the participants in these studies did not enjoy obeying and delivering these shocks. In fact, their actions caused them a good deal of stress, but no lasting emotional harm.

Milgram's obedience studies revealed very valuable insights into the conditions under which people are likely to obey the harmful demands of people in positions of authority. Yet the extreme stress that participants experienced in these studies caused a great deal of concern among many psychologists. Shortly after Milgram published the results of his research the American Psychological Association developed formal guidelines that psychologists must follow when conducting research with human participants (see Chapter 2, page 34). Today, psychologists cannot conduct studies like Milgram's obedience research that cause such high levels of stress in those individuals who are participants. Thus, Milgram's research is important not only for what it revealed about the psychology of obedience. It is also

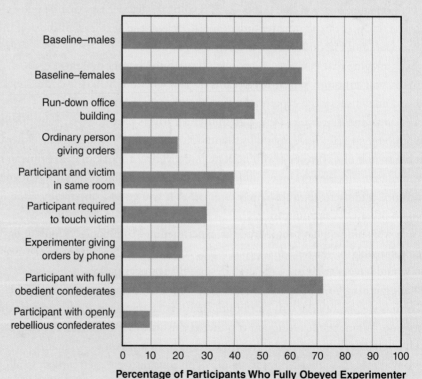

Figure 20-2 FACTORS THAT INFLUENCE OBEDIENCE AND DISOBEDIENCE TO AUTHORITY

What increases or decreases obedience beyond the 65 percent level in Milgram's original study? The location of the experiment, how close the participant is to the victim and the experimenter, and the presence of others who are obedient or disobedient all affect levels of obedience.

Source: Data from S. Milgram, *Obedience to Authority: An Experimental View*, Harper and Row, Publishers, Inc., 1974; and S. Milgram, *The Individual in a Social World: Essays and Experiments*, Addison-Wesley Publishing Company, 1992.

Percentage of Participants Who Fully Obeyed Experimenter

important because it led to the requirement that no psychological research using human subjects can be conducted before its procedures are carefully reviewed by experts to guarantee that the study poses no serious risks to the participants' physical and emotional health.

HAVE OBEDIENCE LEVELS CHANGED?

Because Milgram's research procedures produced unacceptably high levels of stress in participants, the exact study cannot be repeated. However, in 2008 social psychologists partially repeated Milgram's study based on the fact that the 150-volt level was largely a point of no return in the original study. In Milgram's study, nearly 4 out of 5 participants who obeyed the experimenter's instructions at the 150-point level continued to obey his commands all the way to 450 volts. Knowing how Milgram's participants responded up to and including the 150-volt level allowed social psychologists in 2008 to estimate what participants would do if allowed to complete the entire study. Stopping the study after participants decided what to do at the 150-volt level avoided exposing them to the stress in the original studies.

What happened in this new test of people's obedience levels? Results indicate about the same percent of participants as in the original study obeyed up to and at the 150-volt level, and were prepared to read the next item of the test when the experimenter stopped the study. There were also no gender, age, or ethnicity differences in willingness to obey. While this study is not a complete test of the original study, the findings suggest that people's willingness to obey the harmful commands of authority figures may not have changed during the past four decades.

CHECKPOINT › *What is obedience?*

Why is obedience to authority common?

20.1 ASSESSMENT

In Your Own Words

Choose from conformity, compliance, or obedience to explain how you have reacted to a situation in your life. For example, you might say that you bought a specific outfit because all your friends wore that label of clothing. You wanted to be like them and fit in, so you conformed to their style of clothing.

Review Concepts

1. Volunteering to help clean up the school yard because all your friends are doing so is an example of
   a. obedience
   b. conformity
   c. compliance
   d. reciprocity norm

2. Which refers to acting to grant a direct request?
   a. obedience
   b. social norm
   c. social influence
   d. compliance

3. Receiving a gift and feeling the need to give something in return is called
   a. social rule
   b. compliance
   c. social influence
   d. reciprocity norm

4. **True or False** Obedience is granting a direct request.

5. **True or False** Studies indicate that people of all cultures conform equally.

6. **True or False** Other people are more likely to comply with your requests when they are in a good mood.

Think Critically

7. Do you think social influence is stronger among teens than adults? Why or why not?

8. Explain why conformity is necessary in society. Give an example.

9. Explain why Milgram's experiment on obedience cannot be repeated today as it was originally done. Do you agree? Why or why not?

10. List the three factors that increase compliance, and then explain which you think works best in your life. Explain why you chose this factor, and give an example of how it has worked in your life.

11. Why do most people obey a person of high status or authority? List three examples of people you obey.

12. Recall an incident from your past when you behaved a certain way because everyone else was behaving that way. Describe the incident and explain your behavior in terms of the information in this lesson.

13. Why do salespeople try to flatter potential customers when making a sales presentation?

14. Why is it important to give a reason when you are asking someone to grant a request?

OBJECTIVES

- Define the nature of groups.
- Discuss leadership and leadership styles.
- Explain minority influence in a group.

KEY TERMS

- group
- ingroup
- leader
- transformational leader
- minority influence
- minority slowness effect

DISCOVER IT | *How does this relate to me?*

Think about the groups to which you belong. They may be school groups like Da Herd or after-school workplace groups. Your family is a group and so are your friends. Can you identify a leader in each of the groups? Have you noticed that a leader in a soccer group acts differently from a leader in a social club? Feeling close to group members is important for almost everybody. Have you ever had a different opinion on some important issue than the other people in your group? How did that make you feel? Did it threaten that feeling of closeness?

Psychologists have studied how people behave in groups and how leaders lead groups of people. They also have studied how people in groups react when someone disagrees with the majority of the people in the group.

The Nature of Groups

A **group** consists of people who depend on and interact with one another on a regular basis. People often join groups because they want to work on certain tasks and achieve certain goals they cannot achieve alone. For example, you will have a better chance of extinguishing a fire in a burning building or finding shelter for the homeless if you pursue these tasks within the support of a group. People also often join groups to satisfy their desire for approval, belonging, prestige, friendship, and even love. Some groups focus on accomplishing tasks, while others mainly focus on social activities. Examples of *task-oriented groups* are work groups, such as a surgical team operating on patients or postal workers delivering the mail. Examples of *social-oriented groups* are friendship and family groups nurturing and emotionally supporting fellow members or neighbors organizing a summer block party.

group People who depend on and interact with one another on a regular basis

GROUP PRIDE VS. GROUP EMBARRASSMENT

An **ingroup** is a group to which you belong and which forms a part of your social identity. When your group achieves success or when ingroup members are singled out for praise or awards, you tend to respond with pride and satisfaction, even if you had nothing to do with the achievement. This identification with, and embracing of, ingroup success is known as *basking in reflected glory (BIRGing)*. Examples are the joy expressed by citizens following their nation's military and political successes or fan reaction to their sports teams' victories. When such successes occur, group members often describe the success as "our victory." This process of reflected glory increases members' self-esteem because their group identity is an important part of their self-concept.

Although you often readily share your group's successes, what happens following failure? The common reaction is to make excuses ("Our group was treated unfairly!"), while not giving credit to the successful group that defeated your group ("I'm glad our group isn't that vicious!"). By defending your group, you are defending your own self-esteem.

What happens when your group is repeatedly outperformed by other groups? Repeated group failure may cause you to feel embarrassed. To protect self-esteem, you may emotionally distance yourself from the group, a process called *cutting off reflected failure (CORFing)*. CORFing is what many sports fans do when their teams have losing seasons. However, strongly loyal fans do not CORF, but instead, they stay loyal to their losing teams. This describes the actions of Da Herd members. Their loyalty in the face of continuous defeat defined their group identity and was by itself a source of group pride.

A group also can cut its ties to individual members, which often occurs when a member does not go along with the group's way of thinking and behaving. Check out the Closer Look feature on page 603 for more information on this group process of rejecting nonconformists.

ingroup A group to which you belong and which forms a part of your social identity

Your ingroup at school consists of the friends with whom you spend your time.

© ORANGE LINE MEDIA, 2009/USED UNDER LICENSE FROM SHUTTERSTOCK.COM

CHECKPOINT *What is a group?*

How Do Groups Deal with Nonconformists?

Stanley Schachter analyzed how groups deal with members who are nonconformists. Schachter arranged for groups of eight to ten volunteers to form a "case study club" to discuss the case of a juvenile delinquent, Johnny Rocco, and then make a recommendation of what the authorities should do with Johnny. What participants did not know was that each group contained three people who had been instructed to take a particular position in the discussion of Johnny. One, the *dissenter*, argued repeatedly for harsh punishment of Johnny, a position very different from the majority opinion for mild punishment. Another, the *slider*, began arguing for harsh punishment, but then slid toward the majority position of the group during discussion. A third, the *mode*, held the majority opinion of mild punishment throughout the discussion.

How do you think the participants reacted to these three different people? How do you think they dealt with the dissenter, when their best efforts failed to get the dissenter to fall in line? At first, participants communicated a great deal with the dissenter and slider in an attempt to convince them to change their minds about Johnny. During this same time period, little attention was paid to the mode who agreed with them. Once participants concluded that the dissenter was not going to adopt their opinion, and once the slider adopted the group's opinion, communication dropped sharply. These findings suggest that group members focus a great deal of attention on dissenters in the group until they either agree or convince the group that such attempts are fruitless.

At the end of group discussion, Schachter informed everyone that the group was too large for their next discussion and that he wanted them to decide who to keep in the group. Not surprisingly, participants overwhelmingly voted to exclude the dissenter from the group.

Additional studies found that rejecting members who disagree with the group is most likely when the issue involves something that is very important to the group's identity. Although getting people to agree in a group often is an important goal for most members, groups can get into trouble when they ignore contrary opinions and ideas. This is a topic you will learn more about later in this lesson.

Think Critically

Imagine that you are the only dissenter on an issue that is very important to you and the other members with whom you disagree. Can you think of what you might do in this situation to still be accepted by the other members without changing your unpopular position?

Leadership

Members of a group accept influence from others whom they believe have greater ability. The person who has the most influence and provides direction and energy to the group is the **leader**. This is the person who motivates others, gives orders, rewards and punishes other members, settles arguments, and pushes and pulls the group toward its goals. Many groups have only one leader; other groups have two or more individuals with equally high levels of influence. Generally, groups tend to have multiple leaders as their tasks multiply and become more complicated.

TASK LEADERS VS. RELATIONAL LEADERS

In their position of social influence, leaders are called on to perform two basic types of activities—task leadership and relational leadership. *Task leadership* consists of accomplishing the goals of the group. Task leaders have a no-nonsense style where they focus on group goals, give orders, and are not overly warm when dealing with group members. *Relational leadership* involves an attention to the emotions and the relationships within the group. Friendliness, empathy, and an ability to resolve conflicts are important qualities for effective relational leadership. A relational leader's style is democratic, with greater emphasis on dividing up authority among group members and paying attention to their ideas and concerns.

In some groups, one person is the task leader and another person is the relational leader. In other groups, one leader performs both functions. In such instances, the leader must know when to be the taskmaster and when to be the concerned advisor—a difficult job because the two leadership styles often conflict. Research indicates that individuals with a flexible leadership style know when to focus on task production and when to show concern for interpersonal relations. They also tend to receive the highest leadership ratings by other group members.

> **leader** The person who exerts the most influence and provides direction and energy to the group

LAB TEAMS

Leadership Experiment

Successful groups require cooperation, communication, and good leadership. Try this experiment as a group. Write the month and date of your birthday on a sheet of paper, and then tape it on your clothing where it is easily read by other group members. Without talking, organize yourselves into a straight line in the order of your birthdays. When this task is completed, individually write the answers to these questions:

1. Was the task easy or hard to accomplish?

2. Did it seem to you that the group was lost and disorganized or did everyone easily find where they belonged?

3. Which classmates stood out as the leaders? What made you choose these classmates as leaders?

4. What qualities did these leaders show?

When completed, compare your answers with your classmates. How similar are your answers? Did many of you name the same leadership qualities? Did every member of the group have the same experience, or was it different for each of you?

TRANSFORMATIONAL LEADERS

Leaders tend to be more intelligent and taller than nonleaders, and they are more confident and have a higher desire for power. They also tend to be more *charismatic*, a quality of being charming and fascinating. Transformational leaders, in particular, exhibit these qualities. A **transformational leader** is a leader who changes—or transforms—the outlook and behavior of followers so they are unselfish and work for the good of the group or society.

The great leaders throughout history all inspired tremendous changes in their societies by making supporters believe anything was possible if they worked toward a common goal. These leaders include such people as Mahatma Gandhi and Jawaharlal Nehru in India, Abraham Lincoln and Martin Luther King, Jr., in the United States, and Nelson Mandela in South Africa. Transformational leaders can also inspire followers to commit terrible aggression against others, such as Adolf Hitler in Nazi Germany, Idi Amin in Uganda, or Charles Manson in the United States.

The general view of transformational leaders is that they are natural born influence agents who inspire high devotion, motivation, and productivity in group members. Almost all transformational leaders have a captivating way of speaking to people and communicating a vision of the future. They are widely viewed as heroes by those who follow them. Because transformational leaders often use unconventional strategies that put them at risk, it is not uncommon for them to face severe physical hardships—and even death—in moving the group to its goals.

Abraham Lincoln was a transformational leader. As president, he inspired great changes in the United States after the Civil War, reuniting the North and South and bringing an end to slavery in the country.

GENDER AND LEADERSHIP STYLE

Women are assuming larger leadership positions in many countries around the world. Many people believe that women and men have very different leadership styles. Is this true? Research indicates there are more similarities than differences. Female leaders are as task-oriented as male leaders, but they tend to have a more democratic or participative leadership style. Women are more likely than men to invite group members to participate in important group decisions. In contrast, male leaders tend to have a less democratic and a more directive style, in which they give orders rather than make suggestions. Women are friendlier and more likely to recognize and reward group members who perform well. These gender differences may exist because in many cultures women are socialized to be caring and attentive toward others, while men are socialized to be more independent and dominant when dealing with people.

transformational leader A leader who changes the outlook and behavior of followers so they are unselfish and work for the good of the group or society

Highly confident women in leadership roles are helping to change society's beliefs about gender and leaders.

© CARLOSSELLER, 2009/USED UNDER LICENSE FROM SHUTTERSTOCK.COM

One barrier to some women assuming leadership positions is gender stereotypes. In many cultures around the world, the image that people have about a leader is more closely associated with male stereotypes. This "masculinization" of the leader role often results in people assuming that women are less qualified for leadership positions than men. Indeed, there is evidence that people—including women— react more negatively to women than men who adopt a directive leadership style. However, there also is evidence suggesting that women who are highly confident in their leadership abilities can overcome the "women are not natural leaders" stereotype. These highly confident women who succeed as leaders are already changing people's beliefs about who can be an effective leader.

CULTURE AND LEADERSHIP STYLE

How might leadership style operate differently in individualist and collectivist cultures? Research suggests that the ideal leader may be different in these two cultures. A collectivist culture's concern about group needs and interpersonal relations means that nurturing, relationship-oriented leaders are highly desired by group members. In contrast, individualists are socialized to work alone and to be less concerned about how they get along with others while completing tasks. This training may cause individualists to respond better to task-oriented leaders.

What about people living in multicultural societies like the United States and Canada whose family recently arrived as immigrants from a collectivist society? If you are a member of one of these ethnic groups, do you think you sometimes respond to leaders differently based on your collectivist heritage? It's possible. Social psychologists found that first- and second-generation Mexican Americans tend to be more responsive to relationship-oriented work groups than Anglo Americans. These findings raise the possibility that even within an individualist society like the United States, how people respond to task-oriented versus relationship-oriented leaders may be at least influenced by heritage.

CHECKPOINT *What is a leader?*

How Minorities Change Groups

History is filled with stories of individuals and small groups who express unpopular views and endure abuse from the majority of people until the individual or small group's views are adopted by the majority. The Closer Look feature on page 603 examined how dissenters are rejected by the majority, but that is not the full story of group dissent. The way dissenters produce change within a group is called **minority influence**.

Commenting on what it takes to change majority opinions, nineteenth-century feminist Susan B. Anthony said, "Cautious, careful people always casting about to preserve their reputation and social standing never can bring about a reform. Those who are really in earnest must be willing to be anything or nothing in the world's estimation." Social research supports Anthony's statement. Those who oppose the majority generally are thought of as competent, but they often are strongly disliked.

This consequence of being disliked may make some hesitate to voice their opinions. The tendency of those who hold a minority opinion to express that opinion less quickly than people who hold the majority opinion is called the **minority slowness effect**.

For minority members to influence majority members in a group, they must consistently and confidently state their dissenting opinions. However, they cannot appear rigid. Instead, they must be seen as flexible and open-minded. Nelson Mandela, a long-time opponent of the former apartheid government of South Africa, is an excellent example of a minority group leader (a minority in power but not in numbers) whose consistent call for Black equality was combined with a flexible approach to reform that won over many White South Africans. In 1994, he became the first president of a nonapartheid South Africa.

Minority group members have the strongest influence when they take positions similar to the direction the group is going. For example, during the early stages of the civil rights movement in the United States, Martin Luther King, Jr., and other

minority influence The way dissenters produce change within a group

minority slowness effect The tendency of those who hold a minority opinion to express that opinion less quickly than people who hold the majority opinion

Nelson Mandela was a transformational leader who expressed a minority opinion within South African society and eventually was successful in changing the social and political landscape of his country.

JIM BOURG/GETTY IMAGES

civil rights activists talked about equality and human justice. These thoughts were in line with the emerging views within the nation. When majority opinions eventually change due to minority influence, people often forget where they first heard their newly adopted opinions. The efforts of those who first propose minority positions often are not remembered when their influence attempts finally succeed. This is why Susan B. Anthony long ago advised those who hold dissenting opinions not to expect any praise when their opinions are accepted.

CHECKPOINT > *What is minority influence in a group?*

20.2 ASSESSMENT

In Your Own Words

Choose one of the following: define the nature of a group; discuss leadership and leadership styles; or explain minority influence in a group.

Review Concepts

1. Which is an example of a task-oriented group?
   - a. friendship groups
   - b. family groups
   - c. postal workers
   - d. emotional support groups

2. Which leadership style receives the highest leadership rating?
   - a. rigid
   - b. relational
   - c. task
   - d. flexible

3. To which type of leader would a member of a collectivist culture better respond?
   - a. task-oriented leader
   - b. transformational leader
   - c. relationship-oriented leader
   - d. male leader

4. **True or False** BIRGing likely will result when repeated group failure causes you embarrassment and you emotionally distance yourself from the group to protect your self-esteem.

5. **True or False** People share their group's successes but engage in cutting off reflected failure when the group fails.

6. **True or False** Members of a group accept influence from others whom they believe have greater ability.

Think Critically

7. Why do minority group members have the strongest influence when they take positions similar to the direction the group is going?

8. Explain why people join groups, and include a reason you have joined a group.

9. Why is it necessary to defend your ingroup when that group is faced with a failure?

10. Why might an organization need two leaders—a task leader and a relational leader?

20.3 Prejudice and Discrimination

OBJECTIVES

- Explain intolerance between groups and the difference between prejudice and discrimination.
- Discuss breaking the prejudice habit.

KEY TERMS

- stereotypes
- outgroup
- prejudice
- discrimination
- realistic group conflict theory
- ethnocentrism
- implicit prejudice
- intergroup anxiety

DISCOVER IT | *How does this relate to me?*

Have you ever felt someone judged you and even disliked you because of the group to which you belonged? Have you ever felt that others were judging you unfairly based on your gender? The color of your skin? Because you are smart? Because you are not a straight A student? Because you are an athlete? Because you are not athletic? Do you ever form opinions about other people because of the groups to which they belong? That is, you do not really know them as individuals but you think you know some important things about them based on which groups you place them in. The groups could be related to their gender, the color of their skin, or many other qualities. In this lesson you are going to learn about why and how people judge others based on their group membership.

I n trying to understand the psychology of prejudice and discrimination, social psychologists have examined both external factors and internal factors. External factors involve the social conditions that can increase tensions and intolerance between groups. Internal factors involve the thinking and opinions of people from different social groups. It is the interaction of external factors and internal factors that explain both the causes of prejudice and discrimination, as well as the remedies for these social problems.

Intolerance Between Groups

A **stereotype** is a fixed set of beliefs about a group of people that may or may not be accurate. Stereotypes are "shortcuts to thinking" that provide information about individuals not personally known. You learn about the stereotypes associated with different groups from other people. You may have stereotypes about students at your school who are members of different groups, such as those who are on the football versus soccer teams, or those who take mostly college-preparatory courses versus vocational courses. The main advantage of stereotyping is that it speeds up

stereotype A fixed set of beliefs about a group of people that may or may not be accurate

Male nurses do not fit the common stereotype of nurses as warm, caring women.

your judgments of other people. However, because stereotyping involves taking mental shortcuts, its main disadvantage is that it can lead to faulty thinking and mistakes.

Stereotypes can be positive even if they are not always accurate. For example, a common stereotype of nurses are that they are women who are warm, caring, knowledgeable about medicine, and dedicated to helping people who are sick. Yet many nurses are men, not women. There also is a small percentage of nurses who are not competent or caring. Despite the possibility of making mistakes when judging nurses by using this common stereotype, there are many instances when your judgments will be correct. This example illustrates how stereotyped thinking can sometimes help you make accurate—and fast—judgments of others. Unfortunately, there is a very dark side to stereotyping that has nothing to do with accurate judgments.

Research indicates that people are more likely to stereotype outgroup members than ingroup members. An **outgroup** is any group with which you do not share membership. Thus, if you are on the soccer team, you are more likely to stereotype students who are on the football team than you are to stereotype your fellow soccer teammates.

When the stereotypes associated with a particular group are negative and disrespectful, they form the basis for prejudice and discrimination. You know that prejudice and discrimination are socially undesirable behaviors, but what exactly do these terms mean? How do prejudice and discrimination differ?

Prejudice is an attitude and discrimination is a behavior. **Prejudice** is a negative attitude toward members of a specific group. **Discrimination** is a negative action toward members of a specific group. Negative stereotypes can create prejudice, which can then cause discrimination. For example, a store owner may have a negative stereotype about teenagers, believing that they are lazy, irresponsible, and dishonest. Because of this negative stereotype, the storeowner has a negative attitude toward teenagers (prejudice), and thus, refuses to hire them as store workers (discrimination).

Sometimes prejudice does not cause discrimination. Prejudiced people may not discriminate against others because they worry that such discrimination will be judged harshly. For example, a store owner may have a negative stereotype and prejudice against teenagers, but may still hire teenagers in her store because most of her customers are teenagers. In this instance, the store owner does not act on her prejudice and discriminate against teenagers because it would hurt her business.

It also is true that discrimination can occur without prejudice. Sometimes people who are not prejudiced engage in *institutional discrimination* by carrying out the discriminatory guidelines of institutions. For instance, a manager who hires

outgroup Any group with which you do not share membership

prejudice A negative attitude toward members of a specific group

discrimination A negative action toward members of a specific group

workers for a store owned by someone who is prejudiced against teenagers may not be personally prejudiced. Yet by following the hiring guidelines of the owner, this manager engages in age discrimination.

Discrimination is expressed in many ways. Mild forms may be to avoid people toward whom you are prejudiced. Discrimination also may keep people from obtaining desired jobs or housing, or even result in violence.

PREJUDICE CAUSED BY INTERGROUP COMPETITION

Social psychologists investigated factors that cause prejudice and discrimination. One social cause is competition between groups. According to **realistic group conflict theory**, when two groups compete for scarce resources such as territory, jobs, housing, or food, this competition creates prejudice. Realistic group conflict theory states that, when groups are in conflict, two important changes occur. First there is hostility toward the opposing outgroup, and second there is an increase in group loyalty. This pattern of behavior is referred to as **ethnocentrism**.

One of the first studies to test realistic group conflict theory was the Robbers Cave study conducted by Muzafer Sherif and his colleagues in the summer of 1954 at the Robbers Cave State Park in Oklahoma. Participants were 20 well-adjusted 11- and 12-year-old boys who had never met one another. Researchers divided the boys into two groups, with one group leaving for the camp by bus a day before the other. Upon arrival at the camp, each group was assigned a cabin out of sight of the other, so neither knew of the other's existence. The camp counselors were the researchers who secretly recorded day-to-day events.

The study had three phases. The first phase was devoted to *creating ingroups*, the second was devoted to *creating intergroup competition*, and the third involved *encouraging intergroup cooperation*. During the first week, each group engaged in cooperative camp activities and developed its own identity. One group named itself the "Rattlers" while the other group called itself the "Eagles." As the first week drew to a close, each group became aware of the other's existence, and that's when ingroup-outgroup tensions flared: "*They* better not be in *our* swimming hole!" "*Those* guys are using *our* baseball diamond again!"

During the study's second phase, Sherif tested his hypothesis that intergroup competition caused prejudice. He designed a weeklong competition between the groups of ten athletic events such as baseball, football, and tug-of-war. Researchers observed a sudden increase in ethnocentrism by both groups: Name-calling and verbal aggression toward outgroup members increased, while ingroup friction decreased. Both groups went from hostile name calling to physical aggression.

ARCHIVES OF THE HISTORY OF AMERICAN PSYCHOLOGY - THE UNIVERSITY OF AKRON

realistic group conflict theory A theory that intergroup conflict develops from competition for limited resources

ethnocentrism A pattern of increased hostility toward opposing outgroups combined with increased loyalty to one's ingroup

The Robbers Cave study created hostility between two groups of boys at a summer camp by having them compete against one another. What theory explains how prejudice formed between these two groups due to their competitive relationship?

Cooperation between groups became necessary among the boys at camp when there was a common goal to achieve.

ARCHIVES OF THE HISTORY OF AMERICAN PSYCHOLOGY - THE UNIVERSITY OF AKRON

The third phase was designed to reverse the hostility, a task that proved to be more difficult to accomplish. Noncompetitive contact between the groups did not ease tensions. For example, when the two groups ate a meal together, more food was thrown at opposing group members than eaten. To reduce the conflict, researchers created a *superordinate goal*, which is a mutually shared goal that can only be achieved by the two groups cooperating. Over the next six days, the researchers arranged for problems to develop, such as the failure of the camp's water supply or the breakdown of the camp bus. At first, the groups tried to solve the problems on their own. When they discovered that cooperation was necessary, they began to work together. This cooperation gradually eased tensions and new friendships formed between the previously competing group members.

The Robbers Cave study is an example of how prejudice and discrimination can develop when two groups compete for scarce resources. It also demonstrates that having a superordinate goal can lead to peaceful coexistence between previously hostile groups. Although this study used children as participants, similar results were obtained with adults. Check out the Positive Psychology feature on page 613 for how the insights from the Robbers Cave Study were used to reduce prejudice in schools.

IMPLICIT PREJUDICE

Competition among groups often results in open expression of prejudice, but prejudice often is subtle and difficult to detect. One reason is that people who hold prejudicial attitudes may not openly express them, because they realize such attitudes are socially unacceptable. Instead they consciously hide prejudices and publicly express nonprejudiced views. However, when their social guard is down, they unintentionally reveal these prejudices.

Other people's prejudice may be relatively unconscious, meaning they have prejudicial attitudes without being aware of it. **Implicit prejudice** is unconsciously holding prejudicial attitudes. Individuals with implicit prejudice may believe they are not prejudiced, even while they react negatively toward people in certain groups.

How is it possible to react with prejudice toward others without realizing you are doing so? When talking to members of the target group to which they are prejudiced, individuals with implicit prejudice consciously focus on their positive attitudes toward this group. At the same time, they try to ignore their feelings of discomfort created by their implicit prejudice.

How do people from the target group react while conversing with individuals who are implicitly prejudiced? They often notice that these implicitly prejudiced people seem uncomfortable. Nonverbal behaviors related to unconscious negative emotions and tension may include a lot of eye blinking, not looking the person in the eye, and forced smiles. When people from the target group detect these

implicit prejudice
Unconsciously held prejudicial attitudes

behaviors, they often walk away feeling that the person didn't really want to talk to them. How would you feel if people from another group often treated you this way? This is the common reaction that people have when talking to others who have an implicit prejudice toward their group.

CHECKPOINT *What is the difference between prejudice and discrimination?*

POSITIVE PSYCHOLOGY

Can Schools Be Institutions of Social Change?

In 1971, the superintendent of the Austin, Texas schools asked Elliot Aronson to design a plan to reduce interracial tensions in the recently desegregated classrooms. After observing students, Aronson realized the social relationships were similar to those described by Sherif in the Robbers Cave Study (see pages 611–612). Using that study as a guide, Aronson and his colleagues developed a cooperative learning technique that came to be called the *jigsaw classroom*. The technique was so named because students had to cooperate in putting together their daily lessons, the way a jigsaw puzzle is assembled.

In the jigsaw classroom, students were placed in six-person, culturally and academically mixed learning groups. The day's lesson was divided into six subtopics, and each student was responsible for learning one piece of this lesson and then teaching it to the other group members. With the lesson divided up in this way, cooperation was essential for success.

In contrast to traditional classroom learning, in which students compete against one another, the jigsaw classroom promoted superordinate goals. Compared with students in traditional classrooms, students in the jigsaw groups showed a decrease in prejudice and an increase in liking one another. Their liking for school also improved, as did their level of self-esteem. The cooperative learning also improved minority students' academic test scores, while White students' scores were comparable to what they achieved in traditional classrooms. Additional studies find that the jigsaw method offers a promising way to improve race relations in schools by breaking down the out-group barriers that drive a cognitive and emotional wedge between students.

Think Critically
How might cooperative learning break down prejudice?

Breaking the Prejudice Habit

The research discussed so far suggests that prejudice and discrimination are social problems that often are difficult to change. Yet change can and does occur for those who want to reduce their prejudiced responses. For example, imagine that Virginia lives in a society where people in her ingroup grew up believing that the "Snaileen" people are intellectually inferior to her people, and she developed prejudiced views based on this upbringing. Then in school, Virginia meets a number of Snaileen people who do not fit her negative stereotype, so she changes her views. Although Virginia no longer believes the negative stereotype, it is not gone from memory. Because she has used this stereotype so often in the past to judge Snaileen people, it often automatically comes to mind whenever Virginia thinks about people from this outgroup. Trying to block this negative stereotype and not allow it to cause prejudiced thinking takes time and careful attention—like breaking a bad habit.

When trying to become nonprejudiced, stereotypes often are automatically activated from memory, which then triggers a series of unfortunate consequences. However, if you pay attention to how you are thinking, you can break the "prejudice habit."

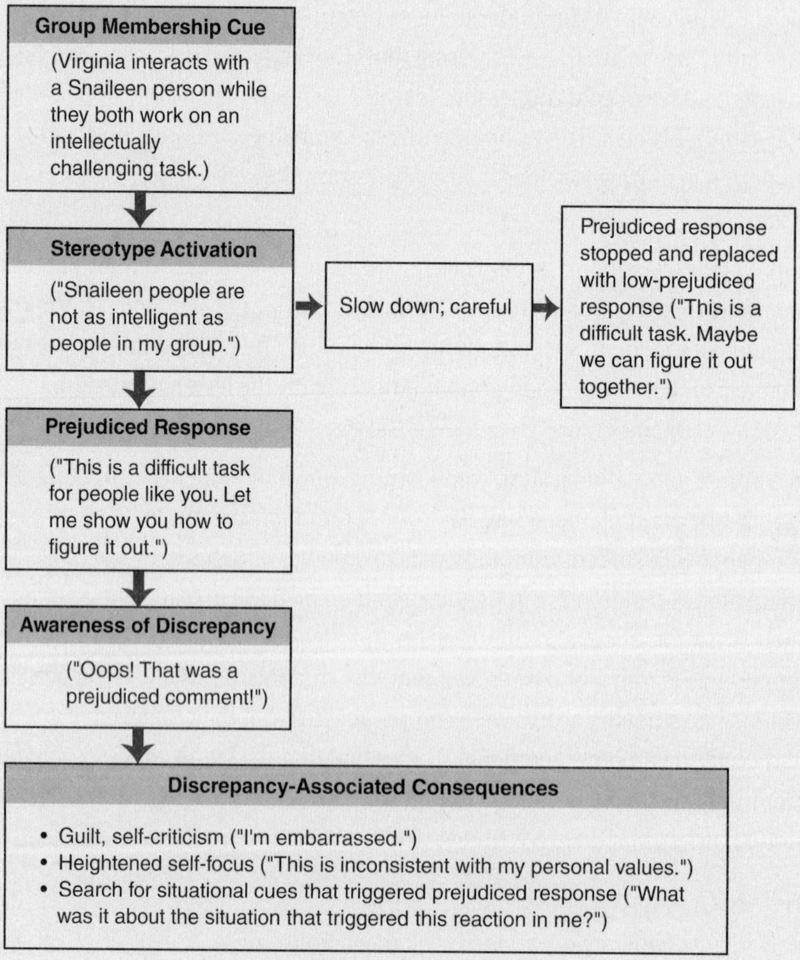

Figure 20-3 **BREAKING THE PREJUDICE HABIT**

Group Membership Cue

(Virginia interacts with a Snaileen person while they both work on an intellectually challenging task.)

↓

Stereotype Activation

("Snaileen people are not as intelligent as people in my group.")

→ Slow down; careful → Prejudiced response stopped and replaced with low-prejudiced response ("This is a difficult task. Maybe we can figure it out together.")

↓

Prejudiced Response

("This is a difficult task for people like you. Let me show you how to figure it out.")

↓

Awareness of Discrepancy

("Oops! That was a prejudiced comment!")

↓

Discrepancy-Associated Consequences

- Guilt, self-criticism ("I'm embarrassed.")
- Heightened self-focus ("This is inconsistent with my personal values.")
- Search for situational cues that triggered prejudiced response ("What was it about the situation that triggered this reaction in me?")

Look at Figure 20-3 on page 614, which outlines how self-awareness and attention reduce prejudiced responses. Whenever Virginia encounters a Snaileen person, the stereotype is automatically activated from memory. If she does not consciously monitor her thoughts, she may slip back into acting as though Snaileen people were intellectually inferior (an inconsistent response). Becoming aware of this inconsistency in her actions, Virginia will feel guilty. In turn, this guilt motivates her to heighten her self-awareness and search her memory for the situations that trigger the prejudiced responses. Through such attention, Virginia will slowly be able to monitor and control her prejudiced responses.

The important lesson here is that you can avoid prejudiced responding by thinking about being nonprejudiced before acting. The more you are committed to reducing your prejudice, the greater care you will take in thinking before acting.

One of the biggest obstacles to breaking the prejudice habit is the tension and distress that many people experience when talking to a person from a different social group. This **intergroup anxiety** occurs because people often have not had positive previous experiences with people from the other group. This lack of experience creates tension about what may happen during the interaction. Due to this intergroup anxiety, people are on guard and try to limit or entirely avoid such encounters. While such avoidance may temporarily reduce anxiety, it does not overcome the anxiety or promote thinking in a nonprejudiced way. What is effective in these situations is to fight the urge to flee, and instead, honestly get to know the other people. If you place yourself in intergroup situations and have positive or even neutral experiences with outgroup members, your intergroup anxiety will decrease.

intergroup anxiety
Anxiety due to expecting negative consequences when interacting with an outgroup member

CHECKPOINT *What is intergroup anxiety?*

PHOTODISC/GETTY IMAGES

Controlling prejudiced responses takes time and attention.

In Your Own Words

Explain the difference between prejudice and discrimination and discuss prejudice caused by intergroup competition, including realistic group conflict theory and ethnocentrism. Give an example of ethnocentrism.

Review Concepts

1. Which refers to a negative action toward members of a specific group?
   - a. stereotype
   - b. outgroup
   - c. prejudice
   - d. discrimination

2. According to realistic group conflict theory, which pattern of behavior occurs when groups are competing for the same thing?
   - a. cooperation
   - b. ethnocentrism
   - c. stereotyping
   - d. disobedience

3. Which refers to anxiety due to expecting negative consequences when interacting with an outgroup member?
   - a. ethnocentrism
   - b. intergroup anxiety
   - c. implicit prejudice
   - d. outgroup anxiety

4. Which refers to a fixed set of beliefs about a group of people that may or may not be accurate?
   - a. stereotype
   - b. ethnocentrism
   - c. discrimination
   - d. prejudice

5. **True or False** Research indicates that people are more likely to stereotype outgroup members than ingroup members.

6. **True or False** A person can be both prejudiced toward and discriminatory against another person at the same time.

7. **True or False** Prejudice can be subtle and difficult to detect.

8. **True or False** Research suggests that prejudice and discrimination are social problems that are difficult to change, but that change is possible for people who want to reduce their prejudiced responses.

Think Critically

9. Explain how a superordinate goal cools hostility between two conflicting groups.

10. How can people with implicit prejudice believe they are not prejudiced even while reacting negatively toward people in certain groups?

11. According to the realistic group conflict theory, what causes conflict? Why do you think this is so?

12. Intergroup anxiety is one of the biggest obstacles to breaking the prejudice habit. What causes this type of anxiety, and how can it be overcome?

Social Psychologist

ealth Science

Are you interested in the social scene—in how people interact with one another and with the environment? Do you wonder how one person's thoughts, feelings, and behaviors are influenced by another person or by group situations? If so, you might be interested in a career as a social psychologist. Social psychologists study social perception and prejudice, and how individuals judge the people and the world around them. They study people's attitudes and analyze the social influence people have on one another.

Many social psychologists specialize in one area of social psychology. One social psychologist might choose to study social perceptions, or the impression one individual or group has of another individual or group. Another social psychologist might choose to specialize in the study of diversity in the workplace, while another might choose to study how students in the same school tend to conform to a specific dress code. A social psychologist might specialize in the study of behaviors that either help or hurt other people, or why people are attracted to one another. Specializations in this field of psychology are varied, but they all have one thing in common—they study the way people live together in the world.

This type of psychologist works mainly in universities, but he or she also can work in organizational consulting firms, market research companies, and other applied psychology fields that are related to people's social interactions.

PHOTODISC/GETTY IMAGES

Employment Outlook

Careers for social psychologists are expected to grow 15 percent until 2016. This is a faster than average rate.

Needed Skills and Education

Most social psychologists have a doctoral degree, a requirement in most states. A doctoral degree usually requires five to seven years of college work after receiving a bachelor's degree. Most states require social psychologists to be licensed if they do not work in a university setting. Requirements vary from state to state. Social psychologists who teach in universities usually have a Ph.D. in psychology or a related field.

Courses that will help you in this career are those in psychology and other related sciences. Courses in sociology are also helpful as are courses in humanities and cross-cultural studies. You need good written and oral communication skills, good interpersonal relationship skills, and good organizational abilities. Computer skills also are helpful.

How You'll Spend Your Day

Social psychologists interview and test individuals and groups and observe individual and group behavior in order to analyze how people interact in their environment. They may write reports for marketing companies, articles for magazines, or undertake research and teach in a university. They may advise firms on how to support diversity or increase leadership among employees.

Most social psychologists work a regular 40-hour work week; however, observation of study participants and analyzing data may include evening or weekends.

Earnings

The median hourly earnings of social psychologists are $59,440. The lowest 10 percent earn $35,280 while the highest 10 percent earn more than $102,730.

What About You?

Does the career of social psychologist sound interesting to you? Interview a social psychologist in person, over the phone, or by e-mail. Write a list of at least 10 questions you want to ask about how the psychologist spends the day. Write an essay on why this career is interesting to you. Be specific and include which type of research you would be most interested in pursuing.

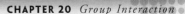

CHAPTER SUMMARY

20.1 Social Influence

- Conformity is a yielding to perceived group pressure.

- Solomon Asch conducted research that demonstrates people find it easier to conform than to challenge the unanimous opinions of others.

- Compliance is acting to grant a direct request. Three factors that increase the likelihood of having a request granted are a positive mood, reciprocity, and a given reason.

- People from collectivist cultures are more concerned than people from individualistic cultures in gaining the approval of their group.

- Obedience is the performance of an action in response to a direct order. Obedience is common because people are taught from a young age to respect and obey people in authority.

- Stanley Milgram's research demonstrated people have a high level of willingness to obey destructive commands of authority figures.

20.2 Group Behavior and Leadership

- A group is people who depend on, and interact with, one another on a regular basis. Task-oriented groups are work groups; social-oriented groups are friendship and family groups.

- With your ingroups, you experience both pride and embarrassment, depending on how well the group is doing.

- A leader is the person who exerts the most influence and provides direction and energy to the group. Leadership styles include task leadership and relational leadership.

- Transformational leaders change the outlook and behavior of followers so they move beyond their self-interests for the good of the group or society.

- Culture and gender influence leadership styles.

- Dissenters can produce change within a group by consistently and confidently stating their dissenting opinions.

20.3 Prejudice and Discrimination

- A stereotype is a fixed set of beliefs about a group of people that may or may not be accurate.

- Research indicates people are more likely to stereotype outgroup members than ingroup members.

- Prejudice is a negative attitude toward members of a specific group; discrimination is a negative action toward a member of a specific group. Prejudice may lead to discrimination but this is not always the case. Discrimination can occur without prejudice, as with institutional discrimination.

- Prejudice can be caused by intergroup competition, but a common goal brings the two competing groups together.

- Individuals may overcome prejudice, but breaking the prejudice habit requires time, motivation, and self-awareness.

CHAPTER ASSESSMENT

Review Psychology Terms

Select the term that best fits the definition. Some terms will not be used.

_____ 1. The exercise of social power by a person or group to change the attitudes or behavior of others in a certain direction

_____ 2. The way dissenters produce change within a group

_____ 3. A fixed set of beliefs about a group of people that may or may not be accurate

_____ 4. Acting to grant a direct request

_____ 5. The performance of an action in response to a direct order

_____ 6. Any group with which you do not share membership

_____ 7. A yielding to perceived group pressure

_____ 8. A pattern of increased hostility toward opposing outgroups combined with increased loyalty to one's ingroup

_____ 9. The expectation that you should return a favor or a good deed

_____ 10. People who depend on, and interact with, one another on a regular basis

_____ 11. An expected way to behave and believe that is established and enforced by a group

_____ 12. A theory that intergroup conflict develops from competition for limited resources

_____ 13. The tendency of those who hold a minority opinion to express that opinion less quickly than people who hold the majority opinion

_____ 14. Unconsciously held prejudicial attitudes

_____ 15. A group to which you belong and which forms a part of your social identity

_____ 16. The person who exerts the most influence and provides direction and energy to the group

_____ 17. Anxiety due to expecting negative consequences when interacting with an outgroup member

a. compliance

b. conformity

c. ethnocentrism

d. group

e. implicit prejudice

f. ingroup

g. intergroup anxiety

h. leader

i. minority influence

j. minority slowness effect

k. obedience

l. outgroup

m. realistic group conflict theory

n. reciprocity norm

o. social influence

p. social norm

q. social power

r. stereotypes

s. superordinate goal

Review Psychology Concepts

18. List three factors that increase the likelihood that others will comply to your request.

19. Describe the differences between relational and task leadership. Which leader would you rather work with? Explain your answer.

20. Compare and contrast the leadership styles of men and women. Analyze why social psychologists suggest these gender differences exist.

21. Define a transformational leader, provide an example of someone you believe is a transformational leader, and explain why you believe this person is a transformational leader.

22. Which of the following is prejudice and which is discrimination: a negative attitude toward a group of young people who dress differently than most teens do; thinking someone is less intelligent because of where they live; an employer refusing to hire someone based on gender or heritage.

23. Evaluate the social power in a group to which you belong. Describe the source of the social power and the behavior that results from the social influence of the leader and other group members.

24. Think about a time when you were able to get someone to comply. Answer the following questions: Who was the other person? What was their relationship to you? What were you asking? Which of the three factors that increases the likelihood of compliance did you use?

25. Why does giving a reason result in greater compliance to requests?

26. List the groups to which you belong, and then categorize them into either a task-oriented or social-oriented group.

27. Describe a time when you were basking in reflected glory of an ingroup and a time when you were cutting off reflected failure of an ingroup. You may use the same group or two different groups. Answer in a way that shows you understand the meaning of *basking in reflected glory* and *cutting off reflected failure.*

28. Compare the leadership styles of people in a collectivist society with those in an individualistic society. Include an evaluation of the role heritage plays when a person with a cultural heritage of a collectivist society lives in an individualistic society.

29. Using the list you made in exercise 26, explain why you joined each of these groups, and what you gain from membership in each group. Are there any outgroups you would consider joining? What benefit would joining provide you?

30. In the Robbers Cave Study, what happened to ingroup friction as aggression toward outgroup members increased?

31. What is the crucial factor in a person's commitment to thinking and acting without prejudice?

32. What is one reason prejudice often is difficult to detect?

33. Are people with collectivist or individualist cultural backgrounds more likely to be concerned with gaining the approval of their group? Explain your answer.

Apply Psychology Concepts

34. Apply the term conformity to a high schooler's life. Give three examples of how conformity can be seen as both a good and a bad behavior.

35. Imagine that you are trying to sell a product of your choice. Identify the product and apply the concepts of positive moods, reciprocity, and giving reasons to your selling strategy.

36. Identify groups in your own life that you associate with using the principle of BIRGing. What reactions do you have when the group is successful and when it is unsuccessful? Explain about a time when you participated in CORFing.

37. Explain how a task leader, a relational leader, and a transformational leader would handle a meeting of 12 jurors trying a murder case where eight believe the accused is guilty and four believe the accused is innocent.

Make Academic Connections

38. **Language Arts** Use the library or Internet to research a transformational leader. Write a biography of that leader. Include personality characteristics that add to the person's leadership qualities. Also include important points of the leader's life that influenced the leader, how the politics of the country where the leader lives or lived influenced the leader, how the family and the leader's upbringing helped create the leader, and any other important influences. You may choose one of the transformational leaders mentioned in the text or someone you discover on your own. Include a photo of the leader with your biography.

39. **English** Write an essay about a time when you felt the need to conform. Explain the situation, discuss why you conformed, and explain the consequences and rewards of doing so. Also analyze the decision you made to conform, and discuss whether you would make the same decision again. Why or why not?

40. **Sociology** Interview 10 to 12 people of different age groups. Ask: Which of society's rules would you prefer to ignore? For example a student might say to drive a vehicle before being old enough to obtain a driver's license; an adult might say to not pay income tax. Write a report on your findings that includes what would happen to society if everyone ignored the rules your respondents chose.

41. **Journalism** Choose a leader in your family, school, or community. Interview the leader, and then write a feature story on that person. Include characteristics that make this person a good leader.

42. **Debate** Choose one side of the following debate: Are leaders born or made? Outline your response. Find a student who chose the other side of the debate and have a discussion on why each of you holds your opinion.

DIGGING DEEPER
with Psychology eCollection

What makes you feel happy? Psychologists and psychiatrists have long studied happiness and the factors that lead to it. Myers' article summarizes some of the findings about the personal characteristics that help people be happy. In general, the results are not surprising: optimistic, outgoing people tend to say they are happy. Access the Gale Psychology eCollection at *www.cengage .com/school/psych/franzoi* and review the characteristics that can lead to happiness that are cited in the article. Write a summary of the article, describing the key elements that lead to happiness and answer the question: Why can't everyone be happy? As an additional project, select one of the characteristics that you or someone you know might improve on and describe how you (or they) could improve it.

Source: Myers, David G. "The secrets of happiness." *Psychology Today*. 25.n4 (July–August 1992): 38(8). Reprinted with permission from *Psychology Today* Magazine, Copyright (c) 1992 Sussec Publishers, LLC.

GLOSSARY

A

Absolute threshold The weakest amount of a given stimulus that a person can detect half of the time (p. 94)

Acceleration Early admission to school and skipping grades (p. 485)

Accommodation The process of changing existing schemas in order to absorb new information (p. 233)

Acculturative stress The stress resulting from the pressure of adapting to a new culture (p. 198)

Acetylcholine Neurotransmitter that sends excitatory messages to your skeletal muscles, which help you to walk, talk, blink your eyes, and breathe (p. 66)

Achievement test A test designed to access what a person has learned (p. 468)

Acquisition Initial learning of a conditioned response (p. 342)

Activation-synthesis theory A theory that dreaming is the forebrain's attempt to interpret random neural activity coming from the midbrain during sleep (p. 444)

Active alert induction Inducing hypnosis while a person dances, spins, or even pedals a stationary bicycle (p. 448)

Activity theory of aging A theory that elderly people are happiest when they remain physically, cognitively, and socially active (p. 291)

Actual self Person you know yourself to be (p. 313)

Adolescence The transition period between childhood and adulthood (p. 247)

Aerobic exercise Sustained exercise that increases heart and lung fitness (p. 202)

Ageism Prejudice or discrimination against people based on their age (p. 290)

Aging The progressive deterioration of the body that ends in death (p. 286)

Agreeableness Describes people who tend to be good-natured, softhearted, courteous, and sympathetic (p. 318)

Alcoholism The tolerance and physical dependence resulting from prolonged abuse of alcohol (p. 455)

Algorithm A problem-solving strategy that involves following a specific rule or step-by-step procedure until you produce the correct solution (p. 423)

Alpha waves Fast, low-amplitude brain waves associated with a relaxed, wakeful state of mind (p. 439)

Altered state of consciousness An awareness of yourself and your surroundings that is noticeably different from your normal state of consciousness (p. 439)

Alzheimer's disease Brain disorder resulting in memory loss caused by a sharp reduction in the supply of acetylcholine (p. 66); fatal disease that destroys areas of the brain that control thought, memory, and language (p. 296)

Amphetamines Stimulant drugs which activate the sympathetic nervous system and increase dopamine and norepinephrine activity (p. 456)

Amplitude Psychological experience of loudness of sound that corresponds to the height of a sound wave (p. 105)

Amygdala The structure in the forebrain's limbic system that controls fear and aggression (p. 75)

Analytical intelligence Intelligence required to solve familiar problems and judge the quality of ideas (p. 479)

Analytical psychology Carl Jung's interpretation of psychoanalysis (p. 311)

Anorexia nervosa An eating disorder in which a person weighs less than 85 percent of her or his expected weight but still expresses an intense fear of gaining weight or becoming fat (p. 161)

Anterograde Forward moving (p. 396)

Anterograde amnesia The inability to form long-term memories due to physical injury to the brain (p. 396)

Antianxiety drugs Drugs that have a calming effect (p. 554)

Antidepressant drugs Drugs that improve mood and energy (p. 554)

Antipsychotic drugs Drugs that reduce schizophrenic symptoms such as auditory hallucinations and paranoia (p. 553)

Antisocial personality disorder Personality disorder in which a person shows a strong disregard for, and violation of, the rights of others; *also called* Psychopathy (p. 524)

Anvil Small vibrating bone in the ear (p. 106)

Anxiety disorders Disorders characterized by distressing, lasting anxiety, and unusual behavior (p. 506)

Aphasia The disruption of language caused by brain damage (p. 405)

Approach-approach conflict Occurs when you must decide between two equally appealing outcomes (p. 185)

Approach-avoidance conflict Involves only one goal choice, but that goal has both desirable and undesirable consequences (p. 185)

Aptitude test A test that predicts a person's capacity for learning (p. 468)

Arranged marriage Occurs when the family of young adults chooses their spouse for them (p. 280)

Artificial intelligence (AI) The science of designing and making intelligent machines, especially intelligent computer programs (p. 412)

Assimilation The process of absorbing new information into existing schemas (p. 233)

Attachment The strong emotional bond young children form with their parents or primary caregivers (p. 222)

Attitudes Positive or negative evaluations of an object (p. 569)

Attribution theory A theory that describes how you decide whether another person's behavior is caused by the person's disposition or the situation (p. 566)

Audience inhibition effect The tendency for people to define a situation as a nonemergency when other bystanders are present (p. 582)

Auditory canal Passageway in the ear that receives sound waves (p. 106)

Auditory nerve Transmits sound information to the brain (p. 106)

Authoritarian parents Parents who impose many rules, demand strict obedience, and harshly punish their children for rule breaking or even questioning their decisions (p. 226)

Authoritative parents Parents who set rules for proper conduct for their children, consistently enforce those rules, yet allow their children a fair amount of freedom (p. 226)

Autonomic nervous system The division of the peripheral nervous system that controls movement of involuntary, nonskeletal muscles (p. 69)

Availability heuristic The tendency to judge the frequency or probability of an event in terms of how easy it is to think of examples of that event (p. 424)

Aversive conditioning A counterconditioning technique in which people are classically conditioned to react with avoidance (or aversion) to a harmful or undesirable stimulus (p. 549)

Axon Tube-like extension in a neuron that carries information down its "tube" in the form of an electrochemical impulse; can range in length from 1/32 of an inch to more than 3 feet (p. 64)

B

Behaviorism An approach to psychology that studies observable behavior rather than hidden mental processes (p. 13)

Behavior therapies Psychotherapies that use learning principles to eliminate unwanted behaviors and replace them with healthier behaviors (p. 546)

Beta waves Very fast, low-amplitude brain waves associated with an active, alert state of mind (p. 439)

Binocular cues Depth cues that require information from both eyes (p. 124)

Biomedical therapy The treatment of psychological disorders by changing the way the brain works, primarily by using drugs, electrical stimulation, or surgery (p. 533)

Biopsychology Studies behavior by examining biological processes, especially those occurring in the brain; *also called* Psychobiology (p. 19)

Bipolar disorder A mood disorder characterized by swings between the emotional extremes of mania and depression (p. 514)

Blind spot The area on the retina where the optic nerve leaves the eye and that contains no receptor cells (p. 101)

Bodily kinesthetic intelligence The ability displayed by gifted athletes, dancers, and surgeons, and used in ordinary activities, such as driving a car or hammering a nail (p. 477)

Bonding signals Behaviors that newborns engage in that adults usually respond to with attention (p. 223)

Broca's aphasia A brain disorder that often causes people to have long pauses between words and to leave out words, such as *and, but,* and *if* (p. 406)

Broca's area A brain area in the left frontal lobe that allows people to speak smoothly and correctly (p. 406)

Bulimia nervosa An eating disorder in which a person engages in recurrent episodes of binge eating followed by drastic measures to remove the food calories from the body (p. 161)

Bystander intervention model A theory that whether bystanders intervene in an emergency is a result of a five-step decision-making process (p. 581)

C

Cannabis Plant from which marijuana is produced (p. 458)

Cannon-Bard theory A theory that emotion-provoking events simultaneously induce both physiological responses and subjective states that are labeled as emotions (p. 169)

Case study A scientific method involving an in-depth analysis of a single subject (p. 40)

Catharsis The release of pent-up emotions that occurs when psychotherapy clients gain insight into underlying troubling memories (p. 541)

Central nervous system The brain and spinal cord (p. 67)

Central route to persuasion This route to persuasion occurs when you are motivated and able to think carefully about the message content (p. 572)

Central tendency A number that describes the central location within a distribution of scores in a sample (p. 48)

Cerebellum The region of the brain important in the regulation and coordination of body movement and learning (p. 74)

Cerebral cortex The thinking center of the brain which coordinates and integrates all areas of the brain into a fully functioning unit (p. 75)

Cerebral hemispheres Two halves of the cerebral cortex (p. 75)

Cerebrospinal fluid Protective fluid that allows the brain to float inside the skull (p. 67)

Child-directed speech Speaking to babies with a high-pitched voice, using short sentences with clearly and slowly pronounced words; *also called* Baby talk (p. 418)

Childhood prodigies Children who are mentally gifted have extraordinary ability in one intellectual area but have relatively normal abilities in other areas (p. 485)

Chromosomes Threadlike structures found in every cell of your body, except in red blood cells (p. 85)

Chronological age The number of years a person has lived (p. 286)

Chunking Combining bits of information into a small number of meaningful groups, or chunks, that can be stored in short-term memory (p. 378)

Circadian rhythms Regular bodily rhythms that occur on a 24-hour cycle (p. 436)

Clairvoyance The supposed ability to perceive objects or events that are not physically present (p. 139)

Classical conditioning A type of learning in which a neutral stimulus triggers a response after being paired with another stimulus that naturally triggers that response (p. 340)

Client-centered therapy A humanistic therapy in which the therapist provides a supportive setting for clients to discover their "true selves" (p. 543)

Clients People who actively work with professional therapists toward the goal of improving their mental health (p. 536)

Clinical psychology Diagnoses and treats people with psychological disorders, such as depression and schizophrenia (p. 20)

Clinical scales Scales that are used to identify psychological difficulties or interests (p. 329)

Cocaine Stimulant drug which activates the sympathetic branch of the autonomic nervous system, raising body temperature, heart rate, and breathing, and reducing the desire for food and sleep (p. 456)

Cochlea The coiled, fluid-filled tube in the inner ear that contains hair-like auditory receptors (p. 106)

Cognition The mental activity of knowing and the process by which knowledge is acquired and problems are solved (p. 232)

Cognitive appraisal Process used to interpret and evaluate stressors in your life (p. 191)

Cognitive-behavior therapy (CBT) The cognitive therapy that identifies and then changes negative thinking and behavior patterns (p. 551)

Cognitive dissonance A feeling of discomfort caused by performing an action inconsistent with your attitude (p. 574)

Cognitive psychology An approach to psychology that studies how the mind organizes and makes sense of information and experiences (p.15); studies all aspects of thinking, including problem solving, decision making, memory, reasoning, and language (p. 19)

Cognitive therapies Psychotherapies that focus on identifying and then fixing troublesome thinking by clients (p. 550)

Collateral growth Rewiring of the brain; process by which the brain can grow new dendrites, which then make new connections with other neurons (p. 78)

Collective unconscious In Jung's personality theory, the part of the unconscious mind containing inherited memories shared by all human beings (p. 311)

Collectivism A philosophy of life stressing that the group is more important than the individual (p. 17)

Color blindness A deficiency in the ability to distinguish among colors (p. 103)

Communication The sending and receiving of information (p. 405)

Companionship love The affection felt for people with whom your lives are deeply entwined (p. 279)

Compliance Acting to grant a direct request (p. 595)

Compulsions Recurring actions or behaviors that cause distress or interfere significantly with ongoing activity (p. 508)

Computerized axial tomograph (CAT) scan A brain-imaging technique that combines thousands of x-ray brain photographs to construct a picture of the brain (p. 72)

Concept A mental grouping of objects, ideas, or events that share common properties (p. 421)

Concrete operational stage Time when children perform mental operations and begin logical reasoning (p. 236)

Conditional positive regard Love and acceptance given to children only when they meet others' standards (p. 543)

Conditioned response (CR) In classical conditioning, the learned response to a previously neutral conditioned stimulus (p. 340)

Conditioned stimulus (CS) In classical conditioning, a previously neutral stimulus that, after repeated pairings with an unconditioned stimulus, comes to bring about a conditioned response (p. 340)

Conduction hearing loss Occurs when there are physical problems sending sound waves through the outer or middle ear; problem often involves a punctured eardrum or damage to any of the three bones in the middle ear (pp. 106–107)

Cones Photoreceptors in the eyes that play a key role in color vision; most cones are concentrated in a small area near the center of the retina known as the fovea, which is the area of central focus (p. 100)

Confirmation bias Tendency to seek only information that supports your beliefs (p. 425)

Conflict Feeling of being pulled between two opposing desires or goals (p. 185)

Conformity A yielding to perceived group pressure (p. 591)

Conscientiousness The measure of your willingness to conform to others' expectations and follow through on what you have agreed to do, even though more tempting options may arise (p. 318)

Conscious mind The relatively small part of your mind that you are aware of in each moment (p. 308)

Consciousness Awareness of yourself and your surroundings (p. 435)

Conservation The understanding that certain physical properties of an object remain unchanged despite changes in its appearance (p. 234)

Contact comfort Direct contact with soft objects (p. 223)

Continuous reinforcement schedule A schedule of reinforcement in which every correct response is followed by a reinforcer (p. 355)

Contrast effect Occurs when people are judged as more attractive after others see an unattractive person of the same gender; similarly, people are judged as less attractive when others see someone who is very attractive (p. 565)

Conventional morality Moral reasoning based on seeking social approval or conforming to authority to maintain social order (p. 257)

Corpus callosum A thick band of more than 200 million white nerve fibers that connects the two hemispheres of the brain and transmits information between them (p. 75)

Correlational research A scientific method that assesses the nature of the relationship between two or more variables that are not controlled by the researcher (p. 41)

Correlation coefficient The statistic, or numerical value, that psychologists use to describe the relationship between two variables (p. 42); statistical measure of the direction and strength of the linear relationship between two variables and ranges from -1.00 to $+1.00$ (p. 472)

Counseling psychology Diagnoses and treats people with personal problems that do not involve psychological disorders, including marriage counseling, social skills training, and career planning (p. 20)

Counterconditioning techniques Therapy techniques in which new responses are conditioned to stimuli that previously triggered unwanted behaviors (p. 547)

Couples therapy A variation of family therapy which focuses on communication and behavior patterns of romantic partners (p. 538)

Creative intelligence Intelligence required to develop new ways of solving problems (p. 479)

Critical thinking The process of deciding what to believe and how to act based on a careful evaluation of the evidence (p. 29)

Cross-sectional research People of different ages are compared with one another (p. 217)

Crystallized intelligence A person's knowledge and verbal skills learned through experience (p. 476)

D

Defense mechanisms The ego's ways of keeping threatening and unacceptable material out of consciousness and thereby reducing anxiety (p. 310)

Deficiency needs Needs where you lack something (p. 155)

Déjà vu A brief eerie feeling of remembering an event that is actually being experienced for the first time (p. 389)

Delta waves Slow, high-amplitude brain waves most typical of stage 4 deep sleep (p. 440)

Delusions Irrational belief systems (p. 521)

Dementia A condition of severe declining mental abilities, especially memory (p. 295)

Dendrites Receive information from other neurons and bring it to the soma (p. 64)

Dependent variable The variable that may change in response to the manipulated changes in the independent variable (p. 43)

Depressants Psychoactive drugs that slow down, or depress, the nervous system and decrease mental and physical activity (p. 455)

Depth perception The ability to perceive objects three-dimensionally (p. 124)

Descriptive statistics Numbers that summarize and describe data in a practical, efficient manner (p. 47)

Desensitization hierarchy A sequence of increasingly anxiety-provoking situations related to a client's phobia (p. 548)

Development The systematic physical, cognitive, and social changes in the individual occurring between conception and death (p. 215)

Developmental psychology Studies how people mature and change physically, cognitively, and socially throughout the life span (p. 19)

Deviation IQ Compares how a person's intelligence test score deviates from the average score of same-age peers (p. 469)

Diagnosis The process of identifying disorders (p. 501)

Diagnostic and Statistical Manual of Mental Disorders (DSM) The classification scheme used by most mental health professionals to diagnose psychological disorders (p. 504)

Difference threshold Smallest difference between two stimuli that can be detected half of the time; *also called* Just-noticeable difference (p. 96)

Difficult temperament Infants with this temperament react negatively to new situations by crying or fussing (p. 224)

Diffusion of responsibility The belief that the presence of other people in an emergency makes you less responsible to help the victim (p. 582)

Discrimination A negative action toward members of a specific group (p. 610)

Disengagement theory of aging Theory that aging naturally leads to a gradual withdrawal from physical and social activities as elderly people spend time reflecting on their lives (p. 291)

Displacement Defense mechanism that redirects your emotions or unacceptable urges toward people, animals, or objects that are less threatening (p. 311)

Dissociative amnesia A dissociative disorder involving a sudden loss of memory of identity and/or other personal information (p. 519)

Dissociative disorders Psychological disorders in which conscious awareness becomes separated (dissociated) from previous memories, including one's identity (p. 518)

Dissociative fugue A dissociative disorder in which people suddenly leave their familiar surroundings and assume a new identity without remembering their real identity (p. 519)

Dissociative identity disorder (DID) A dissociative disorder characterized by the presence of two or more identities or personalities, which take turns controlling the person's behavior (p. 519)

Divorce Legal process by which marriage is ended (p. 282)

DNA Means by which hereditary characteristics pass from one generation to the next (p. 85)

Dopamine Neurotransmitter which controls large muscle movements and influences pleasure and motivation (p. 66)

Down syndrome A form of mental retardation caused by an extra chromosome in the genetic makeup (p. 484)

Dreams Story-like sequences of visual images experienced during sleep (p. 443)

Drive A powerful need in the body, created by a physiological imbalance, that motivates behavior (p. 151)

Drive-reduction theory The idea that an imbalance in homeostasis creates a physiological need, which produces a drive that motivates the organism to satisfy the need (p. 151)

Drug abuse Continued drug use despite it interfering with the drug user's behavior or social relationships (p. 454)

Drug therapy The use of medication to treat psychological disorders (p. 553)

Drug tolerance An effect of drug abuse in which greater amounts of the drug are necessary to produce the same effect once produced by a smaller dose (p. 454)

E

Eardrum A thin, flexible membrane that vibrates in sequence with sound waves (p. 106)

Easygoing temperament Infants with this temperament generally react positively to new situations or stimuli, such as food, people, or toys (p. 224)

Eclectic approach Therapy style based on combining aspects of several different psychotherapy techniques (p. 534)

Ecstasy (MDMA) A stimulant drug that affects the brain cells that produce serotonin, a neurotransmitter that affects mood (p. 457)

Educational and school psychology Assesses and treats both students and the educational environment in order to help students learn and adjust in school (p. 20)

Ego The part of your mind that balances the demands of the id, the superego, and reality (p. 308)

Egocentrism The tendency to view the world from your own perspective without recognizing that others may have different viewpoints (p. 234)

Elaboration likelihood model A theory that people engage in either effortful or effortless thinking after receiving a persuasive message (p. 572)

Elaborative rehearsal The process of thinking about how new information relates to information already stored in long-term memory (p. 379)

Electroconvulsive therapy (ECT) Medical treatment for severe depression in which a brief electric shock is administered to the brain of an anesthetized patient (p. 554)

Electroencephalograph (EEG) A brain-imaging technique that records "waves" of electrical activity in the brain (p. 72)

Electromagnetic energy Energy that is all around you; created by the vibration of electrically charged particles, which are basic units of matter; light is a form of electromagnetic energy (p. 99)

Embryo A developing human organism from the third week after fertilization through the eighth week (p. 216)

Emerging adulthood The age period from the late teens to the mid-twenties in which a person is still free from many adult responsibilities (p. 249)

Emotion A positive or negative feeling state involving physiological arousal, conscious experience, and expressive behavior (p. 167)

Emotional fainting Occurs when the parasympathetic system overreacts and reduces physiological activity too much (p. 169)

Emotion-focused coping Consists of efforts to manage your emotional reactions to stressors (p. 192)

Empty-chair technique A humanistic technique in which clients imagine that the person to whom they would like to speak is sitting in an empty chair facing them (p. 544)

Empty nest syndrome Occurs when middle-aged parents become depressed when their last child leaves home (p. 287)

Encoding The first memory process in which information is organized and interpreted so it can be entered into memory (p. 373)

Endocrine system A network of glands that manufactures and secretes hormones directly into the bloodstream (p. 70)

Endorphins Neurotransmitters important in the experience of pleasure and the control of pain (p. 67)

Enrichment A school program that keeps students in their normal grade level, but supplements course work with advanced material, independent study projects, and other learning experiences (p. 485)

Environment The world around you (p. 84)

Ethnic identity The sense of personal identification with a particular ethnic group (p. 266)

Ethnocentrism A pattern of increased hostility toward opposing outgroups combined with increased loyalty to one's ingroup (p. 611)

Existential intelligence Intelligence that deals with the posing and pondering of philosophical questions (p. 478)

Experiment A scientific method in which researchers manipulate, or change, a variable to observe the effect on some other variable (p. 43)

Experimental psychology Studies basic psychological processes such as sensation, perception, learning, motivation, emotion, and states of consciousness (p. 19)

Explicit memory Memory of previous experiences that you can recollect consciously (p. 381)

External attribution Occurs when your explanation for your description of someone else's behavior is that the behavior is being caused by something outside the person, such as the actions of others, the nature of the situation, or luck (p. 566)

External locus of control A belief that what happens to you is outside your own control (p. 322)

Extinction The gradual weakening and disappearance of the conditioned response (p. 343)

Extrasensory perception (ESP) The ability to perceive events in the world without using the normal senses (p. 139)

Extrinsic motivation The desire to perform a behavior because of promised rewards or the threats of punishment (p. 153)

Extroverts People who focus more attention on the external world, seek out and enjoy others' company, and tend to be confident and socially outgoing (pp. 312, 318)

F

Facial feedback hypothesis Proposes that specific facial expressions trigger the subjective experience of specific emotions (p. 171)

Factor analysis A statistical technique that allows researchers to identify clusters of test items that are related, or correlated, to one another (pp. 316, 475)

Family therapy Therapy designed to constructively change the way in which family members relate to one another (p. 538)

Fetal alcohol syndrome Physical and cognitive abnormalities in children that result when pregnant women consume large quantities of alcohol (p. 216)

Fetus The developing human organism from about nine weeks after fertilization to birth (p. 216)

Fight-or-flight response A rapid physiological reaction by the sympathetic nervous system to threatening events that prepares you either to fight or take flight from an immediate threat (p. 186)

Figure-ground relationship Basic rule of form perception that when you focus on an object, it stands out from its surroundings (p. 122)

Five-Factor Model A trait theory asserting that personality consists of five basic traits (openness to experience, conscientiousness, extroversion, agreeableness, and neuroticism) (p. 317)

Fixed-interval reinforcement schedule Reinforcement occurs for the first response after a fixed time interval has elapsed (p. 357)

Fixed-ratio reinforcement schedule A schedule of reinforcement that reinforces behavior after a certain number of responses (p. 355)

Flashbulb memories Vivid memories of surprising and emotional events that are personally important (p. 387)

Fluid intelligence Involves ability to perform tasks requiring rapid manipulation of ideas, abstract problem solving, and difficult mental effort (p. 294); a person's mental ability to learn or invent strategies (p. 476)

Flynn effect The tendency for performance on IQ tests to improve from one generation to the next (p. 471)

Forebrain The part of the brain above the midbrain that controls emotional reactions, thought processes, movement, sensory information, and body temperature (p. 75)

Formal operational stage Beginning around age 11, children reason abstractly and make predictions about hypothetical situations (p. 237)

Form perception The process by which sensations are organized into meaningful shapes and patterns (p. 121)

Fovea Small area near the center of the retina in which cones are concentrated (p. 100)

Fraternal twins Dizygotic twins develop from the union of two separate sperms and eggs (p. 85)

Free association A psychodynamic therapy technique in which clients say whatever comes to mind (p. 542)

Frequency The number of sound waves that pass through a given point in one second (p. 105)

Freudian slip Occurs when feelings buried within the unconscious are accidentally revealed through statements when the ego's guard is down (pp. 310, 542)

Frontal lobes A section of the cerebral cortex located at the front of the cerebral hemispheres just behind the forehead; involved in the coordination of movement and higher mental processes, such as planning, social skills, emotional control, and abstract thinking (p. 76)

Frustrations Feelings that occur whenever you are hindered or prevented from reaching goals you seek (p. 183)

Functional age A measure of how well you can physically and mentally function in your surroundings (p. 286)

Functional fixedness The tendency to think of objects as functioning in fixed and unchanging ways and ignoring other less obvious ways in which they might be used (p. 426)

Functionalism An early approach to psychology that tried to discover how the conscious mind functions to help humans survive in their environment (p. 7)

Functional magnetic resonance imaging (fMRI) A brain-imaging technique that measures the average neural activity in different brain regions over a few seconds (p. 73)

Fundamental attribution error The tendency to make internal attributions rather than external attributions when trying to explain other people's actions (p. 566)

G

Gate-control theory A theory describing how pain signals open a neurological "pain gate" in the spinal cord and how other touch signals close the gate (p. 112)

Gender Refers to the meanings that a society and the people within it attach to being female and male (p. 228)

Gender identity The knowledge that you are a male or a female (p. 228)

General adaptation syndrome (GAS) Selye's theory that the body responds to stress in three stages: alarm, resistance, and exhaustion (p. 188)

General intelligence factor (g-factor) A general intelligence ability which underlies all mental abilities (p. 475)

Generalized anxiety disorder (GAD) An anxiety disorder involving a constant state of moderate anxiety not associated with an object or situation (p. 508)

Generativity versus stagnation Crisis of middle adulthood, which states that people who fail to contribute and produce something that they feel is worthy of their efforts experience a sense of stagnation, or lack of purpose, in their lives (p. 284)

Generic masculine The use of masculine nouns and pronouns to refer to all people, regardless of their gender (p. 410)

Genes The basic biochemical units of heredity (p. 84)

Geneticists Scientists who study genes, the basic biochemical units of heredity (p. 84)

Genetic preprogramming theory of aging A theory that human cells have a built-in time limit to their ability to copy themselves (p. 293)

Genotype The particular genetic blueprint you inherit from your mother and father (p. 85)

Gerontology The area in psychology and biology that studies late adulthood and aging (p. 289)

Gestalt Meaningful whole (p. 121)

Gestalt psychology An early approach to psychology that studied how the mind actively organizes stimuli into meaningful wholes (p. 7)

Glial cells Supply neurons with support, nutrients, and insulation (p. 65)

Grammar Rules about using sounds and words in a language (p. 408)

Group People who depend on and interact with one another on a regular basis (p. 601)

Group therapy The treatment of several clients at the same time under the guidance of a therapist (p. 538)

H

Habits Activities that are so well learned that you carry them out automatically, without conscious thought (p. 382)

Hallucinations Sensations and perceptions that occur without any external stimulation (p. 456); hearing or seeing things that are not there (p. 521)

Hallucinogens Psychoactive drugs that dramatically alter consciousness and produce hallucinations; *also called* Psychedelics (p. 457)

Hammer Small vibrating bone in the ear (p. 106)

Health psychologists Psychologists who study how people's thoughts and behavior affect their health (p. 183)

Heredity The transmission of genetic characteristics from parents to their children (p. 84)

Heuristic A problem-solving strategy that involves following a general rule of thumb to reduce the number of possible solutions (p. 423)

Hierarchy of needs Maslow's ladder of human needs in which more basic physiological and safety needs must be satisfied before you are motivated to satisfy higher-level psychological needs (p. 155)

Hindbrain The part of the brain found at the rear base of the skull that controls the most basic biological needs for life (p. 74)

Hippocampus The structure in the forebrain's limbic system that is important in memory formation (p. 75)

Histrionic personalities People with this personality disorder are often excessively emotional and attention seeking, frequently turning minor incidents into full-blown dramas (p. 524)

Homeostasis A constant internal body state (p. 75); the tendency to keep physiological systems internally balanced by adjusting them in response to change (p. 151)

Hormones Chemical messengers, carried by the bloodstream, that regulate or stimulate the body (p. 70)

Hostile aggression The intentional use of harmful behavior where the goal is to cause injury or death (p. 578)

Humanistic psychology An approach to psychology that emphasizes human beings' inborn desire for personal growth and their ability to consciously make choices (p. 14)

Humanistic therapies Psychotherapies that help people get in touch with their feelings, their "true selves," and their purpose in life (p. 543)

Hypnosis A state of altered attention and awareness in which a person is unusually responsive to suggestions (p. 448)

Hypnotizability The degree to which a person can enter a deep hypnotic state (p. 450)

Hypochondriasis A somatoform disorder involving an irrational fear of developing some disease (p. 503)

Hypothalamus The brain structure located under the thalamus that provides homeostasis, or a constant internal body state; also regulates eating, drinking, and sexual behavior and controls the release of hormones from the pituitary gland (p. 75)

Hypothesis An educated guess, or prediction, about the nature of things based on a theory (p. 33)

I

Id An unconscious part of your mind that contains the basic drives for reproduction, survival, and aggression (p. 308)

Ideal self Person you want to become (p. 313)

Identical twins Monozygotic twins develop from the union of the same egg and sperm that have split and have exactly the same genotype (p. 85)

Identity achievement Refers to people who are likely to have a feeling of self-acceptance, a high need for achievement, and clear ideas about their personal beliefs and values (p. 265)

Identity diffusion Refers to teenagers who have not explored possible identities and who have made no commitments to any life path (p. 265)

Identity foreclosure Occurs when teenagers have chosen a life path without exploring different identities (p. 265)

Identity status Where an adolescent is in the identity development process (p. 264)

Identity versus role confusion Stage of life where you exercise more complex thinking skills in trying to figure out how to define yourself in your social surroundings (p. 263)

Illusion of transparency False belief that your thoughts, feelings, and emotions are more detectable to others than is actually the case (p. 326)

Imaginary audience A common adolescent belief that other people are constantly focusing their thoughts, feelings, and behavior on you (p. 259)

Immune system Your body's primary defense against disease (p. 189)

Implicit attitude An attitude that is activated automatically from memory, without awareness that you possess it (p. 571)

Implicit memory Memory of previous experiences without conscious recollection (p. 382)

Implicit prejudice Unconsciously held prejudicial attitudes (p. 612)

Impression formation The process of combining information about a person into an overall judgment (p. 563)

Incentive A positive or negative stimulus in the environment that attracts or repels you (p. 153)

Incentive theory A theory proposing that any stimulus that has either positive or negative outcomes for you will become an incentive for behavior (p. 153)

Independent variable The variable that is manipulated in an experiment (p. 43)

Indirect aggression A form of social manipulation in which the aggressor tries to harm another person without a face-to-face encounter (p. 579)

Individualism A philosophy of life stressing that the individual is more important than the group (p. 17)

Industrial–organizational psychology Focuses on ways to select, motivate, and evaluate employees, as well as improving the management structure and working conditions (p. 20)

Inferential statistics Mathematical methods used to determine whether the data support or do not support the research hypothesis (p. 51)

Ingroup A group to which a person belongs and which forms a part of his or her social identity (p. 602)

Inhalants Chemicals whose vapors can be breathed in to produce a mind-altering effect (p. 458)

Initiative The ability to act independently (p. 229)

Insecure attachment style Developed by children with parents who are inattentive to their needs (p. 224)

Insight A problem-solving strategy that involves a sudden realization of how a problem can be solved (p. 424); the process of helping psychotherapy clients understand their own psychological processes (p. 541)

Insomnia The chronic inability to fall or stay asleep (p. 445)

Instinct An unlearned, inherited fixed pattern of behavior (p. 150)

Instinctual drift Instinctual behaviors of animals have that can prevent them from reliably performing certain behaviors (p. 359)

Institutional discrimination Occurs when a person is carrying out the discriminatory guidelines of institutions (p. 610)

Instrumental aggression The intentional use of harmful behavior to achieve some other goal (p. 578)

Insulin A blood hormone that decreases appetite (p. 158)

Integrity versus despair A theory of psychosocial development which states that elderly adults face their last crisis by reviewing their life's accomplishments and failures (p. 291)

Intelligence Mental abilities to adapt to and shape the environment (p. 467)

Intelligence quotient (IQ) Ratio of mental age divided by chronological age, multiplied by 100 (p. 469)

Intergroup anxiety Anxiety due to expecting negative consequences when interacting with an outgroup member (p. 615)

Internal attribution Occurs when your explanation for your description of someone else's behavior is that the behavior is being caused by something inside the person, such as personality traits, moods, attitudes, abilities, or effort (p. 566)

Internal locus of control A belief that things happen because of your own efforts (p. 322)

Interneurons Connect neurons to one another; most important function is to connect the sensory neurons' input signals with the motor neurons' output signals (p. 64)

Interpersonal intelligence The ability to get along well with others and to reliably predict their motives and behavior; this ability is important for salespersons and office managers (p. 477)

Interval schedule Partial reinforcement schedule that is based on the passage of time (p. 355)

Intimacy versus isolation Belief that without close, loving relationships, adults become emotionally isolated and self-absorbed (p. 278)

Intrapersonal intelligence Having insight into your own motives and behavior, which is an ability important for psychologists and religious leaders (p. 477)

Intrinsic motivation The desire to perform a behavior for its own sake (p. 153)

Introspection A procedure used by trained observers to study the mind's structure in which they look at, smell, or touch something and then try to describe in detail what they are experiencing (p. 6)

Introverts People who focus more attention on their inner world and tend to be hesitant and cautious when interacting with people (pp. 312, 318)

Iris A ring of muscles that range in color from light blue to dark brown (p. 100)

J

James-Lange theory A theory that emotion-provoking events produce specific physiological changes that your brain automatically interprets as specific emotions (p. 169)

K

Kinesthetic sense Provides information about the movement and location of different parts of your body (p. 112)

L

Language A way of communicating information using symbols and the rules for combining them (p. 405)

Language acquisition device Noam Chomsky's linguistic theory proposing that an inborn mental program enables children to learn language (p. 415)

Latent content True meaning of the dream which is hidden from the dreamer to avoid anxiety (p. 444)

Latent learning Learning that occurs without any reinforcement but is not demonstrated until reinforcement is provided (p. 360)

Laws of grouping Gestalt principles that describe how you group objects together into a meaningful whole (p. 123)

Leader Person who exerts the most influence and provides direction and energy to the group (p. 604)

Learned helplessness A defeated and helpless state of mind produced by repeatedly being exposed to uncontrollable life events (p. 194)

Learning A change in behavior due to experience (p. 339)

Lens A clear, elastic, disc-shaped structure that refocuses light (p. 100)

Limbic system A series of interrelated doughnut-shaped neural structures in the core of the forebrain; the system's two main structures are the amygdala and hippocampus (p. 75)

Linguistic intelligence The ability to communicate through written and spoken language (p. 477)

Linguistic relativity hypothesis A theory that the structure of language determines the structure of thought, meaning that people who speak different languages also think differently (p. 410)

Lobes The four major sections of both cerebral hemispheres (p. 76)

Locus of control The degree to which you expect that what happens to you in life depends on your own actions and personal qualities versus factors beyond your control (p. 322)

Logical-mathematical intelligence The ability to solve math problems and analyze arguments (p. 477)

Longitudinal studies Research in which the same people are restudied and retested over time (p. 217, 276)

Long-term memory A lasting memory system that holds an enormous amount of information (p. 376)

Looks-for-status exchange The theory stating that women exchange their beauty for social power and men exchange their social power for their partner's beauty (p. 564)

Loose associations Occurs when a person has thoughts that are disconnected from one another and from the world around them (p. 521)

LSD Potent synthesized hallucinogenic drug that is structurally similar to the neurotransmitter serotonin (p. 458)

Lucid dreams Dreams in which you are aware that you are dreaming (p. 443)

M

Magnetic resonance imaging (MRI) A brain-imaging technique that produces three-dimensional images of the brain's soft tissues (p. 73)

Maintenance rehearsal The process of repeating information so it will stay in short-term memory or transfer to long-term memory (p. 379)

Major depressive disorder A mood disorder characterized by extreme and lasting negative moods and the inability to experience pleasure from activities one previously enjoyed (p. 511)

Mania An overly joyful, active emotional state (p. 514)

Manifest content Surface meaning of a dream (p. 444)

Marijuana Psychoactive drug that is made from the Cannabis plant (p. 458)

Mean The arithmetic average of the distribution of scores for a particular variable (p. 48)

Median The middle score in a distribution of scores after you rank the scores from the lowest to highest (p. 48)

Meditation Mental exercises that focus attention and increase awareness (p. 451)

Medulla The part of the hindbrain located at the top of the spinal cord that controls breathing, heart rate, swallowing, and digestion, and allows you to maintain an upright posture (p. 74)

Melatonin Hormone involved in resetting the body's sleep–wake cycle (p. 437)

Memory The mental process by which information is encoded and stored in the brain and later retrieved (p. 373)

Memory illusions False remembering (p. 389)

Menarche The first menstrual period (p. 251)

Menopause The ending of menstruation (p. 286)

Mental age Age that reflects the child's mental abilities in comparison to the average child of the same age (p. 467)

Mental retardation A condition of limited mental ability, indicated by an IQ score at or below 70 and difficulty in adapting to independent living (p. 483)

Mental set Tendency to continue using solutions that have worked in the past, even though better solutions may exist (p. 425)

Mental telepathy The supposed ability to perceive other people's thoughts (p. 139)

Mere exposure effect The tendency to develop positive attitudes toward objects and individuals to which you are repeatedly exposed (p. 569)

Mesmerized Spellbound state of mind; modern form is hypnosis (p. 448)

Methamphetamine (crystal meth) A very addictive stimulant that triggers the release of high levels of dopamine into the brain (p. 457)

Method of loci Visual mnemonic in which you mentally place items to be memorized in specific locations, such as rooms in your house (p. 390)

Microsleep Periods in which you momentarily tune out your surroundings (p. 442)

Midbrain The part of the brain above the hindbrain that plays a role in attention, stimulation, and consciousness (p. 74)

Midlife crisis A stressful period experienced by a few middle-aged adults when they review and reevaluate their lives (p. 287)

Minnesota Multiphasic Personality Inventory (MMPI) An objective personality test consisting of true-false questions that measure various personality dimensions and clinical conditions such as depression (p. 329)

Minority influence The way dissenters produce change within a group (p. 607)

Minority slowness effect The tendency of those who hold a minority opinion to express that opinion less quickly than people who hold the majority opinion (p. 607)

Mirror neurons Specialized brain cells that trigger mimicry (p. 419)

Misinformation effects Changes in memories due to a person being exposed to misleading information (p. 386)

Mnemonics Mental strategies that make it easier to remember information (p. 389)

Mode The score that occurs most frequently in a distribution (p. 48)

Monocular cues Depth cues that require information from only one eye (p. 125)

Mood-congruent memory The tendency to recall experiences that are consistent with your current mood (p. 389)

Mood disorders Psychological disorders characterized by emotional extremes that cause significant disruption in daily functioning (p. 511)

Moon illusion The moon appears to be about 1½ times larger when near the horizon than when high in the sky (p. 134)

Moral reasoning The process of distinguishing between good and bad conduct (p. 256)

Moratorium status Refers to teenagers who are either diffused or foreclosed in their identity status; they believe that they are not yet ready to become adults and are exploring possible identities (p. 265)

Morning people People who wake up early, alert, and full of energy, but go to bed before 10:00 P.M. (p. 442)

Morphemes The smallest units of language that carry meaning (p. 408)

Motivation An inner state that energizes behavior toward a goal (p. 149)

Motor neurons Neurons in the somatic nervous system that send commands from the brain to glands, muscles, and organs (pp. 64, 68)

Müeller-Lyer illusion Misperceiving the length of lines when either inward or outward facing "wings" are placed on the ends of the lines (p. 131)

Multiple intelligences Howard Gardner's theory that there are at least eight separate intelligences all of which are developed differently in each individual (p. 477)

Musical intelligence The ability to analyze, compose, or perform music (p. 477)

Myelin sheath Protective coating of fatty cells that covers neural axons and speeds up the passing of information (pp. 65, 218)

N

Narcissistic personalities People with this personality disorder seek attention, and desire constant admiration (p. 524)

Narcolepsy Sleep disorder characterized by uncontrollable REM sleep attacks during normal waking hours (p. 445)

Naturalistic observation A scientific method that describes how people or animals behave in their natural environment (p. 38)

Naturalist intelligence The ability to see patterns in nature, as found in forest rangers, ecologists, and zoologists (p. 477)

Need for individuation Carl Jung's theory that people are motivated by a desire for psychological growth and wholeness (p. 311)

Need to achieve A desire to overcome obstacles and meet high standards of excellence (p. 164)

Need to belong The need to interact with others and be socially accepted; *also called* Need for affiliation (p. 163)

Negative punishers Weaken a response by removing a positive stimulus after a response (p. 354)

Negative reinforcer Strengthens a response by removing an unpleasant stimulus after a response (p. 352)

Neodissociation theory A theory that hypnosis is an altered state with two streams of consciousness operating at the same time, one actively responding to suggestions and the other passively observing (p. 450)

Neurons Specialized cells in the nervous system that send and receive information throughout the body (p. 63)

Neuroticism Describes how people differ in terms of being anxious, high-strung, insecure, and self-pitying versus relaxed, calm, secure, and content (p. 319)

Neurotics People low in emotional stability (p. 319)

Neurotransmitters Chemical messages that travel between nerve cells and muscles to trigger or prevent an impulse in the receiving cell (p. 65)

Nightmares Common, anxiety-producing dreams that occur during REM sleep among adults and children (p. 445)

Night people People who stay up later in the evening and have a hard time getting up early in the morning (p. 442)

Night terror A panic attack that generally occurs during early-night stage 4 NREM sleep in children between the ages of three and eight (p. 445)

Nonconscious mimicry Adopting the behaviors, postures, or mannerisms of others with whom you are interacting without your awareness (p. 419)

Nonverbal communication Sending and receiving of information using gestures, expressions, and body movements rather than words (p. 418)

Normal distribution The bell-shaped curve that occurs on a graph when the mean, median, and mode are identical in value (p. 48)

Norms The established and approved ways of behaving around others (p. 502)

NREM sleep Non-rapid-eye-movement sleep characterized by slow, regular breathing; absence of body movement; and slow, regular brain activity; *also called* Quiet sleep (p. 441)

O

Obedience The performance of an action in response to a direct order (p. 597)

Obesity The excessive accumulation of body fat (p. 160)

Objective tests A personality test that asks direct, clearly understood questions about your conscious thoughts, feelings, and behavior (p. 328)

Object permanence The realization that an object continues to exist even if you can't see it or touch it (p. 233)

Observational learning Learning by observing and deciding what to imitate in the behavior of others (p. 362)

Obsessions Recurring thoughts or ideas that cause distress or interfere significantly with ongoing activity (p. 508)

Obsessive-compulsive disorder (OCD) An anxiety disorder characterized by recurring, unwanted, and distressing actions and/or thoughts (p. 508)

Occipital lobes The visual regions of the brain located at the back of the cerebral hemispheres that allow you to experience shapes, color, and motion (p. 76)

Off-line dream theory A theory that dreaming is a time for consolidating and storing information gathered during the day (p. 444)

Olfactory nerve The nerve that transmits neural impulses containing smell information from the nose to the brain (p. 109)

Open to experience One of the five basic personality traits that means you are adventurous, sensitive, and passionate, with a childlike wonder at the world (p. 317)

Operant conditioning A type of learning in which behavior is strengthened if followed by reinforcement and weakened if followed by punishment (p. 350)

Operational definition A very clear description of how a variable has been measured (p. 34)

Optic nerve Carries information from the retina to the brain (p. 101)

Optimistic explanatory style Explains negative events as due to external factors that are unstable or changeable and isolated (p. 198)

Outgroup Any group with which you do not share membership (p. 610)

P

Panic disorder An anxiety disorder characterized by episodes of intense anxiety without an apparent reason (p. 506)

Paranoid personalities People with this personality disorder are distrustful and suspicious of others' motives (p. 523)

Paraphrasing Therapy technique in which the therapist summarizes the client's statements (p. 544)

Parapsychology The field that studies ESP and other paranormal phenomena (p. 139)

Parasympathetic nervous system The part of the autonomic nervous system that conserves and maintains the body's energy resources (p. 69)

Parietal lobes A section of the cerebral cortex located in front of the occipital lobes; involved in touch sensation and how you experience yourself in the space around you (p. 76)

Participant observation A scientific method in which a researcher describes behavior as it occurs in its natural environment, and does so as a participant of the group being studied (p. 39)

Particles Electrically charged units of matter (p. 99)

Passionate love A state of intense emotional and physical longing for another person; experienced most strongly during the early stages of a romantic relationship (p. 278)

Peak experiences A fleeting but intense moment when you feel happy, absorbed, and extremely capable (p. 314)

Perception The process that organizes stimuli into meaningful objects and events (p. 121)

Perceptual constancy Perceiving objects as not changing even though there is constantly changing sensory information (p. 127)

Perceptual illusion A misperception of physical reality caused by misapplying one or more perceptual principles (p. 131)

Perceptual set An expectation that creates a tendency to interpret sensory information in a particular way (p. 129)

Peripheral nervous system The nerves that connect the brain and spinal cord with the organs and tissues of the body (p. 68)

Peripheral route to persuasion Occurs when you are unable or unwilling to analyze a persuasive message (p. 573)

Permissive parents Parents who allow their children to set their own rules, make few demands, and submit to their children's desires (p. 227)

Personal fable Teenagers' tendency to believe that no one has ever felt or thought as they do (p. 261)

Personal identity Your understanding of what makes you unique as an individual and different from others; *also called* Self-concept (p. 263)

Personality A person's unique way of thinking, feeling, and acting (p. 307)

Personality disorders Psychological disorders characterized by general styles of living that are ineffective and lead to problems (p. 523)

Personality psychology Studies how people are influenced by relatively stable internal traits (p. 19)

Persuasion The process of trying to change attitudes through communicating a particular message (p. 572)

Pessimistic explanatory style Explains negative events in life as being caused by internal factors that are stable and global (p. 198)

Phobia An object or situation that causes a powerful, irrational fear (p. 547)

Phobic disorder An anxiety disorder characterized by strong irrational fears of specific objects or situations (p. 506)

Phonemes The basic units of sound in speech (p. 408)

Phonology The rules for combining basic sounds into words (p. 408)

Physical attractiveness stereotype The belief that physically attractive individuals have better personalities and lead happier lives than less attractive people (p. 563)

Physical dependence Occurs when a person needs a drug to function normally (p. 454)

Pitch Physical sensation of frequency results in psychological experience of high and low sounds (p. 105)

Pituitary gland Pea-sized structure located in the base of the brain; the pituitary gland is controlled by a nearby brain area called the hypothalamus (p. 70)

Pleasure principle If it feels good, do it, and do it now rather than later (p. 308)

Pons The part of the hindbrain located just above the medulla that is concerned with sleep and arousal (p. 74)

Ponzo illusion Misapplying the monocular distance cue of linear perspective (p. 131)

Population A larger group of research subjects from which a sample is selected (p. 34)

Positive psychology A relatively new approach to psychology that studies how people find mental health and happiness in their everyday living (p. 14)

Positive punishers Weaken a response by presenting an unpleasant stimulus after a response (p. 353)

Positive reinforcer Strengthens a response by presenting a positive stimulus after a response (p. 352)

Positron emission tomography (PET) scan A brain-imaging technique that measures the average neural activity in different brain regions over a few minutes (p. 73)

Postconventional morality Moral reasoning based on abstract principles and values that may conflict with your own interests and societal norms (p. 257)

Post-traumatic stress disorder (PTSD) An anxiety disorder involving flashbacks and recurrent thoughts of life-threatening or other traumatic events (p. 509)

Practical intelligence Intelligence required to use ideas in everyday situations (p. 479)

Precognition The supposed ability to perceive events in the future (p. 139)

Preconscious mind The part of the mind that consists of those mental processes of which you are not currently conscious, but could become so at any moment (p. 308)

Preconventional morality Selfish moral reasoning based on avoiding punishment or seeking rewards (p. 257)

Prejudice A negative attitude toward members of a specific group (p. 610)

Prenatal development The many changes that transform a fertilized egg into a newborn baby (p. 215)

Primacy effect The increased memory for the first bits of information presented in a string of information (p. 376)

Primary appraisal A stage of cognitive appraisal that involves a quick evaluation of the situation (p. 192)

Primary reinforcer Naturally reinforcing because it satisfies some biological need (p. 352)

Primary sex characteristics The reproductive organs (p. 251)

Priming The process by which one memory concept activates another memory concept (p. 384)

Proactive interference Forgetting due to interference from previously learned information (p. 395)

Problem-focused coping A strategy aimed at reducing stress by overcoming the source of the problem (p. 192)

Problem solving Thought process used to overcome obstacles and reach goals (p. 422)

Productive aging The perspective that elderly adults are capable of making valuable contributions to society (p. 290)

Progressive relaxation A relaxation technique that involves progressively relaxing muscle groups in your body (p. 203)

Projection Defense mechanism that involves perceiving your own unacceptable urges or weaknesses, not in yourself, but in others (p. 311)

Projective test A psychological test that asks you to respond to ambiguous stimuli or situations in ways that reveal your unconscious motives and desires (p. 327)

Proprioceptive senses Sources of sensory information that detect body position and movement (p. 112)

Prototype The most representative member of a concept (p. 422)

Psychiatry A branch of medicine concerned with the diagnosis and treatment of psychological disorders (p. 6)

Psychoactive drugs Chemicals that change mental processes and behavior (p. 454)

Psychoanalysis An approach to psychology that studies how human behavior is determined by hidden or unconscious motives and desires (p. 13); Freudian therapy, as originally practiced by Sigmund Freud (p. 541)

Psychobiology An approach to psychology that studies how the brain and other areas of our biology influence behavior (p. 16)

Psychodynamic therapies A variety of psychotherapies based on the work of Sigmund Freud claiming that psychological disorders are caused by unconscious conflict (p. 541)

Psychokinesis The supposed ability to control objects through mental manipulation, such as causing a chair to move or a flipped coin to land either heads or tails (p. 139)

Psychological dependence Occurs when a drug user experiences mental and emotional desires for the drug (p. 454)

Psychological disorder A pattern of unusual behavior that results in personal distress or significant interference in a person's ability to engage in normal daily living (p. 501)

Psychology The scientific study of mental processes and behavior (p. 6)

Psychophysics The study of how physical stimuli are translated into psychological experience (p. 94)

Psychophysiological disorders Stress-related physical illnesses (p. 189)

Psychosurgery A rarely used surgical procedure to treat psychological disorders in which brain tissue thought to be the cause of the disorder is destroyed (p. 555)

Psychotherapy The treatment of psychological disorders using methods that include a personal relationship between a trained therapist and the individual or individuals seeking treatment (p. 533)

Puberty The growth period in which a person reaches sexual maturity and becomes capable of reproducing (p. 250)

Punishment The process by which a stimulus decreases the probability of the behavior it follows (p. 353)

Pupil An opening in the iris that allows light to enter the eye (p. 100)

R

Random assignment A procedure ensuring that all research participants have an equal chance of being exposed to different levels of the independent variable (p. 43)

Random selection A procedure for selecting a sample of people to study in which everyone in the population has an equal chance of being chosen (p. 34)

Rapid smoking Type of aversive conditioning used to help people stop smoking (p. 549)

Rational-emotive therapy (RET) Cognitive therapy in which people are confronted with their irrational beliefs and persuaded to develop a more realistic way of thinking (p. 550)

Rationalization Defense mechanism that occurs when you give what seem like logical explanations for your attitudes, beliefs, or behavior in place of the real, unconscious reasons (p. 310)

Ratio schedule Partial reinforcement schedule that is based on the number of correct responses made between reinforcements (p. 355)

Reaction formation Defense mechanism that occurs when unconscious, unacceptable impulses are consciously expressed as their exact opposite (p. 311)

Reaction range The extent to which genetically determined limits on IQ may increase or decrease due to environmental factors (p. 488)

Realistic group conflict theory A theory that intergroup conflict develops from competition for limited resources (p. 611)

Recall A test of explicit memory in which a person must retrieve and reproduce information from memory (p. 388)

Recency effect The increased memory for the last bits of information presented in a string of information (p. 376)

Reciprocal determinism The social-cognitive belief that your personality emerges from an ongoing mutual interaction among your cognitions and actions, and your environment (p. 320)

Reciprocity norm The expectation that you should return a favor or a good deed (p. 595)

Recognition A test of explicit memory in which a person must decide whether or not the information has been encountered before (p. 388)

Reference group Group with which you identify, using its standards to judge yourself and the world (p. 570)

Reflex An automatic body response to a stimulus that is involuntary (p. 219)

Regression Defense mechanism that occurs when you experience a great deal of anxiety and begin behaving as if you were a very young child (p. 311)

Reinforcement The process by which a stimulus increases the probability of the behavior that it follows (p. 351)

Reinforcer Stimulus that increases the probability that the behavior it follows will be repeated (p. 351)

Relational leadership Involves an attention to the emotions and the relationships within the group (p. 604)

Reliability The degree to which a test yields consistent results (p. 472)

REM (rapid eye movement) sleep Active phase in the sleep cycle during which dreaming occurs, characterized by rapid eye movements; *also called* Active sleep (p. 441)

Replication Repeating an earlier study's scientific procedures, using different participants in an attempt to duplicate the findings (p. 35)

Representational thought The ability to picture (or represent) something in your mind, even when it is not physically present (p. 234)

Repression Defense mechanism which involves the ego banishing into the unconscious any thoughts or feelings that arouse too much anxiety (p. 310); motivated forgetting that occurs when a person unconsciously pushes unpleasant memories out of his or her mind (p. 396)

Resistance Anything clients do that interferes with them understanding their psychological problems (p. 542)

Restrained eater Worrying and trying to control what and how much you eat (p. 158)

Reticular formation A structure in the midbrain that is involved in the regulation and maintenance of consciousness and sleep (p. 74)

Retina The light-sensitive surface at the back of the eye (p. 100)

Retinal disparity Degree of difference between two images which is greater when objects are closer to the viewer (p. 124)

Retrieval The third memory process, which involves recovering stored information from memory so it can be used (p. 374)

Retrieval cue A stimulus that helps you recall information from long-term memory (p. 389)

Retroactive interference Forgetting due to interference from newly learned information (p. 395)

Retrograde Backward moving (p. 396)

Retrograde amnesia The loss of information previously stored in long-term memory due to physical injury to the brain (p. 396)

Ritalin (methylphenidate) A stimulant drug used to treat attention-deficit/hyperactivity disorder (ADHD) in children (p. 457)

Rods Photoreceptors in the eyes that are extremely sensitive to light and are important in detecting patterns of black, white, and gray; rods function best under low-light conditions so are most useful at night (p. 100)

Rorschach Inkblot Test A projective personality test in which you are shown pictures of inkblots and asked what you see in the shapes (p. 327)

S

Sample A group of subjects who are selected to participate in a research study (p. 34)

Schema An organized cluster of knowledge that you use to understand and interpret information (pp. 232–233)

Schizophrenia A psychological disorder characterized by severe problems in thinking, including hallucinations, delusions, or loose associations (p. 521)

Scholastic Assessment Test (SAT) Achievement test that measures a person's learned verbal and mathematical skills; taken by high school students in preparation for entrance into college (p. 468)

Scientific methods A set of procedures used to gather, analyze, and interpret information in a way that reduces error and leads to dependable conclusions (p. 29)

Seasonal affective disorder (SAD) Involves symptoms of depression at particular times of the year, especially during the winter months, when daylight hours are reduced (p. 516)

Secondary appraisal A stage of cognitive appraisal in which you assess whether you have the ability to cope with the stressor (p. 192)

Secondary reinforcer Learned, and becomes reinforcing by being associated with a primary reinforcer (p. 352)

Secondary sex characteristics The non-reproductive physical features that distinguish women and men from one another (p. 251)

Secure attachment style Developed by children with parents who are nurturing and sensitive to their needs (p. 224)

Self-actualization The ultimate goal of human growth (p. 156); the process of fulfilling your potential (p. 313)

Self-awareness A state of mind where you think about yourself (p. 226)

Self-concept The theory or story that you form about yourself through your life experiences and interactions with others (p. 225); your understanding of what makes you unique as an individual and different from others; *also called* Personal identity (p. 263)

Self-efficacy Your belief about your ability to perform behaviors that should bring about a desired outcome (p. 320)

Self-esteem The evaluation of your self-concept as being good, bad, or mediocre (p. 226)

Self-fulfilling prophecy The process by which someone's expectations about a person or group leads to the fulfillment of those expectations (p. 492)

Self-help group Several people regularly meeting and discussing their problems with one another without the guidance of a therapist (p. 538)

Self-report inventory A personality test in which you evaluate yourself (p. 328)

Self-serving bias The tendency to take credit for success while denying blame for failure (p. 321)

Semantics The rules for communicating the meaning of words, phrases, and sentences (p. 408)

Sensation The process that detects stimuli from your body and environment (p. 93)

Sensorimotor stage Stage in which infants develop the ability to coordinate sensory input with motor actions (p. 233)

Sensorineural hearing loss Involves nerve problems in the inner ear; often occurs because hair cells in the cochlea are damaged either by disease, injury, or aging (pp. 106–107)

Sensory adaptation The tendency for sensory receptors to decrease in response to stimuli that continue at the same level (p. 97)

Sensory memory A memory system that very briefly stores a vast amount of information received from your five senses (p. 377)

Sensory neurons Neurons in the somatic nervous system that receive sensory information from the muscles and skin (p. 64); they pick up stimuli inside the body or in the world and send input signals to the brain (p. 68)

Sensory receptor Receptor sites for the senses; connecting neurons in the sense organs send sensory information to the brain (p. 94)

Separation anxiety Fear and distress that infants display when separated from their primary caregiver (p. 223)

Serotonin Neurotransmitter important in regulating emotions, aggression, appetite, and sleep (p. 67)

Set point A level of body weight that the body works to maintain (p. 159)

Sex chromosomes One pair of chromosomes in the body cells that determine the sex of a baby (p. 85)

Shape constancy Tendency to perceive an object as the same shape regardless of the angle from which it is viewed (p. 127)

Shaping The process of teaching a new behavior by reinforcing closer and closer approximations to the desired behavior (p. 358)

Short-term memory A memory system that holds information briefly while you actively work with the information (p. 376)

Signal-detection theory A theory stating that detecting a stimulus is influenced by a person's decision-making strategy (p. 94)

Size constancy Perception of an object as having the same size in spite of changes in the size of its retinal image when it is viewed from different distances (p. 127)

Sleep apnea Sleep disorder in which sleeping individuals briefly stop breathing several times an hour, interrupting sleep without the person's knowledge (p. 446)

Sleep spindles Bursts of rapid, rhythmic brain-wave activity (p. 440)

Sleepwalking A disorder in which a person wanders during early-night NREM sleep (p. 445)

Social-cognitive perspective Personality theory that examines how people analyze and use information about themselves and about others (p. 320)

Social influence The exercise of social power by a person or group to change the attitudes or behavior of others in a certain direction (p. 591)

Social influence theory of hypnosis Theory that hypnosis is a normal state of consciousness in which people act the way they think hypnotized persons are supposed to act (p. 451)

Socialization The process of learning about yourself and your culture and how to live within it (p. 225)

Social learning theory People learn social behaviors mainly by observing and imitating others rather than through direct experience (p. 362)

Social norm An expected way to behave and believe that is established and enforced by a group (p. 592)

Social phobia Phobia which involves a fear of being negatively evaluated by others or acting in ways that are embarrassing (p. 507)

Social psychology The scientific study of how people's thoughts, feelings, and behavior are influenced by others (pp. 19, 563)

Social roles Roles we play in our lives such as the role of son, daughter, student, or employee (p. 227)

Social support Helpful coping resources that friends and other people provide when you are in a stressful situation (p. 201)

Sociocultural psychology An approach to psychology that studies how social surroundings and culture shape thinking and behavior (p. 16)

Soma Central part of a neuron (p. 64)

Somatic nervous system A division of the peripheral nervous system that sends commands to voluntary skeletal muscles and receives sensory information from the muscles and skin (p. 68)

Somatoform disorders Psychological problems that involve some body symptom, even though no actual physical cause of the symptom can be found (p. 503)

Sound waves Vibrations in air, water, or solid material (p. 105)

Spatial intelligence Being skilled at perceiving and arranging objects in the environment (p. 477)

Specific phobia Phobia that involves fear and avoidance of a particular object or situation, such as heights, animals, enclosed spaces, blood, and automobile or air travel (p. 507)

Spermarche Males' first experience of ejaculation (p. 251)

Spinal cord A bundle of nerves that connects the brain to the rest of the body (p. 63)

Split-brain patients Patients who had the nerves of their corpus callosum surgically cut in what was once a treatment for severe epileptic seizures (p. 80)

Spontaneous recovery The reappearance of a response after a period of non-exposure to the conditioned stimulus (p. 344)

Standard deviation A measure of variation that indicates the average difference between the scores in a distribution and their mean (p. 50)

Standardization The process of establishing uniform procedures for administering a test and for interpreting its scores (p. 471)

Statistics A branch of mathematics that allows researchers to organize, describe, and make meaningful judgments from data they collect (p. 47)

Stereotype A fixed set of beliefs about a group of people that may or may not be accurate (p. 609)

Stimulants Drugs that speed up, or stimulate, the nervous system and increase mental and physical activity (p. 456)

Stimulus discrimination In classical conditioning, the tendency for a conditioned response to be elicited by the conditioned stimulus but not to stimuli similar to it (p. 346)

Stimulus generalization In classical conditioning, the tendency for a conditioned response to be triggered by stimuli similar to the conditioned stimulus (p. 344)

Stirrup Small vibrating bone in the ear (p. 106)

Storage The second memory process in which information is entered and maintained in memory for a period of time (p. 374)

Stranger anxiety Fear of strangers developed in infants at the age of six or seven months of age (p. 223)

Stress Response to events that disturb, or threaten to disturb, your physical or psychological balance (p. 183)

Stressors Internal or external events that challenge or threaten you (p. 183)

Stroboscopic movement The illusion of movement produced by a rapid pattern of stimulation on different parts of the retina (p. 132)

Structuralism An early approach to psychology that tried to identify the basic parts, or structure, of the conscious mind (p. 6)

Subliminal perception Processing of information that is below your threshold of conscious awareness (p. 138)

Successful intelligence Knowing when and how to use analytic, creative, and practical abilities (p. 480)

Superego The part of your mind that counterbalances the more primitive demands of the id (p. 309)

Superordinate goal A mutually shared goal that can only be achieved by the two groups cooperating (p. 612)

Suppression Motivated forgetting that occurs when a person consciously tries to forget something (p. 395)

Survey A structured set of questions or statements given to a group of people to measure their attitudes, beliefs, values, or behaviors (p. 41)

Sympathetic nervous system The part of the autonomic nervous system that activates the body's energy resources to deal with threatening situations (p. 69)

Symptom A sign of a disorder (p. 501)

Synapse Space between the axon's terminal buttons and the dendrites; less than a millionth of an inch wide (p. 65)

Synesthesia Rare condition in which people perceive stimuli in other senses, such as tasting color or shapes, hearing someone's touch, or feeling the sounds of musical instruments on their bodies (p. 108)

Syntax The rules for combining words into sentences (p. 408)

Systematic desensitization Counterconditioning technique used to treat phobias in which clients are gradually exposed to feared objects while remaining relaxed (p. 547)

T

Task leadership Consists of accomplishing the goals of the group (p. 604)

Taste buds Sensory receptor organs that contain the receptor cells for taste (p. 110)

Telegraphic speech An early speech phase in which children use short sentences, leaving out all but the important words, like in a telegram (p. 417)

Temporal lobes A section of the cerebral cortex located below the parietal lobes that are important in hearing and language (p. 76)

Tend-and-befriend response Response to stressors that involves women taking action to protect their children or seeking out other people for social support (p. 187)

Test-retest reliability Checking scores on the same test on two or more occasions (p. 472)

Thalamus The brain's sensory relay station that sorts and sends messages from the eyes, ears, tongue, and skin to other parts of the brain (p. 75)

THC Major psychoactive ingredient in marijuana (p. 458)

Thematic Apperception Test (TAT) A personality test in which you "project" your inner feelings and motives through the stories you make up about pictures (p. 328)

Theory An organized system of ideas that seeks to explain why two or more events are related (p. 33)

Theory of mind The commonsense knowledge about other people's thoughts and feelings that allows you to understand and predict their behavior (p. 237)

Theta waves Irregular, small, rapid brain waves associated with stage 1 sleep (p. 440)

Timbre Blending of different waves of different frequencies (p. 106)

Tip-of-the-tongue experience Being unable to remember something you know, followed by the feeling that it is just out of reach (p. 388)

Token economy The reinforcement of desirable behavior by using objects called tokens that can be exchanged for desired items or privileges (p. 549)

Trait A relatively stable tendency to behave in a particular way across a variety of situations (p. 316)

Trait perspective A descriptive approach to personality that identifies stable behavior patterns that a person displays over time and across situations (p. 316)

Transference The process by which the client develops positive or negative feelings for the therapist that represent feelings the client experienced toward others early in life (p. 542)

Transformational leader A leader who changes the outlook and behavior of followers so they are unselfish and work for the good of the group or society (p. 605)

Trial and error A problem-solving strategy that involves trying one possible solution after another until one works (p. 422)

Triarchic theory of intelligence Sternberg's theory that there are three sets of mental abilities making up human intelligence: analytic, creative, and practical (p. 479)

Two-factor theory A theory that experiencing an emotion often is based on becoming physiologically aroused and then attaching a cognitive label to the arousal (p. 170)

Type A behavior pattern A competitive, impatient, ambitious, hostile, hard-driving approach to life (p. 195)

Type B behavior pattern A patient, relaxed, easygoing approach to life, with little hurry or hostility (p. 195)

U

Unconditional positive regard Unquestioning love and acceptance (p. 313); therapists expressing warmth, kindness, and caring for psychotherapy clients without being judgmental (p. 543)

Unconditioned response (UCR) In classical conditioning, the unlearned, automatic response to an unconditioned stimulus (p. 340)

Unconditioned stimulus (UCS) In classical conditioning, a stimulus that naturally and automatically triggers an unconditioned response (p. 340)

Unconscious mind Thoughts, desires, feelings, and memories that are not consciously available to you but that nonetheless shape your everyday behavior (p. 308)

Unrestrained eater Unconcerned about controlling your eating (p. 158)

V

Validity The degree to which a test measures what it is designed to measure (p. 473)

Validity scales Scales that consist of items that detect suspicious response patterns indicating dishonesty, carelessness, defensiveness, or evasiveness (p. 330)

Variable-interval reinforcement schedule Partial reinforcement scale that reinforces the first response after a variable time interval has elapsed (p. 357)

Variable-ratio reinforcement schedule Partial reinforcement schedule that reinforces a response after a variable number of nonreinforced responses (p. 356)

Variables Factors that are capable of changing, or varying (p. 34)

Vestibular sense Provides information on the position of your body by sensing gravity and motion; *also called* Equilibrium (p. 112)

Vitreous humor A clear jelly-like liquid that occupies the space behind the lens of the eye (p. 100)

W

Wavelength The distance between two peaks of light waves (p. 99)

Wear-and-tear theory of aging A theory that human cells gradually wear out after years of damage (p. 293)

Weber's law The principle that to be noticed as different, two stimuli must differ by a constant minimum percentage rather than by a constant amount (p. 96)

Wernicke's aphasia Damage to an area of the brain that often harms people's ability to understand and correctly use language (p. 406)

Wernicke's area A brain area at the back of the left temporal lobe that allows people to recognize and understand spoken words (p. 406)

Wisdom Expert knowledge and judgment about important issues in life (p. 297)

Y

Yerkes-Dodson law A theory that states individuals perform best when maintaining an intermediate level of physiological arousal (p. 152)

Z

Zygote A fertilized human egg during the first two weeks following conception (p. 215)

REFERENCES

A

Aamodt, S., & Wang, S. (2008). *Welcome to your brain: Why you lose your car keys but never forget how to drive and other puzzles of everyday life.* New York: Bloomsbury.

Aarts, H., & Dijksterhuis, A. (2000). Habits as knowledge structures: Automaticity in goal-directed behavior. *Journal of Personality and Social Psychology, 78,* 53–63.

Aarts, H., & Dijksterhuis, A. (2003). The silence of the library: Environment, situational norm, and social behavior. *Journal of Personality and Social Psychology, 84,* 18–28.

Aird, E. (2008). Gather around the children. In K. K. Kline (Ed.). *Authoritative communities: The scientific case for nurturing the whole child* (pp. 369–374). New York: Springer.

Allport, G. W. (1937). *Personality: A psychological interpretation.* New York: Henry Holt.

Allport, G. W. (1961). *Pattern and Growth in Personality.* New York: Holt Rinehart & Winston.

Allport, G. W. (1967). Gordon W. Allport. In E. G. Boring & G. Lindzey (Eds.). *A history of psychology in autobiography* (Vol. 5). New York: Appleton-Century-Crofts.

Allport, G. W., & Odbert, H. S. (1936). Trait-names: A psycholexical study. *Psychological Monographs, 47* (Whole No. 211).

Allport, G. W., & Postman, L. (1945). The basic psychology of rumor. *Transactions of the New York Academy of Sciences, 11,* 61–81.

Allport, G. W., & Postman, L. (1947). *The psychology of rumor.* New York: Henry Holt.

Alwin, D. F., Cohen, R. L., & Newcomb, T. M. (1991). *Political attitudes over the life span: The Bennington women after fifty years.* Madison: University of Wisconsin Press.

Amato, P. R., & Keith, B. (1991). Parental divorce and the well-being of children: A meta-analysis. *Psychological Bulletin, 110,* 26–46.

American Psychiatric Association. (2000). *Diagnostic and statistical manual of mental disorders* (4th ed., Text Revision). Washington, DC: American Psychiatric Press.

Anderson, C. A., & Bushman, B. J. (2001). Effects of violent video games on aggressive behavior, aggressive cognition, aggressive affect, physiological arousal, and prosocial behavior: A meta-analytic review of the scientific literature. *Psychological Science, 12,* 353–359.

Asch, S. E. (1955, November). Opinions and social pressure. *Scientific American,* 31–35.

Asch, S. E. (1956). Studies of independence and conformity: A minority of one against a unanimous majority. *Psychological Monographs, 70* (Whole No. 416).

Aserinsky, E. (1996). Memories of famous neuropsychologists: The discovery of REM sleep. *Journal of the History of the Neurosciences, 5,* 213–227.

Aserinsky, E., & Kleitman, N. (1953). Regularly occurring periods of eye mobility and concomitant phenomena during sleep. *Science, 118,* 273–274.

B

Backer, M., Grossman, P., Schneider, J., Michalsen, A., Knoblauch, N., Tan, L., Niggemeyer, C., Linde, K., Melchart, D., & Dobos, G. J. (2008). Acupuncture in migraine: Investigation of autonomic effects. *Clinical Journal of Pain, 24,* 106–115.

Baltes, P. B., & Kunzmann, U. (2003). Wisdom. *Psychologist, 16,* 131–133.

Bambling, M., King, R., Reid, W., & Wegner, K. (2008). Online counselling: The experience of counsellors providing synchronous single-session counselling to young people. *Counselling & Psychotherapy Research, 8,* 110–116.

Bandura, A. (1965). Influences of models' reinforcement contingencies on the acquisition of initiative responses. *Journal of Personality and Social Psychology, 1,* 589–593.

Bandura, A. (1986). *Social foundations of thought and action: A social-cognitive theory.* Englewood Cliffs, NJ: Prentice Hall.

Bandura, A. (1999). A sociocognitive analysis of substance abuse: An agentic perspective. *Psychological Science, 10,* 214–218.

Bandura, A., Ross, D., & Ross, S. A. (1961). Transmission of aggression through imitation of aggressive models. *Journal of Abnormal and Social Psychology, 63,* 575–582.

Bandura, A., Ross, D., & Ross, S. A. (1963). Vicarious reinforcement and imitative learning. *Journal of Abnormal and Social Psychology, 67,* 601–607.

Bargh, J. A., & Morsella, E. (2008). The unconscious mind. *Perspectives on Psychological Science, 3,* 73–79.

Barlett, C. P., Harris, R. J., & Bruey, C. (2008). The effect of the amount of blood in a violent video game on aggression, hostility, and arousal. *Journal of Experimental Social Psychology, 44,* 539–546.

Beck, A. T. (1991). Cognitive therapy: A 30-year retrospective. *American Psychologist, 46,* 368–375.

Beck, A. T., & Grant, P. M. (2008). Negative self-defeating attitudes: Factors that influence everyday impairment in individuals with schizophrenia. *American Journal of Psychiatry, 165,* 772.

Beekman, M., & Lew, J. B. (2008). Foraging in honeybees—When does it pay to dance? *Behavioral Ecology, 19,* 255–262.

Beeli, G., Esslen, M., & Jancke, L. (2008). Time course of neural activity correlated with colored-hearing synesthesia. *Cerebral Cortex, 18,* 379–385.

Benoit, M., Andrieu, S., Lechowski, L., Gillette-Guyonnet, S., Robert, P. H., & Vellas, B. (2008). Apathy and depression in Alzheimer's disease are associated with functional deficit and psychotropic prescription. *International Journal of Geriatric Psychiatry, 23,* 409–414.

Berkowitz, L. (1989). Frustration-aggression hypothesis: Examination and reformulation. *Psychological Bulletin, 106,* 59–73.

Berkowitz, L. (1993). *Aggression: Its causes, consequences, and control.* New York: McGraw-Hill.

Berscheid, E., Dion, K., Hatfield (Walster), E., & Walster, G. W. (1971). Physical attractiveness and dating choice: A test of the matching hypothesis. *Journal of Experimental Social Psychology, 7,* 173–189.

Berscheid, E., & Hatfield (Walster), E. (1974). A little bit about love. In T. Huston (Ed.), *Foundations of interpersonal attraction* (pp. 355–381). New York: Academic Press.

Biedermann, B., Ruh, N., Nickels, L., & Coltheart, M. (2008). Information retrieval in tip of the tongue states: New data and methodological advances. *Journal of Psycholinguistic Research, 37,* 171–198.

Binet, A., & Simon, T. (1905; reprinted 1916). New methods for the diagnosis of the intellectual level of subnormals. In A. Binet & T. Simon (Eds.), *The development of intelligence in children.* Baltimore: Williams & Wilkins.

Blumenthal, A. L. A. (2002). A reappraisal of Wilhelm Wundt. In W. E. Pickren & D. A. Dewsbury (Eds.), *Evolving perspectives on the history of psychology* (pp. 65–78). Washington, DC: American Psychological Association.

Bransford, J. D., Brown, A. L., & Cocking, R. R. (2008). Mind and brain. In M. H. Immordino-Yang & H. Mary (Eds.), *The Jossey-Bass reader on the brain and learning* (pp. 89–105). San Francisco, CA: Jossey-Bass.

Brendl, C. M., Markman, A. B., & Messner, C. (2001). How do indirect measures of evaluation work? Evaluating the inference of prejudice in the Implicit Association Test. *Journal of Personality and Social Psychology, 81,* 760–773.

Brick, J. (2008). Characteristics of alcohol: Definitions, chemistry, measurement, use, and abuse. In J. Brick (Ed.), *Handbook of the medical consequences of alcohol and drug abuse* (2nd ed., (pp. 1–7). New York: The Haworth Press.

Budney, A. J., Moore, B. A., & Vandrey, R. (2008). Health consequences of marijuana use. In J. Brick (Ed.), *Handbook of the medical consequences of alcohol and drug abuse* (2nd ed., pp. 251–301). New York: The Haworth Press.

Burger, J. M. (2009). Replicating Milgram: Would people still obey today? *American Psychologist. Vol. 64: 1 (Jan),* 1–11.

C

Cacioppo, J. T., & Petty, R. E. (1982). The need for cognition. *Journal of Personality and Social Psychology, 42,* 116–131.

Cacioppo, J. T., Petty, R. E., Feinstein, J. A., & Jarvis, W. B. G. (1996). Dispositional differences in cognitive motivation: The life and times of individuals varying in need for cognition. *Psychological Bulletin, 119,* 197–253.

Cacioppo, J. T., Petty, R. E., Kao, C. F., & Rodriguez, R. (1986). Central and peripheral routes to persuasion: An individual differences perspective. *Journal of Personality and Social Psychology, 51,* 1032–1043.

Capone, G. T., & Kaufmann, W. E. (2008). Human brain development. In P. J. Accardo (Ed.), *Capute and Accardo's neurodevelopmental disabilities in infancy and childhood: Vol 1: Neurodevelopmental diagnosis and treatment* (pp. 27–59). Baltimore, MD: Paul H. Brookes Publishing.

Cattell, R. B. (1963). Theory of fluid and crystallized intelligence: A critical experiment. *Journal of Educational Psychology, 54,* 1–22.

Cattell, R. B. (1965). *The scientific analysis of personality.* Chicago: Aldine.

Cattell, R. B. (1971). *Abilities: Their structure, growth, and action.* Boston: Houghton Mifflin.

Chomsky, N. (1957). *Syntactic structures.* The Hague: Mouton.

Chomsky, N. (1965). *Aspects of the theory of syntax.* Cambridge, MA: Harcourt Brace Jovanovich.

Clark, K. B., & Clark, M. P. (1939). The development of self and the emergence of racial identification in Negro preschool children. *Journal of Social Psychology, 10,* 591–599.

Clark, K. B., & Clark, M. P. (1947). Racial identification and preference in Negro children. In T. M. Newcomb and E. L. Hartley (Eds.), *Readings in social psychology* (pp. 169–178). New York: Holt.

Colombo, J. (1995). Cost, utility, and judgments of institutional review boards. *Psychological Science, 6,* 318–319.

Crandall, C. S., & Eshleman, A. (2003). A justification-suppression of the expression and experience of prejudice. *Psychological Bulletin, 129,* 414–446.

Croen, L. A., Grether, J. K., Yoshida, C. K., Odouli, R., & Van de Water, J. (2005). Maternal autoimmune diseases, asthma and allergies, and childhood autism spectrum disorders: A case-control study. *Archives of Pediatrics and Adolescent Medicine, 159,* 151–157.

Cunningham, W. A., Preacher, K. J., & Bonaji, M. R. (2001). Implicit attitude measures: Consistency, stability, and convergent validity. *Psychological Science, 12,* 163–170.

Cytowic, R. E. (2002). *Synesthesia: A union of the senses* (2nd ed.). Cambridge, MA: MIT Press.

D

Dai, D. Y., & Renzulli, J. S. (2008). Snowflakes, living systems, and the mystery of giftedness. *Gifted Child Quarterly, 52,* 114–130.

Darley, J. M., & Latané, B. (1968). Bystander intervention in emergencies: Diffusion of responsibility. *Journal of Personality and Social Psychology, 8,* 377–383.

Darwin, C. (1872). *Expression of emotion in man and animals.* London: John Murray.

Davachi, L., & Dobbins, I. G. (2008). Declarative memory. *Current Directions in Psychological Science, 17,* 112–118.

Deci, E., Koestner, R., & Ryan, R. (1999). A meta-analytic review of experiments examining the effects of extrinsic rewards on intrinsic motivation. *Psychological Bulletin, 125,* 627–668.

Devine, P. G., Evett, S. R., & Vasquez-Suson, K. A. (1996). Exploring the interpersonal dynamics of intergroup contact. In R. M. Sorrentino & E. T. Higgins (Eds.), *Handbook of motivation and cognition: The interpersonal context* (Vol. 3, pp. 423–464). New York: Guilford.

Diener, E. (2008). Myths in the science of happiness, and directions for future research. In M. Eid & R. J. Larsen (Eds.), *The science of subjective well-being* (pp. 493–514). New York: Guilford Press.

E

Ebbinghaus, H. (1885). *Über das gedächtnis: Untersuchugen zur experimentellen psychologie.* Leipzig: Dunker & Humbolt. Translated by H. A. Ruger & C. E. Byssenine as *Memory: A contribution to experimental psychology.* New York: Dover, 1913.

Eccles, J., Brown, B.V., & Templeton, J. (2008). A developmental framework for selecting indicators of well-being during the adolescent and young adult years. In B. V. Brown (Ed.), *Key indicators of child and youth well-being: Completing the picture* (pp. 197–236). Mahwah, NJ: Lawrence Erlbaum.

Eccles, J., Templeton, J., Barber, B., & Stone, M. (2003). Adolescence and emerging adulthood: The critical passageways to adulthood. In M. H. Bornstein & L. Davidson (Eds.), *Well-being: Positive development across the life course. Crosscurrents in contemporary psychology* (pp. 383–406). Mahwah, NJ: Lawrence Erlbaum.

Edwards, O. W., & Paulin, R. V. (2007). Referred students' performance on the Reynolds Intellectual Assessment Scales and the Wechsler Intelligence Scale for Children—Fourth Edition. *Journal of Psychoeducational Assessment, 25,* 334–340.

Ellis, A. (1962). *Reason and emotion in psychotherapy.* New York: Lyle Stuart.

Ellis, A. (2002). *Overcoming resistance: A rational emotive behavior therapy integrated approach* (2nd ed.). New York: Springer.

Ephraim, D. (2008). Psychocultural system manual. In S. R. Jenkins (Ed.), *A handbook of clinical scoring systems for thematic apperceptive techniques* (pp. 739–760). Mahwah, NJ: Lawrence Erlbaum.

Erikson, E. H. (1950). *Childhood and society.* New York: W. W. Norton.

Erikson, E. H. (1968). *Identity: Youth and crisis.* New York: W. W. Norton.

Erikson, E. H. (1980). *Identity: Youth and crisis.* New York: W. W. Norton.

Evans, S., Ferrando, S., Findler, M., Stowell, C., Smart, C., & Haglin, D. (2008). Mindfulness-based cognitive therapy for generalized anxiety disorder. *Journal of Anxiety Disorders, 22,* 716–721.

F

Fechner, G. T. (1966). *Elements of psychophysics* (H. E. Alder, Trans.). New York: Holt, Rinehart & Winston. (Original work published 1860)

Festinger, L. (1954). A theory of social comparison processes. *Human Relations, 7,* 117–140.

Festinger, L. (1957). *A theory of cognitive dissonance.* Stanford, CA: Stanford University Press.

Festinger, L., Riecken, H. W., & Schachter, S. (1956). *When prophecy fails.* Minneapolis, MN: University of Minnesota Press.

Fiedler, F. E. (1967). *A theory of leadership effectiveness.* New York: McGraw-Hill.

Franzoi, S. L. (2009). *Psychology: A Journey of Discovery.* 4th edition. Mason, OH: Atomic Dog/Cengage Learning.

Franzoi, S. L. (2009). *Social Psychology.* 5th edition. New York: McGraw-Hill.

Freud, S. (1895/1950/1966). Project for a scientific psychology. In J. Strachey (Ed. and Trans.), *The standard edition of the complete psychological works of Sigmund Freud* (Vol. 1, pp. 282–398). London: Hogarth Press.

Freud, S. (1900). *The interpretation of dreams.* In Vols. 4 and 5 of the *Standard edition.* London: Hogarth.

Freud, S. (1900/1953). The interpretation of dreams. In J. Strachey (Ed. and Trans.), *The standard edition of the complete psychological works of Sigmund Freud* (Vols. 4 and 5). London: Hogarth.

Freud, S. (1905). Fragments of an analysis of a case of hysteria. *Collected papers* (Vol. 3). New York: Basic Books. (Reprinted in 1959.)

Freud, S. (1909/1957). Mourning and melancholia. In J. Strachey (Ed. and Trans.), *The standard edition of the complete psychological works of Sigmund Freud* (Vol. 14, pp. 243–258). London: Hogarth.

Freud, S. (1909/1963). Analysis of a phobia in a five-year-old boy. In J. Strachey (Ed. and Trans.), *The standard edition of the complete psychological works of Sigmund Freud* (Vol. 10, pp. 3–149). London: Hogarth.

Freud, S. (1917). Introductory lectures on psychoanalysis. Part III: General theory of the neurosis. In J. Strachey (Ed. and Trans.), *The standard edition of the complete psychological works of Sigmund Freud* (Vol. 16, pp. 243–496). London: Hogarth Press, 1959.

Freud, S. (1926/1959). Inhibitions, symptoms, and anxiety. In J. Strachey (Ed. & Trans.), *The standard edition of the complete psychological works of Sigmund Freud* (Vol. 20, pp. 89–174). London: Hogarth Press.

Freud, S. (1946). *The ego and the mechanisms of defense.* New York: International Universities Press.

Freud, S. (1949). *A general introduction to psychoanalysis.* New York: Penguin.

G

Garcia, J., & Koelling, R. A. (1966). Relation of cue to consequence in avoidance learning. *Psychonomic Science, 4,* 123–124.

Garcia, J., Rusniak, K. W., & Brett, L. P. (1977). Conditioning food-illness aversions in wild animals: Caveat Canonici. In H. Davis & H. M. B. Hurwitz (Eds.), *Operant-Pavlovian interactions.* Hillsdale, NJ: Erlbaum.

Gardner, H. (1993). *Multiple intelligences: The theory in practice.* New York: Basic Books.

Gardner, H. (1999). *Intelligence reframed: Multiple intelligences for the 21st century.* New York: Basic Books.

Gazzaniga, M. S. (1967). The split brain in man. *Scientific American, 217,* 24–29.

Gazzaniga, M. S. (Ed.). (2000). *The new cognitive neuroscience* (2nd ed.). Cambridge, MA: The MIT Press.

Geldard, K., & Geldard, D. (2008). *Personal counseling skills: An integrative approach.* Springfield, IL: Charles C. Thomas.

Gibson, E. J., & Walk, R.D. (1960, April). The "visual cliff." *Scientific American, 202,* 64–71.

Gilbert, A. (2008). *What the nose knows: The science of scent in everyday life.* New York: Crown Publishers.

Gilligan, C. (1982). *In a different voice: Psychological theory and women's development.* Cambridge, MA: Harvard University Press.

Gilman, S. L. (2008). Electrotherapy and mental illness: Then and now. *History of Psychiatry, 19,* 339–357.

Gold, E. K., & Zahm, S. G. (2008). Gestalt therapy. In M. Hersen & A. M. Gross (Eds.), *Handbook of clinical psychology, vol 1: Adults* (pp. 585–616). Hoboken, NJ: John Wiley.

Goldstein, R. B., Grant, B. F., Ruan, W. J., Smith, S. M., & Saha, T. D. (2008). Antisocial personality disorder with childhood- versus adolescence-onset conduct disorder: Results from the National Epidemiologic Survey on Alcohol and Related Conditions: Erratum. *Journal of Nervous and Mental Disease, 196,* 263.

Gosling, S. D. (2008). Personality in non-human animals. *Social and Personality Psychology Compass, 2,* 985–1001.

Greenwald, A. G., Spangenberg, E. R., Pratkanis, A. R., & Eskenazi, J. (1991). Double-blind tests of subliminal self-help audiotapes. *Psychological Science, 2,* 119–122.

H

Hall, J. J., Neal, T. J., & Dean, R. S. (2008). Lateralization of cerebral functions. In A. M. Horton, Jr. & D. Wedding (Eds.), *The neuropsychology handbook* (pp. 183–214). New York: Springer.

Harlow, H. F., & Harlow, M. K. (1962). Social deprivation in monkeys. *Scientific American, 200,* 68–74.

Harlow, H. F., & Zimmermann, R. R. (1959). Affectional responses in the infant monkey. *Science, 130,* 421–432.

Hartmann, P., Kruuse, N. H. S., & Nyborg, H. (2007). Testing the cross-racial generality of Spearman's hypothesis in two samples. *Intelligence, 35,* 47–57.

Hauer, B. J. A., Wessel, I., Geraerts, E., Merckelbach, H., & Dalgleish, T. (2008). Autobiographical memory specificity after manipulating retrieval cues in adults reporting childhood sexual abuse. *Journal of Abnormal Psychology, 117,* 444–453.

Herman, C. P., & Polivy, J. (2004). The self-regulation of eating: Theoretical and practical problems. In R. F. Baumeister & K. D. Vohs (Eds.), *Handbook of self-regulation: Research, theory, and applications* (pp. 492–508). New York: Guilford Press.

Hiatt, K. D., & Dishion, T. J. (2008). Antisocial personality development. In T. P. Beauchaine & S. P. Hinshaw (Eds.), *Child and adolescent psychopathology* (pp. 370–404). Hoboken, NJ: John Wiley.

Higgins, E. T. (2004). Making a theory useful: Lessons handed down. *Personality and Social Psychology Review, 8,* 138–145.

Hilgard, E. R. (1986). *Divided consciousness: Multiple controls in human thought and action.* New York: Wiley.

Hilgard, E. R. (1992). Dissociation and theories of hypnosis. In E. Fromm & M. R. Nash (Eds.), *Contemporary hypnosis research* (pp. 69–101). New York: Guilford Press.

Hilgard, E. R., Leary, D. E., & McGuire, G. R. (1991). History of psychology: A survey and critical assessment. *Annual Review of Psychology, 42,* 79–107.

Hillman, C. H., Erickson, K. I., & Kramer, A. F. (2008). Be smart, exercise your heart: Exercise effects on brain and cognition. *Nature Reviews Neuroscience, 9,* 58–65.

Hobson, J. A. (1995). *Sleep.* New York: Scientific American Library.

Hobson, J. A. (1999). *Consciousness.* New York: Scientific American Library.

Howell, K. K., Coles, C. D., & Kable, J. A. (2008). The medical and developmental consequences of prenatal drug exposure. In J. Brick (Ed.), *Handbook of the medical consequences of alcohol and drug abuse* (2nd ed., pp. 219–249). New York: The Haworth Press.

Howell, R. T., & Howell, C. J. (2008). The relation of economic status to subjective well-being in developing countries: A meta-analysis. *Psychological Bulletin, 134,* 536–560.

Huppert, J. D., Strunk, D. R., Ledley, D. R., Davidson, J. R. T., & Foa, E. B. (2008). Generalized social anxiety disorder and avoidant personality disorder: Structural analysis and treatment outcome. *Depression and Anxiety, 25,* 441–448.

I

Inhelder, B., & Piaget, J. (1958). *The growth of logical thinking from childhood to adolescence.* New York: Basic Books.

J

James, W. (1884). What is an emotion? *Mind, 9,* 188–205.

James, W. (1890). *The principles of psychology* (2 vols.). New York: Henry Holt.

Johnson, H. D., Brady, E., McNair, R., Congdon, D., Niznik, J., & Anderson, S. (2007). Identity as a moderator of gender differences in the emotional closeness of emerging adults' same- and cross-sex friendships. *Adolescence, 42,* 1–23.

Jung, C. G. (1916). *Analytical psychology.* New York: Moffat.

Jung, C. G. (1921). *Psychological types.* New York: Harcourt Brace.

Jung, C. G. (1963). *Memories, dreams, reflections.* New York: Random House.

Jung, C. G. (1964). *Man and his symbols.* New York: Dell.

K

Kaas, J. H. (2008). The evolution of the complex sensory and motor systems of the human brain. *Brain Research Bulletin, 75,* 384–390.

Kâgitçibasi, C. (1994). A critical appraisal of individualism and collectivism: Toward a new formulation. In U. Kim, H. C. Triandis, C. Kâgitçibasi, S. Choi, & G. Yoon (Eds.), *Individualism and collectivism: Theory, method, and applications* (pp. 52–65). Thousand Oaks, CA: Sage.

Karen, R. (2008). Investing in children and society: What we have learned from seven decades of attachment research. In K. K. Kline (Ed.), *Authoritative communities: The scientific case for nurturing the whole child* (pp. 103–120). New York: Springer.

Karremans, J. C., Stroebe, W., & Claus, J. (2006). Beyond Vicary's fantasies: The impact of subliminal priming and brand choice. *Journal of Experimental Social Psychology, 42,* 792–798.

Kiessling, S. G., McClanahan, K. K., & Omar, H. A. (2008). Obesity, hypertension, and mental health evaluation in adolescents: A comprehensive approach. *International Journal of Adolescent Medicine and Health, 20,* 5–15.

Kim, N-G. (2008). The moon illusion and the size-distance paradox. In S. Cummins-Sebree, M. A. Riley, & K. Shockley (Eds.), *Studies in perception and action IX: Fourteenth International Conference on Perception and Action* (pp. 210–213). Mahwah, NJ: Lawrence Erlbaum.

King, L. A. (2008). Personal goals and life dreams: Positive psychology and motivation in daily life. In J. Y. Shah & W. L. Gardner (Eds.), *Handbook of motivation science* (pp. 518–530). New York: Guilford Press.

Kirschenbaum, H. (2004). Carl Rogers's life and work: An assessment on the 100th anniversary of his birth. *Journal of Counseling and Development, 82,* 116–124.

Kleim, J. A., & Jones, T. A. (2008). Principles of experience-dependent neural plasticity: Implications for rehabilitation after brain damage. *Journal of Speech, Language, and Hearing Research, 51,* 225–239.

Klein, R. J. (2008). Ready . . . , set . . . , relax!: Relaxation strategies with children and adolescents. In C. A. Malchiodi (Ed.), *Creative interventions with traumatized children (pp. 302–320). New York: Guilford Press.

Knowlton, B. J., & Foerde, K. (2008). Neural representations of nondeclarative memories. *Current Directions in Psychological Science, 17,* 107–111.

Kohlberg, L. (1981). *Essays on moral development.* New York: Harper & Row.

Kohlberg, L. (1984). *The psychology of moral development: The nature and validity of moral stages.* In *Essays on moral development* (Vol. 2). New York: Harper & Row.

Kübler-Ross, E. (1969). *On death and dying.* New York: Macmillan.

Kübler-Ross, E. (1981). *Living and dying.* New York: Macmillan.

Kurtz, M. M., & Mueser, K. T. (2008). A meta-analysis of controlled research on social skills training for schizophrenia. *Journal of Consulting and Clinical Psychology, 76,* 491–504.

L

Lambert, M. J., & Erekson, D. M. (2008). Positive psychology and the humanistic tradition. *Journal of Psychotherapy Integration, 18,* 222–232.

Latané, B., & Darley, J. M. (1968). Group inhibition of bystander intervention in emergencies. *Journal of Personality and Social Psychology, 10,* 216–221.

Latané, B., & Darley, J. M. (1970). *The unresponsive bystander: Why doesn't he help?* Englewood Cliffs, NJ: Prentice Hall.

Latané, B., Liu, J. H., Nowak, A., & Bonevento, M. (1995). Distance matters: Physical space and social impact. *Personality & Social Psychology Bulletin, 21,* 795–805.

Latané, B., & Nida, S. (1981). Ten years of research on group size and helping. *Psychological Bulletin, 89,* 308–324.

Loftus, E. F. (1993). The reality of repressed memories. *American Psychologist, 48,* 518–537.

Loftus, E. F., Feldman, J., & Dashiell, R. (1995). The reality of illusory memories. In D. L. Schacter (Ed.), *Memory distortion: How minds, brains, and societies reconstruct the past* (pp. 47–68). Cambridge, MA: Harvard University Press.

Loftus, E. F., & Palmer, J. C. (1974). Reconstruction of automobile destruction: An example of the interaction between language and memory. *Journal of Verbal Learning and Verbal Behavior, 13,* 585–589.

Luchins, A. S. (1942). Mechanization in problem solving. *Psychological Monographs, 54* (6, No. 248).

M

Mak, M. H. J. (2002). Accepting the timing of one's death: An experience of Chinese hospice patients. *Omega-Journal of Death & Dying, 45,* 245–260.

Marcia, J. E. (2006). Ego identity and personality disorders. *Journal of Personality Disorders, 20,* 577–596.

Maslow, A. (1970). *Motivation and personality* (2nd ed.). New York: Harper & Row.

Maslow, A. (1971). *The farther reaches of human nature.* New York: Viking Press.

McClelland, D. C. (1985). *Human motivation.* Glenview, IL: Scott, Foresman.

McClelland, D. C., Atkinson, J., Clark, R., & Lowell, E. (1953). *The achievement motive.* New York: Appleton-Century-Crofts.

Mendoza, J. E., & Foundas, A. L. (2008). *Clinical neuroanatomy: A neurobehavioral approach.* New York: Springer.

Milgram, S. (1963). Behavioral study of obedience. *Journal of Abnormal and Social Psychology, 67,* 371–378.

Milgram, S. (1965). Some conditions of obedience and disobedience to authority. *Human Relations, 18,* 57–76.

Milgram, S. (1974). *Obedience to authority: An experimental view.* New York: Harper & Row.

Miller, G. A. (1956). The magical number seven, plus or minus two: Some limits on our capacity to process information. *Psychological Review, 63,* 81–97.

Monteith, M. J. (1993). Self-regulation of prejudiced responses: Implications for progress in prejudice-reduction efforts. *Journal of Personality and Social Psychology, 65,* 469–485.

Morgan, D. L., & Morgan, R. K. (2001). Single-participant research design. *American Psychologist, 56,* 119–127.

Morone, N. E., Greco, C. M., & Weiner, D. K. (2008). Mindfulness meditation for the treatment of chronic low back pain in older adults: A randomized controlled pilot study. *Pain, 134,* 310–319.

Murray, G. K., Corlett, P. R., Clark, L., Pessiglione, M., Blackwell, A. D., Honey, G., Jones, P. B., Bullmore, E. T., Robbins, T. W., & Fletcher, P. C. (2008). How dopamine dysregulation leads to psychotic symptoms. Abnormal mesolimbic and mesostriatal prediction error signalling in psychosis. *Molecular Psychiatry, 13,* 239.

Myers, D., & Diener, E. (1995). Who is happy? *Psychological Science, 6,* 10–19.

N

Nantel-Vivier, A., & Pihl, R. O. (2008). Biological vulnerability to depression. In J. R. Z. Abela & B. L. Hankin (Eds.), *Handbook of depression in children and adolescents* (pp. 103–123). New York: Guilford Press.

Navarro, J., & Karlins, M. (2008). *What everybody is saying: An ex-FBI agent's guide to speed-reading people.* New York: Collins.

Neisser, U., Boodoo, G., Bouchard, T. J., Jr., Boykin, A. W., Brody, N., Ceci, S. J., Halpern, D. F., Loehlin, J. C., Perloff, R., Sternberg, R. J., & Urbina, S. (1996). Intelligence: Knowns and unknowns. *American Psychologist, 51,* 77–101.

Neisser, U., & Harsch, N. (1992). Phantom flashbulbs: False recollections of hearing the news about *Challenger.* In E. Winograd & U. Neisser (Eds.), *Affect and accuracy in recall: Studies of "flashbulb" memories* (pp. 9–31). New York: Cambridge University Press.

Newcomb, T. M. (1943). *Personality and social change: Attitude formation in a student community.* New York: Dryden.

Neyens, D. M., & Boyle, L. N. (2008). The influence of driver distraction on the severity of injuries sustained by teenage drivers and their passengers. *Accident Analysis & Prevention, 40,* 254–259.

O

Okamura, H. (2008). Brain comes to light. *Nature, 452,* 294–295.

O'Kane, G., Kensinger, E. A., & Corkin, S. (2004). Evidence for semantic learning in profound amnesia: An investigation with patient H. M. *Hippocampus, 14,* 417–425.

Ollinger, M., Jones, G., & Knoblich, G. (2008). Investigating the effect of mental set on insight problem solving. *Experimental Psychology, 55,* 269–282.

Oyserman, D., & Lee, S. W. S. (2008). Does culture influence what and how we think? Effects of priming individualism and collectivism. *Psychological Bulletin, 134,* 311–342.

P

Packer, D. J. (2008). Identifying systematic disobedience in Milgram's obedience experiments: A meta-analytic review. *Perspectives on Psychological Science, 3,* 301–304.

Parsons, T. D., & Rizzo, A. A. (2008). Affective outcomes of virtual reality exposure therapy for anxiety and specific phobias: A meta-analysis. *Journal of Behavior Therapy and Experimental Psychiatry, 39,* 250–261.

Pavlov, I. P. (1927). *Conditioned reflexes* (G.V. Anrep, Trans.). London: Oxford University Press.

Pavlov, I. P. (1997). Excerpts from *The work of the digestive glands. American Psychologist, 52,* 936–940. (Original work published 1897)

Perls, F. S. (1969). *Gestalt therapy verbatim.* Lafayette, CA: Real People Press.

Perls, F. S., Heffertine, R. F., & Goodman, P. (1951). *Gestalt therapy.* New York: Julian Press.

Peterson, C. (2006). The Values in Action (VIA) Classification of Strengths: The un-DSM and the real DSM. In M. Csikszentmihalyi & I. Csikszentmihalyi (Eds.), *A life worth living: Contributions to positive psychology* (pp. 29–48). New York: Oxford University Press.

Peterson, C., Maier, S. F., & Seligman, M. E. P. (1993). *Learned helplessness: A theory for the age of personal control.* New York: Oxford University Press.

Peterson, C., Ruch, W., Beermann, U., Park, N., & Seligman, M. E. P. (2007). Strengths of character, orientations to happiness, and life satisfaction. *The Journal of Positive Psychology, 2,* 149–156.

Peterson, C., Park, N., Pole, N., D'Andrea, W., & Seligman, M. E. P. (2008). Strengths of character and posttraumatic growth. *Journal of Traumatic Stress, 21,* 214–217.

Peterson, C., & Seligman, M. E. P. (2004). *Character strengths and virtues: A handbook and classification.* Washington, D. C.: American Psychological Association.

Peterson, C., Seligman, M. E. P., & Vaillant, G. E. (1988). Pessimistic explanatory style is a risk factor for physical illness: A thirty-five-year longitudinal study. *Journal of Personality and Social Psychology, 55,* 23–27.

Peterson, C., & Steen, T. A. (2002). Optimistic explanatory style. In C. R. Snyder & S. J. Shane (Eds.), *Handbook of positive psychology* (pp. 244–256). London: Oxford University Press.

Petty, R. E., & Cacioppo, J. T. (1986). *Communication and persuasion: Central and peripheral routes to attitude change.* New York: Springer-Verlag.

Phinney, J. S. (1993). A three-stage model of ethnic identity development. In M. Bernal & G. Knight (Eds.), *Ethnic identity: Formation and transmission among Hispanics and other minorities* (pp. 61–79). Albany: State University of New York Press.

Phinney, J. S., Cantu, C. L., & Kurtz, D. A. (1997). Ethnic and American identity and self-esteem. *Journal of Youth and Adolescence, 26,* 165–185.

Piaget, J. (1972). Intellectual evolutions from adolescence to adulthood. *Human Development, 15,* 1–12.

Piaget, J., & Inhelder, B. (1969). *The psychology of the child.* New York: Basic Books.

Pisoni, D. B. (2008). Speech perception in deaf children with cochlear implants. In D. B. Pisoni & R. E. Remez (Eds.), *The handbook of speech perception* (pp. 494–523). Malden, MA: Blackwell Publishing.

Pretz, J. E. (2008). Intuition versus analysis: Strategy and experience in complex everyday problem solving. *Memory & Cognition, 36,* 554–566.

R

Restak, R. (2008). How our brain constructs our mental world. In M. H. Immordino-Yang (Ed.), *Jossey-Bass reader on the brain and learning* (pp. 3–11). San Francisco: Jossey-Bass.

Robinson, D. N. (2008). *Consciousness and mental life.* New York: Columbia University Press.

Rogers, C. R. (1951). *Client-centered therapy: Its current practice, implications, and theory.* Boston: Houghton Mifflin.

Rogers, C. R. (1959). A theory of therapy, personality, and interpersonal relationships as developed in the client-centered framework. In S. Koch (Ed.), *Psychology: A study of a science* (Vol. 3, pp. 184–256). New York: McGraw-Hill.

Rogers, C. R. (1961). *On becoming a person.* Boston: Houghton Mifflin.

Rosch, E. H. (1973). Natural categories. *Cognitive Psychology, 4,* 328–350.

Roth, R. M., Koven, N. S., & Pendergrass, J. C. (2008). An introduction to structural and functional neuroimaging. In A. M. Horton, Jr. & D. Wedding (Eds.), *The neuropsychology handbook* (pp. 217–250). New York: Springer.

Rozin, P. (1996). Sociocultural influences on human food selection. In E. Capaldi (Ed.), *Why we eat what we eat: The psychology of eating* (pp. 233–263). Washington, DC: American Psychological Association.

Rusbult, C. E., Morrow, G. D., & Johnson, D. J. (1987). Self-esteem and problem-solving behaviour in close relationships. *British Journal of Social Psychology, 26,* 293–303.

S

Sarwer, D. B., & Crerand, C. E. (2008). Body dysmorphic disorder and appearance enhancing medical treatments. *Body Image, 5,* 50–58.

Schachter, S. (1951). Deviation, rejection and communication. *Journal of Abnormal and Social Psychology, 46,* 190–207.

Schachter, S., & Singer, J. (1962). Cognitive, social, and physiological determinants of emotional state. *Psychological Review, 69,* 379–399.

Sherif, M. (1966). *In common predicament: Social psychology of intergroup conflict and cooperation.* Boston: Houghton Mifflin.

Sherif, M., Harvey, O. J., White, B. J., Hood, W. R., & Sherif, C. (1961). *Intergroup conflict and cooperation: The Robbers' Cave experiment.* Norman, OK: Oklahoma Book Exchange.

Shull, J., & McCarthy, C. (2008). Somatoform disorders. In A. Guerrero & M. Piasecki (Eds.), *Problem-based behavioral science and psychiatry* (pp. 339–351). New York: Springer.

Siskind, D. (2005). Psychotherapy with children and parents during divorce. In L. Gunsberg & P. Hymowitz (Eds.), *A handbook of divorce and custody: Forensic, developmental, and clinical perspectives* (pp. 331–341). Hillsdale, NJ: Analytic Press.

Skaer, T. L., Sclar, D. A., & Robison, L. M. (2008). Trend in anxiety disorders in the USA 1990–2003. *Primary Care & Community Psychiatry, 13,* 1–7.

Skinner, B. F. (1938). *The behavior of organisms.* New York: Appleton-Century-Crofts.

Skinner, B. F. (1948). *Walden two.* New York: Macmillan.

Skinner, B. F. (1957). *Verbal behavior.* New York: Appleton-Century-Crofts.

Skinner, B. F. (1979). *The shaping of a behaviorist.* New York: Knopf.

Skinner, B. F. (1990). Can psychology be a science of the mind? *American Psychologist, 45,* 1206–1210.

Smith, M. L., & Glass, G. V. (1977). Meta-analysis of psychotherapy outcome studies. *American Psychologist, 32,* 752–760.

Spearman, C. E. (1927). *The abilities of man.* London: Macmillan.

Steenbarger, B. N. (2008). Brief therapy. In M. Hersen & A. M. Michel (Eds.), *Handbook of clinical psychology, vol 1: Adults* (pp. 752–775). Hoboken, NJ: John Wiley.

Sternberg, R. J., & Grigorenko, E. L. (2008). Ability testing across cultures. In L. A. Suzuki & J. G. Ponterotto (Eds.), *Handbook of multicultural assessment: Clinical, psychological, and educational applications* (pp. 449–470). San Francisco, CA: Jossey-Bass.

Strack, F., Martin, L. L., & Stepper, S. (1988). Inhibiting and facilitating conditions of facial expressions: A nonobtrusive test of the facial feedback hypothesis. *Journal of Personality and Social Psychology, 54,* 768–777.

Strahan, E. J., Lafrance, A., Wilson, A. E., Ethier, N., Spencer, S. J., & Zanna, M. P. (2008). Victoria's dirty secret: How sociocultural norms influence adolescent girls and women. *Personality and Social Psychology Bulletin, 34,* 288–301.

T

Teigen, K. H. (1994). Yerkes-Dodson: A law for all seasons. *Theory and Psychology, 4,* 525–547.

Thorpe, M. P., & Day, R. D. (2008). Families and obesity: A family process approach to obesity in adolescents. In H. E. Fitzgerald, V. Mousouli, &

H. D. Davies (Eds.), *Obesity in childhood and adolescence, Vol 2: Understanding development and prevention* (pp. 117–140). Westport, CT: Praeger.

Triandis, H. C. (1989). The self and social behavior in differing cultural contexts. *Psychological Review, 96,* 506–520.

Triandis, H. C. (1995). *Individualism & collectivism.* Boulder, CO: Westview Press.

Tulving, E. (1999). Study of memory: Processes and systems. In J. K. Foster & M. Jelicic (Eds.), *Memory: Systems, process, or function?* (pp. 11–30). Oxford, England: Oxford University Press.

Tulving, E. (2002). Episodic memory: From mind to brain. *Annual Review of Psychology, 53,* 1–25.

Tulving, E. (2008). On the law of primacy. In M. A. Gluck, J. R. Anderson, & S. M. Kosslyn (Eds.), *Memory and mind: A festschrift for Gordon H. Bower* (pp. 31–48). Mahwah, NJ: Lawrence Erlbaum.

Tulving, E., & Schacter, D. L. (1990). Priming and human memory systems. *Science, 247,* 301–306.

Tulving, E., & Thomson, D. M. (1973). Encoding specificity and retrieval processes in episodic memory. *Psychological Review, 80,* 352–373.

Turiel, E. (2006). The development of morality. In N. Eisenberg, W. Damon, & R. M. Lerner (Eds.), *Handbook of child psychology: Vol. 3, Social, emotional, and personality development* (6th ed., pp. 789–857). Hoboken, NJ: John Wiley.

V

van Baaren, R. B., Fockenberg, D. A., Holland, R. W., Janssen, L., & van Knippenberg, A. (2006). The moody chameleon: The effect of mood on non-conscious mimicry. *Social Cognition, 24,* 426–437.

van Heck, G. L., & den Oudsten, B. L. (2008). Emotional intelligence: Relationships to stress, health, and well-being. In A. Vingerhoets, I. Nyklicek, & J. Denollet (Eds.), *Emotion regulation: Conceptual and clinical issues* (pp. 97–121). New York: Springer.

W

Watson, J. B. (1913). Psychology as the behaviorist views it. *Psychological Review, 20,* 158–177.

Watson, J. B. (1924). *Behaviorism.* New York: Norton.

Watson, J. B., & Rayner, R. (1920). Conditioned emotional responses. *Journal of Experimental Psychology, 3,* 1–14.

Weber, E. H. (1834). *De pulen, resorptione, auditu et tactu: Annotationes anatomicae et physiologicae.* Leipzig: Koehler.

Whorf, B. L. (1956). Science and linguistics. In J. B. Carroll (Ed.), *Language, thought, and reality: Selected writings of Benjamin Lee Whorf.* Cambridge, MA: MIT Press.

Wickwire, E. M. Jr., Roland, M. M. S., Elkin, T. D., & Schumacher, J. A. (2008). Sleep disorders. In M. Hersen & D. Reitman (Eds.), *Handbook of psychological assessment, case conceptualization, and treatment, Vol 2: Children and adolescents* (pp. 622–651). Hoboken, NJ: John Wiley & Sons Inc.

Wiegand, T., Thai, D., & Benowitz, N. (2008). Medical consequences of the use of hallucinogens: LSD, mescaline, PCP, and MDMA ("ecstasy"). In J. Brick (Ed.), *Handbook of the medical consequences of alcohol and drug abuse* (2nd ed., pp. 461–490). New York: The Haworth Press.

Wittchen, H-U., Nocon, A., Beesdo, K., Pine, D. S., Hofler, M., Lieb, R., & Gloster, A. T. (2008). Agoraphobia and panic. *Psychotherapy and Psychosomatics, 77,* 147–157.

Woolsey, T. A., Hanaway, J., & Gado, M. H. (2008). The brain atlas: A visual guide to the human central nervous system (3rd ed.). Hoboken, NJ: John Wiley.

Wootton, J. (2008). Meditation and chronic pain. In J. F. Audette & A. Bailey (Eds.), *Integrative pain medicine: The science and practice of complementary and alternative medicine in pain management* (pp. 195–209). Totowa, NJ: Humana Press.

INDEX

A

Aarts, Henk, 594
Absolute threshold, 94–95, 137
Academic achievement, valuing, 490–491
Academic Connections
  art, 26, 90, 119, 146, 210, 245 497
  biography, 371
  biology, 335
  business, 59, 335
  careers, 26
  computer science, 91, 244, 561
  computer technology, 588–589
  criminal justice, 530
  cross-cultural, 27, 116, 146, 244, 272, 305, 464
  cultural diversity, 58
  debate, 432, 621
  English, 621
  health, 210, 464
  history, 27, 58, 90, 119, 334, 371, 432, 530
  journalism, 531, 561, 621
  language arts, 26, 58, 147, 181, 245, 403, 432, 464, 589, 621
  marketing, 59, 91, 146, 497
  mathematics, 58, 146
  multimedia, 272
  political science, 305
  research, 91, 119, 210, 370, 403, 432, 497
  science, 26, 58, 91, 117, 146, 272
  social studies, 181, 403
  sociology, 27, 147, 180, 304, 370, 432, 531, 589, 621
  speech, 91, 117, 147
  writing, 26, 58, 90, 180, 210, 245, 335, 370, 432, 496, 530, 561
Acceleration, 485
Acceptance stage of death, 298
Accommodation, 233
Acculturative stress, 198–199
Acetylcholine, 66
Achievement
  academic, 490–491
  need for, 164–165
Achievement test, 468
Ackerman, Diane, 92
Acoustic encoding, 374–375
Acquired immune deficiency syndrome (AIDS), 216
Acquisition, 342–343

Activation-synthesis theory, 444
Active alert induction, form of hypnosis, 448
Active listening skills, 543
Active sleep. *See* REM sleep
Activity theory of aging, 291
Actual control, 193
Actual self, 313
Adams, John, 300
ADHD, 457
Adler, Alfred, 13
Adler, Renata, 500
Adolescence
  complex thinking, 255–258
  defined, 247
  developmental tasks, 248–249
  distinguished from adulthood, 248–250
  emotions/self-consciousness, 259–262
  identity development, 263–264
  identity statuses, 264–265
  moral development, 256–258
  phases of, 249–250
  physical/social effects of puberty, 250–254
  reasoning skills, 256
  schizophrenia and, 522
Adolescent bridge to adulthood, 248, 250
Adoption studies, 488
Adrenal glands, 70, 259
Adrenaline, 70, 188
Adulthood
  developmental tasks signifying, 248–249
  emerging, 249
  psychosocial stages of, 275–276
  See also Adulthood, late; Adulthood, middle; Adulthood, young
Adulthood, late
  activity theory of aging, 291
  aging and the brain, 294–295
  cultural views on aging, 289–290
  death and dying, 297–298
  marriage in later life, 293
  parents/grandparents, 292–293
  peace of mind and meaningfulness, 298
  physical/cognitive changes, 293–297
  psychological stages of dying, 298
  social transitions and roles, 291
  wisdom, 297
Adulthood, middle, 284–287
  aging and, 286–287
  family and work conflicts, 285
  midlife crisis, 287

  parenting and job responsibilities, 284–285
Adulthood, young, 275–282
  divorce and consequences, 282
  love and marriage, 280
  psychosocial stages, 275–276
  romantic conflict, 280–281
  seeking intimacy, 278–279
  theories of, 275–278
Advertising
  persuasion and, 573
  subliminal perception and, 138
Aerobic exercise, 202
Aerosol, as inhalant, 458
Affiliation, need for, 163–164
African Americans
  psychological disorder treatment and, 537
  in psychology, 8–10
Aggression
  in children, 41–44, 366
  gender styles of, 579
  hostile, 578
  indirect, 579
  instrumental, 578
  observational learning and, 363–364
  reducing through role models, 364–365
  ways to reduce, 580–581
Aging, 286–287
  activity theory of, 291
  brain and, 294
  cultural views on, 289–290
  decline in organ function, 294
  depression in older adults, 511
  disengagement theory of, 291
  parents/grandparents, 292–293
  social transitions and roles, 291
  theories of, 293–294
Ageism, 290
Agreeableness, 318
AI. *See* Artificial intelligence
AIDS, 216
Ainsworth, Mary, 223
Alcoholics Anonymous (AA), 538–539
Alcoholism, 455
Algorithms, as problem-solving strategy, 423
ALICE. *See* Artificial Linguistic Internet Computer Entity
Alpha waves, 439
Alston, J. Henry, 8
Altered state of consciousness, 439

Fixed-ratio reinforcement schedules, 355–356
Flashbacks, 458
Flashbulb memories, 387
Fluid intelligence, 47, 294–295
Flynn, James, 471
Flynn effect, 471–472
Food, incentive value of, 158
Forebrain, 75
Forensic psychology, 23
Form perception, 121
Forgetting, 393–397
    curve, 393–394
    interference, 394–395
Formal operational stage, 237, 256
Fovea, 100
Fraternal twins, 85–86, 487
Free association, 542
Frequency, 105
Freud, Sigmund, 13, 40, 307–312, 396, 444
    defense mechanisms, 310–311
    id, ego, and superego, 308–310
    Model of Personality Structure, 309
    psychodynamic therapy and, 541–542
    theory of the mind, 308
Freudian slip, 310, 542
Friedman, Meyer, 195
Frontal lobes, 76
Frosch, Cynthia A., 245
Frustrations, 183
Functional age, 286
Functional fixedness, 426
Functionalism, 7
Functional magnetic resonance imaging (fMRI), 73
Fundamental attribution error, 566–567

G

Gage, Phineas, 79
Galanter, E., 95
Garcia, John, 9, 346–347
Gardner, Howard, 476–478, 480
Gardner's Multiple Intelligences, 477–478
Gases, as inhalant, 458
Gate-control theory, 112
Gender
    bipolar disorder and, 515
    family and work conflict and, 285
    culture, emotions and, 172
    depression rates in, 511, 512, 516
    divorce and, 282
    friendship intimacy and, 268
    leadership style and, 605–606
    psychological disorder treatment and, 535
    puberty and, 252–253

response to stressors, 187
    styles of aggression and, 579
    styles of helping and, 580–581
    terms in language, 410–411
Gender identity, 228–229
Gender socialization, 228–229
General adaptation syndrome (GAS), 188
General intelligence factor, 475
Generalized anxiety disorder, 508
Generativity vs. stagnation, 284
Generic masculine, 410
Genes, behavior and, 84–86
Geneticists, 84
Genetic makeup, 85
Genetics
    building blocks, 85
    causes of personality disorders, 525
    influence on anxiety disorder, 510
    mood disorders and, 515
    personality and, 324
    preprogramming theory of aging, 293
    schizophrenia and, 521–522
Genotype, 85
Germinal stage of prenatal development, 215
Gerontologist, 301
Gerontology, 289, 301
Gestalt psychology, 7–8
    defined, 121
    laws of grouping, 123
    motion parallax and, 120, 126
    principles of, 123
Ghandi, Mahatma, 605
Gibson, Eleanor, 136
Giftedness, 485, 486
Glass, Gene, 540
Glial cells, 65
Global self-description, 228
Goddard, Henry, 468
Goleman, Daniel, 486
Gonads, 70–71
Grammar, 408
Grandparenting styles, 292
Granholm, E., 35
Group, 601
Group behavior
    basking in reflected glory (BIRGing), 602
    competition and prejudice, 611–612
    cutting off reflected failure (CORFing), 602
    dissenter, 603
    ingroup, 602
    intolerance between, 609–616
    leadership and, 604–608
    minorities and, 607–608
    mode, 603
    nature of groups, 601
    nonconformists and, 603
    pride vs. embarrassment, 602
    slider, 603

    social-oriented, 601
    task-oriented, 601
Grouping, laws of, 123
Group therapy, 538
Gunjan, Sinja, 91

H

Habits, 382
Hallucinations, 456, 521
Hallucinogens, 457–458
Hammer, ear bone, 106
Happiness and, GNP and, 22
Harlow, Harry, 223
Harlow, John, 79
Harlow, Margaret, 223
Harris, Judith Rich, 335
Harry Potter, 311–312
Harvard University, early sexism and, 8
Health and safety, of research subjects, 34
Health psychologists, 183
Hearing
    auditory system, 105–108
    ear and, 106–107
    loss of, 106–1078
Heightened selective attention, 449
Helping others
    bystander intervention model, 581–583
    gender styles of, 580–581
Hemispheres, cerebral. See Cerebral hemispheres
Heredity, environment and, 84–86
Heuristics
    decision making and, 424
    as problem-solving strategy, 423
Hierarchy of needs, 155–156
Hilgard, Ernest, 450
Hilts, P. J., 62
Hindbrain, 74
Hippocampus, 75, 382–383, 398
Hispanic Americans
    in psychology, 9
    treatment for psychological disorders and, 537
Histrionic personality, 524
Hitler, Adolf, 605
HIV, 216
Hollon, S. D., 513
Holmes, Thomas, 184
Homeostasis, 75, 151, 188
Hormones, 70–71
Horn, J. L., 476
Horney, Karen, 13
Hostile aggression, 578
Hot flash, 286
Huffing, 458
Human Genome Project, 84